Mc

Modern Literary Theory
A READER
Fourth Edition

Edited by
Philip Rice
and
Patricia Waugh

BLOOMSBURY ACADEMIC

First published by Hodder Education in 1989

Fourth edition published in 2001

This reprint published in 2010 by:

Bloomsbury Academic

An imprint of Bloomsbury Publishing Plc
36 Soho Square, London W1D 3QY, UK
and
175 Fifth Avenue, New York, NY 10010, USA

CIP records for this book are available from the British Library and the Library of Congress

ISBN 978-0-3407-6191-5

This book is produced using paper that is made from wood grown in managed, sustainable
forests.
It is natural, renewable and recyclable. The logging and manufacturing processes conform to
the environmental regulations of the country of origin.

Printed and bound in Great Britain by the MPG Books Group

www.bloomsburyacademic.com

Contents

PART THREE
Critical Debates and Issues   **395**

Acknowledgements

The editors and publishers would like to thank the following for permission to use copyright material in this book.

ADORNO: from *Notes to Literature* by Theodor Adorno, Vol 1, ed. Rolf Tiedmann, tr. Shierry Weber Nicholsen, Columbia University Press, New York, © 1991. Reprinted by permission of the publisher.

BAKHTIN: 'Discourse in the Novel' by M.M. Bakhtin, trans. Carl Emerson and Michael Holquist, from *The Dialogic Imagination: Four Essays by M.M. Bakhtin*. Copyright © 1981 by the University of Texas Press. Reprinted by permission of the publisher.

BALIBAR & MACHEREY: 'Literature as an Ideological Form' by E. Balibar and P. Macherey, from *Oxford Literary review*, vol. 3.1, 1978, pp. 6; 8; 11–12. Reprinted by permission of the publisher.

BARTHES: 'To Write: An Intransative Verb' by Roland Barthes from Richard Macksey and Eugenio Donato, eds. *The Structuralist Controversy: The Languages of Criticism and the Sciences of Man*, pp.134–145 © 1972. Reprinted by permission of The Johns Hopkins University Press. 'The Death of the Author' from *Image-Music-Text* ed. And trans. S. Heath. Reprinted by permission of Editions du Seuil and Collins.

BAUDRILLARD: 'The Orders of Simulcra' by Jean Baudrillard, from *Simulations*, tr. P. Beitchman. © Semiotext(e), 1983. Reprinted by permission of the publisher.

DE BEAUVIOR: from *The Second Sex* by Simone de Beauvior, trans. H M Parshley. Copyright © 1952 and renewed 1980 by Alfred A Knopf, Inc. Reprinted by permission of Alfred A. Knopf, a Division of Random House Inc., and Jonathan Cape, a Division of The Random House Group Ltd.

BHABHA: 'Of Mimicry and Man: The Ambivalence of Colonial Discourse' by Homi Bhabha, *October*, 28 (1984), pp. 125–33. Reprinted by permission of the MIT Press.

BLOOM: 'An Elegy for the Canon' by Harold Bloom from *The Western Canon: The Books and School of the Ages*, copyright © 1994 by Harold Bloom, reprinted by permission of Harcourt, Inc.

BROOKS: 'The Language of Paradox', from *The Well-wrought Urn: Studies in the Structure of Poetry*, copyright 1947 and renewed 1975 by Cleanth Brooks, reprinted by permission of Harcourt, Inc., and Dobson Books Ltd.

BUTLER: 'Critically Queer' by Judith Butler from *Bodies that Matter: On the discursive limits of 'sex'*, Routledge. Copyright © 1993. Reproduced by permission of Taylor & Francis, Inc./Routledge, Inc., http://www.routledge-ny.com

CIXOUS: 'Sorties' by Hélène Cixous. Reprinted by permission of the author.

DERRIDA: Structure, Sign and Play from *Writing and Difference* by Jacques Derrida, translated by Alan Bass © 1966. Reprinted by permission of The University of Chicago Press and Taylor & Francis Books Ltd.

DOLLIMORE: 'Othello: Sexual Difference and Internal Deviation' by Jonathan Dollimore, from *Sexual Dissidence: Augustine to Wilde, Freud to Foucault*, Clarendon Press, 1991. Reprinted by permission of Oxford University Press and the author.

EAGLETON: from *Literary Theory: An Introduction* by Terry Eagleton, 1983. Reproduced by permission of Blackwell Publishers Ltd and the University of Minnesota Press. Extract from *The Illusions of Postmodernism*, Blackwell, 1996. Reprinted by permission of the publisher.

FISH: 'Distinctiveness: Its Achievement and Its Cost' by Stanley Fish from *Professional Correctness: Literary Studies and Political Change*, Clarendon Press, 1995. Reproduced by permission of the author.

FOUCALT: 'The Order of Discourse' by Michel Foucault, trans. Ian McLeod, originally Foucault's inaugural lecture, delivered at the Collège de France, 2 December 1970. In *Untying the Text: A Post-Structuralist Reader*, ed. R. Young (Routledge, 1981). Reprinted by permission.

FREUD: from *Introductory Lectures on Psycho-analysis* by Sigmund Freud, translated by James Strachey. Copyright © 1965, 1954, 1963 by James Strachey. Used by permission of Liveright Publishing Corporation; Sigmund Freud Copyrights, The Institute of Psycho-Analysis and The Hogarth Press for permission to quote from *The Standard Edition of the Complete Psychological Works of Sigmund Freud*, translated and edited by James Strachey.

GENETTE: from *Narrative Discourse Revisited* by Gerard Genette. Translated from the French by Jane E. Lewin. Copyright © 1980 by Cornell University. Used by permission of the publisher, Cornell University Press.

GILBERT & GUBAR: from *The Madwoman in the Attic: The woman writer and the nineteenth-century imagination* by Sandra Gilbert and Susan Gubar, Yale University Press © 1979. Reprinted by permission of the publisher.

GREENBLATT: 'Resonance and Wonder' by Stephen Greenblatt. Fist published in *Bulletin of the American Academy*, January 1990. Reprinted by permission of the author.

HARAWAY: 'A Manifesto for Cyborgs: Science, Technology, and Socialist Feminism in the 1980s' by Donna Haraway from *Feminism/Postmodernism*, ed. Linda Nicholson, Routledge, Copyright © 1989. Reproduced by permission of Taylor & Francis, Inc./Routledge, Inc., http://www.routledge-ny.com

HOOKS: 'Postmodern Blackness' from *Yearning: Race, Gender and Cultural Politics Turnaround* by bell hooks. Reprinted with permission of the publisher, South End Press, 116 Saint Botolph Street, Boston, MA 02115.

IRIGARAY: 'Sexual Difference' by Luce Irigaray, from *French Feminist Thought*, Toril Moi (ed.), Seán Hand (tr.), Blackwell, 1987. Reprinted by permission of the publisher.

KOLODNY: 'Dancing through minefield: some observations on the theory, practice, and politics of a feminist literary criticism' by Annette Kolodny from Showalter, ed., *The New Feminist Criticism*, Virago Press. Reprinted by permission of Little, Brown and Company, and the author Annette Kolodny.

KRISTEVA: 'Women's Time' by Julia Kristeva, from *Signs* 7:1 (1981): pp. 13–35. Reprinted by permission of The University of Chicago Press.

LACAN: 'The Mirror Stage as Formative of the Function of the I as Revealed in Psychoanalytic Experience', from *Ecrits* by Jacques Lacan, translated by Alan Sheridan (Tavistock Publications and W.W. Norton & Company). Copyright © 1977 by Tavistock Publications Ltd. Reprinted by permission of Associated Book Publishers (UK).

LEVINAS: 'Ethics and the Face' by Emmanuel Levinas, from *Totality and Infinity: An essay on Exteriority*, tr. Alphonso Lingis, Duquesne University Press, 1969. Reproduced by permission of the publisher.

LODGE: 'Analysis and Interpretation of the Realist Text' by David Lodge, from *Poetics Today*, vol, 1.4 (Summer 1980), pp. 5–22. Copyright © 1980, Porter Institute for Poetics and Semiotics. All rights reserved. Reprinted by permission of Duke University Press. Extract from 'The Cat in the Rain' by Ernest Hemingway reprinted with permission of Scribner, a Division of Simon & Schuster, from *In Our Time* by Ernest Hemingway. Copyright 1925 by Charles Scribner's Sons. Copyright renewed 1953 by Ernest Hemingway. Copyright © Hemingway Foreign Rights Trust.

LUKACS: 'The Ideology of Modernism' by Georg Lukacs from *The Meaning of Contemporary Realism*, tr. John and Necke Mander, The Merlin Press, London, 1963. Reproduced by permission of the publisher.

LYOTARD: 'Answering the Question: What is Postmodernism?' by Jean-Francois Lyotard from *The Postmodern Condition*, tr. R. Durand, Manchester University Press, 1986. Reprinted by permission of the publisher.

McGANN: 'The Text, the Poem and the Problem of Historical Method' from *The Beauty of Inflections: Literary Investigations in Historical Method and Theory* by Jerome McGann © 1985. Reprinted by permission of Oxford University Press.

DE MAN: 'The Resistance to Theory' by Paul de Man, *Yale French Studies*, 63 (1982), pp. 355–71. Reprinted by permission of the publisher.

MARX & ENGELS: from *The German Ideology* by Karl Marx and Friedrich Engels, ed. R. Pascal, Lawrence & Wishart, London (first published 1938) 1939.

NUSSBAUM: from *Love's Knowledge: Essays on Philosophy and Literature* by Martha C. Nussbaum, copyright © 1990, 1992 by Martha Nussbaum. Used by permission of Oxford University Press, Inc., and Oxford University Press.

RORTY: 'Texts and lumps' by Richard Rorty from *New Literary History* 17 (1985), 1–15. © The University of Virginia. Reprinted by permission of the Johns Hopkins University Press.

SAID: 'Opponents, Audiences, Constituencies and Community' by Edward Said from *Critical Inquiry* 9 (September, 1982), University of Chicago Press. Reproduced by permission of the publisher and the author. Extracts from *Culture and Imperialism*, Chatto & Windus, 1993. © Copyright 1993 Edward Said. Reproduced by permission of the author.

SAUSSURE: from *Course in General Linguistics* by Ferdinand de Saussure, eds Charles Bally and Albert Sechehaye, trans. By Wade Baskin (Peter Owen Ltd). Reprinted by permission of Peter Owen Ltd.

SHKLOVSKY: 'Art as Technique' from *Russian Formalist Criticism: Four Essays* by Victor Shklovsky, trans. By Lee T. Lemon and Marion Reiss. Copyright © 1965 by the University of Nebraska Press. Reprinted by permission of the publisher.

SHOWALTER: 'Towards a Feminist Poetics' by Elaine Showalter from *Women Writing About Women* by Mary Jacobus. Reprinted by permission of Croom Helm Ltd.

SPIVAK: 'The Post-colonial Critic' by Gyatri Chakravorty Spivak, from *The Post-colonial Critic: Interviews Strategies, Dialogues*, ed. Sarah Harasym and Gyatri Chakravorty Spivak. Copyright © 1990. Reproduced by permission of Taylor & Francis, Inc./Routledge, Inc., http://www.routledge-ny.com

WAUGH: 'Postmodernism and Feminism' by Patricia Waugh, from *Contemporary Feminist Theories*, eds. Stevi Jackson and Jackie Jones, Edinburgh University Press, 1998. Reproduced with permission of the publisher.

WHITE: 'The Value of Narrativity in the Representation of Reality' by Hayden White from *The Content of the Form: Narrative Discourse and Historical Representation*, pp.1–25 © 1987. Reproduced by permission of The Johns Hopkins University Press.

WILLIAMS: 'Ideology' from *Marxism and Literature* by Raymond Williams © Oxford University Press, 1977. Reprinted by permission of the publisher.

To the best of our knowledge all copyright holders of material reproduced in this book have been traced. Any rights not acknowledged here will be noted in subsequent printings if notice is given to the publisher.

Preface

The first edition of this anthology appeared in 1989 at the end of a decade when literary theory became established as an important if not yet essential ingredient in the discipline of literary studies. Since then, of course, literary theory has shaped the discipline in far-reaching and unforeseen ways. The success of the first three editions of the anthology has fulfilled original hopes that it would form the basis for a pedagogic introduction to and clarification of the immense volume and diversity of theoretical writing that, over the past thirty years, has so radically questioned our understanding and construction of literature as an object of critical study and of criticism as an organon of methods and reading practices. When Philip Rice and I wrote the first Preface together (in 1988), it was evident that the rapid growth of literary theory since the mid-1960s, and the mass of work devoted to the theoretical discussion of literature, had already transformed literary studies. Critics and philosophers have always theorized about literature and literary criticism, but the sudden erosion of boundaries across philosophy, political theory, psychoanalysis, social theory and literary criticism seemed to represent something of a 'paradigm shift' in literary studies.

Like it or not, a terrible beauty had been born. The very foundations of the Anglo–American tradition had been irrevocably challenged and displaced. Since then, all foundations of Western thought and knowledge have increasingly been held up to critical gaze. The concept of criticism born with modern rational scepticism was always poised to turn introspective, refocusing upon its own discursive constructions. Yet literary theory hardly stands alone as a single instance of such tendencies. What is now often referred to as 'theory' has been part of a more pervasive intellectual movement which has seen modern doubt turn on the instruments of its own articulation and analysis, so that all objects of knowledge seem to be more artefacts constructed through and within language (what Richard Rorty has called 'texts') than they seem to be entities (what he calls 'lumps') on which language reflects. In literary criticism, the notion of the text as an 'object' to be analysed methodically by the empiricist critic has given way to a situation where distinctions between truth and rhetoric, literature and philosophy, history and text, have become increasingly obscure. English has become the site of a new multidisciplinarity which has challenged the methods and assumptions of an earlier literary tradition and those of philosophy and science too.

The crisis in epistemology and controversies about the constitution of literature have brought with them a crisis in value. The postmodern critique of 'grand narratives' has spread its nets over the controversial issue of the canon and the idea that aesthetic value is essential and universal and self-evidentially reflected in a broadly stable tradition of great works of art. Epistemological relativisms have seemed to reinforce cultural relativisms. Recent developments in feminist criticism, in the various new historicisms and in postcolonial criticism have further 'exploded' English and decentred the previously dominant moral – aesthetic and humanist traditions. There has been an increasingly explicit retreat from totalities since the first publication of this book: most explicitly perhaps in the postmodern resistance to universalization, but also in the methods of the new historicists and in postcolonial criticism. Critical practice at the beginning of the new millennium has shifted towards an eclectic mix of methods and positions which tends to avoid any single paradigm or the search for any one systematically explanatory model. Many of the newest schools of criticism, like the New Historicism, for example, are more practices of reading which have assimilated earlier theoretical paradigms than they are 'theories of literature', though they usually aim to be explicit about their theoretical origins and ideological assumptions.

In compiling this fourth edition, the aim has been to retain and to add to those essays and documents which now seem to have a canonical place in the history of modern literary theory; to include for the first time some seminal essays by earlier writers such as Marx and Freud which have helped to shape many of the underlying assumptions of later theorists; and to represent more recent critical material which reflects some of the issues emerging from the retreat from theoretical holism. A new third Part has been added, on critical debates and issues which cut across particular 'schools' and which have engaged critics of many and various intellectual persuasions. Earlier sections have been revised and expanded and new and emerging trends such as the relations between literature and science, the question of ethics and criticism, the issue of the epistemological status of literature and criticism, are now represented. The task of selection has been harder than ever for the field of literary theory is constantly shifting its boundaries and yet, in the last decade, it has become possible to stand back a little and to distinguish clear patterns of influence, intellectual trajectories and hybrid affiliations. The aim of this book is a modest one, however: to introduce a broad and diverse selection of works which might be seen as intellectual 'keys' to the theory 'revolution'; to draw out some of the implications of the theoretical positions represented and to begin to test and sort out their various legacies; and, in particular, to offer an anthology through which the reader might obtain a foothold on the diverse practices which go to make up modern literary theory and become acquainted with some of the principal approaches and theorists.

The book is divided into three Parts. The first two Parts introduce the major movements in modern literary theory and are subdivided into sections, each one representing a major approach or position or set of preoccupations. The aim was to include both purely theoretical statements but also, and where appropriate, contributions which draw on particular theoretical positions to offer interpretations or readings of individual literary texts. Editorial commentary has been kept brief in order to devote as much space as possible to the source material, but commentary is required for the field only partially organizes itself, and then as much on the basis of history as nature. If contemporary theory teaches us anything, it is that the orders of the world are not natural but 'constructed'. Commentary is offered more as an attempt to rationalize the organization of the material rather than to provide a comprehensive intellectual history. It is hoped that the experience of reading the excerpts and essays collected in this book will stimulate further interest and help to clarify the major theoretical positions and their relations to each other. But beyond that (and in the best spirit of contemporary theory) it is hoped that it will encourage readers to contest and challenge the very structures of knowledge and understanding used in its compilation.

The first edition of this reader was initially conceived by myself and Philip Rice in the late eighties and this fourth edition constitutes the most substantial revision and updating since publication of that first edition. Sadly, Philip Rice died shortly after the publication of the second edition. This is the first time that the reader has been extensively revised and I have been very conscious of having to rely on my own judgements about the significant developments in theory and criticism in the last ten years. I very much hope though that Phil would have given his approval. His spirit still shines through the book and as I rewrote and added and subtracted and re-edited I was always conscious of the echoes of all those long conversations we had back in the eighties when the project was first conceived.

General Introduction

As far back as the mid-1950s, and at the height of the revival of positivist scholarship in the Anglo–American tradition, René Wellek and Austin Warren put forward a plea in their seminal text *The Theory of Literature*, for a properly developed theory of literature: 'literary theory, an organon of methods, is the great need of literary scholarship today'.[1] The rapid growth, indeed explosion, of 'theory' since the mid-1960s could hardly have been foreseen in 1956, and since then the mass of work devoted to theoretical discourse about and around literature has produced a radical transformation of the discipline. But is literary theory simply an 'organon of methods', a way of 'doing criticism'? Can there be a pure 'method' which does not imply a substantive account of the nature of literariness, of the function of criticism, and of the very constitution of culture? In its inevitably metacritical relation to the act of criticism itself, theory is more than a method or way of reading: theories carry world-views and 'theory' lays down a challenge to existing or normative views of culture, human nature and existence.

What has most characterized contemporary literary theory has not only been its methodological heterogeneity, but also its fundamental attack on the grounding assumptions of the previously dominant humanistic tradition of Anglo–American criticism and letters. Literary theory, now often simply 'theory', has developed as a curiously hybrid and unstable mix of aesthetics, intellectual history, linguistics, social and political philosophy, anthropology and, most recently, science studies. 'Theory', in this sense, is more than simply speculation or hypothesis, is often analytic, and yet is not subject to the same degree of verificationist or falsificationist rigour, of testing and inference and formulation of laws, which is assumed in the development of any scientific theory. At worst, therefore, 'theory' can degenerate into substantive dogma or an inflexible and *a priori*, pseudo-scientific framework whose interpretative results become as predictable as a well-confirmed scientific explanation: that all texts are 'about' their own condition of indeterminacy, for example, or all texts contain their own subversive strategies, or all texts can be explained as the determined outcome of economic relations – just as water always boils at 100 degrees Centigrade. This is of course to caricature 'theory' in terms which are now the commonplace judgements of its enemies and detractors. Alternatively, and at best, theory is tentative and provisional, self-reflexively critical and cautious, functioning as a thoroughgoing challenge to unexamined common-sense assumptions, those invisible dogmas we inherit from cultural tradition and which close down other possible questions about the world, other ways of seeing and understanding.

Literary studies has always been a pluralistic discipline. The various practices that constituted the Anglo–American tradition, such as literary history, literary biography, moral–aesthetic criticism, and even the New Criticism managed, during the middle decades of the twentieth century, to co-exist in a state of fairly 'stable disequilibrium' based on a broad consensus about the relationship between texts and authors, the nature of the literary work and the purpose of criticism. Critics might argue about the inclusion of this or that piece of writing in the canon of literature or the most effective method of excavating or constituting the meaning or significance of the text, but the notion that a category called 'literature' might have no essential being was never seriously accepted by more than a handful of renegades; nor was the assumption seriously questioned that the author was the expressivist source of the text (whether or not 'his' intentions could be recovered); nor that the act of criticism should serve any other than an explicatory function, as a handmaiden to the text. By the 1980s, of course, each of these assumptions had been thoroughly challenged and re-evaluated from a variety of theoretical positions. The terms of their challenge and repudiation would become the critical commonplaces of the 1990s.

Contemporary critical theory has now established itself comfortably in the everyday life of literary studies, refusing to accept its earlier marginalization by critics such as F.R. Leavis as a peripheral concern more akin to philosophy and inevitably destructive of the plenitudinous and unmediated realization of the meaning and value of the literary text. Contemporary literary theorists now regard their practices as existing at the heart of the critical enterprise, insisting that there is no critical act that can transcend theory. As numerous theorists have pointed out, the traditional forms of criticism through which literature is and has been studied are not 'theory-free' responses to great literary works, nor are they pure scholastic endeavours. All forms of criticism are founded upon a theory, or an admixture of theories, whether they consciously acknowledge that or not. Theory suggests that what are often taken to be 'natural' and 'commonsensical' ways of studying literature actually rest upon a set of theoretical injunctions which have been naturalized to the point at which they no longer have to justify their own practices. And once literary criticism is in dispute or disagreement about the nature, function and constitution of literary criticism itself, then inevitably questions are opened up about the construction of aesthetic values, about the professional and institutional role of criticism and about the kinds of cultural and ideological pressures on canon formation as well as on literary interpretation.

It is surely no coincidence that such metacritical reflections begin to emerge within literary studies at precisely the same moment, the early 1960s, which saw the publication of Thomas Kuhn's immensely influential *The Structure of Scientific Revolutions* (1962).[2] Kuhn sought to demonstrate how all knowledge is produced within communities which implicitly provide the boundaries and the vocabularies within which investigation may take place and also condition the kinds of questions which might be posed. Kuhn referred to such frameworks as 'paradigms'. Every so often, there occurs some revolution in knowledge where an entire paradigm shifts and involves a radical reconstitution of 'facts' within the terms of the new paradigm. According to Kuhn, therefore, even within the scientific institution, facts exist within models agreed by the community and change occurs when the pressure from anomalies in observation and theorizing become so insistent that eventually it forces a revolutionary shift in the entire paradigm: Kuhn's axiomatic example is the shift from Newtonian to post-Einsteinian physics. Kuhn introduced the concept of incommensurability as an account of the way in which, as an entire world-view has shifted, scientific vocabularies regarded as exact and universal, terms such as 'mass', for example, come to carry radically different, indeed incommensurable, meanings within different paradigms. In effect, Kuhn asserted that scientific paradigms constitute irreconcilable 'language games' and non-reconcilable world-views. Furthermore, he argued that there can be no theory-free observation, for there are always underlying and ultimately inarticulatable belief systems and presuppositions which determine the interpretation of the object under observation. Moreover, scientists too inevitably express their 'discoveries' through metaphors and models which help to constitute the object under investigation. Finally, if no theory can be tested against theory-independent facts, then it would seem to be impossible to offer final proof that theoretical constructions are actually in contact with what they set out to explain. It becomes hard to say in what sense one theory is more true than another. Ultimately what is implied here is the notion that even science cannot arrive at knowledge of a mind-independent reality, that its methods are relative to shifting and heterogeneous theoretical frameworks and that the 'objects' of scientific knowledge are thus as intentional as those of the literary text.

If even scientific knowledge began to be subjected to these kinds of metacritical questions, then it is hardly surprising that precisely the same kinds of issues began to be raised in the 1960s about the relationship between the literary text as an 'object' of knowledge in the modern academy and literary criticism as its investigative discourse. One of the tensions which surfaced was between the inherited assumptions of humanist criticism (that literature exemplified in performative mode an experience of concrete particularity, of embodiment and sensuous form, increasingly denied and marginalized by a capitalist and utilitarian culture) and the demands of the professionalized academy where literary criticism is required to conform to a model of systematized knowledge largely derived from the scientific disciplines. Just at the moment when criticism begins to reflect upon such tensions, however (in the various retrospective accounts of the contradictions of the New Criticism with its rigorous and 'scientific' epistemological methods and its ontology of the poem as an organic and irreducible whole), the model of scientific knowledge itself began to be subjected to various kinds of scepticism and relativization. The moment was surely ripe for that explosion within the literary academy of what has come to be referred to (in Kuhnian terms) as the 'theory revolution' and 'English in crisis', the moment when most of the prevailing assumptions about the nature and function of criticism as a means of excavatory interpretation began to be questioned, to be laid bare, made strange, subjected to various kinds of radical critique.

The way that theory subsequently became inflected into the everyday workings of the literary discipline has often proved a source of passionate debate. Responses have taken many forms, from irate dismissal to enthusiastic development. If theory seems to some critics to be deeply implicated in the everyday pursuits and routines of the discipline, to others it seems not to be addressing the object of study directly at all and to be operating in the realms of the abstract and the abstruse, divorced from that close reading and intimate study of literary works that has so characterized the history of the discipline since the early years of the New Criticism. Much literary theory is, of course, highly abstract, confusingly appropriated from a bewildering diversity of other disciplines and discourses which defy mastery, and may be of no pragmatic value in terms of an immediate interpretation of a particular text. Is it worth the sheer effort often involved in trying to understand its often arcane and convoluted grammars and vocabularies? Well, of course, the first thing that theory has taught us is that although literary criticism is largely founded on the assumption of an ideal and immediate relation with its objects of study, this assumption itself is historically determined and not inevitable or natural. Much of the focus of attack on earlier critical orthodoxies has been the undermining of that sense that there is a 'natural' way to study literature. And if literary theory sometimes appears to caricature the tradition it attacks, and to make it seem more singular than it is, that is because the attack has been targeted not so much at the manifest plurality of critical practices which constitute the tradition but at its underlying assumptions which criticism has often obdurately refused to acknowledge as anything other than the 'natural' and 'sensible' way of criticism.

Literary criticism has always been a hybrid mix of practices (literary history, literary biography, myth criticism, psychoanalysis, moral–aesthetic criticism) despite the New Critical attempt to place 'close reading' at its core. Before the advent of 'theory', however, this plurality appeared to be grounded in a broadly consensual conception of relations between authors, texts and readers and upon the aesthetic qualities of the text which constituted its 'literariness' (structural and formal equivalences, fictionality, organic relatedness between parts and whole). Each mode of critical practice tended to foreground a particular feature of the various formal and existential relations constituting the literary experience. Psychoanalytic and biographical approaches emphasized the expressiveness of the author; historical and sociological approaches, the contexts of production and reception; New Criticism, the text-in-itself; moral–aesthetic criticism, the text as a reflection on life or on the question of how one ought to live. However, all accept a broadly mimetic view of the text where literature, in various ways, reflects upon and delivers up truths about life and the human condition (and this is true even when, as with New Criticism, the mimetic view appears to be explicitly repudiated in the name of formal or poetic 'autonomy'). The task of literature is to render life, experience and emotion in a potent way; that of criticism is to reveal the true meaning and value of such a rendition – a rendition at once contained within the literary work and yet requiring the exposition of the critic to reveal and unlock its essential being.

The mimetic perspective is dependent in the end upon a view of language which literary theory would thoroughly challenge: the idea of language as a transparent medium, a medium through which reality can be transcribed and re-presented in aesthetic form, and of reality as self-contained and coherent, always transcending its formulation in words. This is probably the single most important assumption which has been challenged from numerous perspectives within theory. Indeed, the repudiation of the mimeticist premise is the founding move of most contemporary literary theories: deconstructionist, postmodernist, feminist, postcolonialist, New Historicist. It is a view of language related to what Catherine Belsey in 1980 characterized as an 'empiricist–realist' epistemology and which carries with it significant assumptions about the nature of the world and human functioning within it:

> Common sense urges that 'man' is the origin and source of meaning, of action and of history (humanism). Our concepts and our knowledge are held to be the product of experience (empiricism), and this experience is preceded and interpreted by the mind, reason or thought, the property of a transcendent human nature whose essence is the attribute of each individual (idealism).[3]

In this view, the grounding assumptions of humanism presuppose that experience is prior to its expression in language and conceive of language as a mere tool used to express the way that experience is felt and interpreted by the unique individual. Literature thus becomes the expression of especially gifted individuals who are able to capture the elusively universal and timeless truths of the human condition through the sensitive and sensuous use of language. Contemporary literary theory can be seen to begin as an interrogation of this founding assumption, though the critique and challenge has taken a number of forms and orientations.

Probably the key figure in the linguistically sceptical turn which has been at the core of literary theory during the past thirty years, is the Swiss linguist Ferdinand de Saussure. Language, according to Saussure, is not simply a tool devised for the re-presentation of a pre-existing reality. It is rather, a constitutive part of reality, deeply implicated in the way the world is constructed as meaningful. Language is never 'transparent' in the way that correspondence or mimetic theories require it to be. Saussure's ideas about language give rise to an entirely different epistemology which has informed structuralist and post-structuralist theory and, more recently, practices such as the New Historicism or performative theories of gender and sexuality. The implications of this reading of Saussure in the 1970s have been far-reaching and have fed into the political and cultural preoccupations of theory in the last decade or so. If language is constitutive and not simply descriptive, then language is fundamentally unstable, meaning endlessly deferred, and final truths always some form of delusion or ideological power move. T.S. Eliot's observation in the *Four Quartets*, that words, slip, slide and perish, is the informing principle not only of post-structuralism, but of most contemporary political criticism. The capacity to name and thus fix and define the real confers power and suggests that discourse and ideology are intimately bound up with each other. For the contemporary theorist, literature is fascinating in its negotiation of distance from and insight into the relations between ideology, rhetoric and relations of power, but also in the way in which it is unavoidably blind to much of its own ideological complicity.

Part One of this book deals with the attempt to establish a methodological ground for literary studies and with the subsequent and early attempts to break with those founding premises which had been supplied by formalist and structuralist, feminist and Marxist theorizing. Part Two represents the diverse forms taken by literary theory as the implications of post-structuralist challenges to correspondence are assimilated into a variety of cultural and formal perspectives. Part Three presents some long-established but vigorously ongoing debates and controversies within literary studies by offering contrasting and important essays on topics such as ethics and criticism, the literary canon and aesthetic value, criticism and epistemology, and the institutionalization of criticism. Each of the critics gathered together in this section draw substantially on theoretical assumptions developed by writers and critics represented in Parts One and Two. In its most recent manifestations, of course, theory as coherent 'grand narrative' has begun to break down. Instead, a hybrid and shifting mix of models and insights from earlier, often more 'totalizing', theoretical systems are brought together in a new practice of textual criticism or analysis of cultural meaning. In New Historicism and postmodernism or in queer theory or postcolonialism, there is a noticeable shift away from the pleasures of pure and coherent systematizing to an engagement with contingency, plurality, fragmentation and contestation. There is a loss of clear distinction between text and context, depth and surface. Postcolonialism, for example, has drawn extensively on the post-structuralist critique of the centred Subject, on the Gramscian understanding of the concept of hegemony, on Lacanian psychoanalysis, narrative theory, Foucauldian analyses of power and knowledge, feminist critiques of difference and postmodernist challenges to the discourses of the Enlightenment. There is a new emphasis on situatedness, on the provisional and perspectival nature of knowledge, on the problematic relations between the desire for a 'critical' knowledge and the tendency towards an ironist self-subversion of all assumed positions or grounds. The transcendental theoretical 'view from nowhere' has largely disappeared as the object of critical enquiry is seen increasingly to be a discursive construction arising out of specific cultural and institutional practices. The field of literary studies is currently a heterogeneous configuration of competing practices and epistemologies ranging from traditional humanist approaches (and their more formal equivalents such as 'close reading' or their revamped manifestation in, for example, new forms of 'moral criticism') to the newest forms of feminist, postcolonialist and postmodernist critique, and with an ongoing core of scholarly endeavour which has nevertheless been shaped and coloured by the theoretical preoccupations of the last three decades. Indeed, individual critics themselves often occupy multiple, varying and sometimes contradictory positions that go a long way beyond simple disagreements over the interpretation of particular texts. As Terry Eagleton has remarked, 'Literary theory is less an object of intellectual enquiry in its own right than a particular perspective in which to view the history of our time.'[4]

Notes

1 Austin Warren and René Wellek, *Theory of Literature* (New York, Harcourt, Brace and World, 1956), p. 19.
2 Thomas Kuhn, *The Structure of Scientific Revolutions* (2nd ed., University of Chicago Press, 1970).
3 Catherine Belsey, *Critical Practice* (London, Methuen, 1980), p. 7.
4 Terry Eagleton, *Literary Theory: An Introduction* (Oxford, Blackwell, 1990), pp. 194–5.

Part 1

Origins and Foundations

Section 1

Seminal Texts

The essays collected in this section, by Karl Marx and Friedrich Engels, Sigmund Freud, Ferdinand de Saussure and Simone de Beauvoir, may be regarded as foundational discourses for much of the literary theory which emerged in the early 1970s. Collectively, the Marxist analysis of ideology, the Freudian concept of the unconscious, Saussure's notion of the signifier, and de Beauvoir's analysis of the constructedness of gender, have been conceptual planks upon which the modern edifice of literary theory has been built. Though the concepts of ideology, the unconscious, the signifier, and the sex-gender distinction, are often simply assumed as givens in contemporary theory, it is important to recognize their historical emergence and to appreciate the intellectual significance of the writers represented in this introductory section.

Marx and Engels published *The German Ideology* in 1846, shortly before the appearance of *The Communist Manifesto* and some twenty years before the publication of *Capital*. The central thesis of *The German Ideology* for later literary theory is the idea that culture is materially produced. The work constituted a preliminary statement of their later and more developed theory of historical materialism: that consciousness and its products are determined by material conditions. Ideas are not innate or transcendental or universal, but arise out of specific material circumstances. Materialism was not in itself a radically new account of culture or consciousness; nor did Marx and Engels invent the idea that human beings may only realize their full selfhood and freedom through a community. What is new in *The German Ideology*, however, is that a materialist epistemology is developed on a foundation of economic analysis and used to provide the basis for a theory of social relations and of ideology. Relations of production determine social relations which condition the forms of consciousness.

Materialism accounts for events in the world through causal explanation but, again, what is original in Marx and Engels' analysis is their argument that empiricism alone cannot fathom or uncover the true economic relations which determine the forms of culture. These are relations of dominance and inequality which capitalism endeavours to conceal. The epistemological claims of empiricism are thus identified by Marx and Engels as part of the legitimating ideology of capitalism. Marx and Engels believed their work to be 'scientific' but a science grounded in rationalism rather than empirical observation. Their abiding interest in the early work was in the question of why, given that consciousness is historically shaped, there should be so much concern to deny that historical process. Marx and Engels offer an account of ideology as the attempt to deny the material and historical basis of systems of belief and thought and of their own work as that science which might uncover the true historical relations in the foundation of economics. In their view, the dominant ideology serves to legitimate a particular social formation and to confirm the power of the ruling class by making its provisional and particular economic order seem universal or absolute or written into the nature of things. Under capitalism, the working class sells its labour to an entrepreneurial class and such relations of production which arise out of this economic mode of production shape a culture of competition, alienation, control, reification and anomie: people too become commodities, possessions, objects. Ideology functions to disguise the fundamental economic inequalities which give rise to competitive and possessive individualist societies and to legitimate the social order by presenting human nature as eternally competitive and nature as an unjust and survivalist conflict.

Probably the most famous assertion in *The German Ideology* is the belief that under a communist form of social organization – one which would be grounded in the redistribution of wealth, the abolition of private property and the end of class relations – man could be hunter, fisherman, shepherd and critic, and all in the same day. In other words, man could realize his full potential, emancipate his true qualities, and build a world based on co-operation and not competition. *The German Ideology* has little specifically to say about art and certainly does not offer an explicit 'Marxist aesthetics'. It does, however, criticize liberalism as the legitimating ideology of capitalism with its assertion of a universal human nature, of the autonomy and freedom of the individual, and the rational and unencumbered transcendence of mind. Marx and Engels thus provided a foundation for the later development of a Marxist literary theory which would begin to critique the claims of idealist and liberal humanist aesthetics in very much the same terms: repudiating ideas such as autonomy, pure disinterestedness, aesthetic transcendence. Marxists would address the ways in which art is both implicated in and critically distanced from cultural ideologies, recognizing that art is a powerful political force, capable of organizing what Kant referred to as the 'rabble of the senses' through its capacity to give pleasure and to present ideas in the form of embodied experience. Art can encourage conformism with desired models of social cohesion or it can be seized upon as a site for disruption, subversion and challenge. Marx and Engels' account of ideology would be critiqued, developed, finessed by later theorists, but there is no doubt that it is one of the foundation stones of later modern literary theory.

The second essay in this section is Freud's 'The Dream Work' of 1916 which forms lecture 11 of his *Introductory Lectures on Psychoanalysis*. Though published some sixteen years later than *The Interpretation of Dreams*, the lecture essentially offers a summary of Freud's seminal work on the relationship between dreams and the unconscious and is a useful short introduction to his pre-1920 account of the unconscious. In *The Interpretation of Dreams*, Freud had not only offered a new mythology of the mind and symbols through which to represent human behaviour, but also, as he suggested more explicitly in 1915, dealt the third blow to man's naïve self-love and hubristic sense of his relation to himself and nature. The first blow was delivered in the Copernican displacement of earth from the centre of the cosmos, and the second in the Darwinian critique of Creationism and the demonstration of man's ineradicable animal nature. Freud pro-claimed that psychological research (which he defended as a science) had now proved that the human ego is not even master in its own house, that each of us carries a stranger within, the unconscious, which is only partially accessible by the conscious mind and over which we have only limited control. Freud's revolutionary thesis in fact dealt a double blow, first, to that Cartesian rationalist tradition which had attempted to ground all epistemology in the certainty of self-knowledge, and, second, to a naïve empiricism whose assumption was that we might extrapolate from surface manifestations and infer the underlying structures and causes of human behaviour. Freud presents a human self tragically divided and, in addressing the question of how one might know the self, he provided a potent symbolism which must stand in for the inadequacies of empiricist and rationalist accounts of the mind. It is hardly surprising that imaginative writers and literary critics would find in Freudian psychoanalysis, first, a seductive account of the human psyche which grounds it in fundamental biological processes and thus challenges the duality of mind and body and, second, an epistemology which, though claiming to be a science, seems closer to aesthetic practice and mythopoeic symbolism.

Psychoanalysis offered both a new account of representation and a new theory of human subjectivity, though Freud modestly declared on his seventieth birthday that he was not the discoverer of the unconscious for that honour must be accorded to artists and imaginative writers before him. In many ways, Freud's writings on art and literature are highly contradictory for, though he saw the artist as far ahead of the scientist in psychic knowledge, he also saw art as an expression of displaced neurotic conflict: a consoling illusion, symptom, socially acceptable phantasy or substitute gratification which compensates us for the inevitable renunciation of desire involved in the necessary accession to the 'reality principle'. More than his explicit writings on the aesthetic, therefore, it is Freud's general writing on the psyche and, in particular, his work on dreams and sexuality which have most appealed to later literary theorists.

Freud's earliest work on hysteria developed his notion of psychoanalysis as a 'talking cure' which might unlock repressed and painful memories and allow negative energies to be cathartically released. It was this work, conducted before the publication of *The Interpretation of Dreams*, which led him to formulate the idea of the unconscious. Freud began by positing a dynamic factor in the mind which pushes the original painful material out of consciousness, disguising and displacing it so that the hysteric seems to resist all efforts at recall. Psychoanalysis then becomes a dialogic and symbolic method of interpretation which works with a 'manifest' narrative (talk, dream, phantasy) in order to uncover its latent and buried source of meaning. Psychoanalysis is about reading gaps in the text as significant omissions; about understanding how the mind disguises painful material; about how the logic of the primary processes, the basic drives and desires, might be understood through suspending the everyday logic of causality and non-contradiction.

Freud developed two basic models of the mind. The earliest, represented in the essay reprinted here, understands the mind as organized into: (1) consciousness which orders the world and is related to the 'reality principle'; (2) the preconscious, which can be recovered and willed into consciousness; and (3) the unconscious, consisting of instinctual representations regulated by the primary processes and repressed material driven out of consciousness. Freud later (1923) revised this model and posited id, ego and superego as he began to explore the mechanisms of cultural control and the manufacture of morality. Both models, however, posit the idea of a 'pleasure principle' arising out of the biological drives as fundamental to the unconscious and requiring regulation as a condition of entry into human culture. The human infant seeks biological gratification but the 'reality principle' insists that the original psychic energy must be redirected, either through sublimation or repression. In repression, a psychical representative – an idea attached to an instinct – is denied entry into the conscious mind because its impact would be too disturbing, too painful, and the idea then becomes fixated as a measure of energy in the unconscious. At those times when the regulative pressure of the ego is weakened – during sleep or stress, for example – then the unconscious may find a pathway into consciousness but always in disguised form. In the lecture reprinted here, Freud offers an account of the ways in which such material is disguised – through condensation, displacement, symbolization and narrative revision – and develops an interpretative framework for unlocking the dream text.

The earliest forms of psychoanalytic criticism tended to focus on the literary text as a manifestation of unconscious drives rather than focusing on conscious authorial strategies or generic or sociocultural textual determinants. In this sense, psychoanalysis became incorporated into a kind of New Critical reading but where the emphasis is on the expressive source of meaning in the latent structures of the mind rather than on the rhetorical manifestations readily observable in the text as purely stylistic relations. Later psychoanalytic criticism would move away from this expressive model (which draws on Freudian methods in an attempt to locate the 'true' meaning of the text) and towards the recognition of linguistic indeterminacy and the sociocultural and not simply biological construction of the unconscious. Like Marx, Freud posits a model of interpretation where a latent and disguised but 'true' structure may be recovered by a special process of reading through the manifest surfaces of culture. Both regard their practices of reading as forms of scientific enquiry and confer on their own discourses the authority and capacity to stand as metanarratives which can account for the object forms of history and the universal structure of the human mind. Whereas earlier literary criticism largely accepted such claims on their own terms, later appropriations and developments of the ideas of Marx and Freud have subjected them to the kinds of postmodern scepticism turned upon all metanarrative claims. The essays in Part Two of this anthology suggest some of the ways in which this has been achieved.

The work of the Swiss linguist Ferdinand de Saussure has played a crucial and formative role in the recent transformation in literary theory. Saussure's influence rests on a single book which records his seminal theory of language, the *Course in General Linguistics*. This was compiled by students and colleagues, after his death in 1913, from notes taken at lectures he delivered between 1907 and 1911 when he taught at the University of Geneva.

Though not as well known as Marx or Freud, Saussure has been ranked with them in terms of the influence he has had on systems of thought developed in the twentieth century. Like Freud and Marx, Saussure considered the manifest appearance of phenomena to be underpinned and made possible by underlying systems and structures: for Marx, it was the system of economic and social relations; for Freud, the unconscious; for Saussure, the system of language. The most radical implications of their work profoundly disrupt the dominant, humanist conception of the world for they undermine the notion that 'man' is the centre, source and origin of meaning. Saussure's influence on literary theory came to the fore in structuralism and post-structuralism, though his work had significant influence prior to that, notably on the structural linguistics of the Prague Circle and on the structural anthropology of Lévi-Strauss.

It is worth reviewing the main tenets of Saussurean theory since they form the necessary grounding for much of the theory represented in this book. Saussure argued that the object of study for linguistics is the underlying system of conventions (words and grammar) by virtue of which a sign (word) can 'mean'. Language is a system of signs, the sign being the basic unit of meaning. The sign comprises a signifier and signified, the signifier is the 'word image' (visual or acoustic) and the signified the 'mental concept'. Thus the signifier *tree* has the signified *mental concept of a tree*. It is important to note that Saussure is not referring here to the distinction between a name and a thing but to a distinction between the *word-image* and the *concept*. The signifier and signified, however, are only separable on the analytic level, they are not separable at the level of thought – the word-image cannot be divorced from the mental concept and vice versa.

The first principle of Saussure's theory is that the sign is arbitrary. It is useful to consider this at two levels: first, at the level of the signifier; second, at the level of the signified. At the level of the signifier, the sign is arbitrary because there is no *necessary* connection between the signifier *tree* and the signified *concept of tree*; any configuration of sounds or written shapes could be used to signify *tree* – for instance, *arbre, baum, arbor* or even *fnurd*. The relation between the signifier and the signified is a matter of convention; in the English language we conventionally associate the word 'tree' with the concept 'tree'. The arbitrary nature of the sign at this level is fairly easily grasped, but it is the arbitrary nature of the sign at the level of the signified that is more difficult to see and that presents us with the more radical implications of Saussure's theory.

Not only do different languages use different signifiers, they also 'cut up' the phenomenal world differently, articulating it through language-specific concepts – that is, they use different signifieds. The important point to grasp here is that language is not a simple naming process: language does not operate by naming things and concepts that have an independently meaningful existence. Saussure points out that 'if words stood for pre-existing entities they would all have exact equivalents in meaning from one language to the next, but this is not true'. One of the most commonly referred-to illustrations of this is the colour spectrum. The colours of the spectrum actually form a continuum; so, for instance, that part of the spectrum which runs from blue through to red does not consist of a series of different colours – blue, green, yellow, orange, red – existing independently of each other. The spectrum is, rather, a continuum which our language divides up in a particular way.

Just as there is nothing 'natural' about the way we divide up the colour continuum (indeed, other languages divide it up differently), so there is nothing natural or inevitable about the way we divide up and articulate our world in other ways. Each language cuts up the world differently, constructing different meaningful categories and concepts. It is sometimes difficult to see that our everyday concepts are arbitrary and that language does not simply name pre-existing things. We tend to be so accustomed to the world our language system has produced that it comes to seem natural – the correct and inevitable way to view the world. Yet the logic of Saussure's theory suggests that our world is constructed for us by our language and that 'things' do not have fixed essences or cores of meaning which pre-exist linguistic representation.

Returning to the colour spectrum, we can see that orange is not an independently existing colour, not a point on the spectrum but a range on the continuum: we can also see how the colour orange depends, for its existence, on the other colours around it. We can define 'orange' only by what it is not. There is no essence to the colour, only a differentiation. We know that it is orange because it is not yellow and not red. Orange depends for its meaning on what it is not, i.e. orange is produced by the system of difference we employ in dividing up the spectrum.

For Saussure the whole of our language works in this way. It is a system of difference where any one term has meaning only by virtue of its differential place within that system. If we consider the sign 'food', it could not mean anything without the concept of *not* food. In order to 'cut up' the world, even at this crude level, we need a system of difference, i.e. a basic binary system – food/not food. Language is a far more complex version of this simple binary system. This led Saussure to emphasize the *system* of language, for without the system the individual elements (the signs) could not be made to mean.

An important distinction follows from this: that between *langue* and *parole*. Langue is the system of language, the system of forms (the rules, codes, conventions), and parole refers to the actual speech acts made possible by the langue. Utterances (paroles) are many and varied and no linguist could hope to grasp them all. What linguists could do was to study what made them all possible – the latent, underlying system or set of conventions. Saussure then adds a further distinction, that between synchronic and diachronic aspects. The synchronic is the structural aspect of language, the system at a particular moment; the diachronic relates to the history of the language – the changes in its forms and conventions over time. Because signs do not have any essential core of meaning they are open to change, however, in order to 'mean' the sign must exist within a system that is complete at any one moment. This led Saussure to assert that the proper object of study for linguistics was *langue* (the system which made any one act of speech possible), in its synchronic aspect.

The extract chosen to represent the work of Saussure deals, for the most part, with the arbitrary nature of the signified and with that aspect of a sign's meaning which is given by virtue of its place in the system.

First published in French in 1949 and in an English translation by 1953, Simone de Beauvoir's *The Second Sex* offered the first sustained analysis of the construction of woman as 'other'. Borrowing the term from earlier phenomenological and existentialist thought, de Beauvoir developed the implications of situating woman as 'other' within a pervasive dialectic of immanence and transcendence which she saw as structuring the fundamental dualistic codes of Western societies: mind/body, reason/feeling, man/woman, public/private. Her analysis provided the touchstone for much of the feminist theory which followed.

The main thesis of *The Second Sex* is that women are made and not born but, drawing on Marx's account of ideology, she then explores how the powerful myth of the 'Eternal Feminine' has concealed the ways in which woman is defined by her sex always in relation to man. Man is never marked as 'masculine', but is simply the norm and always defined independently of his relation to woman. Her desire is for a world in which all human beings are defined independently of each other but, in a culture where man is the subjective centre, the norm, transcendent and self-defining, woman remains immanent, defined, the 'Eternal Feminine' unable to transcend her discursive imprisonment.

De Beauvoir drew on Sartrean existentialism for her understanding of the fundamental relations between self and other. Like Sartre and Hegel before him, de Beauvoir emphasizes that although each individual desires independence and autonomous self-definition, the simultaneous need for recognition of that independent status paradoxically and inevitably acts to subvert its perfect containment. Human relations therefore inevitably involve an unavoidable struggle for mastery of the gaze and independent self-determination and yet, in a society where men have power, where they occupy the subjective centre, women are inevitably fixed as objects of the gaze, immanent, embodied, opaque and ultimately mysterious as subjects in their own right. If women have never occupied the subjective centre of the gaze, then they have always been named in the terms of exteriority, the terms of the 'Eternal Feminine': Virgin, Whore, Earthmother, Madonna. To resist such naming is to appear to be 'unfeminine' and thus lacking, to conform is to render oneself utterly powerless to resist the gaze and to seek alternative subjectivities.

In its attention to the psychological investments involved in cultural stereotypes, de Beauvoir's analysis provided an enormous incentive for the development of early feminist criticism and a comprehensive examination of the cultural construction of 'Woman' in literary and other kinds of cultural discourse. Like that of Freud, Marx and Saussure, her work also served to challenge the concept of the autonomous Subject, drawing attention to the constructedness of apparently natural categories such as sex. Again, too, it highlighted the inadequacies of naïve empiricist epistemologies in their assumption of a direct correspondence between names and those entities in the world which are named. Although the work of each of these seminal thinkers has a different focus, what unites them and constitutes their most important legacy to modern literary theory is precisely this assault on traditional humanism, on naïve empiricism, and on an earlier rationalism which had failed to take adequate account of the determining pressures of culture and the body.

1 | Karl Marx and Friedrich Engels,

From *The German Ideology* (1846), pp. 70–8

Communism: The Production of the Form of Intercourse Itself

Communism differs from all previous movements in that it overturns the basis of all earlier relations of production and intercourse, and for the first time consciously treats all natural premises as the creatures of men, strips them of their natural character and subjugates them to the power of individuals united. Its organization is, therefore, essentially economic, the material production of the conditions of this unity; it turns existing conditions into conditions of unity. The reality, which communism is creating, is precisely the real basis for rendering it impossible that anything should exist independently of individuals, in so far as things are only a product of the preceding intercourse of individuals themselves. Thus the communists in practice treat the conditions created by production and intercourse as inorganic conditions, without, however, imagining that it was the plan or the destiny of previous generations to give them material, and without believing that these conditions were inorganic for the individuals creating them.

The difference between the individual as a person and what is accidental to him, is not a conceptual difference but a historical fact. This distinction has a different significance at different times – e.g. the estate as something accidental to the individual in the eighteenth century, the family more or less too. It is not a distinction that we have to make for each age, but one which each age makes itself from among the different elements which it finds in existence, and indeed not according to any theory, but compelled by material collisions in life. Of the elements handed down to a later age from an earlier, what appears accidental to the later age as opposed to the earlier, is a form of intercourse which corresponded to a less developed stage of the productive forces. The relation of the productive forces to the form of intercourse is the relation of the form of intercourse to the occupation or activity of the individuals. (The fundamental form of this activity is, of course, material, from which depend all other forms – mental, political, religious, etc. The various shaping of material life is, of course, in every case dependent on the needs which are already developed, and both the production and the satisfaction of these needs is an historical process, which is not found in the case of a sheep or a dog [perversity of Stirner's principal argument *adversus hominem*], although sheep and dogs in their present form certainly, but *malgré eux*, are products of an historical process.) The conditions under which individuals have intercourse with each other, so long as the above-mentioned contradiction is absent, are conditions appertaining to their individuality, in no way external to them; conditions under which these definite individuals, living under definite relationships, can alone produce their material life and what is connected with it; are thus the conditions of their self-activity and are produced by this self-activity. The definite condition under which they produce, thus corresponds, as long as the contradiction has not yet appeared, to the reality of their conditioned nature, their one-sided existence, the one-sidedness of which only becomes evident when the contradiction enters on the scene and thus only exists for the later individuals. Then this condition appears as an accidental fetter, and the consciousness that it is a fetter is imputed to the earlier age as well.

These various conditions, which appear first as conditions of self-activity, later as fetters upon it, form in the whole evolution of history a coherent series of forms of intercourse, the coherence of which consists in this: that in the place of an earlier form of intercourse, which has become a fetter, a new one is put, corresponding to the more developed productive forces and, hence, to the advanced mode of the self-activity of individuals – a form which in its turn becomes a fetter and is then replaced by another. Since these conditions correspond at every stage to the simultaneous development of the productive forces, their history is at the same time the history of the evolving productive forces taken over by each new generation, and is therefore the history of the development of the forces of the individuals themselves.

Since this evolution takes place naturally, i.e. is not subordinated to a general plan of freely combined individuals, it proceeds from various localities, tribes, nations, branches of labour, etc., each of which to start with develops independently of the others and only gradually enters into relation with the others. Furthermore, it takes place only very slowly; the various stages and interests are never completely overcome, but only subordinated to the interest of the victor, and trail along beside the latter for centuries afterwards. It follows from this that within a nation itself the individuals, even apart from their pecuniary circumstances, have quite different developments, and that an earlier interest, the peculiar form of intercourse of which has already been ousted by that belonging to a later interest, remains for a long time afterwards in possession of a traditional power in the illusory community (State, law), which has won an existence independent of the individuals; a power which in the last resort can only be broken by a revolution. This explains why, with reference to individual points which allow of a more general summing-up, consciousness can sometimes appear further advanced than the contemporary empirical relationships, so that in the struggles of a later epoch one can refer to earlier theoreticians as authorities.

On the other hand, in countries which, like North America, begin in an already advanced historical epoch, their development proceeds very rapidly. Such countries have no other natural premises than the individuals, who settled there and were led to do so because the forms of intercourse of the old countries did not correspond to their wants. Thus they begin with the most advanced individuals of the old countries, and therefore with the correspondingly most advanced form of intercourse, before this form of intercourse has been able to establish itself in the old countries.[1] This is the case with all colonies, in so far as they are not mere military or trading stations. Carthage, the Greek colonies, and Iceland in the eleventh and twelfth centuries, provide examples of this. A similar relationship issues from conquest, when a form of intercourse which has evolved on another soil is brought over complete to the conquered country: whereas in its home it was still encumbered with interests and relationships left over from earlier periods, here it can and must be established completely and without hindrance, if only to assure the conquerors' lasting power. (England and Naples after the Norman Conquest, when they received the most perfect form of feudal organization.)

Thus all collisions in history have their origin, according to our view, in the contradiction between the productive forces and the form of intercourse. But also, to lead to collisions in a country, this contradiction need not necessarily come to a head in this particular country. The competition with industrially more advanced countries, brought about by the expansion of international intercourse, is sufficient to produce a similar contradiction in countries with a backward industry (e.g. the latent proletariat in Germany brought into view by the competition of English industry).

This contradiction between the productive forces and the form of intercourse, which, as we saw, has occurred several times in past history without, however, endangering its basis, necessarily on each occasion burst out in a revolution, taking on at the same time various subsidiary forms, such as all-embracing collisions, collisions of various classes, contradiction of consciousness, battle of ideas, etc., political conflict, etc. From a narrow point of view one may isolate one of these subsidiary forms and consider it as the basis of these revolutions; and this is all the more easy as the individuals who started the revolutions made illusions about their own activity according to their degree of culture and the stage of historical development.

The transformation, through the division of labour, of personal powers (relationships) into material powers, cannot be dispelled by dismissing the general idea of it from one's mind, but only by the action of individuals in again subjecting these material powers to themselves and abolishing the division of labour. This is not possible without the community. Only in community with others has each individual the means of cultivating his gifts in all directions; only in the community, therefore, is personal freedom possible. In the previous substitutes for the community, in the State, etc., personal freedom has existed only for the individuals who developed within the relationships of the ruling class, and only in so far as they were individuals of this class. The illusory community, in which individuals have up till now combined, always took on an independent existence in relation to them, and was at the same time, since it was the combination of one class over against another, not only a completely illusory community, but a new fetter as well. In the real community the individuals obtain their freedom in and through their association.

It follows from all we have been saying up till now that the communal relationship into which the individuals of a class entered, and which was determined by their common interests over against a third party, was always a community to which these individuals belonged only as average individuals, only in so far as they lived within the conditions of existence of their class—a relationship in which they participated not as individuals but as members of a class. With the community of revolutionary proletarians on the other hand, who take their conditions of existence and those of all members of society under their control, it is just the reverse; it is as individuals that the individuals participate in it. It is just this combination of individuals (assuming the advanced stage of modern productive forces, of course) which puts the conditions of the free development and movement of individuals under their control—conditions which were previously abandoned to chance and had won an independent existence over against the separate individuals just because of their separation as individuals, and because their combination had been determined by the division of labour, and through their separation had become a bond alien to them. Combination up till now (by no means an arbitrary one, such as is expounded for example in the *Contrat Social*, but a necessary one) was permitted only upon these conditions, within which the individuals were at the mercy of chance (compare, e.g. the formation of the North American State and the South American republics). This right to the undisturbed enjoyment, upon certain conditions, of fortuity and chance has up till now been called personal freedom: but these conditions are, of course, only the productive forces and forms of intercourse at any particular time.

If from a philosophical point of view one considers this evolution of individuals in the common conditions of existence of estates and classes, which followed on one another, and in the accompanying general conceptions forced upon them, it is certainly very easy to imagine that in these individuals the species, or 'man', has evolved, or that they evolved 'man'—and in this way one can give history some hard clouts on the ear.[2] One can conceive these various estates and classes to be specific terms of the general expression, subordinate varieties of the species, or evolutionary phases of 'man'.

This subsuming of individuals under definite classes cannot be abolished until a class has taken shape, which has no longer any particular class interest to assert against the ruling class.

Individuals have always built on themselves, but naturally on themselves within their given historical conditions and relationships, not on the 'pure' individual in the sense of the ideologists. But in the course of historical evolution, and precisely through the inevitable fact that within the division of labour social relationships take on an independent existence, there appears a division within the life of each individual, in so far as it is personal and in so far as it is determined by some branch of labour and the conditions pertaining to it. (We do not mean it to be understood from this that, for example, the rentier, the capitalist, etc., cease to be persons; but their personality is conditioned and determined by quite definite class relation-ships, and the division appears only in their opposition to another class and, for themselves, only when they go bankrupt.)

In the estate (and even more in the tribe) this is as yet concealed: for instance a nobleman always remains a nobleman, a commoner always a commoner, apart from his other relationships, a quality inseparable from his individuality. The division between the personal and the class individual, the accidental nature of the conditions of life for the individual, appears only with the emergence of class, which is itself a product of the bourgeoisie. This accidental character is only engendered and developed by competition and the struggle of individuals among themselves. Thus, in imagination, individuals seem freer under the dominance of the bourgeoisie than before, because their conditions of life seem accidental; in reality, of course, they are less free, because they are more subjected to the violence of things. The difference from the estate comes out particularly in the antagonism between the bourgeoisie and the proletariat. When the estate of the urban burghers, the corporations, etc., emerged in opposition to the landed nobility, their condition of existence – movable property and craft labour, which had already existed latently before their separation from the feudal ties – appeared as something positive, which was asserted against feudal landed property, and therefore in its own way at first took on a feudal form. Certainly the refugee serfs treated their previous servitude as something accidental to their personality. But here they only were doing what every class that is freeing itself from a fetter does; and they did not free themselves as a class but separately. Moreover, they did not rise above the system of estates, but only formed a new estate, retaining their previous mode of labour even in their new situation, and developing it further by freeing it from its earlier fetters, which no longer corresponded to the development already attained.[3]

For the proletarians, on the other hand, the condition of their existence, labour, and with it all the conditions of existence governing modern society, have become something accidental, something over which they, as separate individuals, have no control, and over which no *social* organization can give them control. The contradiction between the individuality of each separate proletarian and labourer, the condition of life forced upon him, becomes evident to him himself, for he is sacrificed from youth upwards and, within his own class, has no chance of arriving at the conditions which would place him in the other class. Thus, while the refugee serfs only wished to be free to develop and assert those conditions of existence which were already there, and hence, in the end, only arrived at free labour, the proletarians, if they are to assert themselves as individuals, will have to abolish the very condition of their existence hitherto (which has, moreover, been that of all society up to the present), namely, labour. Thus they find themselves directly opposed to the form in which, hitherto, individuals have given themselves collective expression, that is, the State. In order, therefore, to assert themselves as individuals, they must overthrow the State.

References

1 Personal energy of the individuals of various nations – Germans and Americans – energy merely through cross-breeding – hence the cretinism of the Germans – in France and England, etc., foreign peoples transplanted to an already developed soil, in America to an entirely new soil – in Germany the natural population quietly stayed where it was.

2 The statement which frequently occurs with Saint Max (Stirner), that each is all that he is through the State, is fundamentally the same as the statement that the bourgeois is only a specimen of the bourgeois species; a statement which presupposes that the *class* of bourgeois existed before the individuals constituting it.

3 N.B. It must not be forgotten that the serfs' very need of existing and the impossibility of a large-sized economy, which involved the distribution of the allotments among the serfs, very soon reduced the services of the serfs to their lord to an average of payments in kind and statute-labour. This made it possible for the serf to accumulate movable property and hence facilitated his escape out of the possession of his lord

and gave him the prospect of prospering as an urban citizen; it also created gradations among the peasants, so that the runaway serfs were already half burghers. It is likewise obvious that the serfs who were masters of a craft had the best chance of acquiring movable property.

---

2 | Sigmund Freud,

From 'The Dream-Work.'[1] *Introductory Lectures on Psychoanalysis* (1916), pp. 204–18

LADIES AND GENTLEMEN,—When you have thoroughly grasped the dream-censorship and representation by symbols, you will not yet, it is true, have completely mastered the distortion in dreams, but you will nevertheless be in a position to understand most dreams. In doing so you will make use of both of the two complementary techniques: calling up ideas that occur to the dreamer till you have penetrated from the substitute to the genuine thing and, on the ground of your own knowledge, replacing the symbols by what they mean. Later on we shall discuss some uncertainties that arise in this connection.

We can now take up once more a task that we tried to carry out previously with inadequate means, when we were studying the relations between the elements of dreams and the genuine things they stood for. We laid down four main relations of the kind: the relation of a part to a whole, approximation or allusion, the symbolic relation and the plastic representation of words. We now propose to undertake the same thing on a larger scale, by comparing the manifest content of a dream *as a whole* with the latent dream as it is revealed by interpretation.

I hope you will never again confuse these two things with each other. If you reach that point, you will probably have gone further in understanding dreams than most readers of my *Interpretation of Dreams*. And let me remind you once again that the work which transforms the latent dream into the manifest one is called the *dream-work*. The work which proceeds in the contrary direction, which endeavours to arrive at the latent dream from the manifest one, is our *work of interpretation*. This work of interpretation seeks to undo the dream-work. The dreams of infantile type which we recognize as obvious fulfilments of wishes have nevertheless experienced some amount of dream-work—they have been transformed from a wish into an actual experience and also, as a rule, from thoughts into visual images. In their case there is no need for interpretation but only for undoing these two transformations. The additional dream-work that occurs in other dreams is called 'dream-distortion', and this has to be undone by our work of interpretation.

Having compared the interpretations of numerous dreams, I am in a position to give you a summary description of what the dream-work does with the material of the latent dream-thoughts. I beg you, however, not to try to understand too much of what I tell you. It will be a piece of description which should be listened to with quiet attention.

The first achievement of the dream-work is *condensation*.[2] By that we understand the fact that the manifest dream has a smaller content than the latent one, and is thus an abbreviated translation of it. Condensation can on occasion be absent; as a rule it is present, and very often it is enormous. It is never changed into the reverse; that is to say, we never find that the manifest dream is greater in extent or content than the latent one. Condensation is brought about (1) by the total omission of certain latent elements (2) by only a fragment of some complexes in the latent dream passing over into the manifest one and (3) by latent elements which have something in common being combined and fused into a single unity in the manifest dream.

If you prefer it, we can reserve the term 'condensation' for the last only of these processes. Its results are particularly easy to demonstrate. You will have no difficulty in recalling instances from your own dreams of different people being condensed into a single one. A composite figure of this kind may look like A perhaps, but may be dressed like B, may do something that we remember C doing, and at the same time we may know that he is D. This composite structure is of course emphasizing something that the four people have in common. It is possible, naturally, to make a composite structure out of things or places in the same way as out of people, provided that the various things and places have in common something which is emphasized by the latent dream. The process is like constructing a new and transitory concept which has this common element as its nucleus. The outcome of this superimposing of the separate elements that have been condensed together is as a rule a blurred and vague image, like what happens if you take several photographs on the same plate.[3]

The production of composite structures like these must be of great importance to the dream-work, since we can show that, where in the first instance the common elements necessary for them were missing, they are deliberately introduced – for instance, through the choice of the words by which a thought is expressed. We have already come across condensations and composite structures of this sort. They played a part in the production of some slips of the tongue. You will recall the young man who offered to *'begleitdigen'* (*'begleiten* [accompany]' + *'beleidigen* [insult])', ... a lady. Moreover, there are jokes of which the technique is based on a condensation like this. But apart from these cases, it may be said that the process is something quite unusual and strange. It is true that counterparts to the construction of these composite figures are to be found in some creations of our imagination, which is ready to combine into a unity components of things that do not belong together in our experience – in the centaurs, for instance, and the fabulous beasts which appear in ancient mythology or in Böcklin's pictures. The 'creative' imagination, indeed, is quite incapable of *inventing* anything; it can only combine components that are strange to one another. But the remarkable thing about the procedure of the dream-work lies in what follows. The material offered to the dream-work consists of thoughts – a few of which may be objectionable and unacceptable, but which are correctly constructed and expressed. The dream-work puts these thoughts into another form, and it is a strange and incomprehensible fact that in making this translation (this rendering, as it were, into another script or language) these methods of merging or combining are brought into use. After all, a translation normally endeavours to preserve the distinctions made in the text and particularly to keep things that are similar separate. The dream-work, quite the contrary, tries to condense two different thoughts by seeking out (like a joke) an ambiguous word in which the two thoughts may come together. We need not try to understand this feature all at once, but it may become important for our appreciation of the dream-work.

But although condensation makes dreams obscure, it does not give one the impression of being an effect of the dream-censorship. It seems traceable rather to some mechanical or economic factor, but in any case the censorship profits by it.

The achievements of condensation can be quite extraordinary. It is sometimes possible by its help to combine two quite different latent trains of thought into one manifest dream, so that one can arrive at what appears to be a sufficient interpretation of a dream and yet in doing so can fail to notice a possible 'over-interpretation'.

In regard to the connection between the latent and the manifest dream, condensation results also in no simple relation being left between the elements in the one and the other. A manifest element may correspond simultaneously to several latent ones, and, contrariwise, a latent element may play a part in several manifest ones – there is, as it were, a criss-cross relationship [...]. In interpreting a dream, moreover, we find that the associations to a single manifest element need not emerge in succession: we must often wait till the whole dream has been interpreted.

Thus the dream-work carries out a very unusual kind of transcription of the dream-thoughts: it is not a word-for-word or a sign-for-sign translation; nor is it a selection made according to fixed rules – as though one were to reproduce only the consonants in a word and to leave out the vowels; nor is it what might be described as a representative selection – one element being invariably chosen to take the place of several; it is something different and far more complicated.

The second achievement of the dream-work is *displacement*.[4] Fortunately we have made some preliminary examination of this: for we know that it is entirely the work of the dream-censorship. It manifests itself in two ways: in the first, a latent element is replaced not by a component part of itself but by something more remote – that is, by an allusion; and in the second, the psychical accent is shifted from an important element on to another which is unimportant, so that the dream appears differently centred and strange.

Replacing something by an allusion to it is a process familiar in our waking thought as well, but there is a difference. In waking thought the allusion must be easily intelligible, and the substitute must be related in its subject-matter to the genuine thing it stands for. Jokes, too, often make use of allusion. They drop the precondition of there being an association in subject-matter, and replace it by unusual external associations such as similarity of sound, verbal ambiguity, and so on. But they retain the precondition of intelligibility: a joke would lose all its efficiency if the path back from the allusion to the genuine thing could not be followed easily. The allusions employed for displacement in dreams have set themselves free from both of these restrictions. They are connected with the element they replace by the most external and remote relations and are therefore unintelligible; and when they are undone, their interpretation gives the impression of being a bad joke or of an arbitrary and forced explanation dragged in by the hair of its head. For the dream-censorship only gains its end if it succeeds in making it impossible to find the path back from the allusion to the genuine thing.

Displacement of accent is unheard-of as a method of expressing thoughts. We sometimes make use of it in waking thought in order to produce a comic effect. I can perhaps call up the impression it produces of going astray if I recall an anecdote. There was a blacksmith in a village, who had committed a capital offence. The Court decided that the crime must be punished; but as the blacksmith was the only one in the village and was indispensable, and as on the other hand there were three tailors living there, one of *them* was hanged instead.

The third achievement of the dream-work is psychologically the most interesting. It consists in transforming thoughts into visual images.[5] Let us keep it clear that this transformation does not affect *everything* in the dream-thoughts; some of them retain their form and appear as thoughts or knowledge in the manifest dream as well; nor are visual images the only form into which thoughts are transformed. Nevertheless they comprise the essence of the formation of dreams; this part of the dream-work is, as we already know, the second most regular one […], and we have already made the acquaintance of the 'plastic' representation of words in the case of individual dream-elements […].

It is clear that this achievement is not an easy one. To form some idea of its difficulties, let us suppose that you have undertaken the task of replacing a political leading article in a newspaper by a series of illustrations. You will thus have been thrown back from alphabetic writing to picture writing.

In so far as the article mentioned people and concrete objects you will replace them easily and perhaps even advantageously by pictures; but your difficulties will begin when you come to the representation of abstract words and of all those parts of speech which indicate relations between thoughts – such as particles, conjunctions and so on. In the case of abstract words you will be able to help yourselves out by means of a variety of devices. For instance, you will endeavour to give the text of the article a different wording, which may perhaps sound less usual but which will contain more components that are concrete and capable of being represented. You will then recall that most abstract words are 'watered-down' concrete ones, and you will for that reason hark back as often as possible to the original concrete meaning of such words. Thus you will be pleased to find that you can represent the 'possession' of an object by a real, physical sitting down on it.[6] And the dream-work does just the same thing. In such circumstances you will scarcely be able to expect very great accuracy from your representation: similarly, you will forgive the dream-work for replacing an element so hard to put into pictures as, for example, 'adultery' ['*Ehebruch*', literally, 'breach of marriage'], by another breach – a broken leg ['*Beinbruch*'].[7] And in this way you will succeed to some extent in compensating for the clumsiness of the picture writing that is supposed to take the place of the alphabetic script.

For representing the parts of speech which indicate relations between thoughts – 'because', 'therefore', 'however', etc. – you will have no similar aids at your disposal; those constituents of the text will be lost so far as translation into pictures goes. In the same way, the dream-work reduces the content of the dream-thoughts to its raw material of objects and activities. You will feel pleased if there is a possibility of in some way hinting, through the subtler details of the pictures, at certain relations not in themselves capable of being represented. And just so does the dream-work succeed in expressing some of the content of the latent dream-thoughts by peculiarities in the *form* of the manifest dream – by its clarity or obscurity, by its division into several pieces, and so on. The number of part-dreams into which a dream is divided usually corresponds to the number of main topics or groups of thoughts in the latent dream. A short introductory dream will often stand in the relation of a prelude to a following, more detailed, main dream or may give the motive for it; a subordinate clause in the dream-thoughts will be replaced by the interpolation of a change of scene into the manifest dream, and so on. Thus the form of dreams is far from being without significance and itself calls for interpretation. When several dreams occur during the same night, they often have the same meaning and indicate that an attempt is being made to deal more and more efficiently with a stimulus of increasing insistence. In individual dreams a particularly difficult element may be represented by several symbols – by 'doublets'.[8]

If we make a series of comparisons between the dream-thoughts and the manifest dreams which replace them, we shall come upon all kinds of things for which we are unprepared: for instance, that nonsense and absurdity in dreams have their meaning. At this point, indeed, the contrast between the medical and the psychoanalytic view of dreams reaches a pitch of acuteness not met with elsewhere. According to the former, dreams are senseless because mental activity in dreams has abandoned all its powers of criticism; according to our view, on the contrary, dreams become senseless when a piece of criticism included in the dream-thoughts – a judgement that 'this is absurd' – has to be represented. The dream you are familiar with of the visit to the theatre ('three tickets for 1 florin 50') [...] is a good example of this. The judgement it expressed was: 'it was absurd to marry so early.'[9]

Similarly, in the course of our work of interpretation we learn what it is that corresponds to the doubts and uncertainties which the dreamer so often expresses as to whether a particular element occurred in a dream, whether it was this or whether, on the contrary, it was something else. There is as a rule nothing in the latent dream-thoughts corresponding to these doubts and uncertainties; they are entirely due to the activity of the dream-censorship and are to be equated with an attempt at elimination which has not quite succeeded.[10]

Among the most surprising findings is the way in which the dream-work treats contraries that occur in the latent dream. We know already [...] that conformities in the latent material are replaced by condensations in the manifest dream. Well, contraries are treated in the same way as conformities, and there is a special preference for expressing them by the same manifest element. Thus an element in the manifest dream which is capable of having a contrary may equally well be expressing either itself or its contrary or both together: only the sense can decide which translation is to be chosen. This connects with the further fact that a representation of 'no' – or at any rate an unambiguous one – is not to be found in dreams.

A welcome analogy to this strange behaviour of the dream-work is provided for us in the development of language. Some philologists have maintained that in the most ancient languages contraries such as 'strong–weak', 'light–dark', 'big–small' are expressed by the same verbal roots. (What we term 'the antithetical meaning of primal words'.) Thus in Ancient Egyptian 'ken' originally meant 'strong' and 'weak'. In speaking, misunderstanding from the use of such ambivalent words was avoided by differences of intonation and by the accompanying gesture, and in writing, by the addition of what is termed a 'determinative' – a picture which is not itself intended to be spoken. For instance, 'ken' meaning 'strong' was written with a picture of a little upright man after the alphabetic signs; when 'ken' stood for 'weak', what followed was the picture of a man squatting down limply. It was only later, by means of slight modifications of the original homologous word, that two distinct representations were arrived at of the contraries included in it. Thus from 'ken' 'strong–weak' were derived 'ken' 'strong' and 'kan' 'weak'. The remains of this ancient antithetical meaning seem to have been preserved not only in the latest developments of the oldest languages but also in far younger ones and even in some that are still living. Here is some evidence of this, derived from K. Abel (1884).[11]

In Latin, words that remained ambivalent in this way are *'altus'* ('high' and 'deep') and *'sacer'* ('sacred' and 'accursed').

As instances of modifications of the same root I may mention *'clamare'* ('to cry'), *'clam'* ('softly', 'quietly', 'secretly'); *'siccus'* ('dry'), *'succus'* ('juice'). And in German: *'Stimme'* ['voice'], *'stumm'* ['dumb'].

If we compare related languages,there are numerous examples. In English, 'to lock'; in German *'Loch'* ['hole'] and *'Lücke'* ['gap']. In English, 'to cleave'; in German, *'kleben'* ['to stick'].

The English word 'without' (which is really 'with–without') is used today for 'without' alone. 'With', in addition to its combining sense, originally had a removing one; this is still to be seen in the compounds 'withdraw ' and 'withhold'. Similarly with the German *'wieder'* ['together with' and *'wider'* 'against'].

Another characteristic of the dream-work also has its counterpart in the development of language. In Ancient Egyptian, as well as in other, later languages, the order of the sounds in a word can be reversed, while keeping the same meaning. Examples of this in English and German are: *'Topf'* ['pot'] –'pot'; 'boat'–'tub'; 'hurry'–*'Ruhe'* ['rest']; *'Balken'* ['beam']–*'Kloben'* ['log'] and 'club'; 'wait'–*'täuwen'* ['tarry']. Similarly in Latin and German: *'capere'*–*'packen'* ['to seize']; *'ren'*–*'Niere'* ['kidney'].

Reversals like this, which occur here with individual words, take place in various ways in the dream-work. We already know reversal of meaning, replacement of something by its opposite [...]. Besides this we find in dreams reversals of situation, of the relation between two people – a 'topsy-turvy' world. Quite often in dreams it is the hare that shoots the sportsman. Or again we find a reversal in the order of events, so that what precedes an event causally comes after it in the dream – like a theatrical production by a third-rate touring company, in which the hero falls down dead and the shot that killed him is not fired in the wings till afterwards. Or there are dreams where the whole order of the elements is reversed, so that to make sense in interpreting it we must take the last one first and the first one last. You will remember too from our study of dream-symbolism that going or falling into the water means the same as coming out of it – that is, giving birth or being born [...], and that climbing up a staircase or a ladder is the same thing as coming down it [...]. It is not hard to see the advantage that dream-distortion can derive from this freedom of representation.

These features of the dream-work may be described as *archaic*. They are equally characteristic of ancient systems of expression by speech and writing and they involve the same difficulties, which we shall have to discuss again later in a critical sense.[12]

And now a few more considerations. In the case of the dream-work it is clearly a matter of transforming the latent thoughts which are expressed in words into sensory images, mostly of a visual sort. Now our thoughts originally arose from sensory images of that kind: their first material and their preliminary stages were sense impressions, or, more properly, mnemic images of such impressions. Only later were words attached to them and the words in turn linked up into thoughts. The dream-work thus submits thoughts to a *regressive* treatment[13] and undoes their development; and in the course of the regression everything has to be dropped that had been added as a new acquisition in the course of the development of the mnemic images into thoughts.

Such then, it seems, is the dream-work. As compared with the processes we have come to know in it, interest in the manifest dream must pale into insignificance. But I will devote a few more remarks to the latter, since it is of it alone that we have immediate knowledge.

It is natural that we should lose some of our interest in the manifest dream. It is bound to be a matter of indifference to us whether it is well put together, or is broken up into a series of disconnected separate pictures. Even if it has an apparently sensible exterior, we know that this has only come about through dream-distortion and can have as little organic relation to the internal content of the dream as the façade of an Italian church has to its structure and plan. There are other occasions when this façade of the dream *has* its meaning, and reproduces an important component of the latent dream-thoughts with little or no distortion. But we cannot know this before we have submitted the dream to interpretation and have been able to form a judgement from it as to the amount of distortion that has taken place. A similar doubt arises when two elements in a dream appear to have been brought into a close relation to each other. This may give us a valuable hint that we may bring together what corresponds to these elements in the latent dream as well; but on other occasions we can convince ourselves that what belongs together in the dream-thoughts has been torn apart in the dream.

In general one must avoid seeking to explain one part of the manifest dream by another, as though the dream had been coherently conceived and was a logically arranged narrative. On the contrary, it is as a rule like a piece of breccia, composed of various fragments of rock held together by a binding medium, so that the designs that appear on it do not belong to the original rocks imbedded in it. And there is in fact one part of the dream-work, known as 'secondary revision',[14] whose business it is to make something whole and more or less coherent out of the first products of the dream-work. In the course of this, the material is arranged in what is often a completely misleading sense and, where it seems necessary, interpolations are made in it.

On the other hand, we must not over-estimate the dream-work and attribute too much to it. The achievements I have enumerated exhaust its activity; it can do no more than condense, displace, represent in plastic form and subject the whole to a secondary revision. What appear in the dream as expressions of judgement, of criticism, of astonishment or of inference– none of these are achievements of the dream-work and they are very rarely expressions of afterthoughts about the dream; they are for the most part portions of the latent dream-thoughts which have passed over into the manifest dream with a greater or less amount of modification and adaptation to the context. Nor can the dream-work compose speeches. With a few assignable exceptions, speeches in dreams are copies and combinations of speeches which one has heard or spoken oneself on the day before the dream and which have been included in the latent thoughts either as material or as the instigator of the dream. The dream-work is equally unable to carry out calculations. Such of them as appear in the manifest dream are mostly combinations of numbers, sham calculations which are quite senseless *quâ* calculations and are once again only copies of calculations in the latent dream-thoughts. In these circumstances it is not to be wondered at that the interest which had turned to the dream-work soon tends to move away from it to the latent dream-thoughts, which are revealed, distorted to a greater or less degree, by the manifest dream. But there is no justification for carrying this shift of interest so far that, in looking at the matter theoretically, one replaces the dream entirely by the latent dream-thoughts and makes some assertion about the former which only applies to the latter. It is strange that the findings of psychoanalysis could be misused to bring about this confusion. One cannot give the name of 'dream' to anything other than the product of the dream-work–that is to say, the *form* into which the latent thoughts have been transmuted by the dream-work. [...]

The dream-work is a process of quite a singular kind, of which the like has not yet become known in mental life. Condensations, displacements, regressive transformations of thoughts into images–such things are novelties whose discovery has already richly rewarded the labours of psychoanalysis. And you can see once more, from the parallels to the dream-work, the connections which have been revealed between psychoanalytic studies and other fields–especially those concerned in the development of speech and thought. You will only be able to form an idea of the further significance of these discoveries when you learn that the mechanism of dream-construction is the model of the manner in which neurotic symptoms arise.

I am also aware that we are not yet able to make a survey of the whole of the new acquisitions which these studies have brought to psychology. I will only point out the fresh proofs they have provided of the existence of unconscious mental acts–for this is what the latent dream-thoughts are–and what an unimaginably broad access to a knowledge of unconscious mental life we are promised by the interpretation of dreams.

But now the time has no doubt come for me to demonstrate to you from a variety of small examples of dreams what I have been preparing you for in the course of these remarks.

Notes

1 The whole of Chapter VI of *The Interpretation of Dreams* (over a third of the entire book) is devoted to the dream-work.
2 Condensation is discussed, with numerous examples, in Section A of Chapter VI of *The Interpretation of Dreams*.

3 Freud more than once compared the result of condensation with Francis Galton's 'composite photographs', e.g. in Chapter IV of *The Interpretation of Dreams*.

4 Displacement is the subject of Section B of Chapter VI of *The Interpretation of Dreams*; but it comes up for discussion at a great many other places in the book.

5 The main discussion of this is in Section C of Chapter VI of *The Interpretation of Dreams*.

6 The German word *'besitzen'* ('to possess') is more obviously connected with sitting than its English equivalent (*'sitzen'* = 'to sit').

7 While I am correcting the proofs of these pages chance has put into my hands a newspaper cutting which offers an unexpected confirmation of what I have written above:

'DIVINE PUNISHMENT

'A Broken Arm for a Broken Marriage

'Frau Anna M., wife of a militiaman, sued Frau Klementine K. for adultery. According to the statement of claim, Frau K. had carried on an illicit relationship with Karl M., while her own husband was at the front and was actually making her an allowance of 70 Kronen [about £ 3.50] a month. Frau K. had already received a considerable amount of money from the plaintiff's husband, while she and her child had to live in hunger and poverty. Fellow-soldiers of her husband had informed her that Frau K. had visited taverns with M. and had sat there drinking till far into the night. On one occasion the defendant had asked the plaintiff's husband in the presence of several other soldiers whether he would not get a divorce soon from "his old woman" and set up with her. Frau K.'s caretaker also reported that she had repeatedly seen the plaintiff's husband in the house most incompletely dressed.

'Before a court in the Leopoldstadt [district of Vienna] Frau K. yesterday denied knowing M., so that there could be no question of her having intimate relations with him.

'A witness, Albertine M., stated, however, that she had surprised Frau K. kissing the plaintiff's husband.

'At a previous hearing, M., under examination as a witness, had denied having intimate relations with the defendant. Yesterday the Judge received a letter in which the witness withdrew the statements he had made on the earlier occasion and admitted that he had a love-affair with Frau K. up till the previous June. He had only denied his relations with the defendant at the former hearing because she had come to him before the hearing and begged him on her knees to save her and say nothing. "Today", the witness wrote, "I feel compelled to make a full confession to the Court, for I have broken my left arm and this seems to me to be a divine punishment for my wrong-doing."

'The Judge stated that the penal offence had lapsed under the statute of limitations. The plaintiff then withdrew her claim and the defendant was discharged.'

8 In philology the term is used of two different words with the same etymology: e.g. 'fashion' and 'faction', both from the Latin *'factio'*.

9 Absurdity in dreams is discussed in Section G of Chapter VI of *The Interpretation of Dreams*.

10 Doubt as a symptom of obsessional neurosis is discussed in Lecture 17.

11 Freud returns to this subject in Lecture 15.

12 See Lecture 13.
13 The subject of 'regression' is discussed at length in Lecture 22.
14 This is the subject of Section I of Chapter VI of *The Interpretation of Dreams*.

3 | Ferdinand de Saussure,

From *Course in General Linguistics* (1915), pp. 111–19, 120–1

1 Language as Organized Thought Coupled with Sound

To prove that language is only a system of pure values, it is enough to consider the two elements involved in its functioning: ideas and sounds.

Psychologically our thought – apart from its expression in words – is only a shapeless and indistinct mass. Philosophers and linguists have always agreed in recognizing that without the help of signs we would be unable to make a clear-cut, consistent distinction between two ideas. Without language, thought is a vague, unchartered nebula. There are no pre-existing ideas and nothing is distinct before the appearance of language.

Against the floating realm of thought, would sounds by themselves yield predelimited entities? No more so than ideas. Phonic substance is neither more fixed nor more rigid than thought; it is not a mold into which thought must of necessity fit but a plastic substance divided in turn into distinct parts to furnish the signifiers needed by thought. The linguistic fact can therefore be pictured in its totality – i.e. language – as a series of contiguous subdivisions marked off on both the indefinite plane of jumbled ideas (*A*) and the equally vague plane of sounds (*B*). The diagram below gives a rough idea of it.

The characteristic role of language with respect to thought is not to create a material phonic means for expressing ideas but to serve as a link between thought and sound, under conditions that of necessity bring about the reciprocal delimitations of units. Thought, chaotic by nature, has to become ordered in the process of its decomposition. Neither are thoughts given material form nor are sounds transformed into mental entities; the somewhat mysterious fact is rather that 'thought sound' implies division and that language works out its units while taking shape between two shapeless masses. Visualize the air in contact with a sheet of water; if the atmospheric pressure changes, the surface of the water will be broken up into a series of divisions, waves; the waves resemble the union or coupling of thought with phonic substance.

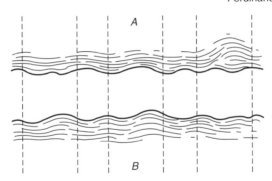

Language might be called the domain of articulations, using the word as it was defined earlier. Each linguistic term is a member, an *articulus* in which an idea is fixed in a sound and a sound becomes the sign of an idea.

Language can also be compared with a sheet of paper: thought is the front and the sound the back; one cannot cut the front without cutting the back at the same time; likewise in language, one can neither divide sound from thought nor thought from sound; the division could be accomplished only abstractedly, and the result would be either pure psychology or pure phonology.

Linguistics then works in the borderland where the elements of sound and thought combine; *their combination produces a form, not a substance.*

These views give a better understanding of what was said before about the arbitrariness of signs. Not only are the two domains that are linked by the linguistic fact shapeless and confused, but the choice of a given slice of sound to name a given idea is completely arbitrary. If this were not true, the notion of value would be compromised, for it would include an externally imposed element. But actually values remain entirely relative, and that is why the bond between the sound and the idea is radically arbitrary.

The arbitrary nature of the sign explains in turn why the social fact alone can create a linguistic system. The community is necessary if values that owe their existence solely to usage and general acceptance are to be set up; by himself the individual is incapable of fixing a single value.

In addition, the idea of value, as defined, shows that to consider a term as simply the union of a certain sound with a certain concept is grossly misleading. To define it in this way would isolate the term from its system; it would mean assuming that one can start from the terms and construct the system by adding them together when, on the contrary, it is from the interdependent whole that one must start and through analysis obtain its elements.

To develop this thesis, we shall study value successively from the viewpoint of the signified or concept (Section 2), the signifier (Section 3), and the complete sign (Section 4).

Being unable to seize the concrete entities or units of language directly, we shall work with words. While the word does not conform exactly to the definition of the linguistic unit, it at least bears a rough resemblance to the unit and has the advantage of being concrete; consequently, we shall use words as specimens equivalent to real terms in a synchronic system, and the principles that we evolve with respect to words will be valid for entities in general.

2 Linguistic Value from a Conceptual Viewpoint

When we speak of the value of a word, we generally think first of its property of standing for an idea, and this is in fact one side of linguistic value. But if this is true, how does *value* differ from *signification*? Might the two words by synonyms? I think not, although it is easy to confuse them, since the confusion results not so much from their similarity as from the subtlety of the distinction that they mark.

From a conceptual viewpoint, value is doubtless one element in signification, and it is difficult to see how signification can be dependent upon value and still be distinct from it. But we must clear up the issue or risk reducing language to a simple naming-process.

Let us first take signification as it is generally understood. As the arrows in the drawing show, it is only the counterpart of the sound-image. Everything that occurs concerns only the sound-image and the concept when we look upon the word as independent and self-contained.

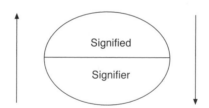

But here is the paradox: on the one hand the concept seems to be the counterpart of the sound-image, and on the other hand the sign itself is in turn the counterpart of the other signs of language.

Language is a system of interdependent terms in which the value of each term results solely from the simultaneous presence of the others, as in the diagram:

How, then, can value be confused with signification, i.e. the counterpart of the sound-image? It seems impossible to liken the relations represented here by horizontal arrows to those represented above by vertical a

Putting it another way – and again taking up the example of the sheet oı paper that is cut in two [...] – it is clear that the observable relation between the different pieces A, B, C, D, etc. is distinct from the relation between the front and back of the same piece as in A/A', B/B', etc.

To resolve the issue, let us observe from the outset that even outside language all values are apparently governed by the same paradoxical principle. They are always composed:

1. of a *dissimilar* thing that can be *exchanged* for the thing of which the value is to be determined; and
2. of *similar* things that can be *compared* with the thing of which the value is to be determined.

Both factors are necessary for the existence of a value. To determine what a five-franc piece is worth one must therefore know: (1) that it can be exchanged for a fixed quantity of a different thing, e.g. bread; and (2) that it can be compared with a similar value of the same system, e.g. a one-franc piece, or with coins of another system (a dollar, etc.). In the same way a word can be exchanged for something dissimilar, an idea; besides, it can be compared with something of the same nature, another word. Its value is therefore not fixed so long as one simply states that it can be 'exchanged' for a given concept, i.e. that it has this or that signification: one must also compare it with similar values, with other words that stand in opposition to it. Its content is really fixed only by the concurrence of everything that exists outside it. Being part of a system, it is endowed not only with a signification but also and especially with a value and this is something quite different.

A few examples will show clearly that this is true. Modern French *mouton* can have the same signification as English *sheep* but not the same value, and this for several reasons, particularly because in speaking of a piece of meat ready to be served on the table, English uses *mutton* and not *sheep*. The difference in value between *sheep* and *mouton* is due to the fact that *sheep* has beside it a second term while the French word does not.

Within the same language, all words used to express related ideas limit each other reciprocally; synonyms like French *redouter* 'dread', *craindre* 'fear', and *avoir peur* 'be afraid' have value only through their opposition: if *redouter* did not exist, all its content would go to its competitors. Conversely, some words are enriched through contact with others: e.g. the new element introduced in *décrépit* (un vieillard *décrépit*) results from the co-existence of *décrépi* (un mur *décrépi*). The value of just any term is accordingly determined by its environment; it is impossible to fix even the value of the word signifying 'sun' without first considering its surrounding: in some languages it is not possible to say 'sit in the *sun*'.

Everything said about words applies to any term of language, e.g. to grammatical entities. The value of a French plural does not coincide with that of a Sanskrit plural even though their signification is usually identical;

Sanskrit has three numbers instead of two (*my eyes, my ears, my arms, my legs*, etc. are dual);[1] it would be wrong to attribute the same value to the plural in Sanskrit and in French; its value clearly depends on what is outside and around it.

If words stood for pre-existing concepts, they would all have exact equivalents in meaning from one language to the next; but this is not true. French uses *louer* (*une maison*) 'let (a house)' indifferently to mean both 'pay for' and 'receive payment for', whereas German uses two words, *mieten* and *vermieten*; there is obviously no exact correspondence of values. The German verbs *Schätzen* and *urteilen* share a number of significations, but that correspondence does not hold at several points.

Inflection offers some particularly striking examples. Distinctions of time, which are so familiar to us, are unknown in certain languages. Hebrew does not recognize even the fundamental distinctions between the past, present, and future. Proto-Germanic has no special form for the future; to say that the future is expressed by the present is wrong, for the value of the present is not the same in Germanic as in languages that have a future along with the present. The Slavic languages regularly single out two aspects of the verb: the perfective represents action as a point, complete in its totality; the imperfective represents it as taking place, and on the line of time. The categories are difficult for a Frenchman to understand, for they are unknown in French; if they were predetermined, this would not be true. Instead of pre-existing ideas then, we find in all the foregoing examples *values* emanating from the system. When they are said to correspond to concepts, it is understood that the concepts are purely differential and defined not by their positive content but negatively by their relations with the other terms of the system. Their most precise characteristic is in being what the others are not.

Now the real interpretation of the diagram of the signal becomes apparent. Thus it means that in French the concept 'to judge' is linked to the sound-image *juger*; in short, it symbolizes signification. But it is quite clear that initially the concept is nothing, that it is only a value determined by its relations with other similar values, and that without them the signification would not exist. If I state simply that a word signifies something when I have in mind the associating of a sound-image with a concept, I am making a statement that may suggest what actually happens, but by no means am I expressing the linguistic fact in its essence and fullness.

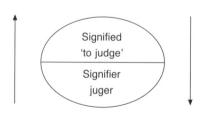

3 Linguistic Value from a Material Viewpoint

The conceptual side of value is made up solely of relations and differences with respect to the other terms of language, and the same can be said of its material side. The important thing in the word is not the sound alone but the phonic differences that make it possible to distinguish this word from all others, for differences carry signification.

This may seem surprising, but how indeed could the reverse be possible? Since one vocal image is no better suited that the next for what it is commissioned to express, it is evident, even *a priori*, that a segment of language can never in the final analysis be based on anything except its noncoincidence with the rest. *Arbitrary* and *differential* are two correlative qualities.

The alteration of linguistic signs clearly illustrates this. It is precisely because the terms *a* and *b* as such are radically incapable of reaching the level of consciousness – one is always conscious of only the *a/b* difference – that each term is free to change according to laws that are unrelated to its signifying function. No positive sign characterizes the genitive plural in Czech *žen*; still the two forms *žena: žen* function as well as the earlier forms *žena: ženb; žen* has value only because it is different.

Here is another example that shows even more clearly the systematic role of phonic differences: in Greek, *éphēn* is an imperfect and *éstēn* an aorist although both words are formed in the same way; the first belongs to the system of the present indicative of *phēmí* 'I say', whereas there is no present *stēmi*; now it is precisely the relation *phēmí : éphēn* that corresponds to the relation between the present and the imperfect (cf. *déiknūmi: edéikūn*, etc.). Signs function, then, not through their intrinsic value but through their relative position.

In addition, it is impossible for sound alone, a material element, to belong to language. It is only a secondary thing, substance to be put to use. All our conventional values have the characteristic of not being confused with the tangible element which supports them. For instance, it is not the metal in a piece of money that fixes its value. A coin nominally worth five francs may contain less than half its worth of silver. Its value will vary according to the amount stamped upon it and according to its use inside or outside a political boundary. This is even more true of the linguistic signifier, which is not phonic but incorporeal – constituted not by its material substance but by the differences that separate its sound-image from all others.

The foregoing principle is so basic that it applies to all the material elements of language, including phonemes. Every language forms its words on the basis of a system of sonorous elements, each element being a clearly delimited unit and one of a fixed number of units. Phonemes are characterized not, as one might think, by their own positive quality but simply by the fact that they are distinct. Phonemes are above all else opposing, relative, and negative entities.

Proof of this is the latitude that speakers have between points of convergence in the pronunciation of distinct sounds. In French, for instance, general use of a dorsal *r* does not prevent many speakers from using a tongue-tip trill; language is not in the least disturbed by it; language requires only that the sound be different and not, as one might imagine, that it have an invariable quality. I can even pronounce the French *r* like German *ch* in *Bach, doch*, etc., but in German I could not use *r* instead of *ch*, for German gives recognition to both elements and must keep them apart.

4 The Sign Considered in its Totality

Everything that has been said up to this point boils down to this: in language there are only differences. Even more important: a difference generally implies positive terms between which the difference is set up; but in language there are only differences *without positive terms*. Whether we take the signified or the signifier, language has neither ideas nor sounds that existed before the linguistic system, but only conceptual and phonic differences that have issued from the system. The idea or phonic substance that a sign contains is of less importance than the other signs that surround it. Proof of this is that the value of a term may be modified without either its meaning or its sound being affected, solely because a neighboring term has been modified [...].

But the statement that everything in language is negative is true only if the signified and the signifier are considered separately; when we consider the sign in its totality, we have something that is positive in its own class. A linguistic system is a series of differences of sound combined with a series of differences of ideas; but the pairing of a certain number of acoustical signs with as many cuts made from the mass of thought engenders a system of values; and this system serves as the effective link between the phonic and psychological elements within each sign. Although both the signified and the signifier are purely differential and negative when considered separately, their combination is a positive fact; it is even the sole type of facts that language has, for maintaining the parallelism between the two classes of differences is the distinctive function of the linguistic institution.

Note

1. The use of the comparative form for two and the superlative for more than two in English (e.g. *may the* better *boxer win: the* best *boxer in the world*) is probably a remnant of the old distinction between the dual and the plural number. [Tr.]

4 | Simone de Beauvoir,

From *The Second Sex* ([1953] 1972), pp. 282–5

The myth of woman plays a considerable part in literature; but what is its importance in daily life? To what extent does it affect the customs and conduct of individuals? In replying to this question it will be necessary to state precisely the relations this myth bears to reality.

There are different kinds of myths. This one, the myth of woman, sublimating an immutable aspect of the human condition–namely, the 'division' of humanity into two classes of individuals–is a static myth. It projects into the realm of Platonic ideas a reality that is directly experienced or is conceptualized on a basis of experience; in place of fact, value, significance, knowledge, empirical law, it substitutes a transcendental Idea, timeless, unchangeable, necessary. This idea is indisputable because it is beyond the given: it is endowed with absolute truth. Thus, as against the dispersed, contingent, and multiple existences of actual women, mythical thought opposes the Eternal Feminine, unique and changeless. If the definition provided for this concept is contradicted by the behaviour of flesh-and-blood women, it is the latter who are wrong: we are told not that Femininity is a false entity, but that the women concerned are not feminine. The contrary facts of experience are impotent against the myth. To pose Woman is to pose the absolute Other, without reciprocity, denying against all experience that she is a subject, a fellow human being.

As group symbols and social types are generally defined by means of antonyms in pairs, ambivalence will seem to be an intrinsic quality of the Eternal Feminine. The saintly mother has for correlative the cruel step-mother, the angelic young girl has the perverse virgin: thus it will be said sometimes that Mother equals Life, sometimes that Mother equals Death, that every virgin is pure spirit or flesh dedicated to the devil.

Thus the paternalism that claims woman for hearth and home defines her as sentiment, inwardness, immanence. In fact every existent is at once immanence and transcendence; when one offers the existent no aim, or prevents him from attaining any, or robs him of his victory, then his transcendence falls vainly into the past–that is to say, falls back into immanence. This is the lot assigned to woman in the patriarchate; but it is in no way a vocation, any more than slavery is the vocation of the slave. The development of this mythology is to be clearly seen in Auguste Comte. To identify Woman with Altruism is to guarantee to man absolute rights in her devotion, it is to impose on women a categorical imperative.

Few myths have been more advantageous to the ruling caste than the myth of woman: it justifies all privileges and even authorizes their abuse. Men need not bother themselves with alleviating the pains and the burdens that physiologically are women's lot, since these are 'intended by Nature'; men use them as a pretext for increasing the misery of the feminine lot still further, for instance by refusing to grant to woman any right to sexual pleasure, by making her work like a beast of burden.[1]

Note

1 Cf. Balzac: *Physiology of Marriage:* 'Pay no attention to her murmurs, her cries, her pains; *Nature has made her for our use* and for bearing everything: children, sorrows, blows and pains inflicted by man. Do not accuse yourself of hardness. In all the codes of so-called civilized nations, man has written the laws that ranged woman's destiny under this bloody epigraph: "*Vae victis*! Woe to the weak!"'

Section 2

Formalism and Structuralism

Introduction

Terry Eagleton has argued in his 1983 introduction to literary theory that if one wanted to put a date on the beginings of modern literary theory, then 1917, the year in which the Russian Formalist Viktor Shklovsky published his pioneering essay 'Art as Device', might be as good a date as any. Though formalist work predates the recent theoretical revolution by some 40 years, its stress on the systematic study of literature links it with the work which initially broke with the traditional critical orthodoxy in the 1960s. Indeed, Formalist work only became more widely available and influential in the post-1960s period.

Russian Formalism is the name now given to a mode of criticism which emerged from two different groups, The Moscow Linguistic Circle (1915) and the Opojaz group (The Society for the Study of Poetic Language) (1916). The main figures in the movement were Roman Jakobson, Viktor Shklovsky, Boris Eichenbaum, Boris Tomashevsky and Yuri Tynyanov. Jakobson was also involved in the later Prague Linguistic Circle (1926–39), which developed some of the Formalist's concerns. Influenced by Futurism and futurist poetry, and reacting against Symbolism's mystificatory poetics (though not against its emphasis on form), they sought to place the study of literature on a scientific basis; their investigation concentrated on the language and the formal devices of the literary work.

Although Russian Formalism is often likened to American New Criticism because of their similar emphasis on close reading, the Russian Formalists regarded themselves as developers of a science of criticism and were more interested in the discovery of a systematic method for the analysis of poetic texts. Russian Formalism emphasized a differential definition of literature, as opposed to the New Critical isolation and objectification of the single text; they were also more emphatic in their rejection of the mimetic/ expressive account of the text. Indeed, Russian Formalism rejected entirely the idea of the text as reflecting an essential unity which is ultimately one of moral or humanistic significance. The central focus of their analysis was not so much literature *per se*, but literariness, that which makes a given text 'literary'. In this sense they sought to uncover the system of literary discourse, the systematic arrangement of language which makes literature possible. Their interest in literary texts tended to centre on the functioning of literary devices rather than on content; literariness was an effect of form.

Shklovsky's essay 'Art as Technique' was one of the first important contributions to the movement. In it he develops the key concept of defamiliarization (*ostranenie*–making strange). Literary language 'makes strange' or defamiliarizes habituated perception and ordinary language. The key to defamiliarization is the literary device, for the device impedes perception, draws attention to the artifice of the text and dehabituates automatized responses. (Formalists tend to be more interested in texts which 'lay bare the device' and which eschew realistic motivation, hence their privileging of difficult or modernist texts.)

One of the most important implications of this view of the literary text is that it logically entails a view of literature as a relational system rather than an absolute or self-contained one, and a system that is bound to change through history. Literary devices cannot remain strange for all time; they too become automatized, fail to retard and break up ordinary perceptions, so that literature continually has to produce new raids on the inarticulate, new defamiliarizational devices to avoid habituated perception. Such a view must see literary tradition not as a seamless continuity, but as discontinuity, where breaks and displacements in form and formal devices continually renew the system. This aspect of the work of the Russian Formalists has proved to be very fertile ground for later transformations in critical practice, influencing later Marxists, for example, in their analysis of literature as a means of defamiliarizing ideologies, and structuralists and post-structuralists in their explorations of intertextuality. In defining the object of enquiry as that of 'literariness', they gave a systematic inflection to the study of literature, one that went beyond intrinsic study of the individual text.

Whereas Russian Formalism aspired to be a 'science' of literature, New Criticism began by explicitly opposing itself to the scientisms of a utilitarian age and arguing that as science reduces the world to types and forms, art must reinvest it with body, the concrete particular, the plenitudinous experience. Although New Criticism also focuses on the formal properties of the literary text, therefore, it parts company with the methods of Russian Formalism in its adherence to an organicist and humanist conception of the function of the literary work which is ultimately derived from Romantic aesthetics. The poem is an object, a formal autonomous entity which, in its unique existence as a for-itself, can restore the world to us. Accordingly, Cleanth Brooks in 1947 attacked the 'heresy of paraphrase' as that critical practice which simply restates the poem in the terms of something else and thus destroys and negates its formal uniqueness. The New Criticism called for a critical practice which could respect the autonomy of the work of art and offer a formal explication which was more than an act of rhetorical transposition.

The New Criticism evolved out of the preoccupations of a group of poets. The Fugitives, writing in the 1930s in the Southern states of America and finding an outlet for their views in two journals of the time, *The Kenyon Review* and *The Sewanee Review*. One of the central early figures in the New Criticism was John Crowe Ransom, perhaps the leading theoretician of the group, who held an almost magical view of poetry as an organization of signs which stood in an iconic relation with nature and offered a concrete and immediate experience which might escape the abstractions of science and the reductionism of the 'Platonic Censor'. Ransom was adamant that literature must be regarded as an object in the world, an entity or for-itself, which criticism must never subjugate to philosophical or scientific systems and reductions. Art preserves the world in its particularity, whereas science looks for universals and works by reduction. Brooks argued similarly that poetry is experience and never simply a statement about or abstraction from experience. Poetry exists to give us back a more refractory original world and thus constitutes an ontologically distinct experience which, nevertheless, can offer a simulacrum of experiential fullness in the world.

In its adherence to an organicist and ultimately expressivist aesthetics, the New Criticism clearly has its origins in Romantic poetics, in the Coleridgean idea of the poem as an organic resolution of oppositions and contradictions and in the Crocean idea of art as a unique and particular way of knowing through embodied and participatory experience. In this sense, therefore, the New Criticism is very different in focus from the work of the Russian Formalists but, like the Formalists, the New Critics too believed that the actual practice of criticism should involve close attention to the formal properties of the work, to those unique structures and organizations of language which conferred upon the literary text its ontological properties. The essay reprinted here, Cleanth Brooks's 'The Language of Paradox', the first chapter of his important book of 1947, *The Well-Wrought Urn: Studies in the Structure of Poetry*, demonstrates both the New Critical adherence to close reading and its concern to differentiate literary from scientific language. Developing the Coleridgean emphasis on organicist resolution, each of the New Critics sought to define a mode of the language of poetry which might adequately define its linguistic otherness: for Brooks, the language of science is a language purged of paradox whereas the truths of poetry may exist in no other form. Poetry is a mode of performance and therefore resists paraphrase. In this essay, Brooks seeks to offer a formal analysis of a variety of poems in order to demonstrate that, whether they flaunt the condition of paradox (as in the poetry of John Donne) or quietly arise out of it (as in Wordsworth's sonnet), poems are always an expression of contradictory truths which may not be apprehended through any other formal arrangement of language.

Structuralism

Though Structuralism developed out of Saussure's pioneering work on language, it was not until the 1960s and 1970s that it found its most widespread influence and application. Generally recognized as 'arriving' in France in the mid-1960s, it gradually made an impact on Anglo–American investigation in the human sciences, including literature. This mode of investigation has been called semiotics as well as Structuralism and though these terms are virtually synonymous some difference in orientation is apparent. Literary Structuralism of this period finds its most powerful advocates in such figures as Roland Barthes, Umberto Eco, Tzvetan Todorov, A.J. Greimas and Gérard Gennette. Saussure's influence is readily apparent in the terms and concepts literary Structuralism deploys, however, the impetus for its development was also provided by such work as the structural anthropology of Lévi-Strauss and Roman Jakobson's studies of language.

In the *Course in General Linguistics*, Saussure had proposed, in a couple of programmatic statements, a 'general science of signs' based on his theory of language. He called this putative science 'semiology' and suggested that the method it inaugurates could be applied to more than just the language system. Recognizing that verbal language, although the most important, was only one among many sign systems, semiology would be widely applicable. Indeed, Saussure's suggestions are taken up in Structuralism, where his theory of language is used as the basis for a critical model which investigates a diverse range of cultural phenomena.

However, Structuralism is more than a methodology; its debt to Saussure goes beyond an analytic model, for inscribed in his theory is the potential for a radical epistemology. Saussure viewed the linguistic sign as arbitrary and as having meaning only because it participates in a system of conventions. Meaning is dependent upon differential relations among elements within a system, i.e. it is *diacritical* not *referential*. In fact, structuralism is not particularly interested in meaning *per se*, but rather in attempting to describe and understand the conventions and modes of signification which make it possible to 'mean'; that is, it seeks to discover the *conditions* of meaning. So *langue* is more important than *parole*– system is more important than individual utterance. Concentration on the system led Todorov to advocate a 'poetics' which would provide a general grammar of literature, or a 'langue' of which the individual work is a 'parole'. Barthes, in *Elements of Semiology* (1964) and *Système de la Mode* (1967), working on broader cultural phenomena, assumes that an individual utterance–whether the wearing of clothes or the articulation of verbal sounds in a conversation–presupposes a system (of fashion or of language) which generates the possibility of meaning for those utterances. The first task of Structuralism is to describe and analyse that system so Structuralists usually begin their analysis by seeking general principles in individual works, though there is also a tendency to explain/interpret individual works by referring to those general principles.

Like Russian Formalism, Structuralism believes in the possibility of a 'science' of literature, one based on form rather than content. For Structuralism, such a science means it could potentially master and explain the world of signs through exhaustive detailing and analysing of the systems that allowed those signs to speak. Though this science would itself have to be carried out in language (the dominant sign system) the language of criticism was deemed to be a 'metalanguage'–that is, a language that can speak about and explain the workings of 'object' languages (languages that seem to speak directly about the world). Structuralism's claim to be operating through a metalanguage cannot, however, overcome the criticism that it is actually no more than a powerful interpretive schema for analysing texts. Moreover, while rejecting the idea of a unified meaning occupying the text, Structuralism still seeks unity or unification in the literary system as a whole, recourse to which can then 'explain' the individual work. It also tends to treat the text as a function of the system of literature, divorcing it from historical and social context.

One focus of this idea of a 'science' of literature was the development of a systematic poetics which could account for the underlying structures of poetic form and narrative. It was Gérard Genette who popularized the term 'narratology' and gave it a structuralist emphasis which moved the study of narrative away from earlier Aristotelian accounts, which emphasize plot or character, and towards the analysis of problems of voice and temporal ordering which develop some of the preoccupations of earlier Jamesian critics such as Percy Lubbock (whose book, *The Craft of Fiction* (1922) was an important attempt to begin to formalize narrative poetics). Genette's work picks up a distinction developed in earlier Russian Formalist writing between the idea of discourse as a connected sequence of narrative statements and the idea of story as an order of events which we extrapolate from discourse in the reading process. Although his work largely focused on the rhetorical uses of voice and temporal ordering in narrative, rather than on questions about the ontology of the text, it did raise the question, seized upon by later post-structuralists and postmodernists, of the extent to which, if the world itself in some sense consists of stories, then narrative might be a fundamental mode of knowledge. For the most part though, Genette's work has been important for its systematic analysis of the complex relationship between the situation of narration and what is narrated. Genette was fascinated by the incredible flexibility of the narrative form of the novel which he saw as inhering in the multiple possibilities of temporal presentation and in the relationship between who speaks (voice) and who sees (perspective or point of view) and the characteristic use of 'focalizers' who blend narratorial voices with characterological perspectives.

The first question raised by Genette is who speaks? He develops the analysis well beyond those theorists of the Anglo–American tradition, deriving from critics such as Lubbock in the 1920s, who offered a breakdown of kinds of narrators (first, third, omniscient, limited omniscient, frame, frame observer, frame participator, camera eye, multiple narrators, unreliable, reliable, etc.) but failed to provide any systematic analysis of the relationship between who speaks and who sees, of who speaks when and to whom and with what authority. The concept of point of view actually conflates voice and perspective and its earlier imprecise use in the analysis of narrative had impeded a full understanding of narrative discourse and the relations between story and discourse. Genette saw that the formal flexibility of the novel rests on its capacity to combine the voice of the narrator (from outside the story) with the perspective or voice (as in free indirect discourse) of the characters (from within the story) who bring the story as discourse into focus. Voice and perspective are, however, only one crucial element in the rhetoric of fiction, for the relations between story and discourse also involve the temporal values of order, duration and frequency, and control effects such as the relationship between the time taken to tell the story and the time taken up by the events narrated (summary, ellipsis, scene, stretch, are some of the possibilities analysed by Genette) or the relationship between the order of events as narrated and the chronology of events in the story. Genette's analyses provided an extremely precise formal vocabulary for trying to understand issues of authority, pace, significance, irony, suspense and curiosity in the reading and interpretation of narrative and they also offered a formal way of understanding related issues such as the differences between realist and modernist texts or between novels and other kinds of narrative.

Like Genette's, the two other essays in this section, Roland Barthes' of 1966 and David Lodge's of 1980, are interesting for the implications they carry about the relations between Structuralist theory as a formal method of reading and Structuralism as a world-view which raises epistemological and ontological questions about the condition of textuality. In the initial break with earlier critical traditions, Structuralism tended to be caught between critical use as a method for the formal analysis of literary texts and adoption as an epistemology, a way of understanding the mode of existence of literature and the text. Genette's writings point in both directions.

Barthes' essay, 'To Write: An Intransitive Verb?', was written at the beginning of the period when his work was undergoing transformation from a Structuralist to a post-structuralist orientation. Its significance lay in the fact that it foregrounded explicitly epistemological questions which began to signal a more radical break with traditional humanist criticism. The essay repudiates mimetic theories of language and correspondence theories of truth, arguing that the modern trajectory has gradually seen the substitution of the 'instance of discourse for the instance of reality' and that 'the field of the writer is nothing but writing itself'. In Barthes' terms, literature is not so much a reflection of the real as an exploration of language. The essay points to the epistemological orientation of structuralism and the way in which the preoccupations of poststructuralism seem inevitably to arise from such reflections. David Lodge's retrospective piece of 1980 has been chosen because its emphasis is explicitly on the formal usefulness of the methods of Formalism and Structuralism as tools for the critical interpretation of texts. Lodge's essay provides a clear and concise summary of the methods and approaches of narratological Structuralist criticism and shows how the tools provided may enhance traditional practices of close reading.

5 | Viktor Shklovsky,

From 'Art as Technique', in L.T. Lemon and M.J. Reis, tr. and ed. *Russian Formalist Criticism: Four Essays* (1917), pp. 11–15; 18

If we start to examine the general laws of perception, we see that as perception becomes habitual, it becomes automatic. Thus, for example, all of our habits retreat into the area of the unconsciously automatic; if one remembers the sensations of holding a pen or of speaking in a foreign language for the first time and compares that with his feeling at performing the action for the ten thousandth time, he will agree with us. Such habituation explains the principles by which, in ordinary speech, we leave phrases unfinished and words half expressed. In this process, ideally realized in algebra, things are replaced by symbols. Complete words are not expressed in rapid speech; their initial sounds are barely perceived. Alexander Pogodin offers the example of a boy considering the sentence 'The Swiss Mountains are beautiful' in the form of a series of letters: $T, S, m, a, b.$[1]

This characteristic of thought not only suggests the method of algebra, but even prompts the choice of symbols (letters, especially initial letters). By this 'algebraic' method of thought we apprehend objects only as shapes with imprecise extensions; we do not see them in their entirety but rather recognize them by their main characteristics. We see the object as though it were enveloped in a sack. We know what it is by its configuration, but we see only its silhouette. The object, perceived thus in the manner of prose perception, fades and does not leave even a first impression; ultimately even the essence of what it was is forgotten. Such perception explains why we fail to hear the prose word in its entirety (see Leo Jakobinsky's article[2] and, hence, why (along with other slips of the tongue) we fail to pronounce it. The process of 'algebrization', the overautomatization of an object, permits the greatest economy of perceptive effort. Either objects are assigned only one proper feature – a number, for example – or else they function as though by formula and do not even appear in cognition:

> I was cleaning a room and, meandering about, approached the divan and couldn't remember whether or not I had dusted it. Since these movements are habitual and unconscious, I could not remember and felt that it was impossible to remember – so that if I had dusted it and forgot – that is, had acted unconsciously, then it was the same as if I had not. If some conscious person had been watching, then the fact could be established. If, however, no one was looking, or looking on unconsciously, if the whole complex lives of many people go on unconsciously, then such lives are as if they had never been.[3]

And so life is reckoned as nothing. Habitualization devours works, clothes, furniture, one's wife, and the fear of war. 'If the whole complex lives of many people go on unconsciously, then such lives are as if they had never been.' And art exists that one may recover the sensation of life; it exists to make one feel things, to make the stone *stony*. The purpose of art is to impart the sensation of things as they are perceived and not as they are known. The technique of art is to make objects *'unfamiliar'*, to make forms difficult, to increase the difficulty and length of perception because the process of perception is an aesthetic end in itself and must be prolonged. *Art is a way of experiencing the artfulness of an object; the object is not important.*

The range of poetic (artistic) work extends from the sensory to the cognitive, from poetry to prose, from the concrete to the abstract: from Cervantes' Don Quixote–scholastic and poor nobleman, half consciously bearing his humiliation in the court of the duke–to the broad but empty Don Quixote of Turgenev; from Charlemagne to the name 'king' (in Russian 'Charles' and 'king' obviously derive from the same root, *korol*). The meaning of a work broadens to the extent that artfulness and artistry diminish; thus a fable symbolises more than a poem, and a proverb more than a fable. Consequently, the least self-contradictory part of Potebnya's theory is his treatment of the fable, which, from his point of view, he investigated thoroughly. But since his theory did not provide for 'expressive' works of art, he could not finish his book. As we know, *Notes on the Theory of Literature* was published in 1905, thirteen years after Potebnya's death. Potebnya himself completed only the section on the fable.[4]

After we see an object several times, we begin to recognize it. The object is in front of us and we know about it, but we do not see it[5]–hence we cannot say anything significant about it. Art removes objects from the automatism of perception in several ways. Here I want to illustrate a way used repeatedly by Leo Tolstoy, that writer who, for Merezhkovsky at least, seems to present things as if he himself saw them, saw them in their entirety, and did not alter them.

Tolstoy makes the familiar seem strange by not naming the familiar object. He describes an object as if he were seeing it for the first time, an event as if it were happening for the first time. In describing something he avoids the accepted names of its parts and instead names corresponding parts of other objects. For example, in 'Shame' Tolstoy 'defamiliarizes' the idea of flogging in this way: 'to strip people who have broken the law, to hurl them to the floor, and to rap on their bottoms with switches', and, after a few lines, 'to lash about on the naked buttocks'. Then he remarks:

> Just why precisely this stupid, savage means of causing pain and not any other–why not prick the shoulders or any part of the body with needles, squeeze the hands or the feet in a vice, or anything like that?

I apologize for this harsh example, but it is typical of Tolstoy's way of pricking the conscience. The familiar act of flogging is made unfamiliar both by the description and by the proposal to change its form without changing its nature. Tolstoy uses this technique of 'defamiliarization', constantly. The narrator of 'Kholstomer', for example, is a horse, and it is the horse's point of view (rather than a person's) that makes the content of the story seem unfamiliar. Here is how the horse regards the institution of private property:

I understood well what they said about whipping and Christianity. But then I was absolutely in the dark. What's the meaning of 'his own', 'his colt'? From these phrases I saw that people thought there was some sort of connection between me and the stable. At the time I simply could not understand the connection. Only much later, when they separated me from the other horses, did I begin to understand. But even then I simply could not see what it meant when they called me 'man's property'. The words 'my horse' referred to me, a living horse, and seemed as strange to me as the words 'my land', 'my air', 'my water'.

But the words made a strong impression on me. I thought about them constantly, and only after the most diverse experiences with people did I understand, finally, what they meant. They meant this: In life people are guided by words, not by deeds. It's not so much that they love the possibility of doing or not doing something as it is the possibility of speaking with words, agreed on among themselves, about various topics. Such are the words 'my' and 'mine', which they apply to different things, creatures, objects, and even to land, people, and horses. They agree that only one may say 'mine' about this, that, or the other thing. And the one who says 'mine' about the greatest number of things is, according to the game which they've agreed to among themselves, the one they consider the most happy. I don't know the point of all this, but it's true. For a long time I tried to explain it to myself in terms of some kind of real gain, but I had to reject that explanation because it was wrong.

Many of those, for instance, who called me their own never rode on me – although others did. And so with those who fed me. Then again, the coachman, the veterinarians, and the outsiders in general treated me kindly, yet those who called me their own did not. In due time, having widened the scope of my observations, I satisfied myself that the notion 'my', not only in relation to us horses, has no other basis than a narrow human instinct which is called a sense of or right to private property. A man says 'this house is mine' and never lives in it; he only worries about its construction and upkeep. A merchant says 'my shop', 'my dry goods shop', for instance, and does not even wear clothes made from the better cloth he keeps in his own shop.

There are people who call a tract of land their own, but they never set eyes on it and never take a stroll on it. There are people who call others their own, yet never see them. And the whole relationship between them is that the so-called 'owners' treat the others unjustly.

There are people who call women their own, or their 'wives', but their women live with other men. And people strive not for the good in life, but for goods they can call their own.

I am now convinced that this is the essential difference between people and ourselves. And therefore, not even considering the other ways in which we are superior, but considering just this one virtue, we can bravely claim to stand higher than men on the ladder of living creatures. The actions of men, at least those with whom I have had dealings, are guided by *words* – ours, by deeds.

The horse is killed before the end of the story, but the manner of the narrative, its technique, does not change:

Much later they put Serpukhovsky's body, which had experienced the world, which had eaten and drunk, into the ground. They could profitably send neither his hide, nor his flesh, nor his bones anywhere.

But since his dead body, which had gone about in the world for twenty years, was a great burden to everyone, its burial was only a superfluous embarrassment for the people. For a long time no one had needed him, for a long time he had been a burden on all. But nevertheless, the dead who buried the dead found it necessary to dress this bloated body, which immediately began to rot, in a good uniform and good boots; to lay it in a good new coffin with new tassels at the four corners, then to place this new coffin in another of lead and ship it to Moscow; there to exhume ancient bones and at just that spot, to hide this putrefying body, swarming with maggots, in its new uniform and clean boots, and to cover it over completely with dirt.

Thus we see that at the end of the story Tolstoy continues to use the technique even though the motivation for it (the reason for its use) is gone.

The technique of defamiliarization is not Tolstoy's alone. I cited Tolstoy because his work is generally known.

Now having explained the nature of this technique, let us try to determine the approximate limits of its application. I personally feel that defamiliarization is found a almost everywhere form is found. In other words, the difference between Potebnya's point of view and ours is this: An image is not a permanent referent for those mutable complexities of life which are revealed through it; its purpose is not to make us perceive meaning, but to create a special perception of the object – *it creates a 'vision' of the object instead of serving as a means for knowing it.*

Notes

1 Alexander Pogodin, *Yazyk kak tvorchestvo* (*Language as Art*) (Kharkov, 1913), p. 42. (The original sentence was in French, '*Les montaignes de la Suisse sont belles*', with the appropriate initials.)
2 Jakubinsky, *Sborniki*, I (1916).
3 Leo Tolstoy's *Diary*, entry dated 1987 February 29. (The date is transcribed incorrectly; it should read 1897 March 1.)
4 Alexander Potebnya, *Iz lektsy po teorii slovesnosti* (*Lectures on the Theory of Language*) (Kharkov, 1914).
5 Victor Shklovsky, *Voskresheniye slova* (*The Resurrection of the Word*) (Petersburg, 1914).

6 | Cleanth Brooks,

From 'The Language of Paradox, *The Well-Wrought Urn* (1947), pp. 292–304

Few of us are prepared to accept the statement that the language of poetry is the language of paradox. Paradox is the language of sophistry, hard, bright, witty; it is hardly the language of the soul. We are willing to allow that paradox is a permissible weapon which a Chesterton may on occasion exploit. We may permit it in epigram, a special subvariety of poetry; and in satire, which though useful, we are hardly willing to allow to be poetry at all. Our prejudices force us to regard paradox as intellectual rather then emotional, clever rather than profound, rational rather than divinely irrational.

Yet there is a sense in which paradox is the language appropriate and inevitable to poetry. It is the scientist whose truth requires a language purged of every trace of paradox; apparently the truth which the poet utters can be approached only in terms of paradox. I overstate the case, to be sure; it is possible that the title of this chapter is itself to be treated as merely a paradox. But there are reasons for thinking that the overstatement which I propose may light up some elements in the nature of poetry which tend to be overlooked.

The case of William Wordsworth, for instance, is instructive on this point. His poetry would not appear to promise many examples of the language of paradox. He usually prefers the direct attack. He insists on simplicity; he distrusts whatever seems sophistical. And yet the typical Wordsworth poem is based upon a paradoxical situation. Consider his celebrated

> It is a beauteous evening, calm and free
> The holy time is quiet as a Nun
> Breathless with adoration . . . .

The poet is filled with worship, but the girl who walks beside him is not worshipping. The implication is that she should respond to the holy time, and become like the evening itself, nunlike; but she seems less worshipful than inanimate nature itself. Yet

> If thou appear untouched by solemn thought,
> Thy nature is not therefore less divine:
> Thou liest in Abraham's bosom all the year;
> And worship'st at the Temple's inner shrine,
> God being with thee when we know it not.

The underlying paradox (of which the enthusiastic reader may well be unconscious) is nevertheless thoroughly necessary, even for that reader. Why does the innocent girl worship more deeply than the self-conscious poet who walks beside her? because she is filled with an unconscious sympathy for *all* of nature, not merely the grandiose and solemn. One remembers the lines from Wordsworth's friend, Coleridge:

> He prayeth best, who loveth best
> All things both great and small.

Her unconscious sympathy is the unconscious worship. She is in communion with nature 'all the year', and her devotion is continual whereas that of the poet is sporadic and momentary. But we have not done with the paradox yet. It not only underlies the poem, but something of the paradox informs the poem, though, since this is Wordsworth, rather timidly. The comparison of the evening to the nun actually has more than one dimension. The calm of the evening obviously means 'worship', even to the dull-witted and insensitive. It corresponds to the trappings of the nun, visible to everyone. Thus, it suggests not merely holiness, but, in the total poem, even a hint of Pharisaical holiness, with which the girl's careless innocence, itself a symbol of her continual secret worship, stands in contrast.

Or consider Wordsworth's sonnet, *Composed upon Westminster Bridge*. I believe that most readers will agree that it is one of Wordsworth's most successful poems; yet most students have the greatest difficulty in accounting for its goodness. The attempt to account for it on the grounds of nobility of sentiment soon breaks down. On this level, the poem merely says: that the city in the morning light presents a picture which is majestic and touching to all but the most dull of souls; but the poem says very little more about the sight: the city is beautiful in the morning light and it is awfully still. The attempt to make a case for the poem in terms of the brilliance of its images also quickly breaks down: the student searches for graphic details in vain: there are next to no realistic touches. In fact, the poet simply huddles the details together:

> . . . silent, bare,
> Ships, towers, domes, theatres, and temples lie
> Open unto the fields . . .

We get a blurred impression – points of roofs and pinnacles along the skyline, all twinkling in the morning light. More than that, the sonnet as a whole contains some very flat writing and some well-worn comparisons.

The reader may ask: Where, then, does the poem get its power? It gets it, it seems to me, from the paradoxical situation out of which the poem arises. The speaker is honestly surprised, and he manages to get some sense of awed surprise into the poem. It is odd to the poet that the city should be able to 'wear the beauty of the morning' at all. Mount Snowdon, Skiddaw, Mont Blanc – these wear it by natural right, but surely not grimy, feverish London. This is the point of the almost shocked exclamation:

> Never did sun more beautifully steep
> In his first splendour, *valley, rock,* or *hill* . . .

The 'smokeless air' reveals a city which the poet did not know existed: man-made London is a part of nature too, is lighted by the sun of nature, and lighted to as beautiful effect.

> The river glideth at his own sweet will . . .

A river is the most 'natural' thing that one can imagine; it has the elasticity, the curved line of nature itself. The poet had never been able to regard this one as a real river – now, uncluttered by barges, the river reveals itself as a natural thing, not at all disciplined into a rigid and mechanical pattern: it is like the daffodils, or the mountain brooks, artless, and whimsical, and 'natural' as they. The poem closes, you will remember, as follows:

Dear God! the very houses seem asleep;
And all that mighty heart is lying still!

The city, in the poet's insight of the morning, has earned its right to be considered organic, not merely mechanical. That is why the stale metaphor of the sleeping houses is strangely renewed. The most exciting thing that the poet can say about the houses is that they are *asleep*. He has been in the habit of counting them dead–as just mechanical and inanimate; to say they are 'asleep' is to say that they are alive, that they participate in the life of nature. In the same way, the tired old metaphor which sees a great city as a pulsating heart of empire becomes revivified. It is only when the poet sees the city under the semblance of death that he can see it as actually alive–quick with the only life which he can accept, the organic life of 'nature'.

It is not my intention to exaggerate Wordsworth's own consciousness of the paradox involved. In this poem, he prefers, as is usual with him, the frontal attack. But the situation is paradoxical here as in so many of his poems. In his preface to the second edition of the *Lyrical Ballads* Wordsworth stated that his general purpose was 'to choose incidents and situations from common life' but so to treat them that 'ordinary things should be preserved to the mind in an unusual aspect'. Coleridge was to state the purpose for him later, in terms which make even more evident Wordsworth's exploitation of the paradoxical: 'Mr Wordsworth . . . was to propose to himself as his object, to give the charm of novelty to things of every day, and to excite a feeling analogous to the supernatural, by awakening the mind's attention from the lethargy of custom, and directing it to the loveliness and the wonders of the world before us . . .' Wordsworth, in short, was consciously attempting to show his audience that the common was really uncommon, the prosaic was really poetic.

Coleridge's terms, 'the charm of novelty to things of every day', 'awakening the mind', suggest the Romantic preoccupation with wonder–the surprise, the revelation which puts the tarnished familiar world in a new light. This may well be the *raison d' être* of most Romantic paradoxes; and yet the neo-classic poets use paradox for much the same reason. Consider Pope's lines from *The Essay on Man*:

In doubt his Mind or Body to prefer;
Born but to die, and reas'ning but to err;
Alike in ignorance, his Reason such,
Whether he thinks too little, or too much . . .

Created half to rise, and half to fall;
Great Lord of all things, yet a Prey to all;
Sole Judge of Truth, in endless Error hurl'd;
The Glory, Jest, and Riddle of the world!

Here, it is true, the paradoxes insist on the irony, rather than the wonder. But Pope too might have claimed that he was treating the things of every day, man himself, and awakening his mind so that he would view himself in a new and blinding light. Thus, there is a certain awed wonder in Pope just as there is a certain trace of irony implicit in the Wordsworth sonnets. There is, of course no reason why they should not occur together, and they do. Wonder and irony merge in many of the lyrics of Blake; they merge in Coleridge's *Ancient Mariner*. The variations in emphasis are numerous. Gray's *Elegy* uses a typical Wordsworth 'situation' with the rural scene and with peasants contemplated in the light of their 'betters'. But in the *Elegy* the balance is heavily tilted in the direction of irony, the revelation an ironic rather than a startling one:

> Can storied urn or animated bust
> Back to its mansion call the fleeting breath?
> Can Honour's voice provoke the silent dust?
> Or Flatt'ry sooth the dull cold ear of Death?

But I am not here interested in enumerating the possible variations; I am interested rather in our seeing that the paradoxes spring from the very nature of the poet's language: it is a language in which the connotations play as great a part as the denotations. And I do not mean that the connotations are important as supplying some sort of frill or trimming, something external to the real matter in hand. I mean that the poet does not use a notation at all—as the scientist may properly be said to do so. The poet, within limits, has to make up his language as he goes.

T. S. Eliot has commented upon 'that perpetual slight alteration of language, *'words perpetually juxtaposed in new and sudden combinations'*, which occurs in poetry. It is perpetual; it cannot be kept out of the poem; it can only be directed and controlled. The tendency of science is necessarily to stabilize terms, to freeze them into strict denotations; the poet's tendency is by contrast disruptive.

The terms are continually modifying each other, and thus violating their dictionary meanings. To take a very simple example, consider the adjectives in the first lines of Wordsworth's evening sonnet: *beauteous, calm, free, holy, quiet, breathless*. The juxtapositions are hardly startling; and yet notice this: the evening is like a nun breathless with adoration. The adjective 'breathless' suggests tremendous excitement; and yet the evening is not only quiet but *calm*. There is no final contradiction, to be sure: it is *that* kind of calm and *that* kind of excitement, and the two states may well occur together. But the poet has no one term. Even if he had a polysyllabic technical term, the term would not provide the solution for his problem. He must work by contradiction and qualification.

We may approach the problem in this way: the poet has to work by analogies. All of the subtler states of emotion, as I. A. Richards has pointed out, necessarily demand metaphor for their expression. The poet must work by analogies, but the metaphors do not lie in the same plane or fit neatly edge to edge. There is a continual tilting of the planes; necessary overlappings, discrepancies, contradictions. Even the most direct and simple poet is forced into paradoxes far more often than we think, if we are sufficiently alive to what he is doing.

But in dilating on the difficulties of the poet's task, I do not want to leave the impression that it is a task which necessarily defeats him, or even that with his method he may not win to a fine precision. To use Shakespeare's figure, he can

> . . . with assays of bias
> By indirections find directions out.

Shakespeare had in mind the game of lawn bowls in which the bowl is distorted, a distortion which allows the skilful player to bowl a curve. To elaborate the figure, science makes use of the perfect sphere and its attack can be direct. The method of art can, I believe, never be direct–is always indirect. But that does not mean that the master of the game cannot place the bowl where he wants it. The serious difficulties will only occur when he confuses his game with that of science and mistakes the nature of his appropriate instrument. Mr Stuart Chase a few years ago, with a touching naïveté, urged us to take the distortion out of the bowl–to treat language like notation.

I have said that even the apparently simple and straightforward poet is forced into paradoxes by the nature of his instrument. Seeing this, we should not be surprised to find poets who consciously employ it to gain a compression and precision otherwise unobtainable. Such a method, like any other, carries with it its own perils. But the dangers are not overpowering: the poem is not predetermined to a shallow and glittering sophistry. The method is an extension of the normal language of poetry, not a perversion of it.

I should like to refer the reader to a concrete case. Donne's *Canonization* ought to provide a sufficiently extreme instance. The basic metaphor which underlies the poem (and which is reflected in the title) involves a sort of paradox. For the poet daringly treats profane love as if it were divine love. The canonization is not that of a pair of holy anchorites who have renounced the world and the flesh. The hermitage of each is the other's body; but they do renounce the world, and so their title to sainthood is cunningly argued. The poem then is a parody of Christian sainthood; but it is an intensely serious parody of a sort that modern man, habituated as he is to an easy yes or no, can hardly understand. He refuses to accept the paradox as a serious rhetorical device; and since he is able to accept it only as a cheap trick, he is forced into this dilemma. Either: Donne does not take love seriously; here he is merely sharpening his wit as a sort of mechanical exercise. Or: Donne does not take sainthood seriously; here he is merely indulging in a cynical and bawdy parody.

Neither account is true; a reading of the poem will show that Donne takes both love and religion seriously; it will show, further, that the paradox is here his inevitable instrument. But to see this plainly will require a closer reading than most of us give to poetry.

The poem opens dramatically on a note of exasperation. The 'you' whom the speaker addresses is not identified. We can imagine that it is a person, perhaps a friend, who is objecting to the speaker's love affair. At any rate, the person represents the practical world which regards love as a silly affectation. To use the metaphor on which the poem is built, the friend represents the secular world which the lovers have renounced.

Donne begins to suggest this metaphor in the first stanza by the contemptuous alternatives which he suggests to the friend:

> . . . chide my palsie, or my gout,
> My five gray haires, or ruin'd fortune flout . . .

The implications are: (1) All right, consider my love as an infirmity, as a disease, if you will, but confine yourself to my other infirmities, my palsy, my approaching old age, my ruined fortune. You stand a better chance of curing those; in chiding me for this one, you are simply wasting your time as well as mine. Why don't you pay attention to your own welfare–go on and get wealth and honour for yourself. What should you care if I do give these up in pursuing my love.

The two main categories of secular success are neatly, and contemptuously epitomized in the line:

> Or the Kings reall, or his stamped face . . .

Cultivate the court and gaze at the king's face there, or, if you prefer, get into business and look at his face stamped on coins. But let me alone.

This conflict between the 'real' world and the lover absorbed in the world of love runs through the poem; it dominates the second stanza in which the torments of love, so vivid to the lover, affect the real world not at all–

> What merchants ships have my sighs drown'd?

It is touched on in the fourth stanza in the contrast between the word 'Chronicle' which suggests secular history with its pomp and magnificence, the history of kings and princes, and the word 'sonnets' with its suggestions of trivial and precious intricacy. The conflict appears again in the last stanza, only to be resolved when the unworldly lovers, love's saints who have given up the world, paradoxically achieve a more intense world. But here the paradox is still contained in, and supported by, the dominant metaphor: so does the holy anchorite win a better world by giving up this one?

But before going on to discuss this development of the theme, it is important to see what else the second stanza does. For it is in this second stanza and the third, that the poet shifts the tone of the poem, modulating from the note of irritation with which the poem opens into the quite different tone with which it closes.

Donne accomplishes the modulation of tone by what may be called an analysis of love-metaphor. Here, as in many of his poems, he shows that he is thoroughly self-conscious about what he is doing. This second stanza he fills with the conventionalized figures of the Petrarchan tradition: the wind of lovers' sighs, the floods of lovers' tears, etc.–extravagant figures with which the contemptuous secular friend might be expected to tease the lover. The implication is that the poet himself recognizes the absurdity of the Petrarchan love metaphors. But what of it? The very absurdity of the jargon which lovers are expected to talk makes for his argument: their love, however absurd it may appear to the world, does no harm to the world. The practical friend need have no fears: there will still be wars to fight and lawsuits to argue.

The opening of the third stanza suggests that this vein of irony is to be maintained. The poet points out to his friend the infinite fund of such absurdities which can be applied to lovers:

> Call her one, mee another flye,
> We're Tapers too, and at our owne cost die . . . .

For that matter, the lovers can conjure up for themselves plenty of such fantastic comparisons: *they* know what the world thinks of them. But these figures of the third stanza are no longer the threadbare Petrarchan conventionalities; they have sharpness and bite. The last one, the likening of the lovers to the phoenix, is fully serious, and with it, the tone has shifted from ironic banter into a defiant but controlled tenderness.

The effect of the poet's implied awareness of the lovers' apparent madness is to cleanse and revivify metaphor; to indicate the sense in which the poet accepts it, and thus to prepare us for accepting seriously the fine and seriously intended metaphors which dominate the last two stanzas of the poem.

The opening line of the fourth stanza,

> Wee can dye by it, if not live by love,

achieves an effect of tenderness and deliberate resolution. The lovers are ready to die to the world; they are committed; they are not callow but confident. (The basic metaphor of the saint, one notices, is being carried on; the lovers, in their renunciation of the world, have something of the confident resolution of the saint. By the bye, the word 'legend'–

> . . . if unfit for tombes and hearse
> Our legend bee –

in Donne's time meant 'the life of a saint'.) The lovers are willing to forego the ponderous and stately chronicle and to accept the trifling and insubstantial 'sonnet' instead; but then if the urn be well wrought, it provides a finer memorial for one's ashes than does the pompous and grotesque monument. With the finely contemptuous, yet quiet phrase, 'halfe-acre tombes', the world which the lovers reject expands into something gross and vulgar. But the figure works further; the pretty sonnets will not merely hold their ashes as a decent earthly memorial. Their legend, their story, will gain them canonization; and approved as love's saints, other lovers will invoke them.

In the last stanza, the theme receives a final complication. The lovers in rejecting life actually win to the most intense life. This paradox has been hinted at earlier in the phoenix metaphor. Here it receives a powerful dramatization. The lovers in becoming hermits, find that they have not lost the world, but have gained the world in each other, now a more intense, more meaningful world. Donne is not content to treat the lovers' discovery as something which comes to them passively, but rather as something which they actively achieve. They are like the saint, God's athlete:

> Who did the whole worlds soule *contract,* and *drove*
>   Into the glasses of your eyes . . . .

The image is that of a violent squeezing as of a powerful hand. And what do the lovers 'drive' into each other's eyes? The 'Countries, Townes', and 'Courts', which they renounced in the first stanza of the poem. The unworldly lovers thus become the most 'worldly' of all.

The tone with which the poem closes is one of triumphant achievement, but the tone is a development contributed to by various earlier elements. One of the more important elements which works towards our acceptance of the final paradox is the figure of the phoenix, which will bear a little further analysis.

The comparison of the lovers to the phoenix is very skilfully related to the two earlier comparisons, that in which the lovers are like burning tapers, and that in which they are like the eagle and the dove. The phoenix comparison gathers up both: the phoenix is a bird, and like the tapers, it burns. We have a selected series of items: the phoenix figure seems to come in a natural stream of association. 'Call us what you will', the lover says, and rattles off in his desperation the first comparisons that occur to him. The comparison to the phoenix seems thus merely another outlandish one, the most outrageous of all. But it is this most fantastic one, stumbled over apparently in his haste, that the poet goes on to develop. It really describes the lovers best and justifies their renunciation. For the phoenix is not two but one, 'we two being one, are it'; and it burns, not like the taper at its own cost, but to live again. Its death is life: 'Wee dye rise the same . . .' The poet literally justifies the fantastic assertion. In the sixteenth and seventeenth centuries to 'die' means to experience the consummation of the act of love. The lovers after the act are the same. Their love is not exhausted in mere lust. This is their title to canonization. Their love is like the phoenix.

I hope that I do not seem to juggle the meaning of *die*. The meaning that I have cited can be abundantly justified in the literature of the period; Shakespeare uses 'die' in this sense; so does Dryden. Moreover, I do not think that I give it undue emphasis. The word is in a crucial position. On it is pivoted the transition to the next stanza,

> Wee can dye by it, if not live by love,
> And if unfit for tombes . . .

Most important of all, the sexual submeaning of 'die' does not contradict the other meanings: the poet is saying: 'Our death is really a more intense life'; 'We can afford to trade life (the world) for death (love), for that death is the consummation of life'; 'After all, one does not expect to live by love, one expects, and wants, to die *by* it'. But in the total passage he is also saying: 'Because our love is not mundane, we can give up the world'; 'Because our love is not merely lust, we can give up the other lusts, the lust for wealth and power'; 'because', and this is said with an inflection of irony as by one who knows the world too well, 'because our love can outlast its consummation, we are a minor miracle, we are love's saints'. This passage with its ironical tenderness and its realism feeds and supports the brilliant paradox with which the poem closes.

There is one more factor in developing and sustaining the final effect. The poem is an instance of the doctrine which it asserts; it is both the assertion and the realization of the assertion. The poet has actually before our eyes built within the song the 'pretty room' with which he says the lovers can be content. The poem itself is the well-wrought urn which can hold the lovers' ashes and which will not suffer in comparison with the prince's 'halfe-acre tomb'.

And how necessary are the paradoxes? Donne might have said directly, 'Love in a cottage is enough'. *The Canonization* contains this admirable thesis, but it contains a great deal more. He might have been as forthright as a later lyricist who wrote, 'We'll build a sweet little nest,/Somewhere out in the West,/And let the rest of the world go by'. He might even have imitated that more metaphysical lyric, which maintains, 'You're the cream in my coffee'. *The Canonization* touches on all these observations, but it goes beyond them, not merely in dignity, but in precision.

I submit that the only way by which the poet could say what *The Canonization* says is by paradox. More direct methods may be tempting, but all of them enfeeble and distort what is to be said. This statement may seem the less surprising when we reflect on how many of the important things which the poet has to say have to be said by means of paradox: most of the language of lovers is such – *The Canonization* is a good example; so is most of the language of religion – 'He who would save his life, must lose it'; 'The last shall be first'. Indeed, almost any insight important enough to warrant a great poem apparently has to be stated in such terms. Deprived of the character of paradox with its twin concomitants of irony and wonder, the matter of Donne's poem unravels into 'facts', biological, sociological, and economic. What happens to Donne's lovers if we consider them 'scientifically', without benefit of the supernaturalism which the poet confers upon them? Well, what happens to Shakespeare's lovers, for Shakespeare uses the basic metaphor of *The Canonization* in his *Romeo and Juliet*? In their first conversation, the lovers play with the analogy between the lover and the pilgrim to the Holy Land. Juliet says:

> For saints have hands, that pilgrims' hands do touch
> And palm to palm is holy palmers' kiss.

Considered scientifically, the lovers become Mr Aldous Huxley's animals, 'quietly sweating, palm to palm'.

For us today, Donne's imagination seems obsessed with the problem of unity; the sense in which the lovers become one – the sense in which the soul is united with God. Frequently, as we have seen, one type of union becomes a metaphor for the other. It may not be too far-fetched to see both as instances of and metaphors for, the union which the creative imagination itself effects. For that fusion is not logical; it apparently violates science and common sense; it welds together the discordant and the contradictory. Coleridge has of course given us the classic description of its nature and power. It

> reveals itself in the balance or reconcilement of opposite or discordant qualities: of sameness, with difference; of the general, with the concrete; the idea, with the image; the individual, with the representative; the sense of novelty and freshness, with old and familiar objects; a more than usual state of emotion, with more than usual order

It is a great and illuminating statement, but is a series of paradoxes. Apparently Coleridge could describe the effect of the imagination in no other way.

Shakespeare, in one of his poems, has given a description that oddly parallels that of Coleridge.

> Reason in it selfe confounded,
> Saw Division grow together,
> To themselves yet either neither,
> Simple were so well compounded.

I do not know what his *The Phoenix and the Turtle* celebrates. Perhaps it *was* written to honour the marriage of Sir John Salisbury and Ursula Stanley; or perhaps the Phoenix is Lucy, Countess of Bedford; or perhaps the poem is merely an essay on Platonic love. But the scholars themselves are so uncertain, that I think we will do little violence to established habits of thinking, if we boldly pre-empt the poem for our own purposes. Certainly the poem is an instance of that magic power which Coleridge sought to describe. I propose that we take it for a moment as a poem about that power;

> So they loved as love in twaine,
> Had the essence but in one,
> Two distincts, Division none,
> Number there in love was slaine.
> Hearts remote, yet not asunder,
> Distance and no space was seene,
> Twixt this *Turtle* and his Queene;
> But in them it were a wonder. . . .
>
> Propertie was thus appalled,
> That the selfe was not the same;
> Single Natures double name,
> Neither two nor one was called.

Precisely! The nature is single, one, unified. But the name is double, and today with our multiplication of sciences, it is multiple. If the poet is to be true to his poetry, he must call it neither two nor one: the paradox is his only solution. The difficulty has intensified since Shakespeare's day: the timid poet, when confronted with the problem of 'Single Nature's double name', has too often funked it. A history of poetry from Dryden's time to our own might bear as its subtitle 'The Half-Hearted Phoenix'.

In Shakespeare's poem, Reason is 'in it selfe confounded' at the union of the Phoenix and the Turtle; but it recovers to admit its own bankruptcy:

Love hath Reason, Reason none,
If what parts, can so remaine. . . .

and it is Reason which goes on to utter the beautiful threnos with which the poem concludes:

Beautie, Truth, and Raritie,
Grace in all simplicitie,
Here enclosde, in cinders lie.

Death is now the *Phoenix* nest,
And the *Turtles* loyall brest,
To eternitie doth rest. . . .

Truth may seeme, but cannot be,
Beautie bragge, but tis not she,
Truth and Beautie buried be.

To this urne let those repaire,
That are either true or faire,
For these dead Birds, sigh a prayer.

Having pre-empted the poem for our own purposes, it may not be too outrageous to go on to make one further observation. The urn to which we are summoned, the urn which holds the ashes of the phoenix, is like the well-wrought urn of Donne's *Canonization* which holds the phoenix-lovers' ashes; it is the poem itself. One is reminded of still another urn, Keats's Grecian urn, which contained for Keats, Truth and Beauty, as Shakespeare's urn encloses 'Beautie, Truth, and Raritie'. But there is a sense in which all such well-wrought urns contain the ashes of a phoenix. The urns are not meant for memorial purposes only, though that often seems to be their chief significance to the professors of literature. The phoenix rises from its ashes; or ought to rise; but it will not arise for all our mere sifting and measuring the ashes, or testing them for their chemical content. We must be prepared to accept the paradox of the imagination itself; else 'Beautie, Truth, and Raritie' remain enclosed in their cinders and we shall end with essential cinders, for all our pains.

The Canonization

For Godsake hold your tongue, and let me love,
    Or chide my palsie, or my gout,
My five gray haires, or ruin'd fortune flout,
    With wealth your state, your minde with Arts improve,
        Take you a course, get you a place,
        Observe his honour, or his grace,
Or the Kings reall, or his stamped face

Contemplate, what you will, approve,
So you will let me love.

Alas, alas, who's injur'd by my love?
What merchants ships have my sighs drown'd?
Who saies my teares have overflow'd his ground?
When did my colds a forward spring remove?
When did the heats which my veines fill
Adde one more to the plaguie Bill?
Soldiers finde warres, and Lawyers finde out still
Litigious men, which quarrels move,
Though she and I do love.

Call us what you will, wee are made such by love;
Call her one, me another flye,
We'are Tapers too, and at our owne cost die,
And wee in us finde the Eagle and the Dove.
The phoenix ridle hath more wit
By us, we two being one, are it.
So to one neutrall thing both sexes fit,
We dye and rise the same, and prove
Mysterious by this love.

Wee can dye by it, if not live by love,
And if unfit for tombes and hearse
Our legend bee, it will be fit for verse;
And if no peece of Chronicle wee prove,
We'll build in sonnets pretty roomes;
As well a well wrought urne becomes
The greatest ashes, as halfe-acre tombes,
And by these hymnes, all shall approve
Us Canoniz'd for Love:

And thus invoke us; You whom reverend love
Made one anothers hermitage;
You, to whom love was peace, that now is rage;
Who did the whole worlds soule contract, and drove
Into the glasses of your eyes
(So made such mirrors, and such spies,
That they did all to you epitomize,)
Countries, Townes, Courts: Beg from above
A patterne or your love!

7 | Gérard Genette,

From *Narrative Discourse*, J. Lewin tr. (1980), pp. 212–27

Voice

The Narrating Instance

'For a long time I used to go to bed early': obviously, such a statement–unlike, let us say, 'Water boils at one-hundred degrees Celsius' or 'The sum of the angles of a triangle is equal to two right angles'–can be interpreted only with respect to the person who utters it and the situation in which he utters it. *I* is identifiable only with reference to that person, and the completed past of the 'action' told is completed only in relation to the moment of utterance. To use Benveniste's well-known terms again, the *story* here is not without a share of *discourse*, and it is not too difficult to show that this is practically always the case.[1] Even historical narrative of the type 'Napoleon died at Saint Helena' implies in its preterite that the story precedes the narrating, and I am not certain that the present tense in 'Water boils at one-hundred degrees' (iterative narrative) is as atemporal as it seems. Nevertheless, the importance or the relevance of these implications is essentially variable, and this variability can justify or impose distinctions and contrasts that have at least an operative value. When I read *Gambara* or *Le Chef-d'oeuvre inconnu*, I am interested in a story, and care little to know who tells it, where, and when; if I read *Facino Cane*, at no time can I overlook the presence of the narrator in the story he tells; if it is *La Maison Nucingen*, the author makes it his business to draw my attention to the person of the talker Bixiou and the group of listeners he addresses; if it is *L'Auberge rouge*, I will undoubtedly give less attention to the foreseeable unfolding of the story Hermann tells than to the reactions of a listener named Taillefer, for the narrative is on two levels, and the second–*where someone narrates*–is where most of the drama's excitement is.

This kind of effect is what we are going to look at under the category of *voice*: 'the mode of action', says Vendryés, 'of the verb considered for its relations to the subject'–the subject here being not only the person who carries out or submits to the action, but also the person (the same one or another) who reports it, and, if need be, all those people who participate, even though passively, in this narrating activity. We know that linguistics has taken its time in addressing the task of accounting for what Benveniste has called *subjectivity in language*,[2] that is, in passing from analysis of statements to analysis of relations between these statements and their generating instance–what today we call their *enunciating*. It seems that poetics is experiencing a comparable difficulty in approaching the generating instance of narrative discourse, an instance for which we have reserved the parallel term *narrating*. This difficulty is shown especially by a sort of hesitation, no doubt an unconscious one, to recognize and respect the autonomy of that instance, or even simply its specificity. On the one hand, as we have already noted, critics restrict questions of narrative enunciating to questions of 'point of view'; on the other hand they identify the narrating instance with the instance of 'writing', the narrator with the author, and the recipient of the narrative with the reader of the work:[3] a confusion that is perhaps legitimate in the case of a historical narrative or a real autobiography, but not when we are dealing with a narrative of fiction, where the role of narrator is itself fictive, even if assumed directly by the author, and where the supposed narrating situation can be very different from the act of writing (or of dictating) which refers to it. It is not the Abbé Prévost who tells the love of Manon and Des Grieux, it is not even the Marquis de Renoncourt, supposed author of the *Mémoires d'un homme de qualité*; it is Des Grieux himself, in an oral narrative where 'I' can designate only him, and where 'here' and 'now' refer to the spatio-temporal circumstances of that narrating and in no way to the circumstances of the writing of *Manon Lescaut* by its real author. And even the references in *Tristram Shandy* to the situation of writing speak to the (fictive) act of Tristram and not the (real) one of Sterne; but in a more subtle and also more radical way, the narrator of *Père Goriot* 'is' not Balzac, even if here and there he expresses Balzac's opinions, for this author-narrator is someone who 'knows' the Vauquer boardinghouse, its landlady and its lodgers, whereas all Balzac himself does is imagine them; and in this sense, of course, the narrating situation of a fictional account is *never* reduced to its situation of writing.

So it is this narrating instance that we have still to look at, according to the traces it has left–the traces it is considered to have left–in the narrative discourse it is considered to have produced. But it goes without saying that the instance does not necessarily remain identical and invariable in the course of a single narrative work. Most of *Manon Lescaut* is told by Des Grieux, but some pages revert to M. de Renoncourt; inversely, most of the *Odyssey* is told by 'Homer' but Books IX–XII revert to Ulysses; and the baroque novel, *The Thousand and One Nights*, and *Lord Jim* have accustomed us to much more complex situations.[4] Narrative analysis must obviously take charge of the study of these modifications–or of these permanences: for if it is remarkable that Ulysses' adventures are told by two different narrators, it is proper to find it just as noteworthy that the loves of Swann and of Marcel are told by the same narrator.

A narrating situation is, like any other, a complex whole within which analysis, or simply description, cannot *differentiate* except by ripping apart a tight web of connections among the narrating act, its protagonists, its spatio-temporal determinations, its relationship to the other narrating situations involved in the same narrative, etc. The demands of exposition constrain us to this unavoidable violence simply by the fact that critical discourse, like any other discourse, cannot say everything at once. Here again, therefore, we will look successively at elements of definition whose actual functioning is simultaneous: we will attach these elements, for the most part, to the categories of *time of the narrating, narrative level*, and *'person'* (that is, relations between the narrator–plus, should the occasion arise, his or their narratee[s][5]–and the story he tells).

Time of the Narrating

By a dissymmetry whose underlying reasons escape us but which is inscribed in the very structures of language (or at the very least of the main 'languages of civilization' of Western culture), I can very well tell a story without specifying the place where it happens, and whether this place is more or less distant from the place where I am telling it; nevertheless, it is almost impossible for me not to locate the story in time with respect to my narrating act, since I must necessarily tell the story in a present, past, or future tense.[6] This is perhaps why the temporal determinations of the narrating instance are manifestly more important than its spatial determinations. With the exception of second-degree narratings, whose setting is generally indicated by the diegetic context (Ulysses with the Phaeacians, the landlady of *Jacques le fataliste* in her inn), the narrating place is very rarely specified, and is almost never relevant:[7] we know more or less where Proust wrote the *Recherche du temps perdu*, but we are ignorant of where Marcel is considered to have produced the narrative of his life, and we scarcely think of worrying about it. On the other hand, it is very important to us to know, for example, how much time elapses between the first scene of the *Recherche* (the 'drama of going to bed') and the moment when it is evoked in these terms: 'Many years have passed since that night. The wall of the staircase, up which I had watched the light of his candle gradually climb, was long ago demolished'; for this temporal interval, and what fills it up and gives it life, is an essential element in the narrative's significance.

The chief temporal determination of the narrating instance is obviously its position relative to the story. It seems evident that the narrating can only be subsequent to what it tells, but this obviousness has been belied for many centuries by the existence of 'predictive' narrative[8] in its various forms (prophetic, apocalyptic, oracular, astrological, chiromantic, cartomantic, oneiromantic, etc.), whose origin is lost in the darkness of time–and has been belied also, at least since *Les Lauriers sont coupés*, by the use of narrative in the present tense. We must consider, further, that a past-tense narrating can to some extent be split up and inserted between the various moments of the story, much like a 'live' running commentary[9] – a common practice with correspondence and private diary, and therefore with the 'novel by letters' or the narrative in the form of a journal (*Wuthering Heights, Journal d' un curé de campagne*). It is therefore necessary, merely from the point of view of temporal position, to differentiate four types of narrating: *subsequent* (the classical position of the past-tense narrative, undoubtedly far and away the most frequent); *prior* (predictive narrative, generally in the future tense, but not prohibited from being conjugated in the present, like Jocabel's dream in *Moyse sauvé*); *simultaneous* (narrative in the present contemporaneous with the action); and *interpolated* (between the moments of the action).

The last type is *a priori* the most complex, since it involves a narrating with several instances, and since the story and the narrating can become entangled in such a way that the latter has an effect on the former. This is what happens particularly in the epistolary novel with several correspondents,[10] where, as we know, the letter is at the same time both a medium of the narrative and an element in the plot.[11] This type of narrating can also be the most delicate, indeed, the one most refractory to analysis, as for example when the journal form loosens up to result in a sort of monologue after the event, with an indefinite, even incoherent, temporal position: attentive readers of *L'Etranger* have not missed these uncertainties, which are one of the audacities – perhaps unintentional – of that narrative.[12] Finally, the extreme closeness of story to narrating produces here, most often,[13] a very subtle effect of friction (if I may call it that) between the slight temporal displacement of the narrative of events ('Here is what happened to me today') and the complete simultaneousness in the report of thoughts and feelings ('Here is what I think about it this evening'). The journal and the epistolary confidence constantly combine what in broadcasting language is called the live and the prerecorded account, the quasi-interior monologue and the account after the event. Here, the narrator is at one and the same time still the hero and already someone else: the events of the day are already in the past, and the 'point of view' may have been modified since then; the feelings of the evening or the next day are fully of the present, and here focalization through the narrator is at the same time focalization through the hero. Cécile Volanges writes to Mme. de Merteuil to tell her how she was seduced, last night, by Valmont, and to confide to her her remorse; the seduction scene is past, and with it the confusion that Cécile no longer feels, and can no longer even imagine; what remains is the shame, and a sort of stupor which is both incomprehension and discovery of oneself: 'What I reproach myself for most, and what, however, I must talk to you about, is that I am afraid I didn't defend myself as much as I could have. I don't know how that happened: surely I don't love M. de Valmont, very much the opposite; and there were moments when I acted as if I did love him . . . .'[14] The Cécile of yesterday, very near and already far off, is seen and spoken of by the Cécile of today. We have here two successive heroines (only) the second of whom is (also) the narrator and gives her point of view, the point of view – displaced just enough to create dissonance – of the immediate *post-event* future.[15] We know how the eighteenth-century novel, from *Pamela* to *Obermann*, exploited that narrative situation propitious to the most subtle and the most 'irritating' counterpoints: the situation of the tiniest temporal interval.

The third type (simultaneous narrating), by contrast, is in principle the simplest, since the rigorous simultaneousness of story and narrating eliminates any sort of interference or temporal game. We must observe, however, that the blending of the instances can function here in two opposite directions, according to whether the emphasis is put on the story or on the narrative discourse. A present-tense narrative which is 'behaviorist' in type and strictly of the moment can seem like the height of objectivity, since the last trace of enunciating that still subsisted in the Hemingway-style narrative (the mark of temporal interval between story and narrating, which the use of the preterite unavoidably comprises) now disappears in a total transparency of the narrative, which finally fades ways in favor of the story. That is how the works that come under the heading of the French 'new novel', and especially Robbe-Grillet's early novels,[16] have generally been received: 'objective literature', 'school of the look' – these designations express well the sense of the narrating's absolute transitivity which a generalized use of the present tense promotes. But inversely, if the emphasis rests on the narrating itself, as in narratives of 'interior monologue', the simultaneousness operates in favor of the discourse; and then it is the action that seems reduced to the condition of simple pretext, and ultimately abolished. This effect was already noticeable in Dujardin, and became more marked in a Beckett, a Claude Simon, a Roger Laporte. So it is as if use of the present tense, bringing the instances together, had the effect of unbalancing their equilibrium and allowing the whole of the narrative to tip, according to the slightest shifting of emphasis, either onto the side of the story or onto the side of the narrating, that is, the discourse. And the facility with which the French novel in recent years has passed from one extreme to the other perhaps illustrates this ambivalence and reversibility.[17]

The second type (prior narrating) has until now enjoyed a much smaller literary investment than the others, and certainly even novels of anticipation, from Wells to Bradbury – which nevertheless belong fully to the prophetic genre – almost always postdate their narrating instances, making them implicitly subsequent to their stories (which indeed illustrates the autonomy of this fictive instance with respect to the moment of actual writing). Predictive narrative hardly appears at all in the literary corpus except on the second level: examples, in Saint-Amant's *Moyse sauvé*, are Aaron's prophetic narrative (sixth part) and Jocabel's long premonitory dream (fourth, fifth, and sixth parts), both of which are connected with Moses' future. [18] The common characteristic of these second narratives is obviously that they are predictive in relation to the immediate narrating instance (Aaron, Jocabel's dream) but not in relation to the final instance (the implied author of *Moyse sauvé*, who explicitly identifies himself with Saint-Amant): clear examples of prediction after the event.

Subsequent narrating (the first type) is what presides over the immense majority of the narratives produced to this day. The use of a past tense is enough to make a narrative subsequent, although without indicating the temporal interval which separates the moment of the narrating from the moment of the story.[19] In classical 'third-person' narrative, this interval appears generally indeterminate, and the question irrelevant, the preterite marking a sort of ageless past:[20] the story can be dated, as it often is in Balzac, without the narrating being so.[21] It sometimes happens, however, that a relative contemporaneity of story time and narrating time is disclosed by the use of the present tense, either at the beginning, as in *Tom Jones*[22] or *Le Pére Goriot*,[23] or at the end , as in *Eugénie Grandet*[24] or *Madame Bovary*.[25] These effects of final convergence (the more striking of the two types) play on the fact that the very length of the story gradually lessens the interval separating it from the moment of the narrating. But the power of these final convergences results from their unexpected disclosure of a temporal isotopy (which, being temporal, is also to a certain extent diegetic) between the story and its narrator, an isotopy which until then was hidden (or, in the case of *Bovary*, long forgotten). In 'first-person'narrative, on the other hand, this isotopy is evident from the beginning, where the narrator is presented right away as a character in the story, and where the final convergence is the rule,[26] in accordance with a mode that the last paragraph of *Robinson Crusoe* can furnish us with a paradigm of: 'And here, resolving to harrass my self no more, I am preparing for a longer Journey than all these, having liv'd 72 Years, a Life of infinite Variety, and learn'd sufficiently to know the Value of Retirement, and the Blessing of ending our Days in Peace.[27] No dramatic effect here, unless the final situation should itself be a violent denouement, as an *Double Indemnity*, in which the hero writes the last line of his confession-narrative before slipping with his accomplice into the ocean where a shark awaits them: 'I didn't hear the stateroom door open, but she's beside me now while I'm writing. I can feel her./The moon.[28]

In order for the story to overtake the narrating in this way, the duration of the latter must of course not exceed the duration of the former. Take Tristram's comic aporia: in one year of writing having succeeded in telling only the first day of his life, he observes that he has gotten 364 days behind, that he has therefore moved backward rather than forward, and that, living 364 times faster than he writes, it follows that the more he writes the more there remains for him to write; that, in short, his undertaking is hopeless.[29] Faultless reasoning, whose premises are not at all absurd. Telling takes time (Scheherazade's life hangs by that one thread), and when a novelist puts on his stage an oral narrating in the second degree, he rarely fails to take that into account: many things happen at the inn while the landlady of *Jacques* tells the story of the Marquis des Arcis, and the first part of *Manon Lescaut* ends with the remark that since the Chevalier spent more than an hour on his tale, he certainly needs supper in order to 'get a little rest'. We have a few reasons to think that Prévost, for his part, spent much more than an hour writing those some one-hundred pages, and we know, for example, that Flaubert needed almost five years to write *Madame Bovary*. Nevertheless – and this is finally very odd – the fictive narrating of that narrative, as with almost all the novels in the world except *Tristram Shandy*, is considered to have no duration; or more exactly, everything takes place as if the question of its duration had no relevance. One of the fictions of literary narrating–perhaps the most powerful one, because it passes unnoticed, so to speak–is that the narrating involves an instantaneous action, without a temporal dimension. Sometimes it is dated, but it is never measured: we know that M. Homais has just received the cross of the Legion of Honor at the moment when the narrator writes that last sentence, but we do not know what was happening while the narrator was writing his first one. Indeed, we even know that this question is absurd: nothing is held to separate those two moments of the narrating instance except the atemporal space of the narrative as text. Contrary to simultaneous or interpolated narrating, which exist through their duration and the relations between that duration and the story's subsequent narrating exists through this paradox: it possesses at the same time a temporal situation (with respect to the past story) and an atemporal essence (since it has no duration proper).[30] Like Proustian reminiscence, it is rapture, 'a moment brief as a flash of lightning', a miraculous syncope, 'a minute freed from the order of [T]ime'.[31]

The narrating instance of the *Recherche* obviously corresponds to this last type. We know that Proust spent more than ten years writing his novel, but Marcel's act of narrating bears no mark of duration, or of division: it is instantaneous. The narrator's present, which on almost every page we find mingled with the hero's various pasts, is a single moment without progression. Marcel Muller thought he found in Germaine Brée the hypothesis of a double narrating instance–before and after the final revelation–but this hypothesis has no basis, and in fact all I see in Germaine Brée is an improper (although common) use of 'narrator' for *hero*, which perhaps led Muller into error on that point.[32] As for the feelings expressed on the final pages of *Swann*, which we know do not correspond to the narrator's final conviction, Muller himself shows very well that they do not at all prove the existence of a narrating instance poir to the revelation;[33] on the contrary, the letter to Jacques Rivière quoted above[34] shows that Proust was anxious to tune the narrator's discourse to the hero's 'errors', and thus to impute to the narrator a belief not his own, in order to avoid disclosing his own mind too early. Even the narrative Marcel produces after the Guermantes soirée, the narrative of his beginnings as a writer (seclusion, rough drafts, first reactions of readers), which necessarily takes into account the length of writing ('like him too, . . . I had something to write. But my task was longer than his, my words had to reach more than a single person. My task was long. By day, the most I could hope for was to try to sleep. If I worked, it would be only at night. But I should need many nights, a hundred perhaps, or even a thousand')[35] and the interrupting fear of death–even this narrative does not gainsay the fictive instantaneousness of its narrating: for the book Marcel then begins to write *in the story* cannot legitimately be identified with the one Marcel has then almost finished writing *as narrative* – and which is the *Recherche* itself. Writing the fictive book, which is the subject of the narrative, is, like writing every book, a 'task [that] was long'. But the actual book the narrative-book, does not have knowledge of its own 'length': it does away with its own duration.

The present of Proustian narrating – from 1909 to 1922 – corresponds to many of the 'presents' of the writing, and we know that almost a third of the book – including, as it happens, the final pages – was written by 1913. The fictive moment of narrating has thus *in fact* shifted in the course of the real writing; today it is no longer what it was in 1913, at the moment when Proust thought his work concluded for the Grasset edition. Therefore the temporal intervals he had in mind – and wanted to signify – when he wrote, for example apropos of the bedtime scene, 'Many years have passed since that night', or apropos of the resurrection of Combray by the madeleine, 'I can measure the resistance, I can hear the echo of great spaces traversed' – these spaces have increased by more than ten years simply because the story's time has lengthened: the signified of these sentences is no longer the same. Whence certain irreducible contradictions like this one: the narrator's *today* is obviously, for us, later than the war, but the 'Paris today' of the last pages of *Swann* remains in its historical determinations (its referential content) a prewar Paris, as it was seen and described in its better days. The novelistic *signified* (the moment of the narrating) has become something like 1925, but the historical *referent*, which corresponds to the moment of the writing, did not keep pace and continues to say: 1913. Narrative analysis must register these shifts – and the resulting discordances – as effects of the actual genesis of the work; but in the end analysis can look at the narrating instance only as it is given in the final state of the text, as a single moment without duration, necessarily placed several years after the last 'scene', therefore after the war, and even, as we have seen,[36] after the death of Marcel Proust. This paradox, let us remember, is not one: Marcel is not Proust, and nothing requires him to die with Proust. What is required, on the other hand, is that Marcel spend 'many years' after 1916 in a clinic, which necessarily puts his return to Paris and the Guermantes matinée in 1921 at the earliest, and the meeting with an Odette 'showing signs of senility' in 1923.[37] That consequence is a must.

Between this single narrating instant and the different moments of the story, the interval is necessarily variable. If 'many years' have elapsed since the bedtime scene in Combray, it is only 'of late' that the narrator has again begun to hear his childhood sobs, and the interval separating the narrating instant from the Guermantes matinée is obviously smaller than the interval separating narrating instant and the hero's first arrival in Balbec. The system of language, the uniform use of the past tense, does not allow this gradual shrinking to be imprinted in the very texture of the narrative discourse, but we have seen that to a certain extent Proust had succeeded in making it felt, by modifications in the temporal pacing of the narrative:

gradual disappearance of the iterative, lengthening of the singulative scenes, increasing discontinuity, accentuation of the rhythm–as if the story time were tending to dilate and make itself more and more conspicuous while drawing near its end, *which is also its origin.*

According to what we have already seen to be the common practice of 'autobiographical' narrating, we could expect to see the narrative bring its hero to the point where the narrator awaits him, in order that these two hypostases might meet and finally merge. People have sometimes, a little quickly, claimed that this is what happens.[38] In fact, as Marcel Muller well notes, 'between the day of the reception at the Princess's and the day when the Narrator recounts that reception there extends a whole era which maintains a gap between the Hero and the Narrator, a gap that cannot be bridged: the verbal forms in the conclusion of the *Temps retrouvé* are all in the past tense.[39] The narrator brings his hero's story–his own story–precisely to the point when, as Jean Rousset says, 'the hero is about to become the narrator';[40] I would say rather, *is beginning to become* the narrator, since he actually starts in on his writing. Muller writes that 'if the Hero overtakes the Narrator, it is like an asymptote: the interval separating them approaches zero, but will never reach it', but his image connotes a Sterneian play on the two durations that does not in fact exist in Proust. There is simply the narrative's halt at the point when the hero has discovered the truth and the meaning of his life: at the point, therefore, when this 'story of a vocation'–which let us remember, is the avowed subject of Proustian narrative–comes to an end. The rest, whose outcome is already known to us by the very novel that concludes here, no longer belongs to the 'vocation' but to the effort that follows it up, and must therefore be only sketched in. The subject of the *Recherche* is indeed 'Marcel becomes a writer', not 'Marcel the writer': the *Recherche* remains a novel of development, and to see it as a 'novel about the novelist', like the *Faux Monnayeurs* [*The Counterfeiters*], would be to distort its intentions and above all to violate its meaning; it is a novel about the future novelist. 'The continuation', Hegel said, precisely apropos of the Bildungsroman, 'no longer has anything novelistic about it. ' Proust probably would have been glad to apply that formulation to his own narrative: what is novelistic is the quest, the *search* [*recherche*], which ends at the discovery (the revelation), not at the use to which that discovery will afterward be put. The final discovery of the truth, the late encounter with the vocation, like the happiness of lovers reunited, can be only a denouement, not an interim stopping place; and in this sense, the subject of the *Recherche* is indeed a traditional subject. So it is necessary that the narrative be interrupted before the hero overtakes the narrator; it is inconceivable for them both together to write: The End. The narrator's last sentence is when– is *that*–the hero finally reaches his first. The interval between the end of the story and the moment of the narrating is therefore the time it takes the hero to write this book, which is and is not the book the narrator, in his turn, reveals to us in a moment brief as a flash of lightning.

Notes

1 On this subject see Gérard Genette, *Figures II*, pp. 61–9.
2 Benveniste, 'Subjectivity in Language', *Problems*, pp. 223–30.
3 For example Todorov, 'Les Catégories du récit littéraire', pp. 146–7
4 On the *Thousand and One Nights*, see Todorov, 'Narrative-Men', in *Poetics of Prose*: 'The record [for embedding] seems to be held by the narrative which offers us the story of the bloody chest. Here

    Scheherazade tells that
        Jaafer tells that
            the tailor tells that
                the barber tells that
                    his brother (and he has six brothers) tells that . . .

The last story is a story to the fifth degree' (p. 71). But the term 'embedding' does not do justice to the fact precisely that each of these stories is at a higher 'degree' than the preceding one, since its narrator is a character in the preceding one; for stories can also be 'embedded' at the same level, simply by digression, without any shift in the narrating instance: see Jacques's parentheses in the *Fataliste*.
5 This is what I will call the receiver of the narrative, patterned after the contrast between *sender* and *receiver* proposed by A.J. Greimas (*Sémantique structurale* [Paris, 1966], p. 177).
6 Certain uses of the present tense do indeed connote temporal indefiniteness (and not simultaneousness between story and narrating), but curiously they seem reserved for very particular forms of narrative (joke, riddle, scientific problem or experiment, plot summary) and literature does not have much investment in them. The case of the 'narrative present' with preterite value is also different.
7 It could be, but for reasons which are not exactly spatial in kind: for a 'first-person' narrative to be produced in prison, on a hospital bed, in a psychiatric institution, can constitute a decisive element of advance notice about the denouement.
8 I borrow the term 'predictive' from Todorov, *Grammaire du Décaméron* (The Hague, 1969), p. 48, to designate any kind of narrative where the narrating precedes the story.
9 Radio or television reporting is obviously the most perfectly live form of this kind of narrative, where the narrating follows so closely on the action that it can be considered practically simultaneous, whence the use of the present tense. We find a curious literary use of simultaneous narrative in Chapter 29 of *Ivanhoe* where Rebecca is telling the wounded Ivanhoe all about the battle taking place at the foot of the castle, a battle she is following from the window.
10 On the typology of epistolary novels according to the number of correspondents, see Rousset, 'Une forme littéraire: le roman par lettres' *Forme et signification*, and Romberg, *Studies*, pp. 51 ff.
11 An example is when, in *Les Liaisons dangereuses*, Mme. de Volanges discovers Danceny's letters in her daughter's writing desk – a discovery whose consequences Danceny is notified of in letter 62, typically 'performative'. Cf. Todorov, *Littérature et signification* (Paris. 1967). pp. 44–6.
12 See B.T. Fitch, *Narrateur et narration dans 'l'Etranger' d' Albert Camus*, 2d rev. ed. (Paris, 1968) pp. 12–26.
13 But there also exist *delayed* forms of journal narrating: for example, the 'first notebook' of the *Symphonie pastorale*, or the complex counterpoint of *L'Emploi du temps*.
14 Letter 97.
15 Compare letter 48, from Valmont to Tourvel, written in Emilie's bed, 'live' and, if I may say so, *at the event*.

16 All written in the present tense except *Le Voyeur*, whose temporal system, as we know, is more complex.

17 An even more striking illustration is *La Jalousie*, which can be read *ad libitum* in the objectivist mode with no jealous person in the narrating, or purely as the interior monologue of a husband spying on his wife and imagining her adventures. Indeed, when this work was published in 1959 it played a pivotal role.

18 See my *Figures II*, pp. 210–11.

19 With the exception of the passé composé, which in French connotes relative closeness: 'The perfect creates a living connection between the past event and the present in which its evocation takes place. It is the tense for the one who relates the facts as a witness, as a participant; it is thus also the tense that will be chosen by whoever wishes to make the reported event ring vividly in our ears and to link it to the present' (Benveniste, 'The Correlations of Tense in the French Verb', *Problems*, p. 210). *L'Etranger*, of course, owes a great deal to the use of this tense.

20 Käte Hamburger (*The Logic of Literature*, trans. Marilynn J. Rose 2nd edn. [Bloomington, Ind., 1973]) has gone so far as to deny any temporal value to the 'epic preterite'. In this extreme and strongly contested position there is a certain hyperbolic truth.

21 On the other hand, Stendhal does like to date, and more precisely to antedate, for reasons of political prudence, the narrating instance of his novels: *Le Rouge* (written in 1829–1830) at 1827, *La Chartreuse* (written in 1839) at 1830.

22 'In that Part of the western Division of this Kingdom, which is commonly called *Somersetshire, there lately lived (and perhaps lives still)* a Gentleman whose Name was *Allworthy*' (*Tom Jones*, Book I, chap. 2 [Norton, p. 27]).

23 'Madame Vauquer, whose maiden name was De Conflans, *is* an elderly woman who for forty years *has* kept, in Paris, a family boardinghouse' (*Père Goriot*, trans. J.M. Sedgwick [New York: Rinehart, 1950], p. 1).

24 'Her face *is* very pale and quiet now, and there *is* a tinge of sadness in the low tones of her voice. She *has* simple manners' (*Eugénie Grandet*, trans. E Marriage [Philadelphia: Gebbie, 1899], p. 223)

25 'The devil himself *doesn't have* a greater following than [M. Homais]: the authorities *treat* him considerately, and public opinion *is* on his side. He *has just been awarded* the cross of the Legion of Honor' (*Madame Bovary*, trans. F. Steegmuller [New York: Random House, 1957,], p. 396). Let us remember that the opening pages (*'we were* in study-hull . . .' [Steegmuller, p. 3]) already indicate that the narrator is contemporary with the hero, and is even one of his fellow students.

26 The Spanish picaresque seems to form a notable exception to this 'rule', at any rate *Lazarillo*, which ends in suspense ('It was the time of my prosperity, and I was at the height of all good fortune'). *Guzman* and *Buscon* also, but while promising a continuation and end, which will not come.

27 *Robinson Crusoe* (Oxford: Blackwell, 1928), III, 220. Or, in a more ironic mode, *Gil Blas*: 'It is three years since then, my friend the reader, that I have been leading a delightful life with such dear people. As a crowning satisfaction, heaven was pleased to bestow on me two children, whose upbringing will become the pastime of my old age, and whose father I dutifully think I am.'

28 James M. Cain, *Double Indemnity*, in *Cain X3* (New York: Knopf, 1969), p. 465

29 Sterne, *Tristram Shandy*, Book IV, Chap. 13.

30 Temporal indications of the kind 'we have *already* said' and 'we will see *later*', etc., do not in fact refer to the temporality of the narrating, but to the space of the text (= *we have said above, we will see further on* . . .) and to the temporality of reading.

31 RH II, 1001 and 1002/P III, 872 and 873.

32 Muller, p. 45; Germaine Brée, *Marcel Proust and Deliverance from Time*, trans. C. J. Richards and A. D. Truitt, 2nd edn. (New Brunswick, N J, 1969), pp. 19–20.
33 Muller, p. 46
34 Pp. 199–200.
35 RH II, 1136/P III, 1043.
36 P. 91
37 This episode takes place (RH II, 1063/P III, 951) 'Less than three years'–thus more than two years–after the Guermantes matinée.
38 In particular Louis Martin-Chauffier: 'As in memoirs, the man who writes and the man whose life we see are distinct in time, but tend to catch up with each other in the long run; they are moving towards the day when the progress of the hero through his life stops at the table, where the narrator, no longer separated from him in time nor tied to him by memory, invites him to sit down beside him so that both together may write: the End' ('Proust and the Double I', *Partisan Review*, 16 [October 1949], 1012).
39 Muller, pp. 49–50. Let us remember, however, that certain anticipations (like the last meeting with Odette) cover a part of that 'era'.
40 Rousset, p. 144.

8 | Roland Barthes,

'To Write: An Intransitive Verb?', in R. Macksey and E. Donato, ed. *The Structuralist Controversy* (1966), pp. 134 – 45

To Write: An Intransitive Verb?[1]

For centuries Western culture conceived of literature not as we do today, through a study of works, authors, and schools, but through a genuine theory of language. This theory, whose name, *rhetoric*, came to it from antiquity, reigned in the Western world from Gorgias to the Renaissance – for nearly two thousand years. Threatened as early as the sixteenth century by the advent of modern rationalism, rhetoric was completely ruined when rationalism was transformed into positivism at the end of the nineteenth century. At that point there was no longer any common ground of thought between literature and language: literature no longer regarded itself as language except in the works of a few pioneers such as Mallarmé, and linguistics claimed very few rights over literature, these being [limited to] a secondary philological discipline of uncertain status – stylistics.

As we know, this situation is changing, and it seems to me that it is in part to take cognizance of this change that we are assembled here: literature and language are in the process of finding each other again. The factors of this *rapprochement* are diverse and complex; I shall cite the most obvious.

On one hand, certain writers since Mallarmé, such as Proust and Joyce, have undertaken a radical exploration of writing, making of their work a search for the total Book. On the other hand, linguistics itself, principally following the impetus of Roman Jakobson, has developed to include within its scope the poetic, or the order of effects linked to the message and not to its referent. Therefore, in my view, we have today a new perspective of consideration which, I would like to emphasize, is common to literature and linguistics, to the creator and the critic, whose tasks until now completely self-contained, are beginning to inter-relate, perhaps even to merge. This is at least true for certain writers whose work is becoming more and more a critique of language. It is in this perspective that I would like to place the following observations (of a prospective and not of a conclusive nature) indicating how the activity of writing can be expressed [énoncée] today with the help of certain linguistic categories.

This new union of literature and linguistics, of which I have just spoken, could be called, provisionally and for lack of a better name, *semio-criticism*, since it implies that writing is a system of signs. Semio-criticism is not to be identified with stylistics, even in a new form; it is much more than stylistics. It has a much broader perspective; its object is constituted not by simple accidents of form, but by the very relationships between the writer [*scripteur, not écrivain*] and language. This perspective does not imply a lack of interest in language but, on the contrary, a continual return to the 'truths' – provisional though they may be – of linguistic anthropology. I will recall certain of these truths because they still have a power of challenge in respect to a certain current idea of literature.

One of the teachings of contemporary linguistics is that there is no archaic language, or at the very least that there is no connection between simplicity and the age of a language: ancient languages can be just as complete and as complex as recent languages; there is no progressive history of languages. Therefore, when we try to find certain fundamental categories of language in modern writing, we are not claiming to reveal a certain archaism of the 'psyche'; we are not saying that the writer is returning to the origin of language, but that language is the origin for him.

A second principle, particularly important in regard to literature, is that language cannot be considered as a simple instrument, whether utilitarian or decorative, of thought. Man does not exist prior to language, either as a species or as an individual. We never find a state where man is separated from language, which he then creates in order to 'express' what is taking place within him: it is language which teaches the definition of man, not the reverse.

Moreover, from a methodological point of view, linguistics accustoms us to a new type of objectivity. The objectivity that has been required in the human sciences up until now is an objectivity of the given, a total acceptance of the given. Linguistics suggests, on the one hand, that we distinguish levels of analysis and that we describe the distinctive elements of each of these levels; in short, that we establish the distinctness of the fact and not the fact itself. On the other hand, linguistics asks us to recognize that unlike physical and biological facts, cultural facts are always double, that they refer us to something else. As Benveniste remarked, the discovery of the 'duplicity' of language gives Saussure's reflection all its value.[2]

These few preliminaries are contained in one final proposition which justifies all semio-critical research. We see culture more and more as a general system of symbols, governed by the same operations. There is unity in this symbolic field: culture, in all its aspects, is a language. Therefore it is possible today to anticipate the creation of a single, unified science of culture, which will depend on diverse disciplines, all devoted to analyzing, on different levels of description, culture as language. Of course semio-criticism will be only a part of this science, or rather of this discourse on culture. I feel authorized by this unity of the human symbolic field to work on a postulate, which I shall call a postulate of *homology*: the structure of the sentence, the object of linguistics, is found again, homologically, in the structure of works. Discourse is not simply an adding together of sentences: it is, itself, one great sentence. In terms of this hypothesis I would like to confront certain categories of language with the situation of the writer in relation to his writing.

The first of these categories is *temporality*. I think we can all agree that there is a linguistic temporality. This specific time of language is equally different from physical time and from what Benveniste calls 'chronicle time' [*temps chronique*], that is, calendar time.[3] Linguistic time finds quite different expression and *découpages* in various languages. For example, since we are going to be interested in the analysis of myths, many languages have a particular past tense of the verb to indicate the past time of myth. Once thing is sure: linguistic time always has its primary center [*centre générateur*] in the present of the statement [*énonciation*]. This leads us to ask whether there is, homological to linguistic time, a specific time of discourse. On this point we may take Benveniste's explanation that many languages, especially in the Indo-European group, have a double system of time. The first temporal system is that of the discourse itself, which is adapted to the temporality of the speaker [*énonciateur*] and for which the *énonciation* is always the point of origin [*moment générateur*]. The second is the system of history or of narrative, which is adapted to the recounting of past events without any intervention by the speaker and which is consequently deprived of present and future (except periphrastically). The specific tense of this second system is the aorist or its equivalent, such as our *passé simple* or the preterite. This tense (the aorist) is precisely the only one missing from the temporal system of discourse. Naturally the existence of this a-personal system does not contradict the essentially logocentric nature of linguistic time that I have just affirmed. The second system simply lacks the characteristics of the first.

Understood thus as the opposition of two radically different systems, temporality does not have the morphological mark of verbs for its only sign; it is marked by all the signs, often very indirect, which refer either to the a-personal tense of the event or to the personal tense of the locutor. The opposition in its fullness permits us first to account for some pure, or we might say classic, cases: a popular story and the history of France retold in our manuals are purely aoristic narratives; on the contrary, Camus' *L'Etranger*, written in the compound past, is not only a perfect form of autobiography (that of the narrator, and not of the author) but, what is more valuable, it permits us to understand better the apparently anomalous cases.[4] Being a historian, Michelet made all historical time pivot around a point of discourse with which he identified himself – the Revolution. His history is a narrative without the aorist, even if the simple past abounds in it; inversely, the preterite can very well serve to signify not the objective *récit*, but the depersonalisation of the discourse – a phenomenon which is the object of the most lively research in today's literature.

What I would like to add to this linguistic analysis, which comes from Benveniste, is that the distinction between the temporal system of discourse and the temporal system of history is not at all the same distinction as is traditionally made between objective discourse and subjective discourse. For the relationship between the speaker [*énonciateur*] and the referent on the one hand and that between the speaker and his utterance [*énonciation*] on the other hand are not to be confused, and it is only the second relationship which determines the temporal system of discourse.

It seems to me that these facts of language were not readily perceptible so long as literature pretended to be a transparent expression of either objective calendar time or of psychological subjectivity, that is to say, as long as literature maintained a totalitarian ideology of the referent, or more commonly speaking, as long as literature was realistic. Today, however, the literature of which I speak is discovering fundamental subtleties relative to temporality. In reading certain writers who are engaged in this type of exploration we sense that what is recounted in the aorist doesn't seem at all immersed in the past, in what has taken place, but simply in the impersonal [*la non-personne*], which is neither history, nor discursive information [*la science*], and even less the one of anonymous writing. (The *one* is dominated by the indefinite and not by the indefinite and not by the absence of person. I would even say that the pronoun *one* is marked in relation to person, while, paradoxically, *he* is not.) At the other extreme of the experience of discourse, the present-day writer can no longer content himself with expressing his own present, according to a lyrical plan for example. He must learn to distinguish between the present of the speaker, which is grounded on a psychological fullness, and the present of what is spoken [*la locution*] which is mobile and in which the event and the writing become absolutely coincidental. Thus literature, at least in some of its pursuits, seems to me to be following the same path as linguistics when, along with Gustave Guillaume (a linguist not presently in fashion but who may become so again), it concerns itself with operative time and the time proper to the utterance [*énonciation*] itself.[5]

A second grammatical category which is equally important in linguistics and in literature is that of *person*. Taking linguists and especially Benveniste as my basis once more, I would like to recall that person (in the grammatical sense of the term) certainly seems to be a universal of language, linked to the anthropology of language. Every language, as Benveniste has shown, organizes person into two broad pairs of opposites: a correlation of personality which opposes person (*I or thou*) to non-person, which is *il* (*he or it*), the sign of absence; and, within this first opposing pair, a correlation of subjectivity (once again in the grammatical sense) which opposes two persons, the *I* and the *non-I* (the *thou*). For our purposes we must, along with Benveniste, make three observations. First, the polarity of persons, a fundamental condition of language, is nevertheless peculiar and enigmatic, for this polarity involves neither equality nor symmetry: *I* always has a position of transcendence with respect to *thou*, I being interior to the *énoncé* and *thou* remaining exterior to it; however, *I* and *thou* are reversible–*I* can always become *thou* and vice versa. This is not true of the non-person (*he or it*) which can never reverse itself into person or vice versa. The second observation is that the linguistic *I* can and must be defined in a strictly a-psychological way: *I* is nothing other than 'la personne qui énonce la présente instance de discours contenant l'instance linguistique *je*' (Benveniste ['the person who utters the present instance of discourse containing the linguistic instance *I*']).[6] The last remark is that the *he* or the non-person never reflects the instance of discourse; *he* is situated outside of it. We must give its full weight to Benveniste's recommendation not to represent the *he* as a more or less diminished or removed person: *he* is absolutely non-person, marked by the absence of what specifically constitutes, linguistically, the *I* and the *thou*.

The linguistic explanation provides several suggestions for an analysis of literary discourse. First, whatever varied and clever forms person may take in passing from the level of the sentence to that of discourse, the discourse of the literary work is rigorously submitted to a double system of person and non-person. This fact may be obscured because classical discourse (in a broad sense) to which we are habituated is a mixed discourse which alternates–very quickly, sometimes within the same sentence–personal and a-personal *énonciation*, through a complex play of pronouns and descriptive verbs. In this type of classical or bourgeois story the mixture of person and non-person produces a sort of ambiguous consciousness which succeeds in keeping the personal quality of what is stated while, however, continuously breaking the participation of the *énonciateur* in the *énoncé*.

Many novelistic utterances, written with *he* (in the third person), are nevertheless discourses of the *person* each time that the contents of the statement depend on its subject. If in a novel we read '*the tinkling of the ice against the glass seemed to give Bond a sudden inspiration*', it is certain that the subject of the statement cannot be Bond himself–not because the sentence is written in the third person, since Bond could very well express himself through a *he*, but because of the verb *seem* which becomes a mark of the absence of person. Nevertheless, in spite of the diversity and often even the ruse of the narrative signs of the person, there is never but one sole and great opposition in the discourse, that of the person and the non-person; every narrative or fragment of a narrative is obliged to join one or the other of these extremes. How can we determine this division? In 're-writing' the discourse. If we can translate the *he* into *I* without changing anything else in the utterance, the discourse is in fact personal. In the sentence which we have cited, this transformation is impossible; we cannot say *'the tinkling of the ice seemed to give me a sudden inspiration'*. The sentence is impersonal. Starting from there, we catch a glimpse of how the discourse of the traditional novel is made; on the one hand it alternates the personal and the impersonal very rapidly, often even in the course of the same sentence, so as to produce, if we can speak thus, a proprietary consciousness which retains the mastery of what it states without participating in it; and on the other hand, in this type of novel, or rather, according to our perspective, in this type of discourse, when the narrator is explicitly an *I* (which has happened many times) there is confusion between the subject of the discourse and the subject of the reported action, as if – and this is a common belief – he who is speaking today were the same as he who acted yesterday. It is as if there were a continuity of the referent and the utterance through the person, as if the declaring were only a docile servant of the referent.

Now if we return to the linguistic definition of the first person (the one who says 'I' in the present instance of discourse), we may better understand the effort of certain contemporary writers (in France I think of Philippe Sollers's latest novel *Drame*) when they try to distinguish, at the level of the story, psychological person and the author of the writing. When a narrator recounts what has happened to him, the *I* who recounts is no longer the same *I* as the one that is recounted. In other words – and it seems to me that this is seen more and more clearly – the *I* of discourse can no longer be a place where a previously stored-up person is innocently restored. Absolute recourse to the instance of discourse to determine person is termed *nyn-egocentrism* by Damourette and Pichon (*nyn* from the Greek *nun*, 'now').[7] Robbe-Grillet's novel *Dans le labyrinthe* begins with an admirable declaration of nyn-egocentrism: 'Je suis seul ici maintenant.' [I am alone here now.][8] This recourse, imperfectly as it may still be practiced, seems to be a weapon against the general 'bad faith' of discourse which would make literary form simply the expression of an inferiority constituted previous to and outside of language.

To end this discussion of person, I would like to recall that in the process of communication the course of the *I* is not homogenous. For example, when I use [*libére*] the sign, *I*, I refer to myself inasmuch as I am talking: here there is an act which is always new, even if it is repeated, an act whose sense is always new. However, arriving at its destination, this sign is received by my interlocutor as a stable sign, product of a complete code whose contents are recurrent. In other words, the *I* of the one who writes *I* is not the same as the *I* which is read by *thou*. This fundamental dissymmetry of language, linguistically explained by Jespersen and then by Jakobson under the name of 'shifter' [*embrayeur*] or an overlapping of message and code, seems to be finally beginning to trouble literature in showing it that intersubjectivity, or rather interlocution, cannot be accomplished simply by wishing, but only by a deep, patient, and often circuitous descent into the labyrinths of meaning.[9]

There remains one last grammatical notion which can, in my opinion, further elucidate the activity of writing at its centre, since it concerns the verb *to write* itself. It would be interesting to know at what point the verb *to write* began to be used in an apparently intransitive manner, the writer being no longer one who writes *something*, but one who writes, absolutely. (How often now we hear in conversations, at least in more or less intellectual circles: 'What is he doing?' – 'He's writing.') This passage from the verb *to write*, transitive, to the verb *to write*, apparently intransitive, is certainly the sign of an important change in mentality. But is it really a question of intransitivity? No writer, whatever age he belongs to, can fail to realise that he always writes *something:* one might even say that it was paradoxically at the moment when the verb *to write* appeared to become intransitive that its object, the book or the text, took on a particular importance. It is not, therefore, in spite of the appearances, on the side of intransitivity that we must look for the definition of the modern verb *to write*. Another linguistic notion will perhaps give us the key: that of *diathesis*, or, as it is called in classical grammars, *voice* (active, passive, middle). Diathesis designates the way in which the subject of the verb is affected by the action [*procès*]; this is obvious for the passive (if I say 'I am beaten', it is quite obvious that I am profoundly affected by the action of the verb *to beat*). And yet linguists tell us that, at least in Indo-European, the diathetical opposition is actually not between the active and the passive, but between the active and the middle. According to the classic example, given by Meillet and Benveniste, the verb *to sacrifice* (ritually) is active if the priest sacrifices the victim in my place for me, and it is middle voice if, taking the knife from the priest's hands, I make the sacrifice for myself.[10] In the case of the active, the action is accomplished outside the subject, because, although the priest makes the sacrifice, he is not affected by it. In the case of the middle voice, on the contrary, the subject affects himself in acting; he always remains inside the action, even if an object is involved. The middle voice does not, therefore, exclude transitivity. Thus defined, the middle voice corresponds exactly to the state of the verb *to write*: today to write is to make oneself the center of the action of speech [*parole*]; it is to effect writing in being affected oneself; it is to leave the writer [*scripteur*] inside the writing, not as a psychological subject (the Indo-European priest could very well overflow with subjectivity in actively sacrificing for his client), but as the agent of the action.

I think the diathetical analysis of the modern verb *to write*, which I have just tried to show a verb of middle voice, can be carried even further. You know that in French – for I am obliged to refer to strictly French examples – certain verbs have an active meaning in the simple form, for example, *aller, arriver, rentrer, sortir* [to go, to arrive, to return, to go out], but, curiously, these active verbs take the passive auxiliary, the verb *être* [to be] in the forms of *the passé composé*. Instead of saying *j'ai allé*, we say *je suis allé, je suis sorti, je suis arrivé, je suis rentré*, etc. To explain this bifurcation peculiar to the middle voice, Guillaume distinguishes between two *passés composés*. The first, which he calls *diriment*, 'separated', is a *passé composé* with the auxiliary *avoir* [to have]; this tense supposes an interruption of the action due to the initiative of the speaker. Take for example the verb *marcher* [to walk], an entirely commonplace active verb: '*je marche; je m'arrête de marcher; j'ai marché* [I walk; I stop walking (by my own initiative); I have walked]– this is the *passé composé diriment*. The other *passé composé* that he calls *intégrant* is constructed with the verb *être* [to be]; it designates a sort of semantic entity which cannot be delivered by the simple initiative of the subject. '*Je suis sorti*' or '*il est mort*' ['I went out' or 'he died'] (for I can't say 'I am dead') never refer to an interruption that would be at all like the *diriment* of the going out or the dying. I believe that this is an important opposition, for we see very well that the verb *to write* was traditionally an active verb and that its past tense is still today, formally a *diriment* past: '*j'écris un livre; je le termine; je l'ai écrit.*' [I write a book; I end it; I have written it.] But in our literature, it seems to me, the verb is changing states, if not form, and the verb *to write* is becoming a middle verb with an *intégrant* past. This is true inasmuch as the modern verb *to write* is becoming a sort of indivisible semantic entity. So that if language followed literature–which, for once perhaps, has the lead–I would say that we should no longer say today '*j'ai écrit*' but, rather, '*je suis écrit*', just as we say '*je suis né, il est mort, elle est éclose.*' There is no passive idea in these expressions, in spite of the verb *to be*, for it is impossible to transform '*je suis écrit*' (without forcing things, and supposing that I dare to use this expression at all) into '*on m'a écrit*' ['I have been written' or 'somebody wrote me']. It is my opinion that in the middle verb *to write* the distance between the writer and the language diminishes asymptotically. We could even say that it is subjective writings, like romantic writing, which are active, because in them the agent is not interior but *anterior* to the process of writing. The one who writes here does not write for himself, but, as if by proxy, for a person who is exterior and antecedent (even if they both have the same name). In the modern verb of middle voice *to write*, however, the subject is immediately contemporary with the writing, being effected and affected by it. The case of the Proustian narrator is exemplary: he exists only in writing.

These remarks suggest that the central problem of modern writing exactly coincides with what we could call the problematic of the verb in linguistics; just as temporality, person, and diathesis define the positional field of the subject, so modern literature is trying, through various experiments, to establish a new status in writing for the agent of writing. The meaning or the goal of this effort is to substitute the instance of discourse for the instance of reality (or of the referent), which has been, and still is, a mythical 'alibi' dominating the idea of literature. The field of the writer is nothing but writing itself, not as the pure 'form' conceived by an aesthetic of art for art's sake, but, much more radically, as the only area [*espace*] for the one who writes.

It seems to me to be necessary to remind those who might be tempted to accuse this kind of inquiry of solipsism, formalism, or, inversely, of scientism, that in returning to the fundamental categories of language, such as person, tense, and voice, we place ourselves at the very heart of a problematic of *inter* locution. For these categories are precisely those in which we may examine the relationships between the *je* and that which is deprived of the mark of *je*. Inasmuch as person, tense, and voice imply those remarkable linguistic beings – the 'shifters' – they oblige us to conceive language and discourse no longer in terms of an instrumental and reified nomenclature but in the very exercise of language [*parole*]. The pronoun, for example, which is without doubt the most staggering of the 'shifters', belongs structurally to speech [*parole*]. That is its scandal, if you like, and it is on this scandal that we must work today, in linguistics and literature. We are all trying, with different methods, styles, perhaps even prejudices, to get to the core of this linguistic pact [*pacte de parole*] which unites the writer and the other, so that – and this is a contradiction which will never be sufficiently pondered – each moment of discourse is both absolutely new and absolutely understood. I think that, with a certain amount of temerity, we could even give a historical dimension to this research. We know that the medieval *septenium*, in its grandiose classification of the universe, prescribed two great areas of exploration: on the one hand, the secrets of nature (the *quadrivium*) and, on the other, the secrets of language [*parole*] (the *trivium: grammatica, rhetorics, dialectica*). From the end of the Middle Ages to the present day, this opposition was lost, language being considered only as an instrument in the service of either reason or the heart. Today, however, something of this ancient opposition lives again: once again the exploration of language, conducted by linguistics, psychoanalysis, and literature, corresponds to the exploration of the cosmos. For literature is itself a science, or at least knowledge, no longer of the 'human heart' but of human language [*parole*]. Its investigation is not, however, addressed to the secondary forms and figures that were the object of rhetoric, but to the fundamental categories of language. Just as in Western culture grammar was not born until long after rhetoric, so it is only after having made its way for centuries through *le beau littéraire* that literature can begin to ponder the fundamental problems of language, without which it would not exist.

Notes

1. 'Ecrire: Verbe intransitif?' The translation which follows is a composite of the communication which M. Barthes distributed in advance to the Symposium participants and the actual transcription of his address. The notes have been supplied by the translator.
2. Emile Benveniste, *Problèmes de la linguistique générale* (Paris, 1966), p 40. 'Qu' estce donc que cet object, que Saussure érige sur une table rase de toutes les notions reçues? Nous touchons ici à ce qu'il y a de primordial dans la doctrine saussurienne,

à un principe qui présume une intuition totale du language, totale à la fois parce qu'elle embrasse la totalité de son objet. Ce principe est que *le langage,* sous quelque point de vue qu'on l'étudie, *est toujours un objet double,* formé de deux parties dont l'une ne vaut que par l'autre.'

3. Cf. Benveniste, 'Les Relations de temps dans le verbe français', ibid., pp. 237–50.
4. Cf. Jean-Paul Sartre, 'Explication de *L'Etranger*', *Situations* I (Paris, 1947), pp. 99–121.
5. Gustave Guillaume, *L'Architectonique du temps dans les langues classiques* (Copenhagen 1945). The work of Guillaume (who died in 1960) toward a 'psycho-systématique' has been continued in the contributions of Roch Valin (*Petite introduction à la psychomécanique du langage* [Québec, 1954]). For a statement by Guillaume about his relation to the tradition of Saussure see *La langue est-elle ou n'est-elle pas un système? Cahiers de linguistique structurale de l'Université de Québec,* I (1952), p. 4.
6. Benveniste, *Problèmes de la linguistique générale,* p. 252.
7. J. Damourette and E. Pichon, *Des mots à la pensée: Essai de grammaire de la langue française* (Paris, 1911–36), V, #1604 and VII, #2958. 'Le langage est naturellement centré sur le moi-ici-maintenant, c'est-à-dire sur la personne qui parle s'envisageant au moment même où elle parle; c'est ce qu'on peut appeler le *nynégocentrisme* naturel du langage' [#1604].
8. *Dans le labyrinthe* (Paris: Editions de Minuit, 1956). For essays by Roland Barthes bearing on the fictional method and theory of Robbe-Grillet, see *Essais critiques* (Paris, 1964), pp. 29–40, 63–70, 198–205.
9. Cf. Jakobson, *Shifters, Verbal Categories, and the Russian Verb* (Cambridge, Mass., 1957). [Translated into French by Nicolas Ruwet in *Essais de linguistique générale* (Paris, 1963, pp. 176–96.] For the origin of the term 'shifter', see Otto Jespersen, *Language, its Nature, Development and Origin* (London, 1922), p. 123, and ibid., *The Philosophy of Grammar* (London, 1923), pp. 83–4.
10. Benveniste, 'Actif et moyen dans le verbe', *Problèmes de la linguistique générale,* pp. 168–75. Cf. the distinction initiated by Pānini (fl. 350 BC): *parasmaipada,* 'word for another', i.e., active, and *āmanepada,* word for self', middle. Thus *yajati* ('he sacrifices' [for another, *qua* priest]) vs. *yajate* ('he sacrifices' [for himself, *qua* offering]). Cf. Berthold Delbrück, *Vergleichende Syntax der Indogermanischen Sprachen* (Strassburg, 1893).

9 | David Lodge,

'Analysis and Interpretation of the Realist Text', *Poetics Today*, vol. 1: 4 (1980),[1] pp. 5–22

I

It is a commonplace that the systematic study of narrative was founded by Aristotle, and scarcely an exaggeration to say that little of significance was added to those foundations until the twentieth century. Narrative theory in the intervening period was mainly directed (or misdirected) at deducing from Aristotle's penetrating analysis of the system of Greek tragedy a set of prescriptive rules for the writing of epic. The rise of the novel as a distinctive and eventually dominant literary form finally exposed the poverty of neoclassical narrative theory, without for a long time generating anything much more satisfactory. The realistic novel set peculiar problems for any formalist criticism because it worked by disguising or denying its own conventionality. It therefore invited – and received – criticism which was interpretative and evaluative rather than analytical. It was not until the late nineteenth and early twentieth centuries that something like a poetics of fiction began to evolve from the self-conscious experiments of novelists themselves, and was elaborated by literary critics. At about the same time, developments in linguistics, folklore and anthropology stimulated a more broad-ranging study of narrative, beyond the boundaries of modern literary fiction. For a long time these investigations were pursued on parallel tracks which seldom converged. In the last couple of decades, however, the Anglo– American tradition of formalist criticism, essentially empirical and text-based, theoretically rather underpowered but critically productive, has encountered the more systematic, abstract, theoretically rigorous and 'scientific' tradition of European structuralist criticism. The result has been a minor 'knowledge explosion' in the field of narrative theory and poetics of fiction.

The question I wish to raise in this paper is whether progress in theory and methodology means progress in the critical reading of texts.[2] Is it possible, or useful, to bring the whole battery of modern formalism and structuralism to bear upon a single text, and what is gained by so doing? Does it enrich our reading by uncovering depths and nuances of meaning we might not otherwise have brought to consciousness, help us to solve problems of interpretation and to correct misreadings? Or does it merely encourage a pointless and self-indulgent academicism, by which the same information is shuffled from one set of categories to another, from one jargon to another, without any real advance in appreciation or understanding? The analysis offered here of a short story by Ernest Hemingway is intended to support a positive answer to the first set of questions, a negative answer to the second set. But first it may be useful to remind ourselves of the range and variety of theories, methodologies and 'approaches' now available to the critic of fiction. I would group them into three categories, according to the 'depth' at which they address themselves to narrative structure.

1 Narratology and Narrative Grammar – i.e., the effort to discover the *langue* of narrative, the underlying system of rules and possibilities of which any narrative *parole* (text) is the realisation. With a few arguable exceptions[3] this enterprise has been almost exclusively dominated by European scholars – Propp, Bremond, Greimas, Lévi-Strauss, Todorov and Barthes, among others. Crucial to this tradition of enquiry are the ideas of function and trans-formation. In the theory of Greimas for instance, all narrative consists essentially of the transfer of an object or value from one actant to another.

An actant performs a certain function in the story which may be classified as Subject or Object, Sender or Receiver, Helper or Opponent, and is involved in doing things which may be classified as performative (tests, struggles, etc.), contractual (establishment and breaking of contracts) and disjunctional (departure and returns). These functions are not simply identifiable from the structure of a narrative text: for instance, several characters may perform the function of one actant, or one character may combine the functions of two actants. All concepts are semantically defined by a binary relationship with their opposites (e.g., Life/Death) or negatives (e.g., Life: Death:: Non-Life: Non-Death), so that all narrative can be seen as the transformation into actants and actions of a thematic four-term homology.[4]

It is often said that this kind of approach is more rewarding when applied to narratives of a traditional, formulaic and orally transmitted type, rather than sophisticated literary narratives; and the exponents of narratology themselves frequently remind us that their aim is not the explication of texts but the uncovering of the system that allows narrative texts to be generated and competent readers to make sense of them. Narratology does, however, bring to the attention of the literary critic factors involved in reading narrative that are important, but in a sense so obvious that they tend to be overlooked. Roland Barthes[5] (1975, 1977) has very fruitfully applied to the analysis of literary fictions the idea, derived from structuralist narratology, that narrative is divisible into sequences that open or close possibilities for the characters, and thus for the reader. The interest of these openings and closures may be either retrospective, contributing to the solution of some enigma proposed earlier in the text (the hermeneutic code) or prospective, making the audience wonder what will happen next (the proairetic code). Suspense and curiosity are therefore the two basic 'affects' aroused by narrative. A story of any sophistication will also, as Kermode points out,[6] make use of what Aristotle called peripeteia, or reversal, when a possibility is closed in a way that is unexpected and yet plausible and instructive. The reversal tends to produce an effect of irony, especially if it is anticipated by the audience.

Two problems arise in applying this kind of approach to realistic fiction. If we segment a text into its smallest units of information, how do we identify those which are functional on the basic narrative level, and what do we do with those units (the majority) which are not? Roland Barthes suggests one solution in his 'Introduction to the Structural Analysis of Narratives' where, drawing his illustrations mainly from. Ian Fleming's *Goldfinger*, he classifies the narrative units as either *nuclei* or *catalyzers*. Nuclei open or close alternatives that are of direct consequence for the subsequent development of the narrative and cannot be deleted without altering the story. Catalyzers are merely consecutive units which expand the nuclei or fill up the space between them. They can be deleted without altering the narrative, though not, in the case of realistic narrative, without altering its meaning and effect, since segments which connect not, or not only, with segments at the same level, but with some more generalized concept such as the psychological make-up of the characters, or the atmosphere of the story, function as *indices*, or (if merely factual) *informants*. Jonathan Culler has suggested that our ability to distinguish nuclei from catalyzers intuitively and to rank them in order of importance is a typical manifestation of reader-competence, verified by the fact that different readers will tend to summarize the plot of a given story in the same way. The intuitive recognition or ranking of nuclei is 'governed by readers' desire to reach an ultimate summary in which plot as a whole is grasped in a satisfying from'.[7] In short, the structural coherence of narratives is inseparable from their meaning, and reading them is inseparable from forming hypotheses about their overall meaning.

2 *Poetics of Fiction*   Under this head I include all attempts to describe and classify techniques of fictional representation. The great breakthrough in this field in the modern era was undoubtedly the Russian Formalists' distinction between *fabula* and *sjuzhet*: on the one hand the story in its most neutral, objective, chronological form – the story as it might have been enacted in real time and space, a seamless continuum of innumerable contiguous events; and on the other hand, the actual text in which this story is imitated, with all its inevitable (but motivated) gaps, elisions, emphases and reorderings. Work along these lines in Europe, culminating in Gérard Genette's Discours du Récit',[8] established two principal areas in which *sjuzhet* significantly modifies *fabula*: time, and what is generally called 'point of view' in Anglo–American criticism – though Genette correctly distinguishes here between 'perspective' (who sees the action) and 'voice' (who speaks the narration of it). He also distinguishes most suggestively three different categories in the temporal organisation (or deformation) of the *fabula* by the *sjuzhet*: order, duration and frequency.

The choices made by the narrative artist at this level are in a sense prior to, or 'deeper' than, his stylistic choices in composing the surface structure of the text, though they place important constraints upon what he can achieve in the surface structure. They are also of manifest importance in the realistic novel which, compared to other, earlier narrative forms, is characterized by a carefully discriminated, pseudo-historical treatment of temporality, and a remarkable depth and flexibility in its presentation of consciousness.

A good deal of Anglo–American critical theorising about the novel, from Percy Lubbock's *The Craft of Fiction* (1921) to Wayne Booth's *The Rhetoric of Fiction* (1961) was implicitly, if unconsciously, based on the same distinction between *fabula* and *sjuzhet*, between 'story' and 'way of telling it'. The cross-fertilization of the two critical traditions has produced much interesting and illuminating work, analyzing and classifying tying novelistic techniques and covering such matters as tense, person, speech and indirect speech in fictional narrative; and we are now, it seems to me, within sight of a truly comprehensive taxonomy of fictional form at this level. Two recent books which have made particularly valuable contributions in this respect are Seymour Chatman[9] and the more narrowly focused work of Dorrit Cohn.[10]

3 *Rhetorical Analysis* By this I mean analyzing the surface structure of narrative texts to show how the linguistic mediation of a story determines its meaning and effect. This is a kind of criticism in which the Anglo–American tradition is comparatively strong, because of the close-reading techniques developed by New Criticism. Mark Shorer's essays are classic statements of this approach.[11] The stylistics that developed out of Romance Philology, represented at its best by Spitzer and Auerbach, also belongs in this category. When I wrote my first book of criticism, *Language of Fiction*,[12] this seemed the best route by which to achieve a formalist critique of the realistic novel.

The underlying aim of this criticism was to demonstrate that what looked like redundant or random detail in realistic fiction was in fact functional contributing to a pattern of motifs with expressive and thematic significance. Much of this criticism was therefore concerned with tracing symbolism and keywords in the verbal texture of novels. Though very few of the New Critics were aware of the work of Roman Jakobson, he provided a theoretical justification for this kind of criticism in his famous definition of literariness, or the poetic function of language, as 'the projection of the principle of equivalence from the axis of selection to the axis of combination'.[13] What the New Critics called 'spatial form'[14] was precisely a pattern of paradigmatic equivalences concealed in the narrative syntagm. Furthermore, as I tried to show in my book *The Modes of Modern Writing*,[15] in his distinction between metaphor and metonymy, Jacobson[16] provided a key to understanding how the realistic novel contrives to build up a pattern of equivalences without violating its illusion of life.

The argument is briefly as follows: metaphor and metonymy (or synecdoche) are both figures of equivalence, but generated by different processes, metaphor according to similarity between things otherwise different, metonymy according to continuity or association between part and whole, cause and effect, thing and attribute, etc. Thus, if I transform the literal sentence 'Ships sail the sea' into 'Keels plough the deep', *plough* is equivalent to 'sail' because of the similarity between the movement of a plough through the earth and/or a ship through the sea, but *keel* is equivalent to 'ship' because it is part of a ship (synecdoche) and *deep* equivalent to 'sea' because it is an attribute of the sea (metonymy). In fact, metonymy is a non-logical (and therefore foregrounded or rhetorical) condensation achieved by transformations of kernel sentences by deletion (*the keels of the ships* condensed to *keels* rather than *ships*, deep sea to *deep* rather than *sea*). Metonymy thus plays with the combination axis of language as metaphor plays with the selection axis of language, and together they epitomize the two ways by which any discourse connects one topic with another: either because they are similar or because they are contiguous. Jackobson's distinction thus allows the analyst to move freely between deep structure and surface structure.

Realistic fiction is dominantly metonymic in a double sense: it connects actions that are contiguous in time and space and connected by cause and effect, but since it cannot describe exhaustively, the narrative *sjuzhet* is always in a metonymic relation to the *fabula*. The narrative text necessarily selects certain details and suppresses or deletes others. The selected details are thus foregrounded by being selected, and their recurrence and interrelation with other selected details in the text become aesthetically significant (what the Prague School calls systematic internal foregrounding). If these selected details are rhetorically mediated, through the use of the actual figures of metonymy and synecdoche, or of metaphor and simile, a denser and more overt pattern of equivalences is generated, but such rhetoric is not essential to the process, which is usually called symbolism in Anglo–American criticism. Barthes defined it as connotation, the device by which one signified acts as the signifier of another signified. Jakobson's distinction enables us to distinguish four different ways in which it operates:

A. Metonymic Signified I metonymically evokes Signified II (e.g., hearth fires in Charlotte Bronte's *Jane Eyre* symbolize domestic comfort, intimacy, security, etc.).
B. Metonymic Signified I metaphorically evokes Signified II (e.g., mud and fog at the beginning of *Bleak House* symbolize obfuscation and degradation of goodness and justice by the law).
C. Metaphoric Signified I metonymically evokes Signified II (e.g., the description of the night in Llaregyb in Dylan Thomas's *Under Milk Wood* as 'bible-black' symbolizes the Protestant chapel-going religious culture of the community).
D. Metaphoric Signified II metaphorically evokes Signified I (e.g., in the opening lines of Yeats's poem, 'The Second Coming'):

> Turning and turning in the widening gyre
> The falcon cannot hear the falconer

The metaphor *gyré* applied to the spiraling movement of the falcon also symbolizes the cyclical movement of history.

Realistic fiction relies principally upon symbolism types A and B.

II

No choice of a text for illustrative purposes is innocent, and no analysis of a single text could possibly provide universally valid answers to the questions posed at the beginning of this paper. These questions will not be settled until we have a significant corpus of synthetic or pluralistic readings of narrative texts of various types. Two distinguished achievements of this kind come to mind: Barthes' *S/Z* and Christine Brooke-Rose's study of *The Turn of the Screw*.[17] The following discussion of Hemingway's short story 'Cat in the Rain'[18] is necessarily much more modest in scope and scale. Two considerations prompted the choice of this story, apart from its convenient brevity: (1) A staff seminar on it in my own Department at Birmingham revealed that it presents certain problems of interpretation, though without being quite so heavily encrusted with the deposits of previous readings and misreadings as *The Turn of the Screw*. (2) It is both realistic and modern, cutting across that historicist and tendentious distinction between the *lisible* and the *scriptible* which I personally find one of the less helpful features of the work of Barthes and his disciples. The implied notion of *vraisemblance* on which Hemingway's story depends, the assumed relationship between the text and reality, is essentially continuous with that of classic bourgeois realism, yet in the experience of readers it has proved ambiguous, polyvalent and resistant to interpretative closure.

This is what Carlos Baker, in the standard critical work on Hemingway, has to say about 'Cat in the Rain' (he discusses it in the context of a group of stories about men–women relationships):

> 'Cat in the Rain', another story taken in part from the woman's point of view, presents a corner of the female world in which the male is only tangentially involved. It was written at Rapallo in May, 1923. From the window of a hotel room where her husband is reading and she is fidgeting, a young wife sees a cat outside in the rain. When she goes to get it, the animal (which somehow stands in her mind for comfortable bourgeois domesticity) has disappeared. This fact is very close to tragic because of the cat's association in her mind with many other things she longs for: long hair she can do in a knot at the back of her neck; a candle-lighted dining table where her own silver gleams; the season of spring and nice weather; and of course, some new clothes. But when she puts these wishes into words, her husband mildly advises her to shut up and find something to read. 'Anyway', says the young wife, 'I want a cat. I want a cat. I want a cat now. If I can't have long hair or any fun, I can have a cat.' The poor girl is the referee in a face-off between the actual and the possible. The actual is made of rain, boredom, a preoccupied husband and irrational yearnings. The possible is made of silver, spring, fun, a new coiffure, and new dresses. Between the actual and the possible stands the cat. It is finally sent up to her by the kindly old innkeeper, whose sympathetic deference is greater than that of the young husband.[19]

There are several things to quibble with in this account of the story. Most important perhaps is Baker's assumption that the cat sent up by the hotel keeper at the end is the same as the one that the wife saw from her window. This assumption is consistent with Baker's sympathy with the wife as a character, implied by his reference to her as 'the poor girl' and his description of the disappearance of the cat as 'very close to tragic'. The appearance of the maid with a cat is the main reversal, in Aristotelian terms, in the narrative. If it is indeed the cat she went to look for, then the reversal is a happy one for her, and confirms her sense that the hotel keeper appreciated her as a woman more than her husband. In Greimas's terms, the wife is the subject of the story and the cat the object. The hotel keeper and the maid enact the role of helper and George is the opponent. The story is disjunctive (departure and return) and concerns the transfer of the cat to the wife.

The description of the tortoiseshell cat as 'big', however, suggests that it is not the same as the one the wife referred to by the diminutive term 'kitty', and which she envisaged stroking on her lap. We might infer that the padrone, trying to humor a client, sends up the first cat he can lay hands on, which is in fact quite inappropriate to the wife's needs. This would make the reversal an ironic one at the wife's expense, emphasizing the social and cultural abyss that separates her from the padrone, and revealing her quasi-erotic response to his professional attentiveness as a delusion.

I shall return to this question of the ambiguity of the ending. One more point about Baker's commentary on the story: he says that the cat 'somehow stands in [the wife's] mind for comfortable bourgeois domesticity', and speaks of its 'association in her mind with many other things she longs for'. In other words, he interprets the cat as a metonymic symbol of type A above. Indeed he sees the whole story as turning on the opposition between two groups of metonymies. 'The actual is made of rain, boredom, a preoccupied husband, and irrational yearnings. The possible is made of silver, spring, fun, a new coiffure, and new dresses.'

John V. Hagopian gives a very different reading of this story. It is, he says, about 'a crisis in the marriage ... involving the lack of fertility, which is symbolically foreshadowed by the public garden (fertility) dominated by the war monument (death)' in the first paragraph. These again are metonymic symbols of type A, effect connoting cause; but Hagopian's reading of the story hinges on the identification of the cat as a symbol of a wanted child, and of the man in the rubber cape (lines 32–3) as a symbol of contraception–symbolism of type B, in which a metonymic signified evokes a second signified metaphorically, i.e., by virtue of similarity.

> As [the wife] looks out into the wet empty square, she sees a man in a rubber cape strolling to the café in the rain .... The rubber cape is a protection from rain, and rain is a fundamental necessity for fertility and fertility is precisely what is lacking in the American wife's marriage. An even more precise interpretation is possible but perhaps not necessary here.[20]

What Hagopian is presumably hinting at is that 'rubber' is an American colloquialism for contraceptive sheath, and that the wife notices the man in the rubber cape because of the subconscious association–a piece of classic Freudian 'symbolism'. It is an ingenious interpretation and all the more persuasive because there seems to be no very obvious reason for introducing the man in the cape into the story–he is not an actant in the narrative but an item of the descriptive background[21] and his appearance does not tell us anything about the weather or the square that we do not know already. Admittedly, the cape does signify, by contrast, the wife's lack of protection from the rain, thus emphasising the padrone's thoughtfulness in sending the maid with the umbrella. But if we accept Hagopian's reading then the umbrella itself, opening with almost comical opportuneness and effortlessness behind her, becomes a symbol of how the wife's way of life comes between her and a vital, fertile, relationship with reality. Her later demands for new clothes, a new hairstyle, a candlelit dining table are, according to Hagopian plan, expressions of a desire that never reaches full consciousness, for 'motherhood, a home with a family, an end to the strictly companionate marriage with George'. And the cat, he says, is by this stage in the story 'an obvious symbol for a child'.[22]

Unlike Baker, Hagopian sees the final reversal in the story as ironic:

The girl's symbolic wish is grotesquely fulfilled in painfully realistic terms. It is George, not the padrone, by whom the wife wants to be fulfilled, but the padrone has sent up the maid with a big tortoise-shell cat, a huge creature that swings down against her body. It is not clear whether this is exactly the same cat as the one the wife had seen from the window – probably not; in any case, it will most certainly not do. The girl is willing to settle for a child-surrogate, but the big tortoise-shell cat obviously cannot serve that purpose.[23]

The reason why this story is capable of providing these two very different interpretations might be expressed as follows: although it is a well-formed narrative, with a clearly defined beginning, middle and end, the primary action is not the primary vehicle of meaning. This can be demonstrated by testing upon the story Jonathan Culler's hypothesis that competent readers will tend to agree on what is and is not essential to the plot of a narrative test. Before the seminar at Birmingham University participants were invited to summarize the action of the story in not more than 30 words of continuous prose.[24] All the contributors mentioned the wife, the cat, the rain, and the hotel manager; most mentioned the nationality of the wife, and her failure to find the cat under the table; about half mentioned the husband, located the story in Italy, and made a distinction between the two cats. None mentioned the maid, or the bickering between husband and wife.

These omissions are particularly interesting. The non-appearance of the maid is easily explained: on the narrative level her function is indistinguishable from that of the manager – both are 'helpers' and the narrative would not be significantly altered *qua* narrative if the maid were deleted from the story and her actions performed by the manager himself. She does contribute to the symmetry of the story both numerically and sexually: it begins by pairing husband and wife, then pairs wife and manager, then wife and maid, then (in the wife's thoughts) maid and manager, then wife and manager again, then wife and husband again, and ends by pairing husband and maid. But this seems to be a purely formal set of equivalences with no significance in the hermeneutic or proairetic codes (such as would obtain if, for instance, there were some intrigue linking the husband with the maid and the manager, the kind of plotting characteristic of the *lisible* text). The main function of the maid in the story is to emphasise the status of the wife as a client and expatriate, and thus to act as a warning or corrective against the wife's tendency to attribute to the padrone a deeply personal interest in herself.

Both Baker and Hagopian agree that the rift between husband and wife is what the story is essentially about, even if they disagree about the precise cause. That none of the synopses should make any allusion to the bickering between the couple is striking evidence that the meaning of the story does not inhere in its basic action. In trying to preserve what is essential to that action in a very condensed summary – the quest for the cat, the failure of the quest, the reversal – one has to discard what seems most important in the story as read: the relationship between husband and wife. Adopting Barthes' terminology in 'The Structural Analysis of Narratives', there are only four nuclei in the story, opening possibilities which might be closed in different ways: will the wife or the husband go to fetch the cat? Will the wife get the cat? Will she get wet? Who is at the door?[25] The rest of the story consists of catalyzers that are indexical or informational, and since most of the information is given more than once, these too become indexical of mood and atmosphere (for instance, we are told more than once that it is raining). One might indeed describe the story generically as indexical: we infer its meaning indexically from its non-narrative components rather than hermeneutically or teleologically from its action. Another way of putting it would be to invoke Seymour Chatman's distinction between the resolved plot and the revealed plot:

> In the traditional narrative of resolution, there is a sense of problem solving … of a kind of ratiocinative or emotional teleology… 'What will happen? is the basic question. In the modern plot of revelation, however, the emphasis is elsewhere, the function of the discourse is not to answer the question or even to pose it … It is not that events are resolved (happily or tragically) but rather that a state of affairs is revealed.[26]

Chatman offers *Pride and Prejudice* and *Mrs. Dalloway* as examples of each kind of plot. 'Cat in the Rain' seems to share characteristics of both: it is, one might say, a plot of revelation (the relationship between husband and wife) disguised as a plot of resolution (the quest for the cat). The ambiguity of the ending is therefore crucial. By refusing to resolve the issue of whether the wife gets the cat she wants, the implied author indicates that this is not the point of the story.

There are several reasons why this ending is ambiguous. One, obviously, is that the story ends where it does, for if it continued for another line or two, or moment or two, it would become apparent from the wife's response whether the cat was the one she had seen from the window, whether she is pleased or disconcerted by its being brought to her, and so on. What I am doing here is comparing the *fabula* with the *sjuzhet*. The *sjuzhet* tantalisingly stops just short of that point in the *fabula* where we should, with our readerly desire for certainty, wish it to. In other respects there is nothing especially striking about the story's treatment of time, though we may admire the smooth transition in the first paragraph from summary of a state of affairs obtaining over a period of days or weeks to the state of affairs obtaining on a particular afternoon, and the subtle condensation of durational time in the final scene between husband and wife, marked by changes in the light outside the window. The order of events is strictly chronological (characteristic, Chatman observes, of the resolved plot (1978: 48)). As regards what Genette calls frequency (the number of times an event is narrated), the story tends toward reiteration rather than summary, telling n times what happened n times or n times what happened once rather than telling once what happened n times. This is important because it reinforces the definition of the characters according to a very limited repertoire of gestures. Thus the wife is frequently described as looking out of the window, the husband as reading, the manager as bowing (and the weather as raining).

The story of the quest for the cat involves four characters, and in theory could be narrated from four points of view, each quite distinct and different in import. The story we have is written from the point of view of the American couple rather than that of the Italian hotel staff, and from the wife's point of view rather than the husband's. We must distinguish here between what Genette calls voice and perspective. The story is narrated throughout by an authorial voice which refers to the characters in the third person and uses the past tense. This is the standard mode of authorial narration and by convention the narrator is authoritative, reliable and within the fictional world of the discourse, omniscient. The authorial voice in this story, however, renounces the privilege of authorial omniscience in two ways: firstly, by abstaining from any comment, judgement or explanation of motive regarding the behaviour of the characters, and secondly by restricting itself to the perspective of only two of the characters, and, for part of the story, to the perspective of only one. By this I mean that the narrator describes nothing that is not seen by either husband or wife or both. Yet it is not quite true to say that the narrator has no independent angle of vision; he has. As in a film, we sometimes see the wife from the husband's angle, and the husband sometimes from the wife's angle, but much of the time we see them both from some independent, impersonal angle.

The first paragraph adopts the common perspective of the American couple, making no distinction between them. With the first sentence of the second paragraph, 'The American wife stood at the window looking out', the narrative adopts her perspective but without totally identifying with it. Note the deictic difference between '*her* husband' in line 18, which closely identifies the narration with her perspective, and '*the* husband' in line 20, '*the* wife' in line 23, which subtly reasserts the independence of the authorial voice. From this point onwards, however, for the next 50 lines the narration identifies itself closely with the wife's perspective, following her out of the room and downstairs into the lobby, and reporting what she thinks as well as what she sees. The anaphoric sequence of sentences beginning 'She liked' (lines 29–31) affects us as being a transcription rather than a description of her thoughts because they could be transposed into monologue (first person/present tense) without any illogicality or stylistic awkwardness. Sentences in free indirect speech, 'The cat would be round to the right. Perhaps she could go along under the eaves' (33–4) and 'of course, the hotel-keeper had sent her' (37–8), mark the maximum degree of identification of the narration with the wife's point of view. When she returns to the room the narration separates itself from her again. There is a lot of direct speech from now on, no report of the wife's thoughts, and occasionally the narration seems to adopt the husband's perspective alone, e.g., 'George looked up and saw the back of her neck, clipped like a boy's' (71), and– very importantly:

> Someone knocked at the door.
> 'Avanti', George said. He looked up from his book.
> In the doorway stood the maid. She held a big tortoise-shell cat … (93–5)

We can now fully understand why the ending of the story is so ambiguous:

it is primarily because the narration adopts the husband's perspective at this crucial point. Since he did not rise from the bed to look: out of the window at the cat sheltering from the rain, he has no way of knowing whether the cat brought by the maid is the same one–hence the non-committal indefinite article '*a* big tortoise-shell cat'. If, however, the wife's perspective had been adopted at this point and the text had read

> 'Avanti,' the wife said. She turned round from the window. In the doorway stood the maid. She held a big tortoise-shell cat...

then it would be clear that this was not the cat the wife had wanted to bring in from the rain (in which case the definite article would be used). It is significant that in the title of the story, there is no article before 'Cat', thus giving no support to either interpretation of the ending.

Carlos Baker's assumption that the tortoise-shell cat and the cat in the rain are one and the same is therefore unwarranted. Hagopian's reading of the ending as ironic is preferable but his assumption that the wife's desire for the cat is caused by childlessness is also unwarranted. Here, it seems to me, the structuralist notion of language as a system of differences and of meaning as the product of structural oppositions can genuinely help to settle a point of interpretation.[27] Hagopian's interpretation of the man in the rubber cape as a symbol of contraception depends in part on the association of rain with fertility. Now rain *can* symbolise fertility, when defined by opposition to drought. In this story, however (and incidentally, throughout Hemingway's work) it is opposed to 'good weather' and symbolises the loss of pleasure and joy, the onset of discomfort and ennui. Hagopian's comments on the disappearance of the artists, 'The rain, ironically, inhibits creativity,[28] is a strained attempt to reconcile his reading with the text: there is no irony here unless we accept his equation, rain = fertility.

The cat as a child-surrogate is certainly a possible interpretation in the sense that it is a recognised cultural stereotype, but again Hagopian tries to enlist in its support textual evidence that is, if anything, negative. He comments on the description of the wife's sensations as she passes the hotel keeper for the second time: "very small and tight inside ... really important ... of supreme importance" all phrases that might appropriately be used to describe a woman who is pregnant'.[29] But not, surely, to describe a woman who merely *wants* to be pregnant. Indeed, if we must have a gynecological reading of the story it is much more plausible to suppose that the wife's whimsical craving for the cat and for other things like new clothes and long hair is the result of her *being* pregnant. There is in fact some extratextual support for this hypothesis. In his biography of Heming-way, Carlos Baker states quite baldly that 'Cat in the Rain' was about Hemingway, his wife Hadley and the manager and chambermaid at the Hotel Splendide in Rapallo, where the story was written in 1923. He also states, without making any connection between the two items, that the Hemingways had left the chilly thaw of Switzerland and gone to Rapallo because Hadley had announced that she was pregnant.[30]

At about the same time, Hemingway was evolving 'a new theory that you could omit anything if you knew what you omitted, and the omitted part would strengthen the story and make people feel something more than they understood.'[31] This is, I think, a very illuminating description by Hemingway of his application of the metonymic mode of classical realism to modernist literary purposes. Metonymy, as I said earlier, is a device of non-logical deletion. Hemingway's word is' omission'. By omitting the kind of motivation that classical realistic fiction provided, he generated a symbolist polysemy in his deceptively simple stories, making his readers 'feel more than they understood'. It would be a mistake, therefore, to look for a single clue, whether pregnancy or barrenness, to the meaning of 'Cat in the Rain'. That the wife's (and, for that matter, the husband's) behaviour is equally intelligible on either assumption is one more confirmation of the story's indeterminacy.

Hemingway's stories are remarkable for achieving a symbolist resonance without the use of rhetorical figures and tropes. Not only does 'Cat in the Rain' contain no metaphors and similes–it contains no metonymies and synecdoches either. The story is 'metonymic' in the structural sense defined above: its minimal semantic units are selected from a single context, a continuum of temporal and spatial contiguities, and are foregrounded simply by being selected, repeated and related to each other oppositionally. Consider, for example, the opening paragraph, which establishes the story's setting in diction that is apparently severely denotative, with no metaphors or metonymies, similes or synecdoches, no elegant variation or pathetic fallacies, yet is nevertheless highly charged with connotative meaning.

There were only two Americans stopping at the hotel. Americans opposed to other nationalities: index of cultural isolation.

They did not know any of the people they passed on the stairs on their way to and from their room. Index of social isolation and mutual dependence–vulnerability to breakdown in relationship.

Their room was on the second floor facing the sea. Culture faces nature.

It also faced the public garden and the war monument. Culture paired with nature (public: garden) and opposed to nature (monument: garden). Pleasure (garden) opposed to pain (war).

There were big palms and green benches in the public garden. Culture and nature integrated. Benches same color as vegetation.

In the good weather there was always an artist with his easel. Artists liked the way the palms grew and the bright colors of the hotels facing the garden and the sea. Culture and nature happily fused. Image of euphoria.

Italians came from a long way off to look up at the war monument. Euphoria qualified. War monument attracts the living but commemorates the dead. Looking associated with absence (of the dead). 'Italian' opposed to 'American'.

It was made of bronze and glinted in the rain. Inert mineral (bronze) opposed to organic vegetable (palm). Rain opposed to good weather. Euphoria recedes.

It was raining. Rain dripped from the palm trees. Euphoria recedes further. Garden uninviting.

Water stood in pools on the gravel paths. Image of stagnation.

The sea broke in a long line in the rain and slipped back down the beach to come up and break again in a long line in the rain. Excess of wetness. Monotony. Ennui.

The motor cars were gone from the square by the war monument. Across the square in the doorway of the café a waiter stood looking out at the square. Images of absence, loss, ennui.

The first paragraph, then, without containing a single narrative nucleus, establishes the thematic core of the story through oppositions between nature and culture, joy and ennui. Joy is associated with a harmonious union of culture and nature. The wife, looking out of the window at a scene made joyless by the rain, sees a cat with whose discomfort she emotionally identifies. Her husband, though offering to fetch it, implies his indifference to her emotional needs by not actually moving. The husband is reading, a 'cultural' use of the eyes. The wife is looking, a 'natural' use of the eyes. Her looking, through the window, expresses a need for communion. His reading of a book is a substitute for communion, and a classic remedy for ennui. It is worth noticing that he is reading on the bed – a place made for sleeping and making love; and the perversity of this behaviour is symbolized by the fact that he is lying on the bed the wrong way round. As the story continues, the contrast between looking and reading, both activities expressing the loss or failure of love, becomes more insistent. Denied the kitty, a 'natural' object (opposed to book) which she could have petted as a substitute for being petted, the wife looks in the mirror, pining for a more natural feminine self. Then she looks out of the window again, while her husband, who has not shifted his position (his immobility opposed to the padrone's punctilious bowing) reads on and impatiently recommends her to 'get something to read'. One could summarize this story in the style of Greimas, as follows: loving is to quarrelling as stroking a cat is to reading a book, a narrative transformation of the opposition between joy and ennui, thus:

Loving (Joy): Quarrelling (Ennui): stroking a cat (Non-joy, a giving but not receiving of pleasure): reading a book (Non-ennui).

Such a summary has this to recommend it: that it brings together the overt action of the story (the quest for the cat) with its implicit subject (the relationship between husband and wife). Whether it, and the preceding comments, enhance our understanding and appreciation of Hemingway's story, I leave others to judge.

Notes

1 Paper presented at *Synopsis* 2: 'Narrative Theory and Poetics of Fiction', an international symposium held at The Porter Institute for Poetics and Semiotics, Tel Aviv University, and the Van Leer Jerusalem Foundation, 16–22 June 1979. For the text of the story, see Appendix.
2 I do not mean to imply that theory can only be justified on such grounds. Theoretical research may have a purpose and value quite independent of its application to particular problems. I merely wish to consider whether exponents of 'practical', or descriptive and interpretative, criticism have anything useful to learn from recent developments in the theory of narrative and poetics of fiction.
3 For example, Northrop Frye, *Anatomy of Criticism* (Princeton, NJ Princeton University Press, 1957) and Frank Kermode, *The Sense of an Ending* (New York and London, Oxford University Press, 1966).

4 A.J. Greimas, *Sémantique structurale* (Paris, Larousse, 1966); *Du Sens* (Paris, Seuil, 1970); *Maupassant. La Sémiologie du texte: exercises practiques* (Paris, Seuil, 1976).

5 Roland Barthes, *S/Z* tr. Richard Miller (London, Cape, 1975 [1970]); 'Introduction to the Structural Analysis of Narratives', in *Image–Music–Text*, ed. and tr. Stephen Heath (London, Fontana, 1977 [1966]).

6 Kermode, *The Sense of an Ending*, p. 18.

7 Jonathan Culler, 'Defining Narrative Units', in Roger Fowler ed., *Style and Structure in Literature* (Oxford, Basil Blackwell, 1975), p. 139.

8 Gérard Genette, 'Discours du récit', in *Figures III* (Paris, Seuil, 1972).

9 Seymour Chatman, *Story and Discourse: Narrative Structure in Fiction and Film* (Ithaca, NY, Cornell University Press, 1978).

10 Dorrit Cohn, *Transparent Minds: Narrative Modes for Presenting Consciousness* (Princeton, NJ, Princeton University Press, 1978).

11 Mark Schorer, 'Technique as Discovery', *Hudson Review* I (1948), pp. 67–86; 'Fiction and the Analogical Matrix', *Kenyon Review* XI (1949), pp. 539–60.

12 David Lodge, *Language of Fiction* (London, Routledge & Kegan Paul, 1966).

13 Roman Jakobson, 'Closing Statement: Linguistics and Poetics', in Thomas A. Sebeok, ed., *Style and Language* (Cambridge, Mass., MIT, 1960), p. 358.

14 Joseph Frank, 'Spatial Form in Modern Literature', in Mark Schorer, Josephine Miles and Gordon McKenzie, eds, *Criticism* (New York, Harcourt Brace, 1948 [1945]).

15 David Lodge, *The Modes of Modern Writing* (London, Arnold, and Ithaca, NY. Cornell University Press, 1977).

16 Roman Jakobson, 'Two Aspects of Language and Two Types of Linguistic Disturbances', in Jakobson and Morris Halle, *Fundamentals of Language* (The Hague, Mouton, 1956).

17 Christine Brooke-Rose, 'The Squirm of the True', *PTL* 1 (1976), pp. 265–94, 513–46; 2 (1977), pp. 517–61.

18 Ernest Hemingway, 'Cat in the Rain', in *In Our Time* (New York, Scribner, 1958 [1925]).

19 Carlos Baker, *Hemingway: The Writer as Artist* (Princeton, NJ, Princeton University Press, 1963 [1952]), pp. 135–6.

20 John V. Hagopian, 'Symmetry in "Cat in the Rain" 'in Jackson J. Benson, ed., *The Short Stories of Ernest Hemingway: Critical Essays* (Durham, NC, Duke University Press, 1975 [1962]), p. 231.

21 Chatman, *Story and Discourse: Narrative Structure in Fiction and Film*, p. 140.

22 Hagopian, 'Symmetry in 'Cat in the Rain'', p. 232.

23 Ibid.

24 My own effort was as follows: 'Bored young American staying with husband at Italian hotel fails to rescue a cat seen sheltering from the rain but is provided with a cat by the attentive manager.'

25 On further reflection I am inclined to think that there is another 'hidden' narrative nucleus in the story, related to the 'marital rift' theme, though it is to be inferred only from George's body language as reported in lines 74–5, and his appreciative speech at line 76: namely, the possibility that he will put aside his book and make love to his wife. This possibility is closed, negatively, at line 86.

26 Chatman, *Story and Discourse: Narrative Structure in Fiction and Film*, p. 48.

27 Perhaps this is overconfident, since it is rarely possible to disprove interpretations. Among the more far-fetched interpretations of 'Cat in the Rain' are Horst Kruse's argument that the man in the rubber cape is an allusion to the mysterious man in the mackintosh in the 'Hades' episode of Joyce's *Ulysses*, and therefore a symbol of death ('The appearance of a man in a raincoat in both *Ulysses* and 'Cat in the Rain' seems clear indication of the dependence of Hemingway's short story on the work

of the Irish writer' (Horst Kruse, 'Hemingway's "Cat in the Rain" and Joyce's *Ulysses'*, *Literatur in Wissenschaft und Unterricht* III (1970), p. 28); and Ramesh Srivastava's suggestion that 'the cat exists only in the imagination of the wife' (Ramesh Srivastava, 'Hemingway's "Cat in the Rain": an interpretation', Literary Criterion IX (1970), p. 83),which presumably entails reading the second sentence in paragraph 2 as free indirect speech.

28 Hagoplan, 'Symmetry in "Cat in the Rain"', p. 230.
29 Ibid., p. 231.
30 Carlos Baker, *Ernest Hemingway* (Harmondsworth, Penguin Books, 1972 [1969]), pp. 159, 161.
31 Ibid., p.165.

Appendix

Cat in the Rain

There were only two Americans stopping at the hotel. They did not know any of the pople they passed on the stairs on their way to and from their room. Their room was on the second floor facing the sea. It also faced the public garden and the war monument. There were big palms and green benches in the public garden. In the good weather there was always an artist with his easel. Artists liked the way the palms grew and the bright colors of the hotels facing the gardens and the sea. Italians came from a long way off to look up at the war monument. It was made of bronze and glistened in the rain. It was raining. The rain dripped from the palm trees. Water stood in pools on the gravel paths. The sea broke in a long line in the rain and slipped back down the beach to come up and break again in a long line in the rain. The motor cars were gone from the square by the war monument. Across the square in the doorway of the café a waiter stood looking out at the empty square.

The American wife stood at the window looking out. Outside right under their window a cat was crouched under one of the dripping green tables. The cat was trying to make herself so compact that she would not be dripped on.

I'm going down and get that kitty,' the American wife said.

'I'll do it', her husband offered from the bed.

'No, I'll get it. The poor kitty out trying to keep dry under a table'.

The husband went on reading, lying propped up with the two pillows at the foot of the bed.

'Don't get wet', he said.

The wife went downstairs and the hotel owner stood up and bowed to her as she passed the office. His desk was at the far end of the office. He was an old man and very tall.

'Il piove', the wife said. She liked the hotel-keeper.

'Si, si, Signora, brutto tempo. It is very bad weather.'

He stood behind his desk in the far end of the dim room. The wife liked him. She liked the deadly serious way he received any complaints. She liked his dignity. She liked the way he wanted to serve her. She liked the way he felt about being a hotelkeeper. She liked his old, heavy face and big hands.

Liking him she opened the door and looked out. It was raining harder. A man in a rubber cape was crossing the empty square to the café. The cat would be around to the right. Perhaps she could go along under the eaves. As she stood in the doorway an umbrella opened behind her. It was the maid who looked after their room.

'You must not get wet,' she smiled, speaking Italian. Of course, the hotelkeeper had sent her.

With the maid holding the umbrella over her, she walked along the gravel path until she was under their window. The table was there, washed bright green in the rain, but the cat was gone. She was suddenly disappointed. The maid looked up at her.

'Ha perduto qualque cosa, Signora?'

'There was a cat,' said the American girl.

'A cat?'

'Si, il gatto.'

'A cat?' the maid laughed. 'A cat in the rain?'

'Yes,' she said, 'under the table.' Then, 'Oh, I wanted it so much. I wanted a kitty.'

When she talked English the maid's face tightened.

'Come, Signora,' she said. 'We must get back inside. You will be wet.'

'I suppose so,' said the American girl.

They went back along the gravel path and passed in the door. The maid stayed outside to close the umbrella. As the American girl passed the office, the padrone bowed from his desk. Something felt very small and tight inside the girl. The padrone made her feel very small and at the same time really important. She had a momentary feeling of being of supreme importance. She went on up the stairs. She opened the door of the room. George was on the bed, reading.

'Did you get the cat?' he asked, putting the book down.

'It was gone.'

'Wonder where it went to,' he said, resting his eyes from reading. She sat down on the bed.

'I wanted it so much,' she said. 'I don't know why I wanted it so much. I wanted that poor kitty. It isn't any fun to be a poor kitty out in the rain.'

George was reading again.

She went over and sat in front of the mirror of the dressing table looking at herself with the hand glass. She studied her profile, first one side and then the other. Then she studied the back of her head and her neck.

'Don't you think it would be a good idea if I let my hair grow out?' she asked, looking at her profile again.

George looked up and saw the back of her neck, clipped close like a boy's.

'I like it the way it is.'

'I get so tired of it,' she said. 'I get so tired of looking like a boy.'

George shifted his position in the bed. He hadn't looked away from her since she started to speak.

'You look pretty darn nice,' he said.

She laid the mirror down on the dresser and went over to the window and looked out. It was getting dark.

'I want to pull my hair back tight and smooth and make a big knot at the back that I can feel,' she said. 'I want to have a kitty to sit on my lap and purr when I stroke her.'

'Yeah?' George said from the bed.

'And I want to eat at a table with my own silver and I want candles. And I want it to be spring and I want to brush my hair out in front of a mirror and I want a kitty and I want some new clothes'.

'Oh, shut up and get something to read,' George said. He was reading again.

His wife was looking out of the window. It was quite dark now and still raining in the palm trees.

'Anyway, I want a cat,' she said, 'I want a cat. I want a cat now. If I can't have long hair or any fun, I can have a cat.'

George was not listening. He was reading his book. His wife looked out of the window where the light had come on in the square.

Someone knocked at the door.

'Avanti,' George said. He looked up from his book.

In the doorway stood the maid. She held a big tortoise-shell cat pressed tight against her and swung down against her body.

'Excuse me,' she said, 'the padrone asked me to bring this for the Signora.'

Section 3

Marxism

Introduction

Broadly speaking, and as we have already seen in the discussion of the work of Marx and Engels, Marxism attempts to understand the relations between the literary text and the social world, recognizing that literature is a process and that the social world involves contexts of production and those of reception. Marxists regard literature as both production and reflection of and on culture and society, and the political aim of Marxist criticism is to understand the social and political world in order to change it. Marx never formulated a complete literary or aesthetic theory, so much of the subsequent debate in Marxist criticism has been over the question of how literature might be seen and understood in Marxist terms. What is not an issue, however, is the idea that literature should be analysed in historical and materialist terms or, in other words, as an integral part of a social structure resting on economic foundations. Where Marxists begin to diverge is in their views about the precise relation between literature and its socio-economic determinants. Their responses tend to involve three areas of debate, in particular: the relationship between form and content; the relative autonomy or otherwise of literary texts and their reworking of ideology; and the problem of value and political correctness.

The essays in this section have been chosen because they illustrate different historical moments of Marxism from the writings of Lukács through to the more formal preoccupations of Adorno and the Frankfurt School, to the Althusserian turn and the emergence of cultural materialism in the work of Raymond Williams. At each of these 'moments' of Marxist criticism, the questions of form and content, of autonomy and value, were revived and addressed within an evolving and increasingly sophisticated vocabulary. Though few Marxists have ever espoused a vulgar reflectionism which would see the literary text as a simple reiteration of class conflict, the question of how and to what extent economic structures finally constrain the forms or content of literary texts is variously approached in the critical essays represented here. The first question perhaps for each of these critics is: how does a literary work take its shape from society as a whole and from its mode of production, without being totally determined by its economic base or superstructure? Marxists agree that literature is produced in material conditions, that it reflects back upon those conditions and can help to change them. What they may disagree about is the nature of the relationship between literature and ideology, for literature may challenge, reflect, refract, mediate, break up, defamiliarize, distance from, expose contradictions in and/or reinforce, ideology. Moreover, different kinds of literature may perform each of these in different ways. Marxist criticism takes its cue from Marx's recognition that consciousness and its products grow out of material conditions so that literature, whatever its relation to ideology, is never completely transcendent and nor may it ever achieve that degree of disinterestedness claimed by the dominant liberal tradition of aesthetics. Yet, because literature has its own internal forms, genres, conventions, which act to mediate or 'reflect life with special mirrors' (as the playwright Bertholt Brecht put it), the literary text is never simply a reflection of class conflict or economic relations or 'dominant ideologies.'

We tend to think, in everyday terms, of ideology as a form of false consciousness, a misrepresentation which obscures the real truth while claiming to be true itself. Many Marxist critics would come to question this definition, however, recognizing that ideologies are lived out as practices and beliefs and are an inevitable aspect of the 'real'. There have been numerous definitions of ideology in Marxist criticism and they have given rise to a number of ways of viewing the relationship between literature and the social and political world. Ideologies have been variously seen as systems of false consciousness, as conspiracies of a ruling class, as ideas which legitimate the power of particular groups, as systems of beliefs and values necessary to the functioning of societies, as that which gives us our sense of cultural identity and allows us to exist as 'subjects' (in all senses of the word) and as the way in which the historically provisional forms of social life are naturalized as essential and universal. Ideology would seem to be a collectively held way of looking at, inhabiting and interpreting the world, and not some solipsistic delusion. To see that literature is contradictorily and complicatedly ideologically rooted in a society is not simply to see it as a tool for social control or as a vehicle for revolutionary subversion.

The first essay in this section, 'The Ideology of Modernism', was chosen because Lukács' work represents one of the earliest attempts within Marxist criticism to address the problem of the relations between form and content in developing a historical materialist account of literature. In the 1930s, Lukács began to develop a Marxist theory of the novel which would draw on Marx's critique of German Idealist aesthetics. Lukács own early work such as *The Theory of the Novel* (1916) was in the tradition of Hegelian aesthetics and embraced the Romantic anti-capitalist critique of industrial society which viewed the modern self as a disembedded subject, homeless in a mechanized world, elevated but unable to participate in the social world. At this point, Lukács looked back to the Ancient Greek *polis* as a model of an organic society which could be held up against industrial capitalism, but he also began to see in art too the possibility of experiencing a reconciled totality which might preserve the dialectical relationship of subject and object which had become split within modernity. Indeed, Lukács developed his famous critique of modernism, the subject of the essay reprinted here, out of this essentially Hegelian insight. For Lukács, modernism was a formal reflection of bourgeois modernity in all its alienation, abstraction, solipsism, fragmentation, and what he referred to as the 'attenuation of actuality'. Incapable of grasping the totality, bourgeois art had diverged into a materialist naturalism, on the one hand, and a subjectivist expressionism, on the other, with no possibility of dialectical relationship between the two. Modernism represented a fetishized immediacy and a denial of history which simply reflected the chaos and anomie of the modern world, its decadence and loss of sense of progress, without attempting critique or analysis. Realism, on the other hand, is regarded by Lukács as a literary mode able to reveal subjective personalities, full 'characters' engaged in practices mediated by the larger forces of the historical process. Great art, which is realistic art, presents a social 'totality' in which the manifest contradictions between subjective experience and objective historical forces are reconciled within the formal structures of the work. The debt to a Coleridgean organicism is evident in this claim for 'reconciliation', but for Lukács such art could function both as a critique of industrial capitalism and as a utopian vision of a better world.

The German dramatist Bertholt Brecht rejected Lukács' reading of realism and modernism, arguing for the socialist appropriation of modernist forms and the capacity of a defamiliarizing art to expose the contradictions and ideologies of bourgeois capitalism. For Brecht, a modernist art, self-reflexive, exposing its own mediating structures, would resist the kind of identification which he saw as part of the ideological naturalization of the world under capitalism. Lukács disagreed. For him, the world was already alienated enough; the individual already fragmented and disidentified. Modernist art, far from offering a critique of capitalist alienation, simply represented another contribution to and facet of it. Brecht championed what he saw as an active aesthetic, an art which could actively transform consciousness in the direction of socialism and release forms for different kinds of uses. Realism, for Brecht, represented a passive reflection of bourgeois ideology, modernism an active attempt to expose the processes of naturalisation. The debate between the two set the agenda for much of the Marxist criticism which developed in the next few decades.

Theodor Adorno, whose essay on lyric poetry and society is the next piece in this section, would follow Brecht in championing modernist and avant-garde art as contributions to socialism. His defence of modernism though would be developed in the context of a powerful critique of mass society and of the burgeoning 'culture industry', regarded as the degradation and commodification of the aesthetic, its final and absolute appropriation by capitalist forces. Adorno was a leading member of the Frankfurt School, associated with the Institute for Social Research, whose energies were largely engaged in developing a critique of Western philosophy and providing analytic studies of contemporary culture. Adorno regarded the culture industry as a potent force for holding the masses in a state of submissive ignorance and believed that only an avant-garde art which utterly repudiated realism might articulate any kind of oppositional position. Brecht had not gone far enough in his modernism.

The essay reprinted here demonstrates Adorno's sociological approach to the literary text. His argument is that even lyric poetry – that seemingly most ethereal of forms – is socially conditioned. Indeed, the very fact that we seem always to want to use poetry to facilitate an escapist withdrawal into the private is, in itself, an implicit comment on a society whose oppressiveness produces a longing for and urge towards transcendence in a variety of forms, including those of art. For Adorno, the aesthetic is the only remaining realm in which a full subjectivity might be preserved and expressed within the structures of a late capitalist society. Like Brecht, Adorno rejected Lukács' reading of modernism and argued that although, and laudably, Lukács situated himself in the great Western philosophical aesthetic tradition which conceives of art as a unique kind of knowledge, the limitation of his work was its failure to take enough account of the formal structures of the artwork. For Adorno, art is not a reflection of society but capable, because of its formal autonomy, of revealing the underlying structures of the real which are veiled by empiricist epistemology and by realism as the vehicle of its aesthetic expression. Art is a form of knowledge, but only avant-garde art is capable of penetrating through the veils of ideology and achieving epistemological authenticity. For Adorno, in art as opposed to science, nothing empirical remains unchanged: empirical 'facts' only begin to take on significance when they are reconciled, as they are in great art, with subjective intentions. Like Lukács, Adorno addresses the problems of production versus reflection, of the relations between subject and object and of form and content, but his conclusions are radically different. For Adorno, Lukács' realism is simply the insipid residue of bourgeois art in its most decadent mode; for Lukács, modernism simply epitomizes the condition of man in modern industrial society: 'solitary, asocial, unable to enter into relations with other human beings'.

The essay by Raymond Williams is included here because it is one of the earliest statements of what would eventually evolve into a fully-fledged cultural materialism. Williams was always interested in negotiating a path between a deterministic Marxism which would view culture simply as the reflection of economic forces, and an idealist aesthetics which has taken insufficient account of the material rootedness of all cultural products, including works of art. Williams borrowed from the Italian Marxist Antonio Gramsci the concept of hegemony, 'the folklore of philosophy', to explain the way in which a prevailing world-view saturates a society, becomes naturalized and established as 'common sense', so that it becomes difficult to think outside of or even to notice its shaping presence. Williams' own term to describe this impalpable form of social consciousness was 'structure of feeling', what he referred to as 'thought as felt and feeling as thought', a kind of practical consciousness without which we could neither think nor meaningfully engage with our fellow human beings. Willams' ideal was a culture in which different kinds of 'structure of feeling' might find expression and he was one of the first theorists to begin to analyse the complex and contradictory nature of social ideologies, drawing attention not only to the existence of contradictions within dominant ideologies, but also to the existence of residual, emergent and alternative ideologies which co-exist in any one culture. Williams saw that if we could come to recognize such contradictions, then it would be possible to move away from economically deterministic models of culture without necessarily embracing an idealist aesthetics. Because ideologies are contradictory, dissidence is possible; because literature reflects, breaks up, exposes and displaces ideology and mediates powerful 'structures of feeling', it is a potent source of emancipatory and critical possibilities.

The final essay in this section by Etienne Balibar and Pierre Macherey has now become one of the classic statements of structuralist Marxism. Marxism in the 1970s and 1980s was dominated for a while by the theories of Louis Althusser and in literary criticism by the work of Pierre Machery. While both claimed not to be structuralists, their theories exhibit striking resemblances to structuralist thought. The initial influence of structuralist Marxism upon literary theory centred mainly around the concept of ideology, though Althusser's notion of ideological State Apparatuses and the construction ('interpellation') of the human subject also influenced much post-structuralist theory. In Althusser's account, ideology reproduces subjects who are willing workers in the capitalist system. Capitalism requires not only the hands of labour, but also the willingness of workers to subject themselves to the system—to accept the status quo—and it is here that ideology works. This conception of ideology is what distinguished Althusser's Marxism from other models.

For Althusser, ideology is not a matter of conscious beliefs, attitudes or values, nor is it a matter of false consciousness (sets of false ideas imposed on individuals to persuade them that there is no real contradiction between capital and labour), it is, rather, a matter of the representation of imaginary versions of the real social relations lived by people. These imaginary versions are seen as necessary for the perpetuation of capitalism. Ideology imposes itself not simply through consciousness nor through disembodied ideas but through systems and structures; ideology is inscribed in the representations (signs) and the practices (rituals) of everyday life. Most importantly though, it is through ideology that individuals are constituted as subjects, misrecognizing themselves as free and autonomous beings with unique personalities. The main agencies for the reproduction of ideology and the subject are what Althusser calls Ideological State Apparatuses (ISAs) which might include the church, the family, the media, schools, art, sports and cultural activities in general.

In the essay reprinted here, Balibar and Macherey take up this notion of ISAs in order to examine the way in which literature functions in the reproduction of ideology within the French educational system. Literature is seen in terms of the acquisition and distribution of what the sociologist Pierre Bourdieu has called 'cultural capital'. However, a residue of Macherey's previous work in *A Theory of Literary Production* (1978) can be seen in the discussion of the relations between the literary text and social reality.

Macherey's earlier book was extremely influential in offering a model of textual analysis based on Althusser's notion of the symptomatic reading. This model involved uncovering the significant absences in texts, the ideological presuppositions on which the text was at once founded but of which it could not speak. In some ways, this work looks forward to the material represented in Part Two of this book, but their belief in a scientific procedure which could yield certain knowledge and the placing of literature between ideology and knowledge, connect them to the kinds of preoccupations which we have seen informing the theories covered in this first part of the anthology.

10 | Georg Lukács,

From *The Meaning of Contemporary Realism*
J. and N. Mander tr., (1972), pp. 19–27, 38–9

What determines the style of a given work of art? How does the intention determine the form? (We are concerned here, of course, with the intention realized in the work; it need not coincide with the writer's conscious intention). The distinctions that concern us are not those between stylistic 'techniques' in the formalistic sense. It is the view of the world, the ideology or *Weltanschauung* underlying a writer's work, that counts. And it is the writer's attempt to reproduce this view of the world which constitutes his 'intention' and is the formative principle underlying the style of a given piece of writing. Looked at in this way, style ceases to be a formalistic category. Rather, it is rooted in content; it is the specific form of a specific content.

Content determines form. But there is no content of which Man himself is not the focal point. However various the *données* of literature (a particular experience, a didactic purpose), the basic question is, and will remain: what is Man?

Here is a point of division: if we put the question in abstract, philosophical terms, leaving aside all formal considerations, we arrive–for the realist school–at the traditional Aristotelian dictum (which was also reached by other than purely aesthetic considerations): Man is *zoon politikon*, a social animal. The Aristotelian dictum is applicable to all great realistic literature. Achilles and Werther, Oedipus and Tom Jones, Antigone and Anna Karenina: their individual existence – their *Sein an sich*, in the Hegelian terminology; their 'ontological being', as a more fashionable terminology has it–cannot be distinguished from their social and historical environment. Their human significance, their specific individuality cannot be separated from the context in which they were created.

The ontological view governing the image of man in the work of leading modernist writers is the exact opposite of this. Man, for these writers, is by nature solitary, asocial, unable to enter into relationships with other human beings. Thomas Wolfe once wrote: 'My view of the world is based on the firm conviction that solitariness is by no means a rare condition, something peculiar to myself or to a few specially solitary human beings, but the inescapable, central fact of human existence.' Man, thus imagined, may establish contact with other individuals, but only in a superficial, accidental manner, only, ontologically speaking, by retrospective reflection. For 'the others ', too, are basically solitary, beyond significant human relationship.

This basic solitariness of man must not be confused with that individual solitariness to be found in the literature of traditional realism. In the latter case, we are dealing with a particular situation in which a human being may be placed, due either to his character or to the circumstances of his life. Solitariness may be objectively conditioned, as with Sophocles' Philoctetes, put ashore on the bleak island of Lemnos. Or it may be subjective, the product of inner necessity, as with Tolstoy's Ivan Ilyitsch or Flaubert's Frédéric Moreau in the *Education Sentimentale*. But it is always merely a fragment, a phase, a climax or anti-climax, in the life of the community as a whole. The fate of such individuals is characteristic of certain human types in specific social or historical circumstances. Beside and beyond their solitariness, the common life, the strife and togetherness of other human beings, goes on as before. In a word, their solitariness is a specific social fate, not a universal *condition humaine*.

The latter, of course, is characteristic of the theory and practice of modernism. I would like, in the present study, to spare the reader tedious excursions into philosophy. But I cannot refrain from drawing the reader's attention to Heidegger's description of human existence as a 'thrownness-into-being' (*Geworfenheit ins Dasein*). A more graphic evocation of the ontological solitariness of the individual would be hard to imagine. Man is 'thrown-into-being'. This implies, not merely that man is constitutionally unable to establish relationships with things or persons outside himself; but also that it is impossible to determine theoretically the origin and goal of human existence.

Man, thus conceived, is an ahistorical being. (The fact that Heidegger does admit a form of 'authentic' historicity in his system is not really relevant. I have shown elsewhere that Heidegger tends to belittle historicity as 'vulgar'; and his 'authentic' historicity is not distinguishable from ahistoricity.) This negation of history takes two different forms in modernist literature. First, the hero is strictly confined within the limits of his own experience. There is not for him – and apparently not for his creator – any pre-existent reality beyond his own self, acting upon him or being acted upon by him. Secondly, the hero himself is without personal history. He is 'thrown-into-the-world': meaninglessly, unfathomably. He does not develop through contact with the world; he neither forms nor is formed by it. The only 'development' in this literature is the gradual revelation of the human condition. Man is now what he has always been and always will be. The narrator, the examining subject, is in motion; the examined reality is static.

Of course, dogmas of this kind are only really viable in philosophical abstraction, and then only with a measure of sophistry. A gifted writer, however extreme his theoretical modernism, will in practice have to compromise with the demands of historicity and of social environment. Joyce uses Dublin, Kafka and Musil the Hapsburg Monarchy, as the locus of their masterpieces. But the locus they lovingly depict is little more than a backcloth; it is not basic to their artistic intention.

This view of human existence has specific literary consequences. Particularly in one category, of primary theoretical and practical importance, to which we must now give our attention: that of *potentiality*. Philosophy distinguishes between *abstract* and *concrete* (in Hegel, 'real') *potentiality*. These two categories, their interrelation and opposition, are rooted in life itself. *Potentiality* – seen abstractly or subjectively–is richer than actual life. Innumerable possibilities for man's development are imaginable, only a small percentage of which will be realized. Modern subjectivism, taking these imagined possibilities for actual complexity of life, oscillates between melancholy and fascination. When the world declines to realize these possibilities, this melancholy becomes tinged with contempt. Hofmannsthal's Sobeide expressed the reaction of the generation first exposed to this experience:

> The burden of those endlessly pored-over
> And now forever perished possibilities . . .

How far were those possibilities even concrete or 'real'? Plainly, they existed only in the imagination of the subject, as dreams or day-dreams. Faulkner, in whose work this subjective potentiality plays an important part, was evidently aware that reality must thereby be subjectivized and made to appear arbitrary. Consider this comment of his: 'They were all talking simultaneously, getting flushed and excited, quarrelling, making the unreal into a possibility, then into a probability, then into an irrefutable fact, as human beings do when they put their wishes into words.' The possibilities in a man's mind, the particular pattern, intensity and suggestiveness they assume, will of course be characteristic of that individual. In practice, their number will border on the infinite, even with the most unimaginative individual. It is thus a hopeless undertaking to define the contours of individuality, let alone to come to grips with a man's actual fate, by means of potentiality. The *abstract* character of potentiality is clear from the fact that it cannot determine development–subjective mental states, however permanent or profound, cannot here be decisive. Rather, the development of personality is determined by inherited gifts and qualities; by the factors, external or internal, which further or inhibit their growth.

But in life potentiality can, of course, become reality. Situations arise in which a man is confronted with a choice; and in the act of choice a man's character may reveal itself in a light that surprises even himself. In literature – and particularly in dramatic literature – the denouement often consists in the realization of just such a potentiality, which circumstances have kept, from coming to the fore. These potentialities are, then, 'real' or concrete potentialities. The fate of the character depends upon the potentiality in question, even if it should condemn him to a tragic end. In advance, while still a subjective potentiality in the character's mind, there is no way of distinguishing it from the innumerable abstract potentialities in his mind. It may even be buried away so completely that, before the moment of decision, it has never entered his mind even as an abstract potentiality. The subject, after taking his decision, may be unconscious of his own motives. Thus Richard Dudgeon, Shaw's Devil's Disciple, having sacrificed himself as Pastor Andersen, confesses: 'I have often asked myself for the motive, but I find no good reason to explain why I acted as I did.'

Yet it is a decision which has altered the direction of his life. Of course, this is an extreme case. But the qualitative leap of the denouement, cancelling and at the same time renewing the continuity of individual consciousness, can never be predicted. The concrete potentiality cannot be isolated from the myriad abstract potentialities. Only actual decision reveals the distinction.

The literature of realism, aiming at a truthful reflection of reality, must demonstrate both the concrete and abstract potentialities of human beings in extreme situations of this kind. A character's concrete potentiality once revealed, his abstract potentialities will appear essentially inauthentic. Moravia, for instance in his novel *The Indifferent Ones*, describes the young son of a decadent bourgeois family, Michel, who makes up his mind to kill his sister's seducer. While Michel, having made his decision, is planning the murder, a large number of abstract – but highly suggestive – possibilities are laid before us. Unfortunately for Michel the murder is actually carried out; and, from the sordid details of the action, Michel's character emerges as what it is – representative of that background from which, in subjective fantasy, he had imagined he could escape.

Abstract potentiality belongs wholly to the realm of subjectivity; whereas concrete potentiality is concerned with the dialectic between the individual's subjectivity and objective reality. The literary presentation of the latter thus implies a description of actual persons inhabiting a palpable, identifiable world. Only in the interaction of character and environment can the concrete potentiality of a particular individual be singled out from the 'bad infinity' of purely abstract potentialities, and emerge as the determining potentiality of just this individual at just this phase of his development. This principle alone enables the artist to distinguish concrete potentiality from myriad abstractions.

But the ontology on which the image of man in modernist literature is based invalidates this principle. If the 'human condition' – man as a solitary being, incapable of meaningful relationships – is identified with reality itself, the distinction between abstract and concrete potentiality becomes null and void. The categories tend to merge. Thus Cesare Pavese notes with John Dos Passos, and his German contemporary, Alfred Döblin, a sharp oscillation between 'superficial *verisme*' and 'abstract Expressionist schematism'. Criticizing Dos Passos, Pavese writes that fictional characters 'ought to be created by deliberate selection and description of individual features – implying that Dos Passos' characterizations are transferable from one individual to another. He describes the artistic consequences: by exalting man's subjectivity, at the expense of the objective reality of his environment, man's subjectivity itself is impoverished.

The problem, once again, is ideological. This is not to say that the ideology underlying modernist writings is identical in all cases. On the contrary: the ideology exists in extremely various, even contradictory forms. The rejection of narrative objectivity, the surrender to subjectivity, may take the form of Joyce's stream of consciousness, or of Musil's 'active passivity', his 'existence without quality', or of Gide's *'action gratuite'*, where abstract potentiality achieves pseudo-realization. As individual character manifests itself in life's moments of decision, so too in literature. If the distinction between abstract and concrete potentiality vanishes, if man's inwardness is identified with an abstract subjectivity, human personality must necessarily disintegrate.

T.S. Eliot described this phenomenon, this mode of portraying human personality, as

Shape without form, shade without colour,
Paralysed force, gesture without motion.

The disintegration of personality is matched by a disintegration of the outer world. In one sense, this is simply a further consequence of our argument. For the identification of abstract and concrete human potentiality rests on the assumption that the objective world is inherently inexplicable. Certain leading modernist writers, attempting a theoretical apology, have admitted this quite frankly. Often this theoretical impossibility of understanding reality is the point of departure, rather than the exaltation of subjectivity. But in any case the connection between the two is plain. The German poet Gottfried Benn, for instance, informs us that 'there is no outer reality, there is only human consciousness, constantly building, modifying, rebuilding new worlds out of its own creativity'. Musil, as always, gives a moral twist to this line of thought. Ulrich, the hero of his *The Man without Qualities*, when asked what he would do if he were in God's place, replies: 'I should be compelled to abolish reality'. Subjective existence 'without qualities' is the complement of the negation of outward reality.

The negation of outward reality is not always demanded with such theoretical rigour. But it is present in almost all modernist literature. In conversation, Musil once gave as the period of his great novel, 'between 1912 and 1914'. But he was quick to modify this statement by adding: 'I have not, I must insist, written a historical novel. I am not concerned with actual events. . . . Events, anyhow, are interchangeable. I am interested in what is typical, in what one might call the ghostly aspect of reality'. The word 'ghostly' is interesting. It points to a major tendency in modernist literature: the attenuation of actuality. In Kafka, the descriptive detail is of an extraordinary immediacy and authenticity. But Kafka's artistic ingenuity is really directed towards substituting his *angst*-ridden vision of the world for objective reality. The realistic detail is the expression of a ghostly un-reality, of a nightmare world, whose function is to evoke *angst*. The same phenomenon can be seen in writers who attempt to combine Kafka's techniques with a critique of society – like the German writer, Wolfgang Koeppen, in his satirical novel about Bonn, *Das Treibhaus*. A similar attenuation of reality underlies Joyce's stream of consciousness. It is, of course, intensified where the stream of consciousness is itself the medium through which reality is presented. And it is carried *ad absurdum* where the stream of consciousness is that of an abnormal subject or of an idiot – consider the first part of Faulkner's *Sound and Fury* or, a still more extreme case, Beckett's *Molloy*.

Attenuation of reality and dissolution of personality are thus interdependent: the stronger the one, the stronger the other. Underlying both is the lack of a consistent view of human nature. Man is reduced to a sequence of unrelated experiential fragments; he is as inexplicable to others as to himself. In Eliot's *Cocktail Party* the psychiatrist, who voices the opinions of the author, describes the phenomenon:

Ah, but we die to each other daily
What we know of other people
Is only our memory of the moments
During which we knew them. And they have changed
since then.

To pretend that they and we are the same
Is a useful and convenient social convention
Which must sometimes be broken. We must also remember
That at every meeting we are meeting a stranger.

The dissolution of personality, originally the unconscious product of the identification of concrete and abstract potentiality, is elevated to a deliberate principle in the light of consciousness. It is no accident that Gottfried Benn called one of his theoretical tracts '*Doppelleben*'. For Benn, this dissolution of personality took the form of a schizophrenic dichotomy. According to him, there was in man's personality no coherent pattern of motivation or behaviour. Man's animal nature is opposed to his denaturized, sublimated thought-processes. The unity of thought and action is 'backwoods philosophy'; thought and being are 'quite separate entities'. Man must be either a moral or a thinking being – he cannot be both at once.

* * * * *

If reality cannot be understood (or no effort is made to understand it), then the individual's subjectivity – alone in the universe, reflecting only itself–takes on an equally incomprehensible and horrific character. Hugo von Hofmannsthal was to experience this condition very early in his poetic career:

> It is a thing that no man cares to think on,
> And far too terrible for mere complaint,
> That all things slip from us and pass away,
>
> And that my ego, bound by no outward force–
> Once a small child's before it became mine–
> Should now be strange to me, like a strange dog.

By separating time from the outer world of objective reality, the inner world of the subject is transformed into a sinister, inexplicable flux and acquires–paradoxically, as it may seem–a static character.

11 | Theodor Adorno,

From 'On Lyric Poetry and Society', R. Tiedemann ed., *Notes to Literature*, Vol. 1 (1991), pp. 45–54

Everything I have said needs to be qualified if it is to avoid misinterpretation. My thesis is that the lyric work is always the subjective expression of a social antagonism. But since the objective world that produces the lyric is an inherently antagonistic world, the concept of the lyric is not simply that of the expression of a subjectivity to which language grants objectivity. Not only does the lyric subject embody the whole all the more cogently, the more it expresses itself; in addition, poetic subjectivity is itself indebted to privilege: the pressures of the struggle for survival allow only a few human beings to grasp the universal through immersion in the self or to develop as autonomous subjects capable of freely expressing themselves. The others, however, those who not only stand alienated, as though they were objects, facing the disconcerted poetic subject but who have also literally been degraded to objects of history, have the same right, or a greater right, to grope for the sounds in which sufferings and dreams are welded. This inalienable right has asserted itself again and again in forms however impure, mutilated, fragmentary, and intermittent–the only forms possible for those who have to bear the burden.

A collective undercurrent provides the foundation for all individual lyric poetry. When that poetry actually bears the whole in mind and is not simply an expression of the privilege, refinement, and gentility of those who can afford to be gentle, participation in this undercurrent is an essential part of the substantiality of the individual lyric as well: it is this undercurrent that makes language the medium in which the subject becomes more than a mere subject. Romanticism's link to the folksong is only the most obvious, certainly not the most compelling example of this. For Romanticism practices a kind of programmatic transfusion of the collective into the individual through which the individual lyric poem indulged in a technical illusion of universal cogency without that cogency characterizing it inherently. Often, in contrast, poets who abjure any borrowing from the collective language participate in that collective undercurrent by virtue of their historical experience. Let me mention Baudelaire again, whose lyric poetry is a slap in the face not only to the *juste milieu* but also to all bourgeois social sentiment, and who nevertheless, in poems like the 'Petites vieilles' or the poem about the servant woman with the generous heart in the *Tableaux Parisiens*, was truer to the masses toward whom he turned his tragic, arrogant mask than any 'poor people's' poetry. Today, when individual expression, which is the pre-condition for the conception of lyric poetry that is my point of departure, seems shaken to its very core in the crisis of the individual, the collective undercurrent in the lyric surfaces in the most diverse places: first merely as the ferment of individual expression and then perhaps also as an anticipation of a situation that transcends mere individuality in a positive way. If the translations can be trusted, García Lorca, whom Franco's henchmen murdered and whom no totalitarian regime could have tolerated, was the bearer of a force of this kind; and Brecht's name comes to mind as a lyric poet who was granted linguistic integrity without having to pay the price of esotericism. I will forgo making a judgment about whether the poetic principle of individuation was in fact sublated to a higher level here, or whether its basis lies in regression, a weakening of the ego. The collective power of contemporary lyric poetry may be largely due to the linguistic and psychic residues of a condition that is not yet fully individuated, a state of affairs that is prebourgeois in the broadest sense – dialect. Until now, however, the traditional lyric, as the most rigorous aesthetic negation of bourgeois convention, has by that very token been tied to bourgeois society.

Because considerations of principle are not sufficient. I would like to use a few poems to concretize the relationship of the poetic subject, which always stands for a far more general collective subject, to the social reality that is its antithesis. In this process the thematic elements, which no linguistic work, even *poésie pure* can completely divest itself of, will need interpretation just as the so-called formal elements will. The way the two interpenetrate will require special emphasis, for it is only by virtue of such interpenetration that the lyric poem actually captures the historical moment within its bounds. I want to choose not poems like Goethe's, aspects of which I commented on without analyzing, but later ones, poems which do not have the unqualified authenticity of the 'Nachtlied'. The two poems I will be talking about do indeed share in the collective undercurrent. But I would like to call your attention especially to the way in which in them different levels of a contradictory fundamental condition of society are represented in the medium of the poetic subject. Permit me to repeat that we are concerned not with the poet as a private person, not with his psychology or his so-called social perspective, but with the poem as a philosophical sundial telling the time of history.

Let me begin by reading you Eduard Mörike's 'Auf einer Wanderung' ['On a Walking Tour']:

> In ein freundliches Städtchen tret' ich ein
> In den Strassen liegt roter Abendschein,
> Aus einem offenen Fenster eben,
> Über den reichsten Blumenflor
> Hinweg, hör man Goldglockentöne schweben,
> Und *eine* Stimme scheint ein Nachtigallenchor,
> Daß die Blüten beben,
> Daß die Lüfte leben,
> Daß in höherem Rot die Rosen leuchten vor.
>
> Lang' hielt ich staunend, lustbeklommen.
> Wie ich hinaus vors Tor gekommen,
> Ich weiss es wahrlich selber nicht,
> Ach hier, wie liegt die Welt so licht!
> Der Himmel wogt in purpurnem Gewühle,
> Rückwärts die Stadt in goldnem Rauch;
> Wie rauscht der Erlenhach, wie rauscht im Grund die Mühle!
> Ich bin wie trunken, irrgeführt –
> O Muse, du hast mein Herz berührt
> Mit einem Liebeshauch!

> [I enter a friendly little town,
> On the streets lies the red evening light,
> From an open window,
> Across the richest profusion of flowers
> One hears golden bell-tones hover,
> And *one* voice seems to be a choir of nightingales,
> So that the blossoms quaver,
> So that the breezes are lively,
> So that the roses glow forth in a higher red.
>
> I stood a long while marvelling, oppressed with pleasure.
> How I got out beyoud the city gate,
> I really do not know myself,
> Oh, how bright the world is here!
> The sky surges in purple turbulence,
> At my back the town in a golden haze;
> How the alder stream murmurs, how the mill roars below!
> I am as if drunken, led astray –
> Oh muse, you have touched my heart,
> With a breath of love!]

Up surges the image of the promise of happiness which the small south German town still grants its guests on the right day, but not the slightest concession is made to the pseudo-Gothic small-town idyll. The poem gives the feeling of warmth and security in a confined space, yet at the same time it is a work in the elevated style, not disfigured by *Gemütlichkeit* and coziness, not sentimentally praising narrowness in opposition to the wide world, not happiness in one's own little corner. Language and the rudimentary plot both aid in skillfully equating the utopia of what is close at hand with that of the utmost distance. The town appears in the narrative only as a fleeting scene, not as a place of lingering. The magnitude of the feeling that results from the speaker's delight in the girl's voice, and not that voice alone but the voice of all of nature, the choir, emerges only outside the confined arena of the town, under the open purple-billowing sky, where the golden town and the rushing brook come together in the *imago*. Linguistically, this is aided by an inestimably subtle, scarcely definable *classical*, ode-like element. As if from afar, the free rhythms call to mind unrhymed Greek stanzas, as does the sudden pathos of the closing line of the first stanza, which is effected with the most discreet devices of transposition of word order: 'Daß in höherem Rot die Rosen leuchten vor'. The single word 'Muse' at the end of the poem is decisive. It is as if this word, one of the most overused in German classicism, gleamed once again, truly as if in the light of the setting sun, by being bestowed upon the *genius loci* of the friendly little town, and as though even in the process of disappearing it were possessed of all the power to enrapture which an invocation of the muse in the modern idiom, comically inept, usually fails to capture. The poem's inspiration proves itself perhaps more fully in this than in any of its other features: that the choice of this most objectionable word at a critical point, carefully prepared by the latent Greek linguistic demeanor, resolves the urgent dynamic of the whole like a musical *Abgesang*.[1] In the briefest of spaces, the lyric succeeds in doing what the German epic attempted in vain, even in such projects as Goethe's *Hermann and Dorothea*.

The social interpretation of a success like this is concerned with the stage of historical experience evidenced in the poem. In the name of humanity, of the universality of the human, German classicism had undertaken to release subjective impulses from the contingency that threatens them in a society where relationships between human beings are no longer direct but instead mediated solely by the market. It strove to objectify the subjective as Hegel did in philosophy and tried to overcome the contradictions of men's real lives by reconciling them in spirit, in the idea. The continued existence of these contradictions in reality, however, had compromised the spiritual solution: in the face of a life not grounded in meaning, a life lived painstakingly amid the bustle of competing interests, a prosaic life, as artistic experience sees it; in the face of a world in which the fate of individual human beings works itself out in accordance with blind laws, art, whose form gives the impression of speaking from the point of view of a realized humanity, becomes an empty word. Hence classicism's concept of the human being withdrew into private, individual existence and its images; only there did humanness seem secure. Of necessity, the idea of humankind as something whole, something self-determining, was renounced by the bourgeoisie, in aesthetic form as in politics. It is the stubborn clinging to one's own restricted sphere, which itself obeys a compulsion, that makes ideals like comfort and *Gemütlichkeit* so suspect. Meaning itself is linked to the contingencies of human happiness; through a kind of usurpation, individual happiness is ascribed a dignity it would attain only along with the happiness of the whole. The social force of Mörike's genius, however, consists in the fact that he combined the two experiences–that of the classicistic elevated style and that of the romantic private miniature–and that in doing so he recognized the limits of both possibilities and balanced them against one another with incomparable tact. In none of his expressive impulses does he go beyond what could be genuinely attained in his time. The much-invoked organic quality of his work is probably nothing other than this tact, which is philosophically sensitive to history and which scarcely any other poet in the German language possessed to the same degree. The alleged pathological traits in Mörike reported by psychologists and the drying up of his production in later years are the negative aspect of his very highly developed understanding of what is possible. The poems of the hypochondriacal clergyman from Cleversulzbach, who is considered one of our naive artists, are virtuoso pieces unsurpassed by the masters of *l'art pour l'art*. He is as aware of the empty and ideological aspects of elevated style as of the mediocrity, petit-bourgeois dullness, and obliviousness to totality of the Biedermeier period, in which the greater part of his lyric work falls. The spirit in him is driven to create, for the last time, images that would betray themselves neither by their classical drapery nor by local color, neither by their manly tones nor by their lip-smacking. As if walking a fine line, the residues of the elevated style that survive in memory echo in him, together with the signs of an immediate life that promised fulfilment precisely at the time when they were already condemned by the direction history was taking; and both greet the poet on his wandering only as they are about to vanish. He already shares in the paradox of lyric poetry in the ascending industrial age. As indeterminate and fragile as his solutions are the solutions of all the great lyric poets who come afterwards, ever those who seem to be separated from him by an abyss–like Baudelaire, of whom Claudel said that his style was a mixture of Racine's and that of the journalists of his time. In industrial society the lyric idea of a self-restoring immediacy becomes–where it does not impotently evoke a romantic past–more and more something that flashes out abruptly, something in which what is possible transcends its own impossibility.

The short poem by Stefan George I would now like to discuss derives from a much later phase in this development. It is one of the celebrated songs from the *Seventh Ring*, a cycle of extremely condensed works which for all their lightness of rhythm are over-heavy with substance and wholly without *Jugendstil* ornament. Their eccentric boldness was rescued from the frightful cultural conservativism of the George circle only when the great composer Anton von Webern set them to music; in George, ideology and social substance are very far apart. The song reads:

Im windes-weben
War meine frage
Nur träumerei.
Nur lächeln war
Was du gegeben.'
Aus nasser nacht
Ein glanz entfacht–
Nun drängt der mai
Nun muss ich gar
Um dein aug und haar
Alle tage
In sehnen leben.
[In the winds-weaving
My question was
Only daydreaming.
Only a smile was
What you gave.
From a moist night
A gleam ignites–
Now May urges
Now I must
For your eyes and hair
Every day
Live in yearning.]

Unquestionably, this is elevated style. Delight in things close at hand, something that still colors Mörike's much earlier poem, has fallen under a prohibition. It has been banished by the Nietzschean pathos of detached reserve which George conceives himself to be carrying on. The remains of Romanticism lie, a deterrent, between him and Mörike; the remains of the idyll are hopelessly outdated and have degenerated to heartwarmers. While George's poetry, the poetry of an imperious individual, presupposes individualistic bourgeois society and the autonomous individual as its preconditions, a curse is put on the bourgeois element of conventional form no less than on the bourgeois contents. But because this poetry can speak from no overarching framework other than the bourgeois, which it rejects not only tacitly and *a priori* but also expressly, it becomes obstructed: on its own initiative and its own authority, it simulates a feudal condition. Socially this is hidden behind what the cliché refers to as George's aristocratic stance. This stance in not the pose that the bourgeois, who cannot reduce these poems to objects of fondling, waxes indignant about. Rather, despite its demeanor of hostility to society, it is the product of the social dialectic that denies the lyric subject identification with what exists and its world of forms, while that subject is nevertheless allied with the status quo in its innermost core: it has no other locus from which to speak but that of a past seigneurial society. The ideal of nobility, which dictates the choice of every word, image, and sound in the poem, is derived from that locus, and the form is medieval in an almost undefinable way, a way that has been virtually imported into the linguistic configuration. To this extent the poem, like George altogether, is neoromantic. But it is not real things and not sounds that are evoked but rather a vanished condition of the soul. The artistically effected latency of the ideal, the absence of any crude archaicism, raise the song above the hopeless fiction it nonetheless offers. It no more resembles the medieval imitations used on wall plaques than it does the repertoire of the modern lyric; the poem's stylistic principle saves it from conformity. There is no more room in it for organic reconciliation of conflicting elements than there was for their pacification in the reality of George's time; they are mastered only through selection, through omission. Where things close at hand, the things one commonly calls concrete immediate experiences, are admitted into George's lyric poetry at all, they are allowed only at the price of mythologization: none may remain what it is. Thus in one of the landscapes of the *Seventh Ring* the child picking berries is transformed, wordlessly, as if with a magic wand, through a magical act of violence, into a fairy-tale child. The harmony of the song is wrested form an extreme of dissonance: it rests on what Valéry called *refus*, on an unyielding renunciation of everything through which the conventions of lyric poetry imagine that they have captured the aura of things. The method retains only the patterns, the pure formal ideas and schemata of lyric poetry itself, which speak with an intensity of expression once again in divesting themselves of all contingency. In the midst of Wilhelmine Germany the elevated style from which that lyric poetry emerged as polemic has no tradition at all to which it may appeal, least of all the legacy of classicism. It is achieved not by making a show of rhetorical figures and rhythms but by an ascetic omission of whatever might diminish its distance from a language sullied by commerce. If the subject is to genuinely resist reification in solitude here, it may no longer even try to withdraw into what is its own as though that were its property; the traces of an individualism that has in the meantime delivered itself over to the market in the form of the feuilleton are alarming. Instead, the subject has to step outside itself by keeping quiet about itself; it has to make itself a vessel, so to speak, for the idea of a pure language. George's greatest poems are aimed at rescuing that language. Formed by the Romance languages, and especially by the extreme simplification of the lyric through which Verlaine made it an instrument of what is most differentiated, the ear of George, the German student of Mallarmé, hears his own language as though it were a foreign tongue. He overcomes its alienation, which is an alienation of use, by intensifying it until it becomes the alienation of a language no longer actually spoken even an imaginary language, and in that imaginary language he perceives what would be possible, but never took place, in its composition. The four lines 'Nun muss ich gar/Um dein aug und haar/Alle tage/In sehnen leben', which I consider some of the most irresistible lines in German poetry, are like a quotation, but a quotation not from another poet but from something language has irrevocably failed to achieve: the medieval German poetry of the *Minnesang* would have succeeded in achieving it if it, if a tradition of the German language–if the German language itself, one is tempted to say–had succeeded. It was in this spirit that Borchardt tried to translate Dante. Subtle ears have taken umbrage at the elliptical 'gar' which is probably used in place of 'ganz und gar' [completely] and to some extent for the sake of the rhyme. One can concede the justice of this criticism and the fact that as used in the line the word has no proper meaning. But great works of art are the ones that succeed precisely where they are most problematic. Just as the greatest works of music may not be completely reduced to their structure but shoot out beyond it with a few superfluous notes or measures, so it is with the 'gar' a Goethean 'residue of the absurd' in which language escapes the subjective intention that occasioned the use of the word. It is probably this very 'gar' that establishes the poem's status with the force of a *déjà vu*: through it the melody of the poem's language extends beyond mere signification. In the age of its decline George sees in language the idea that the course of history has denied it and constructs lines that sound as though they were not written by him but had been there from the beginning of time and would remain as they were forever. The quixotism of this enterprise, however, the impossibility of this kind of restorative writing, the danger of falling into arts and crafts, enriches the poem's substance: language's chimerical yearning for the impossible becomes an expression of the subject's insatiable erotic longing, which finds relief from the self in the other. This tranformation of an individuality intensified to an extreme into self-annihilation–and what was the Maximin cult in the late George but a desperate renunciation of individuality construing itself as something positive–was necessary in creating the phantasmagoria of the folksong, something the German language had been groping for in vain in its greatest masters. Only by virtue of a differentiation taken so far that it can no longer bear its own difference, can no longer bear anything but the universal, freed from the humiliation of isolation, in the particular does lyrical language represent language's intrinsic being as opposed to its service in the realm of ends. But it thereby represents the idea of a free humankind, even if the George School concealed this idea from itself through a base cult of the heights. The truth of George lies in the fact that his poetry breaks down the walls of individuality through its consummation of the particular, through its sensitive opposition both to the banal and ultimately also to the select. The expression of his poetry may have been condensed into an individual expression which his lyrics saturate with substance and with the experience of its own solitude; but this very lyric speech becomes the voice of human beings between whom the barriers have fallen.

Note

1 The *Abgesang* was the closing portion of a stanza in medieval lyric poetry.

12 | Raymond Williams,

From *Marxism and Literature* (1977), pp. 55–71

The concept of 'ideology' did not originate in Marxism and is still in no way confined to it. Yet it is evidently an important concept in almost all Marxist thinking about culture, and especially about literature and ideas. The difficulty then is that we have to distinguish three common versions of the concept, which are all common in Marxist writing. These are, broadly:

(i)   a system of beliefs characteristic of a particular class or group;
(ii) a system of illusory beliefs – false ideas or false consciousness – which can be contrasted with true or scientific knowledge;
(iii) the general process of the production of meanings and ideas.

In one variant of Marxism, senses (i) and (ii) can be effectively combined. In a class society, all beliefs are founded on class position, and the systems of belief of all classes – or, quite commonly, of all classes preceding, and other than, the proletariat, whose formation is the project of the abolition of class society – are then in part or wholly false (illusory). The specific problems in this powerful general proposition have led to intense controversy within Marxist thought. It is not unusual to find some form of the proposition alongside uses of the simple sense (i), as in the characterization, for example by Lenin, of 'socialist ideology'. Another way of broadly retaining but distinguishing senses (i) and (ii) is to use sense (i) of systems of belief founded on class position, including that of the proletariat within class society, and sense (ii) for contrast with (in a broad sense) *scientific* knowledge of all kinds, which is based on reality rather than illusions. Sense (iii) undercuts most of these associations and distinctions, for the ideological process – the production of meanings and ideas – is then seen as general and universal, and ideology is either this process itself or the area of its study. Positions associated with senses (i) and (ii) are then brought to bear in Marxist ideological studies.

   In this situation there can be no question of establishing, except in polemics, a single 'correct' Marxist definition of ideology. It is more to the point to return the term and its variations to the issues within which it and these were formed; and specifically, first, to the historical development. We can then return to the issues as they now present themselves, and to the important controversies which the term and its variations reveal and conceal.

   'Ideology' was coined as a term in the late eighteenth century, by the French philosopher Destutt de Tracy. It was intended to be a philosophical term for the 'science of ideas'. Its use depended on a particular understanding of the nature of 'ideas', which was broadly that of Locke and the empiricist tradition. Thus ideas were not to be and could not be understood in any of the older 'metaphysical' or 'idealist' senses. The science of ideas must be a natural science, since all ideas originate in man's experience of the world. Specifically, in Destutt, ideology is part of zoology:

> We have only an incomplete knowledge of an animal if we do not know his intellectual faculties. Ideology is a part of Zoology, and it is especially in man that this part is important and deserves to be more deeply understood. (*Éléments d' idéologie*, 1801, Preface)

The description is characteristic of scientific empiricism. The 'real elements' of ideology are 'our intellectual faculties, their principal phenomena and their most evident circumstances'. The critical aspect of this emphasis was at once realized by one kind of opponent, the reactionary de Bonald: 'Ideology has replaced metaphysics . . . because modern philosophy sees no other ideas in the world but those of men'. De Bonald correctly related the scientific sense of ideology to the empiricist tradition which had passed from Locke through Condillac, pointing out its preoccupation with 'signs and their influence on thought' and summarizing its 'sad system' as a reduction of 'our thoughts' to 'transformed sensations'. 'All the characteristics of intelligence', de Bonald added, 'disappeared under the scalpel of this ideological dissection'.

The initial bearings of the concept of ideology are then very complex. It was indeed an assertion against metaphysics that there are 'no ideas in the world but those of men'. At the same time, intended as a branch of empirical science, 'ideology' was limited, by its philosophical assumptions, to a version of ideas as 'transformed sensations' and to a version of language as a 'system of signs' (based, as in Condillac, on an ultimately mathematical model). These limitations, with their characteristic abstraction of 'man' and 'the world', and with their reliance on the passive 'reception' and 'systematic association' of 'sensations', were not only 'scientific' and 'empirical' but were elements of a basically bourgeois view of human existence. The rejection of metaphysics was a characteristic gain, confirmed by the development of precise and systematic empirical enquiry. At the same time the effective exclusion of any social dimension – both the practical exclusion of social relationships implied in the model of 'man' and 'the world', and the characteristic displacement of necessary social relationships to a formal system, whether the 'laws of psychology' or language as a 'system of signs' – was a deep and apparently irrecoverable loss and distortion.

It is significant that the initial objection to the exclusion of any active conception of intelligence was made from generally reactionary positions, which sought to retain the sense of activity in its old metaphysical forms. It is even more significant, in the next stage of the development, that a derogatory sense of 'ideology' as 'impractical theory' or 'abstract illusion', first introduced from an evidently reactionary position by Napoleon, was taken over, though from a new position, by Marx.

Napoleon said:

> It is to the doctrine of the ideologues – to this diffuse metaphysics, which in a contrived manner seeks to find the primary causes and on this foundation would erect the legislation of peoples, instead of adapting the laws to a knowledge of the human heart and of the lessons of history – to which one must attribute all the misfortunes which have befallen our beautiful France.[1]

Scott (*Napoleon*, 1827, vi. 251) summarized: 'Ideology, by which nickname the French ruler used to distinguish every species of theory, which, resting in no respect upon the basis of self-interest, could, he thought, prevail with none save hot-brained boys and crazed enthusiasts'.

Each element of this condemnation of 'ideology' – which became very well known and was often repeated in Europe and North America during the first half of the nineteenth century – was taken up and applied by Marx and Engels, in their early writings. It is the substantial content of their attack on their German contemporaries in *The German Ideology* (1846). To find 'primary causes' in 'ideas' was seen as the basic error. There is even the same tone of contemptuous practicality in the anecdote in Marx's Preface:

> Once upon a time an honest fellow had the idea that men were drowned in water only because they were possessed with the idea of gravity. If they were to knock this idea out of their heads, say by stating it to be a superstition, a religious idea, they would be sublimely proof against any danger from water. (*GI*, 2)

Abstract theories, separated from the 'basis of self-interest', were then beside the point.

Of course the argument could not be left at this stage. In place of Napoleon's conservative (and suitably vague) standard of 'knowledge of the human heart and of the lessons of history', Marx and Engels introduced 'the real ground of history' – the process of production and self-production – from which the 'origins and growth' of 'different theoretical products' could be traced. The simple cynicism of the appeal to 'self-interest' became a critical diagnosis of the real basis of all ideas:

> the ruling ideas are nothing more than the ideal expression of the dominant material relationships, the dominant material relationships grasped as ideas. (*GI*, 39)

Yet already at this stage there were obvious complications. 'Ideology' became a polemical nickname for kinds of thinking which neglected or ignored the material social process of which 'consciousness' was always a part:

> Consciousness can never be anything else than conscious existence, and the existence of men is their actual life-process. If in all ideology men and their circumstances appear upside down as in a *camera obscura*, this phenomenon arises just as much from their historical life-process as the inversion of objects on the retina does from their physical life-process. (*GI*, 14)

The emphasis is clear but the analogy is difficult. The physical processes of the retina cannot reasonably be separated from the physical processes of the brain, which, *as a necessarily connected activity*, control and 'rectify' the inversion. The *camera obscura* was a conscious device for discerning proportions; the inversion had in fact been corrected by adding another lens. In one sense the analogies are no more than incidental, but they probably relate to (though in fact, as examples, they work against) an underlying criterion of 'direct positive knowledge'. They are in a way very like the use of 'the idea of gravity' to refute the notion of the controlling power of ideas. If the idea had been not a practical and scientific understanding of a natural force but, say, an idea of 'racial superiority' or of 'the inferior wisdom of women', the argument might in the end have come out the same way but it would have had to pass through many more significant stages and difficulties.

This is also true even of the more positive definition:

> We do not set out from what men say, imagine, conceive, nor from men as narrated, thought of, imagined, conceived, in order to arrive at men in the flesh. We set out from real, active men, and on the basis of their real life-process we demonstrate the development of the ideological reflexes and echoes of this life-process. The phantoms formed in the human brain are also, necessarily, sublimates of their material life-process, which is empirically verifiable and bound to material premises. Morality, religion, metaphysics, all the rest of ideology and their corresponding forms of consciousness, thus no longer retain the semblance of independence. (*GI*, 14)

That 'ideology' should be deprived of its 'semblance of independence' is entirely reasonable. But the language of 'reflexes', 'echoes', 'phantoms', and 'sublimates' is simplistic, and has in repetition been disastrous. It belongs to the naïve dualism of 'mechanical materialism', in which the idealist separation of 'ideas' and 'material reality' had been repeated, but with its priorities reversed. The emphasis on consciousness as inseparable from conscious existence, and then on conscious existence as inseparable from material social processes, is in effect lost in the use of this deliberately degrading vocabulary. The damage can be realized if we compare it for a moment with Marx's description of 'human labour' in *Capital* (i. 185–6):

> We presuppose labour in a form that stamps it as exclusively human . . . What distinguishes the worst architect from the best of bees is this, that the architect raises his structure in imagination before he erects it in reality. At the end of every labour-process, we get a result that already existed in the imagination of the labourer at its commencement.

This goes perhaps even too much the other way, but its difference from the world of 'reflexes', 'echoes', 'phantoms', and 'sublimates' hardly needs to be stressed. Consciousness is seen from the beginning as part of the human material social process, and its products in 'ideas' are then as much part of this process as material products themselves. This, centrally, was the thrust of Marx's whole argument, but the point was lost, in this crucial area, by a temporary surrender to the cynicism of 'practical men' and, even more, to the abstract empiricism of a version of 'natural science'.

What had really been introduced, as a corrective to abstract empiricism, was the sense of material and social history as the real relationship between 'man' and 'nature'. But it is then very curious of Marx and Engels to abstract, in turn, the persuasive 'men in the flesh', at whom we 'arrive'. To begin by presupposing them, as the necessary starting-point, is right while we remember that they are therefore also conscious men. The decision not to set out from 'what men say, imagine, conceive, nor from men as narrated, thought of, imagined, conceived' is then at best a corrective reminder that there is other and sometimes harder evidence of what they have done. But it is also at its worst an objectivist fantasy: that the whole 'real life-process' can be known independently of language ('what men say') and of its records ('men as narrated'). For the very notion of history would become absurd if we did not look at 'men as narrated' (when, having died, they are hardly likely to be accessible 'in the flesh', and on which, inevitably, Marx and Engels extensively and repeatedly relied) as well as at that 'history of *industry* . . . as it objectively exists . . . an *open book of the human faculties* . . . a human *psychology* which can be directly apprehended' (*EPM*, 121), which they had decisively introduced against the exclusions of other historians. What they were centrally arguing was a new way of seeing the total relationships between this 'open book' and 'what men say' and 'men as narrated'. In a polemical response to the abstract history of ideas or of consciousness they made their main point but in one decisive area lost it again. This confusion is the source of the naïve reduction, in much subsequent Marxist thinking, of consciousness, imagination, art, and ideas to 'reflexes', 'echoes', 'phantoms', and 'sublimates', and then of a profound confusion in the concept of 'ideology'.

We can trace further elements of this failure if we examine those definitions of ideology which gain most of their force by contrast with what is not ideology. The most common of these contrasts is with what is called 'science'. For example:

> Where speculation ends – in real life – there real, positive science begins: the representation of the practical activity, of the practical process of development of men. Empty talk about consciousness ceases, and real knowledge has to take its place. When reality is depicted, philosophy as an independent branch of activity loses its medium of existence. (*GI*, 17)

There are several difficulties here. The uses of 'consciousness' and 'philo-sophy' depend almost entirely on the main argument about the futility of separating consciousness and thought from the material social process. It is the separation that makes such consciousness and thought into ideology. But it is easy to see how the point could be taken, and has often been taken, in a quite different way. In a new kind of abstraction, 'consciousness' and 'philosophy' are separated, in their turn, from 'real knowledge' and from the 'practical process'. This is especially easy to do with the available language of 'reflexes', 'echoes', 'phantoms', and 'sublimates'. The result of this separation, against the original conception of an *indissoluble* process, is the farcical exclusion of consciousness from the 'development of men' and from 'real knowledge' of this development. But the former, at least, is impossible by any standard. All that can then be done to mask its absurdity is elaboration of the familiar two-stage model (the mechanical materialist reversal of the idealist dualism), in which there is *first* material social life and then, at some temporal or spatial distance, consciousness and 'its' products. This leads directly to simple reductionism: 'consciousness' and 'its products can be *nothing but* 'reflections' of what has already occurred in the material social process.

It can of course be said from experience (that experience which produced the later anxious warnings and qualifications) that this is a poor practical way of trying to understand 'consciousness and its products': that these continually escape so simple a reductive equation. But this is a marginal point. The real point is that the separation and abstraction of 'consciousness and its products' as a 'reflective' or 'second-stage' process results in an ironic idealization of 'consciousness and its products' at this secondary level.

For 'consciousness and its products' are always, though in variable forms, parts of the material social process itself: whether as what Marx called the necessary element of 'imagination' in the labour process; or as the necessary conditions of associated labour, in language and in practical ideas of relationship; or, which is so often and significantly forgotten, in the real processes – all of them physical and material, most of them manifestly so – which are masked and idealized as 'consciousness and its products' but which, when seen without illusions, are themselves necessarily social material activities. What is in fact idealized, in the ordinary reductive view, is 'thinking' or 'imagining', and the only materialization of these abstracted processes is by a general reference back to the whole (and because abstracted then in effect complete) material social process. And what this version of Marxism especially overlooks is that 'thinking' and 'imagining' are from the beginning social processes (of course including that capacity for 'internalization' which is a necessary part of any social process between actual individuals) and that they become accessible only in unarguably physical and material ways: in voices, in sounds made by instruments, in penned or printed writing, in arranged pigments on canvas or plaster, in worked marble or stone. To exclude these material social processes from *the* material social process is the same error as to reduce all material social processes to mere technical means for some other abstracted 'life'. The 'practical process' of the 'development of men' necessarily includes them from the beginning, and as more than the technical means for some quite separate 'thinking' and 'imagining'.

What can then be said to be 'ideology', in its received negative form? It can of course be said that these processes, or some of them, come in variable forms (which is as undeniable as the variable forms of any production), and that some of these forms are 'ideology' while others are not. This is a tempting path, but it is usually not followed far, because there is a fool's beacon erected just a little way along it. This is the difficult concept of 'science'. We have to notice first a problem of translation. The German *Wissenschaft*, like the French *science*, has a much broader meaning than English *science* has had since the early nineteenth century. The broader meaning is in the area of 'systematic knowledge' or 'organized learning'.

In English this has been largely specialized to such knowledge based on observation of the 'real world' (at first, and still persistently, within the categories of 'man' and 'the world') and on the significant distinction (and even opposition) between the formerly interchangeable words *experience* and *experiment*, the latter attracting, in the course of development, new senses of *empirical* and *positive*. It is then very difficult for any English reader to take the translated phrase of Marx and Engels–'real, positive science' – in anything other than this specialized sense. But two qualifications have then at once to be made. First, that the Marxist definition of the 'real world', by moving beyond the separated categories of 'man' and 'the world' and including, as central, the active material social process, had made any such simple transfer impossible:

> If industry is conceived as an *exoteric* form of the realization of the *essential* human faculties, one is able to grasp also the *human* essence of Nature or the *natural* essence of man. The natural sciences will then abandon their abstract materialist, or rather, idealist, orientation, and will become the basis of a *human* science . . . One basis for life and another for *science* is *a priori* a falsehood. (EPM, 122)

This is an argument precisely against the categories of the English specialization of 'science'. But then, second, the actual progress of scientific rationality, especially in its rejection of metaphysics and in its triumphant escape from a limitation to observation, experiment, and inquiry within received religious and philosophical systems, was immensely attractive as a model for understanding society. Though the object of inquiry had been radically changed–from 'man' and 'the world' to an active, interactive, and in a key sense self-creating material social process–it was supposed, or rather hoped, that the methods, or at least the mood, could be carried over.

This sense of getting free of the ordinary assumptions of social inquiry, which usually began where it should have ended, with the forms and categories of a particular historical *phase* of society, is immensely important and was radically demonstrated in most of Marx's work. But it is very different from the uncritical use of 'science' and 'scientific', with deliberate references to and analogies from 'natural science', to describe the essentially *critical and historical* work which was actually undertaken. Engels, it is true, used these references and analogies much more often than Marx. 'Scientific socialism' became, under his influence, a polemical catchword. In practice it depends almost equally on a (justifiable) sense of systematic knowledge of society, based on observation and analysis of its processes of development (as distinct, say, from 'utopian' socialism, which projected a desirable future without close consideration of the past and present processes within which it had to be attained); and on a (false) association with the 'fundamental' or 'universal' 'laws' of natural science, which, even when they turned out to be 'laws' rather than effective working generalizations or hypotheses, were of a different kind because their objects of study were radically different.

The notion of 'science' has had a crucial effect, negatively, on the concept of 'ideology'. If 'ideology' is contrasted with 'real, positive science', in the sense of detailed and connected knowledge of 'the practical process of development of men', then the distinction may have significance as an indication of the received assumptions, concepts, and points of view which can be shown to prevent or distort such detailed and connected knowledge. We can often feel that this is all that was really intended. But the contrast is of course less simple than it may look, since its confident application depends on a knowable distinction between 'detailed and connected knowledge of the practical process of development' and other kinds of 'knowledge' which may often closely resemble it. One way of applying the distinguishing criterion would be by examining the 'assumptions, concepts, and points of view', whether received or not, by which any knowledge has been gained and organized. But it is just this kind of analysis which is prevented by the *a priori* assumption of a 'positive' method which is not subject to such scrutiny: an assumption based in fact on the received (and unexamined) assumptions of 'positive, scientific knowledge', freed of the 'ideological bias' of all other observers. This position, which has been often repeated in orthodox Marxism, is either a circular demonstration or a familiar partisan claim (of the kind made by almost all parties) that others are biased but that, by definition, we are not.

That indeed was the fool's way out of the very difficult problem which was now being confronted, within historical materialism. Its symptomatic importance at the level of dogma has to be noted and then set aside if we are to see, clearly, a very different and much more interesting proposition, which leads to a quite different (though not often theoretically distinguished) definition of ideology. This begins from the main point of the attack on the Young Hegelians, who were said to 'consider conceptions, thoughts, ideas, in fact all the products of consciousness, to which they attribute an independent existence, as the real chains of men'. Social liberation would then come through a 'change of consciousness'. Everything then turns, of course, on the definition of 'consciousness'. The definition adopted, polemically, by Marx and Engels, is in effect their definition of ideology: not 'practical consciousness' but 'self-dependent theory'. Hence 'really it is only a question of explaining this theoretical talk from the actual existing conditions. The real, practical dissolution of these phrases, the removal of these notions from the consciousness of men, will . . . be effected by altered circumstances, not by theoretical deductions' (*GI*, 15). In this task the proletariat has an advantage, since 'for the mass of men . . . these theoretical notions do not exist'.

If we can take this seriously we are left with a much more limited and in that respect more plausible definition of ideology. Since 'consciousness', including 'conceptions, thoughts, ideas', can hardly be asserted to be non-existent in the 'mass of men', the definition falls back to a kind of consciousness, and certain *kinds* of conceptions, thoughts, and ideas, which are specifically 'ideological'. Engels later sought to clarify this position:

> Every ideology . . . once it has arisen, develops in connection with the given concept-material, and develops this material further; otherwise it would cease to be ideology,

that is, occupation with thoughts as with independent entities, developing independently and subject only to their own laws. That the material life conditions of the persons inside whose heads this thought process goes on, in the last resort determines the course of this process, remains of necessity unknown to these persons, for otherwise there would be an end to all ideology. (*Feuerbach*, 65–6)

Ideology is a process accomplished by the so-called thinker, consciously indeed but with a false consciousness. The real motives impelling him remain unknown to him, otherwise it would not be an ideological process at all. Hence he imagines false or apparent motives. Because it is a process of thought he derives both its form and its content from pure thought, either his own or that of his predecessors.[2]

Taken on their own, these statements can appear virtually psychological. They are structurally very similar to the Freudian concept of 'rationalization' in such phrases as 'inside whose heads'; 'real motives . . . unknown to him'; 'imagines false or apparent motives'. In this form a version of 'ideology' is readily accepted in modern bourgeois thought, which has its own concepts of the 'real'–material or psychological–to undercut either ideology or rationalization. But it had once been a more serious position. Ideology was specifically identified as a consequence of the division of labour:

Division of labour only becomes truly such from the moment when a division of material and mental labour appears . . . From this moment onwards consciousness *can* really flatter itself that it is something other than consciousness of existing practice, that it *really* represents something without representing something real; from now on consciousness is in a position to emancipate itself from the world and to proceed to the formation of 'pure' theory, theology, philosophy, ethics, etc. (*GI*, 51)

Ideology is then 'separated theory', and its analysis must involve restoration of its 'real' connections.

The division of labour . . . manifests itself also in the ruling class as the division of mental and material labour, so that inside this class one part appears as the thinkers of the class (its active, conceptive ideologists, who make the perfecting of the illusion of the class about itself their chief source of livelihood) while the other's attitude to these ideas and illusions is more passive and receptive, because they are in reality the active members of this class and have less time to make up illusions and ideas about themselves. (*GI*, 39–40)

This is shrewd enough, as is the later observation that

each new class . . . is compelled . . . to represent its interest as the common interest of all the members of society, put in an ideal form; it will give its ideas the form of universality, and represent them as the only rational, universally valid ones. (*GI*, 40–1)

But 'ideology' then hovers between 'a system of beliefs characteristic of a certain class' and 'a system of illusory beliefs – false ideas or false consciousness–which can be contrasted with true or scientific knowledge'.

This uncertainty was never really resolved. Ideology as 'separated theory' – the natural home of illusions and false consciousness–is itself separated from the (intrinsically limited) 'practical consciousness of a class'. This separation, however, is very much easier to carry out in theory than in practice. The immense body of direct class-consciousness, directly expressed and again and again directly imposed, can appear to escape the taint of 'ideology', which would be limited to the 'universalizing' philosophers. But then what name is to be found for these powerful direct systems? Surely not 'true' or 'scientific' knowledge, except by an extraordinary sleight-of-hand with the description 'practical'. For most ruling classes have not needed to be 'unmasked'; they have usually proclaimed their existence and the 'conceptions, thoughts, ideas' which ratify it. To overthrow them is ordinarily to overthrow their conscious practice, and this is always very much harder than overthrowing their 'abstract' and 'universalizing' ideas, which also, in real terms, have a much more complicated and interactive relationship with the dominant 'practical consciousness' than any merely dependent or illusory concepts could ever have. Or again, 'the existence of revolutionary ideas in a particular period presupposes the existence of a revolutionary class'. But this may or may not be true, since all the difficult questions are about the development of a pre-revolutionary or potentially revolutionary or briefly revolutionary into a sustained revolutionary class, and the same difficult questions necessarily arise about pre-revolutionary, potentially revolutionary, or briefly revolutionary ideas. Marx and Engels's own complicated relations to the (in itself very complicated) revolutionary character of the European proletariat is an intensely practical example of just this difficulty, as is also their complicated and acknowledged relationship (including the relationship implied by critique) to their intellectual predecessors.

What really happened, in temporary but influential substitution for just this detailed and connected knowledge, was, first, an abstraction of 'ideology', as a category of illusions and false consciousness (an abstraction which as they had best reason to know would prevent examination, not of the abstracted ideas, which is relatively easy, but of the material social process in which 'conceptions, thoughts, ideas', of course in different degrees, become practical). Second, in relation to this, the abstraction was given a categorical rigidity, an *epochal* rather than a genuinely historical consciousness of ideas, which could then be mechanically separated into forms of successive and unified stages of – but which? – both knowledge and illusion. Each stage of the abstraction is radically different, in both theory and practice, from Marx's emphasis on a necessary conflict of real interests, in the material social process, and on the 'legal, political, religious, aesthetic, or philoso-phical – in short ideological – forms in which men become conscious of this conflict and fight it out'. The infection from categorical argument against specialists in categories has here been burned out, by a practical recognition of the whole and indissoluble material and social process. 'Ideology' then reverts to a specific and practical dimension: the complicated process within which men 'become' (are) conscious of their interests and their conflicts. The categorical short-cut to an (abstract) distinction between 'true' and 'false' consciousness is then effectively abandoned, as in all practice it has to be.

All these varying uses of 'ideology' have persisted within the general development of Marxism. There has been a convenient dogmatic retention, at some levels, of ideology as 'false consciousness'. This has often prevented the more specific analysis of operative distinctions of 'true' and 'false' consciousness at the practical level, which is always that of social relationships, and of the part played in these relationships by 'conceptions, thoughts, ideas'. There was a late attempt, by Lukács, to clarify this analysis by a distinction between 'actual consciousness' and 'imputed' or 'potential' consciousness (a full and 'true' understanding of a real social position). This has the merit of avoiding the reduction of all 'actual consciousness' to ideology, but the category is speculative, and indeed *as a category* cannot easily be sustained. In *History and Class-Consciousness* it depended on a last abstract attempt to identify truth with the idea of the proletariat, but in this Hegelian form it is no more convincing than the earlier positivist identification of a category of 'scientific knowledge'. A more interesting but equally difficult attempt to define 'true' consciousness was the elaboration of Marx's point about changing the world rather than interpreting it. What became known as the 'test of practice' was offered as a criterion of truth and as the essential distinction from ideology. In certain general ways this is a wholly consistent projection from the idea of 'practical consciousness', but it is easy to see how its application to specific theories, formulations, and programmes can result either in a vulgar 'success' ethic, masquerading as 'historical truth', or in numbness or confusion when there are practical defeats and deformations. The 'test of practice', that is to say, cannot be applied to 'scientific theory' and 'ideology' taken as abstract categories. The real point of the definition of 'practical consciousness' was indeed to undercut these abstractions, which nevertheless have continued to be reproduced as 'Marxist theory'.

Three other tendencies in twentieth-century concepts of ideology may be briefly noted. First, the concept has been commonly used, within Marxism and outside it, in the relatively neutral sense of 'a system of beliefs characteristic of a particular class or group' (without implications of 'truth' or 'illusion' but with positive reference to a social situation and interest and its defining or constitutive system of meanings and values). It is thus possible to speak neutrally or even approvingly of 'socialist ideology'. A curious example here is that of Lenin:

> Socialism, in so far as it is the ideology of struggle of the proletarian class, undergoes the general conditions of birth, development and consolidation of any ideology, that is to say it is founded on all the material of human knowledge, it presupposes a high level of science, scientific work, etc. . . . In the class struggle of the proletariat which develops spontaneously, as an elemental force, on the basis of capitalist relations, socialism is *introduced* by the ideologists.[3]

Obviously 'ideology' here is not intended as 'false consciousness'. The distinction between a class and its ideologists can be related to the distinction made by Marx and Engels, but one crucial clause of this – 'active, conceptive ideologists, who make the perfecting of the illusion of the class about itself their chief source of livelihood'—has then to be tacitly dropped, unless the reference to a 'ruling class' can be dressed up as a saving clause. More significantly, perhaps, 'ideology' in its now neutral or approving sense is seen as 'introduced' on the foundation of 'all . . . human knowledge, . . . science . . . etc.', of course brought to bear from a class point of view. The position is clearly that ideology is theory and that theory is at once secondary and necessary; 'practical consciousness', as here of the proletariat, will not itself produce it. This is radically different from Marx's thinking, where all 'separate' theory is ideology, and where genuine theory—'real, positive knowledge'—is, by contrast, the articulation of practical consciousness'. But Lenin's model corresponds to one orthodox sociological formulation, in which there is 'social situation' and there is also 'ideology', their relations variable but certainly neither dependent nor 'determined', thus allowing both their separate and their comparative history and analysis. Lenin's formulation also echoes, from a quite opposite political position, Napoleon's identification of 'the ideologists', who *bring ideas* to 'the people', for their liberation or destruction according to point of view. The Napoleonic definition, in an unaltered form, has of course also persisted, as a popular form of criticism of political struggles which are defined by ideas or even by principles. 'Ideology' (the product of 'doctrinaires') is then contrasted with 'practical experience', 'practical politics', and what is known as pragmatism. This general sense of 'ideology' as not only 'doctrinaire' and 'dogmatic' but as *a priori* and abstract has co-existed uneasily with the equally general (neutral or approving) descriptive sense.

Finally there is an obvious need for a general term to describe not only the products but the processes of all signification, including the signification of values. It is intersting that 'ideology' and 'ideological' have been widely used in this sense. Voloŝinov, for example, uses 'ideological' to describe the process of the production of meaning through signs, and 'ideology' is taken as the dimension of social experience in which meanings and values are produced. The difficult relation of so wide a sense to the other senses which we have seen to be active hardly needs stressing. Yet, however far the term itself may be compromised, some form of this emphasis on signification as a central social process is necessary. In Marx, in Engels, and in much of the Marxist tradition the central argument about 'practical consciousness' was limited and frequently distorted by failures to see that the fundamental processes of social signification are intrinsic to 'practical consciousness' and intrinsic also to the 'conceptions, thoughts, and ideas' which are *recognizable* as its products. The limiting condition within 'ideology' as a concept, from its beginning in Destutt, was the tendency to limit processes of meaning and valuation to formed, separable 'ideas' or 'theories'. To attempt to take these back to 'a world of sensations' or, on the other hand, to a 'practical consciousness' or a 'material social process' which has been so defined as to exclude these fundamental signifying processes, or to make them essentially secondary, is the persistent thread of error. For the practical links between 'ideas' and 'theories' and the 'production of real life' are all in this material social process of signification itself.

Moreover, when this is realized, those 'products' which are not ideas or theories, but which are the very different works we call 'art' and 'literature', and which are normal elements of the very general processes we call 'culture' and 'language', can be approached in ways other than reduction, abstraction, or assimilation. This is the argument that has now to be taken into cultural and literary studies, and especially into the Marxist contribution to them, which, in spite of appearances, is then likely to be even more controversial than hitherto. But it is then an open question whether 'ideology' and 'ideological', with their senses of 'abstraction' and 'illusion', or their senses of ideas' and 'theories', or even their senses of a 'system' of beliefs or of meanings and values, are sufficiently precise and practicable terms for so far-reaching and radical a redefinition.

Notes

1 Cited in A. Naess, *Democracy, Ideology, and Objectivity*, (Oslo, 1956), p. 151.
2 Letter to F. Mehring, 14 July 1893, *Marx and Engels: Selected Correspondence* (New York, 1935).
3 *What is to be done?*, (Oxford, 1963, II).

13 | Etienne Balibar and Pierre Macherey,

From 'Literature as an Ideological Form', *Oxford Literary Review*, Vol. 3:1 (1978) pp. 6; 8; 11–12

Literature as an Ideological Form

It is important to 'locate' the production of literary effects historically as part of the ensemble of social practices. For this to be seen dialectically rather than mechanically, it is important to understand that the relationship of 'history' to 'literature' is not like the relationship or 'correspondence' of *two 'branches'*, but concerns the developing forms of an internal *contradiction*. Literature and history are not each set up externally to each other (not even as the history of literature, social and political history), but are in an intricate and connected relationship, the historical conditions of existence of anything like a literature. Very generally, this internal relationship is what constitutes the definition of literature as an ideological form.

But this definition is significant only in so far as its implications are then developed. Ideological forms, to be sure, are not straightforward systems of 'ideas' and 'discourses', but are manifested through the workings and history of determinate *practices* in determinate social relations, what Althusser calls the *Ideological State Apparatus* (ISA). The objectivity of literary production therefore is inseparable from given social practices in a given ISA. More precisely, we shall see that it is inseparable from a given *linguistic practice* (there is a 'French' literature because there is a linguistic practice 'French', i.e., a contradictory ensemble making a national tongue), in itself inseparable from an *academic or schooling practice* which defines both the conditions for the consumption of literature and the very conditions of its production also. By connecting the objective existence of literature to this ensemble of practices, one can define the material anchoring points which *make* literature an historic and social reality.

First, then, literature is historically constituted *in the bourgeois epoch* as an ensemble of language – or rather of specific linguistic practices – inserted in a general schooling process so as to provide appropriate fictional effects, thereby reproducing bourgeois ideology as the dominant ideology. Literature submits to a threefold determination: 'linguistic', 'pedagogic', and 'fictive' [*imaginaire*] (we must return to this point, for it involves the question of a recourse to psycho-analysis for an explanation of literary effects). There is a linguistic determination because the work of literary production depends on the existence of a common language codifying linguistic exchange, both for its material and for its aims – insomuch as literature *contributes* directly to the *maintenance* of a *'common* language'. That it has this starting point is proved by the fact that divergences from the common language are not arbitrary but determined. In our introduction to the work of R. Balibar and D. Laporte,[1] we sketched out an explanation of the historical process by which this 'common language' is set up. Following their thought, we stressed that the common language, i.e. the *national language*, is bound to the political form of 'bourgeois democracy' and is the historical outcome of particular class struggles. Like bourgeois *right*, its parallel, the common national language is needed to unify a new class domination thereby universalising it and providing it with progressive forms throughout its epoch. It refers therefore to a social *contradiction* perpetually reproduced via the process which surmounts it. What is the basis of this contradiction?

It is the effect of the historic conditions under which the bourgeois class established its political, economic and ideological dominance. To achieve hegemony, it had not only to transform the base, the relations of production, but also radically to transform the superstructure the ideological formations. This transformation could be called the bourgeois 'cultural revolution' since it involves not only the formation of a new ideology, but its realisation as the dominant ideology, through new ISAs and the remoulding of the relationships between the different ISAs. This revolutionary transformation, which took more than a century but which was preparing itself for far longer, is characterised by making the school apparatus the means of forcing submission to the dominant ideology – individual submission, but also, and more importantly, the submission of the very ideology of the dominated classes. Therefore in the last analysis, all the ideological contradictions rest on the contradictions of the school apparatus, and become contradictions subordinated to the form of schooling, within the form of schooling itself.

The Specific Complexity of Literary Formations–
Ideological Contradictions and Linguistic Conflicts

The first principle of a materialist analysis would be: literary productions must not be studied from the standpoint of their *unity* which is illusory and false, but from their material *disparity*. One must not look for unifying effects but for signs of the contradictions (historically determined) which produced them and which appear as unevenly resolved conflicts in the text.

So, in searching out the determinant contradictions, the materialist analysis of literature rejects on principle the notion of 'the word'–i.e., the illusory presentation of the unity of a text, its totality, self-sufficiency and perfection (in both senses of the word: success and completion). More precisely, it recognises the notion of 'the work' (and its correlative, 'the author') only in order to identify both as necessary illusions written into the *ideology of literature*, the accompaniment of all literary production. The text is produced under conditions which represent it as a finished work providing a requisite order, expressing either a subjective theme or the spirit of the age, according to whether the reading is a naïve or a sophisticated one. Yet in itself the text is none of these things: on the contrary, it is materially incomplete, disparate and diffuse from being the outcome of the conflicting contradictory effect of superimposing real processes which cannot be abolished in it except in an imaginary way.[2]

To be more explicit: literature is produced finally through the effect of one or more ideological contradictions precisely because these contradictions cannot be solved within the ideology, i.e., in the last analysis through the effect of contradictory class positions within the ideology, as such irreconcilable. Obviously these contradictory ideological positions are not in themselves 'literary'–that would lead us back into the closed circle of 'literature'. They are ideological positions within theory and practice, covering the whole field of the ideological class struggle, i.e. religious, judicial, and political, and they correspond to the conjunctures of the class struggle itself. But it would be pointless to look in the texts for the 'original' bare discourse of these ideological positions, as they were 'before' their 'literary' realisation, *for these ideological positions can only be formed in the materiality of the literary text*. That is, they can only appear in a form which provides their *imaginary solution*, or better still, which displaces them by substituting imaginary contradictions soluble within the ideological practice of religion, politics, morality, aesthetics and psychology.

Let us approach this phenomenon more closely. We shall say that literature 'begins' with the imaginary solution of implacable ideological contradictions, with the representation of that solution: not in the sense of representating i.e. 'figuring' (by images, allegories, symbols or arguments) a solution which is really there (to repeat, literature is produced because such a solution is impossible) but in the sense of providing a 'mise en scène', a *presentation as solution* of the very terms of an insurmountable contradiction, by means of various displacements and substitutions. For there to be a literature, it must be the very terms of the contradiction (and hence of the contradictory ideological elements) that are enunciated in a special language, a language of 'compromise' realising in advance the fiction of a forthcoming conciliation. Or better still, it finds a language of 'compromise' which presents the conciliation as 'natural' and so both necessary and inevitable.

Fiction and Realism: The Mechanism of Identification in Literature

Here we must pause, even if over-schematically, to consider a characteristic literary effect which has already been briefly mentioned: the identification effect. Brecht was the first Marxist theoretician to focus on this by showing how the ideological effects of literature (and of the theatre, with the specific transformations that implies) *materialise* via an identification process between the reader or the audience and the hero or anti-hero, the simultaneous mutual constitution of the fictive 'consciousness' of the character with the ideological 'consciousness' of the reader.

But it is obvious that any process of identification is dependent on the constitution and recognition of the individual as 'subject' – to use a very common ideological notion lifted by philosophy from the juridical and turning up under various forms in all other levels of bourgeois ideology. Now, all ideology, as Althusser shows in his essay 'Ideology and Ideological State Apparatuses',[3] must in a practical way 'hail or interpellate individuals as subjects': so that they perceive themselves as such, with rights and duties, the obligatory accompaniments. Each ideology has its specific mode: each gives to the 'subject' – and therefore to other real or imaginary subjects who confront the individual and present him with his ideological identification in a personal form – one or more appropriate names. In the ideology of literature the nomenclature is: Authors (i.e. signatures), Works (i.e. titles), Readers, and Characters (with their social background, real or imaginary). But in literature, the process of constituting subjects and setting up their relationships of mutual recognition necessarily takes a detour via the fictional world and its values, because that process (i.e. of constitution and setting-up) embraces within its circle the 'concrete' or 'abstract' 'persons' which the text stages. We now reach a classic general problem: what is specifically 'fictional' about literature?

Literature is not fiction, a fictive image of the real, because it cannot define itself simply as a figuration, an appearance of reality. By a complex process, literature is the production of a certain reality, not indeed (one cannot over-emphasise this) an autonomous reality, but a material reality, and of a certain social effect (we shall conclude with this). Literature is not therefore fiction, but *the production of fictions*: or better still, the production of fiction-effects (and in the first place the provider of the material means for the production of fiction-effects).

Similarly, as the 'reflection of the life of a given society', historically given (Mao), literature is still not providing a 'realist' reproduction of it, even and least of all when it proclaims itself to be such, because even then it cannot be reduced to a straight mirroring. But it is true that the text does produce a *reality-effect*. More precisely it produces simultaneously a reality-effect and a fiction-effect, emphasising first one and then the other, interpreting each by each in turn but always *on the basis of their dualism*.

So, it comes to this once more: fiction and realism are not *the concepts for* the production of literature but on the contrary the notions produced by literature. But this leads to remarkable consequences for it means that the *model*, the real referent 'outside' the discourse which both fiction and realism presuppose, has no function here as a non-literary non-discursive anchoring point predating the text. (We know by now that this anchorage, the primacy, of the real, is different from and more complex than a 'representation'.) But it does function as an effect of the discourse. *So, the literary discourse itself institutes and projects the presence of the 'real' in the manner of an hallucination.*

How is this materially possible? How can the text so control what it says, what it describes, what it sets up (or 'those' it sets up) with its sign of hallucinatory reality, or contrastingly, its fictive sign, diverging, infinitesimally perhaps, from the 'real'? On this point too, in parts of their deep analysis, the works we have used supply the material for an answer. Once more they refer us to the effects and forms of the fundamental linguistic conflict.

In a study of 'modern' French literary texts, carefully dated in each case according to their place in the history of the common language and of the educational system, R. Balibar refers to the production of 'imaginary French' [*français fictif*]. What does this mean? Clearly not pseudo-French, elements of a pseudo-language, seeing that these literary instances do also appear in certain contexts chosen by particular individuals, e.g. by compilers of dictionaries who illustrate their rubrics only with literary quotations. Nor is it simply a case of the language being produced *in* fiction (with its own usages, syntax and vocabulary), i.e. that of the characters in a narrative making an imaginary discourse in an imaginary language. Instead, it is a case of expressions which *always* diverge in one or more salient details from those used in practice outside the literary discourse, even when both are grammatically 'correct'. These are linguistic 'compromise formations' compromising between usages which are socially contradictory in practice and hence mutually exclude each other. In these compromise formations there is in essential place, more or less disguised but *recognisable*, for the reproduction of 'simple' language, 'ordinary' language, French 'just like that', i.e. the language which is taught in elementary school as the 'pure and simple' expression of 'reality'. In R. Balibar's book there are numerous examples which 'speak' to everyone, reawakening or reviving memories which are usually repressed (it is their presence, their reproduction – the reason for a character or his words and for what the 'author' makes himself responsible for without naming himself – which produces the effect of 'naturalness' and 'reality', even if it is only by a single phrase uttered as if in passing). In comparison, all other expressions seem 'arguable', 'reflected', in a subjectivity. It is necessary that first of all there should be expressions which seem *objective*: these are the ones which in the text itself produce the imaginary referent of an elusive 'reality'.

Finally, to go back to our starting point: the ideological effect of identification produced by literature or rather by literary texts, which Brecht, thanks to his position as a revolutionary and materialist dramatist, was the first to theorise. But there is only ever identification of *one subject with another* (potentially with 'oneself': 'Madame Bovary, c'est moi', familiar example, signed Gustave Flaubert). And there are only ever subjects through the interpellation of the individual into a subject by a Subject who names him, as Althusser shows: 'tu es un tel, et c'est à toi que je m'adresse': 'Hypocrite lecteur, mon semblable, mon frère', another familiar example, signed Charles Baudelaire. Through the endless functioning of its texts, literature unceasingly 'produces' *subjects*, on display for everyone. So paradoxically using the same schema we can say: literature endlessly transforms (concrete) individuals into subjects and endows them with a quasi-real hallucinatory individuality. According to the fundamental mechanism of the whole of bourgeois ideology, to produce subjects ('persons' and 'characters') *one must oppose them to objects*, i.e. to *things*, by placing them *in* and *against* a world of 'real' things, outside it but always *in relation* to it. The realistic effect is the basis of this interpellation which makes characters or merely discourse 'live' and which makes readers take up an attitude towards imaginary struggles as they would towards real ones, though undangerously. They flourish here, the subjects we have already named: the Author and his Readers, but also the Author and his Characters, and the Reader and his Characters via the mediator, the Author – the Author identified with his Characters, or 'on the contrary' with one of their Judges, and likewise for the Reader. And from there, the Author, the Reader, the Characters opposite their universal abstract subjects: God, History, the People, Art. The list is neither final nor finishable: the work of literature is by definition to prolong and expand it indefinitely.

The Aesthetic Effect of Literature as Ideological Domination-effect

Here is the index of the structure of the process of reproduction in which the literary effect is inserted. What is in fact 'the primary material' of the literary text? (But a raw material which always seems to have been already transformed by it.) It is the ideological contradictions which are *not* specifically literary but political, religious, etc.; in the last analysis, contradictory ideological realisations of determinate class positions in the class struggle. And what is the 'effect' of the literary text? (*At least* on those readers who recognise it as such, those of the *dominant* cultured class.) Its effect is to provoke other ideological discourses which can sometimes be recognised as literary ones but which are usually merely aesthetic, moral, political, religious discourses in which the dominant ideology is realised.

We can now say that the literary test is the *agent* for the *reproduction* of ideology in its ensemble. In other words, it induces by the literary effect the production of 'new' discourses which always reproduce (under constantly varied forms) the *same* ideology with its contradictions). It enables individuals to *appropriate* ideology and make themselves its 'free' *bearers* and even its 'free' *creators*. The literary text is a privileged operator in the concrete relations between the individual and ideology in bourgeois society and ensures its reproduction. To the extent that it induces the ideological discourse to leave its subject matter which has always already been invested as the aesthetic effect, in the form of the work of art, it does not seem a mechanical imposition, forced, revealed like a religious dogma, on individuals who must repeat it faithfully. Instead it appears as if offered for interpretations, a free choice, for the subjective private use of individuals. It is the privileged agent of ideological subjection, in the democratic and 'critical' form of 'freedom of thought.'[4]

Under these conditions, the aesthetic effect is also inevitably an effect of *domination*: the subjection of individuals to the dominant ideology, the dominance of the ideology of the ruling class.

It is inevitably therefore an *uneven* effect which does not operate uniformly on individuals and particularly does not operate in the same way on different and antagonistic social classes. 'Subjection' must be felt by the dominant class as by the dominant but in two different ways. Formally, literature as an ideological formation realised in the common language, is provided and destined for all and makes no distinctions between readers but for their own differing tastes and sensibilities, natural or acquired. But concretely, subjection means one thing for the members of the educated dominant class: 'freedom' to think within ideology, a submission which is experienced and practised as if it were a mastery, another for those who belong to the exploited classes: manual workers or even skilled workers, employees, those who according to official statistics never 'read' or rarely. These find in reading nothing but the confirmation of their inferiority: subjection means domination and repression by the literary discourse of a discourse deemed 'inarticulate' and 'faulty' and inadequate for the expression of complex ideas and feelings.

This point is vital to an analysis. It shows that the difference is not set up *after the event* as a straightforward inequality of reading power and assimilation, conditioned by other social inequalities. It is implicit in the very production of the literary effect and materially inscribed in the constitution of the text.

But one might say, how is it clear that what is implicit in the structure of the text is not just the discourse of those who practice literature but also, *most significantly*, the discourse of those who do not know the text and whom it does not know, i.e. the discourse of those who 'write' (books) and 'read' them, and the discourse of those who do not know how to do it although quite simply they 'know how to read and write' – a play of words and a profoundly revealing double usage. One can understand this only by reconstituting and analysing the linguistic conflict in its determinant place as that which produced the literary text and which opposes two antagonistic usages, equal but inseparable of the common language: on one side, 'literary' French which is studied in higher education (l'enseigne-ment secondaire et supérieur) and on the other 'basic', 'ordinary' French which, far from being natural, is also taught at the other level (à l'école primaire). It is 'basic' only by reason of its *unequal relation* to the other, which is 'literary' by the same reason. This is proved by a comparative and historical analysis of their lexical and syntactical forms – which R. Balibar is one of the first to undertake systematically.

So, if in the way things are, literature can and must be used in secondary education both to fabricate and simultaneously dominate, isolate and repress the 'basic' language of the dominated classes, it is only on condition that that same basic language should be present in literature, as one of the terms of its constitutive contradiction – disguised and masked, but also necessarily given away and exhibited in the fictive reconstructions. And ultimately this is because literary French embodied in literary texts is both tendentially *distinguished from* (and opposed to) the common language and *placed with its* constitution and historic development so long as this process characterises general education because of its material importance to the development of bourgeois society. That is why it is possible to assert that the use of literature in schools and its place in education is only the converse of the *place of education in literature* and that therefore the basis of the production of literary effects is the very structure and historical role of the currently dominant ideological state apparatus. And that too is why it is possible to denounce as a den of their own real practice the claims of the writer and his cultured readers to rise above simple classroom exercises, and evade them.

The effect of domination realised by literary production presupposes the presence of the dominated ideology within the dominant ideology itself. It implies the constant 'activation' of the contradiction and its attendant ideological risk – it thrives on this very risk which is the source of its power. That is why, dialectically, in bourgeois democratic society, the agent of the reproduction of ideology moves tendentially via the effects of literary 'style' and linguistic forms of compromise. Class struggle is not abolished in the literary text and the literary effects which it produces. They bring about the reproduction, as dominant, of the ideology of the dominant class.

Notes

1 R. Balibar and D. Laporte, Le Français National: *constitution de la langue nationale commune à l'époque de la revolution démocratique bourgeoisie*, introduction by E. Balibar and P. Macherey (Paris, Éditions Hachette, 1974), in *Analyses*.
2 Rejecting the mythical unity and completeness of a work of art does not mean adopting a reverse position, i.e. the work of art as anti-nature, a violation of order (cf. *Tel Quel*). Such reversals are characteristic of conservative ideology: 'For oft a fine disorder stems from art' (Boileau)!
3 In *La Pensée* no. 151. June 1970; *Lenin* and *Philosophy*, tr. B. Brewster (London, New Left Books, 1971).

4 One could say that there is no proper *religious literature*; at least that there was not before the bourgeois epoch, by which time religion has been instituted as a form (subordinant and contradictory) of the bourgeois ideology itself. Rather, literature itself and the aesthetic ideology played a decisive part in the struggle against religion, the ideology of the dominant feudal class.

Section 4

Feminism

Introduction

Perhaps more than any other mode of criticism, feminist theory has cut across and drawn on multiple and contradictory traditions while presenting what is arguably one of the most fundamental challenges to previous critical orthodoxies in its revaluation of subjectivity and the category of 'experience'. Like Marxism, feminism is rooted in the political discourses of modernity, inheriting but also challenging its ideas of sovereignty, equality, liberty, rights and rationality. Feminism begins as an Enlightenment discourse founded in the Kantian idea of an autonomous and rational self who is free to choose; in the liberal concept of rights and ownership, and in the idea of citizenship and consensus in the social contract tradition of Hobbes, Rousseau and Locke. Feminism, however, has also been instrumental in exposing some of the contradictions of this legacy and has substantially contributed both to its current development and crisis.

Modern political discourses have been concerned, in particular, with issues of rights, agency, freedom and equality. As earlier writers such as Mary Wollstencraft and Virginia Woolf had recognized, however, many of the political discourses which developed such concepts claimed to be universal but actually excluded women from full citizenship and sovereignty. One of the questions already raised by earlier feminists such as Woolf (in *Three Guineas*, 1938) was whether it was possible to extend to women a system whose very premises involve the naming of femininity as irrational and the exclusion of women from its structures. For liberal modernity could be said to be founded on a fundamental split between the private and the public which relegates women to the demesne of domesticity and deprives them of a political voice while requiring that men identify with a discourse of rationality which splits off and denies the importance of feeling. Were there not inadequacies and flaws in those political discourses of modernity which had already begun to be exposed by thinkers such as Marx and Freud? Although the discourses of feminism clearly arise out of and are made possible by those of Enlightened modernity and its models of reason, justice and autonomous subjectivity as universal categories, feminism has been one of the most powerful movements in thought to expose some of the contradictions and inadequacies of this political legacy. Simply by raising the issue of sexual difference and its construction, feminism weakens the rootedness of Enlightenment thought in the principle of sameness and universality. Feminism has thoroughly exposed the ways in which this 'universal' principle is contradicted by the construction of a public/private split which consigns women to the 'private' realm of feeling, nurturance, intuition, domesticity and the body, in order to clarify a 'public' realm of reason, efficiency and objectivity as masculine.

Gradually what emerged in feminist theory in the 1970s, therefore, was a recognition on the part of feminists of a central contradiction in attempts to define an epistemology and a foundation for its politics: that women seek equality and recognition of a gendered identity which has been constructed through the very culture and ideological formations which feminists were seeking to challenge and dismantle. Woolf herself had begun to articulate this perception in the 1920s, recognizing that if being shut out of a masculine public demesne was frustrating and demeaning, being shut into it might not be the solution either. The aim of feminism must be to break down the public/private split and the binaries of masculinity/femininity, mind/body, reason/feeling and begin to discover a language of politics which might articulate a radically different vision of gender and society.

Developing de Beauvoir's insights into the 'Eternal Feminine', feminists in the 1970s gradually realized the difficulty of talking about a 'woman's identity'. There could be no simple legitimation for feminists in throwing off 'false consciousness' and revealing a 'true' but deeply buried female self if this 'female self' was actually already a construction of patriarchy. However, in order to develop an effective politics in the world, feminism could not afford simply to throw out the concepts of rights, of sovereign subjectivity, agency and universal justice for this would surely be to undermine its effectiveness as an emancipatory politics (again one of the problems recognized by Woolf in her extremely prescient *Three Guineas*). The essays which follow have been chosen to represent the historical development of feminism after *The Second Sex*, but also because they suggest the various strands and tensions within feminism itself as it draws on a variety of modern political and discursive sources including liberalism, Marxism and psychoanalysis.

Early second wave feminist criticism drew extensively on de Beauvoir's work and on Kate Millett's *Sexual Politics* which analysed the system of sex-role stereotyping and the oppression of women under patriarchal social organization. Much of the criticism which drew on these texts and flourished, particularly in America in the 1970s, concentrated its analysis on the 'images of women' represented in and constructed through cultural forms such as literature. Rarely did this writing seek explicitly to question the category of 'literature' *per se* or the dominant expressive-mimetic aesthetics of the time. Accordingly, it has been viewed by later feminists as often failing to offer an adequate analysis of the relationship between ideology and representation, and therefore as inadvertently affirming the universalism and subjectivism of traditional liberal-humanist criticism.

By the mid 1970s, there was increasing attention from both broadly 'liberal' or broadly 'socialist' or 'radical' feminists to texts by women as opposed to the study of the representation of women in texts by male authors. This approach was explicitly advocated, in particular, by Elaine Showalter as the basis of her 'gynocriticism', and her book, *A Literature of their Own* (1977), attempted to construct an alternative tradition of women's writing, focusing specifically on female writing and experience. Although her work challenged the sexist bias of the liberal tradition, it failed to challenge its fundamental conception of the Subject or its underlying assumptions about canonicity. Subjectivity was still conceived of in essential and unitary terms; tradition remained a continuous and seamless process and the text itself remained embedded in expressive-mimetic aesthetics. In many ways, therefore, Showalter's work reaffirmed the orthodox humanist belief in literature as the expression of a universal unity encompassing men and women and known as 'human nature'. The category is simply enlarged rather than radically challenged or deconstructed. Later feminists would challenge this conception of the literary process, drawing on the insights of later Marxism, psychoanalysis and deconstruction.

Gilbert and Gubar's *The Madwoman in the Attic* (1979) was one of the first feminist works to begin this process. Psychoanalysis has been important to feminism because it tries to explain why people invest in behaviours which seem irrational, counter-productive and against their best interests. Psycho-analysis exposes the inadequacy of purely rational or utilitarian accounts of behaviour and tries to analyse the contradictions of desire and the non-rational aspects of human behaviour. De Beauvoir's *The Second Sex* drew on psychoanalytic insights, into the mechanism of 'projection', for example, as it functions in the construction of the 'Eternal Feminine'. The body is denied a place in the rational order of things by being radically split from mind (which comes to be associated with masculinity) and by being projected entirely onto women. Women come to be identified then with everything which is feared as irrational and such fears appear to justify the social control and containment of the female body. Psychoanalysis provided a vocabulary for the description of defences such as splitting and Freud had shown in his work on phobias, for example, how the displaced and split-off entity comes to seem more threatening because it starts outside of the realm of contained knowledge; how it becomes mysterious, irrational and opaque.

Drawing on such insights, Gilbert and Gubar's work suggested some of the reasons why the female body has been controlled and contained, aestheticized, made small, or confined within the domestic space. Women carry the culture's horror of carnal contingency and the female body must therefore be killed into art. Women become bodies or opaque spaces, angels or monsters to be feared or narcissistically revered but hardly regarded as actual, complex human beings in the world. The madwoman in the attic is read as the unconscious articulation of the hidden fears of patriarchy and as the protest of the feminine subject against her exclusion and monstrous distortion.

The remaining essays in this section represent, in the first instance, a plea for the recognition of the differences within feminism and an argument for a continuing and productive pluralism of ideological sources and methods, and in the second, a call for a more rigorous historical materialist account of literary texts and literary institutions which would foreground the largely neglected (as it was then) issue of gender. In Annette Kolodny's 'Dancing through the Minefield', she argues that the strength of feminism is precisely its diversity, that feminists should not feel compelled to aim for the methodological and ideological coherence and homogeneity of Marxism, but should embrace a strategic diversity and range of practices and discourses, a critical language which inserts itself into cultural master narratives to expose their inadequacies and contradictions.

The essay by the British Marxist-Feminist Collective, on the other hand, is an attempt to study the literary text through an analysis of the specific articulations of patriarchy within capitalist society and employs a broadly historically materialist approach. Although Engels had been interested in the extent to which the patriarchal family is necessary as a point of stability within the capitalist economy (and how, in some sense, women are to men within the family as the unit of reproduction, as the worker is to the owner within the realm of productive economic relations), neither Marx nor Engels wrote extensively on gender in their analysis of capitalist relations. The argument of the Marxist-Feminist Collective emphasizes the need to situate the text in relation to an analysis, for example, of the economic position of women as a consequence of the division of labour and the organization of the family; the effects of this on female authorship and reading habits; the control and organization of reproduction and sexuality; the role of cultural forms such as literature in this process, and the specific organization of the institution of literature according to masculine discourses and evaluations.

14 | Elaine Showalter,

'Towards a Feminist Poetics', in M. Jacobus, ed. *Women Writing About Women* (1979), pp. 25–33; 34–6

Feminist criticism can be divided into two distinct varieties. The first type is concerned with *woman as reader* – with woman as the consumer of male-produced literature, and with the way in which the hypothesis of a female reader changes our apprehension of a given text, awakening us to the significance of its sexual codes. I shall call this kind of analysis the *feminist critique*, and like other kinds of critique it is a historically grounded inquiry which probes the ideological assumptions of literary phenomena. Its subjects include the images and stereotypes of women in literature, the omissions and misconceptions about women in criticism, and the fissures in male-constructed literary history. It is also concerned with the exploitation and manipulation of the female audience, especially in popular culture and film; and with the analysis of woman-as-sign in semiotic systems. The second type of feminist criticism is concerned with *woman as writer* – with woman as the producer of textual meaning, with the history, themes, genres and structures of literature by women. Its subjects include the psycho-dynamics of female creativity, linguistics and the problem of a female language; the trajectory of the individual or collective female literary career; literary history; and, of course, studies of particular writers and works. No term exists in English for such a specialised discourse, and so I have adapted the French term *la gynocritique: 'gynocritics'* (although the significance of the male pseudonym in the history of women's writing also suggested the term 'georgics').

The feminist critique is essentially political and polemical, with theoretical affiliations to Marxist sociology and aesthetics; gynocritics is more self-contained and experimental, with connections to other modes of new feminist research. In a dialogue between these two positions, Carolyn Heilbrun, the writer, and Catherine Stimpson, editor of the American journal *Signs: Women in Culture and Society*, compare the feminist critique to the Old Testament, 'looking for the sins and errors of the past', and gynocritics to the New Testament, seeking 'the grace of imagination'. Both kinds are necessary, they explain, for only the Jeremiahs of the feminist critique can lead us out of the 'Egypt of female servitude' to the promised land of the feminist vision. That the discussion makes use of these Biblical metaphors points to the connections between feminist consciousness and conversion narratives which often appear in women's literature; Carolyn Heilbrun comments on her own text, 'when I talk about feminist criticism, I am amazed at how high a moral tone I take'.[1]

The Feminist Critique: Hardy

Let us take briefly as an example of the way a feminist critique might proceed, Thomas Hardy's *The Mayor of Casterbridge*, which begins with the famous scene of the drunken Michael Henchard selling his wife and infant daughter for five guineas at a country fair. In his study of Hardy, Irving Howe has praised the brilliance and power of this opening scene:

> To shake loose from one's wife; to discard the drooping rag of a woman, with her mute complaints and maddening passivity; to escape not by a slinking abandonment but through the public sale of her body to a stranger, as horses are sold at a fair: and thus to wrest, through sheer amoral wilfulness, a second chance out of life – it is with this stroke, so insidiously attractive to male fantasy, that *The Mayor of Casterbridge* begins.[2]

It is obvious that a woman, unless she has been indoctrinated into being very deeply identified indeed with male culture, will have a different experience of this scene. I quote Howe first to indicate how the fantasies of the male critic distort the text; for Hardy tells us very little about the relationship of Michael and Susan Henchard, and what we see in the early scenes does not suggest that she is drooping, complaining or passive. Her role, however, is a passive one; severely constrained by her womanhood, and further burdened by her child, there is no way that *she* can wrest a second chance out of life. She cannot master events, but only accommodate herself to them.

What Howe, like other male critics of Hardy, conveniently overlooks about the novel is that Henchard sells not only his wife but his child, a child who can only be female. Patriarchal societies do not readily sell their sons, but their daughters are all for sale sooner or later. Hardy wished to make the sale of the daughter emphatic and central; in early drafts of the novel Henchard has two daughters and sells only one, but Hardy revised to make it clearer that Henchard is symbolically selling his entire share in the world of women. Having severed his bonds with this female community of love and loyalty, Henchard has chosen to live in the male community, to define his human relationships by the male code of paternity, money and legal contract. His tragedy lies in realising the inadequacy of this system, and in his inability to repossess the loving bonds he comes desperately to need.

The emotional centre of *The Mayor of Casterbridge* is neither Henchard's relationship to his wife, nor his superficial romance with Lucetta Templeman, but his slow appreciation of the strength and dignity of his wife's daughter, Elizabeth-Jane. Like the other women in the book, she is governed by her own heart – man-made laws are not important to her until she is taught by Henchard himself to value legality, paternity, external definitions, and thus in the end to reject him. A self-proclaimed 'woman-hater', a man who has felt at best a 'supercilious pity' for womankind, Henchard is humbled and 'unmanned' by the collapse of his own virile facade, the loss of his mayor's chain, his master's authority, his father's rights. But in Henchard's alleged weakness and 'womanishness', breaking through in moments of tenderness, Hardy is really showing us the man at his best. Thus Hardy's female characters in *The Mayor of Casterbridge*, as in his other novels, are somewhat idealised and melancholy projections of a repressed male self.

As we see in this analysis, one of the problems of the feminist critique is that it is male-oriented. If we study stereotypes of women, the sexism of male critics, and the limited roles women play in literary history, we are not learning what women have felt and experienced, but what men have thought women should be. In some fields of specialisation, this may require a long apprenticeship to the male theoretician, whether he be Althusser, Barthes, Macherey or Lacan; and then an application of the theory of signs or myths or the unconscious to male texts or films. The temporal and intellectual investment one makes in such a process increases resistance to questioning it, and to seeing its historical and ideological boundaries. The critique also has a tendency to naturalise women's victimisation, by making it the inevitable and obsessive topic of discussion. One sees, moreover, in works like Elizabeth Hardwick's *Seduction and Betrayal*, the bittersweet moral distinctions the critic makes between women merely betrayed by men, like Hetty in *Adam Bede*, and the heroines who make careers out of betrayal, like Hester Prynne in *The Scarlet Letter*. This comes dangerously close to a celebration of the opportunities of victimisation, the seduction *of* betrayal.[3]

Gynocritics and Female Culture

In contrast to this angry or loving fixation on male literature, the programme of gynocritics is to construct a female framework for the analysis of women's literature, to develop new models based on the study of female experience, rather than to adapt male models and theories. Gynocritics begins at the point when we free ourselves from the linear absolutes of male literary history, stop trying to fit women between the lines of the male tradition, and focus instead on the newly visible world of female culture. This is comparable to the ethnographer's effort to render the experience of the 'muted' female half of a society, Welch is described in Shirley Ardener's collection, *Perceiving Women*.[4] Gynocritics is related to feminist research in history, anthropology, psychology and sociology, all of which have developed hypotheses of a female subculture including not only the ascribed status, and the internalised constructs of femininity, but also the occupations, interactions and consciousness of women. Anthropologists study the female subculture in the relationships between women, as mothers, daughters, sisters and friends; in sexuality, reproduction and ideas about the body; and in rites of initiation and passage, purification ceremonies, myths and taboos. Michelle Rosaldo writes in *Woman, Culture, and Society*,

> the very symbolic and social conceptions that appear to set women apart and to circumscribe their activities may be used by the women as a basis for female solidarity and worth. When men live apart from women, they in fact cannot control them, and unwittingly they may provide them with the symbols and social resources on which to build a society of their own.[5]

Thus in some women's literature, feminine values penetrate and undermine the masculine systems which contain them; and women have imaginatively engaged the myths of the Amazons, and the fantasies of a separate female society, in genres from Victorian poetry to contemporary science fiction.

In the past two years, pioneering work by four young American feminist scholars has given us some new ways to interpret the culture of nineteenth-century American women, and the literature which was its primary expressive form. Carroll Smith-Rosenberg's essay 'The Female World of Love and Ritual' examines several archives of letters between women, and outlines the homosocial emotional world of the nineteenth century. Nancy Cott's *The Bonds of Womanhood: Woman's Sphere in New England 1780-1835* explores the paradox of a cultural bondage, a legacy of pain and submission, which none the less generates a sisterly solidarity, a bond of shared experience, loyalty and compassion. Ann Douglas's ambitious book, *The Feminization of American Culture*, boldly locates the genesis of American mass culture in the sentimental literature of women and clergymen, two allied and 'disestablished' post-industrial groups. These three are social historians; but Nina Auerbach's *Communities of Women: An Idea in Fiction* seeks the bonds of womanhood in women's literature, ranging from the matriarchal households of Louisa May Alcott and Mrs Gaskell to the women's schools and colleges of Dorothy Sayers, Sylvia Plath and Muriel Spark. Historical and literary studies like these, based on English women, are badly needed; and the manuscript and archival sources for them are both abundant and untouched.[6]

Gynocritics: Elizabeth Barrett Browning and Muriel Spark

Gynocritics must also take into account the different velocities and curves of political, social and personal histories in determining women's literary choices and careers. 'In dealing with women as writers,' Virginia Woolf wrote in her 1929 essay, 'Women and Fiction', 'as much elasticity as possible is desirable; it is necessary to leave oneself room to deal with other things besides their work, so much has that work been influenced by conditions that have nothing whatever to do with art.'[7] We might illustrate the need for this completeness by looking at Elizabeth Barrett Browning, whose verse-novel *Aurora Leigh* (1856) has recently been handsomely reprinted by the Women's Press. In her excellent introduction Cora Kaplan defines Barrett Browning's feminism as romantic and bourgeois, placing its faith in the transforming powers of love, art and Christian charity. Kaplan reviews Barrett Browning's dialogue with the artists and radicals of her time; with Tennyson and Clough, who had also written poems on the 'woman question'; with the Christian Socialism of Fourier, Owen, Kingsley and Maurice; and with such female predecessors as Madame de Staël and George Sand. But in this exploration of Barrett Browning's intellectual milieu, Kaplan omits discussion of the male poet whose influence on her work in the 1850s would have been most pervasive: Robert Browning. When we understand how susceptible women writers have always been to the aesthetic standards and values of the male tradition, and to male approval and validation, we can appreciate the complexity of a marriage between artists. Such a union has almost invariably meant internal conflicts, self-effacement, and finally obliteration for the women, except in the rare cases – Eliot and Lewes, the Woolfs – where the husband accepted a managerial rather than a competitive role. We can see in Barrett Browning's letters of the 1850s the painful, halting, familiar struggle between her womanly love and ambition for her husband and her conflicting commitment to her own work. There is a sense in which she *wants* him to be the better artist. At the beginning of the decade she was more famous than he; then she notes with pride a review in France which praises him more; his work on *Men and Women* goes well; her work on *Aurora Leigh* goes badly (she had a young child and was recovering from the most serious of her four miscarriages). In 1854 she writes to a woman friend,

> I am behind hand with my poem . . . Robert swears he shall have his book ready in spite of everything for print when we shall be in London for the purpose, but, as for mine, it must wait for the next spring I begin to see clearly. Also it may be better not to bring out the two works together.

And she adds wryly; 'If mine were ready I might not say so perhaps.'[8]

Without an understanding of the framework of the female subculture, we can miss or misinterpret the themes and structures of women's literature, fail to make necessary connections within a tradition. In 1852, in an eloquent passage from her autobiographical essay 'Cassandra', Florence Nightingale identified the pain of feminist awakening as its essence, as the guarantee of progress and free will. Protesting against the protected unconscious lives of middle-class Victorian women, Nightingale demanded the restoration of their suffering:

> Give us back our suffering, we cry to Heaven in our hearts–suffering rather than indifferentism–for out of suffering may come the cure. Better to have pain than paralysis: A hundred struggle and drown in the breakers. One discovers a new world.[9]

It is fascinating to see how Nightingale's metaphors anticipate not only her own medical career, but also the fate of the heroines of women's novels in the nineteenth and twentieth centuries. To waken from the drugged pleasant sleep of Victorian womanhood was agonising; in fiction it is much more likely to end in drowning than in discovery. It is usually associated with what George Eliot in *Middlemarch* calls 'the chill hours of a morning twilight', and the sudden appalled confrontation with the contingencies of adulthood. Eliot's Maggie Tulliver, Edith Wharton's Lily Barth, Olive Schreiner's Lyndall, Kate Chopin's Edna Pontellier wake to worlds which offer no places for the women they wish to become; and rather than struggling they die. Female suffering thus becomes a kind of literary commodity which both men and women consume. Even in these important women's novels–*The Mill on the Floss, Story of an African Farm, The House of Mirth*–the fulfilment of the plot is a visit to the heroine's grave by a male mourner.

According to Dame Rebecca West, unhappiness is still the keynote of contemporary fiction by English women.[10] Certainly the literary landscape is strewn with dead female bodies. In Fay Weldon's *Down Among the Women* and *Female Friends*, suicide has come to be a kind of domestic accomplishment, carried out after the shopping and the washing-up. When Weldon's heroine turns on the gas, 'she feels that she has been half-dead for so long that the difference in state will not be very great'. In Muriel Spark's stunning short novel of 1970, *The Driver's Seat*, another half-dead and desperate heroine gathers all her force to hunt down a woman-hating psychopath, and persuade him to murder her. Garishly dressed in a purposely bought outfit of clashing purple, green and white–the colours of the suffragettes (and the colours of the school uniform in *The Prime of Miss Jean Brodie*)–Lise goes in search of her killer, lures him to a park, gives him the knife. But in Lise's careful selection of her death-dress, her patient pursuit of her assassin, Spark has given us the devastated postulates of feminine wisdom: that a woman creates her identity by choosing her clothes, that she creates her history by choosing her man. That, in the 1970s, Mr Right turns out to be Mr Goodbar, is not the sudden product of urban violence, but a latent truth which fiction exposes. Spark asks whether men or women are in the driver's seat, and whether the power to choose one's destroyer is women's only form of self-assertion. To label the violence or self-destructiveness of these painful novels as neurotic expressions of a personal pathology, as many reviewers have done, is to ignore, Annette Kolodny suggests

> the possibility that the worlds they inhabit may in fact be real, or true, and for them the only worlds available, and further, to deny the possibility that their apparently 'odd' or unusual responses, may in fact be justifiable or even necessary.[11]

But women's literature must go beyond these scenarios of compromise, madness and death. Although the reclamation of suffering is the beginning, its purpose is to discover the new world. Happily, some recent women's literature, especially in the United States where novelists and poets have become vigorously involved in the women's liberation movement, has gone beyond reclaiming suffering to its re-investment. This newer writing relates the pain of transformation to history. 'If I'm lonely,' writes Adrienne Rich in 'Song',

> it must be the loneliness
> of waking first, of breathing
> dawn's first cold breath on the city
> of being the one awake
> in a house wrapped in sleep[12]

Rich is one of the spokeswomen for a new women's writing which explores the will to change. In her recent book, *Of Woman Born: Motherhood as Experience and Institution*, Rich challenges the alienation from and rejection of the mother that daughters have learned under patriarchy. Much women's literature in the past has dealt with 'matrophobia' or the fear of becoming one's mother.[13] In Sylvia Plath's *The Bell Jar*, for example, the heroine's mother is the target for the novel's most punishing contempt. When Esther announces to her therapist that she hates her mother, she is on the road to recovery. Hating one's mother was the feminist enlightenment of the fifties and sixties; but it is only a metaphor for hating oneself. Female literature of the 1970s goes beyond matrophobia to a courageously sustained quest for the mother, in such books at Margaret Atwood's *Surfacing*, and Lisa Alther's recent *Kinflicks*. As the death of the father has always been an archetypal rite of passage for the Western hero, now the death of the mother as witnessed and transcended by the daughter has become one of the most profound occasions of female literature. In analysing these purposeful awakenings, these reinvigorated mythologies of female culture, feminist criticism finds its most challenging, inspiriting and appropriate task.

In *A Room of One's Own*, Virginia Woolf argued that economic independence was the essential precondition of an autonomous women's art. Like George

Eliot before her, Woolf also believed that women's literature held the promise of a 'precious speciality', a distinctly female vision.

Feminine, Feminist, Female

All of these themes have been important to feminist literary criticism in the 1960s and 1970s but we have approached them with more historical awareness. Before we can even begin to ask how the literature of women would be different and special, we need to reconstruct its past, to rediscover the scores of women novelists, poets and dramatists whose work has been obscured by time, and to establish the continuity of the female tradition from decade to decade, rather than from Great Woman to Great Woman. As we recreate the chain of writers in this tradition, the patterns of influence and response from one generation to the next, we can also begin to challenge the periodicity of orthodox literary history, and its enshrined canons of achievement. It is because we have studied women writers in isolation that we have never grasped the connections between them. When we go beyond Austen, the Brontës and Eliot, say; to look at a hundred and fifty or more of their sister novelists, we can see patterns and phases in the evolution of a female tradition which correspond to the developmental phases of any subcultural art. In my book on English women writers, *A Literature of Their Own*, I have called these the Feminine, Feminist and Female stages.[14] During the Feminine phase, dating from about 1840 to 1880, women wrote in an effort to equal the intellectual achievements of the male culture, and internalised its assumptions about female nature. The distinguishing sign of this period is the male pseudonym, introduced in England in the 1840s, and a national characteristic of English women writers. In addition to the famous names we all know – George Eliot, Currer, Ellis and Acton Bell – dozens of other women chose male pseudonyms as a way of coping with a double literary standard. This masculine disguise goes well beyond the title page; it exerts an irregular pressure on the narrative, affecting tone, diction, structure and characterisation. In contrast to the English male pseudonym, which signals such clear self-awareness of the liabilities of female authorship, American women during the same period adopted super-feminine, little-me pseudonyms (Fanny Fern, Grace Greenwood, Fanny Forester), disguising behind these nominal bouquets their boundless energy, powerful economic motives and keen professional skills. It is pleasing to discover the occasional Englishwoman who combines both these techniques, and creates the illusion of male authorship with a name that contains the encoded domestic message of femininity – such as Harriet Parr, who wrote under the pen name 'Holme Lee'. The feminist content of feminine art is typically oblique, displaced, ironic and subversive; one has to read it between the lines, in the missed possibilities of the text.

In the Feminist phase, from about 1880 to 1920, or the winning of the vote, women are historically enabled to reject the accommodating postures of femininity and to use literature to dramatise the ordeals of wronged womanhood. The personal sense of injustice which feminine novelists such as Elizabeth Gaskell and Frances Trollope expressed in their novels of class struggle and factory life become increasingly and explicitly feminist in the 1880s, when a generation of New Women redefined the woman artist's role in terms of responsibility to suffering sisters. The purest examples of this phase are the Amazon Utopias of the 1890s, fantasies of perfect female societies set in an England or an America of the future, which were also protests against male government, male laws and male medicine. One author of Amazon Utopias, the American Charlotte Perkins Gilman, also analysed the preoccupations of masculine literature with sex and war, and the alternative possibilities of an emancipated feminist literature. Gilman's Utopian feminism carried George Eliot's idea of the 'precious speciality' to its matriarchal extremes. Comparing her view of sisterly collectivity to the beehive, she writes that

> the bee's fiction would be rich and broad, full of the complex tasks of comb-building and filling, the care and feeding of the young . . . It would treat of the vast fecundity of motherhood, the educative and selective processes of the group-mothers, and the passion of loyalty, of social service, which holds the hives together.[15]

This is feminist Socialist Realism with a vengeance, but women novelists of the period – even Gilman, in her short stories – could not be limited to such didactic formulas, or such maternal topics.

In the Female phase, ongoing since 1920, women reject both imitation and protest – two forms of dependency – and turn instead to female experience as the source of an autonomous art, extending the feminist analysis of culture to the forms and techniques of literature. Representatives of the formal Female Aesthetic, such as Dorothy Richardson and Virginia Woolf, begin to think in terms of male and female sentences, and divide their work into 'masculine' journalism and 'Feminine' fictions, redefining and sexualising external and internal experience. Their experiments were both enriching and imprisoning retreats into the celebration of consciousness; even in Woolf's famous definition of life: 'a luminous halo, a semi-transparent envelope surrounding us from the beginning of consciousness to the end',[16] there is a submerged metaphor of uterine withdrawal and containment. In this sense, the Room of One's Own becomes a kind of Amazon Utopia, population 1.

Notes

I wish to thank Nina Auerbach, Kate Ellis, Mary Jacobus, Wendy Martin, Adrienne Rich, Helen Taylor, Martha Vicinus, Margaret Walters and Ruth Yeazell for sharing with me their ideas on feminist criticism.

1 'Theories of Feminist Criticism' in Josephine Donovan, ed., *Feminist Literary Criticism: Explorations in Theory* (Lexington, 1976), pp. 64, 68, 72.
2 Irving Howe, *Thomas Hardy* (London, 1968), p. 84. For a more detailed discussion of this problem, see my essay 'The Unmanning of the Mayor of Casterbridge' in Dale Kramer, ed., *Critical Approaches to Hardy* (London, 1979).

3 Elizabeth Hardwick, *Seduction and Betrayal* (New York, 1974).

4 Shirley Ardener, ed., *Perceiving Women* (London, 1975).

5 'Women, Culture, and Society: A Theoretical Overview' in Louise Lamphere and Michelle Rosaldo, eds, *Women, Culture and Society* (Stanford, 1974), p. 39.

6 Carroll Smith-Rosenberg, 'The Female World of Love and Ritual: Relations Between Women in Nineteenth-Century America', *Signs: Journal of Women in Culture and Society*, vol. i (Autumn 1975), pp. 1–30; Nancy Cott, *The Bonds of Womanhood* (New Haven, 1977); Ann Douglas, *The Feminization of American Culture* (New York, 1977); Nina Auerbach, *Communities of Women* (Cambridge, Mass., 1978).

7 'Women and Fiction' in Virginia Woolf, *Collected Essays*, vol. ii (London, 1967), p. 141.

8 Peter N. Heydon and Philip Kelley, eds, *Elizabeth Barrett Browning's Letters to Mrs. David Ogilvy* (London, 1974), p. 115.

9 'Cassandra' in Ray Strachey, ed., *The Cause* (London, 1928), p. 398.

10 Rebecca West, 'And They All Lived Unhappily Ever After', *TLS* (26 July 1974), p. 779.

11 Annette Kolodny, 'Some Notes on Defining a 'Feminist Literary Criticism', *Critical Inquiry*, vol. ii (1975), p. 84. For an illuminating discussion of *The Driver's Seat*, see Auerbach, *Communities of Women*, p. 181.

12 Adrienne Rich, *Diving into the Wreck* (New York, 1973), p. 20.

13 The term 'matrophobia' has been coined by Lynn Sukenick; see Rich, *Of Woman Born*, pp. 235 ff.

14 Elaine Showalter, *A Literature of Their Own: British Women Novelists from Brontë to Lessing* (Princeton, NJ, 1977).

15 Charlotte Perkins Gilman, *The Man-made World* (London, 1911), pp. 101–2.

16 Woolf, 'Modern Fiction', *Collected Essays*, vol. ii, p. 106.

15 | Sandra Gilbert and Susan Gubar,
From *The Madwoman in the Attic* (1979), pp. 27–36

If we define a woman like Rossetti's dead wife as indomitably earthly yet somehow supernatural, we are defining her as a witch or monster, a magical creature of the lower world who is a kind of antithetical mirror image of an angel. As such, she still stands, in Sherry Ortner's words, 'both under and over (but really simply outside of) the sphere of culture's hegemony'. But now, as a representative of otherness, she incarnates the damning otherness of the flesh rather than the inspiring otherness of the spirit, expressing what – to use Anne Finch's words – men consider her own 'presumptuous' desires rather than the angelic humility and 'dullness' for which she was designed. Indeed, if we return to the literary definitions of 'authority' with which we began this discussion, we will see that the monster-woman, threatening to replace her angelic sister, embodies intransigent female autonomy and thus represents both the author's power to allay 'his' anxieties by calling their source bad names (witch, bitch, fiend, monster) and, simultaneously, the mysterious power of the character who refuses to stay in her textually ordained 'place' and thus generates a story that 'gets away' from its author.

Because, as Dorothy Dinnerstein has proposed, male anxieties about female autonomy probably go as deep as everyone's mother-dominated infancy, patriarchal texts have traditionally suggested that every angelically selfless Snow White must be hunted, if not haunted, by a wickedly assertive Stepmother: for every glowing portrait of submissive women enshrined in domesticity, there exists an equally important negative image that embodies the sacrilegious fiendishness of what William Blake called the 'Female Will'. Thus, while male writers traditionally praise the simplicity of the dove, they invariably castigate the cunning of the serpent—at least when that cunning is exercised in her own behalf. Similarly, assertiveness, aggressiveness—all characteristics of a male life of 'significant action' — are 'monstrous' in women precisely because 'unfeminine' and therefore unsuited to a gentle life of 'contemplative purity,' Musing on 'The Daughter of Eve,' Patmore's poet-speaker remarks, significantly, that

> The woman's gentle mood o'erstept
>   Withers my love, that lightly scans
> The rest, and does in her accept
>   All her own faults, but none of man's[1].

Luckily, his Honoria has no such vicious defects; her serpentine cunning, as we noted earlier, is concentrated entirely on pleasing her lover. But repeatedly, throughout most male literature, a sweet heroine inside the house (like Honoria) is opposed to a vicious bitch outside.

Behind Thackeray's angelically submissive Amelia Sedley, for instance— an Honoria whose career is traced in gloomier detail than that of Patmore's angel—lurks *Vanity Fair's* stubbornly autonomous Becky Sharp, an independent 'charmer' whom the novelist at one point actually describes as a monstrous and snaky sorceress:

> In describing this siren, singing and smiling, coaxing and cajoling, the author, with modest pride, asks his readers all around, has he once forgotten the laws of politeness, and showed the monster's hideous tail above water? No! Those who like may peep down under waves that are pretty transparent, and see it writhing and twirling, diabolically hideous and slimy, flapping amongst bones, or curling around corpses; but above the water line, I ask, has not everything been proper, agreeable, and decorous . . . .[2]

As this extraordinary passage suggests, the monster may not only be concealed *behind* the angel, she may actually turn out to reside *within* (or in the lower half of) the angel. Thus, Thackeray implies, every angel in the house—'proper, agreeable, and decorous', 'coaxing and cajoling' hapless men—is really, perhaps, a monster, 'diabolically hideous and slimy'.

'A woman in the shape of a monster', Adrienne Rich observes in 'Planetarium', 'a monster in the shape of a woman/the skies are full of them'.[3] Because the skies *are* full of them, even if we focus only on those female monsters who are directly related to Thackeray's serpentine siren, we will find that such monsters have long inhabited male texts. Emblems of filthy materiality, committed only to their own private ends, these women are accidents of nature, deformities meant to repel, but in their very freakishness they possess unhealthy energies, powerful and dangerous arts. Moreover, to the extent that they incarnate male dread of women and, specifically, male scorn of female creativity, such characters have drastically affected the self-images of women writers, negatively reinforcing those messages of submissiveness conveyed by their angelic sisters.

The first book of Spenser's *The Faerie Queene* introduces a female monster who serves as a prototype of the entire line. *Errour* is half woman, half serpent, 'Most lothsom, filthie, foule, and full of vile disdaine' (1.1.126). She breeds in a dark den where her young suck on her poisonous dugs or creep back into her mouth at the sight of hated light, and in battle against the noble Red-crosse Knight, she spews out a flood of books and papers, frogs and toads. Symbolizing the dangerous effect of misdirected and undigested learning, her filthiness adumbrates that of two other powerful females in book 1, Duessa and Lucifera. But because these other women can create false appearances to hide their vile natures, they are even more dangerous.

Like Errour, Duessa is deformed below the waist, as if to foreshadow *Lear*'s 'But to the girdle do the Gods inherit, Beneath is all the fiend's.' When, like all witches, she must do penance at the time of the new moon by bathing with herbs traditionally used by such other witches as Scylla, Circe, and Medea, her 'neather parts' are revealed as 'misshapen, monstrous.'[4] But significantly, Duessa deceives and ensnares men by assuming the shape of Una, the beautiful and angelic heroine who represents Christianity, charity, docility. Similarly, Lucifera lives in what seems to be a lovely mansion, a cunningly constructed House of Pride whose weak foundation and ruinous rear quarters are carefully concealed. Both women use their arts of deception to entrap and destroy men, and the secret, shameful ugliness of both is closely associated with their hidden genitals – that is, with their femaleness.

Descending from Patristic misogynists like Tertullian and St. Augustine through Renaissance and Restoration literature – through Sidney's Cecropia, Shakespeare's Lady Macbeth and his Goneril and Regan, Milton's Sin (and even, as we shall see, his Eve) – the female monster populates the works of the satirists of the eighteenth century, a company of male artists whose virulent visions must have been particularly alarming to feminine readers in an age when women had just begun to 'attempt the pen.' These authors attacked literary women on two fronts. First, and most obviously, through the construction of cartoon figures like Sheridan's Mrs. Malaprop and Fielding's Mrs. Slipslop, and Smollett's Tabitha Bramble, they implied that language itself was almost literally alien to the female tongue. In the mouths of women, vocabulary loses meaning, sentences dissolve, literary messages are distorted or destroyed. At the same time, more subtly but perhaps for that reason even more significantly, such authors devised elaborate anti-romances to show that the female 'angel' was really a female 'fiend', the ladylike paragon really an unladylike monster. Thus while the 'Bluestocking' Anne Finch would find herself directly caricatured (as she was by Pope and Gay) as a character afflicted with the 'poetical Itch' like Phoebe Clinket in *Three Hours After Marriage*,[5] she might well feel herself to be indirectly but even more profoundly attacked by Johnson's famous observation that a woman preacher was like a dog standing on its hind legs, or by the suggestion–embedded in works by Swift, Pope, Gay, and others–that *all* women were inexorably and inescapably monstrous, in the flesh as well as in the spirit. Finally, in a comment like Horace Walpole's remark that Mary Wollstonecraft was 'a hyena in petticoats', the two kinds of misogynistic attacks definitively merged.[6]

It is significant, then, that Jonathan Swift's disgust with the monstrous females who populate so many of his verses seems to have been caused specifically by the inexorable failure of female art. Like disgusted Gulliver, who returns to England only to prefer the stable to the parlor, his horses to his wife, Swift projects his horror of time, his dread of physicality, on to another stinking creature–the degenerate woman. Probably the most famous instance of this projection occurs in his so-called dirty poems. In these works, we peer behind the facade of the angel woman to discover that, say, the idealized 'Caelia, Caelia, Caelia, shits!' We discover that the seemingly unblemished Chloe must 'either void or burst', and that the female 'inner space' of the 'Queen of Love' is like a foul chamber pot.[7] Though some critics have suggested that the misogyny implied by Swift's characterizations of these women is merely ironic, what emerges from his most furious poems in this vein is a horror of female flesh and a revulsion at the inability – the powerlessness–of female arts to redeem or to transform the flesh. Thus, for Swift female sexuality is consistently equated with degeneration, disease, and death, while female arts are trivial attempts to forestall an inevitable end.

Significantly, as if defining the tradition of duplicity in which even Patmore's uxorious speaker placed his heroine, Swift devotes many poems to an examination of the role deception plays in the creation of a saving but inadequate fiction of femininity. In 'A Beautiful Young Nymph', a battered prostitute removes her wig, her crystal eye, her teeth, and her padding at bedtime, so that the next morning she must employ all her 'Arts' to reconstruct her 'scatter'd Parts'.[8] Such as they are, however, her arts only contribute to her own suffering or that of others, and the same thing is true of Diana in 'The Progress of Beauty', who awakes as a mingled mass of dirt and sweat, with cracked lips, foul teeth, and gummy eyes, to spend four hours artfully reconstructing herself. Because she is inexorably rotting away, however, Swift declares that eventually all forms will fail, for 'Art no longer can prevayl/When the Materials all are gone.'[9] The strategies of Chloe, Caelia, Corinna, and Diana – artists manqué all – have no success, Swift shows, except in temporarily staving off dissolution, for like Pope's 'Sex of Queens', Swift's females are composed of what Pope called 'Matter too soft', and their arts are thus always inadequate.[10]

No wonder, then, that the Augustan satirist attacks the female scribbler so virulently, reinforcing Anne Finch's doleful sense that for a woman to attempt the pen is monstrous and 'presumptuous', for she is 'to be dull / Expected and dessigned'. At least in part reflecting male artists' anxieties about the adequacy of their *own* arts, female writers are maligned as failures in eighteenth-century satire precisely because they cannot transcend their female bodily limitations: they cannot *conceive* of themselves in any but reproductive terms. Poor Phoebe Clinket, for instance, is both a caricature of Finch herself and a prototype of the female dunce who proves that literary creativity in women is merely the result of sexual frustration. Lovingly nurturing the unworthy 'issue' of her muse because it attests to the 'Fertility and Readiness' of her imagination, Phoebe is as sensual and indiscriminate in her poetic strainings as Lady Townley is in her insatiable erotic longings.[11] Like mothers of illegitimate or misshapen offspirng, female writers are not producing what they ought, the satirists declare, so that a loose lady novelist is, appropriately enough, the first prize in *The Dunciad*'s urinary contest, while a chamberpot is awarded to the runner-up.

For the most part, eighteenth-century satirists limited their depiction of the female monster to low mimetic equivalents like Phoebe Clinket or Swift's corroding coquettes. But there were several important avatars of the monster woman who retained the allegorical anatomy of their more fantastic precursors. In *The Battle of the Books*, for instance, Swift's 'Goddess Criticism' clearly symbolizes the demise of wit and learning. Devouring numberless volumes in a den as dark as Errour's, she is surrounded by relatives like Ignorance, Pride, Opinion, Noise, Impudence, and Pedantry, and she herself is as allegorically deformed as any of Spenser's females.

> The Goddess herself had claws like a Cat; her Head, and Ears, and Voice, resembled those of an Ass; Her Teeth fallen out before; Her Eyes turned inward, as if she lookt only upon Herself; Her diet was the overflowing of her own Gall: Her Spleen was so large, as to stand prominent like a Dug of the first Rate, nor wanted Excrescencies in forms of Teats, at which a Crew of ugly Monsters were greedily sucking; and what is wonderful to conceive, the bulk of Spleen increased faster than the Sucking could diminish it.[12]

Like Spenser's Errour and Milton's Sin, Criticism is linked by her processes of eternal breeding, eating, spewing, feeding, and redevouring to biological cycles all three poets view as destructive to transcendent, intellectual life. More, since all the creations of each monstrous mother are her excretions, and since all her excretions are both her food and her weaponry, each mother forms with her brood a self-enclosed system, cannibalistic and solipsistic: the creativity of the world made flesh is annihilating. At the same time, Swift's spleen-producing and splenetic Goddess cannot be far removed from the Goddess of Spleen in Pope's *The Rape of the Lock*, and – because she is a mother Goddess – she also has much in common with the Goddess of Dullness who appears in Pope's *Dunciad*. The parent of 'Vapours and Female Wit', the '*Hysteric* or *Poetic* fit', the Queen of Spleen rules over all women between the ages of fifteen and fifty, and thus, as a sort of patroness of the female sexual cycle, she is associated with the same anti-creation that characterizes Errour, Sin, and Criticism.[13] Similarly, the Goddess of Dullness, a nursing mother worshipped by a society of dunces, symbolizes the failure of culture, the failure of art, and the death of the satirist. The huge daughter of Chaos and Night, she rocks the laureate in her ample lap while handing out rewards and intoxicating drinks to her dull sons. A Queen of Ooze, whose inertia comments on idealized Queens of Love, she nods and all of Nature falls asleep, its light destroyed by the stupor that spreads throughout the land in the milk of her 'kindness'.[14]

In all these incarnations – from Errour to Dullness, from Goneril and Regan to Chloe and Caelia – the female monster is a striking illustration of Simone de Beauvoir's thesis that woman has been made to represent all of man's ambivalent feelings about his own inability to control his own physical existence, his own birth and death. As the Other, woman comes to represent the contingency of life, life that is made to be destroyed. 'It is the horror of his own carnal contingence, de Beauvoir notes, 'which [man] projects upon [woman].'[15] In addition, as Karen Horney and Dorothy Dinnerstein have shown, male dread of women, and specifically the infantile dread of maternal autonomy, has historically objectified itself in vilification of women, while male ambivalence about female 'charms' underlies the traditional images of such terrible sorceress-goddesses as the Sphinx, Medusa, Circe, Kali, Delilah, and Salome, all of whom possess duplicitous arts that allow them both to seduce and to steal male generative energy.[16]

The sexual nausea associated with all these monster women helps explain why so many real women have for so long expressed loathing of (or at least anxiety about) their own inexorably female bodies. The 'killing' of oneself into an art object – the pruning and preening, the mirror madness, and concern with odors and aging, with hair which is invariably too curly or too lank, with bodies too thin or too thick – all this testifies to the efforts women have expended not just trying to be angels but trying *not* to become female monsters. More significantly for our purposes, however, the female freak is and has been a powerfully coercive and monitory image for women secretly desiring to attempt the pen, an image that helped enforce the injunctions to silence implicit also in the concept of the *Ewig-Weibliche*. If becoming an *author* meant mistaking one's 'sex and way', if it meant becoming an 'unsexed' or perversely sexed female, then it meant becoming a monster or freak, a vile Errour, a grotesque Lady Macbeth, a disgusting goddess of Dullness, or (to name a few later witches) a murderous Lamia, a sinister Geraldine. Perhaps, then, the 'presumptuous' effort should not be made at all. Certainly the story of Lilith, one more monster woman – indeed, according to Hebrew mythology, both the first woman *and* the first monster – specifically connects poetic presumption with madness, freakishness, monstrosity.

Created not from Adam's rib but, like him, from the dust, Lilith was Adam's first wife, according to apocryphal Jewish lore. Because she considered herself his equal, she objected to lying beneath him, so that when he tried to force her submission, she became enraged and, speaking the Ineffable Name, flew away to the edge of the Red Sea to reside with demons. Threatened by God's angelic emissaries, told that she must return or daily lose a hundred of her demon children to death, Lilith preferred punishment to patriarchal marriage, and she took her revenge against both God and Adam by injuring babies – especially male babies, who were traditionally thought to be more vulnerable to her attacks. What her history suggests is that in patriarchal culture, female speech and female 'presumption' – that is, angry revolt against male domination – are inextricably linked and inevitably daemonic. Excluded from the human community, even from the semidivine communal chronicles of the Bible, the figure of Lilith represents the price women have been told they must pay for attempting to define themselves. And it is a terrible price: cursed both because she is a character who 'got away' and because she dared to usurp the essentially literary authority implied by the act of naming, Lilith is locked into a vengeance (child-killing) which can only bring her more suffering (the killing of her own children). And even the nature of her one-woman revolution emphasizes her helplessness and her isolation, for her protest takes the form of a refusal and a departure, a flight of escape rather than an active rebellion like, say, Satan's. As a paradigm of both the 'witch' and the 'fiend' of Aurora Leigh's 'Ghost, fiend, and angel, fairy, witch and sprite', Lilith reveals, then, just how difficult it is for women even to attempt the pen. And from George MacDonald, the Victorian fantasist who portrayed her in his astonishing *Lilith* as a paradigm of the self-tormenting assertive woman, to Laura Riding, who depicted her in 'Eve's Side of It' as an archetypal woman Creator, the problem Lilith represents has been associated with the problems of female authorship and female authority.[17] Even if they had not studied her legend, literary women like Anne Finch, bemoaning the double bind in which the mutually dependent images of angel and monster had left them, must have gotten the message Lilith incarnates: a life of feminine submission, of 'contemplative purity', is a life of silence, a life that has no pen and no story, while a life of female rebellion, of 'significant action', is a life that must be silenced, a life whose monstrous pen tells a terrible story. Either way, the images on the surface of the looking glass, into which the female artist peers in search of her *self*, warn her that she is or must be a 'Cypher', framed and framed up, indited and indicted.

Notes:

1 *The Correspondence of Gerard Manley Hopkins and Richard Watson Dixon*, ed. C. C. Abbott (London: Oxford University Press, 1935), p. 133.

2 Edward W. Said, *Beginnings: Intention and Method* (New York: Basic Books, 1975), p. 83.

3 Ibid., p. 162. For an analogous use of such imagery of paternity, see Gayatri Chakravorty Spivak's 'Translator's Preface' to Jacques Derrida, *Of Grammatology* (Baltimore: Johns Hopkins University Press, 1976), p. xi: 'to use one of Derrida's structural metaphors, [a preface is] the son or seed . . . caused or engendered by the father (text or meaning).'Also see her discussion of Nietzsche where she considers the 'masculine style of possession' in terms of 'the stylus, the stiletto, the spurs,' p. xxxvi.

4 James Joyce, *Ulysses* (New York: Modern Library, 1934), p. 205.

5 Ibid. The whole of this extraordinarily relevant passage develops this notion further: 'Fatherhood, in the sense of conscious begetting, is unknown to man,' Stephen notes. 'It is a mystical estate, an apostolic succession, from only begetter to only begotten. On that mystery and not on the madonna which the cunning Italian intellect flung to the mob of Europe the church is founded and founded irremovably because founded, like the world, macro- and microcosm, upon the void. Upon incertitude, upon unlikelihood. *Amor matris*, subjective and objective genitive, may be the only true thing in life. Paternity may be a legal fiction' (pp. 204–05).

6 Coleridge, *Biographia Literaria*, chapter 13. John Ruskin, *Modern Painters*, vol. 2, *The Works of John Ruskin*, ed. E. T. Cook and Alexander Wedderburn (London: George Allen, 1903), pp. 250–51. Although Virginia Woolf noted in *A Room of One's Own* that Coleridge thought 'a great mind is androgynous' she added dryly that 'Coleridge certainly did not mean . . . that it is a mind that has any special sympathy with women' (*A Room of One's Own* [New York: Harcourt Brace, 1929], p. 102). Certainly the imaginative power Coleridge describes does not sound 'man-womanly' in Woolf's sense.

7 Shelley, 'A Defense of Poetry.' Keats to John Hamilton Reynolds, 3 February 1818; *The Selected Letters of John Keats*, ed. Lionel Trilling (New York: Doubleday, 1956), p. 121.

8 See E. R. Curtius, *European Literature and the Latin Middle Ages* (New York: Harper Torchbooks, 1963), pp. 305, 306. For further commentary on both Curtius's 'The Symbolism of the Book' and the 'Book of Nature' metaphor itself, see Derrida, *Of Grammatology*, pp. 15–17.

9 'Timon, A Satyr,' in *Poems by John Wilmot Earl of Rochester*, ed. Vivian de Sola Pinto (London: Routledge and Kegan Paul, 1953), p. 99.

10 Bridget Riley, 'The Hermaphrodite,' *Art and Sexual Politics*, ed. Thomas B. Hass and Elizabeth C. Baker (London: Collier Books, 1973), p. 82. Riley comments that she herself would 'interpret this remark as expressing his attitude to his work as a celebration of life.'

11 Norman O. Brown, *Love's Body* (New York: Vintage Books, 1968), p. 134.; John T. Irwin, *Doubling and Incest, Repetition and Revenge* (Baltimore: Johns Hopkins University Press, 1975), p. 163. Irwin also speaks of 'the phallic generative power of the creative imagination' (p. 159).

12 Harold Bloom, *The Anxiety of Influence* (New York: Oxford University Press, 1973), pp. 11, 26.

13 All references to *Persuasion* are to volume and chapter of the text edited by R. W. Chapman, reprinted with an introduction by David Daiches (New York: Norton, 1958).

14 Anne Finch, *Poems of Anne Countess of Winchilsea*, pp. 4–5.

15 Southey to Charlotte Brontë, March 1837. Quoted in Winifred Gérin, *Charlotte Brontë: The Evolution of Genius* (Oxford: Oxford University Press, 1967), p. 110.

16 Finch, *Poems of Anne Countess of Winchilsea*, p. 100. Otto Weininger, *Sex and Character* (London: Heinemann, 1906), p. 286. This sentence is part of an extraordinary passage in which Weininger asserts that 'women have no existence and no essence; they are not, they are nothing,' this because 'woman has no relation to the idea . . . she is neither moral nor anti-moral,' but 'all existence is moral and logical existence.'

17 Richard Chase speaks of the 'masculine *élan*' throughout 'The Brontës, or Myth Domesticated,' in *Forms of Modern Fiction*, ed. William V. O'Connor (Minneapolis: University of Minnesota Press, 1948), pp. 102–13. For a discussion of the 'female eunuch' see Germaine Greer, *The Female Eunuch* (New York: McGraw Hill, 1970). See also Anthony Burgess, 'The Book Is Not For Reading,' *New York Times Book Review*, 4 December 1966, pp. 1, 74, and William Gass, on Norman Mailer's *Genius and Lust*, *New York Times Book Review*, 24 October 1976, p. 2. In this connection, finally, it is interesting (and depressing) to consider that Virginia Woolf evidently defined *herself* as 'a eunuch.' (See Noel Annan, 'Virginia Woolf Fever,' *New York Review*, 20 April 1978, p. 22.)

16 ▎ Annette Kolodny,

'Dancing Through the Minefield: Some Observations on the Theory, Practice, and Politics of a Feminist Literary Criticism', in E. Showalter, ed. *New Feminist Criticism* (1980), pp. 144–5; 159–63

Had anyone had the prescience, in 1969, to pose the question of defining a 'feminist' literary criticism, she might have been told, in the wake of Mary Ellmann's *Thinking About Women*,[1] that it involved exposing the sexual stereotyping of women in both our literature and our literary criticism and, as well, demonstrating the inadequacy of established critical schools and methods to deal fairly or sensitively with works written by women. In broad outline, such a prediction would have stood well the test of time, and, in fact, Ellmann's book continues to be widely read and to point us in useful directions. What could not have been anticipated in 1969, however, was the catalyzing force of an ideology that, for many of us, helped to bridge the gap between the world as we found it and the world as we wanted it to be. For those of us who studied literature, a previously unspoken sense of exclusion from authorship, and a painfully personal distress at discovering whores, bitches, muses, and heroines dead in childbirth where we had once hoped to discover ourselves, could–for the first time–begin to be understood as more than 'a set of disconnected, unrealized private emotions'.[2] With a renewed courage to make public our otherwise private discontents, what had once been 'felt individually as personal insecurity' came at last to be 'viewed collectively as structural inconsistency'[3] within the very disciplines we studied. Following unflinchingly the full implications of Ellmann's percepient observations, and emboldened by the liberating energy of feminist ideology—in all its various forms and guises—feminist criticism very quickly moved beyond merely 'expos[ing] sexism in one work of literature after another',[4] and promised instead that we might at last 'begin to record new choices in a new literary history'[5]. So powerful was that impulse that we experienced it, along with Adrienne Rich, as much more than 'a chapter in cultural history': it became, rather, 'an act of survival'.[6] What was at stake was not so much literature or criticism as such, but the historical, social, and ethical consequences of women's participation in, or exclusion from, either enterprise.

What distinguishes our work from those similarly oriented 'social conscious-ness' critiques, it is said, is its lack of systematic coherence. Pitted against, for example, psychoanalytic or Marxist readings, which owe a decisive share of their persuasiveness to their apparent internal consistency as a system the aggregate of feminist literary criticism appears woefully deficient in system, and painfully lacking in program. It is, in fact, from all quarters, the most telling defect alleged against us, the most explosive threat in the minefield. And my own earlier observation that, as of 1976, feminist literary criticism appeared 'more like a set of interchangeable strategies than any coherent school or shared goal orientation' has been taken by some as an indictment, by others as a statement of impatience. Neither was intended. I felt then, as I do now, that this would 'prove both its strength *and* its weakness',[7] in the sense that the apparent disarray would leave us vulnerable to the kind of objection I have just alluded to; while the fact of our diversity would finally place us securely where, all along, we should have been; camped out, on the far side of the minefield, with the other pluralists and pluralisms.

In our heart of hearts, of course, most critics are really structuralists (whether or not they accept the label) because what we are seeking are patterns (or structures) that can order and explain the otherwise inchoate; thus, we invent, or believe we discover, relational patternings in the texts we read which promise transcendence from difficulty and perplexity to clarity and coherence. But, as I have tried to argue in these pages, to the imputed 'truth' or 'accuracy' of these findings the feminist must oppose the painfully obvious truism that what is attended to in a literary work, and hence what is reported about it, is often determined not so much by the work itself as by the critical technique or aesthetic criteria through which it is filtered or, rather, read and decoded. All the feminist is asserting, then, is her own equivalent right to liberate new (and perhaps different) significances from these same texts; and at the same time, her right to choose which features of a text she takes as relevant because she is, after all, asking new and different questions of it. In the process, she claims neither definitiveness nor structural completeness for her different readings and reading systems, but only their usefulness in recognizing the particular achievements of woman-as-author and their applicability in conscientiously decoding woman-as-sign.

That these alternate foci of critical attentiveness will render alternate readings or interpretations of the same text–even among feminists–should be no cause for alarm. Such developments illustrate only the pluralist contention that 'in approaching a text of any complexity . . . the reader must choose to emphasize certain aspects which seem to him crucial,' and that 'in fact, the variety of readings which we have for many works is a function of the selection of crucial aspects made by the variety of readers'. Robert Scholes, from whom I have been quoting, goes so far as to assert that 'there is no single "right" reading for any complex literary work' and, following the Russian formalist school, he observes that 'we do not speak of readings that are simply true or false, but of readings that are more or less rich, strategies that are more or less appropriate'.[8] Because those who share the term 'feminist' nonetheless practice a diversity of critical strategies, leading, in some cases, to quite different readings, we must acknowledge among ourselves that sister critics, 'having chosen to tell a different story, may in their interpretation identify different aspects of the meanings conveyed by the same passage'.[9]

Adopting a 'pluralist' label does not mean, however, that we cease to disagree; it means only that we entertain the possibility that different readings, even of the same text, may be differently useful, even illuminating, within different contexts of inquiry. It means, in effect, that we enter a dialectical process of examining, testing, even trying out the contexts–be they prior critical assumptions or explicitly stated ideological stances (or some combination of the two)–that led to the disparate readings. Not all will be equally acceptable to every one of us, of course, and even those prior assumptions or ideologies that are acceptable may call for further refinement or clarification. But at the very least, because we will have grappled with the assumptions that led to it, we will be better able to articulate *why* we find a particular reading or interpretation adequate or inadequate. This kind of dialectical process, moreover, not only makes us more fully aware of what criticism is, and how it functions; it also gives us access to its future possibilities, making us conscious, as R. P. Blackmur put it, 'of what we have done', 'of what can be done next, or done again',[10] or, I would add, of what can be done differently. To put it still another way: just because we will no longer tolerate the specifically sexist omissions and oversights of earlier critical schools and methods does not mean that, in their stead, we must establish our own 'party line'.

In my view, our purpose is not and should not be the formulation of any single reading method or potentially Procrustean set of critical procedures nor, even less, the generation of prescriptive categories for some dreamed-of-non-sexist literary canon.[11] Instead, as I see it, our task is to initiate nothing less than a playful pluralism, responsive to the possibilities of multiple critical schools and methods, but captive of none, recognizing that the many tools needed for our analysis will necessarily be largely inherited and only partly of our own making. Only by employing a plurality of methods will we protect ourselves from the temptation of so oversimplifying any text – and especially those particularly offensive to us – that we render ourselves unresponsive to what Scholes has called 'its various systems of meaning and their interaction'.[12] Any text we deem worthy of our critical attention is usually, after all, a locus of many and varied kinds of (personal, thematic, stylistic, structural, rhetorical) relationships. So, whether we tend to treat a text as a *mimesis*, in which words are taken to be re-creating or representing viable worlds; or whether we prefer to treat a text as a kind of equation of communication, in which decipherable messages are passed from writers to readers; and whether we locate meaning as inherent in the text, the act of reading, or in some collaboration between reader and text – whatever our predilection, let us not generate from it a straitjacket that limits the scope of possible analysis. Rather, let us generate an ongoing dialogue of competing potential possibilities – among feminists and, as well, between feminists and non-feminist critics.

The difficulty of what I describe does not escape me. The very idea of pluralism seems to threaten a kind of chaos for the future of literary inquiry while, at the same time, it seems to deny the hope of establishing some basic conceptual model which can organize all data – the hope which always begins any analytical exercise. My effort here, however, has been to demonstrate the essential delusions that inform such objections: if literary inquiry has historically escaped chaos by establishing canons, then it has only substituted one mode of arbitrary action for another – and in this case, at the expense of half the population. And if feminists openly acknowledge ourselves as pluralists, then we do not give up the search for patterns of opposition and connection – probably the basis of thinking itself; what we give up is simply the arrogance of claiming that our work is either exhaustive or definitive. (It is, after all, the identical arrogance we are asking our nonfeminist colleagues to abandon.) If this kind of pluralism appears to threaten both the present coherence of and the inherited aesthetic criteria for a canon of 'greats', then, as I have earlier argued, it is precisely that threat which alone can free us from the prejudices, the strictures, and the blind spots of the past. In feminist hands, I would add, it is less a threat than a promise.

What unites and repeatedly invigorates feminist literary criticism, then, is neither dogma nor method but an acute and impassioned *attentiveness* to the ways in which primarily male structures of power are inscribed (or encoded) within our literary inheritance; the consequences of that encoding for women – as characters, as readers, and as writers; and, with that, a shared analytic *concern* for the implications of that encoding not only for a better understanding of the past but also for an improved reordering of the present and future. If that concern identifies feminist literary criticism as one of the many academic arms of the larger women's movement, then that attentiveness, within the halls of academe, poses no less a challenge for change, generating as it does the three propositions explored here. The critical pluralism that inevitably follows upon those three propositions, however, bears little resemblance to what Robinson has called 'the greatest bourgeois theme of all, the myth of pluralism, with its consequent rejection of ideological commitment as "too simple" to embrace the (necessarily complex) truth'.[13] Only ideological commitment could have gotten us to enter the minefield, putting in jeopardy our careers and our livelihood. Only the power of ideology to transform our conceptual worlds, and the inspiration of that ideology to liberate long-suppressed energies and emotions, can account for our willingness to take on critical tasks that, in an earlier decade, would have been 'abandoned in despair or apathy.'[14] The fact of differences among us proves only that, despite our shared commitments, we have nonetheless refused to shy away from complexity, preferring to disagree openly rather than to give up either intellectual honesty or hard-won insights.

Finally, I would argue, pluralism informs feminist literary inquiry not simply as a description of what already exists but, more importantly, as the only critical stance consistent with the current status of the larger women's movement. Segmented and variously focused, the different women's organizations neither espouse any single system of analysis nor, as a result, express any wholly shared, consistently articulated ideology. The ensuing loss in effective organization and political clout is a serious one, but it has not been paralyzing; in spite of our differences, we have united to act in areas of clear mutual concern (the push for the Equal Rights Amendment is probably the most obvious example). The trade-off, as I see it, has made possible an ongoing and educative dialectic of analysis and proffered solutions, protecting us thereby from the inviting traps of reductionism and dogma. And so long as this dialogue remains active, both our politics and our criticism will be free of dogma – but never, I hope of feminist ideology, in all its variety. For, 'whatever else ideologies may be – projections of unacknowledged fears, disguises for ulterior motives, phatic expressions of group solidarity' (and the women's movement, to date, has certainly been all of these, and more) – whatever ideologies express, they are, as Geertz astutely observes, 'most distinctively, maps of problematic social reality and matrices for the creation of collective conscience'. And despite the fact that 'ideological advocates . . . tend as much to obscure as to clarify the true nature of the problems involved', as Geertz notes, 'they at least call attention to their existence and, by polarizing issues, make continued neglect more difficult. Without Marxist attack, there would have been no labor reform; without Black Nationalists, no deliberate speed'.[15] Without Seneca Falls, I would add, no enfranchisement of women, and without 'consciousness raising' no feminist literary criticism nor, even loss, women's studies.

Ideology, however, only truly manifests its power by ordering the *sum* of our actions.[16] If feminist criticism calls anything into question, it must be that dog-eared myth of intellectual neutrality. For what I take to be the underlying spirit or message of any consciously ideologically premised criticism – that is, that ideas are important *because* they determine the ways we live, or want to live, in the world — is vitiated by confining those ideas to the study, the classroom, or the pages of our books. To write chapters decrying the sexual stereotyping of women in our literature, while closing our eyes to the sexual harassment of our women students and colleagues; to display Katherine Hepburn and Rosalind Russell in our courses on 'The Image of the Independent Career Women in Film', while managing not to notice the paucity of female administrators on our own campus; to study the women who helped make universal enfranchisement a political reality, while keeping silent about our activist colleagues who are denied promotion or tenure; to include segments on 'Women in the Labor Movement' in our American studies or women's studies courses, while remaining willfully ignorant of the department secretary fired for her efforts to organize a clerical workers' union; to glory in the delusions of 'merit', 'privilege' and 'status'which accompany campus life in order to insulate ourselves from the millions of women who labor in poverty—all this is not merely hypocritical; it destroys both the spirit and the meaning of what we are about. It puts us, however unwittingly, in the service of those who laid the minefield in the first place. In my view, it is a fine thing for many of us, individually, to have traversed the minefield; but that happy circumstance will only prove of lasting importance if, together, we expose it for what it is (the male fear of sharing power and significance with women) and deactivate its components, so that others, after us, may literally dance through the minefield.

Notes

'Dancing Through the Minefield' was the winner of the 1979 Florence Howe Essay Contest, which is sponsored by the Women's Caucus of the Modern Language Association.

Some sections of this essay were composed during the time made available to me by a grant from the Rockefeller Foundation, for which I am most grateful.

This essay intentionally deals with white feminist critics only, because it was originally conceived as the first of a two-essay dialogue with myself. A second essay, which was to have dealt with black and Third World American feminist literary critics, is now part of a comprehensive study of feminist criticism in progress, to be called *Dancing Through the Minefield*.

1 Mary Ellman, *Thinking About Women* (New York, Harcourt, Brace & World, 1968).
2 See Clifford Gertz, 'Ideology as a Cultural System' *The Interpretation of Cultures: Selected Essays* (New York, Basic Books, 1973), p. 232.
3 Ibid., p. 204.
4 Lillian S. Robinson, 'Cultural Criticism and the *Horror Vacui*', *College English* 33 (October 1972); reprinted as 'The Critical Task', in her *Sex, Class, and Culture* (Bloomington, Indiana University Press, 1978), p. 51.
5 Elaine Showalter, *A Literature of Their Own: British Women Novelists From Brontë to Lessing* (Princeton, N J Princeton University Press, 1997), p. 36
6 Adrienne Rich, 'When We Dead Awaken: Writing as Re-Vision', *College English* 34 (October 1972); reprinted in *Adrienne Rich's Poetry*, ed. *Barbara* Charles worth Gelpi and Albert Gelpi (New York, W. W. Norton, 1975), p. 90.
7 Annette Kolodny, 'Literary Criticism', Review Essay, *Signs* 2 (Winter 1976): 420.
8 Robert Scholes, *Structuralism in Literature. An introduction* (New Haven, CT. Yale

University Press, 1974). pp. 144–5. These comments appear within his explication of Tzvetan Todorov's theory of reading.

9 I borrow this concise phrasing of pluralistic modesty from M. H. Abrams's 'The Deconstructive Angel' *Critical Inquiry* 3 (Spring 1977); 427. Indications of the pluralism that was to mark feminist inquiry were to be found in the diversity of essays collected by Susan Koppelman Cornillon for her early and groundbreaking anthology, *Images of Women in Fiction: Feminist Perspectives* (Bowling Green, Ohio: Bowling Green University Popular Press, 1972).

10 R. P. Blackmur, 'A Burden for Critics' *Hudson Review* 1 (Summer 1948); 171. Blackmur, of course, was referring to the way in which criticism makes us conscious of how art functions; I use his wording here because I am arguing that that same awareness must also be focused on the critical act itself. 'Consciousness' he avers, 'is the way we feel the critic's burden'.

11 I have earlier elaborated my objection to prescriptive categories for literature in 'The Feminist as Literary Critic' Critical Response, *Critical Inquiry* 2 (Summer 1976): 827–8.

12 Scholes, *Structuralism in Literature*, pp. 151–2.

13 Lillian S. Robinson, 'Dwelling in Decencies: Radical Criticism and the Feminist Perspective', *College English* 32 (May 1971); reprinted in *Sex, Class, and Culture*, p. 11.

14 Ideology bridges the emotional gap between things as they are and as one would have them be, thus ensuring the performance of roles that might otherwise be abandoned in despair or apathy', Geertz comments in 'Ideology as a Cultural System', p. 205.

15 Ibid., pp. 220, 205.

16 I here follow Frederic Jameson's view in *The Prison-House of Language: A Critical Account of Structuralism and Russian Formalism* (Princeton, N. L. Princeton University Press, 1974), p. 107: Ideology would seem to be that grillwork of form, convention, and belief which orders our actions'.

---

17 | The Marxist–Feminist Collective,

From 'Women Writing: Jane Eyre, Shirley, Villette, Aurora Leigh', *Ideology and Consciousness*, 3, Spring (1978), pp. 30–5

In 1859, Charlotte Brontë made a final, impatient plea to Lewes:

> I wish you did not think me a woman. I wish all reviewers believed 'Currer Bell' to be a man; they would be more just to him . . . I cannot, when I write, think always of myself and what you consider elegant and charming in femininity . . .[1]

Criticism of women writers is in general divided between the extremes of gender-disavowal and gender-obsession. The second tendency, which Brontë struggles against in Lewes, patronises women writers as outsiders to literary history, without justifying this apartheid. The Brontës are considered important 'women novelists', not simply novelists. This kind of 'gender criticism' subsumes the text into the sexually-defined personality of its author, and thereby obliterates its literarity. To pass over the ideology of gender, on the other hand, ignores the fact that the conditions of literary production and consumption are articulated, in the Victorian period, in crucially different ways for women and men. Any rigorous Machereyan analysis must account for the ideology of gender as it is written into or out of texts by either sex. Women writers, moreover, in response to their cultural exclusion, have developed a relatively autonomous, clandestine tradition of their own.

Gender and genre come from the same root, and their connection in literary history is almost as intimate as their etymology. The tradition into which the woman novelist entered in the mid-19th century could be polarised as at once that of Mary Wollstonecraft and of Jane Austen, with the attendant polarisation of politics – between revolutionary feminism and conservatism – and of genre – between romanticism and social realism. Wollstonecraft and Austen between them pose the central question of access to male education and discourse on the one hand, on the other the annexing of women's writing to a special sphere, domestic and emotional.

Austen's refusal to write about anything she didn't know is as undermining to the patriarchal hegemony as Wollstonecraft's demand for a widening of women's choices: the very 'narrowness' of her novels gave them a subversive dimension of which she herself was unaware, and which has been registered in critics' bewilderment at what status to accord them.

Bourgeois criticism should be read symptomatically: most of its so-called 'evaluation' is a reinforcement of ideological barriers. Wollstonecraft's, and later Brontë's, ambivalent relation to Romanticism, usually described as clumsy Gothicism, is bound up with their feminism. Romanticism becomes a problem for women writers because of its assumptions about the 'nature of femininity'. The tidal rhythms of menstruation, the outrageous visibility of pregnancy, lead, by a non-sequitur common to all sexual analogy, to the notion that women exist in a state of unreflective bias, the victims of instincts, intuitions, and the mysterious pulsations of the natural world. Intuition is held to be a pre-lapsarian form of knowledge, associated especially with angels, children, idiots, 'rustics' and women. These excluded, or fabulous, groups act for the patriarchy as a mirror onto which it nostalgically projects the exclusions of its discourse. As a glorified, but pre-linguistic communion with nature, intuition lowers women's status while appearing to raise it.

While Wollstonecraft and Brontë are attracted to Romanticism because reluctant to sacrifice, as women writers, their privileged access to feeling, both are aware that full participation in society requires suppression of this attraction. The drive to female emancipation, while fuelled by the revolutionary energy at the origins of Romanticism, has an ultimately conservative aim – successful integration into existing social structures.

Romanticism, after the disappointments of the French Revolution, was gradually depoliticised, and it is only in the mid-nineteenth century, in a period of renewed revolutionary conflict, that it once again becomes a nexus of ideological tension where gender, genre, politics and feminism converge.

Jane Eyre: Her Hand in Marriage

Charlotte Brontë's second preface to *Jane Eyre* states her authorial project as to 'scrutinise and expose' what she calls 'narrow human doctrines' of religion and morality.[2] Our reading of *Jane Eyre* identifies Charlotte Brontë's interrogation of the dominant ideology of love and marriage; but also suggests the Machereyan 'not-said' of the novel – what it is not possible for her to 'scrutinise and expose', woman as a desiring subject, a sexual subject seeking personal fulfilment within the existing structures of class and kinship, i.e. in a patriarchal capitalist society. *Jane Eyre* is *about* kinship, *about* the fact that the social position of a woman, whether rich or poor, pretty or plain, is mediated through the family – to which she may or may not belong.

The text of *Jane Eyre* speaks that desire in the interstices of the debate on woman's social role, between the romance/realism divide, the conflict between Reason and Imagination in her heroine's consciousness. It speaks of women's sexuality in Victorian England, opening the locked room of a tabooed subject – just as that part of the text which concerns Bertha Mason/ Rochester disrupts the realistic narrative of Jane's search for an adequate kinship system, i.e. an opening into the family structure from which she is excluded. Charlotte Brontë's general fictional strategy is to place her heroines in varying degrees of marginality to the normative kinship patterns. Frances Henri, Crimsworth (a female surrogate), Jane, Shirley, Caroline Helstone and Lucy Snowe, all have a deviant socialisation, all confront the problem of a marriage not negotiated by a *pater familias*.

Why? By excluding them from a conventional family situation in which their socialisation and their exchange in marriage cannot follow the practice of Victorian middle-class women, Charlotte Brontë's fiction explores the constraints of the dominant ideology as they bear on female sexual and social identity.

At the centre of Charlotte Brontë's novels is a figure who either lacks or deliberately cuts the bonds of kinship.[3] But Eagleton, although stressing this structural characteristic, discusses it primarily in terms of class-mobility. This treatment of Jane Eyre herself as an asexual representative of the upwardly mobile bourgeoisie leads to a reductionist reading of the text. It neglects gender as a determinant, by subsuming gender under class. The meritocratic vision of 'individual self-reliance', as Eagleton puts its, *cannot* be enacted by a woman character in the same way as it can be by a male. For a woman to become a member of the 'master-class' depends on her taking a sexual master whereby her submission brings her access to the dominant culture.

The social and judicial legitimacy of this relationship – its encoding within the law – is of primary importance; hence Jane's rejection of the role of

Rochester's mistress. She would not merely *not* acquire access–she would forfeit the possibility of ever doing so. The structure of the novel, Jane's development through childhood and adolescence into womanhood does not simply represent an economic and social progression from penniless orphan to member of the landed gentry class; it represents a woman's struggle for access to her own sexual and reproductive potential–in other words, her attempts to install herself as a full subject within a male-dominated culture.

For example, the structure of the five locales of the novel is customarily seen as the articulation of the heroine's progress–a progress described in liberal criticism as the moral growth of the individual, in vulgar sociological terms as 'upward social mobility'. To foreground kinship provides a radically different reading.

Jane's progress is from a dependent orphan to the acquisition of the family necessary for her full integration into mid-nineteenth century culture as a woman. Her cousins, the Rivers, and the Madeira uncle who intervenes twice–once via his agent, Bertha's brother, to save her from becoming a 'fallen woman' as Rochester's bigamous wife, and again at the end of the novel with a legacy which is in effect a dowry–provide Jane with the necessary basis for her exchange into marriage.

Each of the five houses through which the heroine passes traces the variety and instability of a kinship structure at a transitional historical period, and the ideological space this offers to women.

At Gateshead, as the excluded intruder into the Reed family and at Thornfield as the sexually tabooed and socially ambiguous governess, Jane's lack of familial status renders her particularly vulnerable to oppression and exploitation. At Lowood, she acquires a surrogate sister and mother in Helen Burns and Miss Temple–only to lose them through death and marriage. The instability of kinship relations is imaged in the patterns of gain and loss, acceptance and denial, enacted at each 'home'–most dramatically in the loss of a lawful wedded husband, spiritually and sexually akin but socially tabooed. The subsequent flight from Thornfield reduces her to a homeless vagrant lacking both past and identity. Throughout the text, the symmetrical arrangement of Reed and Rivers cousins, the Reed and Eyre uncles, the patterns of metaphors about kinship, affinity and identification articulate the proposition that a woman's social identity is constituted within familial relationships. Without the kinship reading, the River's transformation into long-lost, bona-fide blood-relations at Moor End appears a gross and unmotivated coincidence. This apparently absurd plot manipulation is in fact dictated by the logic of the not-said.

Like such violations of probability, the Gothic elements in the novel are neither clumsy interventions to resolve the narrative problems nor simply the residues of the author's earlier modes of discourse, the childhood fantasies of Angria. Their main function is to evade the censorship of female sexuality within the signifying practice of mid-Victorian realism. For the rights and wrongs of women in social and political terms, there existed a rationalist language, a political rhetoric, inherited from Mary Wollstonecraft. But for the 'unspeakable' sexual desires of women, Charlotte Bornté returned on the one hand to Gothic and Romantic modes, on the other to a metonymic discourse of the human body – hands and eyes for penises, 'vitals' or 'vital organs' for women's genitalia – often to comic effect:

'I am substantial enough – touch me.'. . .
He held out his hand, laughing. 'Is that a dream?' said he, placing it close to my eyes.
He had a rounded, muscular, and vigorous hand, as well as a long, strong arm. [4]

The tale told of women's sexual possibilities is a halting, fragmented and ambivalent one. The libidinal fire of Jane Eyre's 'vital organs' is not denied, not totally repressed, as the refusal of St John Rivers suggests:

At his side, always and always restrained, always checked – forced to keep the fire of my nature continually low, to compel it to burn inwardly, and never utter a cry, though the imprisoned flame consume vital after vital.[5]

The marriage proposed here, significantly, is an inter-familial one which denies the heroine's sexuality. If women's sexuality is to be integrated, reconciled with male patriarchal Law, a compromise must be achieved with the individual Law-bearer, in this case through a return to Edward Rochester.

The alternative to either repression or integration is examined through that part of the text concerned with Bertha Mason/Rochester. Her initial intervention, the uncanny laughter after Jane surveys from the battlements of Thornfield the wider world denied her as a woman, signifies the return of the repressed, the anarchic and unacted desires of women. Bertha's appearances constitute a punctuating device or notation of the not-said – the Pandora's box of unleashed female libido. Bertha's tearing of the veil on the eve of Jane's wedding, for example, is a triumphant trope for the projected loss of Jane's virginity unsanctioned by legitimate marriage. Thus while other spectres were haunting Europe, the spectre haunting Jane Eyre, if not Victorian England, was the insurgence of women's sexuality into the signifying practice of literature.

The myth of unbridled male sexuality is treated through Rochester, whose name evokes that of the predatory Restoration rake, here modified by Byronic sensibility. In the vocabulary of Lacanian psychoanalysis, his maiming by the author is not so much a punitive castration, but represents his successful passage through the castration complex. Like all human subjects he must enter the symbolic order through a necessary acceptance of the loss of an early incestuous love object, a process he initially tries to circumvent through bigamy. His decision to make Jane his bigamous wife attempts to implicate the arch-patriarch God himself ('I know my maker sanctions what I do'). The supernatural lightning which this presumption provokes is less a re-establishing of bourgeois morality than an expression of disapproval by the transcendental phallic signifier of Rochester's Oedipal rivalry. It is God at the end of the novel who refuses to sanction Jane's marriage to St John Rivers when invoked in its support, and who sends Rochester's, supernatural cry to call Jane to him; and it is God's judgement which Rochester, in his maimed condition, finally accepts with filial meekness.

By accepting the Law, he accepts his place in the signifying chain and enters the Symbolic order, as bearer rather than maker of the Law. Sexuality in a reduced and regulated form is integrated – legitimised – within the dominant kinship structure of patriarchy and within the marriage which he (by Bertha's death-by-fire), and Jane (by her acquisition of a family) is now in a position to contract. *Jane Eyre* does not attempt to rupture the dominant kinship structures. The ending of the novel ('Reader, I married him') affirms those very structures. The feminism of the text resides in its 'not-said', its attempt to inscribe women as sexual subjects within this system.

Notes

1 T.J. Wise and J.A. Symington, eds, *The Brontës: Their Lives, Friendships and Correspondence*, 4 Vols (London, Shakespeare Head, 1932), Vol. iii, p. 31.
2 Currer Bell, Preface to the Second Edition of *Jane Eyre* (London, Smith, Elder & Co., 1847).
3 T. Eagleton, *Myths of Power: A Marxist Study of the Brontës* (London, Macmillan, 1988).
4 *Jane Eyre* (Harmondsworth, Penguin, 1966), pp. 306–7.
5 Ibid, p. 433.

Part 2

After Deconstruction

Section 1

Seminal Texts

The material gathered in this introduction to Part Two has been chosen because, like those seminal essays by Marx, Freud, Saussure and de Beauvoir which served to introduce the first part of this anthology, the pieces gathered here, by Barthes, Lacan, Derrida, Foucault and Kristeva, may be regarded as key statements in the final transition from a modernist to a more postmodernist trajectory in literary theory. Each can be seen as developing the key terms – the unconscious, the signifier, ideology and the sex-gender distinction – which appeared at the heart of the work of the earlier thinkers examined in the previous part. This shift, sometimes referred to as post-structuralism (though it is more than that), inaugurated a period of radical questioning of all the previously dominant categories of modernity: the relationship between language and the world, the nature of subjectivity, the possibility of knowledge and the nature and function of the aesthetic.

The term 'post-structuralism' does not refer to a body of work that represents a coherent school or movement. Indeed there is an extensive debate about what constitutes post-structuralism and about its relation to structuralism. For some it is a matter of a more radical reading of Saussure, for others it is the moment at which structuralism becomes self-reflective. It is sometimes taken as a critique of structuralism, sometimes a development of it. In some instances it has almost become synonymous with the name of Derrida and the mode of analysis he inaugurates – 'deconstruction'. However, it is usually used to refer to Derrida and the later Barthes, less certainly to Foucault and Lacan as the principal theorists in the field, and to work which develops out of the writings of these key figures. Our use of the term is related to the body of work that presupposes structuralism, but that distances itself from certain of its features, and that presents a more radical attack on critical orthodoxies (structuralism among them). In other words, while retaining a 'post-Saussurean' definition we have made the category as broad as possible, certainly not restricting it to the Derridean strand.

There are a number of problems with any attempt to classify work as either structuralist or post-structuralist. The material is not naturally self-categorizing, rather, it forms a network: a web of interconnections and antitheses around which it is difficult to draw simple boundaries. Some of the work covered in Part One of this anthology relates more closely at times to the trajectories typical of the work represented in Part Two, and, by the same token, work covered in Part Two often slips back into the kind of mastery of explanation and use of metalanguage characteristic of Part One.

The problem is further complicated by the moments of appearance of structuralism and post-structuralism. If one wanted to date the appearance of post-structuralism then 1966/7 would be a reasonable point to start. At the international symposium, 'The Languages of Criticism and the Sciences of Man', in 1966, a significant post-structuralist impetus emerged.[1] Derrida published three books in 1967, among them *Of Grammatology* and *Writing and Difference*. Barthes's work was undergoing a transition from the structuralism of *Elements of Semiology* (1964) to a post-structuralist position that can be traced in essays written between then and the publication of *S/Z* in 1972. Foucault's *Order of Things* and Lacan's *Ecrits* were published in 1966, and though these latter two might not be fully-fledged works of post-structuralism, they differ significantly from the structuralism represented in Part One of this book.

But if there was a visible post-structuralist impetus it became entangled (in Anglo–American theory at any rate) with structuralism, for the latter was itself only taking significant hold in the mid-1970s. Indeed, the books cited above were not published in English translation until the mid-/late-1970s, while Culler's *Structuralist Poetics* and Hawkes's *Structuralism and Semiotics* had only appeared in the mid-1970s. The moment of structuralism and the moment of post-structuralism almost coincide in terms of their appearance and adoption in Anglo–American literary theory.

Roland Barthes's *S/Z* serves as a good illustration of the convergence and varying appropriations by Anglo–American criticism of structuralist and post-structuralist work. The five codes Barthes had used in his implosive analysis of a short story by Balzac were taken by many critics to be the codes out of which the text was structured and which could therefore be used in textual criticism to reveal an absolute textual structure and meaning. However, a more radical reading of *S/Z* saw it not as providing the structural grid of the text but as *processing* the textual web in an act of structuration. The difference can be captured in the distinction between a 'product' orientation, where criticism sets out to reveal the construction of the product, and a 'process' orientation, where the act of criticism is acknowledged to be a processing act – an act of structuration which is itself an active part of that construction. Here the text is not revealed and explained but worked upon.

While there is a difficulty in simply ascribing certain writings to either a structuralist or a post-structuralist position certain features of post-structuralism do distinguish it from structuralism. Though language remains a central area of interest, post-structuralism takes up a more radical reading and/or critique of Saussurean theory. As we have seen, Saussure argued that 'language is a system of difference, with no positive terms'. Identities do not refer to essences and are not discrete but are articulated in difference; identities are events in language. Structuralism had tended to acknowledge this, but only to a limited degree; it did not extend such reasoning to the foundations of the literary discourse. In post-structuralism everything can be subjected to this formulation. All the categories which literary studies assumes, and which form the basis of the critical act, are open to the re-evaluation and radical scepticism of a post-structuralist perspective, including the category 'Literature' itself. And if the categories of Literature and literary study do not refer to things-in-themselves, but are constructed in difference, then the act of criticism which articulates that difference cannot be viewed as subordinate. Rather, it is of equal importance to the literature it studies, for it is the very act that brings the 'literary' into being; it is the necessary supplement that endows 'literature' with its special and specific existence. In a Derridean inversion, the supplement becomes, paradoxically, the more important term, for without criticism 'Literature' would have no meaning. It is not only the category of literature that can be subjected to such reasoning, but also that of the author and the literary text itself. Post-structuralism effectively undermines all the categories that had previously been taken for granted as having an independent existence.

If this were all that post-structuralism amounted to then it would not be altogether radical. Though identities might be arbitrary, once they had been fixed in language then they would be defined and stable; however, post-structuralism goes further. In the system of difference proposed by Saussure the sign, made up of the signifier and the signified, is arbitrary, fixed by social contract. Once formed, the sign becomes a totality; signifier and signified are inseparable and the sign's form and meaning are self-identical. In other words, Saussure had argued that the continuum of the phenomenal world was 'cut up' by language; but once this process was complete, then the relationship between the arbitrary signifier and the arbitrary signified was fixed and they achieved a stable one-to-one correspon-dence. Post-structuralism questions this assumption, arguing that signifiers do not carry with them well-defined signifieds; meanings are never as graspable or as 'present' as this suggests. Any attempt to define the meaning of a word illustrates the point for it inevitably ends up in a circularity of signifiers, with the signifiers sliding over the continuum of the field of the signified. For example, in the Concise Oxford Dictionary the meaning of the word 'meaning' is given as 'what is meant; significance . . .'; 'meant' in turn refers us to 'mean', 'mean' to 'signify'; meanwhile, 'significance' refers us to 'significant' which is defined as 'having a meaning'. The meaning of 'meaning' does not become present to us, it simply slips beneath a circularity of signifiers. And, of course, these signifiers are open to multiple meaning areas; 'mean' also refers us to 'inferior, poor'; 'not generous'; 'the mathematical mean', etc. Post-structuralism argues, then, that the sign is not stable, that there is an indeterminacy or undecidability about meaning and that it is subject to 'slippage' from signifier to signifier. So, if literature, the author and the text no longer have an identity outside of difference, neither do they have a single, fixed and determinate meaning; they are relativized and unstable.

Post-structuralism, while continuing the attack on humanist ideology and the Anglo–American critical tradition, also applies its perspectives to structuralism. It argues that, in its claim to explain by unveiling an underlying structure, structuralism is in the grip of another form of essentialism in that it presupposes a latent centre or core which gives rise to surface, manifest forms. Structuralism's appeal to a metalanguage of explanation cannot avoid the problems of interpretation and meaning. The signs of that metalanguage are themselves subject to slippage and indeterminacy; they can no more offer a full and final presence of meaning than the signs of an object language. And the metalanguage itself is always open, in its turn, to the gaze of an alternative metalanguage. Indeed, the distinction between an object language and a metalanguage breaks down in post-structuralism. From this position, the claim of structuralism to effect a mastery and explanation of the world through the scientific investigation of sign systems is undermined and compromised.

The radical decentring of identities and an emphasis on the signifier over the signified, form two central characteristics of the post-structuralist shift. However, these characteristics are not evenly distributed over all the movements in thought and criticism which have been influenced by post-structuralist theorising. Each of the sections in this second Part explores different preoccupations and emphases which have arisen broadly out of the questioning of the systems and structures of modernity, whether these are primarily about discourse, history, politics or subjectivity. Postcolonialism, for example, could be seen as developing the post-structuralist critique of difference for political ends, whereas postmodernism has largely focused on the epistemological inadequacies of Enlightenment thought.

Unlike the material in Part One, the work covered in Part Two cannot be seen so easily in terms of movements or schools. However, certain key figures are significant and demand attention. Referring to Lacan, Derrida and Foucault, for example, Robert Young has argued that these are 'the names of problems, not "authors" of doctrines'.[2] Much of the writing in Part Two, however, should be seen as a network of interconnected notions and concepts, and work categorized in one section will often be pertinent to another. Post-structuralism is contradictory in that, on the one hand, grand and overarching theories tend to disappear and yet, on the other, a cluster of preoccupations and assumptions, about language, textuality, subjectivity, difference, tend to drive theorizing in all the most recent critical movements: postmodernism, postcolonialism, gender studies, queer theory, cultural materialism, new historicism.

Indeed, it could be argued that two distinct trajectories have developed in which both the object of enquiry and the way it is conceptualized fundamentally differ: the first, what might be called the trajectory of language, characterizes post-structuralism in its more purely formal deconstructive modes, and the second, which might be called 'discourse', is more concerned with speech communities, ideologies and the political reading of texts. The language trajectory tends to belong to the earliest moments of post-structuralism, to a concern with figures of language in abstraction, with deconstructing the principles of ordering and the 'metaphysics of presence' that seem inescapably built into human language systems. It tends to view all language as a web of signifiers bound up in an endless play of textuality (textuality being the condition of existence of signifiers where they refer endlessly to other textual occurrences, rather than to a pre-text). The discourse trajectory, on the other hand, situates language in the context of use and of speaking and listening subjects. Language is regarded as a practical activity intimately connected with the context in which it appears. Though the sign is unstable in both trajectories, here it is constantly being fixed and unfixed or refixed by different users and communities of users of the language. Language is implicitly still tied to some notion of intentionality and related immediately to the socio-cultural formation in which it appears and to the exercise of power. Of course, few critics subscribe to one or other of these trajectories in any simple way. They represent the two poles of the post-structuralist constellation rather than an exclusive either/or. It is clear though that whereas Derrida, for example, belongs to the language trajectory, Foucault tends towards that of discourse.

Roland Barthes' essay, 'The Death and Return of the Author' has been chosen to open this section, because it provides a short and accessible introduction to many of the preoccupations discussed above and because it has achieved such notoriety for its polemical stance against the prevailing Romantic-humanist tradition which places the author at the centre and source of the work. More difficult, but arguably just as influential, is the essay reprinted here by Jacques Lacan. Lacan's theory of the Subject owes much to Freud; however, he rereads Freud in the light of post-Saussurean linguistics and it is the latter which gives the work its post-structuralist inflection. Language is a crucial element in the theory for it is only in the moment of entry into the symbolic order of language that full subjectivity comes into being.

Lacan argues that before it enters the symbolic through the acquisition of language, the human infant goes through the 'mirror stage', entering the realm of the imaginary (which the subject never entirely leaves). In the mirror stage, Lacan argues, the infant begins to recognize a distinction between its own body and the outside world. This is illustrated in the child's relation to its own image in the mirror; the infant lacks control of its limbs and its experience is a jumbled mass but its image in the mirror appears unified and in control. The child recognizes its image and merges with it in a process of identification, creating an illusory experience of control of the self and the world – an imaginary correspondence of self and image. The two are perceived as self-identical. However, to achieve full distinction of the self, the subject has to enter the symbolic, where identity depends on difference rather than self-identicality. Language, the system of difference which articulates identities, constructs positions for the subject notably the subject position 'I' – which allows differentiation from others, and identity for the self. However, in the necessary acceptance of the subject-positions offered by language, the individual experiences a loss or lack because it is *subject to* the positions that are predefined for it and beyond its control.

The sense of a full and unified subject is contradicted by a sense of being defined by the law of human culture. At this point, desire and the unconscious are also created. The unconscious is, as it were, the repository of that which has to be repressed when the subject takes on the pre-defined positions available in language. Subject-positions, meaning and consciousness, made available through the symbolic order, depend on language as a system of difference and hence they entail a loss of the full presence that seemed to characterize the imaginary realm. The individual desires to control meaning but this is not possible because of the nature of language. Language, Lacan argued, is not a matter of a one-to-one correspondence between signifier and signified. The signifiers of language cannot fix the arbitrary field of the signified; signifiers slide across the continuum and hence the desire for mastery of meaning is unsatisfiable. The unified and stable subject of humanism is contradicted and de-stabilized by this primacy of the signifier and loss of apparent one-to-one correspondence between signifier and signified.

Lacan's work has been criticized for its universalizing and a-historical view of the construction of the subject – in other words, for a residual essentialism. This might seem to put his work into the first part of this book, however, it has provided a starting point for a set of concerns that have become a part of the post-structuralist enterprise and his view of language coincides with the post-structuralist view. Although Lacan's work had been available for some considerable time (indeed the essay reprinted dates from 1949), and had influenced Althusser's notion of interpellation, the attempt to use his psychoanalytic work in literary theory belongs more to the post-structuralist moment and impetus.

In what has here been called the 'language trajectory', the key reference for all theorists has been the work of Jacques Derrida. In this mode of theorizing, the text is taken not as referring to a pre-text but as inscribed within a web of textuality and difference. Its characteristic mode of operation is a spectacular play of language game around the texts it interrogates and its most formidable exponent has been the French philosopher, Derrida.

Derrida has been seen as almost synonymous with the post-structuralist enterprise. He has consistently critiqued and extended structuralism, rigorously following through the most radical implications of the Saussurean theory of language. Though Derrida is perhaps best known for inaugurating 'deconstruction', the various forms of textual analysis that claim to the 'deconstructing the text' often have only tenuous links with his consistent concern to undo the 'logocentric' impulse in texts. 'Logocentrism' is the term Derrida uses to cover that form of rationalism that presupposes a 'presence' behind language and text – a 'presence' such as an idea, an intention, a truth, a meaning or a reference for which language acts as a subservient and convenient vehicle of expression. But at the same time as language and text exhibit logocentric impulses, *writing*, as textuality, undoes that logocentrism through its rhetorical and troping figures; while the text attempts to suppress textuality, textuality inevitably imposes itself on the scene of writing.

Logocentrism, the mark of a 'metaphysics of presence' is, for Derrida, the very foundation of Western thought; it is undermined by Saussure's theory of language in which identities result only from difference. But, as Derrida shows, Saussure himself falls into a logocentrism. In *Of Gramma-tology* Derrida criticizes Saussure on the grounds that he privileges speech over writing. Speech becomes the authentic moment of language where meaning is identical to the speaker's intention and it thus bears the sign of presence, whereas writing is seen as a secondary and inferior form of speech. Typically, Derrida reverses the privileged term of the binary opposition, to show how speech can be seen as a form of writing (rather than vice versa), and how both exist in a mutually reciprocal dependence marked by différance.

Derrida reads Saussure radically, transposing difference to différance – where meaning is a matter of both difference and deferring. Meaning is never self-present in the sign, for if it were then the signifier would simply be the reference for the signified, the signifier 'standing-in' for the absent 'presence' of the concept that lies behind it. Meaning is a result of difference, but it is also deferred, there is always an element of 'undecidability' or 'play' in the unstable sign. This leads to an emphasis on the signifier and on textuality rather than the signified and meaning, since there is no point at which the slippage of signifiers can be stopped, no final resting point where the signifier yields up the truth of the signified, for that signified is just another signifier in a moment in différance.

Deconstruction is a twofold strategy of, on the one hand, uncovering and undoing logocentric rationality and on the other, drawing attention to the language of the text, to its figurative and rhetorical gestures and pointing up the text's existence in a web of textuality, in a network of signifiers where no final and transcendental signified can be fixed. If it is to sustain such a strategy, then it must constantly refuse to set itself up as a systematic analysis independent of the text, a system that explains and masters, since to do so would be to fix the meaning of the text. Deconstruction appears, therefore, not as a rigid method or explanatory metalanguage, but more as a process and a performance closely tied to the texts it deconstructs. However, as Derrida notes, such strategies cannot ultimately escape logocentrism, they can only push at its limits; deconstructionist texts are themselves not beyond deconstruction.

For literary criticism the implications of deconstruction, and of Derrida's work in general, are profound. Literary studies has traditionally been concerned with the interpretation of texts, with revealing the 'meaning' behind the text (be that meaning the author's intention or the 'truth' of the human condition). Deconstructionist logic disrupts that interpretive mode. If the meaning of the text is unstable, undecidable, then the project of literary interpretation is compromised; interpretation is doomed to endlessly repeat the interpretive act, never able to reach that final explanation and understanding of the text – it is haunted by the continual play of différance. What is left to criticism is either a celebration of that play, or a rigorous argumentation around the logocentric versus textuality paradox.

Though Derrida's work has had a formative and direct influence on the American deconstructionists, it has also been highly influential in the development of post-structuralism in general. Indeed, it would be tempting to say that his 'presence' is pervasive in post-structuralist thought – but that would be wilfully logocentric. The essay by Derrida reprinted here interrogates the structuralist project and in particular the work of Lévi-Strauss, taking it to task over the notion of structure, for in structure, structuralism proposes a centre beyond the play of language. This essay is one of Derrida's most widely known pieces, one of the first to be translated into English.

Whereas Derrida's work represents the seminal moment in the shift from structuralism to post-structuralism along the axis of language, the work of the French historian and cultural theorist Michel Foucault has been at the centre of what is here referred to as the 'discourse trajectory'.

For Michel Foucault the 'social' is produced in the network of discourses and discursive practices through which we seem to acquire knowledge about the world. Broadly, Foucault's argument is that it is the modalities of discourses and discursive practices that actually produce both that knowledge and the social itself, and the modalities function differently in different historical 'epistemes'. (An episteme is an historical period that is unified by the rules and procedures – the modalities – for producing knowledge.) The history of epistemes is not a matter of progression or continuity, but of discontinuity. In this earlier work Foucault attempts to uncover the concealed modalities of discourse which govern and produce various 'knowledges'. In *Birth of the Clinic* (1963) and *The Order of Things* (1966) he investigated the 'discursive formations' of medicine and the human sciences, noting how these 'discourses' delimited a field of objects, defined legitimate practices and positions for 'subjects' to adopt, and fixed the norms for producing concepts and theories.

Foucault's work has been concerned primarily with the configuration of discourse, knowledge and power, and it is through these three key notions that he elaborates a complex theory. In his earlier work, he emphasizes discourse; in his later work the emphasis shifts to power. 'The Order of Discourse' is balanced between this shift in emphasis. Where, in earlier work, he had sought to delineate the principles of regularity by which knowledge was produced, here he outlines the forces and technologies of power by which the production of discourse and knowledge is surveyed and controlled; however, if power here appears to be simply repressive, account should be taken of his later writings where he is careful to point out that power is productive – power *produces* discourse, as well as setting its boundaries. This insight, more than any other, was the starting point for that constellation of critical practices which is now referred to as the new historicism.

The final piece in this section is Julia Kristeva's (1971) essay, 'Women's Time'. Kristeva's work is important because she was one of the first feminists to combine linguistics, theories of ideology and psychoanalysis, and to begin to develop post-structuralist critiques of subjectivity for a feminist politics. The essay was published relatively early in the second wave of the feminist movement, but Kristeva already recognizes some of the contra-dictions which would become central to the debates within feminism in the 1980s. She argues strenuously against an essentializing mode of feminism which would simply preserve the categories of 'man' and 'woman' but reverse their evaluation, but equally she recognizes the dangers in that mode of (liberal) feminism which would simply seek to insert women into established masculine-designated subject positions through an extension of rights which leaves the social formation otherwise unchanged. Her argument seeks to undo all forms of adherence to that metaphysics of presence which has the effect of essentializing the categories of masculinity and femininity.

Notes

1 R. Macksey and E. Donato, eds, *The Structuralist Controversy: The Languages of Criticism and the Sciences of Man* (Baltimore, MD, Johns Hopkins University Press, 1972).
2 R. Young, ed., *Untying the Text: A Post-Structuralist Reader* (Boston and London, Routledge, Kegan and Paul, 1981).

18 | Roland Barthes,

'The Death of the Author', S. Heath, tr. and ed. *Image, Music, Text* (1968), pp. 142–8

In his story *Sarrasine* Balzac, describing a castrato disguised as a woman writes the following sentence: *'This was woman, herself, with her sudden fears, her irrational whims, her instinctive worries, her impetuous boldness, her fussings, and her delicious sensibility.'* Who is speaking thus? Is it the hero of the story bent on remaining ignorant of the castrato hidden beneath the woman? Is it Balzac the individual, furnished by his personal experience with a philosophy of Woman? Is it Balzac the author professing 'literary' ideas on femininity? Is it universal wisdom? Romantic psychology? We shall never know, for the good reason that writing is the destruction of every voice, of every point of origin. Writing is that neutral, composite, oblique space where our subject slips away, the negative where all identity is lost, starting with the very identity of the body writing.

No doubt it has always been that way. As soon as a fact is *narrated* no longer with a view to acting directly on reality but intransitively, that is to say, finally outside of any function other than that of the very practice of the symbol itself, this disconnection occurs, the voice loses its origin, the author enters into his own death, writing begins. The sense of this

phenomenon, however, has varied; in ethnographic societies the responsibility for a narrative is never assumed by a person but by a mediator,
shaman or relator whose 'performance' – the mastery of the narrative code –
may possibly be admired but never his 'genius'. The author is a modern
figure, a product of our society insofar as, emerging from the Middle Ages
and English empiricism, French rationalism and the personal faith of the
Reformation, it discovered the prestige of the individual, of, as it is more
nobly put, the 'human person'. It is thus logical that in literature it should
be this positivism, the epitome and culmination of capitalist ideology, which
has attached the greatest importance to the 'person' of the author. The
author still reigns in histories of literature, biographies of writers, interviews,
magazines, as in the very consciousness of men of letters anxious to unite
their person and their work through diaries and memoirs. The image of
literature to be found in ordinary culture is tyrannically centred on the
author, his person, his life, his tastes, his passions, while criticism still
consists for the most part in saying that Baudelaire's work is the failure of
Baudelaire the man, Van Gogh's his madness, Tchaikovsky's his vice. The
explanation of a work is always sought in the man or woman who produced it,
as if it were always in the end, through the more or less transparent allegory
of the fiction, the voice of a single person, the *author* 'confiding' in us.

Though the sway of the Author remains powerful (the new criticism has
often done no more than consolidate it), it goes without saying that certain
writers have long since attempted to loosen it. In France, Mallarmé was
doubtless the first to see and to foresee in its full extent the necessity to
substitute language itself for the person who until then has been supposed
to be its owner. For him, for us too, it is language which speaks, not the
author; to write, is, through a prerequisite impersonality (not at all to be
confused with the castrating objectivity of the realist novelist), to reach
that point, where only language acts, 'performs' and not 'me'. Mallarmé's
entire poetics consists in suppressing the author in the interests of writing
(which is, as will be seen, to restore the place of the reader). Valéry,
encumbered by a psychology of the Ego, considerably diluted Mallarmé's
theory but, his taste for classicism leading him to turn to the lessons of
rhetoric, he never stopped calling into question and deriding the Author;
he stressed the linguistic and, as it were, 'hazardous' nature of his activity,
and throughout his prose works he militated in favour of the essentially
verbal condition of literature, in the face of which all recourse to the writer's
inferiority seemed to him pure superstition. Proust himself, despite the
apparently psychological character of what are called his *analyses*, was
visibly concerned with the task of inexorably blurring, by an extreme
subtilisation, the relation between the writer and his characters; by making
of the narrator not he who has seen and felt nor even he who is writing, but
he who *is going to write* (the young man in the novel – but, in fact, how old
is he and who is he? – wants to write but cannot; the novel ends when
writing at last becomes possible), Proust gave modern writing its epic. By
a radical reversal, instead of putting his life into his novel, as is so often

maintained, he made of his very life a work for which his own book was the model; so that it is clear to us that Charlus does not imitate Montesquiou but that Montesquiou – in his anecdotal, historical reality – is no more than a secondary fragment, derived from Charlus. Lastly, to go no further than this prehistory of modernity, Surrealism, though unable to accord language a supreme place (language being system and the aim of the movement being, romantically, a direct subversion of codes – itself moreover illusory: a code cannot be destroyed, only 'played off'), contributed to the desacrilization of the image of the Author by ceaselessly recommending the abrupt disappointment of expectations of meaning (the famous surrealist 'jolt'), by entrusting the hand with the task of writing as quickly as possible what the head itself is unaware of (automatic writing), by accepting the principle and the experience of several people writing together. Leaving aside literature itself (such distinctions really becoming invalid), linguistics has recently provided the destruction of the Author with a valuable analytical tool by showing that the whole of the enunciation is an empty process, functioning perfectly without there being any need for it to be filled with the person of the interlocutors. Linguistically, the author is never more than the instance writing, just as *I* is nothing other than the instance saying *I*: language knows a 'subject', not a 'person', and this subject, empty outside of the very enunciation which defines it, suffices to make language 'hold together', suffices, that is to say, to exhaust it.

The removal of the Author (one could talk here with Brecht of a veritable 'distancing', the Author diminishing like a figurine at the far end of the literary stage) is not merely an historical fact or an act of writing; it utterly transforms the modern text (or – which is the same thing – the text is henceforth made and read in such a way that at all its levels the author is absent). The temporality is different. The Author, when believed in, is always conceived of as the past of his own book: book and author stand automatically on a single line divided into a *before* and an *after*. The Author is thought to *nourish* the book, which is to say that he exists before it, thinks, suffers, lives for it, is in the same relation of antecedence to his work as a father to his child. In complete contrast, the modern scriptor is born simultaneously with the text, is in no way equipped with a being preceding or exceeding the writing, is not the subject with the book as predicate; there is no other time than that of the enunciation and every text is eternally written *here and now*. The fact is (or, it follows) that *writing* can no longer designate an operation of recording, notation, representation, 'depiction' (as the Classics would say); rather, it designates exactly what linguists, referring to Oxford philosophy, call a performative, a rare verbal form (exclusively given in the first person and in the present tense) in which the enunciation has no other content (contains no other proposition) than the act by which it is uttered – something like the *I declare* of kings or the *I sing* of very ancient poets. Having buried the Author, the modern scriptor can thus no longer believe, as according to the pathetic view of his predecessors, that this hand is too slow for his thought or passion and that consequently, making a law of necessity, he must emphasize this delay and indefinitely 'polish' his form. For him, on the contrary, the hand, cut off from any voice, borne by a pure gesture of inscription (and not of expression), traces a field without origin–or which, at least, has no other origin than language itself, language which ceaselessly calls into question all origins.

We know now that a text is not a line of words releasing a single 'theological' meaning (the 'message' of the Author-God) but a multi-dimensional space in which a variety of writings, none of them original, blend and clash. The text is a tissue of quotations drawn from the innumerable centres of culture. Similar to Bouvard and Pécuchet, those eternal copyists, at once sublime and comic and whose profound ridiculousness indicates precisely the truth of writing, the writer can only imitate a gesture that is always anterior, never original. His only power is to mix writings, to counter the ones with the others, in such a way as never to rest on any one of them. Did he wish to *express himself*, he ought at least to know that the inner 'thing' he thinks to 'translate' is itself only a ready-formed dictionary, its words only explainable through other words, and so on indefinitely; something experienced in exemplary fashion by the young Thomas de Quincey, he who was so good at Greek that in order to translate absolutely modern ideas and images into that dead language, he had, so Baudelaire tells us (in *Paradis Artificiels*), 'created for himself an unfailing dictionary, vastly more extensive and complex than those resulting from the ordinary patience of purely literary themes'. Succeeding the Author, the scriptor no longer bears within him passions, humours, feelings, impressions, but rather this immense dictionary from which he draws a writing that can know no halt: life never does more than imitate the book, and the book itself is only a tissue of signs, an imitation that is lost, infinitely deferred.

Once the Author is removed, the claim to decipher a text becomes quite futile. To give a text an Author is to impose a limit on that text, to furnish it with a final signified, to close the writing. Such a conception suits criticism very well, the latter then allotting itself the important task of discovering the Author (or its hypostases: society, history, psyche, liberty) beneath the work: when the Author has been found, the text is 'explained'–victory to the critic. Hence there is no surprise in the fact that, historically, the reign of the Author has also been that of the Critic, nor again in the fact that criticism (be it new) is today undermined along with the Author. In the multiplicity of writing, everything is to be *disentangled*, nothing *deciphered*; the structure can be followed, 'run' (like the thread of a stocking) at every point and at every level, but there is nothing beneath: the space of writing is to be ranged over, not pierced; writing ceaselessly posits meaning ceaselessly to evaporate it, carrying out a systematic exemption of meaning. In precisely this way literature (it would be better from now on to say *writing*), by refusing to assign a 'secret', an ultimate meaning, to the text (and to the world as text), liberates what may be called an anti-theological activity, an activity that is truly revolutionary since to refuse to fix meaning is, in the end, to refuse God and his hypostases–reason, science, law.

Let us come back to the Balzac sentence. No one, no 'person', says it: its source, its voice, is not the true place of the writing, which is reading. Another–very precise–example will help to make this clear: recent research (J.-P. Vernant[1]) has demonstrated the constitutively ambiguous nature of Greek tragedy, its texts being woven from words with double meanings that each character understands unilaterally (this perpetual misunderstanding is exactly the 'tragic'); there is, however, someone who understands each word in its duplicity and who, in addition, hears the very deafness of the characters speaking in front of him–this someone being precisely the reader (or here, the listener). Thus is revealed the total existence of writing: a text is made of multiple writings, drawn from many cultures and entering into mutual relations of dialogue, parody, contestation, but there is one place where this multiplicity is focused and that place is the reader, not, as was hitherto said, the author. The reader is the space on which all the quotations that make up a writing are inscribed without any of them being lost; a text's unity lies not in its origin but in its destination. Yet this destination cannot any longer be personal: the reader is without history, biography, psychology; he is simply that someone who holds together in a single field all the traces by which the written text is constituted. Which is why it is derisory to condemn the new writing in the name of a humanism hypocritically turned champion of the reader's rights. Classic criticism has never paid any attention to the reader: for it, the writer is the only person in literature. We are now beginning to let ourselves be fooled no longer by the arrogant antiphrastical recriminations of good society in favour of the very thing it sets aside, ignores, smothers, or destroys; we know that to give writing its future, it is necessary to overthrow the myth: the birth of the reader must be at the cost of the death of the Author.

Note

1   Cf. Jean-Pierre Vernant (with Pierre Vidal-Naquet), *Mythe et tragédie en Grèce ancienne* (Paris, 1972), esp. pp. 19–40, 99–131.

19 | Jacques Lacan,

'The Mirror Stage as Formative of the Function of the I as Revealed in Psychoanalytic Experience', Alan Sheridan, tr. *Ecrits, A Selection* (1949), pp. 1–7

The conception of the mirror stage that I introduced at our last congress, thirteen years ago, has since become more or less established in the practice of the French group. However, I think it worthwhile to bring it again to your attention, especially today, for the light it sheds on the formation of the *I* as we experience it in psychoanalysis. It is an experience that leads us to oppose any philosophy directly issuing from the *Cogito*.

Some of you may recall that this conception originated in a feature of human behaviour illuminated by a fact of comparative psychology. The child, at an age when he is for a time, however short, outdone by the chimpanzee in instrumental intelligence, can nevertheless already recognize as such his own image in a mirror. This recognition is indicated in the illuminative mimicry of the *Aha-Erlebnis*, which Köhler sees as the expression of situational apperception, an essential stage of the act of intelligence.

This act, far from exhausting itself, as in the case of the monkey, once the image has been mastered and found empty, immediately rebounds in the case of the child in a series of gestures in which he experiences in play the relation between the movements assumed in the image and the reflected environment, and between this virtual complex and the reality it reduplicates – the child's own body, and the persons and things, around him.

This event can take place, as we have known since Baldwin, from the age of six months, and its repetition has often made me reflect upon the startling spectacle of the infant in front of the mirror. Unable as yet to walk, or even to stand up, and held tightly as he is by some support human or artificial (what, in France, we call a '*trotte-bébé*'), he nevertheless overcomes, in a flutter of jubilant activity, the obstructions of his support and, fixing his attitude in a slightly leaning-forward position, in order to hold it in his gaze, brings back an instantaneous aspect of the image.

For me, this activity retains the meaning I have given it up to the age of eighteen months. This meaning discloses a libidinal dynamism, which has hitherto remained problematic, as well as an ontological structure of the human world that accords with my reflections on paranoiac knowledge.

We have only to understand the mirror stage *as an identification*, in the full sense that analysis gives to the term: namely, the transformation that takes place in the subject when he assumes an image – whose predestination to this phase-effect is sufficiently indicated by the use, in analytic theory, of the ancient term *imago*.

This jubilant assumption of his specular image by the child at the *infans* stage, still sunk in his motor incapacity and nursling dependence, would seem to exhibit in an exemplary situation the symbolic matrix in which the *I* is precipitated in a primordial form, before it is objectified in the dialectic of identification with the other, and before language restores to it, in the universal, its function as subject.

This form would have to be called the Ideal-I,[1] if we wished to incorporate it into our usual register, in the sense that it will also be the source of secondary identifications, under which term I would place the functions of libidinal normalization. But the important point is that this form situates the agency of the ego, before its social determination, in a fictional direction, which will always remain irreducible for the individual alone, or rather, which will only rejoin the coming-into-being (*le devenir*) of the subject asymptotically, whatever the success of the dialectical syntheses by which he must resolve as *I* his discordance with his own reality.

The fact is that the total form of the body by which the subject anticipates in a mirage the maturation of his power is given to him only as *Gestalt*, that is to say, in an exteriority in which this form is certainly more constituent than constitute, but in which it appears to him above all in a contrasting size (*un relief de stature*) that fixes it and in a symmetry that inverts it, in contrast with the turbulent movements that the subject feels are animating him. Thus, this *Gestalt* – whose pregnancy should be regarded as bound up with the species, though its motor style remains scarcely recognizable – by these two aspects of its appearance, symbolizes the mental permanence of the *I*, at the same time as it prefigures its alienating destination; it is still pregnant with the correspondences that unite the *I* with the statue in which man projects himself, with the phantoms that dominate him, or with the automaton in which, in an ambiguous relation, the world of his own making tends to find completion.

Indeed, for the *imagos* – whose veiled faces it is our privilege to see in outline our daily experience and in the penumbra of symbolic efficacity[2] – the mirror-image would seem to be the threshold of the visible world, if we go by the mirror disposition that the *imago of one's own body* presents in hallucinations or dreams, whether it concerns its individual features, or even its infirmities, or its object-projections; or if we observe the role of the mirror apparatus in the appearance of the double, in which psychical realities, however heterogeneous, are manifested.

That a *Gestalt* should be capable of formative effects in the organism is attested by a piece of biological experimentation that is itself so alien to the idea of psychical causality that it cannot bring itself to formulate its results in these terms. It nevertheless recognizes that it is a necessary condition for the maturation of the gonad of the female pigeon that it should see another member of its species, of either sex; so sufficient in itself is this condition that the desired effect may be obtained merely by placing the individual within reach of the field of reflection of a mirror. Similarly, in the case of the migratory locust, the transition within a generation from the solitary to the gregarious form can be obtained by exposing the individual, at a certain stage, to the exclusively visual action of a similar image, provided it is animated by movements of a style sufficiently close to that characteristic of the species. Such facts are inscribed in an order of homeomorphic identification that would itself fall within the larger question of the meaning of beauty as both formative and erogenic.

But the facts of mimicry are no less instructive when conceived as cases of heteromorphic identification, in as much as they raise the problem of the signification of space for the living organism – psychological concepts hardly seem less appropriate for shedding light on these matters than ridiculous attempts to reduce them to the supposedly supreme law of adaptation. We have only to recall how Roger Caillois (who was then very young, and still fresh from his breach with the sociological school in which he was trained) illuminated the subject by using the term *'legendary psychasthenia'* to classify morphological mimicry as an obsession with space in its derealizing effect.

I have myself shown in the social dialectic that structures human knowledge as paranoiac[3] why human knowledge has greater autonomy than animal knowledge in relation to the field of force of desire, but also why human knowledge is determined in that 'little reality' (*ce peu de réalité*), which the Surrealists, in their restless way, saw as its limitation. These reflections lead me to recognize in the spatial captation manifested in the mirror-stage, even before the social dialectic, the effect in man of an organic insufficiency in his natural reality – in so far as any meaning can be given to the word 'nature'.

I am led, therefore, to regard the function of the mirror-stage as a particular case of the function of the *imago*, which is to establish a relation between the organism and its reality – or, as they say, between the *Innenwelt* and the *Umwelt*.

In man, however, this relation to nature is altered by a certain dehiscence at the heart of the organism, a primordial Discord betrayed by the signs of uneasiness and motor unco-ordination of the neo-natal months. The objective notion of the anatomical incompleteness of the pyramidal system and likewise the presence of certain humoral residues of the maternal organism confirm the view I have formulated as the fact of a real *specific prematurity of birth* in man.

It is worth noting, incidentally, that this is a fact recognized as such by embryologists, by the term *foetalization*, which determines the prevalence of the so-called superior apparatus of the neurax, and especially of the cortex, which psycho-surgical operations lead us to regard as the intra-organic mirror.

This development is experienced as a temporal dialectic that decisively projects the formation of the individual into history. The *mirror stage* is a drama whose internal thrust is precipitated from insufficiency to anticipation – and which manufactures for the subject, caught up in the lure of spatial identification, the succession of phantasies that extends from a fragmented body-image to a form of its totality that I shall call orthopaedic – and, lastly, to the assumption of the armour of an alienating identity, which will mark with its rigid structure the subject's entire mental development. Thus, to break out of the circle of the *Innenwelt* into the *Umwelt* generates the inexhaustible quadrature of the ego's verifications.

This fragmented body – which term I have also introduced into our system of theoretical references – usually manifests itself in dreams when the movement of the analysis encounters a certain level of aggressive disintegration in the individual. It then appears in the form of disjointed limbs, or of those organs represented in exoscopy, growing wings and taking up arms for intestinal persecutions – the very same that the visionary

Hieronymus Bosch has fixed, for all time, in painting, in their ascent from the fifteenth century to the imaginary zenith of modern man. But this form is even tangibly revealed at the organic level, in the lines of 'fragilization' that define the anatomy of phantasy, as exhibited in the schizoid and spasmodic symptoms of hysteria.

Correlatively, the formation of the *I* is symbolized in dreams by a fortress, or a stadium–its inner arena and enclosure surrounded by marshes and rubbish-tips, dividing it into two opposed fields of contest where the subject flounders in quest of the lofty, remote inner castle whose form (sometimes juxtaposed in the same scenario) symbolizes the id in a quite startling way. Similarly, on the mental plane, we find realized the structures of fortified works, the metaphor of which arises spontaneously, as if issuing from the symptoms themselves, to designate the mechanisms of obsessional neurosis– inversion, isolation, reduplication, cancellation and displacement.

But if we were to build on these subjective givens alone–however little we free them from the condition of experience that makes us see them as partaking of the nature of a linguistic technique–our theoretical attempts would remain exposed to the charge of projecting themselves into the unthinkable of an absolute subject. This is why I have sought in the present hypothesis, grounded in a conjunction of objective data, the guiding grid for a *method of symbolic reduction*.

It establishes in the *defences of the ego* a genetic order, in accordance with the wish formulated by Miss Anna Freud, in the first part of her great work, and situates (as against a frequently expressed prejudice) hysterical repression and its return at a more archaic stage than obsessional inversion and its isolating processes, and the latter in turn as preliminary to paranoic alienation, which dates from the deflection of the specular *I* into the social *I*.

This moment in which the mirror-stage comes to an end inaugurates, by the identification with the *imago* of the counterpart and the drama of primordial jealousy (so well brought out by the school of Charlotte Bühler in the phenomenon of infantile *transitivism*), the dialectic that will henceforth link the *I* to socially elaborated situations.

It is this moment that decisively tips the whole of human knowledge into mediatization through the desire of the other, constitutes its objects in an abstract equivalence by the co-operation of others, and turns the I into that apparatus for which every instinctual thrust constitutes a danger, even though it should correspond to a natural maturation–the very normalization of this maturation being henceforth dependent, in man, on a cultural mediation as exemplified, in the case of the sexual object, by the Oedipus complex.

In the light of this conception, the term primary narcissism, by which analytic doctrine designates the libidinal investment characteristic of that moment, reveals in those who invented it the most profound awareness of semantic latencies. But it also throws light on the dynamic opposition between this libido and the sexual libido, which the first analysts tried to define when they invoked destructive and, indeed, death instincts, in order to explain the evident connection between the narcissistic libido and the alienating function of the *I*, the aggressivity it releases in any relation to the other, even in a relation involving the most Samaritan of aid.

In fact, they were encountering that existential negativity whose reality is so vigorously proclaimed by the contemporary philosophy of being and nothingness.

But unfortunately that philosophy grasps negativity only within the limits of a self-sufficiency of consciousness, which as one of its premises, links to the *méconnaissances* that constitute the ego, the illusion of autonomy to which it entrusts itself. This flight of fancy, for all that it draws, to an unusual extent, on borrowings from psychoanalytic experience, culminates in the pretension of providing an existential psychoanalysis.

At the culmination of the historical effort of a society to refuse to recognize that it has any function other than the utilitarian one, and in the anxiety of the individual confronting the 'concentrational'[4] form of the social bond that seems to arise to crown this effort, existentialism must be judged by the explanations it gives of the subjective impasses that have indeed resulted from it; a freedom that is never more authentic than when it is within the walls of a prison; a demand for commitment, expressing the impotence of a pure consciousness to master any situation; a voyeuristic-sadistic idealization of the sexual relation; a personality that realizes itself only in suicide; a consciousness of the other that can be satisfied only by Hegelian murder.

These propositions are opposed by all our experience, in so far as it teaches us not to regard the ego as centred on the *perception-consciousness system*, or as organized by the 'reality principle'–a principle that is the expression of a scientific prejudice most hostile to the dialectic of knowledge. Our experience shows that we should start instead from the *function of méconnaissance* that characterizes the ego in all its structures so markedly articulated by Miss Anna Freud. For, if the *Verneinung* represents the patent form of that function, its effects will, for the most part, remain latent, so long as they are not illuminated by some light reflected on to the level of fatality, which is where the id manifests itself.

We can thus understand the inertia characteristic of the formation of the *I*, and find there the most extensive definition of neurosis–just as the captation of the subject by the situation gives us the most general formula for madness, not only the madness that lies behind the walls of asylums, but also the madness that deafens the world with its sound and fury.

The sufferings of neurosis and psychosis are for us a schooling in the passions of the soul, just as the beam of the psychoanalytic scales, when we calculate the tilt of its threat to entire communities, provides us with an indication of the deadening of the passions in society.

At this junction of nature and culture, so persistently examined by modern anthropology, psychoanalysis alone recognises this knot of imaginary servitude that love must always undo again, or sever.

For such a task, we place no trust in altruistic feeling, we who lay bare the aggressivity that underlies the activity of the philanthropist, the idealist, the pedagogue, and even the reformer.

In the recourse of subject to subject that we preserve, psychoanalysis may accompany the patient to the ecstatic limit of the *'Thou art that'*, in which is revealed to him the cipher of his mortal destiny, but it is not in our mere power as practitioners to bring him to that point where the real journey begins.

Notes

1 Throughout this article I leave in its peculiarity the translation I have adopted for Freud's *Ideal-Ich* [i.e., 'je-idéal'], without further comment, other than to say that I have not maintained it since.
2 Cf. Claude Lévi-Strauss, *Structural Anthropology*, Chapter X.
3 Cf. 'Aggressivity in Psychoanalysis', p. 8 and *Écrits*, p. 180.
4 *'Concentrationnaire'*, an adjective coined after World War II (this article was written in 1949) to describe the life of the concentration camp. In the hands of certain writers it became, by extension, applicable to many aspects of 'modern' life [Tr.]

20 | Jacques Derrida,

'Structure, Sign and Play in the Discourse of the Human Sciences', Alan Bass, tr. *Writing and Difference* (1966), pp. 278–95

We need to interpret interpretations more than to interpret things.
(Montaigne)

Perhaps something has occurred in the history of the concept of structure that could be called an 'event', if this loaded word did not entail a meaning which it is precisely the function of structural – or structuralist – thought to reduce or to suspect. Let us speak of an 'event' nevertheless, and let us use quotation marks to serve as a precaution. What would this event be then? Its exterior form would be that of a *rupture* and a *redoubling*.

It would be easy enough to show that the concept of structure and even the word 'structure' itself are as old as the *epistémē* – that is to say, as old as Western science and Western philosophy – and that their roots thrust deep into the soil of ordinary language, into whose deepest recesses the *epistémē* plunges in order to gather them up and to make them part of itself in a metaphorical displacement. Nevertheless, up to the event which I wish to mark out and define, structure – or rather the structurality of structure – although it has always been at work, has always been neutralized or reduced, and this by a process of giving it a center or of referring it to a point of presence, a fixed origin. The function of this center was not only to orient, balance, and organize the structure—one cannot in fact conceive of an unorganized structure—but above all to make sure that the organizing principle of the structure would limit what we might call the *play* of the structure. By orienting and organizing the coherence of the system, the centre of a structure permits the play of its elements inside the total form. And even today the notion of a structure lacking any center represents the unthinkable itself.

Nevertheless, the center also closes off the play which it opens up and makes possible. As center, it is the point at which the substitution of contents, elements, or terms is no longer possible. At the center, the permutation or the transformation of elements (which may of course be structures enclosed within a structure) is forbidden. At least this permutation has always remained *interdicted* (and I am using this word deliberately). Thus it has always been thought that the center, which is by definition unique, constituted that very thing within a structure which while governing the structure, escapes structurality. This is why classical thought concerning structure could say that the center is, paradoxically, *within* the structure and *outside* it. The center is at the center of the totality, and yet, since the center does not belong to the totality (is not part of the totality), the totality *has its center elsewhere*. The center is not the center. The concept of centered structure— although it represents coherence itself, the condition of the *epistēmē* as philosophy or science—is contradictorily coherent. And as always, coherence in contradiction expresses the force of a desire.[1] The concept of centered structure is in fact the concept of a play based on a fundamental ground, a play constituted on the basis of a fundamental immobility and a reassuring certitude, which itself is beyond the reach of play. And on the basis of this certitude anxiety can be mastered, for anxiety is invariably the result of a certain mode of being implicated in the game, of being caught by the game, of being as it were at stake in the game from the outset. And again on the basis of what we call the center (and which, because it can be either inside or outside, can also indifferently be called the origin or end, *archē* or *telos*), repetitions, substitutions, transformations, and permutations are always *taken* from a history of meaning [*sens*]—that is, in a word, a history— whose origin may always be reawakened or whose end may always be anticipated in the form of presence. This is why one perhaps could say that the movement of any archaeology, like that of any eschatology, is an accomplice of this reduction of the structurality of structure and always attempts to conceive of structure on the basis of a full presence which is beyond play.

If this is so, the entire history of the concept of structure, before the rupture of which we are speaking, must be thought of as a series of substitutions of center for center, as a linked chain of determinations of the center. Successively, and in a regulated fashion, the center receives different forms or names. The history of metaphysics, like the history of the West, is the history of these metaphors and metonymies. Its matrix–if you will pardon me for demonstrating so little and for being so elliptical in order to come more quickly to my principal theme–is the determination of Being as *presence* in all senses of this word. It could be shown that all the names related to fundamentals, to principles, or to the center have always designated an invariable presence–*eidos, archē, telos, energeia, ousia* (essence, existence, substance, subject) *alētheia*, transcendentality, consciousness, God, man, and so forth.

The event I called a rupture, the disruption I alluded to at the beginning of this paper, presumably would have come about when the structurality of structure had to begin to be thought, that is to say, repeated, and this is why I said that this disruption was repetition in every sense of the word. Henceforth, it became necessary to think both the law which somehow governed the desire for a center in the constitution of structure, and the process of signification which orders the displacements and substitutions for this law of central presence–but a central presence which has never been itself, has always already been exiled from itself into its own substitute. The substitute does not substitute itself for anything which has somehow existed before it. Henceforth, it was necessary to begin thinking that there was no center, that the center could not be thought in the form of a present-being, that the center had no natural site, that it was not a fixed locus but a function, a sort of nonlocus in which an infinite number of sign-substitutions came into play. This was the moment when language invaded the universal problematic, the moment when, in the absence of a center or origin, everything became discourse–provided we can agree on this word–that is to say, a system in which the central signified, the original or transcendental signified, is never absolutely present outside a system of differences. The absence of the transcendental signified extends the domain and the play of signification infinitely.

Where and how does this decentering, this thinking the structurality of structure, occur? It would be somewhat naïve to refer to an event, a doctrine, or an author in order to designate this occurrence. It is no doubt part of the totality of an era, our own, but still it has always already begun to proclaim itself and begun to *work*. Nevertheless, if we wished to choose several 'names', as indications only, and to recall those authors in whose discourse this occurrence has kept most closely to its most radical formulation, we doubtless would have to cite the Nietzschean critique of metaphysics, the critique of the concepts of Being and truth, for which were substituted the concepts of play, interpretation, and sign (sign without present truth); the Freudian critique of self-presence, that is, the critique of consciousness, of the subject, of self-identity and of self-proximity or self-possession; and, more radically, the Heideggerean destruction of metaphysics, of onto-theology, of the determination of Being as presence. But all these destructive discourses and all their analogues are trapped in a kind of circle. This circle is unique. It describes the form of the relation between the history of metaphysics and the destruction of the history of metaphysics. There is no sense in doing without the concepts of metaphysics in order to shake metaphysics. We have no language – no syntax and no lexicon – which is foreign to this history; we can pronounce not a single destructive proposition which has not already had to slip into the form, the logic, and the implicit postulations of precisely what it seeks to contest. To take one example from many: the metaphysics of presence is shaken with the help of the concept of *sign*. But, as I suggest a moment ago, as soon as one seeks to demonstrate in this way that there is no transcendental or privileged signified and that the domain or play of signification henceforth has no limit, one must reject even the concept and word 'sign' itself – which is precisely what cannot be done. For the signification 'sign' has always been understood and determined, in its meaning, as sign-of, a signifier referring to a signified, a signifier different from its signified. If one erases the radical difference between signifier and signified, it is the word 'signifier' itself which must be abandoned as a metaphysical concept. When Lévi-Strauss says in the preface to *The Raw and the Cooked* that he has 'sought to transcend the opposition between the sensible and the intelligible by operating from the outset at the level of signs,'[2] the necessity, force, and legitimacy of his act cannot make us forget that the concept of the sign cannot in itself surpass this opposition between the sensible and the intelligible. The concept of the sign, in each of its aspects, has been determined by this opposition throughout the totality of its history. It has lived only on this opposition and its system. But we cannot do without the concept of the sign, for we cannot give up this metaphysical complicity without also giving up the critique we are directing against this complicity, or without the risk of erasing difference in the self-identity of a signified reducing its signifier into itself or, amounting to the same thing, simply expelling its signifier outside itself. For there are two heterogenous ways of erasing the difference between the signifier and the signified: one, the classic way, consists in reducing or deriving the signifier, that is to say, ultimately in *submitting* the sign to thought; the other, the one we are using here against the first one, consists in putting into question the system in which the preceding reduction functioned: first and foremost, the opposition between the sensible and the intelligible. For the *paradox* is that the metaphysical reduction of the sign needed the opposition it was reducing. The opposition is systematic with the reduction. And what we are saying here about the sign can be extended to all the concepts and all the sentences of metaphysics, in particular to the discourse on 'structure'. But there are several ways of being caught in this circle. They are all more or less naïve, more or less empirical, more or less systematic, more or less close to the formulation – that is, to the formalization – of this circle. It is these differences which explain the multiplicity of destructive discourses and the disagreement between those who elaborate them. Nietzsche, Freud, and Heidegger, for example, worked within the inherited concepts of metaphysics. Since these concepts are not elements or atoms, and since they are taken from a syntax and a system, every particular borrowing brings along with it the whole of metaphysics. This is what allows these destroyers to destroy each other reciprocally – for example, Heidegger regarding Nietzsche, with as much lucidity and rigor as bad faith and misconstruction, as the last metaphysician, the last 'Platonist'. One could do the same for Heidegger himself, for Freud, or for a number of others. And today no exercise is more widespread.

What is the relevance of this formal schema when we turn to what are called the 'human sciences'? One of them perhaps occupies a privileged place – ethnology. In fact one can assume that ethnology could have been born as a science only at the moment when a decentering had come about: at the moment when European culture – and, in consequence, the history of metaphysics and of its concepts – has been *dislocated*, driven from its locus, and forced to stop considering itself as the culture of reference. This moment is not first and foremost a moment of philosophical or scientific discourse. It is also a moment which is political, economic, technical, and so forth. One can say with total security that there is nothing fortuitous about the fact that the critique of ethnocentrism – the very condition for ethnology – should be systematically and historically contemporaneous with the destruction of the history of metaphysics. Both belong to one and the same era. Now, ethnology – like any science – comes about within the element of discourse. And it is primarily a European science employing traditional concepts, however much it may struggle against them. Consequently, whether he wants to or not – and this does not depend on a decision on his part – the ethnologist accepts into his discourse the premises of ethnocentrism at the very moment when he denounces them. This necessity is irreducible; it is not a historical contingency. We ought to consider all its implications very carefully. But if no one can escape this necessity, and if no one is therefore responsible for giving into it, however little he may do so, this does not mean that all the ways of giving in to it are of equal pertinence. The quality and fecundity of a discourse are perhaps measured by the critical rigor with which this relation to the history of metaphysics and to inherited concepts is thought. Here is a question both of a critical relation to the language of the social sciences and a critical responsibility of the discourse itself. It is a question of explicitly and systematically posing the problem of the status of a discourse which borrows from a heritage the resources necessary for the deconstruction of that heritage itself. A problem of *economy* and *strategy*.

If we consider, as an example, the texts of Claude Lévi-Strauss, it is not only because of the privilege accorded to ethnology among the social sciences, nor even because the thought of Lévi-Strauss weighs heavily on the contemporary theoretical situation. It is above all because a certain choice has been declared in the work of Lévi-Strauss and because a certain doctrine has been elaborated there, and precisely, in a *more or less explicit manner*, as concerns both this critique of language and this critical language in the social sciences.

In order to follow this movement in the text of Lévi-Strauss, let us choose as one guiding thread among others the opposition between nature and culture. Despite all its rejuvenations and disguises, this opposition is congenital to philosophy. It is even older than Plato. It is at least as old as the Sophists. Since the statement of the opposition *physis/nomos, physis/ techne*, it has been relayed to us by means of a whole historical chain which opposes 'nature' to law, to education, to art, to technics – but also to liberty, to the arbitrary, to history, to society, to the mind, and so on. Now, from the outset of his researches, and from his first book (*The Elementary Structures of Kinship*) on, Lévi-Strauss simultaneously has experienced the necessity of utilizing this opposition and the impossibility of accepting it. In the *Elementary Structures*, he begins from this axiom or definition: that which is *universal* and spontaneous, and not dependent on any particular culture or on any determinate norm, belongs to nature. Inversely, that which depends upon a system of *norms* regulating society and therefore is capable of *varying* from one social structure to another, belongs to culture. These two definitions are of the traditional type. But in the very first pages of the *Elementary Structures* Lévi-Strauss, who has begun by giving credence to these concepts, encounters what he calls a *scandal*, that is to say, something which no longer tolerates the nature/culture opposition he has accepted, something which *simultaneously* seems to require the predicates of nature and of culture. This scandal is the *incest prohibition*. The incest prohibition is universal; in this sense one could call it natural. But it is also a prohibition, a system of norms and interdicts; in this sense one could call it cultural:

> Let us suppose then that everything universal in man relates to the natural order, and is characterized by spontaneity, and that everything subject to a norm is cultural and is both relative and particular. We are then confronted with a fact, or rather, a group of facts, which, in the light of previous definitions, are not far removed from a scandal: we refer to that complex group of beliefs, customs, conditions and institutions described succinctly as the prohibition of incest, which presents, without the slightest ambiguity, and inseparably combines, the two characteristics in which we recognize the conflicting features of two mutually exclusive orders. It constitutes a rule, but a rule which, alone among all the social rules, possesses at the same time a universal character.[3]

Obviously there is no scandal except within a system of concepts which accredits the difference between nature and culture. By commencing his work with the *factum* of the incest prohibition. Lévi-Strauss thus places himself at the point at which this difference, which has always been assumed to be self-evident, finds itself erased or questioned. For from the moment when the incest prohibition can no longer be conceived within the nature/ culture opposition, it can no longer be said to be a scandalous fact, a nucleus of opacity within a network of transparent significations. The incest prohibition is no longer a scandal one meets with or comes up against in the domain of traditional concepts; it is something which escapes these concepts and certainly precedes them – probably as the condition of their possibility. It could perhaps be said that the whole of philosophical conceptualization, which is systematic with the nature/culture opposition, is designed to leave in the domain of the unthinkable the very thing that makes this conceptualization possible: the origin of the prohibition of incest.

This example, too cursorily examined, is only one among many others, but nevertheless it already shows that language bears within itself the necessity of its own critique. Now this critique may be undertaken along two paths, in two 'manners'. Once the limit of the nature/culture opposition makes itself felt, one might want to question systematically and rigorously the history of these concepts. This is a first action. Such a systematic and historic questioning would be neither a philological nor a philosophical action in the classic sense of these words. To concern oneself with the founding concepts of the entire history of philosophy, to deconstitute them, is not to undertake the work of the philologist or of the classic historian of philosophy. Despite appearances, it is probably the most daring way of making the beginnings of a step outside of philosophy. The step 'outside philosophy' is much more difficult to conceive than is generally imagined by those who think they made it long ago with cavalier ease, and who in general are swallowed up in metaphysics by the entire body of discourse which they claim to have disengaged from it.

The other choice (which I believe corresponds more closely to Lévi-Strauss's manner), in order to avoid the possibly sterilizing effects of the first one, consists in conserving all these old concepts within the domain of empirical discovery while here and there denouncing their limits, treating them as tools which can still be used. No longer is any truth value attributed to them; there is a readiness to abandon them, if necessary, should other instruments appear more useful. In the meantime, their relative efficacy is exploited, and they are employed to destroy the old machinery to which they belong and of which they themselves are pieces. This is how the language of the social sciences criticizes *itself*. Lévi-Strauss thinks that in this way he can separate *method* from *truth*, the instruments of the method and the objective significations envisaged by it. One could almost say that this is the primary affirmation of Lévi-Strauss; in any event, the first words of the *Elementary Structures* are: 'Above all, it is beginning to emerge that this distinction between nature and society ('nature' and 'culture' seem preferable to us today), while of no acceptable historical significance, does contain a logic, fully justifying its use by modern sociology as a methodo-logical tool.'[4]

Lévi-Strauss will always remain faithful to this double intention: to preserve as an instrument something whose truth value he criticizes.

On the one hand, he will continue, in effect, to contest the value of the nature/culture opposition. More than thirteen years after the *Elementary Structures, The Savage Mind* faithfully echoes the text I have quoted: 'The opposition between nature and culture to which I attached much importance at one time . . . now seems to be of primarily methodological importance.' And this methodological value is not affected by its 'ontological' nonvalue (as might be said, if this notion were not suspect here): 'However, it would not be enough to reabsorb particular humanities into a general one. This first enterprise opens the way for others which . . . are incumbent on the exact natural sciences: the reintegration of culture in nature and finally of life within the whole of its physio-chemical conditions.'[5]

On the other hand, still in *The Savage Mind*, he presents as what he calls *bricolage* what might be called the discourse of this method. The *bricoleur*, says Lévi-Strauss, is someone who uses 'the means at hand', that is, the instruments he finds at his disposition around him, those which are already there, which had not been especially conceived with an eye to the operation for which they are to be used and to which one tries by trial and error to adapt them, not hesitating to change them whenever it appears necessary, or to try several of them at once, even if their form and their origin are heterogenous – and so forth. There is therefore a critique of language in the form of *bricolage*, and it has even been said that *bricolage* is critical language itself. I am thinking in particular of the article of G. Genette, 'Structuralisme et critique littéraire', published in homage to Lévi-Strauss in a special issue of *L'Arc* (no. 26, 1965), where it is stated that the analysis of *bricolage* could 'be applied almost word for word' to criticism, and especially to 'literary criticism'.

If one calls *bricolage* the necessity of borrowing one's concepts from the text of a heritage which is more or less coherent or ruined, it must be said that every discourse is *bricoleur*. The engineer, whom Lévi-Strauss opposes to the *bricoleur*, should be the one to construct the totality of his language, syntax, and lexicon. In this sense the engineer is a myth. A subject who supposedly would be the absolute origin of his own discourse and supposedly would construct it 'out of nothing', 'out of whole cloth', would be the creator of the verb, the verb itself. The notion of the engineer who supposedly breaks with all forms of *bricolage* is therefore a theological idea; and since Lévi-Strauss tells us elsewhere that *bricolage* is mythopoetic, the odds are that the engineer is a myth produced by the *bricoleur*. As soon as we cease to believe in such an engineer and in a discourse which breaks with the received historical discourse, and as soon as we admit that every finite discourse is bound by a certain *bricolage* and that the engineer and the scientist are also species of *bricoleurs*, then the very idea of *bricolage* is menaced and the difference in which it took on its meaning breaks down.

This brings us to the second thread which might guide us in what is being contrived here.

Lévi-Strauss describes *bricolage* not only as an intellectual activity but also as a mythopoetical activity. One reads in *The Savage Mind*, 'Like *bricolage* on the technical plane, mythical reflection can reach brilliant unforeseen results on the intellectual plane. Conversely, attention has often been drawn to the mythopoetical nature of *bricolage*.[6]

But Lévi-Strauss's remarkable endeavor does not simply consist in proposing, notably in his most recent investigations, a structural science of myths and of mythological activity. His endeavour also appears – I would say almost from the outset – to have the status which he accords to his own discourse on myths, to what he calls his 'mythologicals'. It is here that his discourse on the myth reflects on itself and criticises itself. And this moment, this critical period, is evidently of concern to all the languages which share the field of the human sciences. What does Lévi-Strauss say of his 'mythologicals'? It is here that we rediscover the mythopoetical virtue of *bricolage*. In effect, what appears most fascinating in this critical search for a new status of discourse is the stated abandonment of all reference to a *center*, to a *subject*, to a privileged *reference*, to an origin, or to an absolute *archia*. The theme of this decentering could be followed throughout the 'Overture' to his last book, *The Raw and the Cooked*. I shall simply remark on a few key points.

1 From the very start, Lévi-Strauss recognizes that the Bororo myth which he employs in the book as the 'reference myth' does not merit this name and this treatment. The name is specious and the use of the myth improper. This myth deserves no more than any other its referential privilege: 'In fact, the Bororo myth, which I shall refer to from now as the key myth, is, as I shall try to show, simply a transformation, to a greater or lesser extent, of other myths originating either in the same society or in neighboring or remote societies. I could, therefore, have legitimately taken as my starting point any one representative myth of the group. From this point of view, the key myth is interesting not because typical, but rather because of its irregular position within the group.'[7]

2 There is no unity or absolute source of the myth. The focus or the source of the myth are always shadows and virtualities which are elusive, unactualizable, and nonexistent in the first place. Everything begins with structure, configuration, or relationship. The discourse on the acentric structure that myth itself is, cannot itself have an absolute subject or an absolute center. It must avoid the violence that consists in centering a language which describes an acentric structure if it is not to shortchange the form and movement of myth. Therefore it is necessary to forego scientific or philosophical discourse, to renounce the *epistēmē* which absolutely requires, which is the absolute requirement that we go back to the source, to the center, to the founding basis, to the principle, and so on. In opposition to *epistemic* discourse, structural discourse on myths—*mythological* discourse— must itself be *mythomorphic*. It must have the form of that of which it speaks. This is what Lévi-Strauss says in *The Raw and the Cooked*, from which I would now like to quote a long and remarkable passage:

> The study of myths raises a methodological problem, in that it cannot be carried out according to the Cartesian principle of breaking down the difficulty into as many parts as may be necessary for finding the solution. There is no real end to methodological analysis, no hidden unity to be grasped once the breaking-down process has been completed. Themes can be split up *ad infinitum*. Just when you think you have disentangled and separated them, you realize that they are knitting together again in response to the operation of unexpected affinities. Consequently the unity of the myth is never more than tendential and projective and cannot reflect a state or a particular moment of myth. It is a phenomenon of the imagination, resulting from the attempt at interpretation; and its function is to endow the myth with synthetic form and to prevent its disintegration into a confusion of opposites. The science of myths might

therefore be termed 'anaclastic', if we take this old term in the broader etymological sense which includes the study of both reflected rays and broken rays. But unlike philosophical reflection, which aims to go back to its own source, the reflections we are dealing with here concern rays whose only source is hypothetical . . . And in seeking to imitate the spontaneous movement of mythological thought, this essay, which is also both too brief and too long, has had to conform to the requirements of that thought and to respect its rhythm. It follows that this book on myths is itself a kind of myth.[8]

This statement is repeated a little further on: 'As the myths themselves are based on secondary codes (the primary codes being those that provide the substance of language), the present work is put forward as a tentative draft of a tertiary code, which is intended to ensure the reciprocal translatability of several myths. This is why it would not be wrong to consider this book itself as a myth: it is, as it were, the myth of mythology.'[9] The absence of a center is here the absence of a subject and the absence of an author. 'Thus the myth and the musical work are like conductors of an orchestra, whose audience becomes the silent performers. If it is now asked where the real center of the work is to be found, the answer is that this is impossible to determine. Music and mythology bring man face to face with potential objects of which only the shadows are actualized . . . Myths are anonymous.'[10] The musical model chosen by Lévi-Strauss for the composition of his book is apparently justified by this absence of any real and fixed center of the mythical or mythological discourse.

Thus it is at this point that ethnographic *bricolage* deliberately assumes its mythopoetic function. But by the same token, this function makes the philosophical or epistemological requirement of a center appear as mythological, that is to say, as a historical illusion.

Nevertheless, even if one yields to the necessity of what Lévi-Strauss has done, one cannot ignore its risks. If the mythological is mythomorphic, are all discourses on myths equivalent? Shall we have to abandon any epistemological requirement which permits us to distinguish between several qualities of discourse on the myth? A classic, but inevitable question. It cannot be answered – and I believe that Lévi-Strauss does not answer it – for as long as the problem of the relations between the philosopheme or the theorem, on the one hand, and the mytheme or the mythopoem, on the other, has not been posed explicitly, which is no small problem. For lack of explicitly posing this problem, we condemn ourselves to transforming the alleged transgression of philosophy into an unnoticed fault within the philosophical realm. Empiricism would be the genus of which these faults would always be the species. Transphilosophical concepts would be transformed into philosophical naïvetés. Many examples could be given to demonstrate this risk: the concepts of sign, history, truth, and so forth. What I want to emphasize is simply that the passage beyond philosophy does not consist in turning the page of philosophy (which usually amounts to philosophizing badly), but in continuing to read philosophers *in a certain way*. The risk I am speaking of is always assumed by Lévi-Strauss, and it is the very price of this endeavor. I have said that empiricism is the matrix of all faults menacing a discourse which continues, as with Lévi-Strauss in particular, to consider itself scientific. If we wanted to pose the problem of empiricism and *bricolage* in depth, we would probably end up very quickly with a number of absolutely contradictory propositions concerning the status of discourse in structural ethnology. On the one hand, structuralism justifiably claims to be the critique of empiricism. But at the same time there is not a single book or study by Lévi-Strauss which is not proposed as an empirical essay which can always be completed or invalidated by new information. The structural schemata are always proposed as hypotheses resulting from a finite quantity of information and which are subjected to the proof of experience. Numerous texts could be used to demonstrate this double postulation. Let us turn once again to the 'Overture' of *The Raw and the Cooked*, where it seems clear that if this postulation is double, it is because it is a question here of a language on language:

> If critics reproach me with not having carried out an exhaustive inventory of South American myths before analysing them, they are making a grave mistake about the nature and function of these documents. The total body of myth belonging to a given community is comparable to its speech. Unless the population dies out physically or morally, this totality is never complete. You might as well criticise a linguist for compiling the grammar of a language without having complete records of the words pronounced since the language came into being, and without knowing what will be said in it during the future part of its existence. Experience proves that a linguist can work out the grammar of a given language from a remarkably small number of sentences . . . And even a partial grammar or an outline grammar is a precious acquisition when we are dealing with unknown languages. Syntax does not become evident only after a (theoretically limitless) series of events has been recorded and examined, because it is itself the body of rules governing their production. What I have tried to give is an outline of the syntax of South American mythology. Should fresh data come to hand, they will be used to check or modify the formulation of certain grammatical laws, so that some are abandoned and replaced by new ones. But in no instance would I feel constrained to accept the arbitrary demand for a total mythological pattern, since, as has been shown, such a requirement has no meaning.[11]

Totalization, therefore, is sometimes defined as *useless*, and sometimes as *impossible*. This is no doubt due to the fact that there are two ways of conceiving the limit of totalization. And I assert once more that these two determinations coexist implicitly in Lévi-Strauss's discourse. Totalization can be judged impossible in the classical style: one then refers to the empirical endeavor of either a subject or a finite richness which it can never master. There is too much, more than one can say. But nontotalization can also be determined in another way: no longer from the standpoint of a concept of finitude as relegation to the empirical, but from the standpoint of the concept of *play*. If totalization no longer has any meaning, it is not because the infiniteness of a field cannot be covered by a finite glance or a finite discourse, but because the nature of the field–that is, language and a finite language– excludes totalization. This field is in effect that of *play*, that is to say, a field of infinite substitutions only because it is finite, that is to say, because instead of being an inexhaustible field, as in the classical hypothesis, instead of being too large, there is something missing from it: a center which arrests and grounds the play of substitutions. One could say – rigorously using that word whose scandalous signification is always obliterated in French – that this movement of play, permitted by the lack or absence of a center or origin, is the movement of *supplementarity*. One cannot determine the center and exhaust totalization because the sign which replaces the center, which supplements it, taking the center's place in its absence – this sign is added, occurs as a surplus, as a *supplement*.[12] The movement of signification adds something, which results in the fact that there is always more, but this addition is a floating one because it comes to perform a vicarious function, to supplement a lack on the part of the signified. Although Lévi–Strauss in his use of the word 'supplementary' never emphasizes, as I do here, the two directions of meaning which are so strangely compounded within it, it is not by chance that he uses this word twice in his 'Introduction to the Work of Marcel Mauss', at one point where he is speaking of the 'overabundance of signifier, in relation to the signifieds to which this overabundance can refer':

> In this endeavor to understand the world, man therefore always has at his disposal a surplus of signification (which he shares out amongst things according to the laws of symbolic thought – which is the task of ethnologists and linguists to study). This distribution of a *supplementary* allowance [*ration supplémentaire*] – if it is permissible to put it that way – is absolutely necessary in order that on the whole the available signifier and the signified it aims at may remain in the relationship of complementarity which is the very condition of the use of symbolic thought.[13]

(It could no doubt be demonstrated that this *ration supplémentaire* of signification is the origin of the *ratio* itself.) The word reappears a little further on, after Lévi-Strauss has mentioned 'this floating signifier, which is the servitude of all finite thought':

> In other words – and taking as our guide Mauss's precept that all social phenomena can be assimilated to language – we see in *mana, Wakau, oranda* and other notions of the same type, the conscious expression of a semantic function, whose role it is to permit symbolic thought to operate in spite of the contradiction which is proper to it. In this way are explained the apparently insoluble antinomies attached to this notion . . . At one and the same time force and action, quality and state, noun and verb; abstract and concrete, omnipresent and localized – *mana* is in effect all these things. But is it not precisely because it is none of these things that *mana* is a simple form, or more exactly, a symbol in the pure state, and therefore capable of becoming charged with any sort of symbolic content whatever? In the system of symbols constituted by all cosmologies, *mana* would simply be a zero symbolic value, that is to say, a sign marking the necessity of a symbolic content *supplementary* [my italics] to that with which the signified is already loaded, but which can take on any value required, provided only that this value still remains part of the available reserve and is not, as phonologists put it, a group-term.

Lévi-Strauss adds the note:

> Linguists have already been led to formulate hypotheses of this type. For example:

'A zero phoneme is opposed to all other phonemes in French in that it entails no differential characters and no constant phonetic value. On the contrary, the proper function of the zero phoneme is to be opposed to phoneme absence.' (R. Jakobson and J. Lutz, 'Notes on the French Phonemic Pattern', *Word* 5, no. 2 [August 1949]: 155.) Similarly, if we schematise the conception I am proposing here, it could almost be said that the function of notions like *mana* is to be opposed to the absence of signfication, without entailing by itself any particular signification.[14]

The *overabundance* of the signifier, its *supplementary* character, is thus the result of a finitude, that is to say, the result of a lack which must be *supplemented*.

It can now be understood why the concept of play is important in Lévi-Strauss. His references to all sorts of games, notably to roulette, are very frequent, especially in his *Conversations*,[15] in *Race and History*,[16] and in *The Savage Mind*. Further, the reference to play is always caught up in tension.

Tension with history, first of all. This is a classical problem, objections to which are now well worn. I shall simply indicate what seems to me the formality of the problem: by reducing history, Lévi-Strauss has treated as it deserves a concept which has always been in complicity with a teleological and eschatological metaphysics, in other words, paradoxically, in complicity with that philosophy of presence to which it was believed history could be opposed. The thematic of historicity, although it seems to be a somewhat late arrival in philosophy, has always been required by the determination of Being as presence. With or without etymology, and despite the classic antagonism which opposes these significations throughout all of classical thought, it could be shown that the concept of *epistēmē* has always called forth that of *historia*, if history is always the unity of a becoming, as the tradition of truth or the development of science of knowledge oriented toward the appropriation of truth in presence and self-presence, toward knowledge in consciousness-of-self. History has always been conceived as the movement of a resumption of history, as a detour between two presences. But if it is legitimate to suspect this concept of history, there is a risk, if it is reduced without an explicit statement of the problem I am indicating here, of falling back into an ahistoricism of a classical type, that is to say, into a determined moment of the history of metaphysics. Such is the algebraic formality of the problem as I see it. More concretely, in the work of Lévi-Strauss it must be recognized that the respect for structurality, for the internal originality of the structure, compels a neutralisation of time and history. For example, the appearance of a new structure, of an original system, always comes about – and this is the very condition of its structural specificity – by a rupture with its past, its origin, and its cause. Therefore one can describe what is peculiar of the structural organization only by not taking into account, in the very moment of this description, its past conditions: by omitting to posit the problem of the transition from one structure to another, by putting history between brackets. In this 'structuralist' moment, the concepts of chance and discontinuity are indispensable. And Lévi-Strauss does in fact often appeal to them, for example, as concerns that structure of structures, language, of which he says in the 'Introduction to the Work of Marcel Mauss' that it' could only have been born in one fell swoop':

> Whatever may have been the moment and the circumstances of its appearance on the scale of animal life, language could only have been born in one fell swoop. Things could not have set about acquiring signification progressively. Following a transformation the study of which is not the concern of the social sciences, but rather of biology and psychology, a transition came about from a stage where nothing had a meaning to another where everything possessed it.[17]

This standpoint does not prevent Lévi-Strauss from recognizing the slowness, the process of maturing, the continuous toil of factual transformations, history (for example, in *Race and History*). But, in accordance with a gesture which was also Rousseau's and Husserl's, he must 'set aside all the facts' at the moment when he wishes to recapture the specificity of a structure. Like Rousseau, he must always conceive of the origin of a new structure on the model of catastrophe – an overturning of nature in nature, a natural interruption of the natural sequence, a setting aside *of* nature.

Besides the tension between play and history, there is also the tension between play and presence. Play is the disruption of presence. The presence of an element is always a signifying and substitutive reference inscribed in a system of differences and the movement of a chain. Play is always play of absence and presence, but if it is to be thought radically, play must be conceived of before the alternative of presence and absence. Being must be conceived as presence or absence on the basis of the possibility of play and not the other way around. If Lévi-Strauss, better than any other, has brought to light the play of repetition and the repetition of play, one no less perceives in his work a sort of ethic of presence, an ethic of nostalgia for origins, an ethic of archaic and natural innocence, of a purity of presence and self-presence in speech – an ethic, nostalgia, and even remorse, which he often presents as the motivation of the ethnological project when he moves toward the archaic societies which are exemplary societies in his eyes. These texts are well known.[18]

Turned towards the lost or impossible presence of the absent origin, this structuralist thematic of broken immediacy is therefore the saddened, *negative*, nostalgic, guilty, Rousseauistic side of the thinking of play whose other side would be the Nietzschean *affirmation*, that is the joyous affirmation of the play of the world and of the innocence of becoming, the affirmation of a world of signs without fault, without truth, and without origin which is offered to an active interpretation. *This affirmation then determines the noncenter otherwise than as loss of the center*. And it plays without security. For there is a sure play: that which is limited to the *substitution* of *given* and *existing*, *present*, pieces. In absolute chance, affirmation also surrenders itself to *genetic* indetermination, to the *seminal* adventure of the trace.

There are thus two interpretations of interpretation; of structure, of sign, of play. The one seeks to decipher, dreams of deciphering a truth or an origin which escapes play and the order of the sign, and which lives the necessity of interpretation as an exile. The other, which is no longer turned toward the origin, affirms play and tries to pass beyond man and humanism, the name of man being the name of that being who, throughout the history of metaphysics or of ontotheology – in other words, throughout his entire history – has dreamed of full presence, the reassuring foundation, the origin and the end of play. The second interpretation of interpretation, to which Nietzsche pointed the way, does not seek in ethnography, as Lévi-Strauss does, the 'inspiration of a new humanism' (again citing the 'Introduction to the Work of Marcel Mauss').

There are more than enough indications today to suggest we might perceive that these two interpretations of interpretation – which are absolutely irreconcilable even if we live them simultaneously and reconcile them in an obscure economy – together share the field which we call, in such a problematic fashion, the social sciences.

For my part, although these two interpretations must acknowledge and accentuate their difference and define their irreducibility, I do not believe that today there is any question of *choosing* – in the first place because there we are in a region (let us say, provisionally, a region of historicity) where the category of choice seems particularly trivial; and in the second, because we must first try to conceive of the common ground, and the *différance* of this irreducible difference. Here there is a kind of question, let us still call it historical, whose *conception*, *formation*, *gestation*, and *labor* we are only catching a glimpse of today. I employ these words, I admit, with a glance toward the operations of childbearing – but also with a glance toward those who, in a society from which I do not exclude myself, turn their eyes away when faced by the as yet unnamable which is proclaiming itself and which can do so, as is necessary whenever a birth is in the offing, only under the species of the nonspecies, in the formless, mute, infant, and terrifying form of monstrosity.

Notes

1 The reference, in a restricted sense, is to the Freudian theory of neurotic symptoms and of dream interpretation in which a given symbol is understood contradictorily as both the desire to fulfil an impulse and the desire to suppress the impulse. In a general sense the reference is to Derrida's thesis that logic and coherence themselves can only be understood contradictorily, since they presuppose the suppression of *différance*, 'writing' in the sense of the general economy. Cf. 'La pharmacie de Platon', in *La dissemination*, pp. 125–6, where Derrida uses the Freudian model of dream interpretation in order to clarify the contractions embedded in philosophical coherence.

2 *The Raw and the Cooked*, trn. John and Doreen Wightman (New York, Harper & Row, 1969), p. 14. [Translation somewhat modified.]

3 *The Elementary Structures of Kinship*, trn. James Bell, John von Sturmer, and Rodney Needham (Boston, Mass., Beacon Press, 1969), p. 8.

4 Ibid., p. 3.

5 *The Savage Mind* (London, George Weidenfeld & Nicolson; Chicago, The University of Chicago Press, 1966), p. 247.

6 Ibid., p. 17.
7 *The Raw and the Cooked*, p. 2.
8 Ibid., pp. 5–6.
9 Ibid., p. 12.
10 Ibid., pp. 17–18.
11 Ibid., pp. 7–8.
12 This double sense of supplement–to supply something which is missing, or to supply something additional–is at the center of Derrida's deconstruction of traditional linguistics in *De la grammatologie*. In a chapter entitled 'The Violence of the Letter: From Lévi-Strauss to Rousseau' (pp. 149ff.), Derrida expands the analysis of Lévi-Strauss begun in this essay in order further to clarify the ways in which the contradictions of traditional logic 'program' the most modern conceptual apparatuses of linguistics and the social sciences.
13 'Introduction à loeuvre de Marcel Mauss', in Marcel Mauss, *Sociologie et anthropologie* (Paris, P.U.F., 1950), p. xlix.
14 Ibid., pp. xlix–1.
15 George Charbonnier, *Entretiens avec Claude Lévi-Strauss* (Paris, Plon, 1961).
16 *Race and History* (Paris, UNESCO Publications, 1958).
17 'Introduction à l'oeuvre de Marcel Mauss', p. xlvi.
18 The reference is to *Tristes tropiques*, trn. John Russel (London, Hutchinson & Co., 1961).

21 | Michel Foucault,

From 'The Order of Discourse', R. Young, ed. *Untying the Text* (1971), pp. 52–64

II

Here is the hypothesis which I would like to put forward tonight in order to fix the terrain–or perhaps the very provisional theatre–of the work I am doing: that in every society the production of discourse is at once controlled, selected, organised and redistributed by a certain number of procedures whose role is to ward off its powers and dangers, to gain mastery over its chance events, to evade its ponderous, formidable materiality.

In a society like ours, the procedures of exclusion are well known. The most obvious and familiar is the prohibition. We know quite well that we do not have the right to say everything, that we cannot speak of just anything in any circumstances whatever, and that not everyone has the right to speak of anything whatever. In the taboo on the object of speech, and the ritual of the circumstances of speech, and the privileged or exclusive right of the speaking subject, we have the play of three types of prohibition which intersect, reinforce or compensate for each other, forming a complex grid which changes constantly. I will merely note that at the present time the regions where the grid is tightest, where the black squares are most numerous, are those of sexuality and politics; as if discourse, far from being that transparent or neutral element in which sexuality is disarmed and politics pacified, is in fact one of the places where sexuality and politics exercise in a privileged way some of their most formidable powers. It does not matter that discourse appears to be of little account, because the prohibitions that surround it very soon reveal its link with desire and with power. There is nothing surprising about that, since, as psychoanalysis has shown, discourse is not simply that which manifests (or hides) desire – it is also the object of desire; and since, as history constantly teaches us, discourse is not simply that which translates struggles or systems of domination, but is the thing for which and by which there is struggle, discourse is the power which is to be seized.

There exists in our society another principle of exclusion, not another prohibition but a division and a rejection. I refer to the opposition between reason and madness. Since the depths of the Middle Ages, the madman has been the one whose discourse cannot have the same currency as others. His word may be considered null and void, having neither truth nor importance, worthless as evidence in law, inadmissible in the authentification of deeds or contracts, incapable even of bringing about the trans-substantiation of bread into body at Mass. On the other hand, strange powers not held by any other may be attributed to the madman's speech: the power of uttering a hidden truth, of telling the future, of seeing in all naïvety what the others' wisdom cannot perceive. It is curious to note that for centuries in Europe the speech of the madman was either not heard at all or else taken for the word of truth. It either fell into the void, being rejected as soon as it was proffered, or else people deciphered in it a rationality, naïve or crafty, which they regarded as more rational than that of the sane. In any event, whether excluded, or secretly invested with reason, the madman's speech, strictly, did not exist. It was through his words that his madness was recognised; they were the place where the division between reason and madness was exercised, but they were never recorded or listened to. No doctor before the end of the eighteenth century had even thought of finding out what was said, or how and why it was said, in this speech which nonetheless determined the difference. This whole immense discourse of the madman was taken for mere noise, and he was only symbolically allowed to speak, in the theatre, where he would step forward, disarmed and reconciled, because there he played the role of truth in a mask.

You will tell me that all this is finished today or is coming to an end; that the madman's speech is no longer on the other side of the divide; that it is no longer null and void; and on the contrary, it puts us on the alert; that we now look for a meaning in it, for the outline or the ruins of some oeuvre; and that we have even gone so far as to come across this speech of madness in what we articulate ourselves, in that slight stumbling by which we lose track of what we are saying. But all this attention to the speech of madness does not prove that the old division is no longer operative. You have only to think of the whole framework of knowledge through which we decipher that speech, and of the whole network of institutions which permit someone – a doctor or a psychoanalyst–to listen to it, and which at the same time permit the patient to bring along his poor words or, in desperation, to withhold them. You have only to think of all this to become suspicious that the division, far from being effaced, is working differently, along other lines, through new institutions, and with effects that are not at all the same. And even if the doctor's role were only that of lending an ear to a speech that is free at last, he still does this listening in the context of the same division. He is listening to a discourse which is invested with desire, and which–for its greater exaltation or its greater anguish–thinks it is loaded with terrible powers. If the silence of reason is required for the curing of monsters, it is enough for that silence to be on the alert, and it is in this that the division remains.

It is perhaps risky to consider the opposition between true and false as a third system of exclusion, along with those just mentioned. How could one reasonably compare the constraint of truth with divisions like those, which are arbitrary to start with or which at least are organised around historical contingencies; which are not only modifiable but in perpetual displacement; which are supported by a whole system of institutions which impose them and renew them; and which act in a constraining and sometimes violent way?

Certainly, when viewed from the level of a proposition, on the inside of a discourse, the division between true and false is neither arbitrary nor modifiable nor institutional nor violent. But when we view things on a different scale, when we ask the question of what this will to truth has been and constantly is, across our discourses, this will to truth which has crossed so many centuries of our history; what is, in its very general form, the type of division which governs our will to know (notre volonté de savoir), then what we see taking shape is perhaps something like a system of exclusion, a historical, modifiable, and institutionally constraining system.

There is no doubt that this division is historically constituted. For the Greek poets of the sixth century BC, the true discourse (in the strong and valorised sense of the world), the discourse which inspired respect and terror, and to which one had to submit because it ruled, was the one pronounced by men who spoke as of right and according to the required ritual; the discourse which dispensed justice and gave everyone his share; the discourse which in prophesying the future not only announced what was going to happen but helped to make it happen, carrying men's minds along with it and thus weaving itself into the fabric of destiny. Yet already a century later the highest truth no longer resided in what discourse was or did, but in what it said: a day came when truth was displaced from the ritualised, efficacious and just act of enunciations, towards the utterance itself, its meaning, its form, its object, its relation to its reference. Between

Hesiod and Plato a certain division was established, separating true discourse from false discourse: a new division because henceforth the true discourse is no longer precious and desirable, since it is no longer the one linked to the exercise of power. The sophist is banished.

This historical division probably gave our will to know its general form. However, it has never stopped shifting: sometimes the great mutations in scientific thought can perhaps be read as the consequences of a discovery, but they can also be read as the appearance of new forms in the will to truth. There is doubtless a will to truth in the nineteenth century which differs from the will to know characteristic of Classical culture in the forms it deploys, in the domains of objects to which it addresses itself, and in the techniques on which it is based. To go back a little further: at the turn of the sixteenth century (and particularly in England), there appeared a will to know which, anticipating its actual contents, sketched out schemes of possible, observable, measurable, classifiable objects; a will to know which imposed on the knowing subject, and in some sense prior to all experience, a certain position, a certain gaze and a certain function (to see rather than to read, to verify rather than to make commentaries on); a will to know which was prescribed (but in a more general manner than by any specific instrument) by the technical level where knowledges had to be invested in order to be verifiable and useful. It was just as if, starting from the great Platonic division, the will to truth had its own history, which is not that of constraining truths: the history of the range of objects to be known, of the functions and positions of the knowing subject, of the material, technical, and instrumental investments of knowledge.

This will to truth, like the other systems of exclusion, rests on an institutional support: it is both reinforced and renewed by whole strata of practices, such as pedagogy, of course; and the system of books, publishing, libraries; learned societies in the past and laboratories now. But it is also renewed, no doubt more profoundly, by the way in which knowledge is put to work, valorised, distributed, and in a sense attributed, in a society. Let us recall at this point, and only symbolically, the old Greek principle: though arithmetic may well be the concern of democratic cities, because it teaches about the relations of equality, geometry alone must be taught in oligarchies, since it demonstrates the proportions within inequality.

Finally, I believe that this will to truth – leaning in this way on a support and an institutional distribution – tends to exert a sort of pressure and something like a power of constraint (I am still speaking of our own society) on other discourses. I am thinking of the way in which for centuries Western literature sought to ground itself on the natural, the 'vraisemblable', on sincerity, on science as well – in short, on 'true' discourse. I am thinking likewise of the manner in which economic practices, codified as precepts or recipes and ultimately as morality, have sought since the sixteenth century to ground themselves, rationalise themselves, and justify themselves in a theory of wealth and production. I am also thinking of the way in which a body as prescriptive as the penal system sought its bases or its justification, at first of course in a theory of justice, then, since the nineteenth century, in a sociological, psychological, medical, and psychiatric knowledge: it is as if even the word of the law could no longer be authorised, in our society, except by a discourse of truth.

Of the three great Systems of exclusion which forge discourse – the forbidden speech, the division of madness and the will to truth, I have spoken of the third at greatest length. The fact is that it is towards this third system that the other two have been drifting constantly for centuries. The third system increasingly attempts to assimilate the others, both in order to modify them and to provide them with a foundation. The first two are constantly becoming more fragile and more uncertain, to the extent that they are now invaded by the will to truth, which for its part constantly grows stronger, deeper, and more implacable.

And yet we speak of the will to truth no doubt least of all. It is as if, for us, the will to truth and its vicissitudes were masked by truth itself in its necessary unfolding. The reason is perhaps this: although since the Greeks 'true' discourse is no longer the discourse that answers to the demands of desire, or the discourse which exercises power, what is at stake in the will to truth, in the will to utter this 'true' discourse, if not desire and power? 'True' discourse, freed from desire and power by the necessity of its form, cannot recognise the will to truth which pervades it; and the will to truth, having imposed itself on us for a very long time, is such that the truth it wants cannot fail to mask it.

Thus all that appears to our eyes is a truth conceived as a richness, a fecundity, a gentle and insidiously universal force, and in contrast we are unaware of the will to truth, that prodigious machinery designed to exclude. All those who, from time to time in our history, have tried to dodge this will to truth and to put it into question against truth, at the very point where truth undertakes to justify the prohibition and to define madness, all of them, from Nietzsche to Artaud and Bataille, must now serve as the (no doubt lofty) signs for our daily work.

III

There are, of course, many other procedures for controlling and delimiting discourse. Those of which I have spoken up to now operate in a sense from the exterior. They function as systems of exclusion. They have to do with the part of discourse which puts power and desire at stake.

I believe we can isolate another group: internal procedures, since discourses themselves exercise their own control; procedures which function rather as principles of classification, of ordering, of distribution, as if this time another dimension of discourse had to be mastered: that of events and chance.

In the first place, commentary. I suppose – but without being very certain – that there is scarcely a society without its major narratives, which are recounted, repeated, and varied; formulae, texts, and ritualised sets of discourses which are recited in well-defined circumstances; things said once and preserved because it is suspected that behind them there is a secret or a treasure. In short, we may suspect that there is in all societies, with great consistency, a kind of gradation among discourses: those which are said in the ordinary course of days and exchanges, and which vanish as soon as they have been pronounced; and those which give rise to a certain number of new speech-acts which take them up, transform them or speak of them, in short, those discourses which, over and above their formulation, are said indefinitely, remain said, and are to be said again. We know them in our own cultural system: they are religious or juridical texts, but also those texts (curious ones, when we consider their status) which are called 'literary'; and to a certain extent, scientific texts.

This differentiation is certainly neither stable, nor constant, nor absolute, there is not, on the one side, the category of fundamental or creative discourses, given for all time, and on the other, the mass of discourses which repeat, gloss, and comment. Plenty of major texts become blurred and disappear, and sometimes commentaries move into the primary position. But though its points of application may change, the function remains; and the principle of a differentiation is continuously put back in play. The radical effacement of this gradation can only ever be play, utopia, or anguish. The Borges-style play of a commentary which is nothing but the solemn and expected reappearance word for word of the text that is commented on; or the play of a criticism that would speak forever of a work which does not exist. The lyrical dream of a discourse which is reborn absolutely new and innocent at every point, and which reappears constantly in all freshness, derived from things, feelings or thoughts. The anguish of that patient of Janet's for whom the least utterance was gospel truth, concealing inexhaustible treasures of meaning and worthy to be repeated, recommenced, and commented on indefinitely: 'When I think,' he would say when reading or listening, 'when I think of this sentence which like the others will go off into eternity, and which I have perhaps not yet fully understood.'

But who can fail to see that this would be to annul one of the terms of the relation each time, and not to do away with the relation itself? It is a relation which is constantly changing with time; which takes multiple and divergent forms in a given epoch. The juridical exegesis is very different from the religious commentary (and this has been the case for a very long time). One and the same literary work can give rise simultaneously to very distinct types of discourse: the 'Odyssey' as a primary text is repeated, in the same period, in the translation by Bérard, and in the endless 'explications de texte', and in Joyce's 'Ulysses'.

For the moment I want to do no more than indicate that, in what is broadly called commentary, the hierarchy between primary and secondary text plays two roles which are in solidarity with each other. On the one hand it allows the (endless) construction of new discourses: the dominance of the primary text, its permanence, its status as a discourse which can always be re-actualised, the multiple or hidden meaning with which it is credited, the essential reticence and richness which is attributed to it, all this is the basis for an open possibility of speaking. But on the other hand the commentary's only role, whatever the techniques used, is to say at last what was silently articulated 'beyond', in the text. By a paradox which it always displaces but never escapes, the commentary must say for the first time what had, however, never been said. The infinite rippling of commentaries is worked from the inside by the dream of a repetition in disguise: at its horizon there is perhaps nothing but what was at its point of departure – mere recitation. Commentary exorcises the chance element of discourse by giving it its due; it allows us to say something other than the text itself, but on condition that it is this text itself which is said, and in a sense completed. The open multiplicity, the element of chance, are transferred, by the principle of commentary, from what might risk being said, on to the number, the form, the mask, and the circumstances of the repetition. The new thing here lies not in what is said but in the event of its return.

I believe there exists another principle of rarefaction of a discourse, complementary to the first, to a certain extent: the author. Not, of course, in the sense of the speaking individual who pronounced or wrote a text, but in the sense of a principle of grouping of discourses, conceived as the unity and origin of their meanings, as the focus of their coherence. This principle is not everywhere at work, nor in a constant manner: there exist all around us plenty of discourses which circulate without deriving their meaning or their efficacity from an author to whom they could be attributed: everyday remarks, which are effaced immediately; decrees or contracts which require signatories but no author: technical instructions which are transmitted anonymously. But in the domains where it is the rule to attribute things to an author – literature, philosophy, science – it is quite evident that this attribution does not always play the same role. In the order of scientific discourse, it was indispensable during the Middle Ages, that a text should be attributed to an author, since this was an index of truthfulness. A proposition was considered as drawing even its scientific value from its author. Since the seventeenth century, this function has steadily been eroded in scientific discourse: it now functions only to give a name to a theorem, an effect, an example, a syndrome. On the other hand, in the order of literary discourse, starting from the same epoch, the function of the author has steadily grown stronger: all those tales, poems, dramas or comedies which were allowed to circulate in the Middle Ages in at least a relative anonymity are now asked (and obliged to say) where they come from, who wrote them. The author is asked to account for the unity of the texts which are placed under his name. He is asked to reveal or at least carry authentification of the hidden meaning which traverses them. He is asked to connect them to his lived experiences, to the real history which saw their birth. The author is what gives the disturbing language of fiction its unities, its nodes of coherence, its insertion in the real.

I know that I will be told: 'But you are speaking there of the author as he is reinvented after the event by criticism, after he is dead and there is nothing left except for a tangled mass of scribblings; in those circumstances a little order surely has to be introduced into all that, by imagining a project, a coherence, a thematic structure that is demanded of the consciousness or the life of an author who is indeed perhaps a trifle fictitious. But that does not mean he did not exist, this real author, who bursts into the midst of all these worn-out words, bringing to them his genius or his disorder.'

It would, of course, be absurd to deny the existence of the individual who writes and invents. But I believe that—at least since a certain epoch— the individual who sets out to write a text on the horizon of which a possible oeuvre is prowling, takes upon himself the function of the author: what he writes and what does not write, what he sketches out, even by way of provisional drafts, as an outline of the oeuvre, and what he lets fall by way of commonplace remarks—this whole play of differences is prescribed by the author-function, as he receives it from his epoch, or as he modifies it in his turn. He may well overturn the traditional image of the author; nevertheless, it is from some new author-position that he will cut out, from everything he could say and from all that he does say every day at any moment, the still trembling outline of his oeuvre.

The commentary-principle limits the chance-element in discourse by the play of an identity which would take the form of repetition and sameness. The author-principle limits this same element of chance by the play of an identity which has the form of individuality and the self.

We must also recognise another principle of limitation in what is called, not sciences but 'disciplines': a principle which is itself relative and mobile; which permits construction, but within narrow confines.

The organization of disciplines is just as much opposed to the principle of commentary as to that of the author. It is opposed to the principle of the author because a discipline is defined by a domain of objects, a set of methods, a corpus of propositions considered to be true, a play of rules and definitions, of techniques and instruments: all this constitutes a sort of anonymous system at the disposal of anyone who wants to or is able to use it, without their meaning or validity being linked to the one who happened to be their inventor. But the principle of a discipline is also opposed to that of commentary: in a discipline, unlike a commentary, what is supposed at the outset is not a meaning which has to be rediscovered, nor an identity which has to be repeated, but the requisites for the construction of new statements. For there to be a discipline, there must be a possibility of formulating new propositions, ad infinitum.

But there is more; there is more, no doubt, in order for there to be less: a discipline is not the sum of all that can be truthfully said about something; it is not even the set of all that can be accepted about the same data in virtue of some principle of coherence or systematicity. Medicine is not constituted by the total of what can be truthfully said about illness; botany cannot be defined by the sum of all the truths concerning plants. There are two reasons for this: first of all, botany and medicine are made up of errors as well as truths, like any other discipline – errors which are not residues or foreign bodies but which have positive functions, a historical efficacity, and a role that is often indissociable from that of the truths. And besides, for a proposition to belong to botany or pathology, it has to fulfil certain conditions, in a sense stricter and more complex than pure and simple truth: but in any case, other conditions. It must address itself to a determinate plane of objects: from the end of the seventeenth century, for example, for a proposition to be 'botanical' it had to deal with the visible structure of the plant, the system of its close and distant resemblances or the mechanism of its fluids; it could no longer retain its symbolic value, as was the case in the sixteenth century, nor the set of virtues and properties which were accorded to it in antiquity. But without belonging to a discipline, a proposition must use conceptual or technical instruments of a well-defined type; from the nineteenth century, a proposition was no longer medical – it fell 'outside medicine' and acquired the status of an individual phantasm or popular imagery – if it used notions that were at the same time metaphorical, qualitative, and substantial (like those of engorgement, of overheated liquids or of dried-out solids). In contrast it could and had to make use of notions that were equally metaphorical but based on another model, a functional and physiological one (that of the irritation, inflammation, or degeneration of the tissues). Still further: in order to be part of a discipline, a proposition has to be able to be inscribed on a certain type of theoretical horizon: suffice it to recall that the search for the primitive language, which was a perfectly acceptable theme up to the eighteenth century, was sufficient, in the second half of the nineteenth century, to make any discourse fall into – I hesitate to say error – chimera and reverie, into pure and simple linguistic monstrosity.

Within its own limits, each discipline recognises true and false propositions: but it pushes back a whole teratology of knowledge beyond its margins. The exterior of a science is both more and less populated than is often believed; there is of course immediate experience, the imaginary themes which endlessly carry and renew immemorial beliefs; but perhaps there are no errors in the strict sense, for error can only arise and be decided inside a definite practice; on the other hand, there are monsters on the prowl whose form changes with the history of knowledge. In short, a proposition must fulfil complex and heavy requirements to be able to belong to the grouping of a discipline: before it can be called true or false, it must be 'in the true', as Canguilhem would say.

People have often wondered how the botanists or biologists of the nineteenth century managed not to see that what Mendel was saying was true. But it was because Mendel was speaking of objects, applying methods, and placing himself on a theoretical horizon which were alien to the biology of his time. Naudin, before him, had of course posited the thesis that hereditary traits are discrete; yet, no matter how new or strange this principle was it was able to fit into the discourse of biology at least as an enigma. What Mendel did was to constitute the hereditary trait as an absolutely new biological object, thanks to a kind of filtering which had never been used before: he detached the trait from the species and from the sex which transmits it; the field in which he observed it being the infinitely open series of the generations, where it appears and disappears according to statistical regularities. This was a new object which called for new conceptual instruments and new theoretical foundations. Mendel spoke the truth, but he was not 'within the true, of the biological discourse of his time: it was not according to such rules that biological objects and concepts were formed. It needed a complete change of scale, the deployment of a whole new range of objects in biology for Mendel to enter into the true and for his propositions to appear (in large measure) correct. Mendel was a true monster, which meant that science could not speak of him; whereas about thirty years earlier, at the height of the nineteenth century, Scheiden, for example, who denied plant sexuality, but in accordance with the rules of biological discourse, was merely formulating a disciplined error.

It is always possible that one might speak the truth in the space of a wild exteriority, but one is 'in the true' only by obeying the rules of a discursive 'policing' which one has to reactivate in each of one's discourses.

The discipline is a principle of control over the production of discourse. The discipline fixes limits for discourse by the action of an identity which takes the form of a permanent re-actuation of the rules.

We are accustomed to see in an author's fecundity, in the multiplicity of the commentaries, and in the development of a discipline so many infinite resources for the creation of discourses. Perhaps so, but they are nonetheless principles of constraint; it is very likely impossible to account for their positive and multiplicatory role if we do not take into consideration their restrictive and constraining function.

IV

There is, I believe, a third group of procedures which permit the control of discourses. This time it is not a matter of mastering their powers or averting the unpredictability of their appearance, but of determining the condition of their application, of imposing a certain number of rules on the individuals who hold them, and thus of not permitting everyone to have access to them. There is a rarefaction, this time, of the speaking subjects; none shall enter the order of discourse if he does not satisfy certain requirements or if he is not, from the outset, qualified to do so. To be more precise: not all the regions of discourse are equally open and penetrable; some of them are largely forbidden (they are differentiated and differentiating), while others seem to be almost open to all winds and put at the disposal of every speaking subject, without prior restrictions.

In this regard I should like to recount an anecdote which is so beautiful that one trembles at the thought that it might be true. It gathers into a single figure all the constraints of discourse: those which limit its powers, those which master its aleatory appearances, those which carry out the selection among speaking subjects. At the beginning of the seventeenth century, the Shogun heard tell that the Europeans' superiority in matters of navigation, commerce, politics, and military skill was due to their knowledge of mathematics. He desired to get hold of so precious a knowledge. As he had been told of an English sailor who possessed the secret of these miraculous discourses, he summoned him to his palace and kept him there. Alone with him, he took lessons. He learned mathematics. He retained power, and lived to a great old age. It was not until the nineteenth century that there were Japanese mathematicians. But the anecdote does not stop there: it has its European side too. The story has it that this English sailor, Will Adams, was an autodidact, a carpenter who had learnt geometry in the course of working in a shipyard. Should we see this story as the expression of one of the great myths of European culture? The universal communication of knowledge and the infinite free exchange of discourses in Europe, against the monopolised and secret knowledge of Oriental tyranny?

This idea, of course, does not stand up to examination. Exchange and communication are positive figures working inside complex systems of restriction, and probably would not be able to function independently of them. The most superficial and visible of these systems of restriction is constituted by what can be gathered under the name of ritual. Ritual defines the qualification which must be possessed by individuals who speak (and who must occupy such-and-such a position and formulate such-and-such a type of statement, in the play of a dialogue, of interrogation or recitation); it defines the gestures, behaviour, circumstances, and the whole set of signs which must accompany discourse; finally, it fixes the supposed or imposed efficacity of the words, their effect on those to whom they are addressed, and the limits of their constraining value. Religious, judicial, therapeutic, and in large measure also political discourses; finally, it fixes the supposed or imposed efficacity of the words, their effect can scarcely be dissociated from this deployment of a ritual which determines both the particular properties and the stipulated roles of the speaking subjects.

A somewhat different way of functioning is that of the 'societies of discourse', which function to preserve or produce discourses, but in order to make them circulate in a closed space, distributing them only according to strict rules, and without the holders being dispossessed by this distribution. An archaic model for this is provided by the groups of rhapsodists who possessed the knowledge of the poems to be recited or potentially to be varied and transformed. But though the object of this knowledge was after all a ritual recitation, the knowledge was protected, defended and preserved within a definite group by the often very complex exercises of memory which it implied. To pass an apprenticeship in it allowed one to enter both a group and a secret which the act of recitation showed but did not divulge; the roles of speaker and listener were not interchangeable.

There are hardly any such 'societies of discourse' now, with their ambiguous play of the secret and its divulgation. But this should not deceive us: even in the order of 'true' discourse, even in the order of discourse that is published and free from all ritual, there are still forms of appropriation of secrets, and non-interchangeable roles. It may well be that the act of writing as it is institutionalized today, in the book, the publishing-system and the person of the writer, takes place in a 'society of discourse', which though diffuse is certainly constraining. The difference between the writer and any other speaking or writing subject (a difference constantly stressed by the writer himself), the intransitive nature (according to him) of his discourse, the fundamental singularity which he has been ascribing for so long to 'writing', the dissymmetry that is asserted between 'creation' and any use of the linguistic system – all this shows the existence of a certain 'society of discourse', and tends moreover to bring back its play of practices. But there are many others still, functioning according to entirely different schemes of exclusivity and disclosure: e.g., technical or scientific secrets, or the forms of diffusion and circulation of medical discourse, or those who have appropriated the discourse of politics or economics.

At first glance, the 'doctrines' (religious, political, philosophical) seem to constitute the reverse of a 'society of discourse', in which the number of speaking individuals tended to be limited even if it was not fixed; between those individuals, the discourse could circulate and be transmitted. Doctrine, on the contrary, tends to be diffused, and it is by the holding in common of one and the same discursive ensemble that individuals (as many as one cares to imagine) define their reciprocal allegiance. In appearance, the only prerequisite is the recognition of the same truths and the acceptance of a certain rule of (more or less flexible) conformity with the validated discourses. If doctrines were nothing more than this, they would not be so very different from scientific disciplines, and the discursive control would apply only to the form or the content of the statement, not to the speaking subject. But doctrinal allegiance puts in question both the statement and the speaking subject, the one by the other. It puts the speaking subject in question through and on the basis of the statement, as is proved by the procedures of exclusion and the mechanisms of rejection which come into action when a speaking subject has formulated one or several unassimilable statements; heresy and orthodoxy do not derive from a fanatical exaggeration of the doctrinal mechanisms, but rather belong fundamentally to them. And conversely the doctrine puts the statements in question on the basis of the speaking subjects, to the extent that the doctrine always stands as the sign, manifestation and instrument of a prior adherence to a class, a social status, a race, a nationality, an interest, a revolt, a resistance or an acceptance. Doctrine binds individuals to certain types of enunciation and consequently forbids them all others; but it uses, in return, certain types of enunciation to bind individuals amongst themselves, and to differentiate them by that very fact from all others. Doctrine brings about a double subjection: of the speaking subjects to discourses, and of discourses to the (at least virtual) group of speaking individuals.

On a much broader scale, we are obliged to recognise large cleavages in what might be called the social appropriation of discourses. Although education may well be, by right, the instrument thanks to which any individual in a society like ours can have access to any kind of discourse whatever, this does not prevent it from following, as is well known, in its distribution, in what it allows and what it prevents, the lines marked out by social distances, oppositions and struggles. Any system of education is a political way of maintaining or modifying the appropriation of discourses, along with the knowledges and powers which they carry.

I am well aware that it is very abstract to separate speech-rituals, societies of discourse, doctrinal groups and social appropriations, as I have just done. Most of the time, they are linked to each other and constitute kinds of great edifices which ensure the distribution of speaking subjects into the different types of discourse and the appropriation of discourses to certain categories of subject. Let us say, in a word, that those are the major procedures of subjection used by discourse. What, after all, is an education system, other than a ritualisation of speech, a qualification and a fixing of the roles for speaking subjects, the constitution of a doctrinal group, however diffuse, a distribution and an appropriation of discourse with its powers and knowledges? What is 'écriture' (the writing of the 'writers') other than a similar system of subjection, which perhaps takes slightly different forms, but forms whose main rhythms are analogous? Does not the judicial system, does not the institutional system of medicine likewise constitute, in some of their aspects at least, similar systems of subjection of and by discourse?

22 | Julia Kristeva,

From 'Women's Time', *Revolutions of the Word* (1981), pp. 167–70

In the Name of the Father, the Son . . . and the Woman?

These few elements of the manifestations by the new generation of women in Europe seem to me to demonstrate that, beyond the sociopolitical level where it is generally inscribed (or inscribes itself), the women's movement – in its present stage, less aggressive but more artful – is situated within the very framework of the religious crisis of our civilization.

I call 'religion' this phantasmic necessity on the part of speaking beings to provide themselves with a *representation* (animal, female, male, parental, etc.) in place of what constitutes them as such, in other words, symbolization – the double articulation and syntactic sequence of language, as well as its precondition or substitutes (thoughts, affects, etc.) The elements of the current practice of feminism that we have just brought to light seem precisely to constitute such a representation which makes up for the frustrations imposed on women by the anterior code (Christianity or its lay humanist variant). The fact that this new ideology has affinities, often revindicated by its creators, with so-called matriarchal beliefs (in other words, those beliefs characterizing matrilinear societies) should not over-shadow its radical novelty. This ideology seems to me to be part of the broader antisacrificial current which in animating our culture and which, in its protest against the constraints of the sociosymbolic contract, is no less exposed to the risks of violence and terrorism. At this level of radicalism, it is the very principle of sociality which is challenged.

Certain contemporary thinkers consider, as is well known, that modernity is characterized as the first epoch in human history in which human beings attempt to live without religion. In its present form, is not feminism in the process of becoming one?

Or is it, on the contrary and as avant-garde feminists hope, that having started with the idea of difference, feminism will be able to break free of its belief in Woman, Her power, Her writing, so as to channel this demand for difference into each and every element of the female whole, and, finally, to bring out the singularity of each woman, and beyond this, her multiplicities, her plural languages, beyond the horizon, beyond sight, beyond faith itself?

A factor for ultimate mobilization? Or a factor for analysis?

Imaginary support in a technocratic era where all narcissism is frustrated? Or instruments fitted to these times in which the cosmos, atoms, and cells – our true contemporaries – call for the constitution of a fluid and free subjectivity?

The question has been posed. Is to pose it already to answer it?

Another Generation is Another Space

If the preceding can be *said* – the question whether all this is *true* belongs to a different register – it is undoubtedly because it is now possible to gain some distance on these two preceding generations of women. This implies, of course, that a *third* generation is now forming, at least in Europe. I am not speaking of a new group of young women (though its importance should not be underestimated) or of another 'mass feminist movement' taking the torch passed on from the second generation. My usage of the word 'generation' implies less a chronology than a *signifying space*, a both corporeal and desiring mental space. So it can be argued that as of now a third attitude is possible, thus a third generation, which does not exclude – quite to the contrary – the *parallel* existence of all three in the same historical time, or even that they be interwoven one with the other.

In this third attitude, which I strongly advocate – which I imagine? – the very dichotomy man/woman as an opposition between two rival entities may be understood as belonging to *metaphysics*. What can 'identity', even 'sexual identity', mean in a new theoretical and scientific space where the very notion of identity is challenge?[1] I am not simply suggesting a very hypothetical bisexuality which, even if it existed, would only, in fact, be the aspiration toward the totality of one of the sexes and thus an effacing of difference. What I mean is, first of all, the demassification of the problematic of *difference*, which would imply, in a first phase, an apparent dedramatization of the 'fight to the death' between rival groups and thus between the sexes. And this not in the name of some reconciliation–feminism has at least had the merit of showing what is irreducible and even deadly in the social contract–but in order that the struggle, the implacable difference, the violence be conceived in the very place where it operates with the maximum intransigence, in other words, in personal and sexual identity itself, so as to make it disintegrate in its very nucleus.

It necessarily follows that this involves risks not only for what we understand today as 'personal equilibrium' but also for social equilibrium itself, made up as it now is of the counterbalancing of aggressive and murderous forces massed in social, national, religious, and political groups. But is it not the insupportable situation of tension and explosive risk that the existing 'equilibrium' presupposes which leads some of those who suffer from it to divest it of its economy, to detach themselves from it, and to seek another means of regulating difference?

To restrict myself here to a personal level, as related to the question of women, I see arising, under the cover of a relative indifference toward the militance of the first and second generations, an attitude of retreat from sexism (male as well as female) and, gradually, from any kind of anthropomorphism. The fact that this might quickly become another form of spiritualism turning its back on social problems, or else a form of repression[2] ready to support all status quos, should not hide the radicalness of the process. This process could be summarized as an *interiorization of the founding separation of the sociosymbolic contract*, as an introduction of its cutting edge into the very interior of every identity whether subjective, sexual, ideological, or so forth. This in such a way that the habitual and increasingly explicit attempt to fabricate a scapegoat victim as foundress of a society or a countersociety may be replaced by the analysis of the potentialities of *victim/executioner* which characterize each identity, each subject, each sex.

What discourse, if not that of a religion, would be able to support this adventure which surfaces as a real possibility, after both the achievements and the impasses of the present ideological reworkings, in which feminism has participated? It seems to me that the role of what is usually called 'aesthetic practices' must increase not only to counterbalance the storage and uniformity of information by present-day mass media, data-bank systems and, in particular, modern communications technology, but also to demystify the identity of the symbolic bond itself, to demystify, therefore, the *community* of language as a universal and unifying tool, one which totalizes and equalizes. In order to bring out–along with the *singularity* of each person and, even more, along with the multiplicity of every person's possible identifications (with atoms, for example, stretching from the family to the stars) – the *relativity of his/her symbolic as well as biological existence*, according to the variation in his/her specific symbolic capacities. And in order to emphasize the *responsibility* which all will immediately face of putting this fluidity into play against the threats of death which are unavoidable whenever an inside and an outside, a self and an other, one group and another, are constituted. At this level of interiorization with its social as well as individual stakes, what I have called 'aesthetic practices' are undoubtedly nothing other than the modern reply to the eternal question of morality. At least, this is how we might understand an ethics which, conscious of the fact that its order is sacrificial, reserves part of the burden for each of its adherents, therefore declaring them guilty while immediately affording them the possibility for *jouissance*, for various productions, for a life made up of both challenges and differences.

Spinoza's question can be taken up again here: Are women subject to ethics? If not to that ethics defined by classical philosophy – in relationship to which the ups and downs of feminist generations seem dangerously precarious – are women not already participating in the rapid dismantling that our age is experiencing at various levels (from wars to drugs to artificial insemination) and which poses the *demand* for a new ethics? The answer to Spinoza's question can be affirmative only at the cost of considering feminism as but a *moment* in the thought of that anthropomorphic identity which currently blocks the horizon of the discursive and scientific adventure of our species.

(Translated by Alice Jardine and Harry Blake)

Notes

1 See Seminar on *Identity* directed by [Claude] Lévi-Strauss (Paris, Grasset & Fasquelle, 1977).
2 Repression (*le refoulement* or *Verdrangung*) as distinguished from the foreclosure (*la foreclusion* or *Verwerfung*) evoked earlier in the article (see LaPlanche and Pontalis).

Section 2

Subjectivity and Gender

Introduction

The concept of the 'Subject' has proved crucial to literary theory after post-structuralism and acts as a focal point for the various critiques of earlier humanist ideologies. Post-structuralists use the term 'Subject' rather than 'self' or individual' in an attempt to avoid the presupposition that the human being is in some way 'given' and fully-formed, antecedent to the entry into socially symbolic structures. The term plays ambiguously between, on the hand, subject as in the opposition subject/object, or subject as in grammar; and on the other hand, subject as in subject of the state, or subject to the law – that is – subject is both central and at the same time decentred.

Humanist ideologies depend upon a fundamental assumption about the primacy of the autonomous and unified individual. For humanism, 'man' is at the centre of meaning and action; the world is oriented around the individual. Each individual is different, each possesses a unique subjectivity; yet also and paradoxically, each shares a common human nature. The combination of unique individuality and common human essence coheres around the idea of the sovereign self, whose essential core of being transcends the nets of environmental and social conditioning. Post-structuralism has drawn on linguistics, psychoanalysis and political theories to disrupt this man-centred view of the world, arguing that the Subject and that sense of unique subjectivity itself, is constructed in language and discourse; and rather than being fixed and unified, the Subject is split, unstable or fragmented. The introductory section to this second part of the anthology has already introduced the work of Lacan, Derrida and Foucault, Barthes and Kristeva, seminal figures in the post-structuralist critique of the Subject. This section focuses specifically on some of the ways in which this writing has been taken up in order to challenge constructions of gender and sexuality.

The essay by Hélène Cixous, 'Sorties', has been chosen because although clearly influenced by the Lacanian revision of Freudianism, it is also highly sceptical about the possibility of appropriating Freudian or post-Freudian psychoanalytic ideas for a theory of feminine subjctivity. Cixous argues that Freudianism represents another example of patriarchal voyeurism: when everything is reduced to the issue of having or not having the phallus, then woman is also and inevitably either reduced to passivity or non-existence. Woman's libidinal economy has not yet been represented, according to Cixous, because it is outside the reference of the masculine signifying economy. She argues instead for a utopian feminine plurality which abandons altogether the logocentric divide of masculinity/femininity. The essay is written in annunciatory mode: the time has come to exhume the buried feminine and 'invent the other history'.

Luce Irigary's essay addresses the problem of sexual difference in terms recognizably borrowed from the same phenomenological tradition as the work of de Beauvoir. She begins her essay by reiterating the central concept of *The Second Sex*, that even when apparently universal or neutral, the Subject has, in fact, always been written in masculine form. Irigary's essay, like that of Cixous, calls for a radical rethinking of the Subject not simply in relation to discourse, society and culture, but to the very cosmos itself and to the fundamental Kantian categories of space and time. She argues that in the classic Kantian duality, which posits a realm of physical necessity and one of internal and rational freedom, the external realm is conceived in terms of space and the internal in those of time. To be free is to organize external space and to be master of internal temporality (another and earlier French thinker Henri Bergson had already attempted to develop a philosophy of internal temporality or *durée* as freedom, but Bergson's work is in dialogue with Kant as a rationalist and has little to say directly about gender and subjectivity). Accordingly, Irigary suggests that sexual difference has also been set up in relation to these co-ordinates of time and space, so that man subjugates external space (woman) and is master of interiority conceived of as time. In many ways this is a restatement of de Beauvoir's opposition between immanence and transcendence, but Irigary argues not simply for the possibility of woman occupying the transcendent position by escaping her condition of immanent otherness, she calls for an entirely more radical rethinking of the Kantian categories. The piece ends with a plea for the recognition of the importance of wonder in the relations between the sexes, for a recognition of the final impossibility of consummation: one sex is never entirely consumed by the other and the attitude of wonder allows respect for difference, works against the desire to possess or subjugate.

Jonathan Dollimore's work, like Judith Butler's, has always focused on questions of gender and subjectivity and both have become important figures in the development of queer theory. As early as 1984, Dollimore asserted that no issue could be more important to English Studies than that of the Subject. In the essay reprinted here from his book *Sexual Dissidence* (1991), he draws on some of Butler's ideas from *Gender Trouble* to articulate a view of sexual dissidence as working to unsettle oppositions between the dominant and the subordinate. Dollimore is interested in the 'dangerous proximity' of the homosocial to the homosexual where the proximate must be displaced as the 'other' but also works to reveal the sources of the Other in the Same and therefore to unsettle and destabilize fixed relations between Sameness and Otherness, natural and perverse. The perverse, he suggests, originates in the natural as a 'straying from' which becomes a 'contradiction of'. The essay offers an analysis of Shakespeare's *Othello* in these terms, drawing on psychoanalytic concepts such as displacement and condensation to demonstrate how external threats to the symbolic order are recast and replicated as internal deviation across the categories of race, class and nation. Desdemona represents a perverse female desire which turns towards Othello and may turn again, 'nature erring from itself' and from the customs of the Venetian state, while Othello himself 'turns Turk' and discovers the barbarian within. Political and social order is shown to be always internally disordered by the deviations it produces and displaces and defines itself against; political and social order is revealed to be a fragile edifice dependent upon an impossible internal as well as external regulation of 'nature'. Dollimore's essay deconstructs the traditional liberal split between private and public and demonstrates that psychic and social orders are inextricably bound to each other.

From the first, Judith Butler's work has been concerned to revisit the terms of earlier feminist thought and to critique its lurking essentialisms and metaphysical oppositions. She has consistently argued that it does not make sense to talk of an originary body which is somehow acculturated into gender, because gender is itself an originating activity incessantly taking place. In some ways like Irigary, but more explicitly and in a more radical gesture of refusal of the categories of man and woman, she sees the sex/gender distinction as a product of that Cartesian thinking which assumes an absolute split between mind and body, but where body exists effectively in the realm of denial. Butler's anti-idealism led her to be critical of the liberatory essentialism of much French feminist theory and her work has tended to draw on Foucauldian critiques of utopian discourses. She has argued that those feminists who seek to locate an essential femininity in the unexplored spaces of the 'pre-Oedipal', or the unconscious, or some realm of interiority unrepresented in the symbolic order, effectively risk, once again, returning the issue of gender to the category of biological sex, of conflating biology with destiny. In the excerpt reprinted here, the last chapter of her book *Bodies That Matter*, Butler develops her questioning of the issue of whether feminism needs a concept of feminine identity at all and argues that gender is always in fact a performance, not what one is but what one does. To be a subject is to be gendered but given that the performance of gender is never singular but always citational and reiterative there is always scope for pastiche, reformulation, play and resistance.

In this essay, Butler considers the idea of 'queer' as a reworking of abjection into political agency and offers an account of drag as what she sees as an allegory of homosexual melancholy. Deviant sexualities are analysed as parodic and subversive repetitions which displace, defamiliarize and expose heterosexual norms. Parody is a mode which offers critique through complicit performance; it is perhaps the central rhetorical motif of postmodernism and in Butler's hands the Subject becomes a thoroughly postmodern entity with no centre, no depth, no autonomy. Drag is interesting as a performance of the sign of gender which functions to reveal the hyperbolic status of the norm itself, the heterosexual (and impossible!), Man and Woman. Drag reveals that heterosexuality itself can only ever be a performance, for its logic requires exclusive categories of femininity and masculinity. Through the explicit and self-conscious performance which is drag, power is turned against itself but opposition and complicity go hand in hand and the performance must always be a precarious one.

23 | Hélène Cixous,

'Sorties', *New French Feminisms*, Elaine Marks and Isabelle de Courtivoron, eds (1975), pp. 366–71

Where is she?

Activity/passivity,
Sun/Moon,
Culture/Nature,
Day/Night,

Father/Mother,
Head/heart,
Intelligible/sensitive,
Logos/Pathos.

Form, convex, step, advance, seed,
progress.
Matter, concave, ground–which supports
the step, receptacle.
Man

Woman

Always the same metaphor: we follow it, it transports us, in all of its forms, wherever a discourse is organized. The same thread, or double tress leads us, whether we are reading or speaking, through literature, philosophy, criticism, centuries of representation, of reflection.

Thought has always worked by
opposition,
Speech/Writing
High/Low

By dual, *hierarchized*[1] oppositions, Superior/Inferior. Myths, legends, books, Philosophical systems. Wherever an ordering intervenes, a law organizes the thinkable by (dual, irreconcilable; or mitigable, dialectical) oppositions. And all the couples of oppositions are *couples*. Does this mean something? Is the fact that logocentrism subjects thought–all of the concepts, the codes, the values–to a two-term system, related to 'the' couple man/woman?

Nature/History,
Nature/Art,
Nature/Mind,
Passion/Action.

Theory of culture, theory of society, the ensemble of symbolic systems –
are, religion, family, language, – everthing elaborates the same systems.
And the movement by which each opposition is set up to produce meaning
is the movement by which the couple is destroyed. A universal battlefield.
Each time a war breaks out. Death is always at work.

Father/son	Relationships of authority, of privilege, of force.
Logos/writing	Relationships: opposition, conflict, relief, reversion.
Master/slave	Violence. Repression.

And we perceive that the 'victory' always amounts to the same thing; it is
hierarchized. The hierarchization subjects the entire conceptual organization
to man. A male privilege, which can be seen in the opposition by which it
sustains itself, between *activity* and *passivity*. Traditionally, the question of
sexual difference is coupled with the same opposition: activity/passivity.

That goes a long way. If we examine the history of philosophy – in so far
as philosophical discourse orders and reproduces all thought – we perceive[2]
that: it is marked by an absolute constant, the orchestrator of values, which
is precisely the opposition activity/passivity.

In philosophy, woman is always on the side of passivity. Every time the
question comes up; when we examine kinship structures; whenever a family
model is brought into play; in fact as soon as the ontological question is
raised; as soon as you ask yourself what is meant by the question 'What is
it?'; as soon as there is a will to say something. A will: desire, authority, you
examine that, and you are led right back – to the father. You can even fail to
notice that there's no place at all for women in the operation! In the extreme
the world of 'being' can function to the exclusion of the mother. No need
for mother – provided that there is something of the maternal: and it is the
father then who acts as – is – the mother. Either the woman is passive; or
she doesn't exist. What is left is unthinkable, unthought of. She does not
enter into the oppositions, she is not coupled with the father (who is coupled
with the son).

There is Mallarmé's[3] tragic dream, a father lamenting the mystery of
paternity, which mourning tears out of the poet, the mourning of mournings,
the death of the beloved son: this dream of a union between the father and
the son – and no mother then. Man's dream is the face of death. Which
always threatens him differently than it threatens woman.

'an alliance
a union, superb   And dream of
                                      masculine

–and the life	filiation, dream of
	God the father
remaining in me	emerging from
	himself
I shall use it	in his son,–and
to–	no mother then
so no mother then?'	

She does not exist, she may be nonexistent; but there must be something of her. Of woman, upon whom he no longer depends, he retains only this space, always virginal, matter subjected to the desire that he wishes to imprint.

And if you examine literary history, it's the same story. It all refers back to man to his torment, his desire to be (at) the origin. Back to the father. There is an intrinsic bond between the philosophical and the literary (to the extent that it signifies, literature is commanded by the philosophical) and phallocentrism. The philosophical constructs itself starting with the abasement of woman. Subordination of the feminine to the masculine order which appears to be the condition for the functioning of the machine.

The challenging of this solidarity of logocentrism and phallocentrism has today become insistent enough–the bringing to light of the fate which has been imposed upon woman, of her burial–to threaten the stability of the masculine edifice which passed itself off as eternal–natural; by bringing forth from the world of femininity reflections, hypotheses which are necessarily ruinous for the bastion which still holds the authority. What would become of logocentrism, of the great philosophical system, of world order in general if the rock upon which they founded their church were to crumble?

If it were to come out in a new day that the logocentric project has always been, undeniably, to found(fund)[4] phallocentrism, to insure for masculine order a rationale equal to history itself?

Then all the stories would have to be told differently, the future would be incalculable, the historical force would, will, change hands, bodies; another thinking as yet not thinkable will transform the functioning of all society. Well, we are living through this very period when the conceptual foundation of a millenial culture is in process of being undermined by millions of a species of mole as yet not recognized.

When they awaken from among the dead, from among the words, from among the laws ... .

What does one give?

The specific difference that has determined the movement of history as a movement of property is articulated between two economies that define themselves in relation to the problematics of giving.

The (political) economy of the masculine and of the feminine is organized by different requirements and constraints, which, when socialized and metaphorized, produce signs, relationships of power, relationships of production and of reproduction, an entire immense system of cultural inscription readable as masculine or feminine.

I am careful here to use the *qualifiers* of sexual difference, in order to avoid the confusion man/masculine, woman/feminine: for there are men who do not repress their femininity, women who more or less forcefully inscribe their masculinity. The difference is not, of course, distributed according to socially determined 'sexes'. Furthermore, when I speak of political economy and of libidinal economy, in putting the two together, I am not bringing into play the false question of origin, that tall tale sustained by male privilege. We must guard against falling complacently or blindly into the essentialist ideological interpretation, as, for example, Freud and Jones, in different ways, ventured to do; in their quarrel over the subject of feminine sexuality, both of them, starting from opposite points of view, came to support the awesome thesis of a 'natural', anatomical determination of sexual difference-opposition. And from there on, both implicitly support phallocentrism's position of power.

Let us review the main points of the opposing positions: (Ernest) Jones (in *Early Feminine Sexuality*), using an ambiguous approach, attacks the Freudian theses that make of woman an imperfect man.

For Freud:

1 The 'fatality' of the feminine situation is a result of an anatomical 'defectiveness'.
2 There is only one libido, and its essence is male; the inscription of sexual difference begins only with a phallic phase which both boys and girls go through. Until then, the girl has been a sort of little boy: the genital organization of the infantile libido is articulated by the equivalence activity/masculinity; the vagina has not as yet been 'discovered'.
3 The first love object being, for both sexes, the mother, it is only for the boy that love of the opposite sex is 'natural'.

For Jones: Femininity is an autonomous 'essence'

From the outset (starting from the age of six months) the girl has a *feminine* desire for her father; an analysis of the little girl's earliest fantasms would in fact show that, in place of the breast which is perceived as disappointing, it is the penis that is desired, or an object of the same form (by an analogical displacement). It follows, since we are already into the chain of substitutions, that in the series of partial objects in place of the penis, would come the child – for in order to counter Freud, Jones docilely returns to the Freudian terrain. And then some. From the equation breast – penis – child, he concludes that the little girl experiences with regard to the father a primary desire. (And this would include the desire to have a child by the father as well.) And, of course, the girl also has a primary love for the opposite sex. She too, then, has a right to her Oedipal complex as a primary formation, and to the threat of mutilation by the mother. At last she is a woman, anatomically, without defect: her clitoris is not a minipenis. Clitoral masturbation is not, as Freud claims, a masculine practice. And it would seem in light of precocious fantasms that the vagina is discovered very early.

In fact, in affirming that there is a specific femininity (while in other respects preserving the theses of an orthodoxy) it is still phallocentrism that Jones reinforces, on the pretext of taking the part of femininity (and of God, who he recalls created them male and female–!). And bisexuality vanishes into the unbridged abyss that separates the opponents here.

As for Freud, if we subscribe to what he sets forth when he identifies with Napoleon in his article of 1933 on *The Disappearance of the Oedipus Complex*: 'anatomy is destiny', then we participate in the sentencing to death of woman. And in the completion of all History.

That the difference between the sexes may have psychic consequences is undeniable. But they are surely not reducible to those designated by a Freudian analysis. Starting with the relationship of the two sexes to the Oedipal complex, the boy and the girl are oriented toward a division of social roles so that women 'inescapably' have a lesser productivity, because they 'sublimate' less than men and because symbolic activity, hence the production of culture, is men's doing[5].

Freud moreover starts from what he calls the *anatomical* difference between the sexes. And we know how that is pictured in his eyes: as the difference between having/not having the phallus. With reference to these precious parts. Starting from what will be specified, by Lacan, as the transcendental signifier.

But *sexual difference* is not determined by the fantasized relationship to anatomy, which is based, to a great extent, upon the point of view, therefore upon a strange importance accorded [by Freud and Lacan] to exteriority and to the specular in the elaboration of sexuality. A voyeur's theory, of course.

No, it is at the level of sexual pleasure [*jouissance*]in my opinion that the difference makes itself most clearly apparent in as far as woman's libidinal economy is neither identifiable by a man nor referable to the masculine economy.

For me, the question 'What does she want'? that they ask of woman, a question that in fact woman asks herself because they ask it of her, because precisely there is so little place in society for her desire that she ends up by dint of not knowing what to do with it, no longer knowing where to put it, or if she has any, conceals the most immediate and the most urgent question: 'How do I experience sexual pleasure?' What is feminine *sexual pleasure*, where does it take place, how is it inscribed at the level of her body, of her unconscious? And then how is it put into writing?

We can go on at length about a hypothetical prehistory and about a matriarchal era. Or we can, as did Bachofen,[6] attempt to reconstitute a gynecocratic society, and to deduce from it poetic and mythical effects that have a powerfully subversive import with regard to the family and to male power.

All the other ways of depicting the history of power, property, masculine domination, the constitution of the State, the ideological apparatus have their effectiveness. But the change taking place has nothing to do with the question of 'origin'. Phallocentrism *is*. History has never produced, recorded anything but that. Which does not mean that this form is inevitable or natural. Phallocentrism is the enemy. Of *everyone*. Men stand to lose by it, differently but as seriously as women. And it is time to transform. To invent the other history.

There is no such thing as 'destiny', 'nature', or essence, but living structures, caught up, sometimes frozen within historicocultural limits which intermingle with the historical scene to such a degree that it has long been impossible and is still difficult to think or even to imagine something else. At present, we are living through a transitional period – where the classical structure appears as if it might crack.

To predict what will happen to sexual difference – in another time (in two or three hundred years?) is impossible. But there should be no misunderstanding: men and women are caught up in a network of millenial cultural determinations of a complexity that is practically unanalyzable: we can no more talk about 'woman' than about 'man' without getting caught up in an ideological theater where the multiplication of represesntations, images, reflections, myths, identifications constantly transforms, deforms, alters each person's imaginary order and in advance, renders all conceptualization null and void.

There is no reason to exclude the possibility of radical transformations of behavior, mentalities, roles, and political economy. The effects of these transformations on the libidinal economy are unthinkable today. Let us imagine simultaneously a *general* change in all of the structures of formation, education, framework, hence of reproduction, of ideological effects, and let us imagine a real liberation of sexuality, that is, a transformation of our relationship to our body – and to another body), an approximation of the immense material organic sensual universe that we are, this not being possible, of course, without equally radical political transformations (imagine!). Then 'femininity', 'masculinity', would inscribe their effects of difference, their economy, their relationships to expenditure, to deficit, to giving, quite differently. That which appears as 'feminine' or 'masculine' today would no longer amount to the same thing. The general logic of difference would no longer fit into the opposition that still dominates. The difference would be a crowning display of new differences.

But we are still floundering about – with certain exceptions – in the Old order.

The masculine future:

There are exceptions. There always have been those uncertain, poetic beings, who have not let themselves be reduced to the state of coded mannequins by relentless repression of the homosexual component. Men or women, complex, mobile, open beings. Admitting the component of the other sex makes them at once much richer, plural, strong, and to the extent of this mobility, very fragile. We invent only on this condition: thinkers, artists, creators of new values, 'philosophers' of the mad Nietzchean sort, inventors and destroyers of concepts, of forms, the changers of life cannot but be agitated by singularities – complementary or contradictory. This does not mean that in order to create you must be homosexual. But there is no *invention* possible, whether it be philosophical or poetic, without the presence in the inventing subject of an abundance of the other, of the diverse: persons-detached, persons-thought, peoples born of the unconscious, and in each desert, suddenly animated, a springing forth of self that we did not know about – or women, our monsters, our jackals, our Arabs, our fellow – creatures, our fears[7]. But there is no invention of other I's, no poetry, no fiction without a certain homosexuality (interplay therefore of bisexuality) making in me a crystallized work of my ultrasubjectivities. I is this matter, personal, exuberant, lively masculine, feminine or other in which I delights me and distresses me. And in the concert of personalizations called I, at the same time that you repress a certain homosexuality, symbolically, substitutively, it comes out through various signs – traits, comportments, manners, gestures – and it is seen still more clearly in writing.

Thus, under the name of Jean Genet,[8] what is inscribed in the movement of a text which divides itself, breaks itself into bits, regroups itself, is an abundant, maternal, pederastic femininity. A phantasmatical mingling of men, of males, of messieurs, of monarchs, princes, orphans, flowers, mothers, breasts, gravitates around a marvelous 'sun of energy' love, which bombards and distintegrates these ephemeral amorous singularities so that they may recompose themselves in other bodies for new passions.

Notes

1   The translation is faithful to Hélène Cixous's many neologisms. – Translator.
2   This is what all of Derrida's work traversing – investigating the history of philosophy – seeks to make apparent. In Plato, Hegel, Nietzsche, the same process goes on, repression, exclusion, distancing of woman. Murder which intermingles with history as a manifestation and representation of masculine power.
3   *Pour un tombeau d' Anatole* (Paris, Editions du Seuil, 1961, p. 138) tomb in which Mallarmé preserves his son, gurards him, he himself the mother, from death.
4   *Fonder* in French means both 'to found' and 'to fund'. – Translator.
5   Freud's thesis is the following: when the Oedipal complex disappears the superego becomes its heir. At the moment when the boy begins to feel the threat of castration, he begins to overcome the Oedipus complex, with the help of a very severe superego. The Oedipus complex for the boy is a primary process: his first love object, as for the girl, is the mother. But the girl's development is inevitably controlled by the pressure of a less severe superego: the discovery of her castration results in a less vigorous superego. She never completely overcomes the Oedipus complex. The feminine Oedipus complex is not a primary process: the pre-Oedipal attachment to the mother entails for the girl a difficulty from which, says Freud, she never recovers: the necessity of changing objects (to love the father), in midstream is a painful conversion, which

is accompanied by an additional renunciation: the passage from pre-Oedipal sexuality to 'normal' sexuality implies the abandonment of the clitoris in order to move on to the vagina. When this 'destiny' is fulfilled, women have a reduced symbolic activity: they have nothing to lose, to gain, to defend.

6 J.-J. Bachofen (1815–1887) Swiss historian of 'gynecocracy', 'historian' of a nonhistory. His project is to demonstrate that the nations (Greek , Roman, Hebrew) went through an age of 'gynecocracy', the reign of the Mother, before arriving at a patriarchy. This epoch can only be deduced, as it has no history. Bachofen advances that this state of affairs, humiliating for men, must have been repressed, covered over by historical forgetfulness. And he attempts to create (in *Das Mutterrecht* in particular, 1861) an archaeology of the matriarchal system, of great beauty, starting with a reading of the first historical texts, at the level of the symptom, of their unsaid. Gynecocracy, he says, is well-ordered materialism.

7 The French here, *nos semblables, nos frayeurs*, plays on and with the last line of Baudelaire's famous poem 'Au lecteur' [To the reader]: 'Hypocrite lecteur,–mon semblable,–mon frére'.-Translator.

8 Jean Genet, French novelist and playwright, to whose writing Hélène Cixous refers when she gives examples of the inscription of pederastic femininity.–Translator.

24 | Luce Irigaray,

'Sexual Difference', in *Revolutions of the Word* (1977), pp. 170–3

Sexual difference is one of the important questions of our age, if not in fact the burning issue. According to Heidegger, each age is preoccupied with one thing, and one alone. Sexual difference is probably that issue in our own age which could be our salvation on an intellectual level.

For the work of sexual difference to take place, a revolution in thought and ethics is needed. We must re-interpret the whole relationship between the subject and discourse, the subject and the world, the subject and the cosmic, the microcosmic and the macrocosmic. And the first thing to say is that, even when aspiring to a universal or neutral state, this subject has always been written in the masculine form, as man, despite the fact that, at least in French, 'man' is a sexed and not a neutral noun.

It is man who has been the subject of discourse, whether in the field of theory, morality or politics. And the gender of God, the guardian of every subject and discourse, is always *paternal and masculine* in the West. For women, there remain the so-called minor art-forms: cooking, knitting, sewing and embroidery; and in exceptional cases, poetry, painting and music. Whatever their importance, these arts today do not lay down the law, at least not overtly.

We are, of course, presently bearing witness to a certain reversal of values; manual labour and art are both being revalorized. But the relationship of these arts to sexual difference is never really thought through, and properly sorted out, although on occasion it is all related to the class-struggle.

In order to live and think through this difference, we must reconsider the whole question of *space* and *time*.

In the beginning was space and the creation of space, as stated in every theogony. The gods or God first of all creates *space*. And time is there, more or less at the service of space. During the first few days the gods or God organize a world by separating the elements. This world is then peopled, and a rhythmical pattern is established among its inhabitants. God then becomes time itself, lavishing or exteriorizing itself in space or place.

Philosophy confirms this genealogy of the task of the gods or God. Time becomes *interior* to the subject, and space *exterior* (this is developed by Kant in the *Critique of Pure Reason*). The subject, the master of time, becomes the axis, managing the affairs of the world. Beyond him lies the eternal instant of God, who brings about the passage between time and space.

Could it be that this order becomes inverted in sexual difference, such that femininity is experienced as a space that often carries connotations of the depths of night (God being space and light), while masculinity is conceived of in terms of time?

The transition to a new age in turn necessitates a new perception and a new conception of *time and space*, our *occupation of place*, and the different *envelopes known as identity*.[1] It assumes and entails an evolution or transformation of forms, of the relationship of *matter* to *form* and of the interval *between* the two. This trilogy gives us our notion of place. Each age assigns limits to this trinity, be they *matter, form, interval* or *power, act, intermediate–interval*.

Desire occupies or designates the place of the *interval*. A permanent definition of desire would put an end to desire. Desire requires a sense of attraction: a change in the interval or the relations of nearness or distance between subject and object.

The transition to a new age coincides with a change in the economy of desire, necessitating a different relationship between man and god(s), man and man, man and the world, man and woman. Our own age, which is often felt to be the one in which the problem of desire has been brought to the fore, frequently theorizes about this desire on the basis of certain observations about a moment of tension, situated in historical time, whereas desire ought to be thought of as a dynamic force whose changing form can be traced in the past and occasionally the present, but never predicted. Our age will only realize the dynamic potential in desire if the latter is referred back to the economy of the *interval*, that is if it is located in the attractions, tensions, and acts between *form* and *matter*, or characterized as the *residue* of any creation or work, which lies *between* what is already identified and what has still to be identified, etc.

To arrive at the constitution of an ethics of sexual difference, we must at least return to what is for Descartes the first passion: *wonder*.[2] This passion is not opposed to, or in conflict with, anything else, and exists always as though for the first time. Man and woman, woman and man are therefore always meeting as though for the first time since they cannot stand in for one another. I shall never take the place of a man, never will a man take mine. Whatever identifications are possible, one will never exactly fill the place of the other – the one is irreducible to the other:

> When our first encounter with some object surprises us and we find it novel, or very different from what we formerly knew or from what we supposed it ought to be, this causes us to wonder and to be astonished at it. Since all this may happen before we know whether or not the object is beneficial to us, I regard wonder as the first of all the passions. It has no opposite, for, if the object before us has no characteristics that surprise us, we are not moved by it at all and we consider it without passion.[3]

Who or what the other is, I never know. But this unknowable other is that which differs sexually from me. This feeling of wonder, surprise and astonishment in the face of the unknowable ought to be returned to its proper place: the realm of sexual difference. The passions have either been repressed, stifled and subdued, or else reserved for God. Sometimes a sense of wonder is bestowed upon a work of art. But it is never found in the *gap between man and woman*. This space was filled instead with attraction, greed, possession, consummation, disgust, etc., and not with that wonder which sees something as though always for the first time, and never seizes the other as its object. Wonder cannot seize, possess or subdue such an object. The latter, perhaps, remains subjective and free?

This has never happened between the sexes. Wonder might allow them to retain an autonomy based on their difference, and give them a space of freedom or attraction, a possibility of separation or alliance.

All this would happen even before becoming engaged, during their first encounter, which would confirm their difference. The *interval* would never be crossed. There would be no consummation. Such an idea is a delusion. One sex is never entirely consummated or consumed by another. There is always a *residue*.

Notes

1 Irigaray's text has *enveloppe/envelopper* in this and subsequent passages. We have decided to translate 'envelope' and 'envelop', although this translation risks losing something of the concrete sense of enfolding, wrapping, covering, englobing, etc., associated with the French words. While the philosophical idea under discussion is that of the relationship between the container and the contained, there may also be an illusion to certain psychoanalytic theories of an early 'skin-ego', conceptualized as a 'psychic envelope' (Bion, Winnicott, Anzieu). – Ed.

2 The original French expression is *admiration*.

3 René Descartes, *The Passions of the Soul*, article 53 in *The Philosophical Writings of Descartes*, vol. I, J. Cottingham, R. Stoothoff, D. Murdoch. (Cambridge, Cambridge University Press, 1985), p. 350.

25 | Jonathan Dollimore,

From *Sexual Dissidence; Augustine to Wilde, Freud to Foucault* (1991), pp. 148–50; 151–2, 155–8; 162; 164–5

Othello: Sexual Difference and Internal Deviation

The theatre of Elizabethan and Jacobean England provides some especially powerful and intricate enactments of the legitimating power of the natural/ unnatural binary, and of its violent breakdown as well as its equally violent enforcement, and the struggles to demystify it as well as those to reconstitute it. Contradictory notions of nature pushed to an extreme, as in *King Lear,* come to threaten the coherence of the concept itself; it splits apart, disintegrates ideologically, succumbing to the very contradictions it was supposed to contain. By contrast, in *Othello* we witness nature ideologically strained to the point of breaking but still holding. Just. It is at this point that the concept may be at once barely coherent and yet most brutally repressive; with the result that, as in *Othello,* the unnatural is foregrounded, violently demonized, and rendered the object of displacement.

Aberrant Movement

Othello explores that anxious preoccupation with perversity as a disordered and disordering movement. Othello is described as the 'erring barbarian' (I. iii. 343), the 'extravagant and wheeling stranger | Of here and everywhere' (I. i. 135–6). Here 'extravagant' condenses deviation, perversion, and vagrancy. For 'extravagance' the *OED* gives as its first entry, 'A going out of the usual path; an excursion, digression. Also, the position or fact of erring *from* (a prescribed path).' The first *OED* entry for 'extravagant' (as an example of which it cites this same passage from *Othello*) defines it as that which 'wanders out of bounds; straying, roaming vagrant'.

It is not only Othello who is described in terms of a tendency towards aberrant movement; had Brabantio lived to see his daughter murdered it would, says Gratiano, have made him 'do a desperate turn, | Yea, curse his better angel from his side | And fall to reprobance' (V. ii. 206–8). Iago vows to 'serve my turn upon [Othello]'; serving one's turn on one's master is precisely not 'truly' to follow him since 'In following him, I follow but myself'. And yet to follow oneself is to be not oneself: 'I am not what I am' (I. i. 42, 59, 66). In one sense the metaphors of truth, linearity, and deviation point simply to duplicity; but also signified is a wilful disarticulation of traditional relations between authority, service, and identity.

Gratiano's description of Brabantio's 'desperate turn', with its echoes of the Fall, shows that destructive deviation may characterize even the most stolid of patriarchs. But Brabantio's turning would resemble his own conception of the way nature is undermined in the case of his daughter: a deviation pressured by the overwhelming terrible external event, a forcing rather than a succumbing. Likewise with the woman when conceived as passive victim. As Cleopatra says of her honour, it 'was not yielded, | But conquered merely' (III. xiii. 61–2). Brabantio thinks of Desdemona as 'A maiden never bold; | Of spirit so still and quiet that her motion | Blushed at herself' (I, iii. 94–6). When Desdemona is imagined as active she becomes perverse and turning the intrinsic tendency of her will; for her to 'seriously incline' (I. iii. 145) to Othello's tales of mastery over wild and aberrant natures (I. iii. 127 ff.) is strange, but retrospectively less so in one who is supposed to have 'turned to folly, and . . . was a whore' (V. ii. 133).

The opposition of woman as passive/active correlates closely with that of women as madonna/whore. This is not the first time Othello has conceived Desdemona's supposed betrayal in terms of an endless capacity for perverse movement:

> you did wish that I would make her turn.
> Sir, she can turn, and turn, and yet go on,
> And turn again.
>
> (IV. i. 243–5)

This kind of representation of deviant female desire echoes Augustinian privation; its inferiority is marked by a lack which is (perversely and paradoxically) terribly inimical to its masculine superior; Desdemona, in the paranoid masculine imagination, is the lily that festers, the 'weed | Who art so lovely fair, and smell'st so sweet' (IV. ii. 66–7); she harbours an evil inversely proportionate to her apparent goodness:

> OTHELLO. Hang her, I do but say what she is: So delicate with her needle, an admirable musician–O, she will sing the savageness out of a bear–Of so high and plenteous wit and invention–
> IAGO. She's the worse for all this.
> OTHELLO. O, a thousand, thousand times–and then of so gentle a condition!
> IAGO. Ay, too gentle. . . .
> O, 'tis foul in her.
> OTHELLO. With mine officer!
> IAGO. That's fouler.
>
> (IV. i. 177–91)

In such perversity female desire repeatedly echoes its original Fall; thus Desdemona is one who fell when she fell in love with what she feared to look on (I. iii. 98).

* * * * *

Constancy

The opposite of wayward movement is constancy; to remain rather than to turn. In Act V Othello and Emilia dispute as to whether Desdemona was faithful; Emilia reiterates that she was 'true'; Othello denies it. For a woman to be true is of course to be faithful and, more significantly, to be constant, this being the acquiescence-within-allegiance upon which the relationship fundamentally depends (but not only for women: cf. I. i. 43–4: 'all masters | Cannot be truly followed'). Is it only the mobility of language, or is it indicative of some deeper *inconstant*, that Desdemona's defection to the 'gross clasps of a lascivious Moor' can be described by her father, *who has already anticipated the event in his dreams*, as 'too *true* an evil'? (I. i. 125, 159, my emphasis). Whatever, Brabantio's dream that his daughter has betrayed him is the dream of the man who fears he connot control what he possesses. In that, he shares a patriarchal, affinity with Othello–whom, in every other respect, he so despises that he dies of grief when his daughter marries him. In this *Othello* vividly reminds us that patriarchal authority simultaneously violently unites and violently divides men in the domestic as well as the military sphere.

Predictably enough, the concept of nature underwrites constancy. But in crisis nature is seen (like its derivative, kindness) either to harbour its opposite, the unnatural, or to collapse into that which it was supposed to guard against. So Lodovico of the wrecked Othello:

> Is this the nature
> Whom passion could not shake? Whose solid virtue
> The shot of accident nor dart of chance
> Could neither graze nor pierce?
>
> (IV. i. 256–9)

If nature powerfully underwrites constancy it is most significantly at those crucial points where constancy has failed. So for Brabantio it is against 'all rules of nature' that Desdemona could desire Othello; 'For nature so preposterously to err', it must have been overwhelmed by witchcraft– 'practices of cunning hell' (I. iii. 101, 62, 102), with, perhaps, connotations of sexual aberration. But, as already suggested, this is a view of nature beguiled rather than perverted; even though overwhelmed by witchcraft, the integrity of nature holds, and so therefore does the law of racial and cultural differentiation which has its origin in nature's regulation of culture. Hence Brabantio's repeated appeals to nature even after the 'unnatural' event, the violation of natural law.

Fatal Swerve

When Othello recalls Brabantio's words a crucial and fatal transformation occurs: now nature, in the form of female desire, becomes intrinsically perverse, a 'cunning hell' in its own right:

> OTHELLO. And yet, how nature erring from itself–
> IAGO. Ay, there's the point: as (to be bold with you)
> Not to affect many proposèd matches
> Of her own clime, complexion, and degree,
> Whereto we see in all things nature tends–

Foh! one may smell, in such, a will most rank,
Foul disproportion, thoughts unnatural.

(III. iii. 229–35)

'Nature erring from itself': the perverse originates internally to, from within, the natural. Here Othello imagines, and Iago exploits, the paradoxical movement of the perverse: a straying *from* which is also a contradiction of; a divergence which is imagined to subvert that from *which* it departs in the instant that it *does* depart. In short, from within that erring movement of the first line, a perverse divergence within nature, there erupts by the last line its opposite, the 'unnatural'. Additionally, misogyny and xenophobia are rampant in the accusation of perversion, and so too is racism:[2] Iago demonizes Desdemona and Othello, she as the one who has degenerate desire, he as the object of that desire. Desire and object conjoin in the multiple meanings of 'will most rank' where 'will' might denote at once volition, sexual desire, and sexual organs,[3] and 'rank' lust, swollen, smelling, corrupt, foul. All this in seven terrifying lines which effectively sign Desdemona's death warrant. It is a passage in which (among others) the natural/unnatural binary is powerfully active.

* * * * *

External Threat/Internal Deviation

It is extraordinary just how much treachery and insurrection Iago manages to displace on to Desdemona in just six lines. How is this possible? *Othello* is partly a play about impending war. Venetian civilization is at stake, at least to the extent that its military has moved to Cyprus to defend the island against the encroaching Turks. As Simon Shepherd observes in his discussion of how the Elizabethans perceived the Turks, they, along with Moors, Tartars, even Persians, constituted the infidel powers which neighboured and threatened European Christendom. He cites the dedication to the work Thomas Newton translated as the *Notable History of Saracens* (1575): 'They were (indeed) at the first very far off from our clime and region, and therefore the less to be feared, but now they are even at our doors and ready to come into our houses' (Shepherd, *Marlowe*, 142). Alvin Kernan has sketched what he sees as the 'symbolic geography' of *Othello*, and the effect it creates of a beleaguered civilization: its outer limits are defined by the Turks – the infidels, the unbelievers – while Othello himself tells of a beyond inhabited by the barbaric and the monstrous. If Venice stands for order, law, and reason, Cyprus is a vulnerable outpost, a garrison town where civilization is to be defended by Othello, 'himself of savage origins and a converted Christian' (*Othello*, ed. Kernan, pp. xxv–xxvii). Richard Marienstras shows how, at this time, England's xenophobia was increasing in spite of, or probably because of, the fact that it was embarking on colonization and expansion: 'in every domain the foreigner was suspect. . . . Every division, every incoherence, constituted a danger' (*New Perspectives*,

103, and chs. 5, 6). The result was a real tension between the anxieties endemic to nationalism, and the ambitions intrinsic to colonialism.

One consequence of tension was a paranoid search for the internal counterparts of external threats. The famous *Homily against Disobedience and Wilful Rebellion* (1571) is obsessed with internal rebellion, the enemy within, weakening the state and rendering it vulnerable to 'all outward enemies that will invade it, to the utter and perpetual captivity, slavery, and destruction of all their countrymen, their children, their friends, their kinsfolk left alive, whom by their wicked rebellion they procure to be delivered into the hands of foreign enemies' (p. 615). In this *Homily* the sin of rebellion encompasses *all* other sins in one (pp. 609, 611–12). Racism clearly played its part here: a royal edict of 1601 expresses discontent 'at the great number of 'Negars and blackamoors which are crept into the realm'; Queen Elizabeth wanted them transported out of the country. The ostensible reason was overpopulation and unemployment among the English, but the representation of black people 'as satanic, sexual creatures, a threat to order and decency, and a danger to white womanhood' was also a factor.[4] Such considerations meant that, for many in early modern England, the implicit confrontation in *Othello* was between civilization and barbarism, and Othello's blackness becomes crucial in just this respect.

According to Iago, Desdemona's 'thoughts unnatural' involve a threefold transgression of 'clime, complexion, and degree'; that is, region, colour, and rank; or, country, race, and class, three of civilization's most jealously policed domains. The same 'nature' (from within which she errs) plays a key ideological role in demarcating the boundaries of these domains, and it does so through the same double process of discrimination/legitimation already encountered. So it is not coincidence that what Desdemona transgresses – country, race, and class – are all three at risk in the war with the Turks. Country, obviously; race in the sense that the enemy is, in the terms of the play, racially and culturally inferior; class, or degree, in the sense that it is the indispensable basis both of the culture being defended and of the military doing the defending; witness Othello's anger at the fight 'on the court and guard of safety'.

Here then is displacement: an external threat recast or 'condensed' as internal deviation. The perverse subject – the desiring woman – becomes, through imagined sexual transgression, a surrogate alien, a surrogate Turk. Perhaps such displacement and condensation, by reproducing internally an imaginary, demonized counterpart of the enemy without, permit a rehearsal of the violence and retribution not as yet unleashed on that enemy? Quite probably, and the way the foreign is reproduced within the domestic is striking. But no entirely functionalist account of this displacement can be adequate to the full extent of its intensity, destructiveness, and paranoia. That is why I have used psychoanalytic terms to describe it. It is also why to understand it we have to explore the vicissitudes of desire as they inform, deform, and reform the psychic and social 'orders'. And why we need to recall that this displacement of the foreign into the domestic is enabled by

Othello, a domesticated foreigner. Related to this is the way the internal replication of an external threat is itself replicated in the brawl between Cassio and Roderigo, perceived as being the more threatening for being internal to a beleaguered community and, worse still, taking place 'on the court and guard of safety' and in 'a town of war | Yet wild, [where] the people's hearts [are] brimful of fear' (ii. iii. 194–5). The fight risks the *admission* of the alien, not just because the guard is down but because, as a 'barbarous brawl' (154), it is imaged as an internal refiguring of the alien. And the process whereby this external threat reappears as internal disorder is, again, one of *turning*, a perverse deviation into the other: 'Are we turned Turks, and to ourselves do that | Which heaven hath forbid the Ottomites?' (ii. iii. 151–2).

The dominant terms of the several binaries in play at this point (reason/passion, order/chaos, Christian/barbarian) are invoked by Othello as supposed guarantors of order; but they are themselves under threat internally (again, the splitting of the dominant term).[5] The most extreme manifestation of this will be Othello's own sexual jealousy. The instability of desire–even or especially desire harnessed within the confines of legitimate heterosexual love–will be shown to harbour the most 'barbarous' passions of all. And so total is the internal subversion effected by desire, that Othello will finally declare that it is he who has turned Turk, the barbarous thus 'turning out' in the 'highest' rather than the 'lowest'. Thus Robert Burton's observation in *The Anatomy*: the civilized, once perverted, does not so much admit the barbaric, as admit to it, discovering it within itself (above Chapter 8).

Does the fate of Othello confirm, qualify, or discount the charge that this play is racist? Certainly the play enacts a series of displacements of the aberrant and the abhorrent on to the alien. But is it endorsing that process, or re-presenting it for our attention? If the second, then it still remains indeterminate as to whether we, in attending to that process, repudiate or endorse it. Critics and audiences of the play have indisputably done both.

Forget Iago's 'Homosexuality'

The feared internal deviation (Desdemona's perceived identification with the alien) lends urgency to the homosocial alliance[6] between Othello and Iago, whereby masculine honour vows vengeance against both the betraying feminine (Desdemona) and the usurping masculine (Cassio). Within the homosocial perception there is of course a crucial distinction between female betraying and male usurping: whereas Desdemona's supposed betrayal undoes her, makes her 'foul' and 'false', there is a sense in which Cassio's usurpation makes him, albeit threateningly, more of man. To be sure he is described as 'loose of soul' (iii . iii. 417), but that looseness speaks a certain sexual prowess which becomes the focus for male sexual jealousy. According to Iago, Cassio speaks amorously in his sleep, and (mis) identifies Iago as his lover. So is this the moment when Iago's supposed homosexuality is disclosed via a displacement of it on to Cassio? And if so, does this homosexuality then become the real motive for Iago's otherwise motiveless malignity (rendering it, in other words, the less disturbing because now comprehensible)? Iago's and/or Othello's jealousy may well have a homoerotic component, if only because the homoerotic, like other forms of eroticism, might in principle be anywhere, attached to anyone, and in an indeterminate number of contexts. But we would be mistaken to conclude that 'repressed homosexuality' is the 'real' motivation of the homosocial bond since such a conclusion would obscure much and reveal little. Much more significant for understanding the sexual economy at work here is the way Iago's story, intentionally or not, reveals betrayal/usurpation as the typical *double* focus of masculine sexual jealousy, and a major instability in homosocial bonding. Also significant is the way Iago's story superimposes an excessive usurping masculine desire upon a betraying and unnatural female desire, confirming the culpability of both Cassio and Desdemona, usurper and betrayer, but of course hers more than his.

* * * * *

Foul as Slander

Othello explores a kind of disorder, instability, and non-rationality which is never 'chaos' as such because it has very specific causes and predictable effects. This is the ordering within chaos and the chaos within order which the binary order/chaos formally disavows even as in practice it exacerbates it.

As we have seen, the diverse instabilities inherent in the beleaguered state, homosocial bonding, homosocial competition, and racist fear, refigure as the inconstancy of woman. If is not only Iago who facilitates this; Roderigo takes for himself the ideal of feminine virginity – 'In simple and pure soul I come to you' (I. i. 108) – *even* as he convinces Brabantio of his daughter's disobedience. Female constancy is the paradigm to which other kinds of stability, sexual and political, refer, and upon which they depend, dreadfully and of course impossibly:

> EMILIA. For if she be not honest, chaste and true,
>   There's no man happy; the purest of their wives
>   Is foul as slander.
>
> (IV. ii. 16–18)

In one sense – certainly for Emilia – this is merely rhetorical: if she is not true no woman is – i.e. of course she is true. But in another sense, one to which the paranoid imagination is terribly susceptible, the supposition confirms what its manifest absurdity was supposed to preclude: all women cannot be true; therefore all women *are* false; therefore she is false. Such is the 'nature' of the inferior (social, racial, or sexual): one instance of deficiency, imagined or actual, confirms the universal deficiency of the entire group. But notice too how sexual betrayal figures in obsessively public terms: foul as slander. Again, the significant others for the cuckolded male are those other men upon whom his honour is socially dependent. And let us remember that Othello *is* dangerously situated; he certainly misidentifies the source of hostility, but not the hostility itself.

It is via such displacements that ideological formations may not only mask contradictions but, in doing that, also mobilize them. It is also why, when ideology is pushed nearly to incoherence, to the verge of breakdown, those contradictions may be most brutally and effectively mobilized. Such an occurrence is distinct from another wherein ideological legitimation is thrown into such crisis that domination can be sustained only through overt physical force. In practice, however, the two may coexist. 'And yet, how nature, erring from itself . . .': at the moment when the contradictions hitherto contained by the ideological construct surface and threaten it–when it does indeed become susceptible to disarticulation, most vulnerable to its own force being used against it–at that very moment Iago reharnesses and reconstitutes that energy as a force of legitimation/discrimination. At times of crisis there are always massive pressures for restitution. Iago's success in this respect depends precisely on an intensification of the wider instabilities within the state, as well as the social and psychic insecurities of Othello himself. Let us never lose sight of what occurs in those barely incoherent yet violently effective displacements worked by and through Iago: the work of policing boundaries crucial to the maintaining of social domination–boundaries of country, race, and class–is effaced, dissolved into the *a priori* internal regulation of nature.

Notes

1 See Drakakis's analysis of the political and psychological implications of Brabantio's dream in 'The Engendering of Toads', 76.
2 On the alignment of both blackness and femininity with sexual monstrosity, see Newman, 'And Wash the Ethiop White': Femininity and the Monstrous in *Othello*'. In considering the fusion of misogyny and racism in these lines we should remember that neither is a transhistorical category: the changing nature of patriarchy affects the one, the changing history of slavery and colonization the other. But similarities remain: at the time in question, racism relates to beliefs in cultural and national inferiority, while both misogyny and racism would depend on the general belief that unrestrained sexuality, male and female, is destructive, monstrous, perverse; see especially Loomba, *Gender, Race, Renaissance Drama*.
3 Cf. Sonnets 134–6.
4 Jones, *Othello's Countrymen*, esp. 12; Walvin, *Black and White*, esp. 8; Cowhig, 'Blacks in English Renaissance Drama', esp. 4–7, quoted from p. 4; Loomba, *Gender, Race, Renaissance Drama*, esp. 42–5.
5 It is simplistic to say that Othello begins as a rational being who then succumbs to passion. Rather Othello submits himself to the negative term of the reason/passion binary after he initially invokes it in the condemnation of others. And the most pernicious element in all this, what effects the subversion of 'reason', is not passion as such, but Iago's sophisticated rationality. As Greenblatt shows, Iago's so-called evil is of the quintessentially civilized kind, the fashioning of self and others (*Renaissance Self-Fashioning*, ch. 6).

6 'The male homosocial structure', writes Sedgwick, is that 'whereby men's heterosexual desire' or women serves as a more or less perfunctory detour on the way to a closer but homophobically proscribed, bonding with another man' ('A Poem is Being Written', 129–30). For a more extensive exploration of the homosocial, see also Sedgwick's *Between Men*).

26 | Judith Butler,

From *Bodies that Matter* (1993), pp. 237–40, 241–2

Gendered and Sexual Performativity

How then does one link the trope by which discourse is described as 'performing' and that theatrical sense of performance in which the hyperbolic status of gender norms seems central? What is 'performed' in drag is, of course, *the sign* of gender, a sign that is not the same as the body that it figures, but that cannot be read without it. The sign, understood as a gender imperative – 'girl!' – reads less as an assignment than as a command and, as such, produces its own insubordinations. The hyperbolic conformity to the command can reveal the hyperbolic status of the norm itself, indeed, can become the cultural sign by which that cultural imperative might become legible. Insofar as heterosexual gender norms produce inapproximable ideals, heterosexuality can be said to operate through the regulated production of hyperbolic versions of 'man' and 'woman'. These are for the most part compulsory performances, ones which none of us choose, but which each of us is forced to negotiate. I write 'forced to negotiate' because the compulsory character of these norms does not always make them efficacious. Such norms are continually haunted by their own inefficacy; hence the anxiously repeated effort to install and augment their jurisdiction.

The resignification of norms is thus a function of their *inefficacy*, and so the question of subversion, of *working the weakness in the norm*, becomes a matter of inhabiting the practices of its rearticulation. The critical promise of drag does not have to do with the proliferation of genders, as if a sheer increase in numbers would do the job, but rather with the exposure or the failure of heterosexual regimes ever fully to legislate or contain their own ideals. Hence, it is not that drag *opposes* heterosexuality, or that the proliferation of drag will bring down heterosexuality; on the contrary, drag tends to be the allegorization of heterosexuality and its constitutive melancholia. As an allegory that works through the hyperbolic, drag brings into relief what is, after all, determined only in relation to the hyperbolic:

the understated, taken-for-granted quality of heterosexual performativity. At its best, then, drag can be read for the way in which hyperbolic norms are dissimulated as the heterosexual mundane. At the same time these same norms, taken not as commands to be obeyed, but as imperatives to be 'cited', twisted, queered, brought into relief as heterosexual imperatives, are not, for that reason, necessarily subverted in the process.

It is important to emphasize that although heterosexuality operates in part through the stabilization of gender norms, gender designates a dense site of significations that contain and exceed the heterosexual matrix. Although forms of sexuality do not unilaterally determine gender, a non-causal and non-reductive connection between sexuality and gender is nevertheless crucial to maintain. Precisely because homophobia often operates through the attribution of a damaged, failed, or otherwise abject gender to homosexuals, that is, calling gay men 'feminine' or calling lesbians 'masculine' and because the homophobic terror over performing homosexual acts, where it exists, is often also a terror over losing proper gender ('no longer being a real or proper man' or 'no longer being a real and proper woman'), it seems crucial to retain a theoretical apparatus that will account for how sexuality is regulated through the policing and the shaming of gender.

We might want to claim that certain kinds of sexual practices link people more strongly than gender affiliation,[1] but such claims can only be negotiated, if they can, in relation to specific occasions for affiliation; there is nothing in either sexual practice or in gender to privilege one over the other. Sexual practices, however, will invariably be experienced differentially depending on the relations of gender in which they occur. And there may be forms of 'gender' within homosexuality which call for a theorization that moves beyond the categories of 'masculine' and 'feminine'. If we seek to privilege sexual practice as a way of transcending gender, we might ask at what cost the *analytic* separability of the two domains is taken to be a distinction in fact. Is there perhaps a specific gender pain that provokes such fantasies of a sexual practice that would transcend gender difference altogether, in which the marks of masculinity and femininity would no longer be legible? Would this not be a sexual practice paradigmatically fetishistic, trying not to know what it knows, but knowing it all the same? This question is not meant to demean the fetish (where would we be without it?), but it does mean to ask whether it is only according to a logic of the fetish that the radical separability of sexuality and gender can be thought.

In theories such as Catharine MacKinnon's, sexual relations of subordination are understood to establish differential gender categories, such that 'men' are those defined in a sexually dominating social position and 'women' are those defined in subordination. Her highly deterministic account leaves no room for relations of sexuality to be theorized apart from the rigid framework of gender difference or for kinds of sexual regulation that do not take gender as their primary objects (i.e., the prohibition of sodomy, public sex, consensual homosexuality). Hence, Gayle Rubin's influential distinction between the domains of sexuality and gender in 'Thinking Sex' and Sedgwick's reformulation of that position have constituted important theoretical opposition to MacKinnon's deterministic form of structuralism.[2]

My sense is that now this very opposition needs to be rethought in order to muddle the lines between queer theory and feminism.[3] For surely it is as unacceptable to insist that relations of sexual subordination determine gender position as it is to separate radically forms of sexuality from the workings of gender norms. The relation between sexual practice and gender is surely not a structurally determined one, but the destabilizing of the heterosexual presumption of that very structuralism still requires a way to think the two in dynamic relation to one another.

In psychoanalytic terms, the relation between gender and sexuality is in part negotiated through the question of the relationship between identification and desire. And here it becomes clear why refusing to draw lines of causal implication between these two domains is as important as keeping open an investigation of their complex interimplication. For, if to identify as a woman is not necessarily to desire a man, and if to desire a woman does not necessarily signal the constituting presence of a masculine identification, whatever that is, then the heterosexual matrix proves to be an *imaginary* logic that insistently issues forth its own unmanageability. The heterosexual logic that requires that identification and desire be mutually exclusive is one of the most reductive of heterosexism's psychological instruments: if one identifies *as* a given gender, one must desire a different gender. On the one hand, there is no one femininity with which to identify, which is to say that femininity might itself offer an array of identificatory sites, as the proliferation of lesbian femme possibilities attests. On the other hand, it is hardly descriptive of the complex dynamic exchanges of lesbian and gay relationships to presume that homosexual identifications 'mirror' or replicate one another. The vocabulary for describing the difficult play, crossing, and destabilization of masculine and feminine identification within homosexuality has only begun to emerge within theorectical language: the non-academic language historically embedded in gay communities is here much more instructive. The thought of sexual difference *within* homosexuality has yet to be theorized in its complexity.

For one deciding issue will be whether social strategies of regulation, abjection, and normalization will not continue to relink gender and sexuality such that the oppositional analysis will continue to be under pressure to theorize their interrelations. This will not be the same as reducing gender to prevailing forms of sexual relations such that one 'is' the effect of the sexual position one is said to occupy. Resisting such a reduction, it ought to be possible to assert a set of non-causal and non-reductive relations between gender and sexuality, not only to link feminism and queer theory, as one might link two separate enterprises, but to establish their constitutive inter-relationship. Similarly, the inquiry into both homosexuality and gender will need to cede the priority of *both* terms in the service of a more complex mapping of power that interrogates the formation of each in specified racial regimes and geopolitical spatializations. And the task, of course, does not stop here, for no one term can serve as foundational, and the success of any given analysis that centers on any one term may well be the marking of its own limitations as an exclusive point of departure.

The goal of this analysis, then, cannot be pure subversion, as if an undermining were enough to establish and direct political struggle. Rather than denaturalization or proliferation, it seems that the question for thinking discourse and power in terms of the future has several paths to follow: how to think power as resignification together with power as the convergence or interarticulation of relations of regulation, domination, constitution? How to know what might qualify as an affirmative resignification–with all the weight and difficulty of that labor–and how to run the risk of reinstalling the abject at the site of its opposition? But how, also, to rethink the terms that establish and sustain bodies that matter?

* * * * *

Performativity describes this relation of being implicated in that which one opposes, this turning of power against itself to produce alternative modalities of power, to establish a kind of political contestation that is not a 'pure' opposition, a 'transcendence' of contemporary relations of power, but a difficult labor of forging a future from resources inevitably impure.

How will we know the difference between the power we promote and the power we oppose? Is it, one might rejoin, a matter of 'knowing'? For one is, as it were, in power even as one opposes it, formed by it as one reworks it, and it is this simultaneity that is at once the condition of our partiality, the measure of our political unknowingness, and also the condition of action itself. The incalculable effects of action are as much a part of their subversive promise as those that we plan in advance.

The effects of performatives, understood as discursive productions, do not conclude at the terminus of a given statement or utterance, the passing of legislation, the announcement of a birth. The reach of their signifiability cannot be controlled by the one who utters or writes, since such productions are not owned by the one who utters them. They continue to signify in spite of their authors, and sometimes against their authors' most precious intentions.

It is one of the ambivalent implications of the decentering of the subject to have one's writing be the site of a necessary and inevitable expropriation. But this yielding of ownership over what one writes has an important set of political corollaries, for the taking up, reforming, deforming of one's words does open up a difficult future terrain of community, one in which the hope of ever fully recognizing oneself in the terms by which one signifies is sure to be disappointed. This not owning of one's words is there from the start, however, since speaking is always in some ways the speaking of a stranger through and as oneself, the melancholic reiteration of a language that one never chose, that one does not find as an instrument to be used, but that one is, as it were used by, expropriated in, as the unstable and continuing condition of the 'one' and the 'we', the ambivalent condition of the power that binds.

Notes

1 See Eve Kosousky 'Across Gender, Across Sexuality: Willa Cather and Others', *South Atlantic Quarterly*, vol. 88, No. 1 (Winter 1989), pp. 53–72.
2 See Gayle Rubin, 'Thinking Sex: Notes for a Radical Theory of the Politics of Sexuality', in Carole S. Vance, ed., *Pleasure and Danger* (New York, Routledge, 1984), pp. 267–319; Eve Kosofsky Sedgwick, *Epistemology of the Closet*, pp. 27–39.
3 Toward the end of the short theoretical conclusion of 'Thinking Sex' Rubin returns to feminism in a gestural way, suggesting that 'in the long run, feminism's critique of gender hierarchy must be incorporated into a radical theory of sex, and the critique of sexual oppression should enrich feminism. But an autonomous theory and politics specific to sexuality must be developed' (p. 309).

Section 3

Histories and Textuality

Introduction

Since the mid-1980s, literary critics have come to read literary texts more and more as material products of specific historical conditions and circumstances and the terms new historicism, cultural materialism and, more recently, cultural poetics, have all been used to describe a critical practice which has drawn on earlier Marxist, structuralist, post-structuralist and feminist work. In the essays represented in this section, what have been referred to as the 'language' and 'discourse' trajectories combine in different measures to produce a new practice of reading which responds both to what one critic has referred to as 'the textuality of history and the historicity of texts'. The writers gathered here, however, cannot be said to constitute a 'movement' in any coherent sense but, with the exception of Paul de Man, who is important for his theorizing of the relations between the aesthetic and the ideological, they all practise what might be thought of as a form of 'thick description' and all challenge the idea of literature as a sphere of autonomous aesthetic forms sealed off from other kinds of cultural practice.

According to one of its leading proponents, Stephen Greenblatt, new historicism is not so much a theory or doctrine of literary criticism as a textual practice. It is, however, a method of reading informed by and arising out of the theoretical ferment of the 1970s, so that its concern to examine the textual traces of the past is premised on the notion that the past is available to us only in the form of a textuality which is also embedded in that of the present. Old 'historicism', with its Hegelian idealist sense of history as a developing totality or its evolutionary notion of teleology, had produced such classic literary critical accounts of history as Tillyard's *The Elizabethan World Picture* (1943). For new historicists, however, there can be no such seamless, overarching unity, but only the shifting and contradictory representations of numerous 'histories'. History can only be a narrative construction involving a dialectical relationship of past and present concerns. Thus the critic is neither a transcendent commentator nor an objective chronicler because he/she is always implicated in the discourses which help to construct the object of knowledge. Hypothetical grand narratives such as the 'Elizabethan World Picture' are ideological projections based on the exclusivity of sameness. The new historicist is more concerned to focus attention on the multiple and contradictory material practices which embed each historical event or expressive act as contexts of production and reception.

These material practices do not, however, constitute historical 'givens'. Eroding the distinction between text and context, the new historicist views social contexts in themselves as narrative constructions produced through the discursive management of relations of power. There is no 'background' and no absolute and autonomous literary text: literariness as well as cultural value are terms opened to contestation and reconstruction.

The practice of new historicism is mainly associated with two groups of critics, one arising within studies of Romanticism (Marilyn Butler, Marjorie Levinson, Jerome McGann and David Simpson) and the other within Renaissance Studies (Jonathan Goldberg, Stephen Greenblatt and Louis Montrose). The first have been concerned to offer a critique of Romanticism's own self-presentation as aesthetic transcendence, egotistical sublime or poetic autonomy. The second group have used colonialism and theatricality both as political concepts and as looser metaphors to examine strategies of subversion and containment in Renaissance texts.

Stephen Greenblatt named the new historicism in 1988, but the practice had been developing throughout the 1980s, particularly in the pages of the journal *Representations*. In 1987 Marilyn Butler had called for a new historicist practice in her Cambridge lecture 'Repossessing the Past: The Case for an Open Literary History'. In this, she called also for the study of actual literary communities as they function within larger communities in time and in particular places. Butler and Greenblatt emphasize that political and social needs shape literary production and reception and argue that criticism must therefore examine the ways in which traces of social circulation are effaced to produce the illusion of the 'autonomous' literary work: the Ideal Poem.

New historicism follows a trajectory out of American formalist criticism with its close reading practices, through a hybrid mix of 1970s' theory, in order to return to history. Influences include Bakhtin, Althusser, Hayden White, Gadamer, Raymond Williams, Clifford Geertz and Foucault. Specific theoretical insights are derived from: Althusser's notion of ideology as contradictory and lived and his concept of the *relative* autonomy of the text and the interpellation of subjects in history; Gadamer's hermeneutic understanding of the past as ever constructed in relation to a present which is also a development out of that past; Hayden White's view of history as narrative construction or 'stories' and Bakhtin's articulation of all human utterances (including literary lexts) as social acts which are multiaccentual and available for divergent uses.

Probably the most pervasive influence on new historicist practice, however, is the work of Foucault. His writings have consistently shown how so-called objective historical accounts are always products of a will to power enacted through formations of knowledge within specific institutions. His own 'histories' resist the allure of 'total theories 'which offer overarching narratives and instead focus attention on the 'other' excluded by and constructed through such accounts. His view of power as omniscient though not omnipotent has been taken up by Greenblatt, but also by British 'cultural materialists' such as Jonathan Dollimore who also draw on Raymond Williams's later work on ideology. Greenblatt remains pessimistic, however, about the possibilities of subversion, viewing resistance as ultimately always contained. Cultural materialists tend to be more politically optimistic, tracing the potential for radical appropriation of dominant cultural meanings and values.

Though Bakhtin's work belongs to an earlier moment in the evolution of modern literary theory and though he has often been represented as a formalist, he is an important influence on later historicisms. Bakhtin saw, in the social conditions of language use, a variety of temporal provisional and contested attempts to fix meaning, a thesis which looks forward to the new historicist interest in the way in which power seems to produce its own subversion in order finally to better control subversion. His work first emerged alongside Russian Formalism in the 1920s and though Vološinov's concern was primarily with linguistics and Bakhtin's with literature, their work exhibits a number of common features which, along with other evidence, suggest that they were one and the same person, forced by circumstance in Stalin's Russia to publish under two names. In recent years the work undertaken by Vološinov's/Bakhtin has proved fertile ground for literary theorists for though aspects of work mark it as 'of its time', it also contains some remarkably post-structuralist themes.

In *Marxism and the Philosophy of Language* (1929) Vološinov's undertakes a powerful critique of the 'abstract objectivism' of Saussure's theory of language. The basis of his critique is the recognition that language is a social *process*; language is utterance, emerging from concrete social communication not from any abstract, objective system of langue. When viewed in its social contexts language appears not as a closed system of 'self-identical forms' (that is, the one-to-one correspondence of a signifier to a signified) but as a generative and continuous process, as utterances which respond to and anticipate other utterances. These utterances, existing in and as social different 'ideological themes' or meanings for their utterances. So, while acknowledging that the sign is not stable or fixed, Vološinov adds that 'multiplicity of meaning' has to be seen in relation to what he calls 'multi-accentuality'—that is, its openness to different evaluative orientations.

Bakhtin develops this view, seeing language not as singular and monolithic, but as plural and multiple; languages inscribed with various evaluative accents become socio-ideological languages intimately bound up with material and social conditions and with the contexts of their production—i.e. their 'heteroglossia'. Bakhtin applies this to the novel, the form which is exemplary in its ability to represent a dialogic interanimation of socio-ideological languages. The dialogic nature of the novel can be either open or closed; the author can either let the interplay of languages speak for itself or can impose a privileged authorial metalanguage. In Bakhtin the dialogic is closely linked to his notion of carnivalization—to popular forms that disrupt and relativize meaning in opposition to the 'official' discourse and its attempt to close down the polysemy of language.

The American historian Hayden White began to draw on Bakhtinian ideas, on modern narrative theory and on the post-structuralist account of language in order to develop his own critique of positivist historiography, some twenty years before the new historicism began to be named as such. The essay here, taken from a later book of 1987, *The Content of the Form*, draws extensively on earlier narratologists such as Genette for a theory of voice and on the linguist Benveniste for a distinction between discourse and narrative. Hayden White is interested in the way in which historiography aspires to the condition of science by presenting a third-person narrative which appears to be the reflection of events as they are inherently structured by the process of history. Historiography gathers its authority by seeming to dispense with authorial voice, by simulating scientific discourses which appear to reflect the way the world simply is. His essay sets out to show that 'real' events never tell their own stories and that history is always a process of making the real into an object of desire through manipulations of voice and temporality. Hayden White suggests that we desire real events to have a coherence that can, in the end, only ever be imaginary; we need to believe that the world arrives as story in order for moral authority to be established and for it to be perceived as inherent within and not imposed upon the order of nature or history. All narratives, including those of history, are inescapably structures of desire, moral impositions, manifestations of what G.E. Moore called the 'naturalistic fallacy': the belief that we might derive ought from is. Hayden White's essay ends with examples of various forms of narrative history and his critique reveals the ways in which historiography since the Middle Ages has always, in fact, derived is from ought.

Paul de Man was a leading figure in the so-called 'Yale School' of deconstruction and established his reputation with two books, in particular, *Blindness and Insight* (1971) and *Allegories of Reading* (1979), which continued the deconstructive project of revealing how rhetoric inevitably subverts logic. The essay reprinted here has been selected because it provides a good companion piece, from a literary critic, to Hayden White's critique of the uses of narrative in the writing of history. For de Man, literature avoids the kind of bad faith analysed in the accounts of history given by Hayden White, because it is necessarily self-conscious about its own rhetorical status. Theory is important because, though it shares with philosophy a commitment to method, it also shares with literature a recognition of the limitations of systematic method: ultimately texts must acknowledge their own rhetorical performativity, their own linguistic self-referentiality. If no conceptual scheme can explain a text, then in theory too, logic must succumb to rhetoric and a 'subversive element of unpredictability' will inevitably weaken any gesture towards explanatory systematisation. Objections to theory, de Man suggests, may thus be regarded as displaced symptoms of a resistance which is inherent in the theoretical enterprise itself – though inconceivable in the natural sciences and even 'unmentionable' in the social sciences (like history).

Two essays have been chosen to represent the new historicist turn. Jerome McGann's essay demonstrates the move away from formalist concerns or the pursuit of totally coherent theoretical paradigms and advocates a more historically oriented and particularized engagement with the text. McGann argues for the recognition of poetry as a social act and distinguishes between the text which is 'complete' and the poem which is ever open. His focus is on the circulation and reception of texts, arguing against the Kantian sense of the poem as Idea and viewing the critical failure to engage with the materiality of a text as necessarily leading to the blindness of literary critics to the time-bound nature of their own discourses. Greenblatt's essay pursues issues of the same kind, but with a performative panache which seeks to enact the new historicism in a more theatrical rather than sociological mode. The essay appeared in the collection entitled *Learning to Curse* (1990) and is written with a characteristic stylistic blend of wit and lucidity, 'resonance and wonder', which makes Greenblatt perhaps the most entertaining, as well as perspicacious, of the new historicists. Writing partly in response to those critics who have accused him of denying any agency to the human subject and of reading history as a narrative of containment, Greenblatt argues that the new historicism should on the contrary, be regarded as a critical practice concerned to tread a new path between the demand for strict 'relevance' on the one hand and an ahistorical formalism on the other. Neither human subjects nor human artefacts exist outside of history, but to admit therefore that both are historically shaped is not to suggest that they have no power to intervene in the processes of history. He regards his own work as concerned with a process of negotiation and exchange which leaves space for an attitude of 'wonder' (rather than reverence) towards the artefacts of the past which is yet inseparable from a sense of their hermeneutic resonance in the present. The aim is to grasp, simultaneously, 'the historicity of texts and the textuality of history'.

27 | M.M. Bakhtin,

From 'Discourse in the Novel', M. Holquist, ed. *The Dialogic Imagination* (1934), pp. 269–73; 295–6; 301–5

The novel is an artistic genre. Novelistic discourse is poetic discourse, but one that does not fit within the frame provided by the concept of poetic discourse as it now exists. This concept has certain underlying presuppositions that limit it. The very concept – in the course of its historical formulation from Aristotle to the present day – has been oriented toward the specific 'official' genres and connected with specific historical tendencies in verbal ideological life. Thus a whole series of phenomena remained beyond its conceptual horizon.

Philosophy of language, linguistics and stylistics (i.e., such as they have come down to us) have all postulated a simple and unmediated relation of speaker to his unitary and singular 'own' language, and have postulated as well a simple realization of this language in the monologic utterance of the individual. Such disciplines actually know only two poles in the life of language, between which are located all the linguistic and stylistic phenomena they know: on the one hand, the system of a *unitary language*, and on the other the *individual* speaking in this language.

Various schools of thought in the philosophy of language, in linguistics and stylistics have, in different periods (and always in close connection with the diverse concrete poetic and ideological styles of a given epoch), introduced into such concepts as 'system of language', 'monologic utterance', 'the speaking *individuum*', various differing nuances of meaning, but their basic content remains unchanged. This basic content is conditioned by the specific sociohistorical destinies of European languages and by the destinies of ideological discourse, and by those particular historical tasks that ideological discourse has fulfilled in specific social social spheres and at specific stages in its own historical development.

These tasks and destinies of discourse conditioned specific verbal-ideological movements, as well as various specific genres of ideological discourse, and ultimately the specific philosophical concept of discourse itself–in particular, the concept of poetic discourse, which has been at the heart of all concepts of style.

The strength and at the same time the limitations of such basic stylistic categories become apparent when such categories are seen as conditioned by specific historical destinies and by the task that an ideological discourse assumes. These categories arose from and were shaped by the historically *aktuell* forces at work in the verbal-ideological evolution of specific social groups; they comprised the theoretical expression of actualising forces that were in the process of creating a life for language.

These forces are the *forces that serve to unify and centralize the verbal ideological world.*

Unitary language constitutes the theoretical expression of the historical processes of linguistic unification and centralization, an expression of the centripetal forces of language. A unitary language is not something given [*dan*] but is always in essence posited [*zadan*]–and at every moment of its linguistic life it is opposed to the realities of heteroglossia. But at the same time it makes its real presence felt as a force for overcoming this heteroglossia, imposing specific limits to it, guaranteeing a certain maximum of mutual understanding and crystallizing into a real, although still relative, unity– the unity of the reigning conversational (everyday) and literary language, 'correct language'.

A common unitary language is a system of linguistic norms. But these norms do not constitute an abstract imperative; they are rather the generative forces of linguistic life, forces that struggle to overcome the heteroglossia of language, forces that unite and centralize verbal-ideological thought, creating within a heteroglot national language the firm, stable linguistic nucleus of an officially recognized literary language, or else defending an already formed language from the pressure of growing heteroglossia.

What we have in mind here is not an abstract linguistic minimum of a common language, in the sense of a system of elementary forms (linguistic symbols) guaranteeing a *minimum* level of comprehension in practical communication. We are taking language not as a system of abstract grammatical categories, but rather language conceived as ideologically saturated, language as a world view, even as a concrete opinion, insuring a *maximum* of mutual understanding in all spheres of ideological life. Thus a unitary language gives expression to forces working toward concrete verbal and ideological unification and centralization, which develop in vital connection with the processes of sociopolitical and cultural centralization.

Aristotelian poetics, the poetics of Augustine, the poetics of the medieval church, of 'the one language of truth', the Cartesian poetics of neoclassicism, the abstract grammatical universalism of Leibniz (the idea of a 'universal grammar'), Humboldt's insistence on the concrete – all these, whatever their differences in nuance, give expression to the same centripetal forces in socio-linguistic and ideological life; they serve one and the same project of centralizing and unifying the European languages. The victory of one reigning language (dialect) over the others, the supplanting of languages, their enslavement, the process of illuminating them with the True Word, the incorporation of Barbarians and lower social strata into a unitary language of culture and truth, the canonization of ideological systems, philology with its methods of studying and teaching dead languages, languages that were by that very fact 'unities', Indo-European linguistics with its focus of attention, directed away from language plurality to a single proto-language – all this determined the content and power of the category of 'unitary language' in linguistic and stylistic thought, and determined its creative, style-shaping role in the majority of the poetic genres that coalesced in the channel formed by those same centripetal forces of verbal-ideological life.

But the centripetal forces of the life of language, embodied in a 'unitary language', operate in the midst of heteroglossia. At any given moment of its evolution, language is stratified not only into linguistic dialects in the strict sense of the word (according to formal linguistic markers, especially phonetic), but also – and for us this is the essential point – into languages that are socio-ideological: languages of social groups, 'professional' and 'generic' languages, languages of generations and so forth. From this point of view, literary language itself is only one of these heteroglot languages – and in its turn is also stratified into languages (generic, period-bound and others). And this stratification and heteroglossia, once realized, is not only a static invariant of linguistic life, but also what insures its dynamics:

stratification and heteroglossia widen and deepen as long as language is alive and developing. Alongside the centripetal forces, the centrifugal forces of language carry on their uninterrupted work; alongside verbal-ideological centralization and unification, the uninterrupted processes of decentralization and disunification go forward.

Every concrete utterance of a speaking subject serves as a point where centrifugal as well as centripetal forces are brought to bear. The processes of centralization and decentralization, of unification and disunification, intersect in the utterance; the utterance not only answers the requirements of its own language as an individualized embodiment of a speech act, but it answers the requirements of heteroglossia as well; it is in fact an active participant in such speech diversity. And this active participation of every utterance in living heteroglossia determines the linguistic profile and style of the utterance to no less a degree than its inclusion in any normative-centralizing system of a unitary language.

Every utterance participates in the 'unitary language' (in its centripetal forces and tendencies) and at the same time partakes of social and historical heteroglossia (the centrifugal, stratifying forces).

Such is the fleeting language of a day, of an epoch, a social group, a genre, a school and so forth. It is possible to give a concrete and detailed analysis of any utterance, once having exposed it as a contradiction-ridden, tension-filled unity of two embattled tendencies in the life of language.

The authentic environment of an utterance, the environment in which it lives and takes shape, is dialogized heteroglossia, anonymous and social as language, but simultaneously concrete, filled with specific content and accented as an individual utterance.

At the time when major divisions of the poetic genres were developing under the influence of the unifying centralizing, centripetal forces of verbal-ideological life, the novel—and those artistic-prose genres that gravitate toward it—was being historically shaped by the current of decentralizing, centrifugal forces. At the time when poetry was accomplishing the task of cultural, national and political centralization of the verbal-ideological world in the higher official socio-ideological levels, on the lower levels, on the stages of local fairs and at buffoon spectacles, the heteroglossia of the clown sounded forth, ridiculing all 'languages' and dialects; there developed the literature of the *fabliaux* and *Schwänke* of street songs, folksayings, anecdotes, where there was no language-center at all, where there was to be found a lively play with the 'languages' of poets, scholars, monks, knights and others, where all 'languages' were masks and where no language could claim to be an authentic, incontestable face.

Heteroglossia, as organized in these low genres, was not merely hetero-glossial *vis-à-vis* the accepted literary language (in all its various generic expressions), that is, *vis-à-vis* the linguistic center of the verbal-ideological life of the nation and the epoch, but was a heterolossia consciously opposed to this literary language. It was parodic, and aimed sharply and polemically against the official languages of its given time. It was heteroglossia that had been dialogized.

Concrete socio-ideological language consciousness, as it becomes creative – that is, as it becomes active as literature – discovers itself already surrounded by heteroglossia and not at all a single, unitary language, inviolable and indisputable. The actively literary linguistic consciousness at all times and everywhere (that is, in all epochs of literature historically available to us) comes upon 'languages' and not language. Consciousness finds itself inevitably facing the necessity of *having to choose a language*. With each literary-verbal performance, consciousness must actively orient itself amidst heteroglossia, it must move in and occupy a position for itself within it, it chooses, in other words, a 'language'. Only by remaining in a closed environment, one without writing or thought, completely off the maps of socio-ideological becoming, could a man fail to sense this activity of selecting a language and rest assured in the inviolability of his own language, the conviction that his language is predetermined.

Even such a man, however, deals not in fact with a single language, but with languages – except that the place occupied by each of these languages is fixed and indisputable, the movement from one to the other is predetermined and not a thought process; it is as if these languages were in different chambers. They do not collide with each other in his consciousness, there is no attempt to coordinate them, to look at one of these languages through the eyes of another language.

Thus an illiterate peasant, miles away from any urban center, naively immersed in an unmoving and for him unshakable everyday word, nevertheless lived in several language systems: he prayed to God in one language (Church Slavonic), sang songs in another, spoke to his family in a third and, when he began to dictate petitions to the local authorities through a scribe, he tried speaking yet a fourth language (the official-literate language, 'paper' language). All these are *different languages*, even from the point of view of abstract socio-dialectological markers. But these languages were not dialogically coordinated in the linguistic consciousness of the peasant; he passed from one to the other without thinking, automatically: each was indisputably in its own place, and the place of each was indisputable. He was not yet able to regard one language (and the verbal world corresponding to it) through the eyes of another language (that is, the language of everyday life and the everyday world with the language of prayer or song, or vice versa).[1]

As soon as a critical interanimation of languages began to occur in the consciousness of our peasant, as soon as it became clear that these were not only various different languages but even internally variegated languages, that the ideological systems and approaches to the world that were indissolubly connected with these languages contradicted each other and in no way could live in peace and quiet with one another – then the inviolability and predetermined quality of these languages came to an end, and the necessity of actively choosing one's orientation among them began.

The language and world of prayer, the language and world of song, the language and world of labour and everyday life, the specific language and world of local authorities, the new language and world of the workers freshly immigrated to the city–all these languages and worlds sooner or later emerged from a state of peaceful and moribund equilibrium and revealed the speech diversity in each.

Of course the actively literary linguistic consciousness comes upon an even more varied and profound heteroglossia within literary language itself, as well as outside it. Any fundamental study of the stylistic life of the word must begin with this basic fact. The nature of the heteroglossia encountered and the means by which one orients oneself in it determine the concrete stylistic life the word will lead.

The compositional forms for appropriating and organizing heteroglossia in the novel, worked out during the long course of the genre's historical development, are extremely heterogeneous in their variety of genetic types. Each such compositional form is connected with particular stylistic possibilities, and demands particular forms for the artistic treatment of the heteroglot 'languages' introduced into it. We will pause here only on the most basic forms that are typical for the majority of novel types.

The so-called comic novel makes available a form for appropriating and organising heteroglossia that is both externally very vivid and at the same time historically profound; its classic repesentatives in England were Fielding, Smollett, Sterne, Dickens, Thackeray and others, and in Germany Hippel and Jean Paul.

In the English comic novel we find a comic-parodic re-processing of almost all the levels of literary language, both conversational and written, that were current at the time. Almost every novel we mentioned above as being a classic representative of this generic type is an encyclopedia of all strata and forms of literary language: depending on the subject being represented, the story-line parodically reproduces first the forms of parliamentary eloquence, then the eloquence of the court, or particular forms of parliamentary protocol, or court protocol, or forms used by reporters in newspaper articles, or the dry business languages of the City, or the dealings of speculators, or the pedantic speech of scholars, or the high epic style, or Biblical style, or the style of the hypocritical moral sermon or finally the way one or another concrete and socially determined personality, the subject of the story, happens to speak.

This usually parodic stylization of generic, professional and other strata of language is sometimes interrupted by the direct authorial word (usually as an expression of pathos, of Sentimental or idyllic sensibility), which directly embodies (without any refracting) semantic and axiological intentions of the author. But the primary source of language usage in the comic novel is a highly specific treatment of 'common language'. This 'common language'–usually the average norm of spoken and written language for a given social group–is taken by the author precisely as the *common view*, as the verbal approach to people and things normal for a given sphere of society, as the *going point of view* and the going *value*. To one degree or another, the author distances himself from this common language, he steps back and objectifies it, forcing his own intentions to refract and diffuse themselves through the medium of this common view that has become embodied in language (a view that is always superficial and frequently hypocritical).

The relationship of the author to a language conceived as the common view is not static – it is always found in a state of movement and oscillation that is more or less alive (this sometimes is a rhythmic oscillation): the author exaggerates, now strongly, now weakly, one or another aspect of the 'common language', sometimes abruptly exposing its inadequacy to its object and sometimes, on the contrary, becoming one with it, maintaining an almost imperceptible distance, sometimes even directly forcing it to reverberate with his own 'truth', which occurs when the author completely merges his own voice with the common view. As a consequence of such a merger, the aspects of common language, which in the given situation had been parodically exaggerated or had been treated as mere things, undergo change. The comic style demands of the author a lively to-and-fro movement in his relation to language, it demands a continual shifting of the distance between author and language, so that first some, then other aspects of language are thrown into relief. If such were not the case, the style would be monotonous or would require a greater individualization of the narrator – would, in any case, require a quite different means for introducing and organizing heteroglossia.

Against this same backdrop of the 'common language', of the impersonal, going opinion, one can also isolate in the comic novel those parodic stylizations of generic, professional and other languages we have mentioned, as well as compact masses of direct authorial discourse – pathos-filled, moral-didactic, sentimental-elegiac or idyllic. In the comic novel the direct authorial word is thus realized in direct, unqualified stylizations of poetic genres (idyllic, elegiac, etc.) or stylizations of rhetorical genres (the pathetic, the moral-didactic). Shifts from common language to parodying of generic and other languages and shifts to the direct authorial word may be gradual, or may be on the contrary quite abrupt. Thus does the system of language work in the comic novel.

We will pause for analysis on several examples from Dickens, from his novel *Little Dorrit*.

1 The conference was held at four or five o'clock in the afternoon, when all the region of Harley Street, Cavendish Square, was resonant of carriages-wheels and double-knocks. It had reached this point when Mr. Merdle came home from *his daily occupation of causing the British name to be more and more respected in all parts of the civilized globe capable of appreciation of wholewide commercial enterprise and gigantic combinations of skill and capital.* For, though nobody knew with the last precision what Mr. Merdle's business was, except that it was to coin money, these were the terms in which everybody defined it on all ceremonious occasions, and which it was the last new polite reading of the parable of the camel and the needle's eye to accept without inquiry. (Book I, ch. 33)

The italicized portion represents a parodic stylization of the language of ceremonial speeches (in parliaments and at banquets). The shift into this style is prepared for by the sentence's construction, which from the very beginning is kept within bounds by a somewhat ceremonious epic tone. Further on – and already in the language of the author (and consequently in a different style) – the parodic meaning of the ceremoniousness of Merdle's labors becomes apparent: such a characterization turns out to be 'another's speech', to be taken only in quotation marks ('these were the terms in which everybody defined it on all ceremonious occasions').

Thus the speech of another is introduced into the author's discourse (the story) in *concealed form*, that is, without any of the *formal* markers usually accompanying such speech, whether direct or indirect. But this is not just another's speech in the same 'language' – it is another's utterance in a language that is itself 'other' to the author as well, in the archaicized language of oratorical genres associated with hypocritical official celebrations.

> 2 In a day or two it was announced to all the town, that Edmund Sparkler, Esquire, son-in-law of the eminent Mr. Merdle of worldwide renown, was made one of the Lords of the Circumlocution Office; and proclamation was issued, to all true believers, that this admirable *appointment was to be hailed as a graceful and gracious mark of homage, rendered by the graceful and gracious Decimus, to that commercial interest which must ever in a great commercial country – and all the rest of it, with blast of trumpet.* So bolstered by this mark of Government homage, the *wonderful* Bank and all the other *wonderful* undertakings went on and went up; and gapers came to Harley Street, Cavendish Square, only to look at the house where the golden-wonder lived. (Book 2, ch. 12)

Here, in the italicized portion, another's speech in another's (official-ceremonial) language is openly introduced as indirect discourse. But it is surrounded by the hidden, diffused speech of another (in the same official-ceremonial language) that clears the way for the introduction of a form more easily perceived *as* another's speech and that can reverberate more fully as such. The clearing of the way comes with the word 'Esquire', characteristic of official speech, added to Sparkler's name; the final confirmation that this is another's speech comes with the epithet 'wonderful'. This epithet does not of course belong to the author but to that same 'general opinion' that had created the commotion around Merdle's inflated enterprises.

> 3 It was a dinner to provoke an appetite, though he had not had one. The rarest dishes, sumptuously cooked and sumptuously served; the choicest fruits, the most exquisite wines; marvels of workmanship in gold and silver, china and glass; innumerable things delicious to the senses of taste, smell, and sight, were insinuated into its composition. *O, what a wonderful man this Merdle, what a great man, what a master man, how blessedly and enviably endowed – in one word*, what a rich man! (Book 2, ch. 12)

The beginning is a parodic stylization of high epic style. What follows is an enthusiastic glorification of Merdle, a chorus of his admirers in the form of the concealed speech of another (the italicized portion). The whole point here is to expose the real basis for such glorification which is to unmask the chorus' hypocrisy: 'wonderful', 'great', 'master', 'endowed' can all be replaced by the single word 'rich'. This act of authorial unmasking, which is openly accomplished within the boundaries of a single simple sentence, merges with the unmasking of another's speech. The ceremonial emphasis on glorification is complicated by a second emphasis that is indignant, ironic, and this is the one that ultimately predominates in the final unmasking words of the sentence.

We have before us a typical double-accented, double-styled *hybrid construction*.

What we are calling a hybrid construction is an utterance that belongs, by its grammatical (syntactic) and compositional markers, to a single speaker, but that actually contains mixed within it two utterances, two speech manners, two styles, two 'languages', two semantic and axiological belief systems. We repeat, there is no formal–compositional and syntactic–boundary between these utterances, styles, languages, belief systems, the division of voices and languages takes place within the limits of a single syntactic whole, often within the limits of a simple sentence. It frequently happens that even one and the same word will belong simultaneously to two languages, two belief systems that intersect in a hyrid construction–and, consequently, the word has two contradictory meanings, two accents. As we shall see, hybrid constructions are of enormous significance in novel style.

4 But Mr. Tite Barnacle was a buttoned-up man, and *consequently* a weighty one. (Book 2, ch. 12)

The above sentence is an example of *pseudo-objective motivation*, one of the forms for concealing another's speech–in this example, the speech of 'current opinion'. If judged by the formal markers above, the logic motivating the sentence seems to belong to the author, i.e., he is formally at one with it; but in actual fact, the motivation lies within the subjective belief system of his characters, or of general opinion.

Pseudo-objective motivation is generally characteristic of novel style,[2] since it is one of the manifold forms for concealing another's speech in hybrid construction. Subordinate conjunctions and link words ('thus', 'because', 'for the reason that', 'in spite of' and so forth), as well as words used to maintain a logical sequence ('therefore', 'consequently', etc.) lose their direct authorial intention, take on the flavour of someone else's language, become refracted or even completely reified.

Notes

1 We are of course deliberately simplifying: the real life peasant could and did do this to a certain extent.
2 Such a device is unthinkable in the epic.

28 | Hayden White,

From 'The Value of Narrativity in the Representation of
Reality' (1987), pp, 345–8; 401; 403; 405–7.

To raise the question of the nature of narrative is to invite reflection on the
very nature of culture and, possibly, even on the nature of humanity itself.
So natural is the impulse to narrate, so inevitable is the form of narrative
for any report on the way things really happened, that narrativity could
appear problematical only in a culture in which it was absent – or, as in
some domains of contemporary Western intellectual and artistic culture,
programmatically refused. Considered as panglobal facts of culture, narrative
and narration are less problems than simply data. As the late (and profoundly
missed) Roland Barthes remarked, narrative 'is simply there like life
itself . . . international, transhistorical, transcultural'. Far from being a
problem, then, narrative might well be considered a solution to a problem
of general human concern, namely, the problem of how to translate knowing
into telling, the problem of fashioning human experience into a form
assimilable to structures of meaning that are generally human rather than
culture-specific. We may not be able fully to comprehend specific thought
patterns of another culture, but we have relatively less difficulty
understanding a story coming from another culture, however exotic that
culture may appear to us. As Barthes says, 'narrative is *translatable* without
fundamental damage', in a way that a lyric poem or a philosophical discourse
is not.

This suggests that far from being one code among many that a culture
may utilize for endowing experience with meaning, narrative is a meta-
code, a human universal on the basis of which transcultural messages
about the nature of a shared reality can be transmitted. Arising, as Barthes
says, between our experience of the world and our efforts to describe that
experience in language, narrative 'ceaselessly substitutes meaning for the
straightforward copy of the events recounted'. And it would follow that
the absence of narrative capacity or a refusal of narrative indicates an
absence of meaning itself.

But what kind of meaning is absent or refused? The fortunes of narrative
in the history of historical writing give us some insight into this question.
Historians do not have to report their truths about the real world in narrative
form. They may choose other, nonnarrative, even anti-narrative modes of
representation, such as the meditation, the anatomy, or the epitome.
Tocqueville, Burckhardt, Huizinga, and Braudel, to mention only the most
notable masters of modern historiography, refused narrative in certain of
their historiographical works, presumably on the asumption that the meaning

of the events with which they wished to deal did not lend itself to representation in the narrative mode. They refused to tell a story about the past or rather, they did not tell a story with well-marked beginning, middle, and end phases, they did not impose upon the processes that interested them the form that we normally associate with storytelling. While they certainly narrated their accounts of the reality that they perceived, or thought they perceived, to exist within or behind the evidence they had examined, they did not narrativize that reality, did not impose upon it the form of a story. And their example permits us to distinguish between a historical discourse that narrates and a discourse that narrativizes, between a discourse that openly adopts a perspective that looks out on the world and reports it and a discourses that feigns to make the world speak itself and speak itself as a story.

The idea that narrative should be considered less as a form of representation than as a manner of speaking about events, whether real or imaginary, has been recently elaborated within a discussion of the relationship between discourse and narrative that has arisen in the wake of Structuralism and is associated with the work of Jakobson, Benveniste, Genette, Todorov, and Barthes. Here narrative is regarded as a manner of speaking characterized, as Genette expresses it, 'by a certain number of exclusions and restrictive conditions' that the more 'open' form of discourse does not impose upon the speaker. According to Genette, Benveniste showed that certain grammatical forms like the pronoun 'I' (and its implicit reference 'thou'), the pronominal 'indicators' (certain demonstrative pronouns), the adverbial indicators (like 'here', 'now', 'yesterday', 'today', 'tomorrow', etc.) and, at least in French, certain verb tenses like the present, the present perfect, and future, find themselves limited to discourse, while narrative in the strictest sense is distinguished by the exclusive use of the third person and of such forms as the preterite and the pluperfect.

This distinction between discourse and narrative is, of course, based solely on an analysis of the grammatical features of two modes of discourse in which the 'objectivity' of the one and the 'subjectivity' of the other are definable primarily by a 'linguistic order of criteria'. The 'subjectivity' of the discourse is given by the the presence, explicit or implicit, of an 'ego' who can be defined 'only as the person who maintains the discourse'. By contrast, the 'objectivity of narrative is defined by the absence of all reference to the narrator'. In the narrativizing discourse, then, we can say, with Benveniste, that 'truly there is no longer a "narrator"'. The events are chronologically recorded as they appear on the horizon of the story. No one speaks. The events seem to tell themselves'.

What is involved in the production of a discourse in which 'events seem to tell themselves especially when it is a matter of events that are explicitly identified as real rather than imaginary as in the case of historical representative? In a discourse having to do with manifestly imaginary events, which are the 'contents' of fictional discourses, the question poses few problems. For why should not imaginary events be represented as speaking themselves'? Why should not, in the domain of the imaginary, even the stones themselves speak—like Memnon's column when touched by the rays of the sun? But real events should not speak, should not tell themselves. Real events should simply be, they can perfectly well serve as the referents of a discourse, can be spoken about, but they should not pose as the subjects of a narrative. The lateness of the invention of historical discourse in human history and the difficulty of sustaining it in times of cultural breakdown (as in the early Middle Ages) suggest the artificiality of the notion that real events could 'speak themselves' or be represented as 'telling their own story'. Such a fiction would have posed no problems before the distinction between real and imaginary events was imposed upon the storyteller, storytelling becomes a problem only after two orders of events dispose themselves before the storyteller as possible components of stories and storytelling is compelled to exfoliate under the injunction to keep the two orders unmixed in discourse. What we wish to call mythic narrative is under no obligation to keep the two orders of events, real and imaginary, distinct from one another. Narrative becomes a problem only when we wish to give to real events the form of story. It is because real events do not offer themselves as stories that their narrativization is so difficult.

What is involved, then, in that finding of the 'true story', that discovery of the real story within or behind the events that come to us in the chaotic form of 'historical records'? What wish is enacted, what desire is gratified, by the fantasy that real events are properly represented when they can be shown to display the formal coherency of a story? In the enigma of this wish, this desire, we catch a glimpse of the cultural function of narrativizing discourse in general, an intimation of the psychological impulse behind the apparently universal need not only to narrate but to give to events an aspect of narrativity.

Historiography is an especially good ground on which to consider the nature of narration and narrativity because it is here that our desire for the imaginary, the possible, must contest with the imperatives of the real, the actual. If we view narration and narrativity as the instruments with which the conflicting claims of the imaginary and the real are mediated, arbitrated, or resolved in a discourse, we begin to comprehend both the appeal of narrative and the grounds for refusing it. If putatively real events are represented in a nonnarrative form, what kind of reality is it that offers itself, or is conceived to offer itself, to perception in this form? What would a nonnarrative representation of historical reality look like? In answering this question, we do not necessarily arrive at a solution to the problem of the nature of narrative, but we do begin to catch a glimpse of the basis for the appeal of narrativity as a form for the representation of events construed to be real rather than imaginary.

Fortunately, we have examples aplenty of representations of historical reality that are nonnarrative in form. Indeed, the *doxa* of the modern historiographical establishment has it that there are three basic kinds of historical representation – the annals, the chronicle, and the history proper – the imperfect 'historicality' of two of which is evidenced in their failure to attain to full narrativity of the events of which they treat. Needless to say, narrativity alone does not permit the distinction of the three kinds. In order for an account of events, even of past events or of past real events, to count as a proper history, it is not enough that it display all of the features of narrativity. In addition, the account must manifest a proper concern for the judicious handling of evidence, and it must honor the chronological order of the original occurrence of the events of which it treats as a baseline not to be transgressed in the classification of any given event as either a cause or an effect. But by common consent, it is not enough that an historical account deal in real, rather than merely imaginary, events, and it is not enough that the account represents events in its order of discourse according to the chronological sequence in which they originally occurred. The events must be not only registered within the chronological framework of their original occurrence but narrated as well, that is to say, revealed as possessing a structure, an order of meaning, that they do not possess as mere sequence.

Needless to say, also, the annals form lacks completely this narrative component, since it consists only of a list of events ordered in chronological sequence. The chronicle, by contrast, often seems to wish to tell a story, aspires to narrativity, but typically fails to achieve it. More specifically, the chronicle usually is marked by a failure to achieve narrative closure. It does not so much conclude as simply terminate. It starts out to tell a story but breaks off *in media res* , in the chronicler's own present, it leaves things unresolved, or rather, it leaves them unresolved in a storylike way.

While annals represent historical reality as if real events did not display the form of story, the chronicler represents it as if real events appeared to human consciousness in the form of unfinished stories. And the official wisdom has it that however objective a historian might be in his reporting of events, however judicious he has been in his assessment of evidence, however punctilious he has been in his dating of *res gestae,* his account remains something less than a proper history if he has failed to give to reality the form of a story. Where there is no narrative, Croce said, there is no history. And Peter Gay, writing from a perspective directly opposed to the relativism of Croce, puts it just as starkly: 'Historical narration without analysis is trivial, historical analysis without narration is incomplete.' Gay's formulation calls up the Kantian bias of the demand for narration in historical representation, for it suggests, to paraphrase Kant, that historical narratives without analysis are empty, while historical analyses without narrative are blind. Thus we may ask, What kind of insight does narrative give into the nature of real events? What kind of blindness with respect to reality does narrativity dispell?

* * * * *

Modern commentators have remarked on the fact that the annalist recorded the Battle of Poitiers of 732 but failed to note the Battle of Tours which occurred in the same year and which, as every schoolboy knows, was one of 'the ten great battles of world history'. But even if the annalist had known of Tours, what principle or rule of meaning would have required him to record it? It is only from our knowledge of the subsequent history of Western Europe that we can presume to rank events in terms of their world-historical significance, and even then that significance is less world historical than simply Western European, representing a tendency of modern historians to rank events in the record hierarchically from within a perspective that is culture-specific, not universal at all.

It is this need or impulse to rank events with respect to their significance for the culture or group that is writing its own history that makes a narrative representation of real events possible. It is surely much more 'universalistic' simply to record events as they come to notice. And at the minimal level on which the annals unfold, what gets put into the account is of much greater theoretical importance for the understanding of the nature of narrative than what gets left out. But this does raise the question of the function in this text of the recording of those years in which 'nothing happened'. Every narrative, however seemingly 'full', is constructed on the basis of a set of events that might have been included but were left out, this is as true of imaginary narratives as it is of realistic ones. And this consideration permits us to ask what kind of notion of reality authorizes construction of a narrative account of reality in which continuity rather than discountinuity governs the articulation of the discourse.

* * * * *

Interest in the social system, which is nothing other than a system of human relationships governed by law, creates the possibility of conceiving the kinds of tensions, conflicts, struggles, and their various kinds of resolutions that we are accustomed to find in any representation of reality presenting itself to us as a history. This permits us to speculate that the growth and development of historical consciousness, which is attended by a concomitant growth and development of narrative capability (of the sort met with in the chronicle as against the annals form), has something to do with the extent to which the legal system functions as a subject of concern [. . .]

And this suggests that narrativity, certainly in factual storytelling and probably in fictional storytelling as well, is intimately related to, if not a function of, the impulse to moralize reality, that is, to identify it with the social system that is the source of any morality that we can imagine.

* * * * *

I do not offer these reflections on the relation between historiography and narrative as aspiring to anything other than an attempt to illuminate the distinction between story elements and plot elements in the historical discourse. Common opinion has it that the plot of a narrative imposes a meaning on the events that make up its story level by revealing at the end a structure that was immanent in the events all along. What I am trying to establish is the nature of this immanence in any narrative account of real events, events that are offered as the proper content of historical discourse. These events are real not because they occurred but because, first, they were remembered and, second, they are capable of finding a place in a chronologically ordered sequence. In order, however, for an account of them to be considered a historical account, it is not enough that they be recorded in the order of their original occurrence. It is the fact that they can be recorded otherwise, in an order of narrative, that makes them, at one and the same time, questionable as to their authenticity and susceptible to being considered as tokens of reality. In order to qualify as historical, an event must be susceptible to at least two narrations of its occurrence. Unless at least two versions of the same set of events can be imagined, there is no reason for the historian to take upon himself the authority of giving the true account of what really happened. The authority of the historical narrative is the authority of reality itself, the historical account endows this reality with form and thereby makes it desirable by the imposition upon its processes of the formal coherency that only stories possess.

The history, then, belongs to the category of what might be called 'the discourse of the real', as against the 'discourse of the imaginary' or 'the discourse of desire'. The formulation is Lacanian, obviously, but I do not wish to push its Lacanian aspects too far. I merely wish to suggest that we can comprehend the appeal of historical discourse by recognizing the extent to which it makes the real desirable, makes the real into an object of desire, and does so by its imposition, upon events that are represented as real, of the formal coherency that stories possess. Unlike that of the annals, the reality represented in the historical narrative, in 'speaking itself', speaks to us, summons us from afar (this 'afar'is the land of forms), and displays to us a formal coherency to which we ourselves aspire. The historical narrative, as against the chronicle, reveals to us a world that is putatively 'finished', done with, over, and yet not dissolved, not falling apart. In this world, reality wears the mask of a meaning, the completeness and fullness of which we can only imagine, never experience. Insofar as historical stories can be completed, can be given narrative closure, can be shown to have had a plot all along, they give to reality the odor of the ideal. This is why the plot of a historical narrative is always an embarrassment and has to be presented as 'found' in the events rather than put there by narrative techniques [. . .]

This puts us close to a possible characterization of the demand for closure in the history, for the want of which the chronicle form is adjudged to be deficient as a narrative. The demand for closure in the historical story is a demand, I suggest, for moral meaning, a demand that sequences of real events be assessed as to their significance as elements of a moral drama. Has any historical narrative ever been written that was not informed not only by moral awareness but specifically by the moral authority of the narrator? It is difficult to think of any historical work produced during the nineteenth century, the classic age of historical narrative, that was not given the force of a moral judgement on the events it related. [. . .]

But on what other grounds could a narrative of real events possibly conclude? When it is a matter of recounting the concourse of real events, what other 'ending' could a given sequence of such events have than a 'moralizing' ending? What else could narrative closure consist of than the passage from one moral order to another? I confess that I cannot think of any other way of 'concluding' an account of real events, for we cannot say, surely, that any sequence of real events actually comes to an end, that reality itself disappears, that events of the order of the real have ceased to happen. Such events could only seem to have ceased to happen when meaning is shifted, and shifted by narrative means, from one physical or social space to another. Where moral sensitivity is lacking, as it seems to be in an annalistic account of reality, or is only potentially present, as it appears to be in a chronicle, not only meaning but the means to track such shifts of meaning, that is, narrativity, appears to be lacking also. Where, in any account of reality, narrativity is presesnt, we can be sure that morality or a moralizing impluse is present too. There is no other way that reality can be endowed with the kind of meaning that both displays itself in its consummation and withholds itself by its displacement to another story 'waiting to be told' just beyond the confines of 'the end'.

What I have been working around to is the question of the value attached to narrativity itself, especially in representations of reality of the sort embodied in historical discourse. It may be thought that I have stacked the cards in favor of my thesis – that narrativizing discourse serves the purpose of moralizing judgements – by my use of exclusively medieval materials. And perhaps I have, but it is the modern historiographical community that has distinguished between the annals, chronicle, and history forms of discourse on the basis of their attainment of narrative fullness or failure to attain it and this same scholarly community has yet to account for the fact that just when, by its own account, historiography was transformed into an 'objective' discipline, it was the narrativity of the historical discourse that was celebrated as one of the signs of its maturation as a fully 'objective' discipline – a science of a special sort but a science nonetheless. It is historians themselves who have transformed narrativity from a manner of speaking into a paradigm of the form that reality itself displays to a realistic consciousness. It is they who have made narrativity into a value, the presence of which in a discourse having to do with 'real' events signals at once its objectivity, its seriousness, and its realism.

What I have sought to suggest is that this value attached to narrativity in the representation of real events arised out of a desire to have real events display the coherence, integrity, fullness, and closure of an image of life that is and can only be imaginary. The notion that sequences of real events possess the formal attributes of the stories we tell about imaginary events could only have its origin in wishes, daydreams, reveries. Does the world really present itself to perception in the form of well-made stories, with central subjects, proper beginnings, middles, and ends, and a coherence that permits us to see 'the end' in every beginning? Or does it present itself more in the forms that the annals and chronicle suggest, either as mere sequence without beginning or end or as sequences of beginnings that only terminate and never conclude? And does the world, even the social world, ever really come to us as already narrativized, already 'speaking itself' from beyond the horizon of our capacity to make scientific sense of it? Or is the fiction of such a world, capable of speaking itself and of displaying itself as a form of a story, necessary for the establishment of that moral authority without which the notion of a specifically social reality would be unthinkable? If it were only a matter of realism in representation, one could make a pretty good case for both the annals and chronicle forms as paradigms of ways that reality offers iteslf to perception. Is it possible that their supposed want of objectivity, manifested in their failure to narrativize reality adequately, has to do, not at all with the modes of perception that they presuppose, but with their failure to represent the moral under the aspect of the aesthetic? And could we answer that question without giving a narrative account of the history of objectivity itself, an account that would already prejudice the outcome of the story we would tell in favor of the moral in general? Could we ever narrativize without moralizing?

29 | Paul de Man,

'The Resistance to Theory', *Yale French Studies*, 63, (1982) pp. 355–71

This essay was not originally intended to address the question of teaching directly, although it was supposed to have a didactic and an educational function–which it failed to achieve. It was written at the request of the Committee on the Research Activities of the Modern Language Association as a contribution to a collective volume entitled *Introduction to Scholarship in Modern Languages and Literatures*. I was asked to write the section on literary theory. Such essays are expected to follow a clearly determined program: they are supposed to provide the reader with a select but comprehensive list of the main trends and publications in the field, to synthesize and classify the main problematic areas and to lay out a critical and programmatic projection of the solutions which can be expected in the foreseeable future. All this with a keen awareness that, ten years later, someone will be asked to repeat the same exercise.

I found it difficult to live up, in minimal good faith, to the requirements of this program and could only try to explain, as concisely as possible, why the main theoretical interest of literary theory consists in the impossibility of its definition. The Committee rightly judged that this was an inauspicious way to achieve the pedagogical objectives of the volume and commissioned another article. I thought their decision altogether justified, as well as interesting in its implications for the teaching of literature.

I tell this for two reasons. First, to explain the traces in the article of the original assignment which account for the awkwardness of trying to be more retrospective and more general than one can legitimately hope to be. But secondly, because the predicament also reveals a question of general interest: that of the relationship between the scholarship (the key word in the title of the MLA volume), the theory, and the teaching of literature.

Overfacile opinion notwithstanding, teaching is not primarily an intersubjective relationship between people but a cognitive process in which self and other are only tangentially and contiguously involved. The only teaching worthy of the name is scholarly, not personal; analogies between teaching and various aspects of show business or guidance counselling are more often than not excuses for having abdicated the task. Scholarship has, in principle, to be eminently teachable. In the case of literature, such scholarship involves at least two complementary areas: historical and philological facts as the preparatory condition for understanding, and methods of reading or interpretation. The latter is admittedly an open discipline, which can, however, hope to evolve by rational means, despite internal crises, controversies and polemics. As a controlled reflection on the formation of method, theory rightly proves to be entirely compatible with teaching, and one can think of numerous important theoreticians who are or were also prominent scholars. A question arises only if a tension develops between methods and the knowledge which those methods allow one to reach. If there is indeed something about literature, as such, which allows for a discrepancy between truth and method, between *Wahrheit* and *Methode*, then scholarship and theory are no longer necessarily compatible; as a first casualty of this complication, the notion of 'literature as such' as well as the clear distinction between history and interpretation can no longer be taken for granted. For a method that cannot be made to suit the 'truth' of its object can only teach delusion. Various developments, not only in the contemporary scene but in the long and complicated history of literary and linguistic instruction, reveal symptoms that suggest that such a difficulty is an inherent focus of the discourse about literature. These uncertainties are manifest in the hostility directed at theory in the name of ethical and aesthetic values, as well as in the recuperative attempts of theoreticians to reassert their own subservience to these values. The most effective of these attacks will denounce theory as an obstacle to scholarship and, consequently, to teaching. It is worth examining whether, and why, this is the case. For if this is indeed so, then it is better to fail in teaching what should not be taught than to succeed in teaching what is not true.

A general statement about literary theory should not, in theory, start from pragmatic considerations. It should address such questions as the definition of literature (what is literature?) and discuss the distinction between literary and non-literary uses of language, as well as between literary and non-verbal forms of art. It should then proceed to the descriptive taxonomy of the various aspects and species of the literary genus and to the normative rules that are bound to follow from such a classification. Or, if one rejects a scholastic for a phenomenological model, one should attempt a phenomenology of the literary activity as writing, reading or both, or of the literary work as the product, the correlate of such an activity. Whatever the approach taken (and several other theoretically justifiable starting-points can be imagined) it is certain that considerable difficulties will arise at once, difficulties that cut so deep that even the most elementary task of scholarship, the delimitation of the corpus and the *état présent* of the question, is bound to end in confusion, not necessarily because the bibliography is so large but because it is impossible to fix its borderlines. Such predictable difficulties have not prevented many writers on literature from proceeding along theoretical rather than pragmatic lines, often with considerable success. It can be shown however that, in all cases, this success depends on the power of a system (philosophical, religious or ideological) that may well remain implicit but that determines an *a priori* conception of what is 'literary' by starting out from the premises of the system rather than from the literary thing itself–if such a 'thing' indeed exists. This last qualification is of course a real question which in fact accounts for the predictability of the difficulties just alluded to: if the condition of existence of an entity is itself particularly critical, then the theory of this entity is bound to fall back into the pragmatic. The difficult and inconclusive history of literary theory indicates that this is indeed the case for literature in an even more manifest manner than for other verbalized occurrences such as jokes, for example, or even dreams. The attempt to treat literature theoretically may as well resign itself to the fact that it has to start out from empirical considerations.

Pragmatically speaking, then, we know that there has been, over the last fifteen to twenty years, a strong interest in something called literary theory and that, in the United States, this interest has at times coincided with the importation and reception of foreign, mostly but not always continental influences. We also know that this wave of interest now seems to be receding as some satiation or disappointment sets in after the initial enthusiasm. Such an ebb and flow is natural enough, but it remains interesting, in this case, because it makes the depth of the resistance to literary theory so manifest. It is a recurrent strategy of any anxiety to defuse what it considers threatening by magnification or minimization, by attributing to it claims to power of which it is bound to fall short. If a cat is called a tiger it can easily be dismissed as a paper tiger; the question remains, however, why one was so scared of the cat in the first place. The same tactic works in reverse: calling the cat a mouse and then deriding it for its pretence to be mighty. Rather than being drawn into this polemical whirlpool, it might be better to try to call the cat a cat and to document, however briefly, the contemporary version of the resistance to theory in this country.

The predominant trends in North American literary criticism, before the 1960s, were certainly not averse to theory, if by theory one understands the rooting of literary exegesis and of critical evaluation in a system of some conceptual generality. Even the most intuitive, empirical and theoretically low-key writers on literature made use of a minimal set of concepts (tone, organic form, allusion, tradition, historical situation, etc.) of at least some general import. In several other cases, the interest in theory was publicly asserted and practised. A broadly shared methodology, more or less overtly proclaimed, links together such influential text books of the era as *Understanding Poetry* (Brooks and Warren), *Theory of Literature* (Wellek and Warren) and *The Fields of Light* (Reuben Brower) or such theoretically oriented works as *The Mirror and the Lamp*, *Language as Gesture*, and *The Verbal Icon*.

Yet, with the possible exception of Kenneth Burke and, in some respects, Northrop Frye, none of these authors would have considered themselves theoreticians in the post-1960 sense of the term, nor did their work provoke as strong reactions, positive or negative, as that of later theoreticians. There were polemics, no doubt, and differences in approach that cover a wide spectrum of divergencies, yet the fundamental curriculum of literary studies as well as the talent and training expected for them were not being seriously challenged. New Critical approaches experienced no difficulty fitting into the academic establishments without their practitioners having to betray their literary sensibilities in any way; several of its representatives pursued successful parallel careers as poets or novelists next to their academic functions. Nor did they experience difficulties with regard to a national tradition which, though certainly less tyrannical than its European counterparts, is nevertheless far from powerless. The perfect embodiment of the New Criticism remains, in many respects, the personality and the ideology of T.S. Eliot, a combination of original talent, traditional learning, verbal wit and moral earnestness, an Anglo-American blend of intellectual gentility not so repressed as not to afford tantalising glimpses of darker psychic and political depths, but without breaking the surface of an ambivalent decorum that has its own complacencies and seductions. The normative principles of such a literary ambiance are cultural and ideological rather than theoretical, oriented towards the integrity of a social and historical self rather than towards the impersonal consistency that theory requires. Culture allows for, indeed advocates, a degree of cosmopolitanism, and the literary spirit of the American Academy of the fifties was anything but provincial. It had no difficulty appreciating and assimilating outstanding products of a kindred spirit that originated in Europe: Curtius, Auerbach, Croce, Spitzer, Alonso, Valéry and also, with the exception of some of his works, J.P. Sartre. The inclusion of Sartre in this list is important, for it indicates that the dominant cultural code we are trying to evoke cannot simply be assimilated to a political polarity of the left and the right, of the academic and the non-academic, of Greenwich Village and Gambier, Ohio. Politically oriented and predominantly non-academic journals, of which the *Partisan Review* of the fifties remains the best example, did not (after due allowance is made for all proper reservations and distinctions) stand in any genuine opposition to the New Critical approaches. The broad, though negative, consensus that brings these extremely diverse trends and individuals together is their shared resistance to theory. This diagnosis is borne out by the arguments and complicities that have since come to light in a more articulate opposition to the common opponent.

The interest of these considerations would be at most anecdotal (the historical impact of twentieth-century literary discussion being so slight) if it were not for the theoretical implications of the resistance to theory. The local manifestations of this resistance are themselves systematic enough to warrant one's interest.

What is it that is being threatened by the approaches to literature that developed during the sixties and that now, under a variety of designations, make up the ill-defined and somewhat chaotic field of literary theory? These approaches cannot be simply equated with any particular method or country. Structuralism was not the only trend to dominate the stage, not even in France, and structuralism as well as semiology are inseparable from prior tendencies in the Slavic domain. In Germany, the main impulses have come from other directions, from the Frankfurt school and more orthodox Marxists, from post-Husserlian phenomenology and post-Heideg-gerian hermeneutics, with only minor inroads made by structural analysis. All these trends have had their share of influence in the United States, in more or less productive combinations with nationally rooted concerns. Only a nationally or personally competitive view of history would wish to hierarchize such hard-to-label movements. The possibility of doing literary theory, which is by no means to be taken for granted, has itself become a consciously reflected-upon question and those who have progressed furthest in this question are the most controversial but also the best sources of information. This certainly includes several of the names loosely connected with structuralism, broadly enough defined to include Saussure, Jakobson and Barthes as well as Greimas and Althusser, that is to say, so broadly defined as to be no longer of use as a meaningful historical term.

Literary theory can be said to come into being when the approach to literary texts is no longer based on non-linguistic, that is to say historical and aesthetic, considerations or, to put it somewhat less crudely, when the object of discussion is no longer the meaning or the value but the modalities of production and of reception of meaning and of value prior to their establishment – the implication being that this establishment is problematic enough to require an autonomous discipline of critical investigation to consider its possibility and its status. Literary history, even when considered at furthest remove from the platitudes of positivistic historicism, is still the history of an understanding of which the possibility is taken for granted. The question of the relationship between aesthetics and meaning is more complex, since aesthetics apparently has to do with the *effect* of meaning rather than with its content *per se*. But aesthetics is in fact, ever since its development just before and with Kant, a phenomenalism of a process of meaning and understanding, and it may be naive in that it postulates (as its name indicates) a phenomenology of art and of literature which may well be what is at issue. Aesthetics is part of a universal system of philosophy rather than a specific theory. In the nineteenth-century philosophical tradition, Nietzsche's challenge of the system erected by Kant, Hegel and their successors, is a version of the general question of philosophy. Nietzsche's critique of metaphysics includes, or starts out from, the aesthetic, and the same could be argued for Heidegger. The invocation of prestigious philosophical names does not intimate that the present-day development of literary theory is a by-product of larger philosophical speculations. In some rare cases, a direct link may exist between philosophy and literary theory. More frequently, however, contemporary literary theory is a relatively autonomous version of questions that also surface, in a different context, in philosophy, though not necessarily in a clearer and more rigorous form. Philosophy, in England as well as on the Continent, is less freed from traditional patterns than it sometimes pretends to believe and the prominent, though never dominant, place of aesthetics among the main components of the system is a constitutive part of this system. It is therefore not surprising that contemporary literary theory came into being from outside philosophy and sometimes in conscious rebellion against the weight of its tradition. Literary theory may now well have become a legitimate concern of philosophy but it cannot be assimilated to it, either factually or theoretically. It contains a necessarily pragmatic moment that certainly weakens it as theory but that adds a subversive element of unpredictability and makes it something of a wild card in the serious game of the theoretical disciplines.

The advent of theory, the break that is now so often being deplored and that sets it aside from literary history and from literary criticism, occurs with the introduction of linguistic terminology in the metalanguage about literature. By linguistic terminology is meant a terminology that designates reference prior to designating the referent and takes into account, in the consideration of the world, the referential function of language or, to be somewhat more specific, that considers reference as a function of language and not necessarily as an intuition. Intuition implies perception, consciousness, experience, and leads at once into the world of logic and of understanding with all its correlatives, among which aesthetics occupies a prominent place. The assumption that there can be a science of language which is not necessarily a logic leads to the development of a terminology which is not necessarily aesthetic. Contemporary literary theory comes into its own in such events as the application of Saussurian linguistics to literary texts.

The affinity between structural linguistics and literary texts is not as obvious as, with the hindsight of history, it now may seem. Peirce, Saussure, Sapir and Bloomfield were not originally concerned with literature at all but with the scientific foundations of linguistics. But the interest of philologists such as Roman Jakobson or literary critics such as Roland Barthes in semiology reveals the natural attraction of literature to a theory of linguistic signs. By considering language as a system of signs and of signification rather than as an established pattern of meanings, one displaces or even suspends the traditional barriers between literary and presumably non-literary uses of language and liberates the corpus from the secular weight of textual canonization. The results of the encounter between semiology and literature went considerably further than those of many other theoretical models – philological, psychological or classically epistemological – which writers on literature in quest of such models had tried out before. The responsiveness of literary texts to semiotic analysis is visible in that, whereas other approaches were unable to reach beyond observations that could be paraphrased or translated in terms of common knowledge, these analyses revealed patterns that could only be described in terms of their own, specifically linguistic, aspects. The linguistics of semiology and of literature apparently have something in common that only their shared perspective can detect and that pertains distinctively to them. The definition of this something, often referred to as literariness, has become the object of literary theory.

Literariness, however, is often misunderstood in a way that has provoked much of the confusion which dominates today's polemics. It is frequently assumed, for instance, that literariness is another word for, or another mode of, aesthetic response. The use, in conjunction with literariness, of such terms as style and stylistics, form or even 'poetry' (as in 'the poetry of grammar'), all of which carry strong aesthetic connotations, helps to foster this confusion, even among those who first put the term in circulation. Roland Barthes, for example, in an essay properly and revealingly dedicated to Roman Jakobson, speaks eloquently of the writer's quest for a perfect coincidence of the phonic properties of a word with its signifying function.

> We would also wish to insist on the Cratylism of the name (and of the sign) in Proust... Proust sees the relationship between signifier and signified as motivated, the one copying the other and representing in its material form the signified essence of the thing (and not the thing itself)... This realism (in the scholastic sense of the word), which conceives of names as the 'copy' of the ideas, has taken, in Proust, a radical form. But one may well ask whether it is not more or less consciously present in all writing and whether it is possible to be a writer without some sort of belief in the natural relationship between names and essences. The poetic function, in the widest sense of the word, would thus be defined by a Cratylian awareness of the sign, and the writer would be the conveyor of this secular myth which wants language to imitate the idea and which, contrary to the teachings of linguistic science, thinks of signs as motivated signs.[1]

To the extent that Cratylism assumes a convergence of the phenomenal aspects of language, as sound, with its signifying function as referent, it is an aesthetically oriented conception; one could, in fact, without distortion, consider aesthetic theory, including its most systematic formulation in Hegel, as the complete unfolding of the model of which the Cratylian conception of language is a version. Hegel's somewhat cryptic reference to Plato, in the *Aesthetics*, may well be interpreted in this sense. Barthes and Jakobson often seem to invite a purely aesthetic reading, yet there is a part of their statement that moves in the opposite direction. For the convergence of sound and meaning celebrated by Barthes in Proust and, as Gérard Genette has decisively shown,[2] later dismantled by Proust himself as a seductive temptation to mystified minds, is also considered here to be a mere *effect* which language can perfectly well achieve, but which bears no substantial relationship, by analogy or by ontologically grounded imitation, to anything beyond that particular effect. It is a rhetorical rather than an aesthetic function of language, an identifiable trope (paranomasis) that operates on the level of the signifier and contains no responsible pronouncement on the nature of the world – despite its powerful potential to create the opposite illusion. The phenomenality of the signifier, as sound, is unquestionably involved in the correspondence between the name and the thing named, but the link, the relationship between word and thing is not phenomenal but conventional.

This gives the language considerable freedom from referential restraint, but it makes it epistemologically highly suspect and volatile, since its use can no longer be said to be determined by considerations of truth and falsehood, good and evil, beauty and ugliness, or pleasure and pain. Whenever this autonomous potential of language can be revealed by analysis, we are dealing with literariness and, in fact, with literature as the place where this negative knowledge about reliability of linguistic utterance is made available. The ensuing foregrounding of material, phenomenal aspects of the signifier creates a strong illusion of aesthetic seduction at the very moment when the actual aesthetic function has been, at the very least, suspended. It is inevitable that semiology or similarly oriented methods be considered formalistic, in the sense of being aesthetically rather than semantically valorized, but the inevitability of such an interpretation does not make it less aberrant. Literature involves the voiding, rather than the affirmation, of aesthetic categories. One of the consequences of this is that, whereas we have traditionally been accustomed to reading literature by analogy with the plastic arts and with music, we now have to recognise the necessity of a non-perceptual, linguistic moment in painting and in music, and learn to *read* pictures rather than to *imagine* meaning.

If literariness is not an aesthetic quality, it is also not primarily mimetic. Mimesis becomes one trope among others, language choosing to imitate a non-verbal entity just as paranomasis 'imitates' a sound without any claim to identity (or reflection on difference) between the verbal and non-verbal elements. The most misleading representation of literariness, and also the most recurrent objection to contemporary literary theory, considers it as pure verbalism, as a denial of the reality principle in the name of absolute fictions, and for reasons that are said to be ethically and politically shameful. The attack reflects the anxiety of the aggressors rather than the guilt of the accused. By allowing for the necessity of a non-phenomenal linguistics, one frees the discourse on literature from naive oppositions between fiction and reality, which are themselves an offspring of an uncritically mimetic conception of art. In a genuine semiology as well as in other linguistically oriented theories, the referential function of language is not being denied – far from it; what is in question is its authority as a model for natural or phenomenal cognition. Literature is fiction not because it somehow refuses to acknowledge 'reality', but because it is not *a priori* certain that language functions according to principles which are those, or which are *like* those, of the phenomenal world. It is therefore not *a priori* certain that literature is a reliable source of information about anything but its own language.

It would be unfortunate, for example, to confuse the materiality of the signifier with the materiality of what it signifies. This may seen obvious enough on the level of light and sound, but it is less so with regard to the more general phenomenality of space, time or especially of the self: no one in his right mind will try to grow grapes by the luminosity of the word 'day', but it is very difficult not to conceive the pattern of one's past and future existence as in accordance with temporal and spatial schemes that belong to fictional narratives and not to the world. This does not mean that fictional narratives are not part of the world and of reality; their impact upon the world may well be all too strong for comfort. What we call ideology is precisely the confusion of linguistic with natural reality, of reference with phenomenalism. It follows that, more than any other mode of inquiry, including economics, the linguistics of literariness is a powerful and indispensable tool in the unmasking of ideological aberrations, as well as a determining factor in accounting for their occurrence. Those who reproach literary theory for being oblivious to social and historical (that is to say ideological) reality are merely stating their fear at having their own ideological mystifications exposed by the tool they are trying to discredit. They are, in short, very poor readers of Marx's *German Ideology*.

In these all too summary evocations of arguments that have been much more extensively and convincingly made by others, we begin to perceive some of the answers to the initial question: what is it about literary theory that is so threatening that it provokes such strong resistances and attacks? It upsets rooted ideologies by revealing the mechanics of their workings; it goes against a powerful philosophical tradition of which aesthetics is a prominent part; it upsets the established canon of literary works and blurs the borderlines between literary and non-literary discourse. By implication, it may also reveal the links between ideologies and philosophy. All this is ample enough reason for suspicion, but not a satisfying answer to the question. For it makes the tension between contemporary literary theory and the tradition of literary studies appear as a mere historical conflict between two modes of thought that happen to hold the stage at the same time. If the conflict is merely historical, in the literal sense, it is of limited theoretical interest, a passing squall in the intellectual weather of the world. As a matter of fact, the arguments in favor of the legitimacy of literary theory are so compelling that it seems useless to concern oneself with the conflict at all. Certainly, none of the objections to theory, presented again and again, always misinformed or based on crude misunderstandings of such terms as mimesis, fiction, reality, ideology, reference and, for that matter, relevance, can be said to be of genuine rhetorical interest.

It may well be, however, that the development of literary theory is itself over-determined by complications inherent in its very project and unsettling with regard to its status as a scientific discipline. Resistance may be a built-in constituent of its discourse, in a manner that would be inconceivable in the natural sciences and unmentionable in the social sciences. It may well be, in other words, that the polemical opposition, the systematic non-understanding and misrepresentation, the unsubstantial but eternally recurrent objections, are the displaced symptoms of a resistance inherent in the theoretical enterprise itself. To claim that this would be a sufficient reason not to envisage doing literary theory would be like rejecting anatomy because it has failed to cure mortality. The real debate of literary theory is not with its polemical opponents but rather with its own methodological assumptions and possibilities. Rather than asking why literary theory is threatening, we should perhaps ask why it has such difficulty going about its business and why it lapses so readily either into the language of self-justification and self-defence or else into the overcompensation of a program-matically euphoric utopianism. Such insecurity about its own project calls for self-analysis, if one is to understand the frustrations that attend upon its practitioners, even when they seem to dwell in serene methodological self-assurance. And if these difficulties are indeed an integral part of the problem, then they will have to be, to some extent, a-historical in the temporal sense of the term. The way in which they are encountered on the present local literary scene as a resistance to the introduction of linguistic terminology in aesthetic and historical discourse about literature is only one particular version of a question that cannot be reduced to a specific historical situation and called modern, post-modern, post-classical or romantic (not even in Hegel's sense of the term), although its compulsive way of forcing itself upon us in the guise of a system of historical periodization is certainly part of its problematic nature. Such difficulties can be read in the text of literary theory at all times, at whatever historical moment one wishes to select. One of the main achievements of the present theoretical trends is to have restored some awareness of this fact. Classical, medieval and Renaissance literary theory is now often being read in a way that knows enough about what it is doing not to wish to call itself 'modern'.

We return, then, to the original question in an attempt to broaden the discussion enough to inscribe the polemics inside the question rather than having them determine it. The resistance to theory is a resistance to the use of language about language. It is therefore a resistance to language itself or to the possibility that language contains factors or functions that cannot be reduced to intuition. But we seem to assume all too readily that, when we refer to something called 'language', we know what it is we are talking about, although there is probably no word to be found in the language that is as overdetermined, self-evasive, disfigured and disfiguring as 'language'. Even if we choose to consider it at a safe remove from any theoretical model, in the pragmatic history of 'language', not as a concept, but as a didactic assignment that no human being can bypass, we soon find ourselves confronted by theoretical enigmas. The most familiar and general of all linguistic models, the classical *trivium*, which considers the sciences of language as consisting of grammar, rhetoric and logic (or dialectics), is in fact a set of unresolved tensions powerful enough to have generated an infinitely prolonged discourse of endless frustration of which contemporary literary theory, even at its most self-assured, is one more chapter. The difficulties extend to the internal articulations between the constituent parts as well as to the articulation of the field of language with the knowledge of the world in general, the link between the trivium and the *quadrivium*, which covers the non-verbal sciences of number (arithmetic), of space (geometry), of motion (astronomy) and of time (music). In the history of philosophy, this link is traditionally, as well as substantially, accomplished by way of logic, the area where the rigor of the linguistic discourse about itself matches up with the rigor of the mathematical discourse about the world. Seventeenth-century epistemology, for instance, at the moment when the relationship between philosophy and mathematics is particularly close, holds up the language of what it calls geometry (*mos geometricus*), and which in fact includes the homogeneous concatenation between space, time and number, as the sole model of coherence and economy. Reasoning *more geometrico* is said to be 'almost the only mode of reasoning that is infallible, because it is the only one to adhere to the true method, whereas all other ones are by natural necessity in a degree of confusion of which only geometrical minds can be aware.[3] This is a clear instance of the interconnection between a science of the phenomenal world and a science of language conceived as definitional logic, the pre-condition for a correct axiomatic-deductive, synthetic reasoning. The possibility of thus circulating freely between logic and mathematics has its own complex and problematic history as well as its contemporary equivalencies with a different logic and a different mathematics. What matters for our present argument is that this articulation of the sciences of language with the mathematical sciences represents a particularly compelling version of a continuity between a theory of language, as logic, and the knowledge of the phenomenal world to which mathematics give access. In such a system, the place of aesthetics is preordained and by no means alien, provided the priority of logic, in the model of the *trivium*, is not being questioned. For even if one assumes, for the sake of argument and against a great deal of historical evidence, that the link between logic and the natural sciences is secure, this leaves open the question, within the confines of the *trivium* itself, of the relationship between grammar, rhetoric and logic. And this is the point at which literariness, the use of language that foregrounds the rhetorical over the grammatical and the logical function, intervenes as a decisive but unsettling element which, in a variety of modes and aspects, disrupts the inner balance of the model and, consequently, its outward extension to the non-verbal world as well.

Logic and grammar seem to have a natural enough affinity for each other and, in the tradition of Cartesian linguistics, the grammarians of Port-Royal experienced little difficulty at being logicians as well. The same claim persists today in very different methods and terminologies that nevertheless maintain the same orientation toward the universality that logic shares with science. Replying to those who oppose the singularity of specific texts to the scientific generality of the semiotic project, A.J. Greimas disputes the right to use the dignity of 'grammar' to describe a reading that would not be committed to universality. Those who have doubts about the semiotic method, he writes, 'postulate the necessity of constructing a grammar for each particular text. But the essence (*le propre*) of a grammar is its ability to account for a large number of texts, and the metaphorical use of the term…fails to hide the fact that one has, in fact, given up on the semiotic project.[4] There is no doubt that what is here prudently called 'a large number' implies the hope at least of a future model that would in fact be applicable to the generation of all texts. Again, it is not our present purpose to discuss the validity of this methodological optimism, but merely to offer it as an instance of the persistent symbiosis between grammar and logic. It is clear that, for Greimas as for the entire tradition to which he belongs, the grammatical and the logical function of language are co-extensive. Grammar is an isotope of logic.

It follows that, as long as it remains grounded in grammar, any theory of language, including a literary one, does not threaten what we hold to be the underlying principle of all cognitive and aesthetic linguistic systems. Grammar stands in the service of logic which, in turn, allows for the passage to the knowledge of the world. The study of grammar, the first of the *artes liberales*, is the necessary pre-condition for scientific and humanistic knowledge. As long as it leaves this principle intact, there is nothing threatening about literary theory. The continuity between theory and phenomenalism is asserted and preserved by the system itself. Difficulties occur only when it is no longer possible to ignore the epistemological thrust of the rhetorical dimension of discourse, that is, when it is no longer possible to keep it in its place as a mere adjunct, a mere ornament within the semantic function.

The uncertain relationship between grammar and rhetoric (as opposed to that between grammar and logic) is apparent, in the history of the *trivium*, in the uncertain status of figures of speech or tropes, a component of language that straddles the disputed borderlines between the two areas. Tropes used to be part of the study of grammar but were also considered to be the semantic agent of the specific function (or effect) that rhetoric performs as persuasion as well as meaning. Tropes, unlike grammar, pertain primordially to language. They are text-producing functions that are not necessarily patterned on a non-verbal entity, whereas grammar is by definition capable of extra-linguistic generalization. The latent tension between rhetoric and grammar precipitates out in the problem of reading, the process that necessarily partakes of both. It turns out that the resistance to theory is in fact a resistance to reading, a resistance that is perhaps at its more effective, in contemporary studies, in the methodologies that call themselves theories of reading but nevertheless avoid the function they claim as their object.

What is meant when we assert that the study of literary texts is necessarily dependent on an act of reading, or when we claim that this act is being systematically avoided? Certainly more than the tautology that one has to have read at least some parts, however small, of a text (or read some part, however small, of a text about this text) in order to be able to make a statement about it. Common as it may be, criticism by hearsay is only rarely held up as exemplary. To stress the by no means self-evident necessity of reading implies at least two things. First of all, it implies that literature is not a transparent message in which it can be taken for granted that the distinction between the message and the means of communication is clearly established. Second, and more problematically, it implies that the grammatical decoding of a text leaves a residue of indetermination that has to be, but cannot be, resolved by grammatical means, however extensively conceived. The extension of grammar to include para-figural dimensions is in fact the most remarkable and debatable strategy of contemporary semiology, especially in the study of syntagmatic and narrative structures. The codification of contextual elements well beyond the syntactical limits of the sentence leads to the systematic study of metaphrastic dimensions and has considerably refined and expanded the knowledge of textual codes. It is equally clear, however, that this extension is always strategically directed towards the replacement of rhetorical figures by grammatical codes. The tendency to replace a rhetorical by a grammatical terminology (to speak of hypotaxis, for instance, to designate anamorphic or metonymic tropes) is part of an explicit program, a program that is entirely admirable in its intent since it tends towards the mastering and the clarification of meaning. The replacement of a hermeneutic by a semiotic model, of interpretation by decoding, would represent, in view of the baffling historical instability of textual meanings (including, of course, those of canonical texts) a considerable progress. Much of the hesitation associated with 'reading' could thus be dispelled.

The argument can be made, however, that no grammatical decoding, however refined, could claim to reach the determining figural dimensions of a text. There are elements in all texts that are by no means ungrammatical, but whose semantic function is not grammatically definable, neither in themselves nor in context. Do we have to interpret the genitive in the title of Keats' unfinished epic *The Fall of Hyperion* as meaning 'Hyperion's fall', the case story of the defeat of an older by a newer power, the very recognizable story from which Keats indeed started out but from which he increasingly strayed away, or as 'Hyperion falling', the much less specific but more disquieting evocation of an actual process of falling, regardless of its beginning, its end or the identity of the entity to whom it befalls to be falling. This story is indeed told in the later fragment entitled *The Fall of Hyperion*, but it is told about a character who resembles Apollo rather than Hyperion, the same Apollo who, in the first version (called *Hyperion*), should definitely be triumphantly standing rather than falling if Keats had not been compelled to interrupt, for no apparent reason, the story of Apollo's triumph. Does the title tell us that Hyperion is fallen and that Apollo stands, or does it tell us that Hyperion and Apollo (and Keats, whom it is hard to distinguish, at times, from Apollo) are interchangeable in that all of them are necessarily and constantly falling? Both readings are grammatically correct, but it is impossible to decide from the context (the ensuring narrative) which version is the right one. The narrative context suits neither and both at the same time, and one is tempted to suggest that the fact that Keats was unable to complete either version manifests the impossibility, for him as for us, of reading his own title. One could then read the word 'Hyperion' in the title *The Fall of Hyperion* figurally, or, if one wishes, intertextually, as referring not to the historical or mythological character but as referring to the title of Keats' own earlier text (*Hyperion*). But are we then telling the story of the failure of the first text as the success of the second, the Fall of *Hyperion* as the Triumph of *The Fall of Hyperion*? Manifestly yes, but not quite, since the second text also fails to be concluded. Or are we telling the story of why all texts, as texts, can always be said to be falling? Manifestly yes, but not quite, either, since the story of the fall of the first version, as told in the second, applies to the first version only and could not legitimately be read as meaning also the fall of *The Fall of Hyperion*. The undecidability involves the figural or literal status of the proper name Hyperion as well as of the verb falling, and is, thus a matter of figuration and not of grammar. In 'Hyperion's Fall', the word 'fall' is plainly figural, the representation of a figural fall, and we, as readers, read this fall standing up. But in 'Hyperion falling', this is not so clearly the case, for if Hyperion can be Apollo and Apollo can be Keats, then he can also be us and his figural (or symbolic) fall becomes his and our literal falling as well. The difference between the two readings is itself structured as a trope. And it matters a great deal how we read the title, as an exercise not only in semantics, but in what the text actually does to us. Faced with the ineluctable necessity to come to a decision, no grammatical or logical analysis can help us out. Just as Keats had to break off his narrative, the reader has to break off his understanding at the very moment when he is most directly engaged and summoned by the text. One could hardly expect to find solace in this 'fearful symmetry' between the author's and the reader's plight since, at this point, the symmetry is no longer a formal but an actual trap, and the question no longer 'merely' theoretical.

This undoing of theory, this disturbance of the stable cognitive field that extends from grammar to logic to a general science of man and of the phenomenal world, can in its turn be made into a theoretical project of rhetorical analysis that will reveal the inadequacy of grammatical models of non-reading. Rhetoric, by its actively negative relationship to grammar and to logic, certainly undoes the claims of the *trivium* (and by extension, of language) to be an epistemologically stable construct. The resistance to theory is a resistance to the rhetorical or tropological dimension of language, a dimension which is perhaps more explicitly in the foreground in literature (broadly conceived) than in other verbal manifestations or – to be somewhat less vague – which can be revealed in any verbal event when it is read textually. Since grammar as well as figuration is an integral part of reading, it follows that reading will be a negative process in which the grammatical cognition is undone, at all times, by its rhetorical displacement. The model of the *trivium* contains within itself the pseudo-dialectic of its own undoing and its history tells the story of this dialectic.

This conclusion allows for a somewhat more systematic description of the contemporary theoretical scene. This scene is dominated by an increased stress on reading as a theoretical problem or, as it is sometimes erroneously phrased, by an increased stress on the reception rather than on the production of texts. It is in this area that the most fruitful exchanges have come about between writers and journals of various countries and that the most interesting dialogue has developed between literary theory and other disciplines, in the arts as well as in linguistics, philosophy and the social sciences. A straightforward *report* on the present state of literary theory in the United States would have to stress the emphasis on reading, a direction which is already present, moreover, in the New Critical tradition of the forties and the fifties. The methods are now more technical, but the contemporary interest in a poetics of literature is clearly linked, traditionally enough, to the problems of reading. And since the models that are being used certainly are no longer *simply* intentional and centered on an identifiable self, nor *simply* hermeneutic in the postulation of a single originary, pre-figural and absolute text, it would appear that this concentration on reading would lead to the rediscovery of the theoretical difficulties associated with rhetoric. This is indeed the case, to some extent; but not quite. Perhaps the most instructive aspect of contemporary theory is the refinement of the techniques by which the threat inherent in rhetorical analysis is being avoided at the very moment when the efficacy of these techniques has progressed so far that the rhetorical obstacles to understanding, can no longer be mistranslated in thematic and phenomenal commonplaces. The resistance to theory which, as we saw, is a resistance to reading, appears in its most rigorous and theoretically elaborated form among the theoreticians of reading who dominate the contemporary theoretical scene.

It would be a relatively easy, though lengthy, process to show that this is so for theoreticians of reading who, like Greimas or, on a more refined level, Riffaterre or, in a very different mode, H.R. Jauss or Wolfgang Iser –

all of whom have a definite, though sometimes occult, influence on literary theory in this country – are committed to the use of grammatical models or, in the case of *Rezeptionsaesthetik*, to traditional hermeneutic models that do not allow for the problematization of the phenomenalism of reading and therefore remain uncritically confined within a theory of literature rooted in aesthetics. Such an argument would be easy to make because, once a reader has become aware of the rhetorical dimensions of a text, he will not be amiss in finding textual instances that are irreduceable to grammar or to historically determined meaning, provided only he is willing to acknowledge what he is bound to notice. The problem quickly becomes the more baffling one of having to account for the shared reluctance to acknowledge the obvious. But the argument would be lengthy because it has to involve a textual analysis that cannot avoid being somewhat elaborate; one can succinctly suggest the grammatical indetermination of a title such as *The Fall of Hyperion*, but to confront such an undecidable enigma with the critical reception and reading of Keat's text requires some space.

The demonstration is less easy (though perhaps less ponderous) in the case of theoreticians of reading whose avoidance of rhetoric takes another turn. We have witnessed, in recent years, a strong interest in certain elements in language whose function is not only not dependent on any form of phenomenalism but on any form of cognition as well, and which thus excludes, or postpones, the consideration of tropes, ideologies, etc., from a reading that would be primarily performative. In some cases, a link is reintroduced between performance, grammar, logic, and stable referential meaning, and the resulting theories (as in the case of Ohmann) are not in essence distinct from those of avowed grammarians or semioticians. But the most astute practitioners of a speech act theory of reading avoid this relapse and rightly insist on the necessity to keep the actual performance of speech acts, which in conventional rather than cognitive, separate from its causes and effects – to keep, in their terminology, the illocutionary force separate from its perlocutionary function. Rhetoric, understood as persuasion, is forcefully banished (like Coriolanus) from the performative moment and exiled in the affective area of perlocution. Stanley Fish, in a masterful essay, convincingly makes this point.[5] What awakens one's suspicion about this conclusion is that it relegates persuasion, which is indeed inseparable from rhetoric, to a purely affective and intentional realm and makes no allowance for modes of persuasion which are no less rhetorical and no less at work in literary texts, but which are of the order of persuasion by *proof* rather than persuasion by seduction. Thus to empty rhetoric of its epistemological impact is possible only because its tropological, figural functions are being bypassed. It is as if, to return for a moment to the model of the *trivium, rhetoric* could be isolated from the generality that grammar and logic have in common and considered as a mere correlative of an illocutionary power. The equation of rhetoric with psychology rather than with epistemology opens up dreary prospects of pragmatic banality, all the drearier if compared to the brilliance of the performative analysis. Speech act theories of reading in fact repeat, in a much more effective way, the grammatization of the *trivium* at the expense of rhetoric. For the characterization of the performative as sheer convention reduces it in effect to a grammatical code among others. The relationship between trope and performance is actually closer but more disruptive than what is here being proposed. Nor is this relationship properly captured by reference to a supposedly 'creative' aspect of performance, a notion with which Fish rightly takes issue. The performative power of language can be called positional, which differs considerably from conventional as well as from 'creatively' (or, in the technical sense, intentionally) constitutive. Speech act oriented theories of reading read only to the extent that they prepare the way for the rhetorical reading they avoid.

But the same is still true even if a 'truly' rhetorical reading that would stay clear of any undue phenomenalization or of any undue grammatical or performative codification of the text could be conceived – something which is not necessarily impossible and for which the aims and methods of literary theory should certainly strive. Such a reading would indeed appear as the methodical undoing of the grammatical construct and, in its systematic disarticulation of the *trivium*, will be theoretically sound as well as effective. Technically correct rhetorical readings may be boring, monotonous, predictable and unpleasant, but they are irrefutable. They are also totalizing (and potentially totalitarian) for since the structures and functions they expose do not lead to the knowledge of an entity (such as language) but are an unreliable process of knowledge production that prevents all entities, including linguistic entities, from coming into discourse as such, they are indeed universals, consistently defective models of language's impossibility to be a model language. They are, always in theory, the most elastic theoretical and dialectical model to end all models and they can rightly claim to contain within their own defective selves all the other defective models of reading-avoidance, referential, semiological, grammatical, performative, logical, or whatever. They are theory and not theory at the same time, the universal theory of the impossibility of theory. To the extent however that they are theory, that is to say teachable, generalizable and highly responsive to systematization, readings, like the other kinds, still avoid and resist the reading they advocate. Nothing can overcome the resistance to theory since theory is itself this resistance. The loftier the aims and the better the methods of literary theory, the less possible it becomes. Yet literary theory is not in danger of going under; it cannot help but flourish, and the more it is resisted, the more it flourishes, since the language it speaks is the language of self-resistance. What remains impossible to decide is whether this flourishing is a triumph or a fall.

Notes

1 Roland Barthes, 'Proust et les noms' in *To Honor Roman Jakobson* (The Hague, 1967) part I, pp. 157ff.

2 'Proust et le langage indirect' in *Figures* II (Paris, 1969).
3 Pascal, 'De l'esprit géométrique et de l'art de persuader', in *Oeuvres complétes* presented by L. Lafuma (Paris, Editions du Seuil, 1963), pp. 349ff.
4 A.J. Greimas, *Du Sens* (Paris, Editions du Seuil, 1970), p. 13.
5 Stanley Fish, 'How to do things with Austin and Searle: Speech Act Theory and Literary Criticism', *MLN* 91 (1976), pp. 983–1025. See especially p. 1008.

30 ❙ Jerome J. McGann,

'The Text, the Poem, and the Problem of Historical Method', in *The Beauty of Inflections* (1985), pp. 111–32

I

At this point in academic time, the problem of historical method emerges most dramatically at the elementary levels of textual interpretation. The problem appears in two typical forms which are inversely related to each other. On the one hand, intrinsic critics cannot see that historical studies go to the heart of literary objects. Since the latter appear to address problems (and people) which are not historically limited, the 'problem' with historical studies is that they continue to be pursued at all. Why should works which transcend the originary moment require historical analysis and commentary?

On the other hand, historical method is also a problem for scholars and critics who work in any of the areas of extrinsic criticism: in bibliography and textual criticism, in philology, in biography and literary history, and so forth. In this case, the difficulty is that the scholar's work so often does seem irrelevant to the understanding and appreciation of poetry. What is most disturbing about this situation is that so few scholars even acknowledge that their methods require a theoretical grounding in hermeneutics.

These brief remarks will come as news to no one. We are all aware of the situation. Before I try to suggest how we might try to deal with these issues, however, permit me another brief essay into familiar territory. For I believe that we can best come to grips with these problems of historical method if we see more clearly how they came to assume their present form.

It is well known that the most advanced literary studies in the nineteenth century were those which developed and modified the enormous advances in theory and method made in classical and biblical philology and textual criticism. Wolf and Eichhorn are only the most familiar names among that group of brilliant, predominantly German, critics of the late eighteenth century who made the initial breakthrough in transforming literary studies into a modern scientific discipline. These are the scholars who created both the Lower (or textual) Criticism and the Higher (or philological) Criticism. Historical philology in the nineteenth century brought analytic techniques to bear upon previously synthesized material in order to see more clearly the strokes of the tulip and the parts of the rainbow. The most advanced of such critics – in England, men like Coleridge and Arnold hoped to enlist these analytic techniques in the service of a new and higher synthesis: to adapt Coleridge's famous declaration, by dissolving, diffusing, and dissipating, 'to recreate . . . to idealize and to unify'.

In the twentieth century, however, the historical methods of the Lower and Higher Criticism gave way before the advance of several sorts of formal criticism and structural analysis. As we know, the principal impetus behind these critical movements came from language study and especially from linguistics. What Wolf, Lachmann, and Strauss were to nineteenth-century literary criticism, Saussure and Hjelmslev have been to the twentieth century. Hjelmslev's lucid *Prolegomena to a Theory of Language* (1943) accurately describes the shift which took place as a deliberate effort to break free of the descriptive, atomistic, and empirical approaches which flourished in the nineteenth century. 'The study of literature and the study of art', Hjelmslev says, had been carried out under 'historically descriptive rather than systematising disciplines', and his project, which explicitly follows Saussure, proposes a systematic rather than an empirical analytic of humanistic phenomena. *A priori* it would seem to be a generally valid thesis that for *every process* there is a corresponding *system*, by which the process can be analyzed and described by means of a limited number of premises. It must be assumed that any process can be analyzed into a limited number of elements recurring in various combinations.[1] In this passage Hjelmslev prepares the ground for a systematic linguistics, but his words clearly underwrite any number of other twentieth-century programmes of a formal or structural sort (Bultmann in biblical criticism, Lévi-Strauss in anthropology, Propp, Greimas, and many others in literary studies). These new semiological methods can be applied in all humanistic disciplines, as Hjelmslev well knew.

The shift from an empirical to a structural analytic has deeply influenced twentieth-century approaches to literary works, with far-reaching consequences. Before I turn to them, however, and thus reconnect with my initial two-handed 'problem of historical method', let me point out an interesting peripheral remark in Hjelmslev's book. When he attacks the empirical methods of the nineteenth century, its anti-systematic bias, he also explains the particular aesthetic position which underlies that

> humanistic tradition which, in various dress, has till now predominated ... According to this view, humanistic, as opposed to natural, phenomena, are non-recurrent and for that very reason cannot, like natural phenomena, be subjected to exact and generalizing treatment. In the field of the humanities, consequently, there would have to be a different method – namely, mere description, which would be nearer to poetry than to exact science – or, at any event, a method that restricts itself to a

discursive form of presentation, in which the phenomena pass by, one by one, without being interpreted through a system. (pp. 8–9)

As far as the appreciation of poetry is concerned, the nineteenth-century's 'humanistic' methods sought to preserve and illuminate the uniqueness of the poetic object. We would do well to remember this fact about nineteenth-century philology, for in the modern period – as we survey those prelapsarian Germanic tomes of dryasdust scholarship – we do not always recall (indeed, their authors do not always recall) the aesthetic phenomena those critical procedures were designed to illuminate. Our preoccupation with the minute particularities of poetical works emerged from the philological traditions which gave us 'textual criticism'. The contemporary vulgarisation of this philological term eloquently demonstrates the position that modern literary studies takes in relation to its immediate forebears.

The structural and semiological approaches to language and, in particular, to literature provided modern critics with operational procedures for analysing literature in a Kantian mode. In the *Critique of Judgement*, Kant offered a novel philosophy of art grounded in the notion that aesthetic works were integral phenomena whose finality was exhausted in the individual's experience of the work. The modern concept of 'the poem itself' as a self-referential linguistic system is fundamentally Kantian, though twentieth-century developments in linguistics provided this Kantian approach with its basic procedural rules for an actual critical practice.

These procedural rules operated under one fundamental premise: that literary works are special sorts of linguistic 'texts', that every poem is coextensive with its linguistic structure. Twentieth-century literary criticism contains a rich variety of schools and methods – analytical, structural, rhetorical, stylistic – but for all their important differences, they tend to share the conviction that poems are self-subsistent linguistic systems. The function of criticism is to illuminate the operations of those linguistic structures which we now like to call 'texts'. According to the classic formulation of Roman Jakobson: 'Poetics deals with problems of verbal structure . . . Since linguistics is the global science of verbal structure, poetics may be regarded as an integral part of linguistics.'[2]

This idea of the poem as verbal object is so commonplace in modern criticism that we may seem perverse to question it. Still we must do so, for the 'problem of historical method' – whether we approach it from an 'intrinsic' or an 'extrinsic' point of view – will never be opened to solutions until we see one of the signal failures of modern criticism: its inability to distinguish clearly between a concept of the *poem* and a concept of the *text*. Indeed, when we recover this essential analytic distinction, we will begin to reacquire some other, equally crucial distinctions which have fallen into disuse: for example, the distinction between concepts of *poem* and of *poetical work*. For the present I will concentrate on the first of these distinctions, and my analysis will proceed through a series of illustrative examples.[3]

II

When Byron sent the manuscript of *Don Juan* Cantos I and II to his publisher John Murray late in 1818, the poet was not only, with Goethe, the most famous writer in the Western world, his works were the most saleable products on the English literary market. He was not an author Murray wanted to lose. But this new work set Murray back on his heels. He was filled with wonder at its genius and with loathing at its immorality – at its obscenity, its blasphemy, its libellous attacks upon the poet laureate, and its seditious attitude toward the English government's policies at home and abroad.[4]

In the struggle that ensued, Murray and his London circle (which included some of Byron's best and oldest friends) pressed the poet either to withdraw the poem altogether or to revise it drastically and remove its objectionable parts. Byron agreed to some revisions, but his final line of retreat still seemed a fearful one to his publisher. When Byron threatened to take his poem elsewhere, Murray agreed to publish; he did not, however, tell his celebrated author precisely *how* he would publish.

For Murray, the problem was how to issue this inflammatory work without provoking a legal action against himself either by the government directly or by the notorious Society for the Suppression of Vice. His plan of action was ingenious but, in the end, self-defeating. Murray decided to issue a short run (1,500) copies) of the poem in a sumptuous quarto edition and to print it without either Byron's name as author or even his own as publisher. The price – £1 11s. 6d. – was set high in order to ensure a circulation limited alike in numbers and in social class.

The immediate effect of this manoeuvre was successful, for *Don Juan* stole into the world without provoking any moral outcry. The earliest reviewers were generally quite favourable, even from entrenched conservative quarters like *The Literary Gazette*.

But Murray's plan for avoiding the censors failed, in the end, because it was, in the words of Hugh J. Luke, Jr., 'a contradictory one'.[5] Murray avoided prosecution for issuing *Don Juan*, but his method of publication ensured a widespread piratical printing of the poem in the radical press. Thousands of copies of *Don Juan* were issued in cheap pirated editions, and as the work received wider celebrity and distribution, so the moral outcry against it was raised, and spread.

The significance which this story holds for my present purposes – i.e. for my aim to elucidate the problematics of the 'text' – is neatly explained by an anonymous article (possibly by Southey) printed in the conservative *Quarterly Review* in April 1822. In its quarto form, the reviewer notes, *Don Juan*

> would have been confined by its price to a class of readers with whom its faults might have been somewhat compensated by its merits; with whom the ridicule, which it endeavors to throw upon virtue, might have been partially balanced by that with which it covers vice, particularly the vice to which the class of readers to whom we are alluding are most subject – that which pleads romantic sensibility, or

ungovernable passion; to readers, in short, who would have turned with disgust from its indecencies, and remembered only its poetry and its wit.[6]

But the poem was issued in numerous cheap piracies and therein lay the mischief, 'some publishing it with obscene engravings, others in weekly numbers, and all in a shape that brought it within the reach of purchasers on whom its poison would operate without mitigation – who would search its pages for images to pamper a depraved imagination and for a sanction for the insensibility to the sufferings of others, which is often one of the most unhappy results of their own'. In short as the reviewer says so well: 'Don Juan in quarto and on hot-pressed paper would have been almost innocent – in a whity-brown duodecimo it was one of the worst of the mischievous publications that have made the press a snare.'

Several important conclusions follow from this eventful narrative. In this first place, the example illustrates how different texts, in the bibliographical sense, embody different poems (in the aesthetic sense) despite the fact that both are linguistically identical. In the second place, the example also suggests that the method of printing or publishing a literary work carries with it enormous cultural and aesthetic significance for the work itself. Finally, we can begin to see, through this example, that the essential character of a work of art is not determined *sui generis* but is, rather, the result of a process involving the actions and interactions of a specific and socially integrated group of people.[7]

The contemporary fashion of calling literary works 'texts' carries at least one unhappy critical result: it suggests that poems and works of fiction possess their integrity *as poems and works of fiction* totally aside from the events and materials describable in their bibliographies. In this usage we are dealing with 'texts' which transcend their concrete and actual textualities. This usage of the word *text* does not mean anything written or printed in an actual physical state; rather, it means the opposite: it points to an *Ur*-poem or meta-work whose existence is the Idea that can be abstracted out of all concrete and written texts which have ever existed or which ever will exist.[8] All these different texts are what can be called – Ideally – 'The Text'.

This Ideal Text is the object of almost all the critical scrutiny produced in the New Critical and post-New Critical traditions, whether formal, stylistic, or structural.[9] To arrive at such a Text, however, the critic normally obligates himself to make certain that his physical text is 'correct', which is to say that it corresponds, linguistically, to the author's final intentions about what editors call his work's substantive and accidental features. By meeting this obligation the critic pays his dues to the philological traditions of the last three hundred years. At the same time, the critic places himself in a position from which he can treat the literary work as if it were a timeless object, unconnected with history. The Text is viewed *sub specie aeternitatis*, and modern criticism approaches it much as the pre-critical scholar of Sacred Scripture approached the Word of God.

But in fact not even a linguistic uniformity sanctioned by philology can deliver over to us a final, definitive Text which will be the timeless object of critical interpretation and analysis. The example from Byron suggests this, clearly, but that case is merely paradigmatic. No literary work is definable purely in linguistic terms, and the illustration from Byron could easily be replaced by examples from any writer one might choose. It would not be very difficult to show, from the works of William Blake, that linguistic uniformity will hardly serve to establish a definitive Text. Of course everyone knows that Blake's *words* do not comprehend Blake's 'poetical works', so that (Ideally) critics recognize the necessity of 'reading' Blake in facsimile editions: and, in fact, facsimile editions do deliver more of Blake's work to the reader. But a Blake text comprising both words and illustrative matter still falls short of delivering this artist's work to an audience today.

Since Blake's work operates in an integrated verbal and visual medium, we are forced to see that the 'linguistic level' of this work corresponds to the entire mixed medium and not merely to the verbal one. But that Blake's 'poetical works' are not finished and complete in some Ideal mixed-medium Text is apparent if we simply recall the character of Blake's original methods of 'publication'. He is probably the most private and individualistic artist ever to emerge from England, and each of his engraved works was a unique publication by itself. It was part of Blake's artistic project that each of his works *be* unique, and he in fact achieved his purpose – most notoriously, I suppose, in his masterwork *Jerusalem*. Fewer than ten original copies of this work survive, and each is quite distinct. To speak of the Text of *Jerusalem*, then, as if that term comprehended some particular concrete reality rather than a heuristic idea, is manifestly to talk nonsense. One might as well try to speak of the Text of Emily Dickinson's verse. In reality, there is no such Text; there are only texts, of various kinds, prepared by various people (some by the author), at various periods, for particular and various purposes.

Yes the example of Blake carries a moral which takes us beyond the insight that an artist's work is not equivalent to an Ideal Text, nor even to some particular text or edition (say, an especially meticulous one prepared by a skilled editor). For every work of art is the product of an interaction between the artist, on the one hand, and a variety of social determinants on the other. Even the simplest textual problem establishing a work's *linguistic* correctness – can involve other problems that are, quite literally, insoluble. Keats, we recall, wrote two distinct and finished versions of 'La Belle Dame Sans Merci'.[10] But even if one were to set aside these special problems and assume that we can establish 'the author's final intentions' toward the language or even the entire format of a work we would still have, as readers, merely one text of the work, or – as scholars – the means for producing a number of possible editions, or texts.

The fact is that the works of an artist are produced, at various times and places, and by many different sorts of people, in a variety of different textual constitutions (some better than others). Each of these texts is the locus of a process of artistic production and consumption involving the originary author, other people (his audience[s], his publisher, etc.), and certain social institutions. Blake's special way of creating his works emphasizes the presence of these impinging social factors precisely because Blake strove so resolutely, even so obsessively, to produce work that was wholly his own. Each original copy of *Jerusalem* is unique, and in them Blake has achieved an extraordinary degree of artistic freedom. Had his work been reproduced through the procedures maintained by the ordinary publishing institutions of his day, it would have been a very different product altogether (it would have been reviewed, for example, and it would have fallen into many people's hands).[11] Nor are these differences merely accidental, and unimportant for the 'meaning' of Blake's work. Certainly to Blake they seemed immensely consequential; indeed – and he was quite right – they seemed definitive of the difference between one sort of art (free, creative) and another (commonplace, generalized).

In his own day Blake insisted upon having his artistic freedom, and the proper measure of his success in this aim – ironic though it seems lies in his contemporary artistic anonymity. Yet the social life of an artist transcends his particular historical moment, and so Blake, lost to his own age, was 'discovered' by the Pre-Raphaelites, who initiated the process of full social integration which his work has since achieved. Blake's unique works, in consequence, would become mass-produced, and his fierce individuality would itself become deeply integrated into various ideologies and social institutions. We may well see an irony in this event. Even more, however, should we see how it illustrates a fundamental fact about all art: that it is a social product with various, and changing, social functions to perform.

The initial example from Byron and the general case of Blake illustrate very clearly, I think, that a work of art – a poem, in this case – is no more the isolate creation of an artist then 'the poem itself' is defined either by some particular text on the one hand, or by the Ideal Text on the other. Poems are artistic works produced, and maintained, under specific socialized conditions. It is the business of analytic criticism to isolate and categorize the various social factors which meet and interact in various works of art, and finally, to explain those interactions.

In attempting to show how different poetical works have acquired different textual constitutions, I have drawn attention to certain physical characteristics of some texts of *Don Juan* and *Jerusalem*. The physical differences between the several texts stand as signs of a productive process which is different in each case, and which, consequently, produces several different artistic works. The first two cantos of *Don Juan*, as issued by Murray, are not the same work as the first two cantos as issued by the pirates. The fact that Byron's *Don Juan* should have called out these two sorts of edition is one sign of its creative power, just as the poem's long and complex bibliographical history has testified to its trans-historical character and relevance.

Let there be no confusion in this matter, however: when we see that an author's work exists in many different textual constitutions, we do not mean to suggest that, for example, there are as many poems called *Jerusalem* as there are texts or editions. We must resist the modern fashion of referring to poems as 'texts' precisely because this vulgar usage confuses the fundamental difference between a poem's *text*–which is one thing–and a poem–which is quite another. Preserving this distinction is crucial for purposes of critical method, since the distinction facilitates a clear view of a poem's changing life in human society. Speaking of poems as 'texts' implicitly affirms an idea of literary works which involves two contradictory propositions: (1) that a poem is equivalent to its linguistic constitution and (2) that the textual differences in a poem's bibliographical history have no necessary relation to issues of literary criticism as such. The poem-as-text, then, is a critical idea which at once reduces poetry to a verbal construct and inflates it to the level of an immaterial, non-particular pure Idea (the poem as Ideal Text). This result seems paradoxical, but in fact it is the necessary consequence of a view of literary works which is founded on a contradiction.

The example of *Don Juan* must not be taken to suggest, however, that a poetical work is the product of a social engagement entered into, voluntarily or otherwise, by author, printer, and publisher alone. Rather, the local publishing relationship among these three persons is itself a sign needing critical analysis. The fact that Blake deliberately avoided any involvement in this, the normal publishing relationship of his day, is of immense critical significance for his work and especially for a late work like *Jerusalem*. To know the publishing options taken (and refused) by Chaucer, or Donne, or Pope, or Blake, or Byron enables the critic to explain the often less visible, but more fundamental, social engagements which meet in and generate the work in question.

The illustration from Byron is especially illuminating because it brings to our attention another crucial productive figure (anterior to the audience of consumers) who participates in the artistic process initiated by the artist. I mean, of course, the reviewer (or critic), who is the final mediating force between author and audience. It is the function of the (contemporary) reviewer and (subsequent) critic to make explicit the lines of interpretation which exist *in potentia* in their respective audiences. Critics and reviewers– to adapt a phrase from Shelley imagine what students and audiences already know about the works they are to read.

III

At this point in the analysis, though we have, I believe, established the generic functional usefulness of preserving distinctions among texts, poems, and poetical works, the specific value of such distinctions for literary criticism is still unclear. Are these the sort of distinctions which, in the end, make no difference?

In example which follows I mean to illustrate two related points: first (on the negative side), that the failure to maintain these distinctions creates a procedural error which necessarily threatens any subsequent practical criticism with disaster; and second (on the positive side), that the pursuit and elucidation of such distinctions sharply increases our understanding of poetry and poems in both the theoretical and the practical spheres. This second aspect of the demonstration will return us to the 'problem of historical method' which was raised at the outset. By framing these historically self-conscious demonstrations along the traditional 'intrinsic' lines of formal and thematic analysis, I propose to show: (1) that poems are, by the nature of the case (or, as Kant might say, 'transcendentally'), time- and place-specific; (2) that historical analysis is, therefore, a necessary and essential function of any advanced practical criticism.

The case I propose to consider is Allen Tate's famous interpretation of Emily Dickinson's poem 'Because I could not Stop for death'.[12] His discussion raises, once again, the whole range of unresolved problems which lie in wait for any critical method which cannot make serious distinctions between texts and poems.

Tate begins by quoting the poem in full and declaring it to be 'one of the greatest in the English language' and 'one of the perfect poems in English'. His argument for these judgements rests upon T.S. Eliot's famous discussion of the 'dissociation of sensibility'. Dickinson's poem is 'perfect' because it displays a perfect 'fusion of sensibility and thought': 'The framework of the poem is, in fact, the two abstractions, mortality and eternity, which are made to associate in equality with images: she sees the ideas, and thinks the perceptions. She did, of course, nothing of the sort; but we must use the logical distinctions, even to the extent of paradox, if we are to form any notion of this rare quality of mind' (p. 161). Tate argues for this general position by instancing what he sees as the poem's precision and tight structure of rhythm, image, and theme. The poem has nothing to excess; it is marked throughout by 'a restraint that keeps the poet from carrying' her dramatic images too far. As for the peom's ideas, they are something altogether different from 'the feeble poetry of moral ideals that flourished in New England in the eighties':

> The terror of death is objectified through this figure of the genteel driver, who is made ironically to serve the end of Immortality. This is the heart of the poem: she has presented a typical Christian theme in its final irresolution, without making any final statements about it. There is no solution to the problem; there can be only a presentation of it in the full context of intellect and feeling. A construction of the human will, elaborated with all the abstracting powers of the mind, is put to the concrete test of experience: the idea of immortality is confronted with the fact of physical disintegration. We are not told what to think; we are told to look at the situation. (p. 161)

In evaluating this criticism we begin with the text quoted by Tate. When he calls the poem 'The Chariot', as he does at the beginning of his discussion, he tells us what his text shows: Tate is reading the work printed in 1890 by Todd and Higginson. But of course, 'The Chariot' is not what Dickinson wrote, at any time; rather, it is a text which her first editors produced when they carefully worked over the (untitled) text written by the author. Among other, less significant changes, an entire stanza was removed (the fourth) and several lines underwent major alteration.[13] Since Tate's argument for the greatness of the poem depends heavily upon his view of its linguistic perfection, we are faced with a rather awkward situation. Under the circumstances, one would not find it very difficult to embarrass Tate's reading by subjecting it to an ironical inquisition on the subject of textual criticism.

Of course, Tate had no access to the text Dickinson actually wrote. Nevertheless, his critical judgement ought to have been warned that textual problems existed since he did have available to him another–and, as it happens, more accurate–text of Dickinson's work. This text appeared in Martha Dickinson Bianchi's 1924 edition of *The Complete Poems*, and it is the one cited by Yvor Winters in the critique of Tate's essay first published by Winters in *Maule's Curse*.[14] But Tate's critical method could not prepare him to deal with problems in textual criticism. Indeed, he could not even see such problems, much less analyse their critical relevance. In this case, the impoverished historical sense of his general critical method appears as an inability to make critical judgements about poetic texts, to make distinctions between poems and their texts, and to relate those judgements and distinctions to the final business of literary criticism.

We have no call, nor any desire, to ridicule Tate's essay on this matter. Nevertheless, the issue must be faced squarely, for the problems raised by Tate's lack of textual scrupulousness appear at other points, and in other forms, in his discussion, and his example typifies the sorts of problem that remain widespread in Western modes of formal, stylistic, structural, and post-structural procedures. We may observe the congruence of his critical practice–the symmetry between his lack of interest in textual matters and his general interpretive approach–by examining his remarks on the poem's thematic concerns. We shall notice two matters here: first, a tendency to overread the poem at the linguistic level; and second, a reluctance to take seriously, or even notice, either the fact or the importance of the poem's ideological attitudes. In each case we are dealing with something fundamental to Tate's literary criticism and to twentieth-century interpretive approaches generally: their attempt to lift the poem out of its original historical context and to erase the distance between that original context and the immediate context of the critical act.

In this next phase of my analysis, then, I am proposing to extend the discussion from its specific interest in 'the problem of the text' to the more general issue which that problem localizes. Critics who do not or cannot distinguish between the different concrete texts which a poem assumes in its historical passage are equally disinclined to study the aesthetic significance of a poem's topical dimensions, or its didactic, ethical, or ideological materials. Poems that have no textual histories have, at the thematic level, only those meanings and references which 'transcend' the particulars of time and place. The poetry of poems, in this view, is a function not of specific ideology or topical matters but of 'universal' themes and references–and the *most* universal of these universals are a poem's formal, stylistic, or structural excellences. The ultimate consequence of such approaches is that the present critic loses altogether his awareness that his own criticism is historically limited and time-bound in very specific ways. Losing a critical sense of the past, the interpreter necessarily loses his ability to see his own work in a critical light.

Let me return to Tate's analysis and the Dickinson poem, however, where we can study these problems as they emerge in concrete forms. When Tate says, for example, that the poem presents 'the problems of immortality… confronted with the fact of physical disintegration', we observe a critical move characteristic of twentieth-century criticism: that is, the habit of dealing with poetry's substantive concerns at the most abstract and generalized thematic levels. I will have more to say about this sort of critical abstraction in a moment. For now we want most to query Tate's interpretation of the thematic aspects of the Dickinson poem. When he argues, for example, that the poem does not treat 'moral ideas', and that it takes a non-committal ('unresolved') stance toward a serious intellectual problem, we are surely justified in demurring. The civil kindliness of Death is of course ironically presented, but the irony operates at the expense of those who foolishly, the poem implies – regard Death as a fearful thing and and who give all their attention to their mortal affairs ('My labor, and my leisure too') either because of their fear or as a consequence of it. Like the poem's speaker before Death 'stopped' for her, the readers of the poem are assumed to be fearful of Death and too busy with the affairs of their lives to 'stop' for him.[15] The poem does indeed have 'a moral', and it appears in an unmistakable form in the final stanza:

> Since then – 'tis Centuries – and yet
> Feels shorter than the Day
> I first surmised the Horses Heads
> Were toward Eternity –

'We are not told what to think' by the poem, Tate asserts, but his position is only technically correct. Of course the poem does not *tell* us what to think, but its message about the benevolence of Death is plain enough. This message, however, like the poem which carries it, is no simple-minded pronouncement: the message is rich and affecting because it is delivered in human rather than abstract space. Dickinson's poem locates a set of relationships in which Dickinson, her fictive speaker, and her invited readers engage with each other in various emotional and intellectual ways.[16] The focus of these engagements is the poem's commonplace Christian theme: that people who are too busily involved with their worldly affairs give little serious thought to Death and the Afterlife. Criticizing such thoughtlessness, the poem encourages its readers to ponder Death and the Afterlife in a positive way. Its procedure for doing so involves the assumption of another thematic commonplace – that people fear to think about Death – and then undermining its force by a play of wit.

The wit appears most plainly in the rhetorical structure of the poem, which pretends to be spoken by a person already dead. Like some Christian Blessed Damozel from New England, Dickinson's speaker addresses this world from the other side, as it were, and lets us know that Death leads us not to oblivion but to 'Eternity' and 'Immortality'.[17] But the wit goes deeper, for Dickinson does not present her fiction as anything *but* fiction. The playfulness of the poem–which is especially evident in the final stanza, whose quiet good humour has been remarked upon frequently–is the work's most persuasive argument that Death can be contemplated not merely without fear but–more positively–with feelings of civilized affection. The kindliness and civility of the carriage driver are qualities we recognize in the *voice* of the poem's speaker and in the *wit* of its maker.

When we speak of the poem's wit, however, we should not lose ourselves in a hypnotic fascination with its verbal reality alone. The wit is at least as much a function of Dickinson's perspicuous observations of, and comments upon, social reality as it is of her facility with language. We may see this more clearly if we recall the standard critical idea that the figure of Death in this poem is–in the words of a recent critic–a 'gentlemanly suitor'.[18] Tate seems to have initiated this reading when he spoke of the driver as 'a gentleman taking a lady out for a drive', and when he proceeded to notice the 'erotic motive' associated with 'this figure of the genteel driver'. His commentary shows an acute awareness of one of the poem's subtlest and least explicit aspects, but it also displays a failure to see a more obvious but no less important fact about the driver.

This man is not a suitor but an undertaker, as we see quite clearly in the penultimate line's reference to 'Horses Heads'.[19] This small matter of fact has considerable importance for anyone wishing to develop an accurate critical account of the poem. It forces us to see, for example, that the journey being presented is not some unspecified drive in the country, but a funeral ride which is located quite specifically in relation to Emily Dickinson and her Amherst world. The hearse in the poem is on its way out from Pleasant Street, past Emily Dickinson's house, to the cemetery located at the northern edge of the town just beyond the Dickinson homestead.[20] Of course, these details are not verbalized into the Dickinson poem as explicit description. They are only present implicitly, as an originally evoked context which we–at our historical remove–can (and must) reconstitute if we wish to focus and explain the special emotional character of the work.

Consider once again, for example, the undertaker who appears in the poem. The behaviour of this man–his correctness, his rather stiff but kindly formality, his manner of driving the carriage–defines a character-type well-known in nineteenth-century culture, and a favourite one with contemporary caricaturists.[21] Behind the civility and kindly formal behaviour of Emily Dickinson's undertaker lies a tradition which saw in this man a figure of grotesque obsequiousness, as we know from Mark Twain's memorable scene in *Huckleberry Finn*. Indeed, I do not see how one could fully appreciate the finesse of what Tate calls the 'erotic motive' without also seeing just how the poem plays with it, and how Dickinson's poetic style both represents and quietly modifies the contemporary stereotype of this important social functionary so well known to the inhabitants of towns like Amherst. The poem's general ideology, as a work of Christian consolation, would be merely religious claptrap without these 'poetic'[22] elements: and such elements can only escape the critical method which does not seek to grasp the poem at a level more comprehensive than a merely linguistic one.

The power of the poem, then, rests in its ability to show us not merely the thoughts and feelings of Dickinson and her fictive speaker, but the attitudes of her implied readers as well. For all her notorious privacy, Emily Dickinson is, like every poet, a creator of those structures of social energy which we call poems. 'Because I could not Stop for Death' locates not merely an expressive lyrical act, but a significant relationship between the poet and her readers which we, as still later readers, are meant to recognize, enter into, and (finally) extend. Our sympathy with the poem may not be the same as that felt by a Christian reader, whether contemporary with the poem or not; nevertheless, it is *continuous* with the sympathy of such readers (who are consciously and explicitly assumped by the poem) because it takes those readers as seriously as it takes Emily Dickinson and her fictive speaker. Indeed, it must do this, for all are part of the poem in question. Later readers may not share the ideologies of the people represented by this poem, but they cannot read it without recognising and respecting those ideologies – without, in fact, perpetuating them in a critical human memory whose sympathetic powers are drawn from a historical consciousness.

Having discussed the 'ideological set' of this poem – its poetically rendered 'message' – let us return to Allen Tate's essay, where an absence of ideological commitments is imputed to Dickinson's work. We return to ask why Tate should insist upon 'misreading' the poem as he has done.

The reason emerges when we ponder carefully Tate's use of T.S. Eliot. Tate's interpretation shows that he shares Eliot's ideas about how moral concepts should appear in verse (not 'didactically' but dramatically); that he prizes Eliot's views on Metaphysical verse and its excellences; and that he is anxious to deliver his praise of Dickinson's poem in critical terms that will draw her into the company of those poets who illustrate Eliot's standards. In short, Tate reads Emily Dickinson in the same spirit that Eliot read Donne and the Metaphysicals. *Why* Tate, and Eliot before him, should have taken such a position towards the moral aspects of poetry – and especially of Christian poetry in its various forms – is beyond the scope of this analysis, though scholars recognize that the answer lies in the historical factors which generated modernism and its various ideologies.[23]

I have not dwelt upon Tate's discussion in order to debunk it, but rather in order to show the consonance between his interpretation of the Dickinson poem and his ignorance of its textual problems. Tate's eye is no more focused upon Dickinson's poem than it is on the 1890 text of 'The Chariot'. Rather, Tate has 'taken 'The Chariot' for his text', as we might say of one who delivers a sermon or a moral lesson. 'The Chariot' is the occasion for his ideological polemic on behalf of certain aesthetic criteria.

One important lesson to be drawn from this investigation of Tate's essay is that literary criticism – and even the analysis of poems – is not fundamentally a study of verbal structure *per se*. The very existence of Tate's influential and justly admired essay demonstrates that fact. Literary criticism must study poetic texts – the 'verbal structures' of poems – but the analysis of these verbal structures does not comprehend a poetic analysis. This paradox of critical method emerges forcibly in Tate's essay, which dramatizes, in its very limitations, the distinction between text and poem – a distinction, indeed, which Tate's analysis is incapable of making. Yet the distinction must be made – and textual criticism, in the traditional sense, must be revived among literary critics – if our received works of literature are to regain their full human resources – that is to say, if the entire history of poetry and all the potential of specific poems are to be made known and available to each new generation. Poetry and poems are, in this sense, transhistorical, but they acquire this perpetuity by virtue of the particular historical adventures which their texts undergo from their first appearance before their author's eyes through all their subsequent constitutions.

The textual histories of poems, in other words, are paradigm instances of the historically specific character of all poetry. By clarifying the distinction between a poem and its various texts, the examples from Byron and Blake illustrate the need for a systematic theory and method of historical criticism. On the other hand, the example from Dickinson argues, at the level of practical criticism, the specific critical powers inherent in a historical method. These powers appear as a special capacity for elucidating, in a systematic way, whatever in a poem is most concrete, local, and particular to it. Criticism cannot analyse poems, or reveal their special characteristics and values, if it abstracts away from their so-called accidental features. Attending merely to the formal or linguistic phenomena of poems constitutes an initial and massive act of abstraction from what are some of the most crucial particulars of all poems.

Facing the poem and its texts, then, historical criticism tries to define what is most peculiar and distinctive in specific poetical works. Moreover, in specifying these unique features and sets of relationships, it transcends the concept of the-poem-as-verbal-object to reveal the poem as a special sort of communication event. This new understanding of poems takes place precisely because the critical act, occurring in a self-conscious present, can turn to look upon poems created in the past not as fixed objects but as the locus of certain past human experiences. Some of these are dramatized *in* the poems, while others are presented *through* the poetical works, which embody various human experiences *with* the poems, beginning with the author's own experiences. In this way does a historical criticism define poetry not as a formal structure or immediate event but as a continuing human process. That *act* of definition is the fundamental *fact* of literary criticism.

The new fact about *historical* criticism, however, is that it systematically opposes its own reification. Being first of all an *act* of definition rather than a *set* of definitions, historical criticism calls attention to the time-specific and heuristic character of its abstractions. Like the poetry it studies, criticism is always tendentious because it always seeks to define and preserve human values. One of the special values of historical criticism, to my view at any rate, lies in its eagerness to specify and examine its polemical positions. This self-critical aspect of an historical approach seems to be a direct function of its basic method, for in attempting to specify historical distinctions, we set a gulf between our past and our present. It is this gulf which enables us to judge and criticize the past, but it is equally this gulf which enables the past–so rich in its achievements–to judge and criticize us. Thus in our differences do we learn about, and create, a community.

Notes

1 Louis Hjelmslev, *Prolegomena to a Theory of Language*, tr. Francis J. Whitfield (Madison, Wis., 1961), p. 9.

2 Roman Jakobson, 'Linguistics and Poetics', in *Style in Language*, ed. T.A. Sebeok (Cambridge, MA, 1960), p. 350. In the latest, post-structural phase of these traditions the models are more generically semiological than linguistic. The shift in emphasis– from specific 'text' to the process of 'textuality'–marks the increased self-consciousness in this tradition, but not a departure from its fundamental premises.

3 Literary criticism in general would benefit if certain clear distinctions were preserved when using words (and concepts) like *text, poem*, and *poetical work*. In the present essay, the word *text* is used as a purely bibliographical concept which means to deal with the material of poetry in a purely physical or impersonal frame of reference. The term deliberately abstracts away the critic's or the reader's immediate (social) point of view. Poetry is a social phenomenon, but the concept of *text* withholds from consideration all matters that relate to the involvement of reader or audience in the reproduction of the work. It does so, of course, for analytic purposes, and *only provisionally*. I propose that we use the term *text* when we deal with poems as they are part of a productive (or reproductive) process, but when we are with-holding from consideration all matters that relate to the process of consumption. *Poem*, on the other hand, is the term I will use to refer to the work as it is the locus of a specific process of production (or reproduction) and consumption. *Poetical work* is my term for the global history of some particular work's process of production/reproduction and consumption. I use the term *poetry* to refer generically to imaginative literary works without respect to any specific social or historical factors. The terms *text* and *Ideal Text* also appear in this essay, and these refer to various (non-historical and non-sociological) twentieth-century critical concepts.

   I hope it is clear that these distinctions mean to counter the semiological approach to the concepts of *text* and *textuality*. A paradigm example of the latter approach will be found in Roland Barthes's famous essay 'From Work to Text'.

4 See *Don Juan: A Variorum Edition*, ed. T.G. Steffan and W.W. Pratt (Austin, Tx 1957), i. 11–32 and iv. 293–308.

5 'The Publishing of *Don Juan*', *PMLA* lxxx (June 1965), p. 200.

6 For the *Quarterly Review* quotations see ibid., p. 202.

7 Cf. Levin Schüking, *The Sociology of Literary Taste* (London, 1966).

8 Post-structural critiques of their own (formalist) tradition have been widespread during the past ten years and have contributed to the break-up of the academic consensus which developed between 1935 and 1965. See John Fekete, *The Critical Twilight* (London, 1978). The attacks upon the New Criticism have tended to accuse it of an arrogant and technocratic empiricism, with its insistence upon taking the

poem as *sui generis*. These attacks–see Richard Palmer, *Hermeneutics* (Evanston, Ill., 1969), for example–charge the New Criticism with a crude theory of the poem as 'object' or 'thing'. This sort of attack is deeply misguided and misses entirely the fundamental Idealism of both the New Criticism in particular and its later formalist context in general. A revisionist commentator like Gerald Graff has been able to see the mistake in such critiques and to suggest what is in fact the case: that New Criticism and its academic inheritors (including many of its recent antagonists) are part of a single tradition (*Literature Against Itself*, Chicago, 1979, chap. 5). As Graff notes, New Criticism was marked throughout by contradictions along an Ideal/ Empirical fault-line; nor could it have been otherwise with a fundamentally Idealist theory which was seeking to establish its authority in a scientific, rational, and technological world. Graff's views have been anticipated by a number of trenchant critiques put out from relatively orthodox Marxist writers: see, e.g. Robert Weimann, 'Past Significance and Present Meaning in Literary History', in *New Directions in Literary History*, ed. Ralph Cohen (Baltimore, 1974), esp. pp. 43–50.

9   That an Ideal Text is the object of contemporary 'textual' interpreters is patent: see also Tony Bennett, *Formalism and Marxism* (London, 1979), pp. 70–1.

10 For a more thorough discussion see chap. I of *Keats and the Historical Method in Literary Criticism*, pp. 15–67, by McGann in the same book *The Beauty of Inflections*.

11 As is well known, Blake purchased his artistic freedom at a fearful personal cost, for his conscious artistic policies ensured his contemporary isolation. Appealing to what Byron called 'the Avenger, Time', Blake's work had to wait for the justice of history. Cf. the discussion in J.W. Saunders, *The Profession of Letters* (London, 1964) pp. 146–73 *passim* and, on Blake particularly, pp. 164–6; see also Jerome J. McGann, *A Critique of Modern Textual Criticism* (Chicago, 1983), pp. 44–7.

12 This is poem no. 172 in *The Poems of Emily Dickinson*, ed. Thomas H. Johnson (Cambridge, MA., 1955) ii. 546–7. For Tate's discussion, see his 'New England Culture and Emily Dickinson', in *The Recognition of Emily Dickinson*, ed. C.E. Blake and C.F. Wells (Ann Arbor, MI, 1968), pp. 153–67, esp. pp. 160–2, from which the quotations below are taken.

13 See *Poems by Emily Dickinson*, ed. Mabel Loomis Todd and Thomas W. Higginson (Boston, 1890). Also see Johnson's edition, where the textual issues are succinctly presented.

14 Winters' essay is reprinted in Blake and Wells, eds, *The Recognition of Emily Dickinson*; see esp. pp. 192–3.

15 This motif is an ancient one in the tradition of Christian art and poetry. For its biblical sources see Matt. 24:43 and I Thess. 5:2–4. An excellent contemporary example is to be found in Alan Dugan's 'Tribute to Kafka for Someone Taken'.

16 See V.N. Vološinov (i.e. M.M. Bakhtin), 'Discourse in Life and Discourse in Art', in *Freudianism, A Marxist Critique*, tr. I.R. Titunik (New York, 1976), where Bakhtin distinguishes among the author, the reader, and the figure he calls 'the hero' or the 'third participant'.

17 In adopting this rhetorical model Dickinson was following a literary practice that had grown extremely popular in the nineteenth century. See Ann Douglas, 'Heaven Out Home: Consolation Literature in the Northern United States 1830–1880', in *Death in America*, ed. Daniel Stannard, (Philadelphia, 1974); see esp. pp. 58–9, 61–2. But the procedure is deeply traditional: see also Rosemary Woolf, *English Religious Lyric in the Middle Ages* (Oxford, 1963), chap. 9 *passim*.

18 Robert Weisbuch, *Emily Dickinson's Poetry* (Chicago, 1972), p. 114.

19 That is to say, a suitor's carriage would have had only one horse.

20 The hearse's journey to the Amherst cemetery–one of the new, so-called rural

cemeteries – must have been appallingly familiar to Emily Dickinson. The mortality rate in Amherst was high, and Emily Dickinson's room overlooked the cemetery route. See Millicent Todd Bingham, *Emily Dickinson's Home* (New York, 1955), the map facing p. 62 and pp. 179–80; also Jay Leyda, *The Years and Hours of Emily Dickinson* (New Haven, 1969), ii. 2–3. Emily Dickinson's bedroom was the best vantage in the house for observing the stately procession of the funeral hearse as it moved out from Pleasant Street to the cemetery. The special location of the Dickinson house meant that the funeral hearse would always pass by, no matter where the deceased person had lived in town. One should also note that the poem's references to the 'School' and the 'Fields of Gazing Grain' are precise. In point of fact, 'Because I could not Stop for Death' narrates the imagined (non imaginary) journey of the hearse from somewhere in the central part of Amherst out along Pleasant Street, past the schoolhouse on the left, and out to the beginning of the 'Fields of Gazing Grain', at which point the undertaker would have turned to the right and driven past more fields to the gravesite. For a general discussion of the rural cemetery see Neil Harris, 'The Cemetery Beautiful', in *Passing: The Vision of Death in America*, ed. Charles O. Jackson (Westport, CT., 1977), pp. 103–11.

21 See Alfred Scott Warthen, 'The Period of Caricature' and 'The Modern Dance of Death', in *The Physician of the Dance of Death* (New York, 1934). Twain was fond of presenting the undertaker from a comic point of view. See *Huckleberry Finn*, chap. 27, and his essay 'The Undertaker's Chat'.

22 What makes them 'poetic' is their ability to dramatize the relationships which exist between specific social realities and a complex set of related – and often antagonistic – ideological attitudes and formations.

23 See Richard Ohmann. 'Studying Literature at the End of Ideology', in *The Politics of Literature*, ed. Louis Kampf and Paul Lauter (New York, 1973), esp. pp. 13–49; Renato Poggioli, *The Theory of the Avant-Garde*. tr. Gerald Fitzgerald (New York, 1971); and see nn. 3 and 8 above.

31 | Stephen Greenblatt,

'Resonance and Wonder', *Bulletin of the American Academy of the Arts and Sciences*, 43, (1990), pp. 11–34

In a small glass case in the library of Christ Church, Oxford, there is a round, broad-brimmed cardinal's hat; a note card identifies it as having belonged to Cardinal Wolsey. It is altogether appropriate that this hat should have wound up at Christ Church, for the college owed its existence to Wolsey, who had decided at the height of his power to found in his own honor a magnificent new Oxford college. But the hat was not a direct bequest; historical forces, as we sometimes say – in this case, taking the ominous form of Henry VIII – intervened, and Christ Church, like Hampton Court Palace, was cut off from its original benefactor. Instead, as the note informs us, after it had passed through the hands of various owners– including Bishop Burnet, Burnet's son, Burnet's son's housekeeper, the Dowager Countess of Albemarle's butler, the countess herself, and Horace Walpole–the hat was acquired for Christ Church in the nineteenth century, purchased, we are told, for the sum of sixty-three pounds, from the daughter of the actor Charles Kean. Kean is said to have worn the hat when he played Wolsey in Shakespeare's *Henry VIII*. If this miniature history of an artifact is too slight to be of much consequence, it nonetheless evokes a vision of cultural production that I find compelling. The peregrinations of Wolsey's hat suggest that cultural artifacts do not stay still, that they exist in time, and that they are bound up with personal and institutional conflict, negotiations, and appropriations.

The term culture has, in the case of the hat, a convenient material referent– a bit of red cloth stitched together–but that referent is only a tiny element in a complex symbolic construction that originally marked the transformation of Wolsey from a butcher's son to a prince of the church. Wolsey's gentleman usher, George Cavendish, has left a remarkably circumstantial contemporary account of that construction, an account that enables us even to glimpse the hat in its place among all the other ceremonial regalia:

> And after Mass he would return in his privy chamber again and, being advertised of the furniture of his chamber without with noblemen and gentlemen . . . , would issue out into them apparelled all in red in the habit of a Cardinal; which was either of fine scarlet or else of crimson satin, taffeta, damask, or caffa [a rich silk cloth], the best that he could get for money; and upon his head a round pillion with a neck of black velvet, set to the same in the inner side. . . . There was also borne before him first the Great Seal of England, and then his Cardinal's hat by a nobleman or some worthy gentleman right solemnly, bareheaded. And as soon as he was entered into his chamber of presence where was attending his coming to await upon him to Westminister Hall, as well noblemen and other worthy gentlemen as noblemen and gentlemen of his own family; thus passing forth with two great crosses of silver borne before him, with also two great pillars of silver, and his sergeant at arms with a great mace of silver gilt. Then his gentlemen ushers cried and said, 'Oh my lords and masters, make way for my lord's grace!'[1]

The extraordinary theatricality of this manifestation of clerical power did not escape the notice of the Protestant reformers who called the Catholic church 'the Pope's playhouse'. When the Reformation in England dismantled the histrionic apparatus of Catholicism, they sold some of its gorgeous properties to the professional players–not only a mark of thrift but a polemical gesture, signifying that the sanctified vestments were in reality mere trumpery whose proper place was a disreputable word of illusion-mongering. In exchange for this polemical sesrvice, the theatrical joint-stock companies received more than an attractive, cut-rate wardrobe; they acquired the tarnished but still potent charisma that clung to the old vestments, charisma that in paradoxical fashion the players at once emptied out and heightened. By the time Wolsey's hat reached the library at Christ Church, its charisma must have been largely exhausted, but the college could confer upon it the prestige of an historical curiosity, as a trophy of the distant founder. And in its glass case it still radiates a tiny quantum of cultural energy.

Tiny indeed—I may already have seemed to make much more of this trivial relic than it deserves. But I am fascinated by transmigrations of the kind I have just sketched here—from theatricalized rituals to the stage to the university library or museum—because they seem to reveal something critically important about the *textual* relics with which my profession is obsessed. They enable us to glimpse the social process through which objects, gestures, rituals, and phrases are fashioned and moved from one zone of display to another. The display cases with which I am most involved—books—characteristically conceal this process, so that we have a misleading impression of fixity and little sense of the historical transactions through which the great texts we study have been fashioned. Let me give a literary example, an appropriately tiny textual equivalent of Wolsey's hat. At the close of Shakespeare's *Midsummer Night's Dream*, the Fairy King Oberon declares that he and his attendants are going to bless the beds of the three couples who have just been married. This ritual of blessing will ensure the happiness of the newlyweds and ward off moles, harelips, and other prodigious marks that would disfigure their offspring. 'With this field-dew consecrate,' the Fairy King concludes,

> Every fairy take his gait,
> And each several chamber bless,
> Through this palace, with sweet peace,
> And the owner of it blest
> Ever shall in safety rest.
>
> (5.1.415–20)

Oberon himself, we are told, will conduct the blessing upon the 'best bridebed', that of the ruler Theseus and his Amazon queen Hippolyta.

The ceremony—manifestly the sanctification of ownership and caste, as well as marriage—is a witty allusion to the traditional Catholic blessing of the bride-bed with holy water, a ceremony vehemently attacked as pagan superstition and banned by English Protestants. But the conventional critical term 'allusion' seems inadequate, for the term usually implies a bloodless, bodiless thing, while even the tiny, incidental detail of the field dew bears a more active charge. Here, as with Wolsey's hat, I want to ask what is at stake in the shift from one zone of social practice to another, from the old religion to public theater, from priests to fairies, from holy water to field dew, or rather to theatrical fairies and theatrical field drew on the London stage. When the Catholic ritual is made into theatrical representation, the transposition at once naturalises, denaturalises mocks, and celebrates. It naturalises the ritual by transforming the specially sanctified water into ordinary dew; it denaturalises the ritual by removing it from human agents and attributing it to the fairies; it mocks Catholic practice by associating it with notorious superstition and then by enacting it on the stage where it is revealed as a histrionic illusion; and it celebrates such practice by reinvesting it with the charismatic magic of the theater.

Several years ago, intending to signal a turn away from the formal, decontextualized analysis that dominates new criticism, I used the term 'new historicism' to describe an interest in the kinds of issues I have been raising – in the embeddedness of cultural objects in the contingencies of history – and the term has achieved a certain currency. But like most labels, this one is misleading. The new historicism, like the Holy Roman Empire, constantly belies its own name. *The American Heritage Dictionary* gives three meanings for the term 'historicism':

1   The belief that processes are at work in history that man can do little to alter.
2   The theory that the historian must avoid all value judgements in his study of past periods or former cultures.
3   Veneration of the past or of tradition.

Most of the writing labelled new historicist, and certainly my own work, has set itself resolutely against each of these positions.

1 *The belief that processes are at work in history that man can do little to alter.* This formulation rests upon a simultaneous abstraction and evacuation of human agency. The men and women who find themselves making concrete choices in given circumstances at particular times are transformed into something called 'man'. And this colorless, nameless collective being cannot significantly intervene in the 'processes . . . at work in history' processes that are thus mysteriously alienated from all of those who enact them.

New historicism, by contrast, eschews the use of the term 'man'; interest lies not in the abstract universal but in particular, contingent cases, the selves fashioned and acting according to the generative rules and conflicts of a given culture. And these selves, conditioned by the expectations of their class, gender, religion, race and national identity, are constantly effecting changes in the course of history. Indeed if there is any inevitability in the new historicism's vision of history it is this insistence on agency, for even inaction or extreme marginality is understood to possess meaning and therefore to imply intention. Every form of behavior, in this view, is a strategy: taking up arms or taking flight is a significant social action, but so is staying put, minding one's business, turning one's face to the wall. Agency is virtually inescapable.

Inescapable but not simple; new historicism, as I understand it, does not posit historical processes as unalterable and inexorable, but it does tend to discover limits or constraints upon individual intervention. Actions that appear to be single are disclosed as multiple; the apparently isolated power of the individual genius turns out to be bound up with collective, social energy; a gesture of dissent may be an element in a larger legitimation process, while an attempt to stabilise order on things may turn out to subvert it. And political valences may change, sometimes abruptly; there are no guarantees, no absolute, formal assurances that what seems progressive in one set of contingent circumstances will not come to seem reactionary in another.

The new historicism's insistence on the pervasiveness of agency has apparently led some of its critics to find in it a Nietzchean celebration of the ruthless will to power, while its ironic and skeptical reappraisal of the cult of heroic individualism has led others to find in it a pessimistic doctrine of human helplessness. Hence, for example, from a Marxist perspective one critic characterises the new historicism as a 'liberal disillusionment' that finds that 'any apparent site of resistance ultimately serves the interests of power', while from a liberal humanist perspective, another critic proclaims that 'anyone who, like me, is reluctant to accept the will to power as the defining human essence will probably have trouble with the critical procedures of the new historicists and with their interpretive conclusion'.[2] But the very idea of 'defining human essence' is precisely what new historicists find vacuous and untenable, as I do the counter-claim that love rather than power makes the world go round. The Marxist critique is more plausible, but it rests upon an assertion that new historicism argues that '*any* apparent site of resistance' is ultimately coopted. Some are, some aren't.

I argued in an essay published some years ago that the sites of resistance in Shakespeare's second tetralogy are coopted in the play's ironic, complex, but finally celebratory affirmation of charismatic kingship. That is, the formal structure and rhetorical strategy of the plays make it difficult for audiences to withhold their consent from the triumph of Prince Hal. Shakespeare shows that the triumph rests upon a claustrophobic narrowing of pleasure, a hypocritical manipulation of appearances, and a systematic betrayal of friendship, and yet these manifestations of bad faith only contrive to heighten the spectators' knowing pleasure and the ratification of applause. The subversive perceptions do not disappear, but insofar as they remain within the structure of the play, they are contained and indeed serve to heighten a power they would appear to question.

I did not propose that all manifestations of resistance in all literature (or even in all plays by Shakespeare) were coopted – one can readily think of plays where the forces of ideological containment break down. And yet characterisations of this essay in particular, and new historicism in general, repeatedly refer to a supposed argument that any resistance is impossible[3]. A particularizing argument about the subject position projected by a set of plays is at once simplified and turned into a universal principle from which contingency and hence history itself is erased.

Moreover, even my argument about Shakespeare's second tetralogy is misunderstood if it is thought to foreclose the possibility of dissent or change or the radical alteration of the processes of history. The point is that certain aesthetic and political structures work to contain the subversion perceptions they generate, not that those perceptions simply wither away.

On the contrary, they may be pried loose from the order with which they were bound up and may serve to fashion a new and radically different set of structures. How else could change ever come about? No one is forced – except perhaps in school – to take aesthetic or political wholes as sacrosanct. The order of things is never simply a given: it takes labor to produce, sustain, reproduce, and transmit the way things are, and this labor may be withheld or transit formed. Structures may be broken in pieces, the pieces altered, inverted, rearranged. Everything can be different than it is; eveything could have been different than it was. But it will not do to imagine that this alteration is easy, automatic, without cost or obligation. My objection was to the notion that the rich ironies in the history plays were themselves inherently liberating, that to savor the tetralogy's skeptical cunning was to participate in an act of political resistance. In general I find dubious the assertion that certain rhetorical features in much-loved literary works constitute authentic acts of political liberation; the fact that this assertion is now heard from the left, where in my college days it was more often heard from the right, does not make it in most instances any less fatuous and presumptuous. I wished to show, at least in the case of Shakespeare's histories and in several analogous discourses, how a set of representational and political practices in the late sixteenth century could produce and even batten upon what appeared to be their own subversion.

To show this is not to give up on the possibility of altering historical processes – if this is historicism I want no part of it – but rather to eschew an aestheticized and idealised politics of the imagination.

2 *The theory that the historian must avoid all value judgements in his study of past periods or former cultures.* Once again, if this is an essential tenet of historicism, then the new historicism belies its name. My own critical practice and that of many others associated with new historicism was decisively shaped by the American 1960s and early 70s, and especially by the opposition to the Viet Nam War. Writing that was not enagaged, that withheld judgements, that failed to connect the present with the past seemed worthless. Such connection could be made either by analogy or causality; that is, a particular set of historical circumstances could be represented in such a way as to bring out homologies with aspects of the present or, alternatively, those circumstances could be analyzed as the generative forces that led to the modern condition. In either mode, value judgements were implicated, because a neutral or indifferent relation to the present seemed impossible. Or rather it seemed overwhelmingly clear that neutrality was itself a political position, a decision to support the official policies in both the state and the academy.

To study the culture of sixteenth-century England did not present itself as an escape from the turmoil of the present; it seemed rather an intervention, a mode of relation. The fascination for me of the Renaissance was that it seemed to be powerfully linked to the present both analogically and causally. This doubled link at once called forth and qualified my value judgements:

called them forth because my response to the past was inextricably bound up with my response to the present; qualified them because the analysis of the past revealed the complex, unsettling historical genealogy of the very judgements I was making. To study Renaissance culture then was simultaneously to feel more rooted and more estranged in my own values.[4]

Other critics associated with the new historicism have written directly and forcefully about their own subject position and have made more explicit than I the nature of this engagement.[5] If I have not done so to the same extent, it is not because I believe that my values are somehow suspended in my study of the past but because I believe they are pervasive: in the textual and visual traces I choose to analyze, in the stories I choose to tell, in the cultural conjunctions I attempt to make, in my syntax, adjectives, pronouns. 'The new historicism', someone has written in a lively critique, 'needs at every point to be more overtly self-conscious of its methods and its theoretical assumptions, since what one discovers about the historical place and function of literary texts is in large measure a function of the angle from which one looks and the assumptions that enable the investigation.'[6] I am certainly not opposed to methodological self-consciousness, but I am less inclined to see overtness – an explicit articulation of one's values and methods – as inherently necessary or virtuous. Nor, though I believe that my values are everywhere engaged in my work, do I think that there need be a perfect integration of those values and the objects I am studying. On the contrary, some of the most interesting and powerful ideas in cultural criticism occur precisely at moments of disjunction, disintegration, unevenness. A criticism that never encounters obstacles, that celebrates predictable heroines and rounds up the usual suspects, that finds confirmation of its values everywhere it turns, is quite simply boring.[7]

3. *Veneration of the past or of tradition.* The third definition of historicism obviously sits in a strange relation to the second, but they are not simply alternatives. The apparent eschewing of value judgements was often accompanied by a still more apparent admiration, however cloaked as objective description, of the past. One of the more irritating qualities of my own literary training had been its relentlessly celebratory character: literary criticism was and largely remains a kind of secular theodicy. Every decision made by a great artist could be shown to be a brilliant one; works that had seemed flawed and uneven to an earlier generation of critics bent on displaying discriminations in taste were now revealed to be organic masterpieces. A standard critical assignment in my student years was to show how a text that seemed to break in parts was really a complex whole: thousands of pages were dutifully churned out to prove that the bizarre subplot of *The Changeling* was cunningly integrated into the tragic mainplot or that every tedious bit of clowning in *Doctor Faustus* was richly significant. Behind these exercises was the assumption that great works of art were triumphs of resolution, that they were, in Bakhtin's term, monological – the mature expression of a single artistic intention. When this formalism was

combined, as it often was, with both ego psychology and historicism, it posited aesthetic integration as the reflection of the artist's psychic integration and posited that psychic integration as the triumphant expression of a healthy, integrated community. Accounts of Shakespeare's relation to Elizabethan culutre were particularly prone to this air of veneration, since the Romantic cult of poetic genius could be conjoined with the still older political cult that had been created around the figure of the Virgin Queen.

Here again new historicist critics have swerved in a different direction. They have been more interested in unresolved conflict and contradiction than in integration; they are as concerned with the margins as with the center; and they have turned from a celebration of achieved aesthetic order to an exploration of the ideological and material bases for the production of this order. Traditional formalism and historicism, twin legacies of early nineteenth-century Germany, shared a vision of high culture as a harmonising domain of reconciliation based upon an aesthetic labor that transcends specific economic or political determinants. What is missing is psychic, social, and material resistance, a stubborn, unassimilable otherness, a sense of distance and difference. New historicism has attempted to restore this distance, hence its characteristic concerns have seemed to some critics off-center or strange. 'New historicists', writes a Marxist observer, 'are likely to seize upon something out of the way, obscure, even bizarre: dreams, popular or aristocratic festivals, denunciations of witchcraft, sexual treatises, diaries and autobiographies, descriptions of clothing, reports on disease, birth and death records, accounts of insanity.'[8] What is fascinating to me is that concerns like these should have come to seem bizarre, especially to a critic who is committed to the historical understanding of culture. That they have done so indicates how narrow the boundaries of historical understanding had become, how much these boundaries needed to be broken.

For none of the cultural practices on this list (and one could extend it considerably) is or should be 'out of the way' in a study of Renaissance literature or art; on the contrary, each is directly in the way of coming to terms with the period's methods of regulating the body, its conscious and unconscious psychic strategies, its ways of defining and dealing with marginals and deviants, its mechanisms for the display of power and the expression of discontent, its treatment of women. If such concerns have been rendered 'obscure', it is because of a disabling idea of causality that confines the legitimate field of historical agency within absurdly restrictive boundaries. The world is parcelled out between a predictable group of stereotypical causes and a large, dimly lit mass of raw materials that the artist chooses to fashion.

The new historicist critics are interested in such cultural expressions as witchcraft accusations, medical manuals, or clothing not as raw materials but as 'cooked'–complex symbolic and material articulations of the imaginative and ideological structures of the society that produced them. Consequently, there is a tendency in at least some new historicist writings (certainly in my own) for the focus to be partially displaced from the work of art that is their formal occasion onto the related practices that had been adduced ostensibly in order to illuminate that work. It is difficult to keep those practices in the background if the very concept of historical background has been called into question.

I have tried to deal with the problem of focus by developing a notion of cultural negotiation and exchange, that is, by examining the points at which one cultural practice intersects with another, borrowing its forms and intensities or attempting to ward off unwelcome appropriations or moving texts and artifacts from one place to another. But it would be misleading to imagine that there is a complete homogenization of interest; my own concern remains centrally with imaginative literature, and not only because other cultural structures resonate powerfully within it. If I do not approach works of art in a spirit of veneration, I do approach them in a spirit that is best described as wonder. Wonder has not been alien to literary criticism, but it has been associated (if only implicitly) with formalism rather than historicism. I wish to extend this wonder beyond the formal boundaries of works of art, just as I wish to intensify resonance within those boundaries.

It will be easier to grasp the concepts of resonance and wonder if we think of the way in which our culture presents to itself not the textual traces of its past but the surviving visual traces, for the latter are put on display in galleries and museums specially designed for the purpose. By resonance I mean the power of the object displayed to reach out beyond its formal boundaries to a larger world, to evoke in the viewer the complex, dynamic cultural forces from which it has emerged and for which as metaphor or more simply as metonymy it may be taken by a viewer to stand. By wonder I mean the power of the object displayed to stop the viewer in his tracks, to convey an arresting sense of uniqueness, to evoke an exalted attention.

The new historicism obviously has distinct affinities with resonance; that is, its concern with literary texts has been to recover as far as possible the historical circumstances of their original production and consumption and to analyse the relationship between these circumstances and our own. New historicist critics have tried to understand the intersecting circumstances not as a stable, prefabricated background against which the literary texts can be placed, but as a dense network of evolving and often contradictory social forces. The idea is not to find outside the work of art some rock onto which literary interpretation can be securely chained but rather to situate the work in relation to other representational practices operative in the culture at a given moment in both its history and our own. In Louis Montrose's convenient formulation, the goal has been to grasp simultaneously the historicity of texts and the textuality of history.

Insofar as this approach, developed for literary interpretation, is at all applicable to visual traces, it would call for an attempt to reduce the isolation of individual 'masterpieces', to illuminate the condition of their making, to disclose the history of their appropriation and the circumstances in which they come to be displayed, to restore the tangibility, the openness, the permeability of boundaries that enabled the objects to come into being in the first place. An actual restoration of tangibility is obviously in most cases impossible, and the frames that enclose pictures are only the ultimate formal confirmation of the closing of the borders that marks the finishing of a work of art. But we need not take that finishing so entirely for granted; museums can and on occasion do make it easier imaginatively to recreate the work in its moment of openness.

That openness is linked to a quality of artifacts that museums obviously dread, their precariousness. But though it is perfectly reasonable for museums to protect their objects – I would not wish it any other way – precariousness is a rich source of resonance. Thomas Greene, who has written a sensitive book on what he calls the 'vulnerable texts', suggests that the symbolic wounding to which literature is prone may confer upon it power and fecundity. 'The vulnerability of poetry', Greene argues, 'stems from four basic conditions of language: its historicity, its dialogic function, its referential function, and its dependence on figuration.'[9] Three of these conditions are different for the visual arts, in ways that would seem to reduce vulnerability: painting and sculpture may be detached more readily than language from both referentiality and figuration, and the pressures of contextual dialogue are diminished by the absence of an inherent *logos*, a constitutive word. But the fourth condition – historicity – is in the case of material artifacts vastly increased, indeed virtually literalized. Museums function, partly by design and partly in spite of themselves, as monuments to the fragility of cultures, to the fall of sustaining institutions and noble houses, the collapse of rituals, the evacuation of myths, the destructive effects of warfare, neglect, and corrosive doubt.

I am fascinated by the signs of alteration, tampering, even destructiveness which many museums try simply to efface: first and most obviously, the act of displacement that is essential for the collection of virtually all older artifacts and most modern ones – pulled out of chapels, peeled off church walls, removed from decaying houses, seized as spoils of war, stolen, 'purchased' more or less fairly by the economically ascendent from the economically naive, the poor, the hard-pressed heirs of fallen dynasties and impoverished religious orders. Then too there are the marks on the artifacts themselves: the attempt to scratch out or deface the image of the devil in numerous late-medieval and Renaissance paintings, the concealing of the genitals in sculptured and painted figures, the iconoclastic smashing of human or divine representations, the evidence of cutting or reshaping to fit a new frame or purpose, the cracks or scorch marks or broken-off noses that indifferently record the grand disasters of history and the random accidents of trivial incompetence. Even these accidents – the marks of a literal fragility – can have their resonance: the climax of an absurdly hagiographical Proust exhibition several years ago was a display case holding a small, patched, modest vase with a notice, 'This vase broken by Marcel Proust'.

As this comical example suggests, wounded artifacts may be compelling not only as witnesess to the violence of history but as signs of use, marks of the human touch, and hence links with the openness to touch that was the condition of their creation. The most familar way to recreate the openness of aesthetic artifacts without simply renewing their vulnerability is through a skillful deployment of explanatory texts in the catalogue, on the walls of the exhibit, or on cassettes. The texts so deployed introduce and in effect stand in for the context that has been effaced in the process of moving the object into the museum. But insofar as that context is partially, often primarily, visual as well as verbal, textual contextualism has its limits. Hence the mute eloquence of the display of the palette, brushes, and other implements that an artist of a given period would have employed or of objects that are represented in the exhibited paintings or of materials and images that in some way parallel or intersect with the formal works of art.

Among the most resonant moments are those in which the supposedly contextual objects take on a life of their own, make a claim that rivals that of the object that is formally privileged. A table, a chair, a map, often seemingly placed only to provide a decorative setting for a grand work, become oddly expressive, significant not as 'background' but as compelling representational practices in themselves. These practices may in turn impinge upon the grand work, so that we begin to glimpse a kind of circulation: the cultural practice and social energy implicit in map-making drawn into the aesthetic orbit of a painting which has itself enabled us to register some of the representational significance of the map. Or again the threadbare fabric on the old chair or the gouges in the wood of a cabinet juxtapose the privileged painting or sculpture with marks not only of time but of use, the imprint of the human body on the artifact, and call attention to the deliberate removal of certain exalted aesthetic objects from the threat of that imprint.

For the effect of resonance does not necessarily depend upon a collapse of the distinction between art and non-art; it can be achieved by awakening in the viewer a sense of the cultural and historically contingent construction of art objects, the negotiations, exchanges, swerves, exclusions by which certain representational practices come to be set apart from other representational practices that they partially resemble. A resonant exhibition often pulls the viewer away from the celebration of isolated objects and toward a series of implied, only half-visible relationships and questions. How have the objects come to be displayed? What is at stake in categorizing them as of 'museum-quality'? How were they originally used? What cultural and material conditions made possible their production? What were the feelings of those who originally held these objects, cherished them, collected them, possessed them? What is the meaning of my relationship to these same objects now that they are displayed here, in this museum, on this day?

It is time to give a more sustained example. Perhaps the most purely resonant museum I have ever seen is the State Jewish Museum in Prague. This is housed not in a single building but in a cluster of old synagogues scattered through the city's former Jewish Town. The oldest of these–known as the Old-New Synagogue – is a twin-nave medieval structure dating to the last third of the 13th century; the others are mostly Renaissance and Baroque. In these synagogues are displayed Judaica from 153 Jewish communities throughout Bohemia and Moravia. In one there is a permanent exhibition of synagogue silverworks, in another there are synagogue textiles, in a third there are Torah scrolls, ritual objects, manuscripts and prints illustrative of Jewish beliefs, traditions, and customs. One of the synagogues shows the work of the physician and artist Karel Fleischmann, principally drawings done in the Terezin concentration camp during his months of imprisonment prior to his deportation to Auschwitz. Next door in the Ceremonial Hall of the Prague Burial Society there is a wrenching exhibition of children's drawings from Terezin. Finally, one synagogue, closed at the time of my visit to Prague, has simply a wall of names – thousands of them – to commemorate the Jewish victims of Nazi persecution in Czechoslovakia.

'The Museum's rich collections of synagogue art and the historic synagogue buildings of Prague's Jewish town', says the catalogue of the State Jewish Museum, 'form a memorial complex that has not been preserved to the same extent anywhere else in Europe.' 'A memorial complex' – this museum is not so much about artifacts as about memory, and the form the memory takes is a secularised kaddish, a commemorative prayer for the dead. The atmosphere has a peculiar effect on the act of viewing. It is mildly interesting to note the differences between the mordant Grosz-like lithographs of Karel Fleischmann in the pre-war years and the tormented style, at once detached and anguished, of the drawings in the camps, but aesthetic discriminations feel weird, out-of-place. And it seems wholly absurd, even indecent, to worry about the relative artistic merits of the drawings that survive by children who did not survive.

The discordance between viewing and remembering is greatly reduced with the older, less emotionally charged artifacts, but even here the ritual objects in their glass cases convey an odd and desolate impression. The oddity, I suppose, should be no greater than in seeming a Mayan god or, for that matter, a pyx or a ciborium, but we have become so familiarized to the display of such objects, so accustomed to considering them works of art, that even pious Catholics, as far as I know, do not necessarily feel disconcerted by their transformation from ritual function to aesthetic exhibition. And until very recently the voices of the tribal peoples who might have objected to the display of their religious artifacts have not been heard and certainly not attended to.

The Jewish objects are neither sufficiently distant to be absorbed into the detached ethos of anthropological display nor sufficiently familiar to be framed and encased alongside the altarpieces and reliquaries that fill Western museums. And moving as they are as mnemonic devices, most of the ritual objects in the State Jewish Museum are not, by contrast with Christian liturgical art, particularly remarkable either for their antiquity or their extraordinary beauty. They are the products of a people with a resistance to joining figural representation to religious observance, a strong anti-iconic bias. The objects have, as it were, little will to be observed; many of them are artifacts–ark curtains, Torah crowns, breastplates, pointers, and the like–whose purpose was to be drawn back or removed in order to make possible the act that mattered: not vision but reading.

But the inhibition of viewing in the Jewish Museum is paradoxically bound up with its resonance. This resonance depends not upon visual stimulation but upon a felt intensity of names, and behind the names, as the very term resonance suggests, of voices: the voices of those who chanted, studied, muttered their prayers, wept, and then were forever silenced. And mingled with these voices are others–of those Jews in 1389 who were murdered in the Old-New Synagogue where they were seeking refuge; of the great sixteenth-century Kabbalist, Jehuda ben Bezalel, known as Rabbi Loew, who is fabled to have created the Golem; of the twentieth-century's ironic Kabbalist, Franz Kafka.

It is Kafka who would be most likely to grasp imaginatively the State Jewish Museum's ultimate source of resonance: the fact that most of the objects are located in the museum–were displaced, preserved, and transformed categorically into works of art–because the Nazis stored the articles they confiscated in the Prague synagogues that they chose to preserve for this very purpose. In 1941 the Nazi Hochschule in Frankfurt had established an Institute for the Exploration of the Jewish Question which in turn had initiated a massive effort to confiscate Jewish libraries, archives, religious artifacts, and personal property. By the middle of 1942 Heydrich, as Hitler's chief officer within the so-called Protectorate of Bohemia and Moravia, had chosen Prague as the site of the Central Bureau for Dealing with the Jewish Question, and an SS officer, Untersturmführer Karl Rahm, had assumed control of the small existing Jewish museum, founded in 1912, which was renamed the Central Jewish Museum. The new charter of the museum announced that 'the numerous, hitherto scattered Jewish possessions of both historical and artistic value, on the territory of the entire Protectorate, must be collected and stored.'[10]

During the following months, tens of thousands of confiscated items arrived, the dates of the shipments closely coordinated with the 'donors' deportation to the concentration camps. The experts formally exployed by the original Jewish museum were compelled to catalogue the items, and the Nazis compounded this immense task by also ordering the wretched, malnourished curators to prepare a collections guide and organize private exhibitions for SS staff. Between September 1942 and October 1943 four major exhibitions were mounted. Since these required far more space than the existing Jewish Museum's modest location, the great old Prague synagogues – made vacant by the Nazi prohibition of Jewish public worship – were partially refurbished for the occasion. Hence in March 1943, for example, in the seventeenth-century Klaus Synagogue there was an exhibition of Jewish festival and life-cycle observances; 'when Sturmbannführer Günther first toured the collection on April 6, he demanded various changes, including the translation of all Hebrew texts and the addition of an exhibit on kosher butchering' (*Precious Legacy*, p. 36). Plans were drawn up for other exhibitions, but the curators–who had given themselves to the task with a strange blend of selflessness, irony, helplessness, and heroism–were themselves at this point sent to concentration camps and murdered.

After the war, the few survivors of the Czech Jewish community apparently felt they could not sustain the ritual use of the synagogues or maintain the large collections. In 1949 the Jewish Community Council offered as a gift to the Czechoslovak government both the synagogues and their contents. These became the resonant, impure 'memorial complex' they are–a cultural machine that generates an uncontrollable oscillation between homage and desecration, longing and hopelessness, the voices of the dead and silence. For resonance, like nostalgia, is impure, a hybrid forged in the barely acknowledged gaps, the cesurae, between words like State, Jewish, and Museum.

I want to avoid the implication that resonance must be necessarily linked to destruction and absence; it can be found as well in unexpected survival. The key is the intimation of a larger community of voices and skills, an imagined ethnographic thickness. Here another example will serve: in the Yucatan there is an extensive, largely unexcavated late-Classic Maya site called Coba, whose principal surviving feature is a high pyramid known as Nahoch Mul. After a day of tramping around the site, I was relaxing in the pool of the nearby Club Med Archaeological Villa in the company of a genial structural engineer from Little Rock. To make conversation, I asked my pool-mate what he as a structural engineer thought of Nahoch Mul. 'From an engineer's point of view', he replied, 'a pyramid is not very interesting–it's just an enormous gravity structure.' 'But', he added, 'did you notice that Coca-Cola stand on the way in? That's the most impressive example of contemporary Maya architecture I've ever seen.' I thought it quite possible that my leg was being pulled, but I went back the next day to check–I had, of course, completely blocked out the Coke stand on my first visit. Sure enough, some enterprising Mayan had built a remarkably elegant shelter with a soaring pyramidal roof constructed out of ingeniously intertwining sticks and branches. Places like Coba are thick with what Spenser called the Ruins of Time–with a nostalgia for a lost civilisation, in a state of collapse long before Cortés or Montejo cut their paths through the jungle. But, despite frequent colonial attempts to drive them or imagine them out of existence, the Maya have not in fact vanished, and a single entrepreneur's architectural improvisation suddenly had more resonance for me than the mounds of the 'lost' city.

My immediate thought was that the whole Coca-Cola stand could be shipped to New York and put on display in the Museum of Modern Art. And that impulse moves us away from resonance and toward wonder. For the MOMA is one of the great contemporary places not for the hearing of intertwining voices, not for historical memory, not for ethnographic thickness, but for intense, indeed enchanting looking. Looking may be called enchanted when the act of attention draws a circle around itself from which everything but the object is excluded, when intensity of regard blocks out all circumambient images, stills all murmuring voices. To be sure, the viewer may have purchased a catalogue, read an inscription on the wall, switched on a cassette, but in the moment of wonder all of this apparatus seems mere static.

The so-called boutique lighting that has become popular in recent years – a pool of light that has the surreal effect of seeming to emerge from within the object rather than to focus upon it from without – is an attempt to provoke or to heighten the experience of wonder, as if modern museum designers feared that wonder was increasingly difficult to arouse or perhaps that it risked displacement entirely onto the windows of designer dress shops and antique stores. The association of that lighting – along with transparent plastic rods and other devices to create the magical illusion of luminous, weightless suspension – with commerce would seem to suggest that wonder is bound up with acquisition, and possession, yet the whole experience of most art museums is about *not* touching, *not* carrying home, *not* owning the marvelous objects. Modern museums in effect at once evoke the dream of possession and evacuate it.[11] (Alternatively, we could say that they displace that dream onto the museum gift shop, where the boutique lighting once again serves to heighten acquisition, now of reproductions that stand for the unattainable works of art.)

That evacuation or displacement is an historical rather than structural aspect of the museum's regulation of wonder: that is, collections of objects calculated to arouse wonder arose precisely in the spirit of personal acquisition and were only subsequently detached from it. In the Middle Ages and Renaissance we characteristically hear about wonders in the context of those who possessed them (or who gave them away). Hence, for example, in his *Life of Saint Louis*, Joinville writes that 'during the king's stay at Saida someone brought him a stone that split into flakes';

> It was the most marvelous stone in the world, for when you lifted one of the flakes you found the form of a sea-fish between the two pieces of stone. This fish was entirely of stone, but there was nothing lacking in its shape, eyes, bones, or colour to make it seem otherwise than if it had been alive. The king gave me one of these stones. I found a tench inside; it was brown in colour, and in every detail exactly as you would expect a tench to be.[12]

The wonder-cabinets of the Renaissance were at least as much about possession as display. The wonder derived not only from what could be seen but from the sense that the shelves and cases were filled with unseen wonders, all the prestigious property of the collector. In this sense, the cult of wonder originated in close conjunction with a certain type of resonance, a resonance bound up with the evocation not of an absent culture but of the great man's superfluity of rare and precious things. Those things were not necessarily admired for their beauty; the marvelous was bound up with the excessive, the surprising, the literally outlandish, the prodigious. They were not necessarily the manifestations of the artistic skill of human makers: technical virtuosity could indeed arouse admiration, but so could nautilus shells, ostrich eggs, uncannily large (or small) bones, stuffed crocodiles, fossils. And, most importantly, they were not necessarily objects set out for careful viewing.

The experience of wonder was not initially regarded as essentially or even primarily *visual*; reports of marvels had a force equal to the seeing of them. Seeing was important and desirable, of course, but precisely in order to make reports possible, reports which then circulated as virtual equivalents of the marvels themselves. The great medieval collections of marvels are almost entirely textual: Friar Jordanus's *Marvels of the East*, Marco Polo's *Book of Marvels*, Mandeville's *Travels*. Some of the manuscripts, to be sure, were illuminated but these illuminations were almost ancillary to the textual record of wonders, just as emblem books were originally textual and only subsequently illustrated. Even in the sixteenth century, when the power of direct visual experience was increasingly valued, the marvelous was principally theorised as a textual phenomenon, as it had been in the antiquity. 'No one can be called a poet', writes the influential Italian critic Minturno in the 1550s, 'who does not excel in the power of arousing wonder'.[13] For Aristotle wonder was associated with pleasure as the end of poetry, and in the *Poetics* he examined the strategies by which tragedians and epic poets employ the marvelous to arouse wonder. For the Platonists too wonder was conceived as an essential element in literary art: in the sixteenth century, the Neo-Platonist Francesco Patrizi defined the poet as principal 'maker of the marvelous,' and the marvelous is found, as he put it, when men 'are astounded, ravished in ecstasy'. Patrizi goes so far as to posit marvelling as a special faculty of the mind, a faculty which in effect mediates between the capacity to think and the capacity to feel'.[14]

Modern art museums reflect a profound transformation of the experience: the collector – a Getty or a Mellon – may still be celebrated, and market value is even more intensely registered, but the heart of the mystery lies with the uniqueness, authenticity, and visual power of the masterpiece, ideally displayed in such a way as to heighten its charisma, to compel and reward the intensity of the viewer's gaze, to manifest artistic genius. Museums display works of art in such a way as to imply that no one, not even the nominal owner or donor, can penetrate the zone of light and actually possess the wonderful object. The object exists not principally to be owned but to be viewed. Even the *fantasy* of possession is no longer central to the museum-gaze, or rather it has been inverted, so that the object in its essence seems not to be a possession but rather to be itself the possessor of what is most valuable and enduring.[15] What the work possesses is the power to arouse wonder, and that power, in the dominant aesthetic ideology of the West, has been infused into it by the creative genius of the artist.

It is beyond the scope of this essay to account for the transformation of the experience of wonder from the spectacle of proprietorship to the mystique of the object – an exceedingly complex, overdetermined history centering on institutional and economic shifts – but I think it is important to say that at least in part this transformation was shaped by the collective project of

Western artists and reflects their vision. Already in the early sixteenth century, when the marvelous was still principally associated with the prodigious, Dürer begins, in a famous journal entry describing Mexican objects sent to Charles V by Cortés, to reconceive it:

> I saw the things which have been brought to the King from the new golden land: a sun all a gold a whole fathom broad, and a moon all of silver of the same size, also two rooms full of the armour of the people there, and all manner of wondrous weapons of theirs, harness and darts, wonderful shields, strange clothing, bedspreads, and all kinds of wonderful objects of various uses, much more beautiful to behold than prodigies. These things were all so precious that they have been valued at one hundred thousand gold florins. All the days of my life I have seen nothing that has gladdened my heart so much as these things, for I saw amongst then wonderful works of art, and I marvelled at the subtle *ingenia* of men in foreign lands. Indeed, I cannot express all that I thought there.[16]

Dürer's description is full of the conventional marks of his period's sense of wonder: he finds it important that the artifacts have been brought as a kind of tribute to the king, that large quantities of precious metals have been used, that their market value has been reckoned; he notes the strangeness of them, even as he uncritically assimilates that strangeness to his own culture's repertory of objects (which include harness and bedspreads). But he also notes, in perceptions highly unusual for his own time, that these objects are 'much more beautiful to behold than prodigies', Dürer relocates the source of wonder from the outlandish to the aesthetic, and he understands the effect of beauty as a testimony to creative genius: 'I saw amongst them wonderful works of art, and I marvelled at the subtle *ingenia* of men in foreign lands'.

It would be misleading to strip away the relations of power and wealth that are encoded in the artist's response, but it would be still more misleading, I think, to interpret that response as an unmediated expression of those relations. For Dürer gives voice to an aesthetic understanding–a form of wondering and admiring and knowing–that is at least partly independent of the structures of politics and the marketplace.

This understanding–by no means autonomous and yet not reducible to the institutional and economic forces by which it is shaped–is centered on a certain kind of looking, a looking whose origins lie in the cult of the marvelous and hence in the art work's capacity to generate in the spectator surprise, delight, admiration, and intimations of genius. The knowledge that derives from this kind of looking may not be very useful in the attempt to understand another culture, but is vitally important in the attempt to understand our own. For it is one of the distinctive achievements of our culture to have fashioned this type of gaze, and one of the most intense pleasures that it has to offer. This pleasure does not have an inherent and necessary politics, either radical or imperialist, but Dürer's remarks suggest that it originates at least in respect and admiration for the *ingenia* of others. This respect is a response worth cherishing and enhancing. Hence, for all of my academic affiliations and interests, I am skeptical about the recent attempt to turn our museums from temples of wonder into temples of resonance.

Perhaps the most startling instance of this attempt is the transfer of the paintings in the Jeu de Paume and the Louvre to the new Musée d'Orsay. The Musée d'Orsay is at once a spectacular manifestation of French cultural *dépense* and a highly self-conscious, exceptionally stylish generator of resonance, including the literal resonance of voices in an enormous vaulted railway station. By moving the Impressionist and Post-Impressionist masterpieces into proximity with the work of far less well-known painters – Jean Béraud, Guillaume Dubuffe, Paul Sérusier, and so forth – and into proximity as well with the period's sculpture and decorative arts, the museum remakes a remarkable group of highly individuated geniuses into engaged participants in a vital, conflict-ridden, immensely productive period in French cultural history. The reimagining is guided by many well-designed informative boards – cue cards, in effect – along, of course, with the extraordinary building itself.

All of this is intelligently conceived and dazzlingly executed – on a cold winter day in Paris, the museum-goer may look down from one of the high balconies by the old railway clocks and savor the swirling pattern formed by the black and gray raincoats of the spectators below, as they pass through the openings in the massive black stone partitions of Gay Aulenti's interior. The pattern seems spontaneously to animate the period's style – if not Manet, then at least Caillebotte; it is as if a painted scene had recovered the power to move and to echo.

But what has been sacrificed on the altar of cultural resonance is visual wonder centered on the aesthetic masterpiece. Attention is dispersed among a wide range of lesser objects that collectively articulate the impressive creative achievement of French culture in the late nineteenth century, but the experience of the old Jeu de Paume – intense looking at Manet, Monet, Cézanne and so forth – has been radically reduced. The paintings are there, but they are mediated by the resonant contextualism of the building itself and its myriad objects and its descriptive and analytical plaques. Moreover, many of the greatest paintings have been demoted, as it were, to small spaces where it is difficult to view them adequately – as if the design of the museum were trying to assure the triumph of resonance over wonder.

But is a triumph of one over the other necessary? I have, for the purposes of this exposition, obviously exaggerated the extent to which these are alternative models for museums (or for the reading of texts): in fact, almost every exhibition worth the viewing has strong elements of both. I think that the impact of most exhibitions is likely to be greater if the initial appeal is wonder, a wonder that then leads to the desire for resonance, for it is easier to pass from wonder to resonance than from resonance to wonder. Why this should be so is suggested by a remarkable passage in his *Commentary on the Metaphysics of Aristotle* by Aquinas's teacher, Albert the Great:

> wonder is defined as a constriction and suspension of the heart caused by amazement at the sensible appearance of something so portentous, great, and unusual, that the

heart suffers a systole. Hence wonder is something like fear in its effect on the heart. This effect of wonder, then, this constriction and systole of the heart, spring from an unfulfilled but felt desire to know the cause of that which appears portentous and unusual: so it was in the beginning when men, up to that time unskilled, began to philosophize. . . . Now the man who is puzzled and wonders apparently does not know. Hence wonder is the movement of the man who does not know on his way to finding out, to get at the bottom of that at which he wonders and to determine its cause. . . . Such is the origin of philosophy.[17]

Such too, from the perspective of the new historicism, is the origin of a meaningful desire for cultural resonance. But while philosophy would seek to supplant wonder with secure knowledge, it is the function of the new historicism continually to renew the marvelous at the heart of the resonant.

Notes

1 George Cavendish, *The Life and Death of Cardinal Wolsey*, in *Two Early Tudor Lives*, ed. Richard S. Sylvester and Davis P. Harding (New Haven and London, Yale University Press, 1962), pp. 24-5. We get another glimpse of the symbolism of hats later in the text, when Wolsey is beginning his precipitous fall from power: 'And talking with Master Norris upon his knees in the mire, he would have pulled off his under cap of velvet, but he could not undo the knot under his chin. Wherefore with violence he rent the laces and pulled it from his head and so kneeled bareheaded' (p. 106). I am grateful to Anne Barton for correcting my description of the hat in Christ Church and for transcribing the note card that details its provenance.

2 Walter Cohen, 'Political Criticism of Shakespeare', in *Shakespeare Reproduced: The Text in History and Ideology*, ed. Jean E. Howard and Marion F. O' Connor (New York and London, Methuen, 1987), p. 33; Edward Pechter, 'The New Historicism and Its Discontents', in *PLMA* 102 (1987), p. 301.

3 'The new historicists and cultural materialists', one typical summary puts it, 'represent, and by representing, reproduce in their *new* history of ideas, a world which is hierarchical, authoritarian, hegemonic, unsubvertable. . . . In this world picture, Stephen Greenblatt has poignantly asserted, there can be no subversion– and certainly not for us!' Poignantly or otherwise, I asserted no such thing; I argued that the spectator of the history plays was continually tantalized by a resistance simultaneously powerful and deferred.

4 See my *Renaissance Self-Fashioning: from More to Shakespeare* (Chicago, University of Chicago Press, 1980), pp. 174-5: 'We are situated at the close of the cultural movement initiated in the Renaissance; the places in which our social and psychological world seems to be cracking apart are those structural joints visible when it was first constructed'.

5 Louis Adrian Montrose, 'Renaissance Literary Studies and the Subject of History', in *English Literary Renaissance* 16 (1986), pp. 5–12; Don Wayne, 'Power, Politics, and the Shakespearean Text: Recent Criticism in England and the United States', in *Shakespeare Reproduced*, ed. Howard and O'Connor, pp. 47–67; Catherine Gallagher, 'Marxism and the New Historicism', in *The New Historicism*, ed. Harold Veeser (New York and London, Routledge, 1989).

6 Jean E. Howard, 'The New Historicism in Renaissance Studies', in *Renaissance Historicism: Selections from 'English Literary Renaissance'*, ed. Arthur F. Kinney and Dan S. Collins (Amherts: University of Massachusetts Press, 1987), pp. 32–3.

7 If there is then no suspension of value judgements in the new historicism, there is

at the same time a complication of those judgements, what I have called a sense of estrangement. This estrangement is bound up with the abandonment, the values of the present could no longer seem the necessary outcome of an irreversible teleological progression, whether of enlightenment or decline. An older historicism that proclaimed self-consciously that it had avoided all value judgements in its account of the past – that it had given us historical reality *wie es eigentlilich gewesen* – did not thereby avoid all value judgements; it simply provided a misleading account of what it had actually done. In this sense the new historicism, for all its acknowledgment of engagement and partiality, may be slightly less likely than the older historicism to impose its values belligerently on the past, for those values seem historically contingent.

8 Cohen, in *Shakespeare Reproduced*, pp. 33–4.
9 Thomas Greene, The *Vulnerable Text: Essays on Renaissance Literature* (New York, Columbia University Press, 1986), p. 100.
10 Quoted in Linda A. Altshuler and Anna R. Cohn, 'The Precious Legacy', in David Altshuler, ed., *The Precious Legacy: Judaic Treasures from the Czechoslovak State Collections* (New York, Summit Books, 1983), p. 24. My sketch of the genesis of the State Jewish Museum is largely paraphrased from this chapter.
11 In effect that dream of possessing wonder is at once aroused and evacuated in commerce as well, since the minute the object – shoe or dress or soup tureen – is removed from its magical pool of light, it loses its wonder and returns to the status of an ordinary purchase.
12 Joinville, *Life of Saint Louis*, in *Chronicles of the Crusades*, tr. M.R.B. Shaw (Harmondsworth, Penguin, 1963), p. 315.
13 Quoted in J.V. Cunningham, *Woe or Wonder: The Emotional Effect of Shakespearean Tragedy* (Denver, Alan Swallow, 1960: orig. edn 1951), p. 82.
14 Hathaway, pp. 66–9. Hathaway's account of Patrizi is taken largely from Bernard Weinberg, *A History of Literary Criticism in the Italian Renaissance*, 2 vols (Chicago, University of Chicago Press, 1961).
15 It is a mistake then to associate the gaze of the museum-goer with the appropriative male gaze about which so much has been written recently. But then I think that the discourse of the appropriative male gaze is itself in need of considerable qualification.
16 Quoted in Hugh Honour, *The New Golden Land: European Images of America from the Discoveries to the Present Time* (New York, Pantheon Books, 1975), p. 28.
17 Quoted in Cunningham, *Woe or Wonder*, pp. 77–8.

Section 4

Postmodernism

Introduction

For the American novelist John Barth, commenting on the term in 1980, Postmodernism was essentially a continuation but modification of cultural modernism, a way of 'telling stories'. By 1990, although the term had spilled out of the boundaries of literary critical debate, it still carried with it this earlier sense, but the stories are now indistinguishable from what was once assumed to be knowledge: scientific truth, ethics, law, history. Somewhere in the 1980s, the term shifted from functioning primarily as a description of a range of aesthetic practices involving irony, parody, self-consciousness, fragmentation, playful self-reflexivity and parataxis, to a use encompassing a more general shift of thought and registering a pervasive loss of faith in the progressivist and rationalist discourses of Enlightened modernity. It is now used variously as a term to describe the cultural epoch through which we are living (often apocalyptically, sometimes as the logic of Late Capitalism); an aesthetic practice (viewed as co-extensive with the commodified surfaces of this culture or as a disruption of its assumptions from within through a 'micropolitics' or 'politics of desire') or as a critique of the foundationalist assumptions of Enlightened political and philosophical thought. Lyotard's *The Postmodern Condition* (1979), marked the point where the specifically literary critical debate began to be dissolved into the larger theoretical and cultural one, though post-structuralists had already undermined the concept of grand- and metanarratives, the unity and autonomy of the subject and the ability of discourses to stabilize and contain cultural meanings.

Postmodernism is a 'mood' expressed theoretically across a diverse range of theoretical discourses and involving: a focus on the collapse of grand narratives into local incommensurable language games or 'little narratives'; a Foucauldian emphasis on the discontinuity and plurality of history as discursively produced and formulated, and a tendency to view the discourses of Enlightenment reason as complicit with the instrumental rationalization of modern life. The historian Arnold Toynbee first used the term in 1947 to describe the current, fourth and final, phase of Western history, dominated by anxiety and irrationalism. In the contemporary version, there is no longer a transcendent space from which to offer a critique of this culture: only disruption from within, micropolitics, language games, parody and fragmentation. Postmodernism wages war on totality. Postmodernists claim the exhaustion of all metanarratives which claim to legitimate foundations for truth, though some surreptitiously import new foundationalisms (the body, the aesthetic, desire). History becomes a plurality of islands of discourse arising out of the institutionally produced languages which we bring to bear on it. Or it is a network of agonistic language games where surface phenomena can no longer be 'explained' as the manifestations of deeper underlying truths. Absolute systems of knowledge give way to contingencies and ironies, aesthetic fictionality displaces philosophical certainty.

Whether influenced by post-Heideggerian hermeneutics, Nietzschean perspectivism or Wittgensteinian language games, Postmodernists such as Lyotard, Baudrillard and Rorty see knowledge of the world as indissociable from being-in-the-world: knowledge and experience are inextricably bound to each other and always culturally situated. There can be no transcendental 'view from nowhere', no position from outside culture from which to offer a criticism of it. Implication is all. We live in a pluralized culture surrounded by a multiplicity of styles, knowledges, stories that we tell ourselves about the world. To attempt to impose an overarching narrative on such experience is to perpetuate the violences of modernity with their exclusions and terrors. The relativization of styles which is postmodernism, throws into doubt the claims of any one discourse or story to be offering the 'truth' about the world or an authoritative version of the real. Issues of ethics, law, equality and authority become deeply problematic in such a context: how is one to legitimate knowledge and where to locate value?

Central to the 'postmodern condition' is a recognition and account of the way in which the 'grand narratives' of Western history, and in particular of enlightened modernity, have broken down. Counter-Enlightenment, of course, is as old as Enlightenment itself but, whereas in Romantic thought the critique of reason is accompanied by an assertion of an alternative foundationalist paradigm based on imaginative knowing and the truth of the human heart, postmodernists claim abandonment of all metanarratives which claim to legitimate foundations for knowledge or truth. This argument was first and most explicitly put forward in Jean-François Lyotard's *The Postmodern Condition* (translated into English in 1984) where Lyotard claimed that instrumental conceptions of reason and belief in 'totalities', systematic metaphysical systems, had produced totalitarianism, reigns of terror. Lyotard's book welcomed the collapse of grand theory and of legitimating metanarratives and advocated context-specific agon, heterogeneity, difference.

The essay reprinted here appeared as a post-script to the English translation of *The Postmodern Condition*. It is included because its emphasis on the sublime makes explicit the aestheticist assumptions of Lyotard's thought and a strong assertion of his belief in the collapse, and the desirability of the collapse, of Enlightened modernity and its rational systems. The essay is implicitly in dialogue with those defenders of the Enlightenment such as the German social theorist Jürgen Habermas who had argued that Enlightenment is not exhausted but simply unfinished, requiring a reworking of its modes of reason from an instrumental conception towards a more communicative mode. Habermas had argued that art can enhance life by allowing us to reconnect with pre-reflective and bodily aspects of experience but only as one aspect of our expansion of the concept of reason. Habermas argues against the collapse of knowledge and ethics into the aesthetic and defends the modern, Kantian argument for the separation of these spheres of discourse.

Lyotard's essay begins with the Kantian notion of the sublime as confirming the incommensurability of reality as pure Idea to concept as a tool of human understanding. This is in contradistinction to the beautiful which has the effect of seeming to affirm a realizable correspondence between internal and external orders. Sublimity, for Kant, is that experience of an object which evokes an idea of pure reason, but one which is radically indeterminate and cannot be formulated or known. Kant suggests that the imagination, in this mode, can excite in us ideas which cannot be realized in sensory form, though the experience in itself liberates us into a sense of the magnitude of the human mind. Lyotard's sublime is a self-consciously postmodern mode in which all striving for correspondence between Real and concept is abandoned; the aesthetic is not to be projected onto the social in the shape of a dangerous metaphysical totality. Lyotard thus embraces an aestheticist irony which entirely repudiates the notion of correspondence not simply for art but for all forms of knowledge including science. Lyotard's aesthetic of the sublime welcomes dissensus, radical incommensurability. It refuses to provide solutions or comfort but exists as a mode of resistance to the banal and automatizing effects of contemporary culture. Existence may be aestheticized, but the aesthetic must not be used to underpin political ideologies which offer blueprints for cultural revolution. For Lyotard, irony becomes a kind of fundamentalism.

Baudrillard's postmodern scenario is perhaps the bleakest of them all. To live in the postmodern condition for Baudrillard is not so much to inhabit a world saturated with consumer logic (as for Fredric Jameson or Terry Eagleton) as one entirely processed through technological reproduction. Earlier theorists, such as the American sociologist Daniel Bell, had argued that the condition of late capitalism could be defined as the shift from a production to a knowledge economy, but for Baudrillard the defining feature of the age is that we have entered the culture of the 'simulacrum'. Since the 1970s, Baudrillard's work has moved entirely away from an analysis of political economy (where he began, under the influence of Marxist theory) to a concern with what he calls the culture of 'hyperreality': models replace the real and determine the real. Disneyland becomes America; hyperreality is everyday reality. Media messages saturate the cultural field so entirely that the 'masses' are reduced, through an overload of information, to an inert and silent majority as all meaning disappears into the black hole of the simulacra in Baudrillard's work, the poststructuralist critique of reference is taken to a nihilistic limit.

Terry Eagleton has consistently criticized postmodern theory from a Marxist position, regarding it as a poststructuralist embrace of 'desire' as that which can explode out of history in order to deny its own historicity. For Eagleton, postmodernism is simply co-extensive with the depthless surfaces of consumer culture and reflects the commodification of all things in the culture of late capitalism. In a commercially driven world, art is simply an aesthetic reflection of already aestheticized images; postmodern art, in particular, is entirely complicit with this thrust of commodification. Eagleton reads postmodernism as a debasement of earlier and genuine avant-garde energies, seeing it as an exacerbation of modernist tendencies towards the refusal of engagement with history, as everything becomes 'text'. Eagleton regards its strategies as a desperate and decadent pastiche of genuine political discourses of emancipation which require either a concept of subjectivity as a coherent and intentional agency and/or a structural understanding of cultural, economic and political realities which can provide a foundation for collective agreements about the nature of the good.

In his book *The Illusions of Postmodernism*, from which this excerpt is taken, Eagleton sees postmodernism failing on both these counts. On the one hand, it merely represents an absurd and facile *reductio ad absurdam* of the classic liberal principle of negative liberty into the restless and empty libertarianism of a subjectivity without a self caught in the ever-spiralling dialectic of need and desire of a self-perpetuating freemarket economy. On the other hand, it collapses into a paranoid neo-Hegelianism where the positive liberty of citizenship or the republican ideal of discovering the self within the practices of civil society is turned into a monolithic cultural determinism from which the only escape must be into a textualist void of freedom as *jouissance*, consumer hedonism or criticism as free play. Postmodernism is here diagnosed as a manic-depressive cultural disorder, oscillating between the poles of textualist euphoria and constructivist dystopia, both underlyingly expressive of a desiring but culturally and economically decentred subjectivity obssessed with freedom but with nothing to be free for, in a society which can only be regarded as an oppressive constraint and curb on such free-floating desire. In this flimsy dream of escape, the ironist theorist takes over the negative associations of modern autonomy understood as the Romantic-modernist artist's pursuit of silence, exile and cunning. Language is fetishized and a rampant culturalism hijacks genuine political energies for a purely textualist and empty utopianism. In Eagleton's reading, postmodernism is intellectual decadence and even its more politically useful concern with 'difference' is purely empty if difference simply becomes an end in itself with no other purposive goals. Eagleton's critique continues to be one of the strongest theoretical condemnations of postmodernism.

The final essay in this section offers an outline of the history of relations between feminists and postmodern theorising. In particular, it addresses the implications for political movements like feminism of the dismantling of foundationalist arguments and of the concepts of universal justice, unity and liberation. The essay offers an historical overview but also seeks to discriminate between different orientations in postmodern thinking: deconstructionist and reconstructionist, strong and weak, and to consider the implications of each for feminist politics and understanding of gender relations.

32 | Jean-François Lyotard,

From 'Answering the Question: What is Postmodernism?'
in *The Postmodern Condition*, R. Durand tr., (1986),
pp. 71–82

A Demand

This is a period of slackening – I refer to the color of the times. From every
direction we are being urged to put an end to experimentation, in the arts
and elsewhere. I have read an art historian who extols realism and is militant
for the advent of a new subjectivity. I have read an art critic who packages
and sells 'Transavantgardism' in the marketplace of painting. I have read
that under the name of postmodernism, architects are getting rid of the
Bauhaus project, throwing out the baby of experimentation with the bathwater
of functionalism. I have read that a new philosopher is discovering what
he drolly calls Judaeo-Christianism, and intends by it to put an end to the
impiety which we are supposed to have spread. I have read in a French
weekly that some are displeased with *Mille Plateaux* [by Deleuze and Guattari]
because they expect, especially when reading a work of philosophy, to be
gratified with a little sense. I have read from the pen of a reputable historian
that writers and thinkers of the 1960 and 1970 avant-gardes spread a reign
of terror in the use of language, and that the conditions for a fruitful exchange
must be restored by imposing on the intellectuals a common way of speaking,
that of the historians. I have been reading a young philosopher of language
who complains that Continental thinking, under the challenge of speaking
machines, has surrendered to the machines the concern for reality, that it
has substituted for the referential paradigm that of 'adlinguisticity' (one
speaks about speech, writes about writing, intertextuality), and who thinks
that the time has now come to restore a solid anchorage of language in the
referent. I have read a talented theatrologist for whom postmodernism,
with its games and fantasies, carries very little weight in front of political
authority, especially when a worried public opinion encourages authority
to a politics of totalitarian surveillance in the face of nuclear warfare threats.

I have read a thinker of repute who defends modernity against those he
calls the neoconservatives. Under the banner of postmodernism, the latter
would like, he believes, to get rid of the uncompleted project of modernism,
that of the Enlightenment. Even the last advocates of *Aufklärung*, such as
Popper or Adorno, were only able, according to him, to defend the project
in a few particular spheres of life – that of politics for the author of *The
Open Society*, and that of art for the author of *Ästhetische Theorie*. Jürgen
Habermas (everyone had recognized him) thinks that if modernity has
failed, it is in allowing the totality of life to be splintered into independent
specialities which are left to the narrow competence of experts, while the

concrete individual experiences 'desublimated meaning' and 'destructured form', not as a liberation but in the mode of that immense *ennui* which Baudelaire described over a century ago.

Following a prescription of Albrecht Wellmer, Habermas considers that the remedy for this splintering of culture and its separation from life can only come from 'changing the status of aesthetic experience when it is no longer primarily expressed in judgements of taste', but when it is 'used to explore a living historical situation', that is, when 'it is put in relation with problems of existence.' For this experience then 'becomes a part of a language game which is no longer that of aesthetic criticism'; it takes part 'in cognitive processes and normative expectations'; 'it alters the manner in which those different moments *refer* to one another.' What Habermas requires from the arts and the experiences they provide is, in short, to bridge the gap between cognitive, ethical, and political discourses, thus opening the way to a unity of experience.

My question is to determine what sort of unity Habermas has in mind. Is the aim of the project of modernity the constitution of sociocultural unity within which all the elements of daily life and of thought would take their places as in an organic whole? Or does the passage that has to be charted between heterogeneous language games – those of cognition, of ethics, of politics – belong to a different order from that? And if so, would it be capable of effecting a real synthesis between them?

The first hypothesis, of a Hegelian inspiration, does not challenge the notion of a dialectically totalizing *experience*; the second is closer to the spirit of Kant's *Critique of Judgement*; but must be submitted, like the *Critique*, to that severe reexamination which postmodernity imposes on the thought of the Enlightenment, on the idea of a unitary end of history and of a subject. It is this critique which not only Wittgenstein and Adorno have initiated, but also a few other thinkers (French or other) who do not have the honor to be read by Professor Habermas – which at least saves them from getting a poor grade for their neoconservatism.

Realism

The demands I began by citing are not all equivalent. They can even be contradictory. Some are made in the name of postmodernism, others in order to combat it. It is not necessarily the same thing to formulate a demand for some referent (and objective reality), for some sense (and credible transcendence), for an addressee (and audience), or an addressor (and subjective expressiveness) or for some communicational consensus (and a general code of exchanges, such as the genre of historical discourse). But in the diverse invitations to suspend artistic experimentation, there is an identical call for order, a desire for unity, for identity, for security, or popularity (in the sense of *Öffentlichkeit*, of 'finding a public'). Artists and writers must be brought back into the bosom of the community, or at least, if the latter is considered to be ill, they must be assigned the task of healing it.

There is an irrefutable sign of this common disposition: it is that for all those writers nothing is more urgent than to liquidàte the heritage of the avant-gardes. Such is the case, in particular, of the so-called transavant-gardism. The answers given by Achille Bonito Oliva to the questions asked by Bernard Lamarche-Vadel and Michel Enric leave no room for doubt about this. By putting the avant-gardes through a mixing process, the artist and critic feel more confident that they can suppress them than by launching a frontal attack. For they can pass off the most cynical eclecticism as a way of going beyond the fragmentary character of the preceding experiments; whereas if they openly turned their backs on them, they would run the risk of appearing ridiculously neoacademic. The *Salons* and the *Académies*, at the time when the bourgeoisie was establishing itself in history, were able to function as purgation and to grant awards for good plastic and literary conduct under the cover of realism. But capitalism inherently possesses the power to derealize familiar objects, social roles, and institutions to such a degree that the so-called realistic representations can no longer evoke reality except as nostalgia or mockery, as an occasion for suffering rather than for satisfaction. Classicism seems to be ruled out in a world in which reality is so destabilized that it offers no occasion for experience but one for ratings and experimentation.

This theme is familiar to all readers of Walter Benjamin. But it is necessary to assess its exact reach. Photography did not appear as a challenge to painting from the outside, any more than industrial cinema did to narrative literature. The former was only putting the final touch to the program of ordering the visible elaborated by the quattrocento; while the latter was the last step in rounding off diachronies as organic wholes, which had been the ideal of the great novels of education since the eighteenth century. That the mechanical and the industrial should appear as substitutes for hand or craft was not in itself a disaster–except if one believes that art is in its essence the expression of an individuality of genius assisted by an elite craftsmanship.

The challenge lay essentially in that photographic and cinematographic processes can accomplish better, faster, and with a circulation a hundred thousand times larger than narrative or pictorial realism, the task which academicism had assigned to realism: to preserve various consciousnesses from doubt. Industrial photography and cinema will be superior to painting and the novel whenever the objective is to stabilize the referent, to arrange it according to a point of view which endows it with a recognizable meaning, to reproduce the syntax and vocabulary which enable the addressee to decipher images and sequences quickly, and so to arrive easily at the consciousness of his own identity as well as the approval which he thereby receives from others–since such structures of images and sequences constitute a communication code among all of them. This is the way the effects of reality, or if one prefers, the fantasies of realism, multiply.

If they too do not wish to become supporters (of minor importance at that) of what exists, the painter and novelist must refuse to lend themselves to such therapeutic uses. They must question the rules of the art of painting or of narrative as they have learned and received them from their predecessors. Soon those rules must appear to them as a means to deceive, to seduce, and to reassure, which makes it impossible for them to be 'true.' Under the common name of painting and literature, an unprecedented split is taking place. Those who refuse to reexamine the rules of art pursue successful careers in mass conformism by communicating, by means of the 'correct rules,' the endemic desire for reality with objects and situations capable of gratifying it. Pornography is the use of photography and film to such an end. It is becoming a general model for the visual or narrative arts which have not met the challenge of the mass media.

As for the artists and writers who question the rules of plastic and narrative arts and possibly share their suspicions by circulating their work, they are destined to have little credibility in the eyes of those concerned with 'reality' and 'identity'; they have no guarantee of an audience. Thus it is possible to ascribe the dialectics of the avant-gardes to the challenge posed by the realisms of industry and mass communication to painting and the narrative arts. Duchamp's 'ready made' does nothing but actively and parodistically signify this constant process of dispossession of the craft of painting or even of being an artist. As Thierry de Duve penetratingly observes, the modern aesthetic question is not 'What is beautiful?' but 'What can be said to be art (and literature)?'

Realism, whose only definition is that it intends to avoid the question of reality implicated in that of art, always stands somewhere between academicism and kitsch. When power assumes the name of a party, realism and its neoclassical complement triumph over the experimental avant-garde by slandering and banning it – that is, provided the 'correct' images, the 'correct' narratives, the 'correct' forms which the party requests, selects, and propagates can find a public to desire them as the appropriate remedy for the anxiety and depression that public experiences. The demand for reality – that is, for unity, simplicity, communicability, etc. – did not have the same intensity nor the same continuity in German society between the two world wars and in Russian society after the Revolution: this provides a basis for a distinction between Nazi and Stalinist realism.

What is clear, however, is that when it is launched by the political apparatus, the attack on artistic experimentation is specifically reactionary: aesthetic judgement would only be required to decide whether such or such work is in conformity with the established rules of the beautiful. Instead of the work of art having to investigate what makes it an art object and whether it will be able to find an audience, political academicism possesses and imposes *a priori* criteria of the beautiful, which designate some works and a public at a stroke and forever. The use of categories in aesthetic judgement would thus be of the same nature as in cognitive judgement. To speak like Kant, both would be determining judgements: the expression is 'well formed' first in the understanding, then the only cases retained in experience are those which can be subsumed under this expression.

When power is that of capital and not that of a party, the 'transavantgardist' or 'postmodern' (in Jencks's sense) solution proves to be better adapted than the antimodern solution. Eclecticism is the degree zero of contemporary general culture: one listens to reggae, watches a western, eats McDonald's food for lunch and local cuisine for dinner, wears Paris perfume in Tokyo and 'retro' clothes in Hong Kong; knowledge is a matter for TV games. It is easy to find a public for eclectic works. By becoming kitsch, art panders to the confusion which reigns in the 'taste' of the patrons. Artists, gallery owners, critics, and public wallow together in the 'anything goes', and the epoch is one of slackening. But this realism of the 'anything goes' is in fact that of money; in the absence of aesthetic criteria, it remains possible and useful to assess the value of works of art according to the profits they yield. Such realism accommodates all tendencies, just as capital accommodates all 'needs', providing that the tendencies and needs have purchasing power. As for taste, there is no need to be delicate when one speculates or entertains oneself.

Artistic and literary research is doubly threatened, once by the 'cultural policy' and once by the art and book market. What is advised, sometimes through one channel, sometimes through the other, is to offer works which, first, are relative to subjects which exist in the eyes of the public they address, and second, works so made ('well made') that the public will recognize what they are about, will understand what is signified, will be able to give or refuse its approval knowingly, and if possible, even to derive from such work a certain amount of comfort.

The interpretation which has just been given of the contact between the industrial and mechanical arts, and literature and the fine arts is correct in its outline, but it remains narrowly sociologizing and historicizing – in other words, one-sided. Stepping over Benjamin's and Adorno's reticences, it must be recalled that science and industry are no more free of the suspicion which concerns reality than are art and writing. To believe otherwise would be to entertain an excessively humanistic notion of the mephistophelian functionalism of sciences and technologies. There is no denying the dominant existence today of techno-science, that is, the massive subordination of cognitive statements to the finality of the best possible performance, which is the technological criterion. But the mechanical and the industrial, especially when they enter fields traditionally reserved for artists, are carrying with them much more than power effects. The objects and the thoughts which originate in scientific knowledge and the capitalist economy convey with them one of the rules which supports their possibility: the rule that there is no reality unless testified by a consensus between partners over a certain knowledge and certain commitments.

This rule is of no little consequence. It is the imprint left on the politics of the scientist and the trustee of capital by a kind of flight of reality out of the metaphysical, religious, and political certainties that the mind believed it held. This withdrawal is absolutely necessary to the emergence of science and capitalism. No industry is possible without a suspicion of the Aristotelian theory of motion, no industry without a refutation of corporatism, of mercantilism, and of physiocracy. Modernity, in whatever age it appears, cannot exist without a shattering of belief and without discovery of the 'lack of reality' of reality, together with the invention of other realities.

What does this 'lack of reality' signify if one tries to free it from a narrowly historicized interpretation? The phrase is of course akin to what Nietzsche calls nihilism. But I see a much earlier modulation of Nietzschean perspectivism in the Kantian theme of the sublime. I think in particular that it is in the aesthetic of the sublime that modern art (including literature) finds its impetus and the logic of avant-gardes finds its axioms.

The sublime sentiment, which is also the sentiment of the sublime, is, according to Kant, a strong and equivocal emotion: it carries with it both pleasure and pain. Better still, in it pleasure derives from pain. Within the tradition of the subject, which comes from Augustine and Descartes and which Kant does not radically challenge, this contradiction, which some would call neurosis or masochism, develops as a conflict between the faculties of a subject, the faculty to conceive of something and the faculty to 'present' something. Knowledge exists if, first, the statement is intelligible, and second, if 'cases' can be derived from the experience which 'corresponds' to it. Beauty exists if a certain 'case' (the work of art), given first by the sensibility without any conceptual determination, the sentiment of pleasure independent of any interest the work may elicit, appeals to the principle of a universal consensus (which may never be attained).

Taste, therefore testifies that between the capacity to conceive and the capacity to present an object corresponding to the concept, an undetermined agreement, without rules, giving rise to a judgement which Kant calls reflective, may be experienced as pleasure. The sublime is a different sentiment. It takes place, on the contrary, when the imagination fails to present an object which might, if only in principle, come to match a concept. We have the idea of the world (the totality of what is), but we do not have the capacity to show an example of it. We have the idea of the simple (that which cannot be broken down, decomposed), but we cannot illustrate it with a sensible object which would be a 'case' of it. We can conceive the infinitely great, the infinitely poweful, but every presentation of an object destined to 'make visible' this absolute greatness or power appears to us painfully inadequate. Those are ideas of which no presentation is possible. Therefore, they impart no knowledge about reality (experience); they also prevent the free union of the faculties which gives rise to the sentiment of the beautiful; and they prevent the formation and the stabilization of taste. They can be said to be unpresentable.

I shall call modern the art which devotes its 'little technical expertise' (*son 'petit technique'*), as Diderot used to say, to present the fact that the unpresentable exists. To make visible that there is something which can be conceived and which can neither be seen nor made visible: this is what is at stake in modern painting. But how to make visible that there is something which cannot be seen? Kant himself shows the way when he names 'formlessness the absence of form,' as a possible index to the unpresentable. He also says of the empty 'abstraction' which the imagination experiences when in search for a presentation of the infinite (another unpresentable): this abstraction itself is like a presentation of the infinite, its 'negative presentation.' He cites the commandment, 'Thou shalt not make graven images' (*Exodus*), as the most sublime passage in the Bible in that it forbids all presentation of the Absolute. Little needs to be added to those observations to outline an aesthetic of sublime paintings. As painting, it will of course 'present' something though negatively; it will therefore avoid figuration or representation. It will be 'white' like one of Malevitch's squares; it will enable us to see only by making it impossible to see; it will please only by causing pain. One recognizes in those instructions the axioms of avant-gardes in painting, inasmuch as they devote themselves to making an allusion to the unpresentable by means of visible presentations. The systems in the name of which, or with which, this task has been able to support or to justify itself deserve the greatest attention; but they can originate only in the vocation of the sublime in order to legitimize it, that is, to conceal it. They remain inexplicable without the incommensurability of reality to concept which is implied in the Kantian philosophy of the sublime.

It is not my intention to analyze here in detail the manner in which the various avant-gardes have, so to speak, humbled and disqualified reality by examining the pictorial techniques which are so many devices to make us believe in it. Local tone, drawing, the mixing of colors, linear perspective, the nature of the support and that of the instrument, the treatment, the display, the museum: the avant-gardes are perpetually flushing out artifices of presentation which make it possible to subordinate thought to the gaze and to turn it away from the unpresentable. If Habermas, like Marcuse, understands the task of derealization as an aspect of the (repressive) 'desublimation' which characterizes the avant-garde, it is because he confuses the Kantian sublime with Freudian sublimation, and because aesthetics has remained for him that of the beautiful.

The Postmodern

What, then, is the postmodern? What place does it or does it not occupy in the vertiginous work of the questions hurled at the rules of image and narration? It is undoubtedly a part of the modern. All that has been received, if only yesterday (*modo, modo*, Petronius used to say), must be suspected. What space does Cézanne challenge? The Impressionists'. What objects do Picasso and Braque attack? Cézanne's. What presupposition does Duchamp break with in 1912? That which says one must make a painting, be it cubist. And Buren questions that other presupposition which he believes had survived untouched by the work of Duchamp: the place of presentation of the work. In an amazing acceleration, the generations precipitate themselves. A work can become modern only if it is first postmodern. Postmodernism thus understood is not modernism at its end but in the nascent state, and this state is constant.

Yet I would like not to remain with this slightly mechanistic meaning of the word. If it is true that modernity takes place in the withdrawal of the real and according to the sublime relation between the presentable and the conceivable, it is possible, within this relation, to distinguish two modes (to use the musician's language). The emphasis can be placed on the powerlessness of the faculty of presentation, on the nostalgia for presence felt by the human subject, on the obscure and futile will which inhabits him in spite of everything. The emphasis can be placed, rather, on the power of the faculty to conceive, on its 'inhumanity' so to speak (it was the quality Apollinaire demanded of modern artists), since it is not the business of our understanding whether or not human sensibility or imagination can match what it conceives. The emphasis can also be placed on the increase of being and the jubilation which result from the invention of new rules of the game, be it pictorial, artistic, or any other. What I have in mind will become clear if we dispose very schematically a few names on the chessboard of the history of avant-gardes: on the side of melancholia, the German Expressionists, and on the side of *novatio*, Braque and Picasso, on the former Malevitch and on the latter Lissitsky, on the one Chirico and on the other Duchamp. The nuance which distinguishes these two modes may be infinitesimal; they often coexist in the same piece, are almost indistinguishable; and yet they testify to a difference (*un différend*) on which the fate of thought depends and will depend for a long time, between regret and assay.

The work of Proust and that of Joyce both allude to something which does not allow itself to be made present. Allusion, to which Paolo Fabbri recently called my attention, is perhaps a form of expression indispensable to the works which belong to an aesthetic of the sublime. In Proust, what is being eluded as the price to pay for this allusion is the identity of consciousness, a victim to the excess of time (*au trop de temps*). But in Joyce, it is the identity of writing which is the victim of an excess of the book (*au trop de livre*) or of literature.

Proust calls forth the unpresentable by means of a language unaltered in its syntax and vocabulary and of a writing which in many of its operators still belongs to the genre of novelistic narration. The literary institution, as Proust inherits it from Balzac and Flaubert, is admittedly subverted in that the hero is no longer a character but the inner consciousness of time, and in that the diegetic diachrony, already damaged by Flaubert, is here put in question because of the narrative voice. Nevertheless, the unity of the book, the odyssey of that consciousness, even if it is deferred from chapter to chapter, is not seriously challenged: the identity of the writing with itself throughout the labyrinth of the interminable narration is enough to connote such unity, which has been compared to that of *The Phenomenology of Mind*.

Joyce allows the unpresentable to become perceptible in his writing itself, in the signifier. The whole range of available narrative and even stylistic operators is put into play without concern for the unity of the whole, and new operators are tried. The grammar and vocabulary of literary language are no longer accepted as given; rather they appear as academic forms, as rituals originating in piety (as Nietzsche said) which prevent the unpresentable from being put forward.

Here, then, lies the difference: modern aesthetics is an aesthetic of the sublime, though a nostalgic one. It allows the unpresentable to be put forward only as the missing contents; but the form, because of its recognizable consistency, continues to offer to the reader or viewer matter for solace and pleasure. Yet these sentiments do not constitute the real sublime sentiment, which is in an intrinsic combination of pleasure and pain: the pleasure that reason should exceed all presentation, the pain that imagination or sensibility should not be equal to the concept.

The postmodern would be that which, in the moderns puts forward the unpresentable in presentation itself; that which denies itself the solace of good forms, the consensus of a taste which would make it possible to share collectively the nostalgia for the unattainable; that which searches for new presentations, not in order to enjoy them but in order to impart a stronger sense of the unpresentable. A postmodern artist or writer is in the position of a philosopher: the text he writes, the work he produces are not in principle governed by preestablished rules, and they cannot be judged according to a determining judgement, by applying familiar categories to the text or to the work. Those rules and categories are what the work of art itself is looking for. The artist and the writer, then, are working without rules in order to formulate the rules of what *will have been done*. Hence the fact that work and text have the characters of an *event*; hence also, they always come too late for their author, or, what amounts to the same thing, their being put into work, their realization (*mise en oeuvre*) always begin too soon. *Post modern* would have to be understood according to the paradox of the future (*post*) anterior (*modo*).

It seems to me that the essay (Montaigne) is postmodern, while the fragment (*The Athaeneum*) is modern.

Finally, it must be clear that it is our business not to supply reality but to invent allusions to the conceivable which cannot be presented. And it is not to be expected that this task will effect the last reconciliation between language games (which, under the name of faculties, Kant knew to be separated by a chasm), and that only the transcendental illusion (that of Hegel) can hope to totalize them into a real unity. But Kant also knew that the price to pay for such an illusion is terror. The nineteenth and twentieth centuries have given us as much terror as we can take. We have paid a high enough price for the nostalgia of the whole and the one, for the reconciliation of the concept and the sensible, of the transparent and the communicable experience. Under the general demand for slackening and for appeasement, we can hear the mutterings of the desire for a return of terror for the realization of the fantasy to seize reality. The answer is: let us wage a war on totality; let us be witnesses to the unpresentable; let us activate the differences and save the honor of the name.

33 | Jean Baudrillard,

From 'The Orders of Simulacra', in *Simulations*, P. Beitchman tr. (1983), pp. 142–56

The very definition of the real becomes: *that of which it is possible to give an equivalent reproduction*. This is contemporaneous with a science that postulates that a process can be perfectly reproduced in a set of given conditions, and also with the industrial rationality that postulates a universal system of equivalency (classical representation is not equivalence, it is transcription, interpretation, commentary). At the limit of this process of reproductibility, the real is not only what can be reproduced, but *that which is always already reproduced*. The hyperreal.

And so: end of the real, and end of art, by total absorption one into the other? No: hyperrealism is the limt of art, and of the real, by respective exchange, on the level of the simulacrum, of the privileges and the prejudices which are their basis. The hyperreal transcends representation (cf. J.F. Lyotard, *L'Art Vivant*, number on hyperrealism) only because it is entirely in simulation. The tourniquet of representation tightens madly, but of an implosive madness, that, far from eccentric (marginal) inclines towards the center to its own infinite repetition. Analogous to the distancing characteristic of the dream, that makes us say that we are only dreaming; but this is only the game of censure and of perpetuation of the dream. Hyperrealism is made an integral part of a coded reality that it perpetuates, and for which it changes nothing.

In fact, we should turn our definition of hyperrealism inside out: *It is reality itself today that is hyperrealist*. Surrealism's secret already was that the most banal reality could become surreal, but only in certain privileged moments that nevertheless are still connected with art and the imaginary. Today it is quotidian reality in its entirety – political, social, historical and economic – that from now on incorporates the simulatory dimension of hyperrealism. We live everywhere already in an 'esthetic' hallucination of reality. The old slogan 'truth is stranger than fiction', that still corresponded to the surrealist phase of this estheticization of life, is obsolete. There is no more fiction that life could possibly confront, even victoriously – it is reality itself that disappears utterly in the game of reality – radical disenchantment, the cool and cybernetic phase following the hot stage of fantasy.

It is thus that for guilt, anguish and death there can be substituted the total joy of the signs of guilt, despair, violence and death. It is the very euphoria of simulation, that sees itself as the abolition of cause and effect, the beginning and the end, for all of which it substitutes reduplication. In this manner all closed systems protect themselves at the same time from the referential – as well as from all metalanguage that the system forestalls in playing at its own metalanguage; that is to say in duplicating itself in its own critique of itself. In simulation, the metalinguistic illusion duplicates and completes the referential illusion (pathetic hallucination of the sign and pathetic hallucination of the real).

'It's a circus', 'It's theatre', 'It's a movie', old adages, old naturalistic denunciation. These sayings are now obsolete. The problem now is that of the *satellization of the real*, the putting into orbit of an indefinable reality without common measure to the fantasies that once used to ornament it. This satellization we find further naturalized in the two-rooms-kitchen shower that they have launched into orbit – to the powers of space, you could say – with the last lunar module. The banality of the earthly habitat lifted to the rank of cosmic value, of absolute decor – hypostatized in space – this is the end of metaphysics, the era of hyperreality that begins.[1] But the spatial transcendence of the banality of the two-rooms, like its cool and mechanical figuration of hyperrealism,[2] says only one thing: that this module, such as it is, participates in a hyperspace of representation – where each is already technically in possession of the instantaneous reproduction of his own life, where the pilots of the Tupolev that crashed at Bourget could see themselves die live on their own camera. This is nothing else than the short-circuit of the response by the question in the test, instantaneous process of re-conduction whereby reality is immediately contaminated by its simulacrum.

There used to be, before, a specific class of allegorical and slightly diabolical objects: mirrors, images, works of art (concepts?) – simulacra, but transparent and manifest (you didn't confuse the counterfeit with the original), that had their characteristic style and savoir-faire. And pleasure consisted then rather in discovering the 'natural' in what was artificial and counterfeit. Today, when the real and the imaginary are confused in the same operational totality, the esthetic fascination is everywhere. It is a subliminal perception (a sort of sixth sense) of deception, montage, scenaria – of the overexposed reality in the light of the models – no longer a production space, but a reading strip, strip of coding and decoding, magnetized by the signs – esthetic reality – no longer by the premeditation and the distance of art, but by its elevation to the second level, to the second power, by the anticipation and the immanence of the code. A kind of non-intentional parody hovers over everything, of technical simulation, of indefinable fame to which is attached an esthetic pleasure, that very one of reading and of the rules of the game. Travelling of signs, the media, of fashion and the models, of the blind and brilliant ambiance of the simulacra.

A long time ago art prefigured this turning which is that today of daily life. Very quickly the work turns back on itself as the manipulation of the signs of art: over-signification of art, 'academism of the signifier', as Lévi-Strauss would say, who interprets it really as the form-sign. It is then that art enters into its indefnite *reproduction:* all that reduplicates itself, even if it be the everyday and banal reality, falls by the token under the sign of art, and becomes esthetic. It's the same thing for production, which you could say is entering today this esthetic reduplication , this phase when, expelling all content and finality, it becomes somehow abstract and non-figurative. It expresses then the pure form of production, it takes upon itself, as art, the value of a finality without purpose. Art and industry can then exchange their signs. Art can become a reproducing machine (Andy Warhol) without ceasing to be art, since the machine is only a sign. And production can lose all social finality so as to be verified and exalted finally in the prestigious, hyperbolic signs that are the great industrial combines, the 1/4-mile-high towers or the number mysteries of the GNP.

And so art is everywhere, since artifice is at the very heart of reality. And so art is dead, not only because its critical transcendence is gone, but because reality itself, entirely impregnated by an esthetic which is inseparable from its own structure, has been confused with its own image. Reality no longer has the time to take on the appearance of reality. It no longer even surpasses fiction: it captures every dream even before it takes on the appearance of a dream. Schizophrenic vertigo of these serial signs, for which no counterfeit, no sublimation is possible, immanent in their repetition–who could say what the reality is that these signs simulate? They no longer even repress anything (which is why, if you will, simulation pushes us close to the sphere of psychosis). Even the primary processes are abolished in them. The cool universe of digitality has absorbed the world of metaphor and metonymy. The principle of simulation wins out over the reality principle just as over the principle of pleasure.

Notes

1　The coefficient of reality is proportional to the imaginary in reverse which gives its specific density. This is true of geographical and spatial exploration also. When there is no more territory virgin and therefore available for the imaginary, when the map covers the whole territory, then something like a principle of reality disappears. The conquest of space constitutes in this sense an irreversible threshold in the direction of the loss of the earthly referential. This is precisely the hemorrhage of reality as internal coherence of a limited universe when its limits retreat infinitely. The conquest of space follows that of the planet as the same fantastic enterprise of extending the jurisdiction of the real–to carry for example the flag, the technique, and the two-rooms-and-kitchen to the moon–same tentative to substantiate the concepts or to territorialize the unconscious–the latter equals making the human race unreal, or to reversing it into a hyperreality of simulation.

2　Or that of the metal-plated caravan or supermarket dear to hyperrealists, or Campbell's Soup dear to Andy Warhol, or the Mona Lisa, since she too has been satellized around the planet, as absolute model of earthly art, no longer a work of art but a planetary simulacrum where everyone comes to witness himself (really his own death) in the gaze of the future.

34 | Terry Eagleton,

From *The Illusions of Postmodernism* (1997), pp. 109–14

The rejection of so-called metanarratives is definitive of postmodern philosophy, but the options it poses here are sometimes rather narrow. Either you are enthused by a particular metanarrative, such as the story of technological progress or the march of Mind, or you find these fables oppressive and turn instead to a plurality of tales. But we have seen already that these are not the only choices available, as indeed the more intelligent postmodernist recognizes. Socialism holds to a sort of metanarrative, but it is by no means the kind of bedtime story one would recount to a child given to nightmares. It has its more upbeat aspects, but in other ways it is a horror story. The sooner it is over the better; it is just that proclaiming it over already, as postmodernists tend to do, it likely to help perpetuate it.

The other misleading choice offered by some (though not all) postmodernism is to imagine that there is either a single metanarrative or a multiplicity of micronarratives. The same goes for the postmodern concept of foundations: either there is one of them, or none at all. This all-or-nothingism ill befits a supposedly non-binary theory. What if there were a plurality of metanarratives? There are basically two kinds of activity which keep the human species going, one of them to do with material reproduction and the other with sexual reproduction. Without these two stories, human history would have ground to a halt and postmodernism would have nothing to be posterior to. And both of these stories have been chronicles of ceaseless warfare. To call them 'metanarratives' is not to suggest that they each encompass everything that ever happened (how could either, since we already have two of them?), or that some unruptured thread of continuity runs through them both, or that they are in every respect the most valuable or interesting tales one can tell. Interesting in what sense? They may be what keep the species going, but they are both fairly sordid anecdotes, and for value one would be well advised to turn to culture, which in its narrower sense is not central to the survival of the species at all. There would, to be sure, be no culture at all without these grander chronicles, but that makes them more fundamental than culture only in the sense that Dickens's having a pen was fundamental to *Little Dorrit*. These particular *grands récits* are significant for two reasons: first, because they are the cause today as in the past of a good deal of misery which needs to be put to rights, and secondly because if we do not do so they shall go on demanding enormous investments of energy and hence distract us from the pleasures of talking about something more interesting for a change. These stories bulk so large in our lives, precisely because they have proved so problematic, that they weigh burdensomely upon many of our micronarratives too, skewing them from the inside and leaving their bleak inscription upon them. If one wanted a fresh understanding of the Marxist model of base and superstructure, one could perhaps find it here.

These are not metanarratives in the sense of being stories of which all other stories are a mere function. Marxism has very little of interest to say about the virtues of Icelandic cuisine in contrast to Bulgarian. Why should it? It is not some sort of cosmic philosophy along the lines of Rosicrucianism. It has had fairly little of interest to say about feminism either, partly because much of it has been conventionally patriarchal, but also because it is a restricted narrative which was never intended to be a Theory of Everything. It is not a fault of feminist theory that it has made few major contributions to Marxist thought; why should it have done? There is a difference between a theory from which everything else can be supposedly deduced, as in the more megalomaniac forms of high rationalism, and a narrative which is 'grand' in the sense of providing the matrix within which many, but not all, of our other practices take shape. And there are, arguably, other grand narratives besides the ones I have mentioned, such as the global story of imperialism and colonialism. In denying that this constitutes a metanarrative, one should be careful as a Westerner that one is not subtly defusing it. It is curious that so much postcolonial theory should want to deny the systematic, world-historical nature of the imperial history it examines, its repetitions as well as its differences, thus in some sense letting it off the hook. But none of these fables is 'grand' because it operates by a single logic, any more than *Middlemarch* does.

Postmodernism, wedded as it is to the particular, would be reluctant to accept that there are propositions which are true of all times and places, yet which are not simply vacuous or trivial. The statement 'In all times and places, most men and women have led lives of fairly futile labour, usually for the profit of a few' seems one such utterance. 'Women have always suffered oppression' is another. To narrativize these propositions is to help defamiliarize them – to recover something of our naive astonishment at what we had taken for granted. There is a sense in which we can forget or deny what is most common exactly because it *is* so common, as in Roland Barthes's celebrated example of those names of countries which march across the map in such huge capitals that they are effectively invisible. Grand narratives are in this sense a bit like transcendental conditions, so much the very framework of our perception that it is hard to stare at them straight.

Similarly, it is difficult for us to recapture the imaginative excitement which must have burst upon the world with the concept of universality. What could have sounded more scandalous to a profoundly particularist culture, one in which what you were was bound up with your region, function, social rank, than the extraordinary notion that everyone was entitled to individual respect quite independently of these things? This outlandish new doctrine was of course launched into philosophical orbit from a highly specific postion, that of a wing of the European bourgeoisie, but so is every doctrine, universal or otherwise. Whether Jean Baudrillard's ideas are true or false is not to be determined by the fact that he is a Frenchman working in California, even if these facts may have some relevance to their formation. The exotic new thesis was abroad that you were entitled to freedom, autonomy, justice, happiness, political equality and the rest not because you were the son of a minor Prussian count but simply on account of your humanity. We now had rights, obligations and responsibilities which put in brackets all of our most intimately individuating features. Postmodernism is in general allergic to any such trampling on the particular, and this ferocious abstraction trampled on it with a vengeance. It was also one of the greatest emancipatory ideas of world history, one which postmodernism has come so much to take for granted that it can apparently only identify it by its blindspots. It was not at all true in practice that everyone–women, for example, or non-Europeans or the lower peasantry–was accorded equal respect. But everyone's freedom mattered in theory, and 'in theory' is a sizeable improvement on its not mattering even as that. It is an improvement not least because middle-class society could now be challenged by those it suppressed *according to its own logic*, caught out in a performative contradiction between what it said and what it did. And this is always a far sharper form of critique than measuring a social order against values whose validity it would not even acknowledge.

This great revolutionary concept was of course thoroughly essentialist. It was by virtue of our shared human nature that we had ethical and political claims upon one another, not for any more parochial, paternalist or sheerly cultural reason. These matters were too important to be left to the tender mercies of custom or tradition, to the whim of your masters or the tacit codes of your community. The respect you had been contingently granted could be just as contingently withdrawn, and this was too feeble a basis for an ethics. Justice had to be indifferent; it was the *anciens régimes* which were the great apologists for difference, in the sense that how you were treated depended on how you were ranked. Difference was now a reactionary idea, and sameness or identity a revolutionary one. If you wanted to reject elitism or autocracy on any thing stronger than pragmatic grounds, you had to go universalist. Postmodernism, which tends to both anti-elitism and anti-universalism, thus lives a certain tension between its political and philosophical values. It seeks to resolve this by short-circuiting universality and returning in a sense of pre-modern particularism, but now to a particularism without privilege, which is to say to a difference without hierarchy. Its problem is how a difference without hierarchy is not to collapse into pure *in*difference, so becoming a kind of inverted mirror-image of the universalism it repudiates.

35 | Patricia Waugh,

'Postmodernism and Feminism?', in S. Jackson and J. Jones eds, *Contemporary Feminist Theories* (1998), pp. 177–92

The term postmodernism has come to seem definitive of our end-of-millennium consciousness, along with all the other 'post-' phenomena which emerged in the 1970s and 1980s: post-industrialism, post-Marxism, post-humanism and, of course, so-called 'post-feminism'. The term exerts an enormous grip upon our intellectual climate and upon contemporary debates within feminism. A crucial problem in trying to assess the relations between postmodernism and feminism is that, although feminism can be broadly defined as a political movement whose objectives are ultimately emancipatory, postmodernism cannot be described so easily. The term 'postmodernism' has now come to designate a bewilderingly diverse array of cultural practices, writers, artists, thinkers and theoretical accounts of late modernity. In also refers to a more general sense of radical change in the ways of thinking we have inherited from the eighteenth-century European Enlightenment.

The Enlightenment has been characterised as a project definitively committed to 'develop objective science, universal morality and law, and autonomous art according to their own inner logic' (Habermas 1981: 9). Postmodernists, however, have argued that science, ethics and art are or no longer should be seen as separable. Hence postmodernism denies the possibility of an 'objective' science discovering the laws of an independently existing reality; it repudiates the pursuit of universal and rational ethical principles; it rejects the existence of a separate category of the 'aesthetic' which is removed from the realms of science, ethics or everyday cultural practice.

Many feminists remain sceptical about the likely political consequences of a total abandonment of the Enlightenment project. Yet feminism has been drawn into that postmodern critique which accuses Enlightenment thinkers of setting up so-called 'universal' categories of knowledge and value which actually exclude entire communities or groups of people, and of claiming 'objectivity' for knowledge which actually reflects vested interests. Feminism has in fact always contributed its own critique of the Enlightenment, arguing that the notion of a universal rational Subject is implicitly masculine, as is its understanding of history as a grand narrative of progress. By the same token, the ideal that knowledge was an objective reflection of an independently existing world fell by the wayside. Recently, feminist theory has come to manifest a number of overt postmodern symptoms: an infatuation with such concepts as the sublime, with the idea of radical alterity (otherness) or the possibility of a feminine 'space' outside of rationality and patriarchal hierarchies, and a fondness for images suggestive of fluidity or hybridity such as the cyborg or the nomad.

Postmodernism and Feminism: A Brief History

The term 'postmodernism' was first used in the 1950s by critics concerned to describe what they perceived to be new kinds of literary experiment arising out of but moving beyond those of cultural modernism. By the early eighties, however, the term shifts from the description of a range of aesthetic practices involving playful irony, parody, self-consciousness and fragmentation, to a use which encompasses a more general shift in thought and seems to register a pervasive cynicism about the progressivist ideals of the Enlightenment. 'Postmodernism' is now used to designate a new cultural epoch in which capitalism, in its latest consumerist phase, invades everything, leaving no remaining oppositional space (Jameson 1991). Postmodernism thus comes to encompass a constellation of preoccupations involving repudiations of foundationalism (the idea that knowledge can be grounded in secure *a priori* principles), a range of aesthetic practices which disrupt the modernist concept of artistic autonomy, and a variety of attempts to describe the present cultural mood or condition. The term is now variously used to describe both the contemporary cultural condition *per se* and a diverse range of intellectual responses which appear in part actually to construct that condition.

Perhaps postmodernism is best thought of as a 'mood' arising out of a sense of the collapse of all those foundations of modern thought which seemed to guarantee a reasonably stable sense of Truth, Knowledge, Self and Value. The refusal to separate domains of knowledge has, in fact, absorbed both knowledge and experience into the realm of the aesthetic. Even scientific knowledge becomes a fiction: there are no objective 'facts', for 'facts' too are produced through forms of observation and discourse determined by theoretical (fictional) frames. Indeed, Jean Baudrillard has described postmodernism as a condition of hyperinflation of the aesthetic, for 'art is everywhere, since artifice is at the very heart of reality' (Baudrillard 1983: 151).

Ihab Hassan has usefully offered an epochal definition of postmodernism as an: 'antinomian movement that assumes a vast unmaking of the Western mind' (in Wellmer 1985: 338). He uses the term 'unmaking', to cover terms such as deconstruction, decentring, demystification, discontinuity and difference, which feature prominently in postmodern discourse. These terms assume or imply a rejection of the idea of a rational coherent subject, and the end of 'grand narratives' of universal truth or of ideas such as Marx's theory of the progressive development of productive forces. If the search for universal truth requires confidence in the ability of the rational enquirer to arrive at fundamental, generally applicable knowledge, then it would seem that the demise of the rational subject also entails the collapse of the notion of 'Truth'. Similarly, therefore (the argument runs), without a foundation in universal and objective knowledge, there cannot be a political project of universal emancipation through the rational pursuit of such knowledge because no such knowledge is achievable.

For some, particularly those influenced by the thought of Michel Foucault, to continue to believe in the Enlightenment project is either to ignore everything which it excludes, or to be guilty of perpetrating totalitarian violences under the banner of freedom and progress. The crisis in knowledge – the idea that all knowledge is constructed and reflects relations of power – is seen to entail a crisis in the political orientation of the Enlightenment. With the rejection of Descartes' move to found Reason in individual subjectivity comes the argument that individual subjectivity is not a basis, but a result of historically variable discursive operations. Consequently, the focus shifts towards an emphasis on relativity, and a receptiveness to ideas of 'difference', plurality, fragmentation, non-totality, aesthetic self-fashioning, contingency and 'language games'.

Postmodernism thus entails a pervasive crisis in the modern understanding of selfhood as founded upon a unitary coherent subjectivity. Much of this 'crisis' was actually formulated within the discourse of modernity. For example, the Marxist critique of individualism had already anticipated much of this argument. It was later extended by post-structuralist thinkers such as Althusser, Lacan and Derrida through an engagement with Saussure's structural linguistics. Here language 'far from reflecting an already given social reality, constitutes social reality for us' (Weedon 1987: 22). This approach has implications for subjectivity. Against the idea of subjectivity as 'an essence at the heart of each individual which is unique, fixed and coherent', poststructuralism 'proposes a subjectivity which is precarious, contradictory and in process, constantly being reconstituted in discourse every time we think or speak' (1987: 32–3).

The crisis in the understanding of selfhood and knowledge has produced a radical uncertainty which has infected feminism as much as any other emancipatory movement. Historically, the rise of second-wave feminism coincided with a growing incredulity towards universal truth-claims. Yet feminism has, to some extent, always been 'postmodern'. Feminists have shown how Enlightenment discourses universalise white, Western, middle-class male experience and have thus exposed the buried strategies of domination implicit in the ideal of objective knowledge. Feminists as well as postmodernists have long recognised the need for a new ethics responsive to technological changes and shifts in the understanding between the relations of power and knowledge. Feminism has provided its own critique of essentialist and foundationalist assumptions, arguing, for example, that gender is not a consequence of anatomy and that social institutions do not reflect universal truths about human nature. Simply in articulating issues of sexual difference, feminist discourse weakens the rootedness of Enlightenment thought in the principle of ungendered sameness and universalism. Once knowledge is regarded as constructed and situated, as produced within a specific context, then, so the argument goes, Truth can no longer be envisaged as discoverable by objective, rational thought.

Both critiques suggest that earlier models of knowledge may have been complicit with those very forms of oppression they were designed to supplant (Foucault 1981; Butler 1990). Indeed, some feminists have argued that Enlightenment discourses of emancipation have functioned as much to oppress as to liberate women. Contemporary feminists have analysed the ways in which 'universal' principles were always contradicted by the Enlightenment's construction of a public/private split–which consigned women to the 'private' realm of embodiment and domesticity in order to demarcate a public realm of reason and subjective sovereignty as essentially abstract, disinterested and, above all, male. In recent years, debates on identity and 'difference', the recognition that there is no universal 'woman' for whom feminism can speak, also resonate with the radical uncertainty of postmodernism.

Yet feminist ideas clearly arise out of and are made possible by those of modernity and its models of reason, justice and autonomous subjectivity. Feminists have fought for the extension of Enlightenment discourses and sovereign rights to women as full human subjects. Feminist critics of postmodernism have cautioned against an unthinking acceptance of an epistemological critique which might amount to no more than a revolt of secure but ungrateful bourgeois sons against their more authoritarian Enlightenment fathers. It seems unlikely that feminism can sustain itself as a political and emancipatory movement unless it continues to acknowledge and to interrrogate its relation to the discourses of Enlightenment. At the risk of sounding essentialist, I would still argue that, never having experienced the kind of subjective sovereignty and political security of the average white, Western, male postmodernist, it would seem that feminists may have more to lose in a premature renunciation of the goals and methods of Enlightenment thought. For, to accept the arguments of strong postmodernism is to raise uncertainty even about the existence of a specifically female subject and inevitably, therefore, about the very possibility of political agency for women.

The crucial question in the relations between feminism and postmodernism would seem to be whether it is possible to preserve the emancipatory ideals of modernity which seem necessary to the very endeavour of feminism, whilst dispensing with those absolute epistemological foundations which have been so thoroughly and variously challenged. Alternatively, how far is it possible to modify those foundations rather than urging their total abandonment? As a political practice, surely feminism must continue to posit some belief in the notion of effective human agency, the necessity for historical continuity in formulating identity and a belief in some kind of historical progress. All along it would seem that feminism has been engaged in an effort to reconcile context-specific difference or situatedness with universal political aims: to modify the Enlightenment in the context of late modernity and according to the specific needs and perspectives of women, but not to capitulate to the nihilistic and ultra-relativist positions of postmodernism as a celebration of the disembodied 'view from everywhere' (Bordo 1990: 133).

Feminists, like other commentators on postmodernism, remain deeply divided: most are either for it or against it. Some feminists dismiss postmodernism as mystificatory academic pretentiousness, while others see it as the only viable future for a rejuvenated political philosophy:

> feminism and postmodernism are the only contemporary theories that present a truly radical critique of the Enlightenment legacy of modernism. No other approaches on the contemporary intellectual scene offer a means of displacing and transforming the masculinist epistemology of modernity.
>
> (Hekman 1990: 189)

Evaluations of postmodern art and literature tend to line up in similarly polarised camps. Terry Eagleton (1985), for example, dismisses postmodernism as a perversion of the radical energies of an earlier avant-garde, and sees it as a cultural practice which merely reflects the superficiality of late capitalist consumer society. Linda Hutcheon (1988) on the other hand, sees in the postmodern the only possibility of critique and opposition from the margins which gives a voice to feminists, post-colonials, ethnic, racial and sexual minorities. According to some critics, such as Fredric Jameson (1991), this tendency to praise or condemn postmodernism is simply beside the point: for we are *in* the condition of postmodernity and simply have no choice but to resign ourselves to that condition. For Jameson, therefore, postmodernism is best thought of as a periodising concept which serves to correlate the formal and stylistic features of contemporary culture with the underlying economic structures of late consumer capitalism.

A Map of the Postmodern

If we are to begin to map the relations between feminism and postmodernism, we need to break down the global version of the postmodern condition into more analytically manageable categories and units. For the moment I will propose that we maintain a distinction between postmodernism as an aesthetic practice and postmodernism as a critique of knowledge. I shall argue that one way in which to begin to disentangle the relations between feminism and postmodernism (as theoretical critiques and cultural practices) is to view postmodernism as existing in two generic varieties; one I shall refer to as 'strong' and the other 'weak', and then to see both varieties in turn operating in 'reconstructive' and 'deconstructive' modes. Broadly, deconstructive modes tend to be more concerned with a critique of the legacy of the Enlightenment and in their strong forms to recommend its entire abandonment; reconstructive modes are more concerned with imagining alternative futures which either transform or attempt to break entirely with those of modernity, again depending on whether the vision is what I have called 'weak' or 'strong'.

If we break down postmodernism in this way, we may discover that a particular form of the postmodern which has been productive for feminism in the aesthetic sphere may be problematic for feminist critiques of knowledge and for feminist politics. This suggests, contrary to globalising accounts of the postmodern condition, that feminism is free to take a strategic stance on postmodernism, selecting those aspects which might be useful to a particular goal at a particular time.

Strong Postmodernism

'Strong' deconstructive postmodernism probably begins with Nietzsche's critique of metaphysics. In a famous statement in *The Genealogy of Morals*, he declared that 'there is only a perspectival knowing' (Nietzsche 1969: 111, 3). He suggests that we are deluded in our belief that we can find universal metanarratives which may ground knowledge or ethics. Following this, strong postmodernism tends to champion perspectivism and thus 'difference' (which is potentially endless); exhibits, therefore, a tendency towards nominalism–refusing the idea that there is 'a reality', out in the real world, to which 'concepts' actually refer, assuming that 'concepts' construct and even produce the reality they pretend to describe. Postmodernism, furthermore, tends towards a preference for performance and rhetoric over intrinsic or universal truth or right, towards models of dissensus rather than consensus as the basis for political action, and calls for an acknowledgement of the incommensurability of the various language games, or 'little narratives', which reflect the specific perspectives and interests of particular groups in society. Strong postmodernists reject any claim to knowledge which makes 'an explicit appeal to some grand narrative, such as the dialectic of the Spirit, the hermeneutic of meaning, the emancipation of the rational or working subject or the creation of wealth' (Lyotard 1984: xxiii). Such claims are regarded as disguised manifestations of a totalising will-to-power where 'man', seeking his destiny in the conquest of nature, has sought to impose his ideal blueprints on the rest of the human race and, in so doing, has produced the violences, wars, totalitarianisms and pogroms of the last two hundred or so years. On the one hand, this kind of critique has exposed the gendered exclusiveness of the so-called 'universal' narratives of progressive modernity, but, on the other, it seems to entail the view that feminism has no more legitimacy than any other political language game. Within the terms of 'strong' postmodernism one could not even make an unconditional claim that it is wrong to oppress women. Indeed, for postmodern feminists such as Judith Butler (1990), the term 'woman' is merely a signifier with no substance, referring to nothing, simply a token in the particular language game in which it happens to be deployed.

Strong reconstructive postmodernism begins with similar premises to the deconstructive variety, but produces a number of 'aestheticised' and sometimes utopian accounts of knowledge and culture. One of the best-known is that of Richard Rorty. Though Rorty's project of cultural reconstruction requires the centrality of notions of consensus, his version of 'little narratives' suggests that political and social solidarity do not require universal epistemological foundations or 'grand' and monocausal narratives and that progress is actually impeded by the continued search for such absolute guarantees: 'solidarity has to be constructed out of little pieces, rather than found already waiting' (Rorty 1989: 94). What makes Rorty 'strong' in his postmodernism, however, is his insistence that society can only be transformed without violence through *vocabularies*. Rather than searching for scientific proof or metaphysical certainty, or a structural analysis of economic or social inequality, we should now recognise that the way to understand and to change our world is through the artificial mutation and manipulation of vocabularies. There is no truth awaiting our discovery, only 'truths' to be invented through the creative uses of language. For Rorty, the Enlightenment represents an adherence to an outmoded scientism which should now give way to a post-Nietzschean cultural aestheticism in which 'the method is to redescribe lots and lots of things in new ways, until you have created a pattern of linguistic behaviour which will tempt the rising generation to adopt it, thereby causing them to look for appropriate forms of non-linguistic behaviour' (1989: 9). Rorty's project is another example of what might be called strong linguistic determinism. Once everything is conceived in terms of language, here 'vocabularies', then the revolution of the word is claimed to be inseparable from revolution in the world: only irony can save us.

That such a position raises enormous difficulties for any emancipatory collective movement concerned with profound economic and social inequalities is immediately obvious. But perhaps even more problematic for feminists (though paradoxically more seductive) is a pervasive rhetoric of the 'sublime' which I would also categorise as another aestheticist version of strong reconstructive postmodernism. Rhetorics of the sublime usually take the form of positing a utopian 'space' outside of rationality, consciousness or language, to be set against a world conceived in the terms of linguistic determinism. If we cannot step outside of our systems of signification, not even to criticise one language game from within the terms of another, then there is no empirical means of comparing linguistic systems, of evaluating them or of understanding one from the perspective of another. Once this incommensurability thesis is accepted, then it is not surprising that so many postmodernists have invoked some version of the sublime as a space of the 'other' outside of publicly avilable modes of discourse or knowledge, opaque to rational methodologies. There was a dangerous tendency in the various postmodern critiques of reason which circulated in the 1980s, to regard alterity as a sublime space outside the law, recoverable through madness, hysteria, or some metaphorised return to the body. If physical space could not be politically transformed, the power of the imaginary or a new supra-rational sublime must be heightened and politicised. Indeed the work of French feminists such as Luce Irigaray was quickly appropriated for this postmodern reading of the sublime (see, for example, Deleuze and

Guattari 1983). But analogy may all too easily be mistaken for causality and a revolutionary political significance claimed for a semi-mystical notion of otherness. This space was often designated 'feminine', but in the hands of male theorists rarely had very much to do with actual women and even threatened, in continuing to identify femininity with a mysterious, irrational and unrepresentable 'otherness', to keep real women locked in a prisonhouse of (postmodern) language: a condition which might seem disturbingly similar to that earlier state of eternal femininity challenged by the entire tradition of modern (i.e. Enlightened) feminism.

Strong Postmodern Feminism: From Lyotard to Haraway

Contemporary 'strong' postmodernism, in both its deconstructive and reconstructive modes, owes much to Jean-François Lyotard's *The Postmodern Condition* (1984). This has been the most influential text in establishing the antifoundationalist thrust of the strong postmodern critique of knowledge in its axiomatic assumption of the exhaustion of Enlightenment meta-narratives and of the so-called emancipatory project of modernity. In this section, I wish to examine its significance for feminists and to examine the work of one 'strong' postmodern feminist, Donna Haraway, whose critique of science and politics bears many resemblances to Lyotard's position.

Lyotard's argument is that the commitment of post-Enlightenment thinkers to the instrumental uses of science and technology in the cause of social justice, and to the pursuit of objective knowledge as the foundation of social progress, is no longer a viable or desirable objective: 'the society of the future falls less within the province of a Newtonian anthropology (such as structuralism or system theory) than a pragmatics of language particles. There are many different language games—a heterogeneity of elements' (Lyotard 1984: xxiv).

Lyotard claims that there can be no objective grounds for truth, because science and philosophy are discourses whose 'truths' make sense only in terms of their own internal organisation; there is no external truth to which they refer. He is saying, therefore, that rationalism fails because it cannot ground its own rational procedures and requires another kind of discourse, narrative knowledge or 'customary' knowledge, in order to achieve a sense of grounding. In the postmodern world, however, this customary knowledge has now fragmented into a multiplicity of heterogeneous language games with their own internal rules.

There can no longer be belief, therefore, in privileged meta-discourses such as Nature, History, Spirit or Pure Reason which transcend local and contingent conditions and in which truth can be grounded. What follows from this, for feminism, is that gender, like class, or race, or ethnicity, can no longer be regarded as an essential or even a stable category, nor can it be used to explain the practices of human societies as a whole. It is no longer legitimate to appeal to the category 'women' to ground a meta-narrative of political practice—even in the name of emancipation.

According to the logic of Lyotard's argument, therefore, the continued adherence to metanarratives of gender must necessarily blind feminist theorists to the oppressive ethnocentricity and heterocentricity lurking in all essentialist truth claims about the nature of 'woman' or feminine experience. Moreover, Lyotard's argument implies that any recourse to trans-historical structures as a means of explaining political oppression will simply re-enact those forms of oppression in reverse mode. Political communities founded on the solidarity of shared experience might only exist legitimately in local, provisional and attenuated forms. Indeed, the publication of Lyotard's book coincided with a shift within feminism itself to an assault on essentialism and a problematisation of the notion of difference.

Lyotard's strong deconstructive critique has certainly been valuable in alerting feminists to essentialism and ethnocentrism in their own thought and his notion of heterogeneity does seem to hold out some possibility of pragmatic 'dialogue' across groups (see Fraser and Nicholson 1988). We might wish to contest the proclaimed 'openness' of Lyotard's thought, however, for his thesis contains its own (hidden) authoritarian structures of legitimation. This impinges very directly on my chosen example of strong postmodern feminism: Haraway's (1990) work on the cyborg. Lyotard, like all strong postmodernists insists the pre-emptive Doubt of Cartesianism (Descartes' idea that we should doubt everything until reason delivers certainty) should be renounced for an ever open-ended postmodern Uncertainty. What follows is that first, the dialectical pursuit of truth through rational critique, must therefore give way to endless postmodern 'dialogue'; and, second, that the assumptions underpinning classic scientific methodology – that the truth of a hypothesis can be verified by testing it against observable phenomena – must be abandoned for the acceptance of fictionality and indeterminacy. But the very examples used to proclaim that the legitimacy of scientific method is now exhausted, are simultaneously mobilised to provide the scientific legitimacy of Lyotard's own position.

He achieves this by substituting a model of knowledge derived from the New Science for the supposedly discredited epistemologies of classic realist science. He highlights those aspects of the New Science (particularly quantum physics' attempts to describe and formulate the nature of sub-atomic particles) which appear to exist in the manner of aesthetic objects: as indeterminate structures given realisation through the act of an intentional consciousness (the Uncertainty Principle). Scientific knowledge thus becomes indistinguishable from aesthetic knowing: science is used to deny the hegemony of science. Where once Enlightenment thought produced a scientised world, now postmodernism offers a thoroughly aestheticised one. Lyotard achieves this sleight of hand by representing New Science so that it corresponds with his postmodernist argument. He emphasises its concern with 'undecidables', with a radically uncertain world characterised as 'discontinuous, catastrophic, non-rectifiable and paradoxical (Lyotard 1984: 60). Curiously enough, the New Science comes to share the postmodern condition in all its details of undecideability and indeterminacy. Uncertainty is not simply a consequence of the limitations on us as knowers, but is the very condition of the universe itself and inherent in the structure of matter. Moreover, this condition now becomes paradoxically reassuring. Once we recognise that materialism is dead: we can give up the painful and searching condition of modern Doubt and re-identify ourselves in a world where cells and stars, consciousness and matter, are similarly constituted, open-ended, radically Uncertain.

In Donna Haraway's 'Manifesto for Cyborgs' we see a similar conflation of the organic and the inorganic, of science with art and of fictionality with fact, in a strong reconstructive postmodern feminist version of Lyotard's reading of science. For Donna Haraway the cyborg is an answer to the question of what might fill the void left by postmodern feminists' necessary sense of exile from all those (masculinist) Utopian dreams of Enlightenment which sought to return to an original wholeness, an ultimate reconciliation of cosmos and consciousness. Haraway informs us that 'a cyborg is a cybernetic organism, a hybrid of machine and organism, a creature of social reality as well as a creature of fiction' (1990: 191). More pertinently, for feminism, a cyborg is 'a creature in a postgender world; it has no truck with bisexuality, pre-Oedipal symbiosis, unalienated labour, or other seductions to organic wholeness through a final appropriation of all the powers of the parts into a higher unity . . . . The cyborg skips the step of original unity, of identification with nature in the Western sense' (Haraway 1990: 192).

The myth which, according to Haraway, is refuted by the image of the cyborg is nothing less than the founding myth of modernity: the search for reconciliation, in the absence of belief in a transcendent Deity, of all those dualisms, of mind and body, consciousness and cosmos, art and science, custom and reason, associated with the Enlightenment. For the very moment which brought modern science to birth also delivered its twin: a redemptive humanist aesthetic which might compensate for all that science would abstract from the world, disenchanting its inhabitants, disembedding them from a unified lifeworld, offering the cold comfort of spectatorship at a world picture of pure mechanical design. Haraway, however, will have no truck with such notions of the machine in the garden. In her postmodern landscape of urban technological and post-industrial space, 'machine is us, our processes, an aspect of our embodiment' (1990: 222), open to the possibility of regeneration but not rebirth, collapsing the myth of the two realms of science and humanistic culture, cutting across the fundamental distinctions which differentiate human from machine, man from woman, nature from nurture.

The cyborg is offered as a way out of the dualisms of modernity in which women have always discovered themselves on the weaker or negated side. The cyborg is intended to explode the delusions of the Cartesian rational subject in its search for a bedrock of knowledge located in an autonomous and unitary consciousness, which turns out to be nothing more than an endless, fictional projection. Yet, in a peculiar way, and as with Lyotard's image of Uncertainty, the cyborg promises ultimate reconciliation in a postmodernist and post-humanist world. The cyborg offers a different kind of radical fictionality: that there is no truth to discover, no unitary consciousness to which we might return; there is only endless fictionality, endless construction of shifting subjectivities, technological productiveness, only an absolute condition of Uncertainty. The cyborg, too, is science as art, machine as human, a hybrid and unstable constellation of fact and fiction which denies any privileged epistemological status to biologism *or* mentalism.

Haraway thus exhorts us to renounce our nostalgia for the old myths of wholeness (much as Lyotard insists we give up the pursuit of 'grand narratives' and our aching for totality), and recognise that the shift from organic to industrial to postindustrial society carries with it the liberatory potential of the postmodern, polymorphously perverse information systems to explode concepts of subjectivity and truth which have functioned within the paradigms of modernity to oppress women. Her argument, of course, is fraught with all those problems about ethics and agency which have already been rehearsed during the course of this chapter. The cyborg is another image of the postmodern sublime, of a radical alterity which seduces with utopian promise yet presents enormous problems for a feminist politics. Not the least of these problems is its tendency to romanticise the marginal as unrepresentable and therefore to repeat as a gesture of liberation those very patriarchal discourses which have been used to control women in the first place: biologically fixed Woman might now become technologically (and infinitely) manipulable Woman.

Indeed, the cyborg is a concretised image of that impossible 'view from everywhere', of partial, multiple, floating subjectivities, which is advocated by some postmodernists as an alternative to a discredited 'view from nowhere' (the idea of an 'objective' point of reference from which to view the world). What they share, of course, is a sublime dis-embodiment: the idea of a disembodied 'knower' is replaced in the postmodern version by the 'body-in-bits', the protean being whose negative capability extends to an ability to occupy numerous subject positions. Haraway shares with Lyotard the postmodern retreat from the regulative ideal of a unified rational subjectivity whose capacity to generate a view from nowhere becomes the guarantee of an 'objective' knowing, and she too substitutes a perspectival constructivism claimed to be ethically superior in its refusal of the violences of 'totalising' knowledge. Yet, as I have already suggested, this 'view from everywhere' bears no relation to the constraints imposed on our actual being in the world. Moreover, without the capacity to stand back, to believe in the view from nowhere as a kind of regulative priniciple underpinning our attempts to know and judge, we would be unable to discriminate amongst different points of view. Postmodern hybridity, nomadism, fragmentation and endless fictionality may seem to offer an escape route from biological, social and cosmic determinism. However, if they preclude the possibility of discrimination between, and negotiation across, multiple positions and discourses, then it is difficult to see how such a radical or strong postmodernism could form the basis for any kind of politics, ethics or epistemology which assumes the necessity for personal and collective agency and responsibility.

Weak Postmodernism

At this point (or impasse?), I will turn to examine some examples of 'weak postmodernism' and consider what, if anything, they may offer feminists reluctant to embrace strong postmodernism in either or both its aesthetic and philosophical modes. Unlike strong postmodernism, the weak version may accept the human need to invest in grand narratives, though its proponents would reject monocausal varieties and insist that all knowledge is embedded or situated in particular cultures or cultural traditions. According to weak postmodernism, understanding arises through the practices, customs, traditions and textures of a particular culture and we may arrive at a shared structure of values, a sense of personal significance, and the possibility of belief in historical progress through collective engagements which do not require foundations of truth or value. In some versions of 'weak postmodernism', however, the ideal of objectivity or the impulse toward the 'view from nowhere' is to be preserved but is brought to earth and combined with the perspective of the culturally situated and embodied subject. In this way, weak postmodernism resists the utopian seductiveness of the strong postmodern 'view from everywhere' and the fluid, disembodied and centreless subject which underpins it.

The starting point for weak postmodernism is Martin Heidegger and the tradition of hermeneutic theory. For Heidegger, modernity is characterised by a denial or disavowal of being-in-the-world. A detached subjectivity has come to stand over an inert nature, looking, speculating, fixing and judging; its instrumental rationalism radically distanced from the world it surveys, distorted into the shape of its own fictionally projected ends. But, says Heidegger, 'in clarifying being-in-the-world we have shown that a bare subject without a world never . . . is . . . given' (Heidegger 1962: 152). Heidegger's influence on weak deconstructive postmodernism is most obviously felt in the work of Hans-Georg Gadamer. The central thesis of Gadamer's *Truth and Method* (1960) is that there can be no Archimedean point outside of culture from which to achieve 'objective knowledge', for understanding exists only in relation to the perspectives (or 'prejudice' as he calls it) provided for us through our cultural traditions and these perspectives can never be brought to full rational consciousness.

Though seemingly close to Heidegger's position, Gadamer's version of being-in-the-world does allow for greater intervention and agency, for though we can never achieve full knowledge, we may become aware of our prejudices and therefore begin to modify them through exposure to experiences of truth which seem to contradict our own–though neither self nor world can ever be rationally conceptualised in any final sense. However, if strong postmodernism seems not to anchor subjectivity at all, raising all the problems for feminism of ethical accountability and political agency, weak postmodernism may seem to raise the same difficulties through the provision of too much anchorage. Yet, Gadamer's elaboration of 'embodied' knowledge does function to remove the gendered polarities of mind and body written into the history of modernist philosophy. Gadamer's work suggests the extent to which *all* human understanding is actually rooted and embodied in profound cultural relations and traditions: we can neither separate 'reason' from 'custom', nor should we seek to do so.

The varieties of reconstructive postmodernism which have emerged from the hermeneutic critique may be regarded as 'weak' in that they never entirely abandon the importance of agency, of the need to experience the self as a coherent and consistent, if revisable entity, nor do they dispute the assumption that ethics requires a subject. Some of the more recent communitarian versions of this model of self and society, however, may seen as 'strong' as the centreless worlds of the cyborg. So Alasdair MacIntyre's (1985) work, for example, has in common with strong postmodernism, an insistence that truth and value are only ever internal to the conditions of particular communities or enclosed institutional frameworks.

MacIntyre advocates an ethical system based on a return to a pre-modern model of virtue and practical wisdom, but tempered by a modern, aesthetic sense of how we might reformulate and rewrite the scripts of tradition. In such a world, we would not be subjected to stagnatory anchorage, but neither would we float dangerously adrift. MacIntyre tends to conceive of culture in homogenous terms and to ignore the fact that most of us move daily between multiple groups and communities each with different preoccupations and often non-complementary goals, values and aims. There are elements of MacIntyre's work which have appealed to feminists, but it remains to be seen whether it is possible to reconcile this kind of contextualism with the modern imperative of freedom, emancipation and the desire, simply, to change the script. MacIntyre does allow that we may become authors (or active agents) but, like those postmodernists who emphasise existing culture, or language, or biology, as final determinants of our being in the world, he too seems to offer only a script which has finally already been written.

Feminism and Weak Postmodernism

In its communitarian aspects, 'weak' postmodernism is becoming increasingly attractive to feminism as a way of dealing with the impasses of postmodernism in its 'strong' forms. The work of Seyla Benhabib (1992) represents the most forceful recent feminist attempt to come to terms with postmodernism whilst resisting the implications and the Uncertainty of its 'strong' versions. Indeed, she has explicitly argued that strong post-modernism threatens the entire identity of feminism as a politics and tries to discredit the emancipatory ideals which have guided it in the past. Whilst recommending a contextualist theory of knowledge or understanding, she nevertheless insists on the need to sustain a commitment to Enlightenment models of rationality as a regulative principle guiding our enquiries and beliefs. She argues for the need also to continue to envisage the possibility of Utopia (and therefore progress) as an inspiration for political practice and has put forward a persuasive case that social critics cannot afford to abandon the philosophical ideal of 'objectivity', for we need to able to detach ourselves from immediate contexts, to stand back, reflect upon, compare, and analyse cross-culturally. For this, we need at times to inhabit the detached stance of the rationalist philosopher:

> social criticism needs philosophy precisely because the narratives of our culture are so conflictual and irreconcilable that, even when one appeals to them, a certain ordering of one's normative priorities, a statement of the methodological assumptions guiding one's choice of narratives, and a clarification of those principles in the name of which one speaks is unavoidable.
>
> (Benhabib 1992: 226)

Benhabib seems to suggest that we need both a contextual sense of our perspective from the place in the world where we find ourselves, but also the discipline of imagining that world from outside but with ourselves inside it: an attenuated version of the View from Nowhere.

Of course, Nowhere is not just an image for a regulative ideal governing rationalist thought; it may also suggest No-place as Utopia. The 'View from Nowhere's is our capacity to imagine otherwise, to project an ideal beyond what is. Strong deconstructive postmodernism bears witness to an historical retreat from such utopian visions, and to a disillusionment with the Enlightenment hopes for rational planning of the perfect society. However, substituted in their place is the 'Nowhere' of its own strong reconstructive mode, a non-rationalist space of the sublime filled with cyborgs and nomads, chaos and catastrophe. It is assumed here that because we cannot arrive at absolute knowledge, there is nothing out there to know except the spectral shapes of our own projected fictional constructions.

In presenting my own account of postmodernism, I do not wish to deny the importance of both the 'Nowhere' of fictional space and the 'Nowhere' of rational thought as modes which enable the projection of ourselves beyond our own immediate preoccupations, but I would argue against the tendency of strong postmodernism to regard the two as identical procedures. Surely, in the 'Nowhere' of aesthetic fictions there is no responsibility for accurate depiction of historical reality, whereas in the 'Nowhere' of the ideal realm of objective knowledge, the aim is to describe and explain material realities. Strong postmodernism would deny that there is any distinction to be made between these ways of knowing, but my own argument has been that feminism may discover a viable relation with postmodernism only if wary of such 'strong' readings.

It would seem that the appropriate place for sublime fantasy, for the imagination of a No-Place unencumbered by physical or biological or historical limitation, is in works of fiction. In novels by Jeanette Winterson, Toni Morrison and Angela Carter, for example, history may be deconstructed as an endless regress of mirrors or reinvented in fantastic form. In Winterson's novel *Sexing the Cherry* (1989), for instance, ideas and images from postmodern science are used imaginatively to develop the theme of division and its overcoming: divisions which are directly presented as a consequence of Cartesian dualism and Newtonian science and which separate mind and matter, man and woman, feeling and reason. Set at the moment of the beheading of Charles I, the novel fantastically explores the beginnings of a historical and cultural divide where a feminised nature is transformed into a mechanical universe requiring dissection, demystification and naming of parts. The fictional universe of Winterson's novel postmodernistically breaks free of such determinism, however, in its narrative and formal re-enactment of the post-Einsteinian account of a universe where imaginative hypothesis and material reality are no longer opposed poles and where Nature becomes the flickering pictures of our relation to what must always exceed our conceptual categories. But all this takes place in the designated space of aesthetic fiction: as trial without the consequences of error. Such No-Places constitute one important kind of Utopianism. The Nowhere of the aesthetic, however, may provide imaginary visions, but only the Nowhere at the end of, and guiding rational thought, can attempt to determine the historical consequences of their actual realisation. For a feminist politics committed to the futures of actual women in the world, the rather more earth-bound and situated reason of weak postmodernism may complement the stronger postmodernist impulses at work in experimental art and literature.

In the chapter I have suggested that feminism can benefit from the postmodern, both in its cultural-aesthetic and in its epistemological modes, but that feminism should beware of their easy conflation and continue to explore the consequences of, and the alternatives to, the abandonment of the discourses of modernity. We do have choices and our relation to postmodernism is never one of necessary symbiosis, but always of strategic selection and a reasonable, if never purely rational, process of decision-making. If feminism, like some versions of the postmodern self, is an ever-revisable narrative project, then, like a good author, it needs a sense of the appropriate moment to stand back from its creations, to decide what is worth retaining and what has had its moment, what is of lasting value and what is simply pandering to fashion.

References

Baudrillard, J. (1983) *Simulations*, (New York, Semiotext(e)).
Benhabib, S. (1992) *Situating the Self* (Cambridge, Polity Press).
Bordo, S. (1990) 'Feminism, Postmodernism and Gender-Scepticism', in L.J. Nicholson (ed.) *Feminism/Postmodernism* (New York and London, Routledge).
Butler, J. (1990) *Gender Trouble* (New York, Routledge).
Deleuze, G. and Guattari, F. (1983) *Anti-Oedipus* (Minneapolis, University of Minnesota Press).

Eagleton, T. (1985) 'Capitalism, Modernism and Postmodernism', *New Left Review* 152: 60–73.

Foucault, M. (1981) *The History of Sexuality. Volume 1: The Will to Truth* (Harmondsworth, Penguin).

Fraser, N. and Nicholson, L. (1988) 'Social Criticism without Philosophy: An Encounter between Feminism and Postmodernism', *Theory, Culture and Society* 5, 2–3: 373–94.

Gadamer, H.-G. [1960] (1975) *Truth and Method*, in G. Barden and J. Cumming (eds) (New York, Continuum).

Habermas, J. (1981) 'Modernity v. Postmodernity', *New German Critique*, 22.

Haraway, D. (1990) 'A Manifesto for Cyborgs: Science, Technology, and Socialist Feminism in the 1980s', in, Nicholson (ed.).

Heidegger, M. (1962) *Being and Time* (New York, Harper and Row).

Hekman, S. (1990) *Gender and Knowledge: Elements of a Postmodern Feminism*, (Cambridge, Polity Press).

Hutcheon, L. (1988) *A Poetics of Postmodernism: History, Theory, Fiction* (London, Routledge).

Jameson, F. (1991) *Postmodernism* (London, Verso).

Lyotard, J.-F. (1984) *The Postmodern Condition: A Report on Knowledge*, (Manchester, Manchester University Press).

MacIntyre, A. (1985) *After Virtue: A Study in Moral Theory*, (London, Duckworth).

Nietzsche, F. (1969) *The Genealogy of Morals*, W. Kaufmann tr. (New York, Random House).

Rorty, R. (1989) *Contingency, Irony, Solidarity*, (Cambridge, Cambridge University Press).

Weedon, C. (1987) *Feminist Practice and Poststructuralist Theory* (Oxford, Blackwell).

Wellmer, A. (1985) 'The Dialectic of Modernism and Postmodernism', *Praxis International 4*.

Winterson, J. (1989) *Sexing the Cherry* (London, Bloomsbury).

Section 5

Postcolonialism

Introduction

bell hooks's essay 'Postmodern blackness' provides a useful bridge between the consideration of postmodernism and gender, on the one hand, and postmodernism and race, on the other. She suggests that the postmodern concept of difference is too often used as a vague umbrella term to refer to a Western sense of the exhaustion of high modernism and a crisis in the legacy of the Enlightenment. In its unspecified and unsituated appropriation and as a gesture of radical chic, the term merely reproduces the blindnesses of modernism, though in reverse and negative mode. Her argument is that the concepts of otherness and difference must be anchored more specifically to the politics of race and gender. Just as the black movement of the 1960s largely failed to connect with feminist critiques of patriarchy, so postmodernists have tended to ignore issues of race.

The specific space of 'postcolonialism', however, was first articulated in Edward Said's book *Orientalism*, published in 1978. Like 'postmodernism', the term has come to refer both to a condition (here postcoloniality) and to the discourses which theorize that condition. As a condition, however, postcolonialism is hardly new. In the excerpt reprinted here from Said's later book, *Culture and Imperialism* (1993), the analysis of Conrad's *Heart of Darkness* reminds us that postcoloniality may refer as much to the Roman conquest of Britain and its aftermath as to the more recent historical recovery from the 'scramble for Africa' in the nineteenth century. 1974, however, saw the beginning of the formal dissolution of the European colonial empires and the granting of independence after world-wide campaigns of anti-colonial resistance. The contemporary postcolonial situation begins, therefore, in 1947, though postcolonialism as a discursive and theoretical space is not named until 1978. In his earlier book, Said examined those forms of Western scholarship and cultural representation which codified knowledge about non-metropolitan cultures under colonial control. The book drew eclectically on Foucauldian post-structuralism and on the Gramscian concept of hegemony in order to demonstrate that Europe's construction of the Orient is a paradigm of all colonial and imperial structures. In each case, the mysterious and duplicitous 'other' which is the colonized culture functions as a means of stabilizing and affirming the identity of the imperialist power. Said's book emphasized the centrality of cultural repersentation in this process. If colonized peoples are to become subjects of history then 'postcolonialism' must strengthen as well as analyse the discursive process of resistance to colonialist perspectives. In his own analysis of Conrad, Said shows how imperialism maintains power through the designation of a discursive space which makes silent and invisible all those perspectives which are excluded by and from its frame. He shows, through an analysis of Conrad's representation of Africa, how the construction of 'them' is necessary for the affirmation of 'us'.

A similar preoccupation with relations between power and knowledge in the construction of 'otherness' and, in particular, in the construction of the colonial Subject is the focus of the two pieces here by Homi Bhabha and Gayatri Spivak. Like hooks's essay, these writings consider and enact a constellation of concerns and concepts which cut across many of the discourses represented in the second part of this anthology; the critique of essentialism; the deconstruction of Enlightenment models of the Subject; the crisis in Western rationalism and its discourses of authority; the analysis of the cultural nexus of power and knowledge. In different ways, both Spivak and Bhabha articulate anxieties about voice and authority in the context of colonial and postcolonial discourses. Bhabha's subject is the ambivalence of colonial discourse. When discourse is translated into a colonial context, the result is a mimicry which constitutes both resemblance and menace, a kind of hybridisation which exposes the lie of universalism that underwrites colonial authority. Spivak too addresses the problem of 'voice' and authority for the postcolonial intellectual in terms of ambivalence. To be a teacher of English in a postcolonial context is to occupy a marginal position where, ironically, the only power accrues from one's facility as a speaker of a Western liberal discourse even as one exposes the contradictions and exclusions in Western liberal discourse. Again the postcolonial intellectual appears in a situation that is somewhere between mimicry and mockery, where the menace of mimicry lies in its dualism in disclosing the ambivalence of colonial discourse and thereby disrupting its authority. In some ways, the postcolonialist strategies of both Spivak and Bhabha resemble those of Butler and Dollimore (see Part Two, Section One, Subjectivity and Gender) in their articulation of relations between the dominant and the deviant in constructions of sexuality. Butler's analysis of 'queer' as a reverse discourse and of 'drag' as a performance which exposes heterosexual performance, and Dollimore's sense of the deviant as a movement proceeding out of and thus becoming part of the dominant, are also analyses of ambivalence and mimicry, of the impossibility of a pure voice or view from nowhere or non-complicitous discourse.

36 | bell hooks,

'Postmodern Blackness', in *Yearning: Race, Gender, and Cultural Politics* (1991), pp. 23–31

Postmodernist discourses are often exclusionary even as they call attention to, appropriate even, the experience of 'difference' and 'Otherness' to provide oppositional political meaning, legitimacy and immediacy when they are accused of lacking concrete relevance. Very few African-American intellectuals have talked or written about postmodernism. At a dinner party I talked about trying to grapple with the significance of postmodernism for contemporary black experience. It was one of those social gatherings where only one other black person was present. The setting quickly became a field of contestation. I was told by the other black person that I was wasting my time, that 'this stuff does not relate in any way to what's happening with black people'. Speaking in the presence of a group of white onlookers, staring at us as though this encounter were staged for their benefit, we engaged in a passionate discussion about black experience. Apparently, no one sympathized with my insistence that racism is perpetuated when blackness is associated solely with concrete gut level experience conceived as either opposing or having no connection to abstract thinking and the production of critical theory. The idea that there is no meaningful connection between black experience and critical thinking about aesthetics or culture must be continually interrogated.

My defense of postmodernism and its relevance to black folks sounded good, but I worried that I lacked conviction, largely because I approach the subject cautiously and with suspicion.

Disturbed not so much by the 'sense' of postmodernism but by the conventional language used when it is written or talked about and by those who speak it, I find myself on the outside of the discourse looking in. As a discursive practice it is dominated primarily by the voices of white male intellectuals and/or academic elites who speak to and about one another with coded familiarity. Reading and studying their writing to understand postmodernism in its multiple manifestations, I appreciate it but feel little inclination to ally myself with the academic hierarchy and exclusivity pervasive in the movement today.

Critical of most writing on postmodernism, I perhaps am more conscious of the way in which the focus on 'Otherness and difference' that is often alluded to in these works seems to have little concrete impact as an analysis or standpoint that might change the nature and direction of postmodernist theory. Since much of this theory has been constructed in reaction to and against high modernism, there is seldom any mention of black experience or writings by black people in this work's specifically black women (though in more recent work one may see a reference to Cornel West, the black male scholar who has most engaged postmodernist discourse). Even if an aspect of black culture is the subject of postmodern critical writing, the works cited will usually be those of black men. A work that comes immediately to mind is Andrew Ross's chapter 'Hip, and the long front of color' in *No Respect: Intellectuals and Popular Culture*; while it is an interesting reading, it constructs black culture as though black women have had no role in black cultural production. At the end of Meaghan Morris' discussion of postmodernism in her collection of essays *The Pirate's Fiancé: Feminism and Postmodernism*, she provides a bibliography of works by women, identifying them as important contributions to a discourse on postmodernism that offer new insight as well as challenging male theoretical hegemony. Even though many of the works do not directly address postmodernism, they address similar concerns. There are no references to works by black women.

The failure to recognize a critical black presence in the culture and in most scholarship and writing on postmodernism compels a black reader, particularly a black female reader, to interrogate her interest in a subject where those who discuss and write about it seem not to know black women exist or even to consider the possibility that we might be somewhere writing or saying something that should be listened to, or producing art that should be seen, heard, approached with intellectual seriousness. This is especially the case with works that go on and on about the way in which postmodernist discourse has opened up a theoretical terrain where 'difference and Otherness' can be considered legitimate issues in the academy. Confronting both the absence of recognition of black female presence that much postmodernist theory re-inscribes and the resistance on the part of most black folks to hearing about real connection between postmodernism and black experience, I enter a discourse, a practice, where there may be no ready audience for my words, no clear listener, uncertain, then, that my voice can or will be heard.

During the sixties, the black power movement was influenced by perspectives that could easily be labeled modernist. Certainly many of the ways black folks addressed issues of identity conformed to a modernist universalizing agenda. There was little critique of patriarchy as a master narrative among black militants. Despite the fact that black power ideology reflected a modernist sensibility, these elements were soon rendered irrelevant as militant protest was stifled by a powerful, repressive postmodern state. The period directly after the black power movement was a time when major news magazines carried articles with cocky headlines like 'Whatever happened to Black America?' This response was an ironic reply to the aggressive, unmet demand by decentered, marginalized black subjects who had at least momentarily successfully demanded a hearing, who had made it possible for black liberation to be on the national political agenda. In the wake of the black power movement, after so many rebels were slaughtered and lost, many of these voices were silenced by a repressive state; others became inarticulate. It has become necessary to find new avenues to transmit the messages of black liberation struggle, new ways to talk about racism and other politics of domination. Radical postmodernist practice, most powerfully conceptualized as a 'politics of difference', should incorporate the voices of displaced, marginalized, exploited and oppressed black people. It is sadly ironic that the contemporary discourse which talks the most about heterogeneity, the decentered subject, declaring breakthroughs that allow recognition of otherness, still directs its critical voice primarily to a specialized audience that shares a common language rooted in the very master narratives it claims to challenge. If radical postmodernist thinking is to have a transformative impact, then a critical break with the notion of 'authority' as 'mastery over' must not simply be a rhetorical device. It must be reflected in habits of being, including styles of writing as well as chosen subject matter. Third world nationals, elites and white critics who passively absorb white supremacist thinking, and therefore never notice or look at black people on the streets or at their jobs, who render us invisible with their gaze in all areas of daily life, are not likely to produce liberatory theory that will challenge racist domination, or promote a breakdown in traditional ways of seeing and thinking about reality, ways of constructing aesthetic theory and practice. From a different standpoint, Robert Storr makes a similar critique in the global issue of *Art in America* when he asserts:

> To be sure, much postmodernist critical inquiry has centered precisely on the issues of 'difference' and 'Otherness'. On the purely theoretical plane the exploration of these concepts has produced some important results, but in the absence of any sustained research into what artists of color and others outside the mainstream might be up to, such discussions become rootless instead of radical. Endless second guessing about the latent imperialism of intruding upon other cultures only compounded matters, preventing or excusing these theorists from investigating what black, Hispanic, Asian and Native American artists were actually doing.

Without adequate concrete knowledge of and contact with the non-white 'Other', white theorists may move in discursive theoretical directions that are threatening and potentially disruptive of that critical practice which would support radical liberation struggle.

The postmodern critique of 'identity', though relevant for renewed black liberation struggle, is often posed in ways that are problematic. Given a pervasive politic of white supremacy which seeks to prevent the formation of radical black subjectivity, we cannot cavalierly dismiss a concern with identity politics. Any critic exploring the radical potential of postmodernism as it relates to racial difference and racial domination would need to consider the implications of a critique of identity for oppressed groups. Many of us are struggling to find new strategies of resistance. We must engage decolonization as a critical practice if we are to have meaningful chances of survival even as we must simultaneously cope with the loss of political grounding which made radical activism more possible. I am thinking here about the postmodernist critique of essentialism as it pertains to the construction of identity as one example.

Postmodern theory that is not seeking to simply appropriate the experience of 'Otherness' to enhance the discourse or to be radically chic should not separate the 'politics of difference' from the politics of racism. To take racism seriously one must consider the plight of underclass people of color, a vast majority of whom are black. For African-Americans our collective condition prior to the advent of postmodernism and perhaps more tragically expressed under current postmodern conditions has been and is characterized by continued displacement, profound alienation and despair. Writing about blacks and postmodernism, Cornel West describes our collective plight:

> There is increasing class division and differentiation, creating on the one hand a significant black middle-class, highly anxiety-ridden, insecure, willing to be co-opted and incorporated into the powers that be, concerned with racism to the degree that it poses constraints on upward social mobility; and on the other, a vast and growing black underclass, an underclass that embodies a kind of walking nihilism of pervasive drug addiction, pervasive alcoholism, pervasive homicide, and an exponential rise in suicide. Now because of the deindustrialization, we also have a devastated black industrial working class. We are talking here about tremendous hopelessness.

This hopelessness creates longing for insight and strategies for change that can renew spirits and reconstruct grounds for collective black liberation struggle. The overall impact of postmodernism is that many other groups now share with black folks a sense of deep alienation, despair, uncertainty, loss of a sense of grounding even if it is not informed by shared circumstance. Radical postmodernism calls attention to those shared sensibilities which cross the boundaries of class, gender, race, etc., that could be fertile ground for the construction of empathy–ties that would promote recognition of common commitments, and serve as a base for solidarity and coalition.

Yearning is the word that best describes a common psychological state shared by many of us, cutting across boundaries of race, class, gender and sexual practice. Specifically, in relation to the postmodernist reconstruction of 'master' narratives, the yearning that wells in the hearts and minds of those whom such narratives have silenced is the longing for critical voice. It is no accident that 'rap' has usurped the primary position of rhythm and blues music among young black folks as the most desired sound or that it began as a form of 'testimony' for the underclass. It has enabled underclass black youth to develop a critical voice, as a group of young black men told me, a 'common literacy'. Rap projects a critical voice, explaining, demanding, urging. Working with this insight in his essay 'Putting the pop back into postmodernism', Lawrence Grossberg comments:

> The postmodern sensibility appropriates practices as boasts that announce their own– and consequently our own–existence, like a rap song boasting of the imaginary (or real–it makes no difference) accomplishments of the rapper. They offer forms of empowerment not only in the face of nihilism but precisely through the forms of nihilism itself: an empowering nihilism, a moment of positivity through the production and structuring of affective relations.

Considering that it is as subject one comes to voice, then the postmodernist focus on the critique of identity appears at first glance to threaten and close down the possibility that this discourse and practice will allow those who have suffered the crippling effects of colonization and domination to gain or regain a hearing. Even if this sense of threat and the fear it evokes are based on a misunderstanding of the postmodernist political project, they nevertheless shape responses. It never surprises me when black folks respond to the critique of essentialism, especially when it denies the validity of identity politics, by saying, 'Yeah, it's easy to give up identity, when you got one'. Should we not be suspicious of postmodern critiques of the 'subject' when they surface at a historical moment when many subjugated people feel themselves coming to voice for the first time. Though an apt and oftentimes appropriate comeback, it does not really intervene in the discourse in a way that alters and transforms.

Criticisms of directions in postmodern thinking should not obscure insights it may offer that open up our understanding of African-American experience. The critique of essentialism encouraged by postmodernist thought is useful for African-Americans concerned with reformulating outmoded notions of identity. We have too long had imposed upon us from both the outside and the inside a narrow, constricting notion of blackness. Postmodern critiques of essentialism which challenge notions of universality and static over-determined identity within mass culture and mass consciousness can open up new possibilities for the construction of self and the assertion of agency.

Employing a critique of essentialism allows African-Americans to acknowledge the way in which class mobility has altered collective black experience so that racism does not necessarily have the same impact on our lives. Such a critique allows us to affirm multiple black identities, varied black experience. It also challenges colonial imperialist paradigms of black identity which represent blackness one-dimensionally in ways that reinforce and sustain white supremacy. This discourse created the idea of the 'primitive' and promoted the notion of an 'authentic' experience, seeing as 'natural' those expressions of black life which conformed to a pre-existing pattern or stereotype. Abandoning essentialist notions would be a serious challenge to racism. Contemporary African-American resistance struggle must be rooted in a process of decolonization that continually opposes re-inscribing notions of 'authentic' black identity. This critique should not be made synonymous with a dismissal of the struggle of oppressed and exploited peoples to make ourselves subjects. Nor should it deny that in certain circumstances this experience affords us a privileged critical location from which to speak. This is not a re-inscription of modernist master narratives of authority which privilege some voices by denying voice to others. Part of our struggle for radical black subjectivity is the quest to find ways to construct self and identity that are oppositional and liberatory. The unwillingness to critique essentialism on the part of many African-Americans is rooted in the fear that it will cause folks to lose sight of the specific history and experience of African-Americans and the unique sensibilities and culture that arise from that experience. An adequate response to this concern is to critique essentialism while emphasizing the significance of 'the authority of experience'. There is a radical difference between a repudiation of the idea that there is a black 'essence' and recognition of the way black identity has been specifically constituted in the experience of exile and struggle.

When black folks critique essentialism, we are empowered to recognize multiple experiences of black identity that are the lived conditions which make diverse cultural productions possible. When this diversity is ignored, it is easy to see black folks as falling into two categories: nationalist or assimilationist, black-identified or white-identified. Coming to terms with the impact of postmodernism for black experience, particularly as it changes our sense of identity, means that we must and can rearticulate the basis for collective bonding. Given the various crises facing African-Americans (economic, spiritual, escalating racial violence, etc.), we are compelled by circumstance to reassess our relationship to popular culture and resistance struggle. Many of us are as reluctant to face this task as many non-black postmodern thinkers who focus theoretically on the issue of 'difference' are to confront the issue of race and racism.

Music is the cultural product created by African-Americans that has most attracted postmodern theorists. It is rarely acknowledged that there is far greater censorship and restriction of other forms of cultural production by black folks – literary, critical writing, etc. Attempts on the part of editors and publishing houses to control and manipulate the representation of black culture, as well as the desire to promote the creation of products that will attract the widest audience, limit in a crippling and stifling way the kind of work many black folks feel we can do and still receive recognition. Using myself as an example, that creative writing I do which I consider to be most reflective of a postmodern oppositional sensibility, work that is abstract, fragmented, non-linear narrative, is constantly rejected by editors and publishers. It does not conform to the type of writing they think black women should be doing or the type of writing they believe will sell. Certainly I do not think I am the only black person engaged in forms of cultural production, especially experimental ones, who is constrained by the lack of an audience for certain kinds of work. It is important for postmodern thinkers and theorists to constitute themselves as an audience for such work. To do this they must assert power and privilege within the space of critical writing to open up the field so that it will be more inclusive. To change the exclusionary practice of postmodern critical discourse is to enact a postmodernism of resistance. Part of this intervention entails black intellectual participation in the discourse.

In his essay 'Postmodernism and Black America', Cornel West suggests that black intellectuals 'are marginal – usually languishing at the interface of Black and white cultures or thoroughly ensconced in Euro-American settings'. He cannot see this group as potential producers of radical postmodernist thought. While I generally agree with this assessment, black intellectuals must proceed with the understanding that we are not condemned to the margins. The way we work and what we do can determine whether or not what we produce will be meaningful to a wider audience, one that includes all classes of black people. West suggests that black intellectuals lack 'any organic link with most of Black life' and that this 'diminishes their value to Black resistance'. This statement bears traces of essentialism. Perhaps we need to focus more on those black intellectuals, however rare our presence, who do not feel this lack and whose work is primarily directed towards the enhancement of black critical consciousness and the strengthening of our collective capacity to engage in meaningful resistance struggle. Theoretical ideas and critical thinking need not be transmitted solely in written work or solely in the academy. While I work in a predominantly white institution, I remain intimately and passionately engaged with black community. It's not like I'm going to talk about writing and thinking about postmodernism with other academics and/or intellectuals and not discuss these ideas with underclass non-academic black folks who are family, friends and comrades. Since I have not broken the ties that bind me to underclass poor black community, I have seen that knowledge, especially that which enhances daily life and strengthens our capacity to survive, can be shared. It means that critics, writers and academics have to give the same critical attention to nurturing and cultivating our ties to black community that we give to writing articles, teaching and lecturing. Here again I am really talking about cultivating habits of being that reinforce awareness that knowledge can be disseminated and shared on a number of fronts. The extent to which knowledge is made available, accessible, etc., depends on the nature of one's political commitments.

Postmodern culture with its decentered subject can be the space where ties are severed or it can provide the occasion for new and varied forms of bonding. To some extent, ruptures, surfaces, contextuality, and a host of other happenings create gaps that make space for oppositional practices which no longer require intellectuals to be confined by narrow separate spheres with no meaningful connection to the world of the everyday. Much postmodern engagement with culture emerges from the yearning to do intellectual work that connects with habits of being, forms of artistic expression and aesthetics that inform the daily life of writers and scholars as well as a mass population. On the terrain of culture, one can participate in critical dialogue with the uneducated poor, the black underclass who are thinking about aesthetics. One can talk about what we are seeing, thinking or listening to; a space is there for critical exchange. It's exciting to think, write, talk about and create art that reflects passionate engagement with popular culture, because this may very well be 'the' central future location of resistance struggle, a meeting place where new and radical happenings can occur.

37 | Edward Said,

From *Culture and Imperialism* (1993), pp. 20–35

Two Visions in *Heart of Darkness*

Domination and inequities of power and wealth are perennial facts of human society. But in today's global setting they are also interpretable as having something to do with imperialism, its history, its new forms. The nations of contemporary Asia, Latin America, and Africa are politically independent but in many ways are as dominated and dependent as they were when ruled directly by European powers. On the one hand, this is the consequence of self-inflicted wounds, critics like V.S. Naipaul are wont to say: *they* (everyone knows that 'they' means coloureds, wogs, niggers) are to blame for what 'they' are, and it's no use droning on about the legacy of imperialism. On the other hand, blaming the Europeans sweepingly for the misfortunes of the present is not much of an alternative. What we need to do is to look at these matters as a network of interdependent histories that it would be inaccurate and senseless to repress, useful and interesting to understand.

The point here is not complicated. If while sitting in Oxford, Paris, or New York you tell Arabs or Africans that they belong to a basically sick or unregenerate culture, you are unlikely to convince them. Even if you prevail over them, they are not going to concede to you your essential superiority or your right to rule them despite your evident wealth and power. The history of this stand-off is manifest throughout colonies where white masters were once unchallenged but finally driven out. Conversely, the triumphant natives soon enough found that they needed the West and that the idea of *total* independence was a nationalist fiction designed mainly for what Fanon calls the 'rationalist bourgeoisie', who in turn often ran the new countries with a callous, exploitative tyranny reminiscent of the departed masters.

And so in the late twentieth century the imperial cycle of the last century in some way replicates itself, although today there are really no big empty spaces, no expanding frontiers, no exciting new settlements to establish. We live in one global environment with a huge number of ecological, economic, social, and political pressures tearing at its only dimly perceived, basically uninterpreted and uncomprehended fabric. Anyone with even a vague consciousness of this whole is alarmed at how such remorselessly selfish and narrow interests – patriotism, chauvinism, ethnic, religious, and racial hatreds – can in fact lead to mass destructiveness. The world simply cannot afford this many more times.

One should not pretend that models for a harmonious world order are ready at hand, and it would be equally disingenuous to suppose that ideas of peace and community have much of a chance when power is moved to action by aggressive perceptions of 'vital national interests' or unlimited sovereignty. The United States' clash with Iraq and Iraq's aggression against Kuwait concerning oil are obvious examples. The wonder of it is that the schooling for such relatively provincial thought and action is still prevalent unchecked, uncritically accepted, recurringly replicated in the education of generation after generation. We are all taught to venerate our nations and admire our traditions: we are taught to pursue their interests with toughness and in disregard for other societies. A new and in my opinion appalling tribalism is fracturing societies, separating peoples, promoting greed, bloody conflict, and uninteresting assertions of minor ethnic or group particularity. Little time is spent not so much in 'learning about other cultures' – the phrase has an inane vagueness to it – but in studying the map of interactions, the actual and often productive traffic occurring on a day-by-day, and even minute-by-minute basis among states, societies, groups, identities.

No one can hold this entire map in his or her head, which is why the geography of empire and the many-sided imperial experience that created its fundamental texture should be considered first in terms of a few salient configurations. Primarily, as we look back at the nineteenth century, we see that the drive toward empire in effect brought most of the earth under the domination of a handful of powers. To get hold of part of what this means, I propose to look at a specific set of rich cultural documents in which the interaction between Europe or America on the one hand and the imperialized world on the other is animated, informed, made explicit as an experience for both sides of the encounter. Yet before I do this, historically and systematically, it is a useful preparation to look at what still remains of imperialism in recent cultural discussion. This is the residuum of a dense, interesting history that is paradoxically global and local at the same time, and it is also a sign of how the imperial past lives on, arousing argument and counter-argument with surprising intensity. Because they are contemporary and easy at hand, these traces of the past in the present point the way to a study of the histories – the plural is used advisedly – created by empire, not just the stories of the white man and woman but also those of the non-whites whose lands and very being were at issue, even as their claims were denied or ignored.

One significant contemporary debate about the residue of imperialism – the matter of how 'natives' are represented in the Western media – illustrates the persistence of such interdependence and overlapping, not only in the debate's content but in its form, not only in what is said but also in how it is said, by whom, where, and for whom. This bears looking into, although it requires a self-discipline not easily come by, so well-developed, tempting, and ready at hand are the confrontational strategies. In 1984, well before *The Satanic Verses* appeared, Salman Rushdie diagnosed the spate of films and articles about the British Raj, including the television series *The Jewel in the Crown* and David Lean's film of *A Passage to India*. Rushdie noted that the nostalgia pressed into service by these affectionate recollections of British rule in India coincided with the Falklands War, and that 'the rise of Raj revisionism, exemplified by the huge success of these fictions, is the artistic counterpart to the rise of conservative ideologies in modern Britain'. Commentators responded to what they considered Rushdie's wailing and whining in public and seemed to disregard his principal point. Rushdie was trying to make a larger argument, which presumably should have appealed to intellectuals for whom George Orwell's well-known description of the intellectual's place in society as being inside and outside the whale no longer applied; modern reality in Rushdie's terms was actually 'whaleless, this world without quiet corners [in which] there can be no easy escapes from history, from hullabaloo, from terrible, unquiet fuss'.[1] But Rushdie's main point was *not* the point considered worth taking up and debating. Instead the main issue for contention was whether things in the Third World hadn't in fact declined after the colonies had been emancipated, and whether it might not be better on the whole to listen to the rare – luckily, I might add, extremely rare – Third World intellectuals who manfully ascribed most of their present barbarities, tyrannies, and degradations to their own native histories, histories that were pretty bad before colonialism and that reverted to that state after colonialism. Hence, ran *this* argument, better a ruthlessly honest V.S. Naipaul than an absurdly posturing Rushdie.

One could conclude from the emotions stirred up by Rushdie's own case, then and later, that many people in the West came to feel that enough was enough. After Vietnam and Iran – and note here that these labels are usually employed equally to evoke American domestic traumas (the student insurrections of the 1960s, the public anguish about the hostages in the 1970s) as much as international conflict and the 'loss' of Vietnam and Iran to radical nationalisms – after Vietnam and Iran, lines had to be defended. Western democracy had taken a beating, and even if the physical damage had been done abroad, there was a sense, as Jimmy Carter once rather oddly put it, of 'mutual destruction'. This feeling in turn led to Westerners rethinking the whole process of decolonization. Was it not true, ran their new evaluation, that 'we' had given 'them' progress and modernization? Hadn't we provided them with order and a kind of stability that they haven't been able since to provide for themselves? Wasn't it an atrocious misplaced trust to believe in their capacity for independence, for it had led to Bokassas and Amins, whose intellectual correlates were people like Rushdie? Shouldn't we have held on to the colonies, kept the subject or inferior races in check, remained true to our civilizational responsibilities?

I realize that what I have just reproduced is not entirely the thing itself, but perhaps a caricature. Nevertheless it bears an uncomfortable resemblance to what many people who imagined themselves speaking for the West said. There seemed little scepticism that a monolithic 'West' in fact existed, any more than an entire ex-colonial world described in one sweeping generalization after another. The leap to essences and generalization was accompanied by appeals to an imagined history of Western endowments and free hand-outs, followed by a reprehensible sequence of ungrateful bitings of that grandly giving 'Western' hand. Why don't they appreciate us, after what we did for them?[2]

How easily so much could be compressed into that simple formula of unappreciated magnanimity! Dismissed or forgotten were the ravaged colonial peoples who for centuries endured summary justice, unending economic oppression, distortion of their social and intimate lives, and a recourseless submission that was the function of unchanging European superiority. Only to keep in mind the millions of Africans who were supplied to the slave trade is to acknowledge the unimaginable cost of maintaining that superiority. Yet dismissed most often are precisely the infinite number of traces in the immensely detailed, violent history of colonial intervention – minute by minute, hour by hour – in the lives of individuals and collectivities, on both sides of the colonial divide.

The thing to be noticed about this kind of contemporary discourse, which assumes the primacy and even the complete centrality of the West, is how totalizing is its form, how all-enveloping its attitudes and gestures, how much it shuts out even as it includes, compresses, and consolidates. We suddenly find ourselves transported backward in time to the late nineteenth century.

This imperial attitude is, I believe, beautifully captured in the complicated and rich narrative form of Conrad's great novella *Heart of Darkness*, written between 1898 and 1899. On the one hand, the narrator Marlow acknowledges the tragic predicament of all speech – that 'it is impossible to convey the life-sensation of any given epoch on one's existence – that which makes its truth, its meaning – its subtle and penetrating essence . . . . We live, as we dream – alone'[3] – yet still manages to convey the enormous power of Kurtz's African experience through his own overmastering narrative of his voyage into the African interior towards Kurtz. This narrative in turn is connected directly with the redemptive force, as well as the waste and horror, of Europe's mission in the dark world. Whatever is lost or elided or even simply made up in Marlow's immensely compelling recitation is compensated for in the narrative's sheer historical momentum, the temporal forward movement – with digression, descriptions, exciting encounters, and all. Within the narrative of how he journeyed to Kurtz's Inner Station whose source and authority he now becomes, Marlow moves backward and forward materially in small and large spirals, very much the way episodes in the course of his journey up-river are then incorporated by the principal forward trajectory into what he renders as 'the heart of Africa'.

Thus Marlow's encounter with the improbably white-suited clerk in the middle of the jungle furnishes him with several digressive paragraphs, as does his meeting later with the semi-crazed, harlequin-like Russian who has been so affected by Kurtz's gifts. Yet underlying Marlow's inconclusiveness, his evasions, his arabesque meditations on his feelings and ideas, is the unrelenting course of the journey itself, which, despite all the many obstacles, is sustained through the jungle, through time, through hardship, to the heart of it all, Kurtz's ivory-trading empire. Conrad wants us to see how Kurtz's great looting adventure, Marlow's journey up the river, and the narrative itself all share a common theme: Europeans performing acts of imperial mastery and will in (or about) Africa.

What makes Conrad different from the other colonial writers who were his contemporaries is that, for reasons having partly to do with the colonialism that turned him, a Polish expatriate, into an employee of the imperial system, he was so self-conscious about what he did. Like most of his other tales, therefore, *Heart of Darkness* cannot just be a straightforward recital of Marlow's adventures: it is also a dramatization of Marlow himself, the former wanderer in colonial regions, telling his story to a group of British listeners at a particular time and in a specific place. That this group of people is drawn largely from the business world is Conrad's way of emphasizing the fact that during the 1890s the business of empire, once an adventurous and often individualistic enterprise, had become the empire of business. (Coincidentally we should note that at about the same time Halford Mackinder, an explorer, geographer, and Liberal Imperialist, gave a series of lectures on imperialism at the London Institute of Bankers:[4] perhaps Conrad knew about this.) Although the almost oppressive force of Marlow's narrative leaves us with a quite accurate sense that there is no way out of the sovereign historical force of imperialism, and that it has the power of a system representing as well as speaking for everything within its dominion, Conrad shows us that what Marlow does is contingent, acted out for a set of like-minded British hearers, and limited to that situation.

Yet neither Conrad nor Marlow gives us a full view of what is *outside* the listeners on the deck of the *Nellie*, and Conrad. By that I mean that *Heart of Darkness* works so effectively because its politics and aesthetics are, so to speak, imperialist, which in the closing years of the nineteenth century seemed to be at the same time an aesthetic, politics, and even epistemology inevitable and unavoidable. For if we cannot truly understand someone else's experience and if we must therefore depend upon the assertive authority of the sort of power that Kurtz wields as a white man in the jungle or that Marlow, another white man, wields as narrator, there is no use looking for other, non-imperialist alternatives; the system has simply eliminated them and made them unthinkable. The circularity, the perfect closure of the whole thing is not only aesthetically but also mentally unassailable.

Conrad is so self-conscious about situating Marlow's tale in a narrative moment that he allows us simultaneously to realize after all that imperialism, far from swallowing up its own history, was taking place in and was circumscribed by a larger history, one just outside the tightly inclusive circle of Europeans on the deck of the *Nellie*. As yet, however, no one seemed to inhabit that region, and so Conrad left it empty.

Conrad could probably never have used Marlow to present anything other than an imperialist world-view, given what was available for either

Conrad or Marlow to see of the non-European at the time. Independence was for whites and Europeans; the lesser or subject peoples were to be ruled; science, learning, history emanated from the West. True, Conrad scrupulously recorded the differences between the disgraces of Belgian and British colonial attitudes, but he could only imagine the world carved up into one or another Western sphere of dominion. But because Conrad also had an extraordinarily persistent residual sense of his own exilic marginality, he quite carefully (some would say maddeningly) qualified Marlow's narrative with the provisionality that came from standing at the very juncture of this world with another, unspecified but different. Conrad was certainly not a great imperialist entrepreneur like Cecil Rhodes or Frederick Lugard, even though he understood perfectly how for each of them, in Hannah Arendt's words, to enter 'the maelstrom of an unending process of expansion, he will, as it were, cease to be what he was and obey the laws of the process, identify himself with anonymous forces that he is supposed to serve in order to keep the whole process in motion, he will think of himself as mere function, and eventually consider such functionality, such an incarnation of the dynamic trend, his highest possible achievement'.[5] Conrad's realization is that if, like narrative, imperialism has monopolized the entire system of representation – which in the case of *Heart of Darkness* allowed it to speak for Africans as well as for Kurtz and the other adventurers, including Marlow and his audiences – your self-consciousness as an outsider can allow you actively to comprehend how the machine works, given that you and it are fundamentally not in perfect synchrony or correspondence. Never the wholly incorporated and fully acculturated Englishman, Conrad therefore preserved an ironic distance in each of his works.

The form of Conrad's narrative has thus made it possible to derive two possible arguments, two visions, in the post-colonial world that succeeded his. One argument allows the old imperial enterprise full scope to play itself out conventionally, to render the world as official European or Western imperialism saw it, and to consolidate itself after World War Two. Westerners may have physically led their old colonies in Africa and Asia, but they retained them not only as markets but as locales on the ideological map over which they continued to rule morally and intellectually. 'Show me the Zulu Tolstoy', as one American intellectual has recently put it. The assertive sovereign inclusiveness of this argument courses through the words of those who speak today for the West and for what the West did, as well as for what the rest of the world is, was, and may be. The assertions of this discourse exclude what has been represented as 'lost' by arguing that the colonial world was in some ways ontologically speaking lost to begin with, irredeemable, irrecusably inferior. Moreover, it focuses not on what was shared in the colonial experience, but on what must never be shared, namely the authority and rectitude that come with greater power and development. Rhetorically, its terms are the organization of political passions, to borrow from Julien Benda's critique of modern intellectuals, terms which, he was sensible enough to know, lead inevitably to mass slaughter, and if not to literal mass slaughter then certainly to rhetorical slaughter.

The second argument is considerably less objectionable. It sees itself as Conrad saw his own narratives, local to a time and place, neither unconditionally true nor unqualifiedly certain. As I have said, Conrad does not give us the sense that he could imagine a fully realized alternative to imperialism: the natives he wrote about in Africa, Asia, or America were incapable of independence, and because he seemed to imagine that European tutelage was a given, he could not foresee what would take place when it came to an end. But come to an end it would, if only because–like all human effort, like speech itself–it would have its moment, then it would have to pass. Since Conrad *dates* imperialism, shows its contingency, records its illusions and tremendous violence and waste (as in *Nostromo*), he permits his later readers to imagine something other than an Africa carved up into dozens of European colonies, even if, for his own part, he had little notion of what that Africa might be.

To return to the first line out of Conrad, the discourse of resurgent empire proves that the nineteenth-century imperial encounter continues today to draw lines and defend barriers. Strangely, it persists also in the enormously complex and quietly interesting interchange between former colonial partners, say between Britain and India, or between France and the Francophone countries of Africa. But these exchanges tend to be over-shadowed by the loud antagonisms of the polarized debate of pro- and anti-imperialists, who speak stridently of national destiny, overseas interests, neo-imperialism, and the like, drawing like-minded people–aggressive Westerners and, ironically, those non-Westerners for whom the new nationalist and resurgent Ayatollahs speak–away from the other ongoing interchange. Inside each regrettably constricted camp stand the blameless, the just, the faithful, led by the omnicompetent, those who know the truth about themselves and others; outside stands a miscellaneous bunch of querulous intellectuals and wishy-washy sceptics who go on complaining about the past to little effect.

An important ideological shift occurred during the 1970s and 1980s, accompanying this contraction of horizons in what I have been calling the first of the two lines leading out of *Heart of Darkness*. One can locate it, for instance, in the dramatic change in emphasis and, quite literally, direction among thinkers noted for their radicalism. The later Jean-François Lyotard and Michel Foucault, eminent French philosophers who emerged during the 1960s as apostles of radicalism and intellectual insurgency, describe a striking new lack of faith in what Lyotard calls the great legitimizing narratives of emancipation and enlightenment. Our age, he said in the 1980s, is post-modernist, concerned only with local issues, not with history but with problems to be solved, not with a grand reality but with games.[6] Foucault also turned his attention away from the oppositional forces in modern society which he had studied for their undeterred resistance to exclusion and confinement–delinquents, poets, outcasts, and the like–and decided that since power was everywhere it was probably better to concentrate on the local micro-physics of power that surround the individual.

The self was therefore to be studied, cultivated, and, if necessary, refashioned and constituted.[7] In both Lyotard and Foucault we find precisely the same trope employed to explain the disappointment in the politics of liberation: narrative, which posits an enabling beginning point and a vindicating goal, is no longer adequate for plotting the human trajectory in society. There is nothing to look forward to: we are stuck within our circle. And now the line is enclosed by a circle. After years of support for anti-colonial struggles in Algeria, Cuba, Vietnam, Palestine, Iran, which came to represent for many Western intellectuals their deepest engagement in the politics and philosophy of anti-imperialist decolonization, a moment of exhaustion and disappointment was reached.[8] One began to hear and read how futile it was to support revolutions, how barbaric were the new regimes that came to power, how – this is an extreme case – decolonization had benefited 'world communism'.

Enter now terrorism and barbarism. Enter also the ex-colonial experts whose well-publicized message was: these colonial peoples deserve only colonialism or, since 'we' were foolish to pull out of Aden, Algeria, India, Indochina, and everywhere else, it might be a good idea to reinvade their territories. Enter also various experts and theoreticians of the relationship between liberation movements, terrorism, and the KGB. There was a resurgence of sympathy for what Jeane Kirkpatrick called authoritarian (as opposed to totalitarian) regimes who were Western allies. With the onset of Reaganism, Thatcherism, and their correlates, a new phase of history began.

However else it might have been historically understandable, peremptorily withdrawing 'the West' from its own experiences in the 'peripheral world' certainly was and is not an attractive or edifying activity for an intellectual today. It shuts out the possibility of knowledge and of discovery of what it means to be outside the whale. Let us return to Rushdie for another insight:

> We see that it can be as false to create a politics-free fictional universe as to create one in which nobody needs to work or eat or hate or love or sleep. Outside the whale it becomes necessary, and even exhilarating, to grapple with the special problems created by the incorporation of political material, because politics is by turns farce and tragedy, and sometimes (e.g., Zia's Pakistan) both at once. Outside the whale the writer is obliged to accept that he (or she) is part of the crowd, part of the ocean, part of the storm, so that objectivity becomes a great dream, like perfection, an unattainable goal for which one must struggle in spite of the impossibility of success. Outside the whale is the world of Samuel Beckett's famous formula: *I can't go on, I'll go on.*[9]

The terms of Rushdie's description, while they borrow from Orwell, seem to me to resonate even more interestingly with Conrad. For here is the second consequence, the second line leading out of Conrad's narrative form; in its explicit references to the outside, it points to a perspective outside the basically imperialist representations provided by Marlow and his listeners. It is a profoundly secular perspective, and it is beholden neither to notions about historical destiny and the essentialism that destiny always seems to entail, nor to historical indifference and resignation. Being on the inside shuts out the full experience of imperialism, edits it and subordinates it to the dominance of one Eurocentric and totalizing view; this other perspective suggests the presence of a field without special historical privileges for one party.

I don't want to overinterpret Rushdie, or put ideas in his prose that he may not have intended. In this controversy with the local British media (before *The Satanic Verses* sent him into hiding), he claimed that he could not recognize the truth of his own experience in the popular media representations of India. Now I myself would go further and say that it is one of the virtues of such conjunctures of politics with culture and aesthetics that they permit the disclosure of a common ground obscured by the controversy itself. Perhaps it is especially hard for the combatants directly involved to see this common ground when they are fighting back more than reflecting. I can perfectly understand the anger that fuelled Rushdie's argument because like him I feel outnumbered and outorganized by a prevailing Western consensus that has come to regard the Third World as an atrocious nuisance, a culturally and politically inferior place. Whereas we write and speak as members of a small minority of marginal voices, our journalistic and academic critics belong to a wealthy system of interlocking informational and academic resources with newspapers, television networks, journals of opinion, and institutes at its disposal. Most of them have now taken up a strident chorus of rightward-tending damnation, in which they separate what is non-white, non-Western, and non-Judeo-Christian from the acceptable and designated Western ethos, then herd it all together under various demeaning rubrics such as terrorist, marginal second-rate, or unimportant. To attack what is contained in these categories is to defend the Western spirit.

Let us return to Conrad and to what I have been referring to as the second, less imperialistically assertive possibility offered by *Heart of Darkness*. Recall once again that Conrad sets the story on the deck of a boat anchored in the Thames; as Marlow tells his story the sun sets, and by the end of the narrative the heart of darkness has reappeared in England; outside the group of Marlow's listeners lies an undefined and unclear world. Conrad sometimes seems to want to fold that world into the imperial metropolitan discourse represented by Marlow, but by virtue of his own dislocated subjectivity he resists the effort and succeeds in so doing, I have always believed, largely through formal devices. Conrad's self-consciously circular narrative forms draw attention to themselves as artificial constructions, encouraging us to sense the potential of a reality that seemed inaccessible to imperialism, just beyond its control, and that only well after Conrad's death in 1924 acquired a substantial presence.

This needs more explanation. Despite their European names and mannerisms, Conrad's narrators are not average unreflecting witnesses of European imperialism. They do not simply accept what goes on in the name of the imperial idea: they think about it a lot, they worry about it, they are actually quite anxious about whether they can make it seem like a routine thing. But it never is. Conrad's way of demonstrating this discrepancy between the orthodox and his own views of empire is to keep drawing attention to how ideas and values are constructed (and reconstructed) through dislocations in the narrator's language. In addition, the recitations are meticulously staged: the narrator is a speaker whose audience and the reason for their being together, the quality of whose voice, the effect of what he says – are all important and even insistent aspects of the story he tells. Marlow, for example, is never straightforward. He alternates between garrulity and stunning eloquence, and rarely resists making peculiar things seem more peculiar by surprisingly misstating them, or rendering them vague and contradictory. Thus, he says, a French warship fires 'into a continent'; Kurtz's eloquence is enlightening as well as fraudulent; and so on – his speech so full of these odd discrepancies (well discussed by Ian Watt as 'delayed decoding'[10]) that the net effect is to leave his immediate audience as well as the reader with the acute sense that what he is presenting is not quite as it should be or appears to be.

Yet the whole point of what Kurtz and Marlow talk about is in fact imperial mastery, white Europeans *over* black Africans and their ivory, civilization *over* the primitive dark continent. By accentuating the discrepancy between the official 'idea' of empire and the remarkably disorienting actuality of Africa, Marlow unsettles the reader's sense not only of the very idea of empire but of something more basic, reality itself. For if Conrad can show that all human activity depends on controlling a radically unstable reality to which words approximate only by will or convention, the same is true of empire, of venerating the idea, and so forth. With Conrad, then, we are in a world being made and unmade more or less all the time. What appears stable and secure – the policeman at the corner, for instance – is only slightly more secure than the white men in the jungle, and requires the same continuous (but precarious) triumph over an all-pervading darkness, which by the end of the tale is shown to be the same in London and in Africa.

Conrad's genius allowed him to realize that the ever-present darkness could be colonized or illuminated – *Heart of Darkness* is full of references to the *mission civilisatrice*, to benevolent as well as cruel schemes to bring light to the dark places and peoples of this world by acts of will and deployments of power – but that it also had to be acknowledged as independent. Kurtz and Marlow acknowledge the darkness, the former as he is dying, the latter as he reflects retrospectively on the meaning of Kurtz's final words. They (and of course Conrad) are ahead of their time in understanding that what they call 'the darkness' has an autonomy of its own, and can reinvade and reclaim what imperialism had taken for *its* own. But Marlow and Kurtz are also creatures of their time and cannot take the next step, which would be to recognise that what they saw, disablingly and disparagingly, as a non-European 'darkness' was in fact a non-European world *resisting* imperialism so as one day to regain sovereignty and independence, and not, as Conrad reductively says, to reestablish the darkness. Conrad's tragic limitation is that even though he could see clearly that on one level imperialism was essentially pure dominance and land-grabbing, he could not then conclude that imperialism had to end so that 'natives' could lead lives free from European domination. As a creature of his time, Conrad could not grant the natives their freedom, despite his severe critique of the imperialism that enslaved them.

The cultural and ideological evidence that Conrad was wrong in his Eurocentric way is both impressive and rich. A whole movement, literature, and theory of resistance and response to empire exists, and in greatly disparate post-colonial regions one sees tremendously energetic efforts to engage with the metropolitan world in equal debate so as to testify to the diversity and differences of the non-European world and to its own agendas, priorities, and history. The purpose of this testimony is to inscribe, reinterpret, and expand the areas of engagement as well as the terrain contested with Europe. Some of this activity – for example, the work of two important and active Iranian intellectuals, Ali Shariati and Jalal Ali i-Ahmed, who by means of speeches, books, tapes, and pamphlets prepared the way for the Islamic Revolutions – interprets colonialims by asserting the absolute opposition of the native culture: the West is an enemy, a disease, an evil. In other instances, novelists like the Kenyan Ngugi and the Sudanese Tayib Salih appropriate for their fiction such great *topoi* of colonial culture as the quest and the voyage into the unknown, claiming them for their own, post-colonial purposes. Salih's hero in *Season of Migration to the North* does (and is) the reverse of what Kurtz does (and is): the Black man journeys north into white territory.

Between classical nineteenth-century imperialism and what it gave rise to in resistant native cultures, there is thus both a stubborn confrontation and a crossing over in discussion, borrowing back and forth, debate. Many of the most interesting post-colonial writers bear their past within them – as scars of humiliating wounds, as instigation for different practices, as potentially revised visions of the past tending towards a new future, as urgently reinterpretable and redeployable experiences, in which the formerly silent native speaks and acts on territory taken back from the empire. One sees these aspects in Rushdie, Derek Walcott, Aimé Céasire, Chinua Achebe, Pablo Neruda, and Brian Friel. And now these writers can truly read the great colonial masterpieces, which not only misrepresented them but assumed they were unable to read and respond directly to what had been written about them, just as European ethnography presumed the natives' incapacity to intervene in scientific discourse about them.

Notes

1 Salman Rushdie, 'Outside the Whale', in *Imaginary Homelands: Essays and Criticism 1981–1991* (London, Viking/Granta, 1991), pp. 92, 101.
2 This is the message of Conor Cruise O'Brien's 'Why the Wailing Ought to Stop,' *The Observer*, 3 June 1984.
3 Joseph Conrad, 'Heart of Darkness,' in *Youth and Two Other Stories* (Garden City, NY, Doubleday, Page, 1925), p. 82.

4 For Mackinder, see Neil Smith, *Uneven Development: Nature, Capital and the Production of Space* (Oxford, Blackwell, 1984), pp. 102–3. Conrad and triumphalist geography are at the heart of Felix Driver, 'Geography's Empire: Histories of Geographical Knowledge,' *Society and Space*, 1991.

5 Hannah Arendt, *The Origins of Totalitarianism* (1951; new ed., New York, Harcourt Brace Jovanovich, 1973), p. 215. See also Fredric Jameson. *The Political Unconscious: Narrative as a Socially Symbolic Act* (Ithaca, NY, Cornell University Press, 1981).

6 Jean-François Lyotard, *The Postmoden Condition: A Report on Knowledge*, Geoff Bennington and Brian Massumi tr. (Minneapolis, University of Minnesota Press, 1984), p. 37.

7 See especially Foucault's late work, *The Care of the Self*, Robert Hurley tr. (New York, Pantheon, 1986). A bold new interpretation arguing that Foucault's entire *œuvre* is about the self, and his in particular, is advanced in *The Passion of Michel Foucault* by James Miller (New York, Simon & Schuster, 1993).

8 See, for example, Gérard Chaliand, *Revolution in the Third World* (Harmondsworth, Penguin, 1978).

9 Rushdie, 'Outside the Whale,' pp. 100–1.

10 Ian Watt, *Conrad in the Nineteenth Century* (Berkeley, University of California Press, 1979), pp. 175–9.

38 | Homi Bhabha,

'Of Mimicry and Man: The Ambivalence of Colonial Discourse', October, no. 28, Spring (1983)*, pp. 125–33

Mimicry reveals something in so far as it is distinct from what might be called an itself that is behind. The effect of mimicry is camouflage . . . . It is not a question of harmonizing with the background, but against a mottled background, of becoming mottled – exactly like the technique of camouflage practised in human warfare.

Jacques Lacan,
'The Line and Light', *Of the Gaze*

It is out of season to question at this time of day, the original policy of conferring on every colony of the British Empire a mimic representation of the British Constitution. But if the creature so endowed has sometimes forgotten its real insignificance and under the fancied importance of speakers and maces, and all the paraphernalia and ceremonies of the imperial legislature, has dared to defy the mother country, she has to thank herself for the folly of conferring such privileges on a condition of society that has no earthly claim to so exalted a position. A fundamental principle appears to have been forgotten or overlooked in our system of colonial policy – that of colonial dependence. To give to a colony the forms of independence is a mockery; she would not be a colony for a single hour if she could maintain an independent station.

Sir Edward Cust,
'Reflections on West African Affairs . . . addressed to the Colonial
Office', Hatchard, London 1839

The discourse of post-Enlightenment English colonialism often speaks in a tongue that is forked, not false. If colonialism takes power in the name of history, it repeatedly exercises its authority through the figure of farce. For the epic intention of the civilizing mission, 'human and not wholly human' in the famous words of Lord Rosebery, 'writ by the finger of the Divine'[1] often produces a text rich in the traditions of *trompe l' œil*, irony, mimicry, and repetition. In this comic turn from the high ideals of the colonial imagination to its low mimetic literary effects, mimicry emerges as one of the most elusive and effective strategies of colonial power and knowledge.

Within that conflictual economy of colonial discourse which Edward Said[2] describes as the tension between the synchronic panoptical vision of domination – the demand for identity, stasis – and the counter-pressure of the diachrony of history – change, difference – mimicry represents an *ironic* compromise. If I may adapt Samuel Weber's formulation of the marginalizing vision of castration,[3] then colonial mimicry is the desire for a reformed, recognizable Other, as *a subject of a difference that is almost the same, but not quite*. Which is to say, that the discourse of mimicry is constructed around an *ambivalence*; in order to be effective, mimicry must continually produce its slippage, its excess, its difference. The authority of that mode of colonial discourse that I have called mimicry is therefore stricken by an indeterminacy: mimicry emerges as the representation of a difference that is itself a process of disavowal. Mimicry is, thus, the sign of a double articulation; a complex strategy of reform, regulation, and discipline, which 'appropriates' the Other as it visualizes power. Mimicry is also the sign of the inappropriate, however, a difference of recalcitrance which coheres the dominant strategic function of colonial power, intensifies surveillance, and poses an immanent threat to both 'normalized' knowledges and disciplinary powers.

The effect of mimicry on the authority of colonial discourse is profound and disturbing. For in 'normalizing' the colonial state or subject, the dream of post-Enlightenment civility alienates its own language of liberty and produces another knowledge of its norms. The ambivalence which thus informs this strategy is discernible, for example, in Locke's Second Treatise which *splits* to reveal the limitations of liberty in his double use of the word 'slave': first simply, descriptively as the locus of a legitimate exercise of power. What is articulated in that distance between the two uses of the absolute, imagined difference between the 'Colonial' State of Carolina and the Original State of Nature.

It is for this area between mimicry and mockery, where the reforming, civilizing mission is threatened by the displacing gaze of its disciplinary double, that my instances of colonial imitation come. What they all share is a discursive process by which the excess or slippage produced by the *ambivalence* of mimicry (almost the same, *but not quite*) does not merely 'rupture' the discourse, but becomes transformed into an uncertainty which fixes the colonial subject as a 'partial' presence. By 'partial' I mean both 'incomplete' and 'virtual'. It is as if the very emergence of the 'colonial' is dependent for its representation upon some strategic limitation or prohibition *within* the authoritative discourse itself. The success of colonial appropriation depends on a proliferation of inappropriate objects that ensure its strategic failure, so that mimicry is at once resemblance and menace.

A classic text of such partiality is Charles Grant's 'Observations on the State of Society among the Asiatic Subjects of Great Britain' (1792)[4] which was only superseded by James Mills's *History of India* as the most influential early nineteenth-century account of Indian manners and morals. Grant's dream of an evangelical system of mission education conducted uncompromisingly in English was partly a belief in political reform along Christian lines and partly an awareness that the expansion of company rule in India required a system of 'interpellation' – a reform of manners, as Grant put it, that would provide the colonial with 'a sense of personal identity as we know it.' Caught between the desire for religious reform and the fear that the Indian might become turbulent for liberty, Grant implies that it is, in fact the 'partial' diffusion of Christianity, and the 'partial' influence of moral improvements which will construct a particularly appropriate form of colonial subjectivity. What is suggested is a process of reform through which Christian doctrines might collude with divisive caste practices to prevent dangerous political alliances. Inadvertently, Grant produces a knowledge of Christianity as a form of social control which conflicts with the enunciatory assumptions which authorize his discourse. In suggesting, finally, that 'partial reform' will produce an empty form of 'the *imitation* of English manners which will induce them [the colonial subjects] to remain under our protection',[5] Grant mocks his moral project and violates the Evidences of Christianity–a central missionary tenet–which forbade any tolerance of heathen faiths.

The absurd extravagance of Macaulay's *Infamous Minute* (1835)–deeply influenced by Charles Grant's *Observation*–makes a mockery of Oriental learning until faced with the challenge of conceiving of a 'reformed' colonial subject. Then the great tradition of European humanism seems capable only of ironizing itself. At the intersection of European learning and colonial power, Macaulay can conceive of nothing other than 'a class of interpreters between us and the millions whom we govern–a class of persons Indian in blood and colour, but English in tastes, in opinions, in morals and in intellect'[6]–in other words a mimic man raised 'through our English School', as a missionary educationist wrote in 1819, 'to form a corps of translators and be employed in different departments of Labour',[7] The line of descent of the mimic man can be traced thorugh the works of Kipling, Forster, Orwell, Naipaul, and to his emergence, most recently, in Benedict Anderson's excellent essary on nationalism, as the anomalous Bipin Chandra Pal.[8] He is the effect of a flawed colonial mimesis, in which to be Anglicized, is *emphatically* not to be English.

The figure of mimicry is locatable within what Anderson describes as 'the inner incompatability of empire and nation.'[9] It problematizes the signs of racial and cultural priority, so that the 'national' is no longer naturalizable. What emerges between mimesis and mimicry is a *writing*, a mode of representation, that marginalizes the monumentality of history, quite simply mocks its power to be a model, that power which supposedly makes it imitable. Mimicry *repeats* rather than *re-presents* and in that diminishing perspective merges Decoud's displayed European vision of Sulaco as

> the endlessness of civil strife where folly seemed even harder to bear than its ignominy . . . the lawlessness of a populace of all colours and races, barbarism, irremediable tyranny . . . . America is ungovernable.[10]

Or Ralph Singh's apostasy in Naipaul's *The Mimic Men*:

> We pretended to be real, to be learning, to be preparing ourselves for life, we mimic men of the New World, one unknown corner of it, with all its reminders of the corruption that came so quickly to the new.[11]

Both Decoud and Singh, and in their different ways Grant and Macaulay, are the parodists of history. Despite their intentions and invocations they inscribe the colonial text erratically, eccentrically across a body politic that refuses to be representative, in a narrative that refuses to be representational. The desire to merge as 'authentic' through mimicry – through a process of writing and repetition – is the final irony of partial representation.

What I have called mimicry is not the familiar exercise of *dependent* colonial relations through narcissistic identification so that, as Fanon has observed,[12] the black man stops being an actional person for only the white man can represent his self-esteem. Mimicry conceals no presence or identity behind its mask: it is not what Césaire describes as 'colonization-thingification'[13] behind which there stands the essence of the *présence Africaine*. The *menace* of mimicry is its *double* vision which in disclosing the ambivalence of colonial discourses also disrupts its authority. And it is a double-vision that is a result of what I've described as the partial representation/recognition of the colonial object. Grant's colonial as partial imitator, Macaulay's translator, Naipaul's colonial politician as playactor, Decoud as the scene setter of the *opéra bouffe* of the New World, these are the appropriate objects of a colonialist chain of command, authorized versions of otherness. But they are also, as I have shown, the figures of a doubling, the part-objects of a metonymy of colonial desire which alienates the modality and normality of those dominant discourses in which they emerge as 'inappropriate' colonial subjects. A desire that, through the repetition of *partial presence*, which is the basis of mimicry, articulates those disturbances of cultural, racial, and historical difference that menace the narcissistic demand of colonial authority. It is a desire that reverses 'in part' the colonial appropriation by now producing a partial vision of the colonizer's presence. A gaze of otherness, that shares the acuity of the genealogical gaze which, as Foucault describes it, liberates marginal elements and shatters the unity of man's being through which he extends his sovereignty.[14]

I want to turn to this process by which the look of surveillance returns as the displacing gaze of the disciplined, where the observer becomes the observed and 'partial' representation rearticulates the whole notion of *identity* and alienates it from essence. But not before observing that even an exemplary history like Eric Stokes's *The English Utilitarians in India* acknowledges the anomalous gaze of otherness but finally disavows it in a contradictory utterance:

> Certainly India played *no* central part in fashioning the *distinctive* qualities of English civilisation. In many ways it acted as a disturbing force, a magnetic power placed at the periphery tending to distort the natural development of Britain's character . . . .[15]

What is the nature of the hidden threat of the partial gaze? How does mimicry emerge as the subject of the scopic drive and the object of colonial surveillance? How is desire disciplined, authority displaced?

If we turn to a Freudian figure to address these issues of colonial textuality, that form of difference that is mimicry – *almost the same but not quite* – will become clear. Writing of the partial nature of fantasy, caught *inappropriately*, between the unconscious and the preconscious, making problematic, like mimicry, the very notion of 'origins', Freud has this to say:

> Their mixed and split origin is what decides their fate. We may compare them with individuals of mixed race who taken all round resemble white men but who betray their coloured descent by some striking feature or other and on that account are excluded from society and enjoy none of the privileges.[16]

Almost the same but not white: the visibility of mimicry is always produced at the site of interdiction. It is a form of colonial discourse that is uttered *inter dicta*: a discourse at the crossroads of what is known and permissible and that which though known must be kept concealed; a discourse uttered between the lines and as such both against the rules and within them. The question of the representation of difference is therefore always also a problem of authority. The 'desire' of mimicry, which is Freud's *striking feature* that reveals so little but makes such a big difference, is not merely that impossibility of the Other which repeatedly resists signification. The desire of colonial mimicry – an interdictory desire – may not have an object, but it has strategic objectives which I shall call the *metonymy of presence*.

Those inappropriate signifiers of colonial discourse – the difference between being English and being Anglicized; the identity between stereotypes which, through repetition, also become different; the discriminatory identities constructed across traditional cultural norms and classifications, the Simian Black, the Lying Asiatic – all these are metonymies of presence. They are strategies of desire in discourse that make the anomalous representation of the colonized something other than a process of 'the return of the repressed', what Fanon unsatisfactorily characterized as collective catharsis.[17] These instances of metonymy are the nonrepressive productions of contradictory and multiple belief. They cross the boundaries of the culture of enunciation through a strategic confusion of the metaphoric and metonymic axes of the cultural production of meaning. For each of these instances of 'a difference that is almost the same but not quite' inadvertently creates a crisis for the cultural priority given to the *metaphoric* as the process of repression and substitution which negotiates the difference between paradigmatic systems and classifications. In mimicry, the representation of identity and meaning is rearticulated along the axis of metonymy. As Lacan reminds us, mimicry is like camouflage, not a harmonization or repression of difference, but a form of resemblance that differs/defends presence by displaying it in part, metonymically. Its threat, I would add, comes from the prodigious and strategic production of conflictual, fantastic, discriminatory 'identity effects' in the play of a power that is elusive because it hides no essence, no 'itself'. And that form of *resemblance* is the most terrifying thing to behold, as Edward Long testifies in his *History of Jamaica* (1774). At the end of a tortured, negrophobic passage, that shifts anxiously between piety, prevarication, and perversion, the text finally confronts its fear; nothing other than the repetition of its resemblance 'in part':

> (Negroes) are represented by all authors as the vilest of human kind, to which they have little more pretension of resemblance *than what arises from their exterior forms* (my italics).[18]

From such a colonial encounter between the white presence and its black semblance, there emerges the question of the ambivalence of mimicry as a problematic of colonial subjection. For if Sade's scandalous theatricalization of language repeatedly reminds us that discourse can claim 'no priority', then the work of Edward Said will not let us forget that the 'ethnocentric and erratic will to power from which texts can spring'[19] is itself a theater of war. Mimicry, as the metonymy of presence is, indeed, such an erratic, eccentric strategy of authority in colonial discourse. Mimicry does not merely destroy narcissistic authority through the repetitious slippage of difference and desire. It is the process of the *fixation* of the colonial as a form of cross-classificatory, discriminatory knowledge in the defiles of an interdictory discourse, and therefore necessarily raises the question of the *authorization* of colonial representations. A question of authority that goes beyond the subject's lack of priority (castration)to a historical crisis in the conceptuality of colonial man as an *object* of regulatory power, as the subject of racial, cultural, national representation.

'This culture . . . fixed in its colonial status', Fanon suggests, '[is] both present and mummified, it testified against its members. It defines them in fact without appeal.'[20] The ambivalence of mimicry—almost but not quite—suggests that the fetishized colonial culture is potentially and strategically an insurgent counter-appeal. What I have called its 'identify-effects', are always crucially split. Under cover of camouflage, mimicry, like the fetish, is a part-object that radically revalues the normative knowledges of the priority of race, writing, history. For the fetish mimes the forms of authority at the point at which it deauthorizes them. Similarly, mimicry rearticulates presence in terms of its 'otherness', that which it disavows. There is a crucial difference between this *colonial* articulation of man and his doubles and that which Foucault describes as 'thinking the unthought'[21] which, for nineteenth-century Europe, is the ending of man's alienation by reconciling him with his essence. The colonial discourse that articulates an *interdictory* 'otherness' is precisely the 'other scense' of this nineteenth-century European desire for an authentic historical consciousness.

The 'unthought' across which colonial man is articulated is that process of classificatory confusion that I have described as the metonymy of the substitutive chain of ethical and cultural discourse. This results in the *splitting* of colonial discourse so that two attitudes towards external reality persist; one takes reality into consideration while the other disavows it and replaces it by a product of desire that repeats, rearticulates 'reality'as mimicry.

So Edward Long can say with authority, quoting variously, Hume, Eastwick, and Bishop Warburton in his support, that:

> Ludicrous as the opinion may seem I do not think that an orangutang husband would be any dishonour to a Hottentot female.[22]

Such contradictory articulations of reality and desire–seen in racist stereo-types, statements, jokes, myths–are not caught in the doubtful circle of the return of the repressed. They are the effects of a disavowal that denies the differences of the other but produces in its stead forms of authority and multiple belief that alienate the assumptions of 'civil' discourse. If, for a while, the ruse of desire is calculable for the uses of discipline soon the repetition of guilt, justification, pseudoscientific theories, superstition, spurious authorities, and classifications can be seen as the desperate effort to 'normalize' *formally* the disturbance of a discourse of splitting that violates the rational, enlightened claims of its enunciatory modality. The ambivalence of colonial authority repeatedly turns from *mimicry*–a difference that is almost nothing but not quite–to *menace*–a difference that is almost total but not quite. And in that other scene of colonial power, where history turns to farce and presence to 'a part', can be seen the twin figures of narcissism and paranoia that repeat furiously, uncontrollably.

In the ambivalent world of the 'not quite/not white', on the margins of metropolitan desire, the *founding objects* of the Western world become the erratic, eccentric, accidental *objets trouvés* of the colonial discourse–the part–objects of presence. It is then that the body and the book loose their re-presentational authority. Black skin splits under the racist gaze, displaced into signs of bestiality, genitalia, grostesquerie, which reveal the phobic myth of the undifferentiated whole white body. And the holiest of books–the Bible–bearing both the standard of the cross and the standard of empire finds itself strangely dismembered. In May 1817 a missionary wrote from Bengal:

> Still everyone would gladly receive a Bible. And why?–that he may lay it up as a curiosity for a few pice; or use it for waste paper. Such it is well known has been the common fate of these copies of the Bible . . . . Some have been bartered in the markets, others have been thrown in snuff shops and used as wrapping paper.[23]

Notes

*This paper was first presented as a contribution to a panel of 'Colonialist and Post-Colonialist Discourse', organized by Gayatri Chakravorty Spivak for the Modern

Language Association Convention in New York, December 1983. I would like to thank Professor Spivak for inviting me to participate on the panel and Dr Stephen Feuchtwang for his advice in the preparation of the paper.

1 Cited in Eric Stokes, *The Political Ideas of English Imperialism* (Oxford, Oxford University Press, 1960), pp. 17–18.
2 Edward Said, *Orientalism* (New York, Pantheon Books, 1978), p. 240.
3 Samuel Weber: 'The Sideshow, Or: Remarks on a Canny Moment', *Modern Language Notes*, vol. 88, no. 6 (1973), p. 1112.
4 Charles Grant, 'Observations on the State of Society among the Asiatic Subjects of Great Britian', *Sessional Papers 1812-13*, X (282), East India Company.
5 Ibid., chap. 4, p. 104.
6 T.B. Macaulay, 'Minute on Education', in *Sources of Indian Tradition*, vol. II, ed. William Theodore de Bary (New York, Columbia University Press, 1958), p. 49.
7 Mr Thomason's communication to the Church Missionary Society, 5 September 1819, in *The Missionary Register*, 1821, pp. 54–5.
8 Benedict Anderson, *Imagined Communities* (London, Verso, 1983), p. 88.
9 Ibid., pp. 88–9.
10 Joseph Conrad, *Nostromo* (London, Penguin, 1979), p. 161.
11 V.S. Naipaul, *The Mimic Men* (London, Penguin, 1967), p. 146.
12 Frantz Fanon, *Black Skin, White Masks* (London, Paladin, 1970), p. 109.
13 Aimé Césaire, *Discourse on Colonialism* (New York, Monthly Review Press, 1972), p. 21.
14 Michel Foucault, 'Nietzsche, Genealogy, History', in *Language, Counter-Memory, Practice*, Donald F. Bouchard and Sherry Simon tr. (Ithaca, Ny, Cornell University Press), p. 153.
15 Eric Stokes, *The English Utilitarians and India*, (Oxford, Oxford University Press, 1959), p. xi.
16 Sigmund Freud, 'The Unconscious' (1915), *SE*, XIV, pp. 190–1.
17 Fanon, *Black Skin, White Masks*, P. 103.
18 Edward Long, *A History of Jamaica* (1774), vol. II, p. 353.
19 Edward Said, 'The Text, the World, the Critic', in *Textual Strategies*, ed. J.V. Harari (Ithaca, NY, Cornell University Press, 1979), p. 184.
20 Frantz Fanon, 'Racism and Culture', in *Toward the African Revolution* (London, Pelican, 1967), p. 44.
21 Michel Foucault, *The Order of Things* (New York, Pantheon, 1970), part II, chap. 9.
22 Long, *A History of Jamaica*, p. 364.
23 *The Missionary Register*, May 1817, p. 186.

39 | Gayatri Chakravorty Spivak,

From *The Post-Colonial Critic* (1990), pp. 67–74

Q There are several questions that arise out of the way you perceive yourself ('The post-colonial diasporic Indian who seeks to decolonize the mind'), and the way you constitue us (for convenience, 'native' intellectuals):

a. Your commitment to rendering visible the historical and institutional structures from within which you speak explains your explorations of the diasporic condition of the post-colonial Indian academic in the US. What are the theories or explanations, the narratives of affiliation and disaffiliation that you bring to the politically contaminated and ambivalent function of the non-resident Indian (NRI) who comes back to India, however temporarily, upon the winds of progress?
b. Are you privileging exile as a vantage point for a clearer perspective on the scene of post-colonial cultural politics?
c. Would you say that your pedagogic practice here in the classroom, say at JNU, conveys the terms of your engagement with the Indian scene?

Gayatri Spivak (GCS)   In the first place, your description of how I constitute you does not seem quite correct. I though I constituted you, equally with the diasporic Indian, as a post-colonial intellectual!

As for how I came to be in Delhi, these were for reasons that were not sufficiently clear me to then, reasons that have more to do with an unexamined life than with exile. I'd like to say that an exile is some one who is obliged to stay away–I am not in that sense an exile.

The space I occupy might be explained by my history. It is a position into which I have been written. I am not privileging it, but I do want to use it. I can't fully construct a position that is different from the one I am in.

As for my engagement with the Indian scene, I don't think one can construct an engagement out of a visiting professorship!

And I am not sure why I am more 'politically contaminated' than you.

Rashmi Bhatnagar (RB) and Rajeshwari Sunder Rajan (RS)   The sense in which we used the notion of contamination was not to suggest a degree of purity for ourselves. Perhaps the relationship of distance and proximity between you and us is that what we write and teach has political and other actual consequences for us that are in a sense different from the consequences, or lack of consequences, for you. In this context, how is it possible to work against the grain of one's space?

GCS   No one can quite articulate the space she herself inhabits. My attempt has been to describe this relatively ungraspable space in terms of what might be its history. I'm always uneasy if I'm asked to speak for my space– it's the thing that seems to be most problematic, and something that one really only learns from other people. I was really therefore most interested in your notion of the 'freedom' involved with being an NRI. One never quite understands this 'freedom'.

It's also difficult for me to make claims for working against the grain. In my second lecture at JNU, I specified my position only because I was asked to, and since then I have found myself foregrounding it rather more than I anticipated having to.

RB   I recall that in the essay 'French Feminism in an International Frame',[1] you claimed for yourself only the negotiations operative for an 'academic feminist'–the crucial definition for you arising from the workplace.

GCS I call myself an academic feminist so as to make my claim minimal. If one has to define oneself irreducibly, it must be in minimal terms.

Mine really has been a small effort to come to an understanding of these problems, and the effort has been influenced by the site of the university.

I really am here because I wanted to learn a little more about how objects of historical investigation are made when there is not enough evidence, and what consequences that has for cultural explanations. Being an Indian by birth and citizenship, I find that this inquiry and the terms of this inquiry somehow get articulated into a place from which I can speak to others. I have never travelled anywhere without a job because it seems to be one way of finding out what the problems with one's space might be, and of involving oneself in the place one visits.

It is my conviction that you probably understand the complexities of my space as diasporic Indian intellectual better than I can. That too is part of the instruction I want to receive.

Lola Chatterjee (LC) The NRI is defined here primarily in economic terms – the Indian abroad invests money in India because it is more profitable!

GCS That kind of economic definition is closer to the point. I certainly have no money to invest here, and I don't fit in with the Indian community abroad. I like to think that the drunken father in 'My Beautiful Laundrette' offers a stereotype that is closest to the space I occupy. He uses an outdated 'socialist' language in a colonial accent while the actual NRIs are integrated into the chicaneries of local small capital.

Q In the process of investigating 'the matter of the colonies' using First World elite theory, you have said that you use the resistance of the matter to theory as a way of opening up theory.

a. Now there is a certain uneasiness here about the ideological contamination of theory by the specific historical origins which produce it and therefore about the implications of employing it in our own context. Would you defend the post-colonial intellectual dependence upon Western models as historical necessity?

b. This question is inevitable: what are the possibilities of discovering/ promoting indigenous theory?

GCS I don't use only First World theory – I have intervened, for instance, in the debate on the use of Sanskrit (in my lectures on 'Didi', as well as 'Standayini'[2]). I believe in using what one has, and this has nothing to do with privileging First World theories. What is an indigenous theory?

RB Well, that was the question. Take something like Gandhism, even though it is a highly synthesized model . . . .

GCS I cannot understand what indigenous theory there might be that can ignore the reality of nineteenth-century history. As for syntheses: syntheses have more problems than answers to offer. To construct indigenous theories one must ignore the last few centuries of historical involvement. I would rather use what history has written for me.

I am not interested in defending the post-colonial intellectual's dependence on Western models: my work lies in making clear my disciplinary predicament. My position is generally a reactive one. I am viewed by the Marxists as too codic, by feminists as too male-identified, by indigenous theorists as too committed to Western theory. I am uneasily pleased about this. One's vigilance is sharpened by the way one is perceived, but it does not involve defending oneself.

Q   Why does your theory lever the woman question via homologies and analogies? Why is it necessary to have a series of discontinuous displacements of the concept–metaphors from, say, Marx's text to, say, a text of Mahasweta Devi's? Why is there a structure of postponements in your work which you have yourself noticed in Derrida and Foucault? So we have read and assented to your cautionary narratives for a readership of First World feminists.[3] What is it you now say to us?

GCS   I'm very glad that you gave me a sense of how you perceive the woman question in the hierarchy of my theory. I think this structure of postponements that you have noticed relates to what I've been saying in the classroom. I see my charge as teaching post-structuralist theory.

My own feeling is that the constituency of feminism is one that even when I work with feminists and for them, it is inevitably from above. I perceive that constituency as my judges. However even as I acknowledge their judgement, I can't accept their judgement to the extent of changing myself in response to it. When I speak about my position, I really speak only to women like you who are, by my understanding, in as much of the predicament of the post-colonial intellectual as I am.

This is one of the reasons why I seem to be working within a structure of postponements. I think the hardest lesson for me to learn–and I have not learnt it, one attempts to learn it everyday–is that the word 'woman' is not after all something for which one can find a literal referent without looking into the looking glass. And as you have yourself realized, what I see in the looking glass is not particularly the constituency of feminism. In a situation like that I think one has to postpone indefinitely even as one constantly indicates possibilities of connections and practice. And I am afraid of speaking too quickly in academic situations about the women–the tribal subaltern, the urban sub-proletariat, the unorganized peasant–to whom I have not learnt to make myself acceptable other than as a concerned benevolent person who is free to come and go. And this is a condition which you share with me. I find that to be a much more difficult problem to work at than all of the differences between living abroad and living at home.

As far as my theoretical interventions go–I don't want to be confessional or autobiographical–but all my invited lectures here[4] were about women (perhaps not woman). I have, for instance, tried to write about the loneliness of the gendered woman in Mahasweta Devi's Stanadayini, about how unexpectedly and singularly the other woman is located in her 'Hunter', and offered an examination of our own production as emancipated female readers in my discussion of Tagore's 'Didi'.

Q   The regulative psychobiography for Indian women, according to you, is sanctioned suicide.[5] Now the notion of alternative psychobiographies – alternative to the Freudian family romance – is an attractive and powerful idea and not just for academic mileage, but in the arena of Indian women's cultural self representations.

But is there a danger in sanctioned suicide being the regulative psychobiography, that there are other realities and other myths that you will overlook? Is there a danger in sanctioned suicide becoming the master key, and of regulative psychobiography becoming prey to a kind of negativeness?

GCS   When I began to discover the argument of sanctioned suicide, what I was trying to do was to find an alternatve regulative psychobiography at work outside of both psychoanalysis and counterpsychoanalysis. Of course sanctioned suicide is not a master key, and of course it can become dangerously starting, but that was for me only a diagnostic point.

Q   Would you like to discuss the pragmatic political usefulness of your own recent work which has focussed on the subaltern gendered subject?

GCS   I cannot get a hold on what is meant by a direct pragmatic political usefulness which might be unrelated to the classroom. In Ameica some people say their pedagogy is their politics – I think it can be a kind of alibi. In the long run, and I am sorry if I seem too reactive here, I would like to learn about the political usefulness of my work, whatever it might be, from the outside, and from an outside which I inhabit myself. If you ask me directly what its pragmatic political usefulness is, I would say very little . . . as little as anyone else's.

Q   In terms of reading critical procedures you recommended, in your lecture on 'The Burden of English Studies in the Colonies', negotiating with the structures of violence. This produced at once a level of assert and a number of problems that we put to you in very naive fashion: how does one negotiate from a position which some of us English teachers often see as a position of political impotence, cultural irrelevance, ideological distortion – our only power being the power of the hegemonic, Western-educated liberalism that inhabits us? Furthermore, is there in your notion of 'negotiation' something of the rarefied and oversubtle which may emanate from the complexities of your own position as diasporic intellectual, and which we would buy at our cost since our realities surely need connotations of a stronger and more formal intervention? Would you like elaborate the theory of negotiation in the face of such unease and such interest?

GCS   Well, if it is rarefield and oversubtle, you would know how better than I.

As far as I can understand, in order to intervene one must negotiate. If there is anything I have learnt in and through the last 23 years of teaching, it is that the more vulnerable your position, the more you have to negotiate. We are not talking about discursive negotiations, or negotiation between equals, not even a collective bargaining. It seems to me that if you are in a position where you are, as you have said, being constituted by Western liberalism, you have to negotiate to see what positive role you can play from within the constraints of Western liberalism (which is a very broad term) breaking it open. I am not sure what formal intervention in your question might mean. If you mean that you have to make interventions in the structure of which you are part, it seems to me that is the most negotiated position, because you must intervene even as you inhabit those structures.

Since I really don't understand what the oversubtlety of it is I guess all I mean by negotiation here is that one tries to change something that one is obliged to inhabit, since one is not working from the outside. In order to keep one's effectiveness, one must also preserve those structures – not cut them down completely. And that, as far as I can understand, is negotiation. You inhabit the structures of violence and violation, here defined by you as Western liberalism.

Here again, I don't think the difference is between rarefaction and super subtlety on one side, and the need for stronger interventions on the other. Once again I would look at the ethico-political agenda that creates such a differentiation, such as defining of one's self.

I notice in your questions a kind of warning which, pared down to the essentials, is: don't talk at us, you are in a different position. I would think again, since this is the kind of thing I meditate on, of what the other person defines me as in order to define herself. You might want to think and mediate on your own desires in that matter.

RS Instead of the solipsism of meditation, is it possible to achieve a dialogue, an exchange? I think the attempt has been from our side to communicate to you something of our conditions of work.

GCS Since we have been talking about elite theory, let me suggest that, that is the kind of position Jürgen Habermas articulates: a neutral communication situation of free dialogue. Well, it is not a situation that ever comes into being – there is no such thing. The desire for neutrality and dialogue, even as it should not be repressed, must always mark its own failure. To see how desire articulates itself, one must read the text in which that desire is expressed. The idea of neutral dialogue is an idea which denies history, denies structure, denies the positioning of subjects. I would try to look how, in fact, the demand for a dialogue is articulated.

Q When you speak of the 'burden' of English studies, we recognise the double burden upon the third world woman teacher of English literature. Because of course this is her enclave and her privilege it is the 'suitable' profession, and the suitable undergraduate course for Indian women. So there are at many levels simulations of a gendered perspective – this even while the woman teacher of English negotiates, or hopes she negotiates, with the epistemic violence visited on her women students and on her own self in the family, in the workplace and on the street. How does all this translate into pedagogic practice? What kind of dialogue do we set up between the teaching of English and the women's movement here, so that reality is not outside the classroom?

GCS The two areas you mention, English literature and the Women's Movement–are discontinous, through not unrelated. They would bring each other to crisis.

The teaching of English literature, if one looks at its definition, has very little involvement with the Women's Movement–not just in India, but elsewhere too. Literature occupies a kind of enchanted space within intellectual history since at least the end of the eighteenth century in Europe.

In terms of teaching English (not in terms of the Women's Movement), I think that what I have been trying to do in my small way is to show how they–the makers of English literature–need us.

For example, the place of widow sacrifice in Jane Eyre as an unacknowledged metaphor leads to an extremely odd reading of the novel.[6] But I wanted to push that odd reading, since it shows how the English nineteenth century needed the axiomatics of imperialism in order to construct itself. I think that is about all we can do within the pedagogy of English literature.

I also try to look at the subject position of the colonial intellectual within texts produced in the colonies at the same time as British or French texts: so I try to teach *Kim* and *Gora* at the same time. I am not supporting either– there is no dialogue between the two, and they are both constructed out of situations of power, and constructed differently. I think these are the two things, with my limited training, that I can do in the English literature classroom: to see how the master texts need us in the construction of their texts without acknowledging that need; and to explore the difference and similarities between texts coming from the two sides which are engaged with the same problem at the same time. The connection between this and the Women's Movement is discontinuous, through not unrelated, as I said, and brings the other to crisis.

Notes

1 *Yale French Studies: Feminist Readings*, French Texts/American Contexts, No. 62, 1981.

2 'The Burden of English Studies in the Colonies: Tagore's Didi' the V. Krishna Memorial Lecture delivered at Miranda House, Delhi University, in February 1987. Paper on Mahasweta Devi's 'Stanadyini' read at a symposium, constructing women held at the Department of Sociology, Delhi University, in February 1987.

3 'Draupadi': by Mahasweta Devi in *Writing and Sexual Difference,* ed. Elizabeth Alsel (Chicago: University of Chicago Press,1982).

4 See (3) above. Also lecture on Mahasweta Devi's 'The Hunter' delivered to the Comparative Literature Association, Delhi University, in March 1987.

5 'Can the Subaltern Speak? Speculation on Widow Sacrifice', *Wedge* 7/8, Winter/ Spring, 1985.

6 'Three Women's Texts and a Critique of Imperialism', *Critical Inquiry* 12, Autumn 1985.

Part 3

Critical Debates and Issues

Section 1

Canonicity and Value

A self-conscious preoccupation with the reformulation of literary, like any cultural tradition, seems always to surface when 'tradition', no longer tacit or self-evident, has thereby been opened up to critical debate. In the past 20 years, this debate has come to focus most insistently on questions of canonicity and literary value. The idealist aesthetics which informed literary criticism until the 'theory revolution' of the 1970s broadly claimed that aesthetic values are essential and universal and thus self-evidentially reflected in a fundamentally stable canon of great works of art. Within the pluralist programme of Romantic–humanist aesthetics, there is and was some disagreement about how such values might be described, but as long as there was consensus about the definition of literature and literariness, some disagreement might be afforded about the nature of literary value. For some critics, such values were to be intuited in a subliminal way, though their transcendence or resistance to the categories of conceptual thought suggested that literary criticism might only apprehend them through the development of its own creative vocabulary. For others, aesthetic values inhere in the formal and structural complexity unique to works of high art and which guarantee its endless interpretability. Although a range of meanings might be attributed to such works in different ages, their essential trans-historical aesthetic value remains stable. Moreover, if it is a property of form, then this gives to criticism its own proper method, an intrinsic criticism which can describe the rhetorical and formal dispositions of the language of literariness.

With the advent of the 'theory revolution', these assumptions were increasingly and variously challenged. The development of feminist, Marxist, postcolonialist, new historicist, postmodernist and cultural materialist theory, together with the shift towards cultural relativism, the development of alternative artistic forms around new technologies, and the erosion of boundaries between 'high' and 'popular' art forms, have all contributed to an explosion of the identities of high art. Such changes have given rise to a variety of materialist accounts of canonicity and arguments which represent the canon as an ideological formation bound up with relations of power within those institutions which are seen to regulate cultural value and taste (Althusser's ISAs): the academy, the publishing industry, arts councils, schools and ministries for the arts.

The term 'canon' originates in debates within the Christian Church about the authenticity of the Hebrew Bible and the books of the New Testament.

This ecclesiastical use goes back to the fourth century and was concerned to establish which books of the bible and writings of the early Fathers were to be preserved as bearing the fundamental truths of Christianity. Etymologically, then, the canon, an instrument of measurement, becomes an orthodoxy for keeping out heretics, for establishing universal truth and absolute authority. If a Church were to announce that its canons were provisional, that they simply represented the interests and historical circumstances and needs of a particular group at a particular time, then that announcement would fundamentally undermine ecclesiastical authority and power. The same is not true if the Church admits there may be some differences in interpretative perspective: as long as there is agreement about the constitution of the canon, there can be some disagreement about its evaluation and interpretation.

This is Harold Bloom's starting point with reference to the broad literary church in his book *The Western Canon*. Indeed, to write a book which claims to define and defend the Western literary canon is at bottom a gesture which enacts the belief that ultimately the canon is the only entity unique to the discipline of English literature, and which, as far as Bloom is concerned, is therefore the only remaining disciplinary bastion against the inevitable and degenerative onslaught of Cultural Studies. Bloom envisages an immanent cultural dusk of nations as he sees a natural entropy where all things fall from greatness meshing with the contemporary barbarisms and political correctnesses, misplaced guilt, and furious *ressentiment* of a deluded literary academy worm-eaten by theorists unable to appreciate the essence of great literature. Bloom's argument is against all those theorists who make the claim that canonicity is a function of ideology which operates to construct a value system which legitimates as good those artefacts which mediate or represent those with cultural power.

The literary canon provokes so much debate because, since the nineteenth century, it has been viewed as the place where the English language achieves its finest expression, the nation its consummate articulation, and its people a sense of community. From Coleridge to Arnold to Leavis, the literary properties of organic form are seen to provide a model for social harmony and cultural integration. In fact, the literary canon has been continuously reformulated ever since its functional origins in the eighteenth century with the establishment of a vernacular English literature, though its conceptual and ideological underpinnings were not seriously challenged until the theory revolution of the late twentieth century. The challenge from theory came from a number of perspectives: the post-structuralist critique of the mimetic–expressivist view of literature as reflecting permanent truths about human nature; the analysis of the relations between ideology and cultural artefacts in the work of Marxists, feminists, cultural materialists and, more recently, postcolonialists; and the recognition of the function of the state and its institutions in the work of writers such as Michel Foucault and Pierre Bourdieu.

The pieces by Harold Bloom and Terry Eagleton offer opposing positions on these questions. Eagleton's 1983 book, *Literary Theory: An Introduction* forcibly argued for a view of literature as an institutionalized part of the modern state and the capitalist economy. In other words, a view of literature as both an aspect and productive of broader ideological politics. For Eagleton, the importance of theory lies in its capacity to expose and critique and challenge dominant values and to reveal the ways in which literature is a chimerical entity, neither an objective nor subjective category but a structure of values which are transitive and always in the process of production and reproduction. Eagleton even dares to envisage a future society which might be unable to derive any sense of value from the works of Shakespeare. His position is underpinned by an epistemological argument which rejects the positivist separation of fact and value. He is anxious to demonstrate the ways in which interests are constitutive of knowledge and how beliefs about what is or is not true are bound up with the reproduction of social power. Not only is the canon a construct, a provisional structure of value reflecting vested interests and struggles over cultural authority, literature itself is a transitive category with no essential core.

Bloom adamantly and flamboyantly rejects such arguments, though he writes in an heroic–apocalyptic vein which foresees a time when the political infection of criticism will have transformed it entirely into a moralizing discourse and in which the free and pure aestheticist spirits like himself will have been driven underground in a kind of inversion of Wells's fable of the Morlocks and the Eloi (*The Time Machine*). For Bloom, criticism should be unashamedly elitist and he castigates the entire moral–aesthetic tradition from Plato to postcolonialism for succumbing to a misplaced guilt complex which renders it ever in flight from the aesthetic, ever bent on reducing the aesthetic to ideological investment and criticism to democratic social improvement. For Bloom, there is no such thing as society, only individuals and their private reading and writing experiences.

Agon is central both to Bloom's theory of tradition and to his relations with his fellow critics. The survival of the self is dependent on never-ending mortal combat: all great poems are the traces of gladiatorial verbal wrestling to overcome the influence of earlier great poems. The quest of the poetic *ēphebē* must be to evade the power of the precursor and to discover self-identity through the annihilation of the impulse to repeat by strong and creative misprision. The strength of any poem is the poem it has managed to exclude; of any self, those other selves which have been evaded. Bloom's argument, a version of T.S. Eliot's famous 'Tradition and the Individual Talent' essay of 1919, is a Romantic–apocalyptic thesis about the creation of art and the construction of tradition which, for a critic like Eagleton, might alternatively be viewed as an assertion of possessive individualism and competitive entrepreneurialism to be understood as a mirror of its liberal capitalist age. For Bloom, poems are made from poems as a struggle for self-identity and poetry, as a genre subversive of all values, has nothing to teach us about politics, ethics, history or citizenship; we cannot turn to art for a programme of social salvation. But in Bloom's view, contemporary criticism, particularly in our theory-driven times, has entirely sacrificed art as the beauty and sublimity of self-expression to a 'relevance' once moral (Leavisism) and now dispiritingly and overwhelmingly political.

For Bloom, the canon consists of those great works of literature which stand in their unique beauty and perpetual strangeness evoking our awe and wonder. Just as the canon began life with ecclesiastical reference, so Bloom returns it to its origins. In his hands, the canon of Western literature becomes a Holy Book or shrine wherein his own critical practice becomes a lonely and dark vigil, a nightly battle with the tenebrous regions of the soul and a daily offensive to keep out the infidel and the heretic. Reading, for Bloom, is private meditation, a confrontation of the unique self with its own mortality and isolation; only those literary works which function, Charon-like, as 'ministers of death' are fit to enter the exclusive preserve of the Bloomian Pantheon.

40 | Terry Eagleton,

From *Literary Theory: An Introduction* (1983), pp. 10–16

We have still not discovered the secret, then, of why Lamb, Macaulay and Mill are literature but not, generally speaking, Bentham, Marx and Darwin. Perhaps the simple answer is that the first three are examples of 'fine writing', whereas the last three are not. This answer has the disadvantage of being largely untrue, at least in my judgement, but it has the advantage of suggesting that by and large people term 'literature' writing which they think is *good*. An obvious objection to this is that if it were entirely true there would be no such thing as 'bad literature'. I may consider Lamb and Macaulay overrated, but that does not necessarily mean that I stop regarding them as literature. You may consider Raymond Chandler 'good of his kind', but not exactly literature. On the other hand, if Macaulay were a *really* bad writer – if he had no grasp at all of grammar and seemed interested in nothing but white mice – then people might well not call his work literature at all, even bad literature. Value-judgements would certainly seem to have a lot to do with what is judged literature and what isn't – not necessarily in the sense that writing has to be 'fine' to be literary, but that it has to be *of the kind* that is judged fine: it may be an inferior example of a generally valued mode. Nobody would bother to say that a bus ticket was an example of inferior literature, but someone might well say that the poetry of Ernest Dowson was. The term 'fine writing', or *belles lettres*, is in this sense ambiguous: it denotes a sort of writing which is generally highly regarded, while not necessarily committing you to the opinion that a particular specimen of it is 'good'.

With this reservation, the suggestion that 'literature' is a highly valued kind of writing is an illuminating one. But it has one fairly devastating consequence. It means that we can drop once and for all the illusion that the category 'literature' is 'objective', in the sense of being eternally given and immutable. Anything can be literature, and anything which is regarded as unalterably and unquestionably literature–Shakespeare, for example–can cease to be literature. Any belief that the study of literature is the study of a stable, well-definable entity, as entomology is the study of insects, can be abandoned as a chimera. Some kinds of fiction are literature and some are not; some literature is fictional and some is not; some literature is verbally self-regarding, while some highly-wrought rhetoric is not literature. Literature, in the sense of a set of works of assured and unalterable value, distinguished by certain shared inherent properties, does not exist. When I use the words 'literary' and 'literature' from here on in this book, then, I place them under an invisible crossing-out mark, to indicate that these terms will not really do but that we have no better ones at the moment.

The reason why it follows from the definition of literature as highly valued writing that it is not a stable entity is that value-judgements are notoriously variable. 'Times change, values don't,' announces an advertisement for a daily newspaper, as though we still believed in killing off infirm infants or putting the mentally ill on public show. Just as people may treat a work as philosophy in one century and as literature in the next, or vice versa, so they may change their minds about what writing they consider valuable. They may even change their minds about the grounds they use for judging what is valuable and what is not. This, as I have suggested, does not necessarily mean that they will refuse the title of literature to a work which they have come to deem inferior: they may still call it literature, meaning roughly that it belongs to the *Type* of writing which they generally value. But it does mean that the so-called 'literary canon', the unquestioned 'great tradition' of the 'national literature', has to be recognized as a *construct*, fashioned by particular people for particular reasons at a certain time. There is no such thing as a literary work or tradition which is valuable *in itself*, regardless of what anyone might have said or come to say about it. *'Value'* is a transitive term: it means whatever is valued by certain people in specific situations, according to particular criteria and in the light of given purposes. It is thus quite possible that, given a deep enough transformation of our history, we may in the future produce a society which was unable to get anything at all out of Shakespeare. His works might simply seem desperately alien, full of styles of thought and feeling which such a society found limited or irrelevant. In such a situation, Shakespeare would be no more valuable than much present-day graffiti. And though many people would consider such a social condition tragically impoverished, it seems to me dogmatic not to entertain the possibility that it might arise rather from a general human enrichment. Karl Marx was troubled by the question of why ancient Greek art retained an 'eternal charm', even though the social conditions which produced it had long passed; but how do we know that it will remain 'eternally' charming, since history has not yet ended? Let us imagine that by dint of some deft archaeological research we discovered a great deal more about what ancient Greek tragedy actually meant to its original audiences, recognized that these concerns were utterly remote from our own, and began to read the plays again in the light of this deepened knowledge. One result might be that we stopped enjoying them. We might come to see that we had enjoyed them previously because we were unwittingly reading them in the light of our own preoccupations; once this became less possible, the drama might cease to speak at all significantly to us.

The fact that we always interpret literary works to some extent in the light of our own concerns – indeed that in one sense of 'our own concerns' we are incapable of doing anything else – might be one reason why certain works of literature seem to retain their value across the centuries. It may be, of course, that we still share many preoccupations with the work itself; but it may also be that people have not actually been valuing the 'same' work at all, even though they may think they have. 'Our' Homer is not identical with the Homer of the Middle Ages, nor 'our' Shakespeare with that of his contemporaries; it is rather that different historical periods have constructed a 'different' Homer and Shakespeare for their own purposes, and found in these texts elements to value or devalue, though not necessarily the same ones. All literary works, in other words, are 'rewritten', if only unconsciously, by the societies which read them; indeed there is no reading of a work which is not also a 're-writing'. No work, and no current evaluation of it, can simply be extended to new groups of people without being changed, perhaps almost unrecognizably, in the process; and this is one reason why what counts as literature is a notably unstable affair.

I do not mean that it is unstable because value-judgements are 'subjective'. According to this view, the world is divided between solid facts 'out there' like Grand Central station, and arbitrary value-judgements 'in here' such as liking bananas or feeling that the tone of a Yeats poem veers from defensive hectoring to grimly resilient resignation. Facts are public and unimpeachable, values are private and gratuitous. There is an obvious difference between recounting a fact, such as 'This cathedral was built in 1612', and registering a value-judgement, such as 'This cathedral is a magnificent specimen of baroque architecture.' But suppose I made the first kind of statement while showing an overseas visitor around England, and found that it puzzled her considerably. Why, she might ask, do you keep telling me the dates of the foundation of all these buildings? Why this obsession with origins? In the society I live in, she might go on, we keep no record at all of such events: we classify our buildings instead according to whether they face north-west or south-east. What this might do would be to demonstrate part of the unconscious system of value-judgements which underlies my own descriptive statements. Such value-judgements are not necessarily of the same kind as 'This cathedral is a magnificent specimen of baroque architecture,' but they are value-judgements nonetheless, and no factual pronouncement I make can escape them. Statements of fact are after all *statements*, which presumes a number of questionable judgements: that those statements are worth making, perhaps more worth making than certain others, that I am the sort of person entitled to make them and perhaps able to guarantee their truth, that you are the kind of person worth making them to, that something useful is accomplished by making them, and so on. A pub conversation may well transmit information, but what also bulks large in such dialogue is a strong element of what linguists would call the 'phatic', a concern with the act of communication itself. In chatting to you about the weather I am also signalling that I regard conversation with you as valuable, that I consider you a worthwhile person to talk to, that I am not myself anti-social or about to embark on a detailed critique of your personal appearance.

In this sense, there is no possibility of a wholly disinterested statement. Of course stating when a cathedral was built is reckoned to be more disinterested in our own culture than passing an opinion about its architecture, but one could also imagine situations in which the former statement would be more 'value-laden' than the latter. Perhaps 'baroque' and 'magnificent' have come to be more or less synonymous, whereas only a stubborn rump of us cling to the belief that the date when a building was founded is significant, and my statement is taken as a coded way of signalling this partisanship. All of our descriptive statements move within an often invisible network of value-categories, and indeed without such categories we would have nothing to say to each other at all. It is not just as though we have something called factual knowledge which may then be distorted by particular interests and judgements, although this is certainly possible; it is also that without particular interests we would have no knowledge at all, because we would not see the point of bothering to get to know anything. Interests are *constitutive* of our knowledge, not merely prejudices which imperil it. The claim that knowledge should be 'value-free' is itself a value-judgement.

It may well be that a liking for bananas is a merely private matter, though this is in fact questionable. A thorough analysis of my tastes in food would probably reveal how deeply relevant they are to certain formative experiences in early childhood, to my relations with my parents and siblings and to a good many other cultural factors which are quite as social and 'non-subjective' as railway stations. This is even more true of that fundamental structure of beliefs and interests which I am born into as a member of a particular society, such as the belief that I should try to keep in good health, that differences of sexual role are rooted in human biology or that human beings are more important than crocodiles. We may disagree on this or that, but we can only do so because we share certain 'deep' ways of seeing and valuing which are bound up with our social life, and which could not be changed without transforming that life. Nobody will penalize me heavily if I dislike a particular Donne poem, but if I argue that Donne is not literature at all then in certain circumstances I might risk losing my job. I am free to vote Labour or Conservative, but if I try to act on the belief that this choice itself merely masks a deeper prejudice – the prejudice that the meaning of democracy is confined to putting a cross on a ballot paper every few years – then in certain unusual circumstances I might end up in prison.

The largely concealed structure of values which informs and underlies our factual statements is part of what is meant by 'ideology'. By 'ideology' I mean, roughly, the ways in which what we say and believe connects with the power-structure and power-relations of the society we live in. It follows from such a rough definition of ideology that not all of our underlying judgements and categories can usefully be said to be ideological. It is deeply ingrained in us to imagine ourselves moving forwards into the future (at least one other society sees itself as moving backwards into it), but though this way of seeing *may* connect significantly with the power-structure of our society, it need not always and everywhere do so. I do not mean by 'ideology' simply the deeply entrenched, often unconscious beliefs which people hold; I mean more particularly those modes of feeling, valuing, perceiving and believing which have some kind of relation to the maintenance and reproduction of social power. The fact that such beliefs are by no means merely private quirks may be illustrated by a literary example.

In his famous study *Practical Criticism* (1929), the Cambridge critic I.A. Richards sought to demonstrate just how whimsical and subjective literary value-judgements could actually be by giving his undergraduates a set of poems, withholding from them the titles and authors' names, and asking them to evaluate them. The resulting judgements, notoriously, were highly variable: time-honoured poets were marked down and obscure authors celebrated. To my mind, however, much the most interesting aspect of this project, and one apparently quite invisible to Richards himself, is just how tight a consensus of unconscious valuations underlies these particular differences of opinion. Reading Richards' undergraduates' accounts of literary works, one is struck by the habits of perception and interpretation which they spontaneously share – what they expect literature to be, what assumptions they bring to a poem and what fulfilments they anticipate they will derive from it. None of this is really surprising: for all the participants in this experiment were, presumably, young, white, upper- or upper middle-class, privately educated English people of the 1920s, and how they responded to a poem depended on a good deal more than purely 'literary' factors. Their critical responses were deeply entwined with their broader prejudices and beliefs. This is not a matter of *blame*: there is no critical response which is not so entwined, and thus no such thing as a 'pure' literary critical judgement or interpretation. If anybody is to be blamed it is I.A. Richards himself, who as a young, white, upper-middle-class male Cambridge don was unable to objectify a context of interests which he himself largely shared, and was thus unable to recognize fully that local, 'subjective' differences of evaluation work within a particular, socially structured way of perceiving the world.

If it will not do to see literature as an 'objective', descriptive category, neither will it do to say that literature is just what people whimsically choose to call literature. For there is nothing at all whimsical about such kinds of value-judgement: they have their roots in deeper structures of belief which are as apparently unshakeable as the Empire State building. What we have uncovered so far, then, is not only that literature does not exist in the sense that insects do, and that the value-judgements by which it is constituted are historically variable, but that these value-judgements themselves have a close relation to social ideologies. They refer in the end not simply to private taste, but to the assumptions by which certain social groups exercise and maintain power over others. If this seems a far-fetched assertion, a matter of private prejudice, we may test it out by an account of the rise of 'literature' in England.

41 | Harold Bloom,
The Western Canon (1995), pp. 15–18, 23–5

Originally the canon meant the choice of books in our teaching institutions, and despite the recent politics of multiculturalism, the Canon's true question remains: What shall the individual who still desires to read attempt to read, this late in history? The Biblical three-score years and ten no longer suffice to read more than a selection of the great writers in what can be called the Western tradition, let alone in all the world's traditions. Who reads must choose, since there is literally not enough time to read everything, even if one does nothing but read. Mallarmé's grand line – 'the flesh is sad, alas, and I have read all the books' – has become a hyperbole. Overpopulation, Malthusian repletion, is the authentic context for canonical anxieties. Not a moment passes these days without fresh rushes of academic lemmings off the cliffs they proclaim the political responsibilities of the critic, but eventually all this moralizing will subside. Every teaching institution will have its department of cultural studies, an ox not to be gored, and an aesthetic underground will flourish, restoring something of the romance of reading.

Reviewing bad books, W.H. Auden once remarked, is bad for the character. Like all gifted moralists, Auden idealized despite himself, and he should have survived into the present age, wherein the new commissars tell us that reading good books is bad for the character, which I think is probably true. Reading the very best writers – let us say Homer, Dante, Shakespeare, Tolstoy – is not going to make us better citizens. Art is perfectly useless, according to the sublime Oscar Wilde, who was right about everything. He also told us that all bad poetry is sincere. Had I the power to do so, I would command that these words be engraved above every gate at every university, so that each student might ponder the splendor of the insight.

President Clinton's inaugural poem, by Maya Angelou, was praised in a *New York Times* editorial as a work of Whitmanian magnitude, and its sincerity is indeed overwhelming; it joins all the other instantly canonical achievements that flood our academies. The unhappy truth is that we cannot help ourselves; we can resist, up to a point, but past that point even our own universities would feel compelled to indict us as racists and sexists. I recall one of us, doubtless with irony, telling a *New York Times* interviewer that 'We are all feminist critics'. That is the rhetoric suitable for an occupied country, one that expects no liberation from liberation. Institutions may hope to follow the advice of the prince in Lampedusa's *The Leopard*, who counsels his peers, 'Change everything just a little so as to keep everything exactly the same.'

Unfortunately, nothing ever will be the same because the art and passion of reading well and deeply, which was the foundation of our enterprise, depended upon people who were fanatical readers when they were still small children. Even devoted and solitary readers are now necessarily beleaguered, because they cannot be certain that fresh generations will rise up to prefer Shakespeare and Dante to all other writers. The shadows lengthen in our evening land, and we approach the second millennium expecting further shadowing.

I do not deplore these matters; the aesthetic is, in my view, an individual rather than a societal concern. In any case there are no culprits, though some of us would appreciate not being told that we lack the free, generous, and open societal vision of those who come after us. Literary criticism is an ancient art; its inventor, according to Bruno Snell, was Aristophanes, and I tend to agree with Heinrich Heine that 'There is a God, and his name is Aristophanes.' Cultural criticism is another dismal social science, but literary criticism, as an art, always was and always will be an elitist phenomenon. It was a mistake to believe that literary criticism could become a basis for democratic eduction or for societal improvement. When our English and other literature departments shrink to the dimensions of our current Classics departments, ceding their grosser functions to the legions of Cultural Studies, we will perhaps be able to return to the study of the inescapable, to Shakespeare and his few peers, who after all, invented all of us.

The Canon, once we view it as the relation of an individual reader and writer to what has been preserved out of what has been written, and forget the canon as a list of books for required study, will be seen as identical with the literary Art of Memory, not with the religious sense of canon. Memory is always an art, even when it works involuntarily. Emerson opposed the party of Memory to the party of Hope, but that was in a very different America. Now the party of Memory *is* the party of Hope, though the hope is diminished. But it has always been dangerous to institutionalize hope, and we no longer live in a society in which we will be allowed to institutionalize memory. We need to teach more selectively, searching for the few who have the capacity to become highly individual readers and writers. The others, who are amenable to a politicized curriculum, can be abandoned to it. Pragmatically, aesthetic value can be recognized or experienced, but it cannot be conveyed to those who are incapable of grasping its sensations and perceptions. To quarrel on its behalf is always a blunder.

What interests me more is the flight from the aesthetic among so many in my profession, some of whom at least began with the ability to experience aesthetic value. In Freud, flight is the metaphor for repression, for unconscious yet purposeful forgetting. The purpose is clear enough in my profession's flight: to assuage displaced guilt. Forgetting, in an aesthetic context, is ruinous, for cognition, in criticism, always relies on memory. Longinus would have said that pleasure is what the resenters have forgotten. Nietzsche would have called it pain; but they would have been thinking of the same experience upon the heights. Those who descend from there, lemminglike, chant the litany that literature is best explained as a mystification promoted by bourgeois institutions.

This reduces the aesthetic to ideology, or at best to metaphysics. A poem cannot be read *as a poem*, because it is primarily a social document or, rarely yet possibly, an attempt to overcome philosophy. Against this approach I urge a stubborn resistance whose single aim is to preserve poetry as fully and purely as possible. Our legions who have deserted represent a strand in our traditions that has always been in flight from the aesthetic: Platonic moralism and Aristotelian social science. The attack on poetry either exiles it for being destructive of social well-being or allows it sufferance if it will assume the work of social catharsis under the banners of the new multiculturalism. Beneath the surfaces of academic Marxism, Feminism, and New Historicism, the ancient polemic of Platonism and the equally archaic Aristotelian social medicine continue to course on. I suppose that the conflict between these strains and the always beleaguered supporters of the aesthetic can never end. We are losing now, and doubtless we will go on losing, and there is a sorrow in that, because many of the best students will abandon us for other disciplines and professions, an abandonment already well under way. They are justified in doing so, because we could not protect them against our profession's loss of intellectual and aesthetic standards of accomplishment and value. All that we can do now is maintain some continuity with the aesthetic and not yield to the lie that what we oppose is adventure and new interpretations.

* * * * *

The flight from or repression of the aesthetic is endemic in our institutions of what still purport to be higher education. Shakespeare, whose aesthetic supremacy has been confirmed by the universal judgement of four centuries, is now 'historicized' into pragmatic diminishment, precisely because his uncanny aesthetic power is a scandal to any ideologue. The cardinal principle of the current School of Resentment can be stated with singular bluntness: what is called aesthetic value emanates from class struggle. This principle is so broad that it cannot be wholly refuted. I myself insist that the individual self is the only method and the whole standard for apprehending aesthetic value. But 'the individual self', I unhappily grant, is defined only against society, and part of its agon with the communal inevitably partakes of the conflict between social and economic classes. Myself the son of a garment worker, I have been granted endless time to read and meditate upon my reading. The institution that sustained me, Yale University, is ineluctably part of an American Establishment, and my sustained meditation upon literature is therefore vulnerable to the most traditional Marxist analyses of class interest. All my passionate proclamations of the isolate selfhood's aesthetic value are necessarily qualified by the reminder that the leisure for meditation must be purchased from the community.

No critic, not even this one, is a hermetic Prospero working white magic upon an enchanted island. Criticism, like poetry, is (in the hermetic sense) a kind of theft from the common stock. And if the governing class, in the days of my youth, freed one to be a priest of the aesthetic, it doubtless had its own interest in such a priesthood. Yet to grant this is to grant very little. The freedom to apprehend aesthetic value may rise from class conflict, but the value is not identical with the freedom, even if it cannot be achieved without that apprehension. Aesthetic value is by definition engendered by an interaction between artists, an influencing that is always an interpretation. The freedom to be an artist, or a critic, necessarily rises out of social conflict. But the source or origin of the freedom to perceive, while hardly irrelevant to aesthetic value, is not identical with it. There is always guilt in achieved individuality; it is a version of the guilt of being a survivor and is not productive of aesthetic value.

Without some answer to the triple question of the agon–more than, less than, equal to? – there can be no aesthetic value. That question is framed in the figurative language of the Economic, but its answer will be free of Freud's Economic Principle. There can be no poem in itself, and yet something irreducible does abide in the aesthetic. Value that cannot be altogether reduced constitutes itself through the process of interartistic influence. Such influence contains psychological, spiritual, and social components, but its major element is aesthetic. A Marxist or Foucault-inspired historicist can insist endlessly that the *production* of the aesthetic is a question of historical forces, but production is not in itself the issue here. I cheerfully agree with the motto of Dr. Johnson–'No man but a blockhead ever wrote, except for money'–yet the undeniable economics of literature, from Pindar to the present, do not determine questions of aesthetic supremacy. And the openers-up of the Canon and the traditionalists do not disagree much on where the supremacy is to be found: in Shakespeare. Shakespeare *is* the secular canon, or even the secular scripture; forerunners and legatees alike are defined by him alone for canonical purposes. This is the dilemma that confronts partisans of resentment: either they must deny Shakespeare's unique eminence (a painful and difficult matter) or they must show why and how history and class struggle produced just those aspects of his plays that have generated his centrality in the Western Canon.

Here they confront insurmountable difficulty in Shakespeare's most idiosyncratic strength: he is always ahead of you, conceptually and imagistically, whoever and whenever you are. He renders you anachronistic because he *contains* you; you cannot subsume him. You cannot illuminate him with a new doctrine, be it Marxism or Freudianism or Demanian Linguistic skepticism. Instead, he will illuminate the doctrine, not by prefiguration but by postfiguration as it were: all of Freud that matters most is there in Shakespeare already, with a persuasive critique of Freud besides. The Freudian map of the mind is Shakespeare's; Freud seems only to have prosified it. Or, to vary my point, a Shakespearean reading of Freud illuminates and overwhelms the text of Freud; a Freudian reading of Shakespeare reduces Shakespeare, or would if we could bear a reduction that crosses the line into absurdities of loss. *Coriolanus* is a far more powerful reading of Marx's *Eighteenth Brumaire of Louis Napoleon* than any Marxist reading of *Coriolanus* could hope to be.

Shakespeare's eminence is, I am certain, the rock upon which the School of Resentment must at last founder. How can they have it both ways? If it is arbitrary that Shakespeare centers the Canon, then they need to show why the dominant social class selected him rather than, say, Ben Jonson, for that arbitrary role. Or if history and not the ruling circles exalted Shakespeare, what was it in Shakespeare that so captivated the mighty Demiurge, economic and social history? Clearly this line of inquiry begins to border on the fantastic; how much simpler to admit that there is a *qualitative* difference, a difference in kind, between Shakespeare and every other writer, even Chaucer, even Tolstoy, or whoever. Originality is the great scandal that resentment cannot accommodate, and Shakespeare remains the most original writer we will ever know.

Section 2

Criticism and Ethics

A central notion which has recurred throughout this anthology and which is specifically addressed in the debates about the canon, is the idea that if there can be no consensus about the category of literature, then there is unlikely to be agreement about the nature of aesthetic or other kinds of value. Whereas the debates about the canon raise the issue of the nature of aesthetic value, the current epistemological crisis referred to as 'postmodernism' has also raised questions about the relationship between knowledge and ethical values, a relationship first systematically analysed in Plato's dialogues and particularly in his *Republic*.

Kuhn's idea of knowledge communities, variously developed by postmodernists, pragmatists and post-Marxists, insisted that truth and value are finally only ever internal to particular communities or within particular institutional frameworks. According to this perspective, literary works are neither 'true for all time', reflecting universal insights into the human condition, nor can they tell us how we should live, for beliefs and values can only be mediated through particular institutional frameworks with their own knowledge and value agendas. From the postmodernist perspective, knowledge and value exist as incommensurable 'language games' where the values of one language game are entirely enclosed within its peculiar frame and cannot be addressed or challenged from the perspective of any other. One of the consequences of this assault on the Enlightenment grand narratives of universal justice, on its teleological accounts of history, and its view of the relations between knowledge and the good, is that it seems to plunge us into a situation of endless difference and of epistemological and cultural relativism which approaches a condition of nihilism. Ever since Nietzsche announced, in *The Genealogy of Morals*, that there can only be a perspectival knowing, the idea that rationality can provide the basis for ethics, that through reason we can arrive at an understanding of nature or ourselves that will provide a reliable guide as to how we should live, has been under attack from a variety of philosophical positions.

Shortly before Kuhn published his seminal *The Structure of Scientific Revolutions* (1962), Hans Georg Gadamer had also published a groundbreaking book, *Truth and Method* (1960), in which he challenged the idea that from the certain knowledge derived through scientific method, we can deduce a rational structure of ethics and values. Instead, Gadamer argued that there can be no Archimedean point outside of culture from which to achieve 'objective knowledge' for understanding exists only in relation to the perspectives (or 'prejudices') provided for us through our cultural traditions: perspectives which can never be brought to full consciousness. Knowledge is already bound up with ethical values and can never be entirely separated from them. In Gadamer's version of Heideggerian being-in-the-world, we can never achieve full rational knowledge, the kind of knowledge which becomes an absolute foundation and model for argumentative and other kinds of rational procedures (such as ethical debate). However, through exposure to forms of relative otherness we may become aware of our prejudices, able then partially to define and to see our values and even to repossess our sense of self expanded through other ways of seeing. Prejudice thus becomes a precondition of Enlightenment and of any way of knowing. We are shaped through tradition and our situatedness in a *sensus communis* which gives us the substance of our inextricably confounded epistemologies and ethics. In this model, scientific knowledge is displaced as the dominant epistemological paradigm by aesthetic knowing. Readers acquire knowledge of literary texts through immersion in an experience made meaningful by the values they bring to the process and in terms of the expansion of those values as they are modified in the encounter with the partial otherness of the text. For Gadamer, however, texts are never radically other, because they are part of a tradition that has already shaped what we are and in the reading experience we come to understand some of the sources of those values and some of their limitations.

Gadamer's work became important to later literary theorists seeking to negotiate a path between the absolutes of Enlightenment rationalist ethics and postmodernist relativism and nihilism. For the moral philosopher Alisdair MacIntyre, for example, Enlightenment models of knowledge and ethics with their formal proceduralism (Kantian and utilitarian arguments for the mathematical formulation of justice and rights) might offer us a 'blind' model of justice as equality, but they had singularly failed in offering us any substantive vision of the good, an account of how to live or how to shape our values or sense of what is a good life. For MacIntyre, it is precisely this vacuum at the heart of liberal modernity which has produced the kind of emotivism, subjectivism and even nihilism foreshadowed in Nietzsche's work and coming to full fruition in the postmodernism of writers such as Lyotard and Rorty.

Questions of the good, as opposed to the formulation of abstract rights were, of course, central to an Ancient understanding of the Good Life, to a 'virtue' ethics displaced by what MacIntyre sees as the scientistic formalisms of the modern and specifically Enlightenment and post-Enlightenment era. MacIntyre's work has been hugely influential for critics such as Nussbaum, represented here, in calling for a return to a specifically Aristotelian model of virtue and practical wisdom, but tempered by a modern aesthetic sense of how we might reformulate and rewrite the scripts of tradition. One of the problems, of course, with this call for a return to a virtue ethics (the basis of one powerful model of contemporary communitarian thought) is that Aristotle's ethics arose out of the enclosed community of the Greek *polis*, a slave society and extremely restricted democracy by modern standards. It is hard to see how this reconstruction of ethics could have direct application to a multicultural and heterogeneous modern society in which most of us move daily between and amongst different groups and communities, different 'subject' positions, each with its own preoccupations and imperatives.

In some ways, the aesthetic has always been adduced as a complement and corrective to scientific modernity. If science provided a world-picture governed by the certainty of mechanical law but with no place within its material parameters for human consciousness, purpose and value, no foundation therefore for a vision of the good which might be translated into substantial cultural values, modern literature has always been looked to as a source of such vision and value. Kantian idealism seemed to extend rational method to the discovery of the 'moral law within' as Right, but understood as an empty proceduralism governed by the categorical imperative and incapable of legislating for specific values or of offering a vision of how best to live. In the eighteenth and nineteenth centuries, literature came more and more to be read as offering this function and the literary critic to be regarded as a moral interpreter and arbiter. In the Leavisite moral–aesthetic, for example, art exists to provide an embodied vision of the good and the experience of great art is one of moral as well as rhetorical discrimination. Procedural liberalism, which has made the formal idea of Right the basis of its understanding of justice, has inevitably turned to art to supply a vision of the good which has been eradicated from its own formal systems of 'rational' ethics. Art can give visions of the good and the beautiful, but art is outside of rationality and therefore useful in the education of feeling but increasingly regarded as irrelevant to the important and practical business of life, and to be kept safely therefore in its own enclaves within the university and the English Department.

Martha Nussbaum's work needs to be understood in the context of such debates for, in calling for the importance of literature as an ethical experience and a lesson in ethical evaluation, she returns not only to the Leavisian notion of the moral function of art within the broader community, but more specifically to the ancient idea that art can teach us how to live and is not a remote or sublime or academic exercise but an experience fully integrated into the complete life. Along with other broadly communitarian critics such as Charles Taylor and Alisdair MacIntyre, she has been consistently critical of post-structuralism, regarding its decentring of the subject and of consciousness as a dehumanizing move which plays into the hands of current scientifically imperialist attempts to wrest the realm of value from the humanities by claiming to account for consciousness and ethics in terms of evolutionary biology or computer models of the mind. Nussbaum wishes to defend the humanities by extending humanistic understanding. She sees literature as completing moral philosophy in its formal capacity to present embodied and concrete experience, individual perception and universal rule.

There are a number of difficulties with Nussbaum's position: first, the question of to what extent literature actually constitutes in itself a form of practical wisdom or whether it is simply her own reading which imposes an ethical order upon the text; second, the question of how far this is simply a return to a mimetic–expressivist aesthetics not so far removed from that of the Leavisite tradition; and third, there is surely the problem, already raised with reference to MacIntyre's work, about the validity of returning to an Aristotelian model of virtue.

If Nussbaum places literature at the centre of her plea for a return to practical wisdom as an alternative to the postmodern critique of Enlightenment, Emmanuel Levinas is suspicious of the idea that there can be anything ethical at all in the experience of literature. For Levinas, as representation and not presence, literature can no more partake of the ethical as an experience than it can provide an educational model or simulacrum of it. For Nussbaum, literature is an experience we step into and which has existential effects beyond its ontological frame. In her understanding of this process, Nussbaum revises but does not abandon rationality: literature is an embodied experience but one which necessarily carries with it a metacritical function. Literature is both experience and reflection upon experience; it is simultaneously experience and knowledge of that experience. Levinas, however, argues that only the unmediated presence, an absolute quiddity, the raw encounter with the full presence of the other, can constitute ethical experience.

Levinas, born in Lithuania in 1906, was an early exponent of German phenomenology and an influence on important existentialist philosophers such as Jean-Paul Sartre. His starting point, like Nussbaum's, is with the question of the relation between knowledge and the good, the question, for him, of whether it is possible to have an ethics without a rational or any other kind of foundation. Like Nussbaum, he too is opposed to the anti-humanism of post-structuralist thought, though not to its assault on traditional ideas of the Subject. Whereas Nussbaum is interested in returning the concept of rationality to the idea of practical wisdom rooted in a more communitarian understanding of the Subject, Levinas is a metaphysical and ultimately religious thinker. For him, all Western systems of thought have operated to incorporate otherness into sameness in a denial of the full ethical relation. Levinas refers to this kind of rationality as a form of totality and he calls for a philosophical phenomenology of the other, an impulse towards the infinite and not the total, in a face-to-face encounter where the other is not incorporated into the same, does not become an alter ego but is left with its otherness intact. This idea has been an important influence on a variety of theoretical positions (particularly feminism, postcolonialism and new historicism) and has prompted a similar variety of critiques (though mostly focused on the problem of how one would even begin to recognize an other who is so radically other or even to begin to empathize and feel the kind of compassion central to most other non-rational ethical accounts).

Levinas's fundamental question is: how can I co-exist with the other and leave his otherness intact? His answer is that only a concept of infinity and not totality can allow for this kind of relationship. The face-to-face encounter with the other lies outside of conceptual definition or construction: an epiphany, an experience where the other is solicited but remains finally irreducible. Levinas's ethics, in some sense existentialist, lie outside of traditional accounts derived from Socratic, Aristotelian and Kantian arguments. Despite his resistance to the notion of literature as an ethical encounter, his thinking has been enormously influential on those critics seeking to articulate an ethics without rational foundation which can avoid the nihilisms of some postmodernist thinking. Like Nussbaum, he shares the search for an alternative source of ethical wisdom to the Kantian and rationalist tradition, but whereas she reaches towards a mode of practical wisdom, or *phronesis*, which grounds reason in community and reads literature as an expression of a *sensus communis*, Levinas posits a non-rational ethical encounter which reaches beyond the human altogether in order finally to return to something more fully human.

42 | Martha Nussbaum,

From *Love's Knowledge: Essays on Philosophy and Literature* (1990), pp. 23–9

The Starting Point: 'How Should One Live?'

It is no chance matter we are discussing, but how one should live.

Plato, *Republic*

Here, as in all other, cases, we must set down the appearances and, first working through the puzzles, in this way go on to show, if possible, the truth of all the deeply held beliefs about these experiences; and, if this is not possible, the truth of the greatest number and the most authoritative.

Aristotle, *Nicomachean Ethics*

The 'ancient quarrel' had an exemplary clarity, since the participants shared a view of what the quarrel was about. However much Plato and the poets disagreed, they agreed that the aim of their work was to provide illumination concerning how one should live. Of course they were at odds concerning what the ethical truth was, and also concerning the nature of understanding. But still, there was some roughly single goal, however much in need of further specification, that they did share, some question to which they could be seen as offering competing answers.

One obstacle to any contemporary version of the ancient project is the difficulty of arriving at any account of what we are looking for that will be shared by the various parties. My aim is to establish that certain literary texts (or texts similar to these in certain relevant ways) are indispensable to a philosophical inquiry in the ethical sphere: not by any means sufficient, but sources of insight without which the inquiry cannot be complete. But then it is important to have some conception, however general and flexible, of the inquiry inside which I wish to place the novels, the project in which I see them as helping to state a distinctive alternative to Kantian and Utilitarian conceptions. A difficulty here is that some influential accounts of what moral philosophy includes are cast in the terms of one or another of the competing ethical conceptions; thus they will prove unsuitable, if we want to organize a fair comparison among them. For example, if we begin with the Utilitarian's organizing question, 'How can one maximize utility?', we accept, already, a certain characterization of what is salient in the subject matter of ethics, of the right or relevant descriptions for practical situations – one that would rule out from the start, as irrelevant, much of what the novels present as highly relevant. Similarly, reliance on a Kantian characterization of the domain of the moral, and of its relation to what happens in the empirical realm, together with reliance on the Kantian's organizing question 'What is my moral duty?', would have the effect of artificially cutting off from the inquiry some element of life that the novels show as important and link to others – all in advance of a sensitive study of the sense of life that the novels themselves have to offer. So we would, it seems, be ill advised to adopt either of these methods and questions as architectonic guides to the pursuit of a comparison among different conceptions, different senses of life – among these the views of life expressed in the novels. It seems that we should see whether we can find an account of the methods, subject matter, and questions of moral philosophy (ethical inquiry) that is more inclusive.

And here, it must be stressed, what we really want is an account of ethical inquiry that will capture what we actually do when we ask ourselves the most pressing ethical questions. For the activity of comparison I describe is a real practical activity, one that we undertake in countless ways when we ask ourselves how to live, what to be; one that we perform together with others, in search of ways of living together in a community, country, or planet. To bring novels into moral philosophy is not – as I understand this proposal – to bring them to some academic discipline which happens to ask ethical questions. It is to bring them into connection with our deepest practical searching, for ourselves and others, the searching in connection with which the influential philosophical conceptions of the ethical were originally developed, the searching we pursue as we compare these conceptions, both with one another and with our active sense of life. Or rather, it is to recognize that the novels are in this search already: to insist on and describe, the connections the novels have already for readers who love them and who read, like David Copperfield, for life.

No starting point is altogether neutral here. No way of pursuing the search, putting the question, fails to contain some hint as to where the answers might lie.[1] Questions set things up one way or another, tell us what to include, what to look for. Any procedure implies some conception or conceptions of how we come to know, which parts of ourselves we can trust. This does not mean that all choices of procedure and starting-point are merely subjective and irrational.[2] It does mean that in order to attain to the rationality that *is* available (as the chimera of total detachment is not) we need to be alert to those aspects of a procedure that might bias it unduly in one direction or another, and to commit ourselves to the serious investigation of alternative positions.

Here both life and the history of philosophy combine to help us. For we do, in life, bring our experience, our active sense of life, to the different conceptions we encounter, working through them, comparing the alternatives they present, with, reference to our developing sense of what is important and what we can live with, seeking a fit between experience and conception. And in the history of moral philosophy we also find an account of an inclusive starting point, and an open and dialectial method, that is, in effect, the philosophial description of this real-life activity and how it goes, when done with thoroughness and sensitivity. For the proponents of rival philosophical conceptions in ethics have usually not concluded that their inquiries and results were non-comparable with those of their opponents, or comparable only by a method of comparison that already throws judgement to one or another side. They have, instead, frequently appealed to the inclusive dialectical method first described by Aristotle, as one that (continuous with the active searching of life) can provide an overarching or framing procedure in which alternative views might be duly compared, with respect for each, as well as for the evolving sense of life to which each is a response. Philosophers as different as Utilitarian Henry Sidgwick and Kantian John Rawls have appealed to Aristotle's conception of philosophical procedure as one that can, in its inclusiveness, be fair to the competing positions. [3] I concur in this judgement and follow this example–insisting, as well, that one of the salient virtues of this method is its continuity with 'our actual adventure' as we search for understanding. (It is important to distinguish the Aristotelian procedure and starting point from Aristotle's own ethical conception, which is just one of the conceptions it considers.)

The Aristotelian procedure in ethics begins with a very broad and inclusive question: 'How should a human being live?'[4] This question presupposes no specific demarcation of the terrain of human life, and so, *a fortiori*, not its demarcation into separate moral and nonmoral realms. It does not, that is, assume that there is, among the many ends and activities that human beings cherish and pursue, some one domain, the domain of moral value, that is of special importance and dignity, apart from the rest of life. Nor does it assume, as do utility theorists, that there is a more or less unitary something that a good agent can be seen as maximizing in every act of choice. It does not assume the denial of these claims either; it holds them open for inquiry within the procedure–with the result that, so far, we are surveying everything that Aristotle surveys, that we do actually survey: humor alongside justice, grace in addition to courage.

The inquiry (as I describe it more fully in 'Perceptive Equilibrium') is both empirical, and practical: empirical, in that is concerned with, takes its 'evidence' from, the experience of life; practical, in that its aim is to find a conception by which human beings can live, and live together.

The inquiry proceeds by working through the major alternative positions including Aristotle's own, but others as well), holding 'them up against one another and also against the participants' beliefs and feelings, their active sense of life. Nothing is held unrevisable in this process, except the very basic logical idea that statement implies negation, that to assert something is to rule out something else. The participants look not for a view that is true by correspondence to some extra-human reality, but for the best overall fit betwen a view and what is deepest in human lives. They are asked to imagine, at each stage, what they can least live well without, what lies deepest in their lives; and, again, what seems more superficial, more dispensable. They seek for coherence and fit in the web of judgement, feeling, perception, and principle, taken as a whole.

In this enterprise, literary works play a role on two levels.[5] First, they can intervene to make certain that we get a sufficiently rich and inclusive conception of the opening question and of the dialectical procedure that pursues it–inclusive enough to hold all that our sense of life urges us to consider. 'Perceptive Equilibrium' discusses this question, showing how John Rawls's conception of the Aristotelian procedure might be enlarged by consideration of our literary experience.[6] And the style of this Introduction illustrates the inclusiveness of the Aristotelian approach.

But according to the terms of the ancient quarrel the very choice to write a tragic drama–or, we can now say, a novel–expresses already certain evaluative commitments. Among these seem to be commitments to the ethical significance of uncontrolled events, to the epistemological value of emotion, to the variety and non-commensurability of the important things. Literary works (and from now on [. . .] we shall focus on certain novels) are not neutral instruments for the investigation of all conceptions. Built into the very structure of a novel is a certain conception of what matters. In the novelists we study here, when we do find a Kantian character, or some other exponent of an ethical position divergent from the one that animates the narrative taken as a whole (James's Mrs. Newsome, Dickens's Agnes and Mr. Gradgrind[7]), those characters are not likely to fare well with the reader. And we are made aware that if the events in which we, as readers, participate had been described to us by those characters, they would not have had the literary form they now do, and would not have constituted a novel at all. A different sense of salience would have dictated a different form. In short, by consenting to see the events in the novel's world as the novel presents them, we are, as readers, already breaking ethically with Gradgrind, Mrs. Newsome, and Agnes.

My second interest in the novels, then, is an interest in this link between a distinctive conception of life (or a family of conceptions) and the structures of these novels. I shall argue, in fact, that there is a distinctive ethical conception (which I shall call the Aristotelian conception) that requires, for its adequate and complete investigation and statement, forms and structures such as those that we find in these novels. Thus if the enterprise of moral philosophy is understood as we have understood it as a thetic investigation of all major ethical alternatives and the comparison of each with our active sense of life, then moral philosophy requires such literary texts, and the experience of loving and attentive novel-reading, for its own completion. This involves, clearly, an expansion and reconstruction of what moral philosophy has a long time been taken to be and to include.

Nothing could be further from my intentions than to suggest that we *substitute* the study of novels for the study of the recognized great works of the various philosophical traditions in ethics. Although this may disappoint some who find moderate positions boring, I have no interest in dismissive assaults on systematic ethical theory, or on 'Western rationality', or even on Kantianism or Utilitarianism, to which the novels, to be sure, display their own oppositions. I make a proposal that should be acceptable even to Kantians or Utilitarians, if, like Rawls and Sidgwick, they accept the Aristotelian question and the Aristotelian dialectical procedure as good overall guides in ethics, and are thereby methodologically committed to the sympathetic study of alternative conceptions. The proposal is that we should *add* the study of certain novels to the study of these works, on the grounds that without them we will not have a fully adequate statement of a powerful ethical conception, one that we ought to investigate. It will be clear that I sympathize with this ethical conception and that I present, in alliance with the novels, the beginning of a defense of it. But that's just it, it is the beginning, not the completion. And in the full working out of the inquiry the investigation of alternative views, in their own styles and structures, would play a central role. In fact, work on this larger inquiry will, as 'Perceptive Equilibrium' argues, play a role even in the understanding of the novels, since one sees something more deeply and clearly when one understands more clearly that to which it is opposed.

There will be those who will object that no question and no procedure can possibly be fair both to the sense of life we find in a novel of James and to the very different view of, say, Kant's second Critique. And of course we have admitted that the procedure is not empty of content. In fact, the procedures of Aristotelian dialectic and the insights of the Aristotelian ethical view, though importantly distinct, are in many ways continuous with one another, in that the sense of life that leads us to build into the overall procedure an attention to particulars, a respect for the emotions, and a tentative and non-dogmatic attitude to the bewildering multiplicities of life will incline us also to have some sympathy with the Aristotelian conception, which emphasizes these features. But, first of all, the procedure as a whole simply *includes* these features: it does not, yet, tell us how to value them. And it instructs us to consider sympathetically all the significant positions, not only this one. In its inclusiveness and its flexibility, and above all its open-endedness, it can plausibly claim to be a balanced philosophical inquiry into all alternatives, not simply a partisan defense of this one. Furthermore, the procedure did not include these features for arbitrary theoretical reasons: it got them from life, and it included them because our sense of life seemed to include them. So if a procedure that includes what life includes is distant from certain theoretical alternatives, this is, or may be, a sign of narrowness in those theoretical alternatives.

But surely, some will say, any conception of procedure that has any content at all will incorporate a conception of rationality that belongs to one tradition of thought rather than another, and which cannot therefore contain or sympathetically explore the thoughts of any other traditon. Traditions each embody norms of procedural rationality that are part and parcel of the substantive conclusions they support.[8] This is no small worry; but I think that a great deal, here, depends on what one makes of it, how determined one is or is not to make progress on the opening question. The Aristotelian procedure tells us to be respectful of difference; but it also instructs us to look for a consistent and sharable answer to the 'how to live' question, one that will capture what is deepest and most basic, even though it will, of necessity, to achieve that aim, have to give up certain other things. To this extent its flexibility is qualified by a deep commitment to getting somewhere. It is built into the procedure itself that we will not simply stop with an enumeration of difference and with the verdict that we cannot fairly compare, cannot rationally decide. It instructs us to do what we can to compare and choose as best we can, in the knowledge that no comparison is, perhaps, altogether above somebody's reproach, since we must translate each of the alternatives, in effect, into our own evolving terms and hold them up against the resoruces of our own imaginations, our own admittedly incomplete sense of life. (We must note here that it is exactly that determination to compare and to arrive at something sharably that motivates both Rawls's and Sidgwick's choice of the Aristotelian procedure.) So why pursue this flawed method, instead of simply concluding that every ethical tradition is altogether noncomparable with every other, and that there is no single starting point, no single procedure?

The Aristotelian's answer to this is that this is what we actually do—and what we must most urgently do more, and do better. We do ask how to live. We do compare and assess one tradition, one way, one answer against another—though each one contains norms of procedural rationality— undeterred, in our neediness, by the messiness of that enterprise. What I propose here is not a merely theoretical undertaking, but one that is urgently practical, one that we conduct every day, and must conduct.[9] If we wish to regard the obstacles against fair comparison of alternatives as insuperable for reasons of methodological purity, we can always do so; but at enormous practical cost. And our common experiences, our active practical questions, give a unity and focus to the search that it might not seem to have when we regard it solely on the plane of theory. As Aristotle said, 'All people seek, not the way of their ancestors, but the good.'[10] The Aristotelian procedure gives explicit form to that search and urges its continuation. We want to know how the different ethical conceptions – including those distant from us in time and place – do or do not fit with our experience and our wishes. And in a world in which practical discourse is and must be increasingly international, we need to do this all the more urgently, as flexibly and attentively as we can, no matter how hard it is to do this well. As Charlotte Stant says to the Prince (before embarking on a project that is messy, urgent, and full of love), 'What else can we do, what in all the world else?'[11]

But why, a different objector might ask, do I wish to dragoon literature into this practical/philosophical enterprise? And must this enterprise not make too many concessions to the philosophical demand for explanation to be altogether fair to literature? Isn't literature being turned, here, into a chapter in a textbook on ethics, and thus flattened and reduced? To this, the reply must first of all be that literature is there in the practical search already; and that it is not ordinary readers, but theorists, who have sometimes felt that the pressure of a practical question would, rather like a sweaty hand on an exquisite leather binding, sully the text's purity of finish.[12] Our actual relation to the books we love is already messy, complex, erotic. We do 'read for life', bringing to the literary texts we love (as to texts admittedly philosophical) our pressing questions and perplexities, searching for images of what we might do and be, and holding these up against the images we derive from our knowledge of other conceptions, literary, philosophical, and religious. And the further pursuit of this enterprise through explicit comparison and explanation is not a diminution of the novels at all, but rather an expression of the depth and breadth of the claims that those who love them make for them. Depth, because the Aristotelian practical procedure shows with what they are to be compared, to what they are taken to be the rivals: namely, to the best and deepest of the other philosophical conceptions. Breadth, because the result of the dialectical enterprise should be to convince not only people of an already Jamesian sensibility, but all people interested in serious ethical reflection and in fair scrutiny of alternatives, that works like these contain something that cannot be fully stayed otherwise and should not be omitted.

Nor, we must insist again, does this dialectical approach to works of literature convert them from what they are into systematic treatises, ignoring in the process their formal features and their mysterious, various, and complex content. It is, in fact, just this that we wish to preserve and to bring into philosophy – which means, for us, just the pursuit of truth, and which therefore must become various and mysterious and unsystematic if, and insofar as, the truth is so. The very qualities that make the novel so unlike dogmatic abstract treatises are, for us, the source of their *philosophical* interest.

Notes

1 See the further discussion of this in 'Perceptive Equilibrium': also 'Therapeutic Arguments'. And see Cora Diamond, 'Having a Rough Story: About What Moral Philosophy Is'. *New Literary History* 15 (1983). 155–70.

2 See 'Therapeutic Arguments'.

3 John Rawls, *A Theory of Justice*, 46–53; Henry Sidgwick, *The Methods of Ethics*, 7th ed. (London, 1907), especially the preface to the sixth edition (republished in the seventh).

4 Bernard Williams presents an effective defense of this starting point in *Ethics and the Limits* of Philosophy (Cambridge, MA, 1983): see also *Fragility*, chap. 1, and 'Perceptive Equilibrium'.

5 A third function for literature in this inquiry is described in the Notes to 'Plato on Commensurability,'.

6 See also H. Richardson, 'The Emotions of Reflective Equilibrium', forthcoming.

7 On Mrs. Newsome, see 'Perceptive Equilibrium'; on Agnes, 'Steerforth's Arm', on Mr. Gradgrind 'Discernment'.

8 For this challenge, see Alasdair MacIntyre, *Whose Justice? Which Rationality?* (Notre Dame, 1988); I discuss MacIntyre's argument in a review article in *The New York Review of Books*, (December 7, 1989).

9 See also Nussbaum, 'Non-Relative Virtues: an Aristotelian Approach', *Midwest Studies in Philosophy* 13 (1988), 32–53; 'Aristotle on Human Nature and the Foundations of Ethics', in a volume on the philosophical work of Bernard Williams, ed. J. Altham and R. Harrison, (Cambridge University Press, 1991). For one sketch of the political outcome of such an inquiry, see Nussbaum, 'Aristotelian Social Democracy', in *Liberalism and the Good*, ed. H. Richardson and G. Mara (New York, 1990).

10 Aristotle, *Politics*, 1268a 39ff, discussed in 'Non-Relative Virtues' (above, n. 9).

11 James, *The Golden Bowl*. III, 5.

12 It is striking that in the last few years literary theorists allied with deconstruction have taken a marked turn toward the ethical. Jacques Derrida, for example, chose to address the American Philosophical Association on the topic of Aristotle's theory of friendship (*Journal of Philosophy* 85 (1988), 632–44); Barbara Johnson's *A World of Difference* (Baltimore, 1987) argues that Deconstruction can make valuable ethical and social contributions; and in general there seems to be a return to the ethical and practical – if not, perhaps, to the rigorous engagement with ethical thought characteristic of the best work in moral philosophy, whether 'philosophical' or 'literary'. No doubt a part of this change can be traced to the scandal over the political career of Paul de Man, which has made theorists anxious to demonstrate that Deconstruction does not imply a neglect of ethical and social considerations.

43 | Emmanuel Levinas,

From *Totality and Infinity*. A. Lingis tr. (1969), pp. 194–202

Ethics and the Face

1. Infinity and the Face

Inasmuch as the access to beings concerns vision, it dominates those beings, exercises a power over them. A thing is *given*, offers itseslf to me. In gaining access to it I maintain myself within the same.

The face is present in its refusal to be contained. In this sense it cannot be comprehended, that is, encompassed. It is neither seen nor touched – for in visual or tactile sensation the identity of the I envelops the alterity of the object, which becomes precisely a content.

The Other is not other with a relative alterity as are, in a comparison, even ultimate species, which mutually exclude one another but still have their place within the community of a genus–excluding one another by their definition, but calling for one another by this exclusion, across the community of their genus. The alterity of the Other does not depend on any quality that would distinguish him from me, for a distinction of this nature would precisely imply between us that community of genus which already nullifies alterity.

And yet the Other does not purely and simply negate the I; total negation, of which murder is the temptation and the attempt, refers to an antecedent relation. The relation between the Other and me, which dawns forth in his expression, issues neither in number nor in concept. The Other remains infinitely transcendent, infinitely foreign; his face in which his epiphany is produced and which appeals to me breaks with the world that can be common to us, whose virtualities are inscribed in our *nature* and developed by our existence. Speech proceeds from absolute difference. Or, more exactly, an absolute difference is not produced in a process of specification descending from genus to species, in which the order of logical relations runs up against the given, which is not reducible to relations. The difference thus encountered remains bound up with the logical hierarchy it contrasts with, and appears against the ground of the common genus.

Absolute difference, inconceivable in terms of formal logic, is established only by language. Language accomplishes a relation between terms that breaks up the unity of a genus. The terms, the interlocutors, absolve themselves from the relation, or remain absolute within relationship. Language is perhaps to be defined as the very power to break the continuity of being or of history.

The incomprehensible nature of the presence of the Other, which we spoke of above, is not to be described negatively. Better than comprehension, *discourse* relates with what remains essentially transcendent. For the moment we must attend to the formal work of language, which consists in presenting the transcendent; a more profound signification will emerge shortly. Language is a relation between separated terms. To the one the other can indeed present himself as a theme, but his presence is not reabsorbed in his status as a theme. The word that bears on the Other as a theme seems to contain the Other. But already it is said to the Other who, as interlocutor, has quit the theme that encompassed him, and upsurges inevitably behind the said. Words are said, be it only by the silence kept, whose weight acknowledges this evasion of the Other. The knowledge that absorbs the Other is forthwith situated within the discourse I address to him. Speaking, rather than 'letting be', solicits the Other. Speech cuts across vision. In knowledge or vision the object seen can indeed determine an act, but it is an act that in some way appropriates the 'seen' to itself, integrates it into a world by endowing it with a signification, and, in the last analysis, constitutes it. In discourse the divergence that inevitably opens between the Other as my theme and the Other as my interlocutor, emancipated from the theme that seemed a moment to hold him, forthwith contests the meaning I ascribe to my interlocutor. The formal structure of language thereby announces the ethical inviolability of the Other and, without any odor of the 'numinous', his 'holiness'.

The fact that the face maintains a relation with me by discourse does not range him in the same; he remains absolute within the relation. The solipsist dialectic of consciousness always suspicious of being in captivity in the same breaks off. For the ethical relationship which subtends discourse is not a species of consciousness whose ray emanates from the I; it puts the I in question. This putting in question emanates from the other.

The presence of a being not entering into, but overflowing, the sphere of the same determines its 'status' as infinite. This overflowing is to be distinguished from the image of liquid overflowing a vessel, because this overflowing presence is effectuated as a position *in face of* the same. The facing position, opposition par excellence, can be only as a moral summons. This movement proceeds from the other. The idea of infinity, the infinitely more contained in the less, is concretely produced in the form of a relation with the face. And the idea of infinity alone maintains the exteriority of the other with respect to the same, despite this relation. Thus a structure analogous to the ontological argument is here produced: the exteriority of a being is inscribed in its essence. But what is produced here is not a reasoning, but the epiphany that occurs as a face. The metaphysical desire for the absolutely other which animates intellectualism (or the radical empiricism that confides in the teaching of exteriority) deploys its *en-ergy* in the vision of the face [vision du visage], or in the idea of infinity. The idea of infinity exceeds my powers (not quantitatively, but, we will see later, by calling them into question); it does not come from our *a priori* depths–it is consequently experience *par excellence*.

The Kantian notion of infinity figures as an ideal of reason, the projection of its exigencies in a Beyond, the ideal completion of what is given incomplete–but without the imcomplete being confronted with a privileged *experience* of infinity, without it drawing the limits of its finitude from such a confrontation. The finite is here no longer conceived by relation to the infinite; quite the contrary, the infinite presupposes the finite, which it amplifies infinitely (although this passage to the limit or this projection implicates in an unacknowledged form the idea of infinity, with all the consequences Descartes drew from it, and which are presupposed in this idea of projection). The Kantian finitude is described positively by sensibility, as the Heideggerian finitude by the being for death. This infinity referring to the finite marks the most anti-Cartesian point of Kantian philosophy as, later, of Heideggerian philosophy.

Hegel returns to Descartes in maintaining the positivity of the infinite, but excluding all multiplicity from it; he posits the infinte as the exclusion of every 'other' that might maintain a relation with the infinite and thereby limit it. The infinite can only encompass all relations. Like the god of Aristotle it refers only to itself, though now at the term of a history. The relation of a particular with infinity would be equivalent to the entry of this particular into the sovereignty of a State. It becomes infinite in negating its own finitude. But this outcome does not succeed in smothering the protestation of the private individual, the apololgy of the separated being (though it be called empirical and animal), of the individual who experiences as a tyranny the State willed by his reason, but in whose impersonal destiny he no longer recognizes his reason. We recognize in the finitude to which the Hegelian infinite is opposed, and which it encompasses, the finitude of man before the elements, the finitude of man invaded by the *there is*, at each instant traversed by faceless gods against whom labor is pursued in order to realize the security in which the 'other' of the elements would be revealed as the same. But the other absolutely other–the Other–does not limit the freedom of the same; calling it to responsibility, it founds it and justifies it. The relation with the other as face heals allergy. It is desire, teaching received, and the pacific opposition of discourse. In returning to the Cartesian notion of infinity, the 'idea of infinity' put in the separated being by the infinite, we retain its positivity, its anteriority to every finite thought and every thought of the finite, its exteriority with regard to the finite; here there was the possibility of separated being. The idea of infinity, the overflowing of finite thought by its content, effectuates the relation of thought with what exceeds its capacity, with what at each moment it learns without suffering shock. This is the situation we call welcome of the face. The idea of infinity is produced in the *opposition* of conversation, in sociality. The relation with the face, with the other absolutely other which I can not contain, the other in this sense infinite, is nonetheless my Idea, a commerce. But the relation is maintained without violence, in peace with this absolute alterity. The 'resistance' of the other does not do violence to me, does not act negatively; it has a positive structure: ethical. The first revelation of the other, presupposed in all the other relations with him, does not consist in grasping him in his negative resistance and in circumventing him by ruse. I do not struggle with a faceless god, but I respond to his expression, to his revelation.

2 Ethics and the Face

The face resists possession, resists my powers. In its epiphany, in expression, the sensible, still graspable, turns into total resistance to the grasp. This mutation can occur only by the opening of a new dimension. For the resistance to the grasp is not produced as an insurmountable resistance, like the hardness of the rock against which the effort of the hand comes to naught, like the remoteness of a star in the immensity of space. The expression the face introduces into the world does not defy the feebleness of my powers, but my ability for power.[1] The face, still a thing among things, breaks through the form that nevertheless delimits it. This means concretely: the face speaks to me and thereby invites me to a relation incommensurate with a power exercised, be it enjoyment or knowledge.

And yet this new dimension opens in the sensible appearance of the face. The permanent openness of the contours of its form in expression imprisons this openness which breaks up form in a caricature. The face at the limit of holiness and caricature is thus still in a sense exposed to powers. In a sense only: the depth that opens in this sensibility modifies the very nature of power, which henceforth can no longer take, but can kill. Murder still aims at a sensible datum, and yet it finds itself before a datum whose being can not be *suspended* by an appropriation. It finds itself before a datum absolutely non-neutralizable. The 'negation' effected by appropriation and usage remained always partial. The grasp that contests the independence of the thing preserves it 'for me'. Neither the destruction of things, nor the hunt, nor the extermination of living beings aims at the face, which is not of the world. They still belong to labor, have a finality, and answer to a need. Murder alone lays claim to total negtation. Negation by labor and usage, like negation by representation, effect a grasp or a comprehension, rest on or aim at affirmation; they can. To kill is not to dominate but to annihilate; it is to renounce comprehension absolutely. Murder exercises a power over what escapes power. It is still a power, for the face expresses itself in the sensible, but already impotency, because the face rends the sensible. The alterity that is expressed in the face provides the unique 'matter' possible for total negation. I can wish to kill only an existent absolutely independent, which exceeds my powers infinitely, and therefore does not oppose them but paralyzes the very power of power. The Other is the sole being I can wish to kill.

But how does this disproportion between infinity and my powers differ from that which separates a very great obstacle from a force applied to it? It would be pointless to insist on the banality of murder, which reveals the quasi-null resistance of the obstacle. This most banal incident of human history corresponds to an exceptional possibility – since it claims the total negation of a being. It does not concern the force that this being may possess as a part of the world. The Other who can sovereignly say *no* to me is exposed to the point of the sword or the revolver's bullet, and the whole unshakeable firmness of his 'for itself' with that intransigent *no* he opposes is obliterated because the sword or the bullet has touched the ventricles or auricles of his heart. In the contexture of the world he is a quasi-nothing. But he can oppose to me a struggle, that is, oppose to the force that strikes him not a force of resistance, but the very *unforeseeableness* of his reaction. He thus opposes to me not a greater force, an energy assessable and consequently presenting itself as though it were part of a whole, but the very transcendence of his being by relation to that whole; not some superlative of power, but precisely the infinity of his transcendence. This infinity, stronger than murder, already resists us in his face, is his face, is the primordial *expression,* is the first word: 'you shall not commit murder'. The infinite paralyses power by its infinite resistance to murder, which, firm and insurmountable, gleams in the face of the Other, in the total nudity of his defenceless eyes, in the nudity of the absolute openness of the Transcedent. There is here a relation not with a very great resistance, but with something absolutely *other*: the resistance of what has no resistance – the ethical resistance. The epiphany of the face brings forth the possibility of gauging the infinity of the temptation to murder, not only as a temptation to total destruction, but also as the purely ethical impossibility of this temptation and attempt. If the resistance to murder were not ethical but real, we would have a *perception* of it, with all that reverts to the subjective in perception. We would remain within the idealism of a *consciousness* of struggle, and not in relationship with the Other, a relationship that can turn into struggle, but already overflows the consciousness of struggle. The epiphany of the face is ethical. The struggle this face can threaten *presupposes* the transcendence of expression. The face threatens the eventuality of a struggle, but this threat does not exhaust the epiphany of infinity, does not formulate its first word. War presupposes peace, the antecedent and non-allergic presence of the Other: it does not represent the first event of the encounter.

The impossibility of killing does not have a simply negative and formal signification; the relation with infinity, the idea of infinity in us, conditions it positively. Infinity presents itself as a face in the ethical resistance that paralyses my powers and from the depths of defenceless eyes rises firm and absolute in its nudity and destitution. The comprehension of this destitution and this hunger establishes the very proximity of the other. But thus the epiphany of infinity is expression and discourse. The primordial essence of expression and discourse does not reside in the information they would supply concerning an interior and hidden world. In expression a being presents itself; the being that manifests itself attends its manifestation and consequently appeals to me. This attendance is not the *neutrality [le neutre]* of an image, but a solicitation that concerns me by its destitution and its Height. To speak to me is at each moment to surmount what is necessarily plastic in manifestation. To manifest oneself as a face is to *impose onself* above and beyond the manifested and purely phenomenal form, to present oneself in a mode irreducible to manifestation, the very straight-forwardness of the face to face, without the intermediary of any image, in one's nudity, that is, in one's destitution and hunger. In *Desire* are conjoined the movements unto the Height and unto the Humility of the Other.

Expression does not radiate as a splendor that spreads unbeknown to the radiating being–which is perhaps the definition of beauty. To manifest oneself in attending one's own manifestation is to invoke the interlocutor and expose oneself to his response and his questioning. Expression does not impose itself as a true representation or as an action. The being offered in true representation remains a possibility of appearance. The world which invades me when I engage myself in it is powerless against the 'free thought' that suspends that engagement, or even refuses it interiorly, being capable of living hidden. The being that expresses itself imposes itself, but does so precisely by appealing to me with its destitution and nudity–its hunger– without my being able to be deaf to that appeal. Thus in expression the being that imposes itself does not limit but promotes my freedom, by arousing my goodness. The order of responsibility, where the gravity of ineluctable being freezes all laughter, is also the order where freedom is ineluctably invoked. It is thus the irremissible weight of being that gives rise to my freedom. The ineluctable has no longer the inhumanity of the fateful, but the severe seriousness of goodness.

This bond between expression and responsibility, this ethical condition or essence of language, this function of language prior to all disclosure of being and its cold splendor, permits us to extract language from subjection to a preexistent thought, where it would have but the servile function of translating that preexistent thought on the outside, or of universalizing its interior movements. The presentation of the face is not true, for the true refers to the non-true, its eternal contemporary, and ineluctably meets with the smile and silence of the skeptic. The presentation of being in the face does not leave any logical place for its contradictory. Thus I cannot evade by silence the discourse which the epiphany that occurs as a face opens, as Thrasymachus, irritated, tries to do, in the first book of the *Republic* (moreover without succeeding). 'To leave men without food is a fault that no circumstance attenuates; the distinction between the voluntary and the involuntary does not apply here', says Rabbi Yochanan.[2] Before the hunger of men responsibility is measured only 'objectively'; it is irrecusable. The face opens the primordial discourse whose first word is obligation, which no 'interiority' permits avoiding. It is that discourse that obliges the entering into discourse, the commencement of discourse rationalism prays for, a 'force' that convinces even 'the people who do not wish to listen'[3] and thus founds the true universality of reason.

Preexisting the disclosure of being in general taken as basis of knowledge and as meaning of being is the relation with the existent that expresses himself; preexisting the plane of ontology is the ethical plane.

3. Reason and the Face

Expression is not produced as the manifestation of an intelligible form that would connect terms to one another so as to establish, across distance, the assemblage of parts in a totality, in which the terms joined up already derive their meaning from the situation created by their community, which, in its turn, owes its meaning to the terms combined. This 'circle of understanding' is not the primordial event of the logic of being. Expression precedes these coordinating effects visible to a third party.

The event proper to expression consists in bearing witness to oneself, and guaranteeing this witness. This attestation of oneself is possible only as a face, that is, as speech. It produces the commencement of intelligibility, initiality itself, principality, royal sovereignty, which commands unconditionally. The principle is possible only as command. A search for the influence that expression would have undergone or an unconscious source from which it would emanate would presuppose an inquiry that would refer to new testimonies, and consequently to an original sincerity of an expression.

Language as an exchange of ideas about the world, with the mental reservations it involes, across the vicissitudes of sincerity and deceit it delineates, presupposes the originality of the face without which, reduced to an action among actions whose meaning would require an infinite psychoanalysis or sociology, it could not commence. If at the bottom of speech there did not subsist this originality of expression, this break with every influence, this dominant position of the speaker foreign to all compromises and all contamination, this straightforwardness of the face to face, speech would not surpass the plane of activity, of which it is evidently not a species—even though language can be integrated into a system of acts and serve as an instrument. But language is possible only when speaking precisely renounces this function of being action and returns to its essence of being expression.

Expression does not consist in *giving* us the Other's interiority. The Other who expresses himself precisely does not *give* himself, and accordingly retains the freedom to lie. But deceit and veracity already presuppose the absolute authenticity of the face—the privileged case of a presentation of being foreign to the alternative of truth and non-truth, circumventing the ambiguity of the true and the false which every truth risks—an ambiguity, moreover, in which all values move. The presentation of being in the face does not have the status of a value. What we call the face is precisely this exceptional presentation of self by self, incommensurable with the presentation of realities simply given, always suspect of some swindle, always possibly dreamt up. To seek truth I have already established a relationship with a face which can guarantee itself, whose epiphany itself is somehow a word of honor. Every language as an exchange of verbal signs refers already to this primordial word of honour. The verbal sign is placed where someone signifies something to someone else. It therefore already presupposes an authentification of the signifier.

Notes

1 'Mon pouvoir de pouvoir.'
2 Treatise *Synhedrin*, 104 b.
3 Plato, *Republic*, 327 b.

Section 3

Criticism and the Institution

Debates about the institutional function and construction of criticism arose in the 1970s and 1980s as a consequence of the increasing professionalization of the discipline and in response to the preoccupations of two theoretical orientations, in particular: Althusserian Marxism's analysis of ideological State Apparatuses and the development of an aesthetics of reception concerned with the material constraints on and frameworks of reading. A general account of Marxism and the relations between ideology and literature have been offered in earlier section introductions, so some account will be given here of the development of reception aesthetics and the issue of professionalization, in order to provide a context for the essays by Stanley Fish and Edward Said.

The question of how we read and interpret texts and how the institutional framework of criticism conditions the kinds of reading which are possible, began to be raised by two schools of reader theory in the early 1970s. The first, 'reader response theory' was largely American in origin and included figures such as Norman Holland, a psychoanalytic critic, David Bleitch who advocated a subjectivist aesthetics and Stanley Fish, in one of his earlier incarnations as an 'affective stylistician', concentrating on reading as a subjective, experiential and temporal process. Fish later revised his earlier position as he recongnized that the process he was describing could not be extrapolated out as *the* reading process, only as *a* reading process. In his reworking, he developed the notion of 'interpretative communities'–a version of Kuhn's knowledge communities–which named communities of readers with shared practices and competences. For Fish, it is the interpretative community which determines interpretations rather than the intrinsic textual features of the work. Given that modern literary criticism is almost entirely insitutionalized within the academy, this earlier work soon led to a focus on the professional structures of the modern university, its definitions of knowledge and constructions of value.

Aesthetics of reception was earlier dominated by two figures, in particular, the German theorists Wolfgang Iser and Hans Robert Jauss. Iser drew extensively on the work of the phenomenologist aesthetician Roman Ingarden, sharing his view of the text as a potential structure which is 'concretized' by the reader in the act of reading. For Iser, this is a process which takes place in relation to extra-literary norms and values through which the reader makes sense of experience. Iser's writings reveal a considerable degree of ambiguity about the extent of the reader's freedom to fill in the gaps in the texts' 'schemata' according to his or her own experiential norms, and the extent to which the text controls or determines the way it will be read. What is clear, however, is Iser's commitment to a phenomenological view of the reading experience; the reader realizes the text as an aesthetic object according to his or her own experience, but the norms which structure that experience will inevitably be modified by the reading experience itself. As we read we continually re-evaluate events with regard to our expectations of what will happen in the text, and against the background of what has already happened. Unexpected textual occurrences, however, will require us to reformulate our expectations and to reinterpret the significance which we have attributed to what has gone before. Iser sees the reader as someone who, above all, seeks coherence as the basis of sense-making and who will reconnect the different schemata of the text according to continual revisions which guarantee an overall meaning.

Iser's thesis was influential, but it soon became apparent to theorists that it lacked any account of history of the specific material contexts of reading and seeming to posit an ideal reader, like Joyce's, suffering from an ideal insomnia. Jauss's reception theory responded by offering a more historically situated understanding of the concretization process, positing an 'horizon of expectations' which lays down the criteria in each historical period according to which people read and evaluate literary works. The horizon of expectations at the original moment of production can only tell us something about how the work was understood and received at that time; it does not establish its absolute or universal meaning. Jauss here drew substantially on the ideas of Gadamer, who also viewed the text as in an endless dialogue between past and present in which the present position of the interpreter will always influence how the past is understood and received. In attempting to make sense of the past we can only know it in the light of the present cultural horizon and so Jauss argues for a 'fusion of horizons' which will unite past and present.

Jauss's analysis began to situate the reception of texts in the context of communities of readers, but his account differs substantially from that of Fish in that Jauss ultimately posits a seamless and hermeneutic continuity between past and present so that each horizon takes its shape on the back of the previous one. This is a very different account of interpretation from that inspired by Kuhn's idea of knowledge communities where there is a radical disjunction between the frameworks of communities of knowledge at different times and in different places and to the extent that even shared vocabularies might actually signify incommensurable meanings from one community to another. Stanley Fish began to develop his ideas about critical and reading communities in the contexts of these debates about knowledge and interpretation. His essay and that of Edward Said, reprinted here, take up the issue of the function of criticism and the nature of interpretation in the modern professionalized academy. They ask questions about the cultural role of the critic and the relations between the academic and the wider community.

That literary criticism has been increasingly professionalized in the twentieth century is evident from the growing separation between literary criticism and other kinds of writing on literature such as reviews, journalism and the kinds of commentary which writers make on their own work. Professionalization is, of course, a double-edged process: part of a broadening democracy and involving issues such as accountability, fairness, standards, but also part of the modern capitalist state and concerned with efficiency, expertise and specialization, and careerism. The profession, and Fish would argue that this is as true for the profession of literary criticism as it is for the law or the civil service, sets the terms for training, objectives, goals and vocationalism. The position of the profession is double-edged too in the sense that professionalization involves a public profile and management by the state, but also allows for a certain degree of self-management, of functioning as a protected enclave. Professionalization can be said to involve a degree of 'relative autonomy' to use Althusser's phrase.

Most professions have drawn on a vocabulary of service and higher goals, some notion of an Arnoldian best self, and the profession of literary criticism is no exception, with its talk of high-minded disinterestedness and its general use of a rhetoric of selflessness which might cynically be deconstructed as simultaneously self-serving and self-aggrandizing. Literary criticism has come under pressure in the twentieth century to reconcile a vocabulary inherited from an idealist Romantic–humanist tradition with the knowledge vocabularies of the modern university, largely derived from the natural sciences. Throughout the twentieth century, the pressure of this research model has produced controversies and insecurities about the appropriate 'method' for literary criticism as a discipline and the function of criticism as a form of knowledge within the university and the wider community. The situation has also produced conflict because, whereas the Arnoldian tradition down to Leavis saw the humanities in general and criticism in particular as concerned with values and purposes, the various cultural relativisms and political movements of the late twentieth century have, as we have seen, produced a breakdown in the earlier consensus about the nature of such values.

The essay reprinted here from Stanley Fish's book *Professional Correctness* argues that the professionalization of criticism has inevitably led to a disappearance of the relationship between art and civic virtue. Criticism is now a self-enclosed game with rules and structural moves and those who learn to play it well and work creatively within the rules will be guaranteed their professional rewards (presumably Fish would include himself in this analysis). Fish argues that this was not always the case, and that in the seventeenth century, for example, action and expression were regarded as equally potent forms of political and cultural intervention. What changed, according to this analysis, is that, with the development of liberalism from Locke onwards, the idea of free speech gradually prises action apart from expression so that freedom of speech is purchased at the expense of efficacy. Literature, in particular, is inevitably marginalized and allowed to speak freely within its own enclaves and according to rules which are increasingly divorced from forms of expression connected to practical action in the world. Criticism can thus claim what it likes – the death of God, of the author, of the phallus, or even claim to be a cure for the common cold – but it is entirely unable to make good any of these claims in the world. Criticism is simply an institutionalized game with its own internal rules.

Though Edward Said might and has agreed with some of Stanley Fish's arguments about the pressures of professionalization and institutionalization, and though he shares his anti-idealist view of the academy, Said would certainly distance himself from Fish's easy-going and complacent pragmatism. Said recognizes that the pressures of professionalization produce a drive towards conformity, a need for recognition and inclusion by the group. There will always be those whose success is founded on the appearance of being maverick because the appeal is actually to an orthodoxy which does not acknowledge itself as such. To this extent, Said would go along with some of Fish's arguments. But Said is certainly not content to rest there. His desired model of the literary critic is of the modern intellectual, a figure who can connect a specialized and academic knowledge with the needs and concerns of the wider culture, challenging its norms and exposing its complacencies. Said's analysis of modern criticism is of the gradual formation of a special branch of civil servants who speak the language of a wider democracy (as in some of the early statements of the New Criticism, for example, with its promise to open up a method of reading which would be free to all and not dependent upon the specialized and costly scholarly library), but who have actually hardened into a self-serving and enclosed guild speaking only to each other and serving the petrified monuments of an exclusive tradition. His essay is essentially a call for the revival of the concept of the intellectual, for literary critics to use their skills in order actively to intervene in the wider culture: to escape from the academicism which infects even the so-called 'radical' schools of political criticism, and to connect so-called 'cultural politics' with actual politics in the world. Both Said and Fish view the humanities as having come to represent a humane marginality, an enclave of decencies and arcane language, of free expression and Byzantine theorizing, which have very little connection with the world outside of the academy. Fish is happy with the situation insofar as literary critics recognize their condition and stop pretending to be anything else; Said most certainly is not.

44 | Stanley Fish,

From *Political Correctness* (1995), pp. 32–9

In our time the relationship between art and the production of civic virtue is thin to the point of vanishing. At most one can claim, with Shelley, that poets are the unacknowledged legislators of the world; the ambition is grand, but it is much more abstract and less capable of verification than the ambition felt and sometimes realized by poets whose influence on the acknowledged legislators was defining of their project. Deprived of a secure if unofficial place in the corridors of government and commerce, literary activity is increasingly pursued in the academy where proficiency is measured by academic standards and rewarded by the gatekeepers of an academic guild. The name for this is professionalization, a form of organization in which membership is acquired by a course of special training whose end is the production of persons who recognize one another not because they regularly meet at the same ceremonial occasions (unless one equates an MLA meeting with the Elizabethan court), but because they perform the same 'moves' in the same 'game'. That is, they participate in the same 'immanent intelligibility' whose content is the same set of 'internal'– not foreign–purposes.

It would not be too much to say that these purposes are exactly the opposite of those informing the intelligibility of literary activity before the Enlightenment. The 'foreign ideals' against which the literary–from both the production and consumption ends–now defines itself are the very ideals that would have been named as internal and constitutive by someone like Milton: contribution to civic harmony and public aspiration, guidance to princes and generals, education of the children of the ruling class, celebration of royal birthdays, inculcation of religious sentiments. All of these are now understood (except by new historicists and cultural materialists) as appropriate to the purposes animating *other* enterprises: politics, warfare, educational planning, theology.

Here I can imagine someone saying 'those were the days' and urging us to work for the reintegration of the literary with the political and the social. To that urging I would respond, first, that it's not that easy, and, second, that even if a reintegration should somehow be effected, it would not compromise or blur the distinctiveness of tasks as I have been arguing for it. My introduction of a historical dimension at this point should not be taken to suggest that if we could only recover the conditions obtaining in the Renaissance, literary activity and political activity could again be one and the same. They were not one and the same then. To be sure, in the sixteenth and seventeenth centuries literary actors could *also* be political actors, and could, as part of their political activity, make use of their literary credentials; but even when they did so, they had a strong sense of distinctive abilities whose exercise could at times be put into a double harness. For Milton and the others, even in their state of cultural integration, thinking to compose a poem was an act conditioned by the history and presupposed imperatives of poetic practice as embodied in the texts of accepted exemplars (Virgil, Homer, etc.). What distinguishes them from us is that they could then contemplate incorporating that literary intention into a political one by, say, writing a poem intended to influence military or diplomatic policy. They would then be putting to political effect a competence that was not, in and of itself, political at all. In short, they could reasonably intervene in political matters by exercising literary skills. In so far as there survives any sense of the literary as an interventionary project, it takes the form of a claim that it is the purpose of the literary to provide a space of critique – a vantage-point of clear-eyed, astringent interrogation – from which the apparent coherence of familiar discourses can be problematized and challenged. But in this view of literary effectivity the work is understood to be done at the level of conceptual analysis and does not involve the urging of any particular agenda, except the agenda of continual sceptical scrutiny.

That is why the pre-eminent question of literary interpretation – what does this poem (or novel or play) *mean*? – is properly answered not by a proposition ('This poem means that war is hell' or 'This poem means that infant mortality is a national disgrace'), but by a *refusal directly to answer it*. Something must always be left over, unaccounted for, open to still another turn of the interpretive screw; were this not so, the work could be said to have engaged in totalizing – in telling (or claiming to tell) the truth about the world once and for all – and thereby forfeited its right to be called 'literary'. To be sure, literary works are full of propositions of the kind one finds in philosophy or history ('This is so' or 'This is what happened'), but in a literary performance, either at the production end or at the reception end, propositions and accounts of facts do not come into primary focus; rather they provide the material, or 'stuff', on which the literary impulse – the impulse to probe ever deeper the incorrigible duplicity of assertion even as it presents itself as univocal and single – can be exercised. (I hasten to say again that I am not here giving my own answer to the question 'What is literature?', but reporting on the answer most practitioners would today give if they were asked.)

In so distinguishing the literary or literariness from the workings of philosophy and history respectively I may have reminded you of an earlier effort along the same lines. In his *Defense of Poesy*, Philip Sidney identifies philosophy with the giving of general precepts and opposes it to history, which offers us an undifferentiated mass of particular examples. It is the excellence of the poet, says Sidney, to do *both* 'for whatsoever the philosopher says should be done, he gives a perfect picture of it by someone by whom he presupposes it was done, so as he couples the general notion with the particular example' (Sir Philip Sidney's *Defense of Poesy*, ed. Lewis Soens, Lincoln, Nebr., 1970,17). Like his modern counterpart, then, Sidney puts poetry in a special category, but there is a crucial difference. Whereas twentieth-century critics distinguish poetry from history and philosophy in order to sequester artistic production and reception from the contigencies of politics, Sidney locates poetry's distinctiveness in its superior ability to prosecute a moral/political task. In his account philosophy, history, and poetry are all in the same line of public work–telling and promulgating the truth; it is just that poetry does it better, 'not only . . . furnishing the mind with knowledge, but . . . setting it forward to that which deserves to be called and accounted good', for 'it is not knowing, but doing must be the fruit' (23).

By linking poetry so strongly to action, Sidney implicitly authorizes poets (and literary people in general) to intervene in the realm of public affairs, where they might perform as advisers to princes, as ambassadors, as churchmen, as legislators, as diplomats, as the leaders of commerical and military expeditions, in short, in all the ways taken up by Sidney, Spenser, Raleigh, Donne, Marvell, and Milton. One should note that this expansive understanding of the arenas into which poets can intrude themselves has as its corollary a correspondingly expansive understanding of the dangers awaiting them in those arenas. Service to a king or a prelate, even if it is largely verbal, carries with it risks (of dismissal, banishment, incarceration, death) from which the poet as Sidney conceives him cannot be insulated. In 1992 by contrast, insulation is assured (who *cares* what poets do?) but at the price of the wide entry and influence to which Sidney and his friends could reasonably aspire.

This shift from an aesthetic that puts poetry in the world to one that quarantines it is accompanied by (and reflected in) a shift in attitudes toward censorship. Even so staunch a defender of free expression as Milton protested only against 'prior restraint', the suppressing of speech or writing before it appears on the world's stage; once something has been published, however, 'it is of greatest concernment in the church and commonwealth, to have a vigilant eye how books demean themselves as well as men; and therefore to confine, imprison, and do sharpest justice on them as malefactors' (*Areopagitica*). What will seem strange to the modern reader of this passage is the absence of the distinction between action, the proper object of judicial attention, and expression which, because it is merely verbal and without real-world consequences, should be exempt from regulation. It is this distinction that Milton specifically rejects, insisting on the 'potency' of words no less than of deeds and therefore holding them to a standard of accountability that not only allows but demands state scrutiny. To do otherwise, he would have said, would be to imply that verbal actions do not matter or that they matter only in a realm wholly distanced from political life, a realm called, perhaps, 'the life of the mind'or 'the world of the imagination.'

This of course is exactly what is not merely implied but stated in many twentieth-century accounts of the matter: verbal productions except when they cross a line and become incitements to action – and when they cross that line they cease to be truly expressive or truly literary – are to be regarded as the effusions of essentially free minds; and therefore any attempt to police them is an infringement upon that freedom. The development of this argument, which is at the heart of liberalism's disinclination either to authorize or to condemn anyone's opinions, has provided the artist with his strongest bulwark against state regulation (although, as many would complain, it is a bulwark continually being breached by overreaching statists), but at the same time the argument deprives the artist of any rationale for intervening in precincts that have been assigned to other agents whose franchise is held no less exclusively than his.

It is by now a familiar paradox: artistic freedom is purchased at the expense of artistic efficacy. As Norman Mailer has put it,

> Every gain of freedom carries its price. There's a wonderful moment when you go from oppression to freedom, there in the middle, when one's still oppressed but one's achieved the first freedoms. There's an extraordinary period that goes from there until the freedoms begin to outweigh the oppression. By the time you get over to complete freedom, you begin to look back almost nostalgically on the days of oppression, because in those days you were ready to become a martyr, you had a sense of importance, you could take yourself seriously, you were fighting the good fight. (Quoted in Edward de Grazia, *Girls Lean Back Everywhere: The Law of Obscenity and the Assault on Genius*, New York, 1992, 495.)

Recently, Mailer's words have been echoed (and confirmed) by Russian poet Aleksandr Kushner. In the good old days, Kushner explains, the writer was 'like an uncrowned prince'. Now, he laments, 'this is gone':

> Why? In those days, literature was the one real door open to people of a certain kind. Now there are lots of doors to walk through. You can go into business, play on the Israeli soccer team, play for a New York hockey team, make your fortune in Greece, or even go into poltics if you choose. At the same time, literature in the eyes of many has lost its exceptional importance. Literature will always have a place, as it does in America. Marginal, but important. Small but beautiful. Of course, if a monster, a fascist, like Vladimir Zhironovsky is ever elected President of Russia, literature might have to assume its old role. But for now, no. (*New Yorker*, 18 July 1994, 52)

Notice that in Kushner's mind the resumption by literature of its 'old role' will have to wait upon events external to the literary culture. If the battle for artistic freedom has been won, but is now seen to bring with it losses that had not been contemplated, you cannot, by yourself or in the company of your fellows, turn back the clock and reinstitute the condition (of there being a good fight to fight) that once gave your project its excitement and consequentiality. Turning the clock back would not be the preferred self-description of those who call today for a more interventionary literary scholarship; but it is no accident that such calls often issue from scholars who work in the sixteenth and seventeenth centuries and who have argued, persuasively in my view, for an Elizabethan–Jacobean culture in which the boundaries betwen the literary and non-literary are permeable. What is curious is that the insights of these scholars into the material conditions which made intervention possible and even inescapable in the period they study have not been matched by a recognition that these conditions no longer exist and a realization that their return cannot be willed either by an individual or by the collective of a gathered practice. If no one critic can, by himself, declare a change in the basic gestures by which he signals and validates his entry into an ongoing practice, no one practice can, by itself, rearrange the map of responsibilities, efficacies, relevancies, and possible consequences that marks out the spheres assigned (by no one and everyone) to all the games currently in play. Any announcement by one of these practices that it will now enlarge the territory within which its agents are understood to operate will be met with resistance and incredulity.

Imagine, if you will, a meeting of all the literary and cultural critics in the world at a single conference, and imagine an overwhelming vote to the effect that from now on we shall address our analyses not to the small number of our professional peers but to the public at large and that we expect an alerted public to pay us the kind of attention it mistakenly reserves for politicians, political pundits, and basketball players. Such a proclamation would have its brief moment of impact as newspapers reported on one more instance of academic hubris and absurdity; but when the laughter had died down, little, if anything, will have changed. This is not to say that the division of labour and its attendant parcelling out of responsibilities and rewards cannot be changed, only that the change will be structural, effected not by an isolated act of will, whether perfomed by an individual or by the collective of a particular practice, but by shifts in the cultural consciousness that are glacially slow and overdetermined. This point is not understood by those like Bruce Robbins who believe that because literary criticism has shifted (ar least in some avantgarde quarters) from an aesthetic to a socio-political justification of its project, it is now 'able to claim a more public role' (*Secular Vocations*, London, 1993, 97). This internal change (were it to be effected on a large scale, a matter still in doubt) will certainly alter both the rhetoric and the practice of criticism, but it will not alter the world, unless the world has been altered already. Criticism can 'claim' anything it likes; it can claim to be a cure for the common cold; but making good on its claims will depend on forces it cannot even muster, never mind control.

45 | Edward Said,

'Opponents, Audiences, Constituencies and Community', in *Postmodern Culture* H. Foster ed., (1985), pp. 137–43; 155–9

At a recent MLA convention, I stopped by the exhibit of a major university press and remarked to the amiable sales representative on duty that there seemed to be no limit to the number of highly specialized books of advanced literary criticism his press put out. 'Who reads these books?' I asked, implying of course that however brilliant and important most of them were they were difficult to read and therefore could not have a wide audience – or at least an audience wide enough to justify regular publication during a time of economic crisis. The answer I received made sense, assuming I was told the truth. People who write specialized, advanced (i.e., New New) criticism faithfully read each other's books. Thus each such book could be assured of, but wasn't necessarily always getting, sales of around three thousand copies, 'all other things being equal'. The last qualification struck me as ambiguous at best, but it needn't detain us here. The point was that a nice little audience had been built and could be routinely mined by this press; certainly, on a much larger scale, publishers of cookbooks and exercise manuals apply a related principle as they churn out what may seem like a very long series of unnecessary books, even if an expanding crowd of avid food and exercise aficionados is not quite the same thing as a steadily attentive and earnest crowd of three thousand critics reading each other.

What I find peculiarly interesting about the real or mythical three thousand is that whether they derive ultimately from the Anglo-American New Criticism (as formulated by I.A. Richards, William Empson, John Crowe Ransom, Cleanth Brooks, Allen Tate, and company, beginning in the 1920s and continuing for several decades thereafter) or from the so-called New New Criticism (Roland Barthes, Jacques Derrida, *et al.*, during the 1960s), they vindicate, rather than undermine, the notion that intellectual labor ought to be divided into progressively narrower niches. Consider very quickly the irony of this. New Criticism claimed to view the verbal object as in itself it really was, free from the distractions of biography, social message, even paraphrase. Matthew Arnold's critical program was thereby to be advanced not by jumping directly from the text to the whole of culture but by using a highly concentrated verbal analysis to comprehend cultural values available only through a finely wrought literary structure finely understood.

Charges made against the American New Criticism that its ethos was clubby, gentlemanly or Episcopalian are, I think, correct only if it is added that in practice New Criticism, for all its elitism, was strangely populist in intention. The idea behind the pedagogy, and of course the preaching, of Brooks and Robert Penn Warren was that everyone properly instructed could feel, perhaps even act, like an educated gentleman. In its sheer projection this was by no means a trivial ambition. No amount of snide mocking at their gentility can conceal the fact that, in order to accomplish the conversion, the New Critics aimed at nothing less than the removal of *all* of what they considered the specialized rubbish–put there, they presumed, by professors of literature–standing between the reader of a poem and the poem. Leaving aside the questionable value of the New Criticism's ultimate social and moral messge, we must concede that the school deliberately and perhaps incongruously tried to create a wide community of responsive readers out of a very large, potentially, unlimited, constituency of students and teachers of literature.

In its early days, the French *nouvelle critique*, with Barthes as its chief apologist, attempted the same kind of thing. Once again the guild of professional literary scholars was characterized as impeding responsiveness to literature. Once again the antidote was what seemed to be a specialized reading technique based on a near jargon of linguistic, psychoanalytic and Marxist terms, all of which proposed a new freedom for writers and literature readers alike. The philosophy of *écriture* promised wider horizons and a less restricted community, once an initial (and as it turned out painless) surrender to structuralist activity had been made. For despite structuralist prose, there was no impulse among the principal structuralists to exclude readers; quite the contrary, as Barthes's often abusive attacks on Raymond Picard show, the main purpose of critical reading was to create new readers of the classics who might otherwise have been frightened off by their lack of professional literary accreditation.

For about four decades, then, in both France and the United States, the schools of 'new' critics were committed to prying literature and writing loose from confining institutions. However much it was to depend upon carefully learned technical skills, reading was in very large measure to become an act of public depossession. Texts were to be unlocked or decoded, then handed on to anyone who was interested. The resources of symbolic language were placed at the disposal of readers who it was assumed suffered the debilitations of either irrelevant 'professional' information or the accumulated habits of lazy inattention.

Thus French and American New Criticism were, I believe, competitors for authority within mass culture, not other-worldly alternatives to it. Because of what became of them, we have tended to forget the original missionary aims the two schools set for themselves. They belong to precisely the same moment that produced Jean-Paul Sartre's ideas about an engaged literature and a committed writer. Literature was about the world, readers were in the world; the question was not *whether* to be but *how* to be, and this was best answered by carefully analyzing language's symbolic enactments of the various existential possibilities available to human beings. What the Franco-Ameican critics shared was the notion that verbal discipline could be self-sufficient once you learned to think pertinently about language stripped of unnecessary scaffolding; in other words, you did not need to be a professor to benefit from Donne's metaphors or Saussure's liberating distinction between *langue* and *parole*. And so the New Criticism's precious and cliquish aspect was mitigated by its radically anti-institutional bias, which manifested itself in the enthusiastic therapeutic optimism to be observed in both France and the United States. Join humankind against the schools: this was a message a great many people could appreciate.

How strangely perverse, then, that the legacy of both types of New Criticism is the private-clique consciousness embodied in a kind of critical writing that has virtually abandoned any attempt at reaching a large, if not a mass, audience. My belief is that both in the United States and in France the tendency toward formalism in New Criticism was accentuated by the academy. For the fact is that a disciplined attention to language can only thrive in the rarefied atmosphere of the classroom. Linguistics and literary analysis are features of the modern school, not of the marketplace. Purifying the language of the tribe–whether as a project subsumed within modernism or as a hope kept alive by embattled New Criticisms surrounded by mass culture–always moved further from the really big existing tribes and closer toward emerging new ones, comprised of the acolytes of a reforming or even revolutionary creed who in the end seemed to care more about turning the new creed into an intensely separatist orthodoxy than about forming a large community of readers.

To its unending credit, the university protects such wishes and shelters them under the umbrella of academic freedom. Yet advocacy of *close reading* or of *écriture* can quite naturally entail hostility to outsiders who fail to grasp the salutary powers of verbal analysis; moreover, persuasion too often has turned out to be less important than purity of intention and execution. In time the guild adversarial sense grew as the elaborate techniques multiplied, and an interest in expanding the consituency lost out to a wish for abstract correctness and methodological rigor within a quasi-monastic order. Critics read each other and cared about little else.

The parallels between the fate of a New Criticism reduced to abandoning universal literacy entirely and that of the school of F.R. Leavis are sobering. As Francis Mulhern reminds us in *The Moment of Scrutiny*, Leavis was not a formalist himself and began his career in the context of generally Left politics. Leavis argued that great literature was fundamentally opposed to a class society and to the dictates of a coterie. In his view, English studies ought to become the cornerstone of a new, fundamentally democratic outlook. But largely because the Leavisites concentrated their work both in and for the university, what began as a healthy oppositional participation in modern industrial society changed into a shrill withdrawal from it. English studies became narrower and narrower, in my opinion, and critical reading degenerated into decisions about what should or should not be allowed into the great tradition.

I do not want to be misunderstood as saying that there is something inherently pernicious about the modern university that produces the changes I have been describing. Certainly there is a great deal to be said in favor of a university manifestly not influenced or controlled by coarse partisan politics. But one thing in particular about the university – and here I speak about the modern university without distinguishing between European, American, or Third World and socialist universities – does appear to exercise an almost totally unrestrained influence: the principle that knowledge ought to exist, be sought after and disseminated in a very divided form. Whatever the social, political, economic and ideological reasons underlying this principle, it has not long gone without its challengers. Indeed, it may not be too much of an exaggeration to say that one of the most interesting motifs in modern world culture has been the debate between proponents of the belief that knowledge can exist in a synthetic universal form and, on the other hand, those who believe that knowledge is inevitably produced and nurtured in specialized compartments. Georg Lukács's attack on reification and his advocacy of 'totality', in my opinion, very tantalizingly resemble the wide-ranging discussions that have been taking place in the Islamic world since the late nineteenth century on the need for mediating between the claims of a totalizing Islamic vision and modern specialized science. These epistemological controversies are therefore centrally important to the workplace of knowledge production, the university, in which *what* knowledge is and how it ought to be discovered are the very lifeblood of its being.

The most impressive recent work concerning the history, circumstances and constitution of modern knowledge has stressed the role of social convention. Thomas Kuhn's 'paradigm of research', for example, shifts attention away from the individual creator to the communal restraints upon personal initiative. Galileos and Einsteins are infrequent figures not just because genius is a rare thing but because scientists are borne along by agreed-upon ways to do research, and this consensus encourages uniformity rather than bold enterprise. Over time this uniformity acquires the status of a discipline, while its subject matter becomes a field or territory. Along with these goes a whole apparatus of techniques, one of whose functions is, as Michel Foucault has tried to show in *The Archaeology of Knowledge*, to protect the coherence, the territorial integrity, the social identity of the field, its adherents and its institutional presence. You cannot simply choose to be a sociologist or a psychoanalyst; you cannot simply make statements that have the status of knowledge in anthropology; you cannot merely suppose that what you say as a historian (however well it may have been researched) enters historical discourse. You have to pass through certain rules of accreditation, you must learn the rules, you must speak the language, you must master the idioms and you must accept the authorities of the field – determined in many of the same ways – to which you want to contribute.

In this view of things, expertise is partially determined by how well an individual learns the rules of the game, so to speak. Yet it is difficult to determine in absolute terms whether expertise is *mainly* constituted by the social conventions governing the intellectual manners of scientists or, on the other hand, mainly by the putative exigencies of the subject matter itself. Certainly convention, tradition and habit create ways of looking at a subject that transform it completely; and just as certainly there are generic differences between the subjects of history, literature and philology that require different (albeit related) techniques of analysis, disciplinary attitudes and commonly held views. Elsewhere I have taken the admittedly aggressive position that Orientalists, area-studies experts, journalists and foreign-policy specialists are not always sensitive to the dangers of self-quotation, endless repetition, and received ideas that their fields encourage, for reasons that have more to do with politics and ideology than with any 'outside' reality. Hayden White has shown in his work that historians are subject not just to narrative conventions but also to the virtually closed space imposed on the interpreter of events by verbal retrospection, which is very far from being an objective mirror of reality. Yet even these views, although they are understandably repugnant to many people, do not go as far as saying that everything about a 'field' can be reduced either to an interpretive convention or to political interest.

Let us grant, therefore, that it would be a long and potentially impossible task to prove empirically that, on the one hand, there could be objectivity so far as knowledge about human society is concerned or, on the other, that all knowledge is esoteric and subjective. Much ink has been spilled on both sides of the debate, not all of it useful, as Wayne Booth has shown in his discussion of scientism and modernism, *Modern Dogma and the Rhetoric of Assent*. An instructive opening out of the impasse—to which I want to return a bit later—has been the body of techniques developed by the school of reader-response critics: Wolfgang Iser, Norman Holland, Stanley Fish, and Michael Riffaterre, among others. These critics argue that since texts without readers are no less incomplete than readers without texts, we should focus attention on what happens when both components of the interpretive situation interact. Yet with the exception of Fish, reader-response critics tend to regard interpretation as an essentially private, interiorized happening, thereby inflating the role of solitary decoding at the expense of its just as important social context. In his latest book, *Is There a Text in This Class?*, Fish accentuates the role of what he calls interpretive communities, groups as well as institutions (principal among them the classroom and pedagogues) whose presence, much more than any unchanging objective standard or correlative of absolute truth, controls what we consider to be knowledge. If, as he says, 'interpretation is the only game in town,' then it must follow that interpreters who work mainly by persuasion and not scientific demonstration are the only players.

I am on Fish's side there. Unfortunately; though, he does not go very far in showing why, or even how, some interpretations are more persuasive than others. Once again we are back to the quandary suggested by the three thousand advanced critics reading each other to everyone else's unconcern. Is it the inevitable conclusion to the formation of an interpretive community that its constituency, its specialized languge and its concerns tend to get tighter, more airtight, more self-enclosed as its own self-confirming authority acquires more power, the solid status of orthodoxy and a stable constituency? What is the acceptable humanistic antidote to what one discovers, say among sociologists, philosophers and so-called policy scientists who speak only to and for each other in a language oblivious to everything but a well-guarded, constantly shrinking fiefdom forbidden to the uninitiated?

For all sorts of reasons, large answers to these questions do not strike me as attractive or convincing. For one, the universalizing habit by which a system of thought is believed to account for everything too quickly slides into a quasi-religious synthesis. This, it seems to me, is the sobering lesson offered by John Fekete in *The Critical Twilight,* an account of how New Criticism led directly to Marshall McLuhan's 'technocratic-religious eschatology.' In fact, interpretation and its demands add up to a rough game, once we allow ourselves to step out of the shelter offered by specialized fields and by fancy all-embracing mythologies. The trouble with visions, reductive answers and systems is that they homogenize evidence very easily. Criticism as such is crowded out and disallowed from the start, hence impossible; and in the end one learns to manipulate bits of the system like so many parts of a machine. Far from taking in a great deal, the universal system as a universal type of explanation either screens out everything it cannot directly absorb or it repetitively churns out the same sort of thing all the time. In this way it becomes a kind of conspiracy theory. Indeed, it has always seemed to me that the supreme irony of what Derrida has called logocentrism is that its critique, deconstruction, is as insistent, as monotonous and as inadvertently systematizing as logocentrism itself. We may applaud the wish to break out of departmental divisions, therefore, without at the same time accepting the notion that one single method for doing so exists.

* * * * *

The particular mission of the humanities is, in the aggregate, to represent *noninterference* in the affairs of the everyday world. As we have seen, there has been a historical erosion in the role of letters since the New Criticism, and I have suggested that the conjuncture of a narrowly based university environment for technical language and literature studies with the self-policing, self-purifying communities erected even by Marxist, as well as other disciplinary, discourses, produced a very small but definite function for the humanities: to represent humane marginality, which is also to preserve and if possible to conceal the hierarchy of powers that occupy the center, define the social terrain, and fix the limits of use functions, fields, marginality and so on. Some of the corollaries of this role for the humanities generally and literary criticism in particular are that the institutional presence of humanities guarantees a space for the deployment of free-floating abstractions (scholarship, taste, tact, humanism) that are defined in advance as indefinable; that when it is not easily domesticated, 'theory' is employable as a discourse of occultation and legitimation; that self-regulation is the ethos behind which the institutional humanities allow and in a sense encourage the unrestrained operation of market forces that were traditionally thought of as subject to ethical and philosophical review.

Very broadly stated, then, noninterference for the humanist means laissez-faire: 'they' can run the country, we will explicate Wordsworth and Schlegel. It does not stretch things greatly to note that noninterference and rigid specialization in the academy are directly related to what has been called a counterattack by 'highly mobilized business elites' in reaction to the immediately preceding period during which national needs were thought of as fulfilled by resources allocated collectively and democratically. However, working through foundations, think tanks, sectors of the academy, and the government, corporate elites according to David Dickson and David Noble 'proclaimed a new age of reason while remystifying reality.' This involved a set of 'interrelated'epistemological and ideological imperatives, which are an extrapolation from the noninterference I spoke about earlier. Each of these imperatives is in congruence with the way intellectual and academic 'fields' view themselves internally and across the dividing lines:

1. The rediscovery of the self-regulating market, the wonders of free enterprise, and the classical liberal attack on government regulation of the economy, all in the name of liberty.
2. The reinvention of the idea of progress, now cast in terms of 'innovation' and 'reindustrialization,' and the limitation of expectations and social welfare in the quest for productivity.
3. The attack on democracy, in the name of 'efficiency,' 'manageability,' 'governability,' 'rationality,' and 'competence.'
4. The remystification of science through the promotion of formalized decision methodologies, the restoration of the authority of expertise, and the renewed use of science as legitimation for social policy through deepening industry ties to universities and other 'free' institutions of policy analysis and recommendation.[1]

In other words, (1) says that literary criticism minds its own business and is 'free' to do what it wishes with no community responsibility whatever. Hence at one end of the scale, for instance, is the recent succesful attack on the NEH for funding too many socially determined programs and, at the other end, the proliferation of private critical lanuages with an absurdist bent presided over paradoxically by 'big name professors,' who also extoll the virtues of humanism, pluralism and humane scholarship. Retranslated, (2) has meant that the number of jobs for young graduates has shrunk dramatically as the 'inevitable' result of market forces, which in turn prove the marginality of scholarship that is premised on its own harmless social obsolescence. This has created a demand for sheer innovation and indiscriminate publication (e.g., the sudden increase in advanced critical journals; the departmental need for experts and courses in theory and structuralism), and it has virtually destroyed the career trajectory and social horizons of young people within the system. Imperatives (3) and (4) have meant the recrudescence of strict professionalism for sale to any client, deliberately oblivious of the complicity between the academy, the government and the corporation, decorously silent on the large questions of social, economic and foreign policy.

Very well: if what I have been saying has any validity, then the politics of interpretation demand a dialectical response from a critical consciousness worthy of its name. Instead of noninterference and specialization, there must be *interference,* crossing of borders and obstacles, a determined attempt to generalize exactly at those points where generalizations seem impossible to make. One of the first interferences to be ventured, then is a crossing from literature, which is supposed to be subjective and powerless, into those exactly parallel realms, now covered by journalism and the production of information, that employ representation but are supposed to be objective and powerful. Here we have a superb guide in John Berger, in whose most recent work there is the basis of a major critique of modern representation. Berger suggests that if we regard photography as coeval in its origins with sociology and positivism (and I would add the classic realistic novel), we see that

> what they shared was the hope that observable quantifiable facts, recorded by experts, would constitute the proven truth that humanity required. Precision would replace metaphysics; planning would resolve conflicts. What happened, instead, was that the way was opened to a view of the world in which everything and everybody could be reduced to a factor in a calculation, and the calculation was profit.[2]

Much of the world today is represented in this way: as the McBride Commission Report has it, a tiny handful of large and powerful oligarchies control about ninety percent of the world's information and communication flows. This domain, staffed by experts and media executives, is, as Herbert Schiller and others have shown, affiliated to an even smaller number of governments, at the very same time that the rhetoric of objectivity, balance, realism and freedom covers what is being done. And for the most part, such consumer items as 'the news' – a euphemism for ideological images of the world that determine political reality for a vast majority of the world's population – hold forth, untouched by interfering secular and critical minds, who for all sorts of obvious reasons are not hooked into the systems of power.

This is not the place, nor is there time, to advance a fully articulated program of interference. I can only suggest in conclusion that we need to think about breaking out of the disciplinary ghettos in which as intellectuals we have been confined, to reopen the blocked social processes ceding objective representation (hence power) of the world to a small coterie of experts and their clients, to consider that the audience for literacy is not a closed circle of three thousand professional critics but the community of human beings living in society, and to regard social reality in a secular rather than a mystical mode, despite all the protestations about realism and objectivity.

Two concrete tasks – again adumbrated by Berger – strike me as particularly useful. One is to use the visual faculty (which also happens to be dominated by visual media such as television, news photography and commercial film, all of them fundamentally immediate, 'objective' and ahistorical) to restore the nonsequential energy of lived historical memory and subjectivity as fundamental components of meaning in representation. Berger calls this an alternative use of photograph: using photomontage to tell other stories than the official sequential or ideological ones produced by institutions of power. (Superb examples are Sarah Graham-Brown's photoessay *The Palestinians and Their Society* and Susan Meisalas's *Nicaragua*.) Second is opening the culture to experiences of the Other which have remained 'outside' (and have been repressed or framed in a context of confrontational hostility) the norms manufactured by 'insiders.' An excellent example is Malek Alloula's *Le Harem colonial,* a study of early twentieth-century postcards and photographs of Algerian harem women. The pictorial capture of colonized people by colonizer, which signifies power, is reenacted by a young Algerian sociologist, Alloula, who sees his own fragmented history in the pictures, then reinscribes this history in his text as the result of understanding and making that intimate experience intelligible for an audience of modern European readers.

In both instances, finally, we have the recovery of a history hitherto either misrepresented or rendered invisible. Stereotypes of the Other have always been connected to political actualities of one sort or another, just as the truth of lived communal (or personal) experience has often been totally sublimated in official narratives, institutions and ideologies. But in having attempted – and perhaps even successfully accomplishing – this recovery, there is the crucial next phase: connecting these more politically vigilant forms of interpretation to an ongoing political and social praxis. Short of making that connection, even the best-intentioned and the cleverest interpretive activity is bound to sink back into the murmur of mere prose. For to move from interpretation to its politics is in large measure to go from undoing to doing, and this, given the currently accepted divisions between criticism and art, is risking all the discomfort of a great unsettlement in ways of seeing and doing. One must refuse to believe, however, that the comforts of specialized habits can be so seductive as to keep us all in our assigned places.

Notes

1   David Dickson and David Noble, 'By Force of Reason: The Politics of Science and Policy,' in *The Hidden Election,* ed. Thomas Ferguson and Joel Rogers (New York, Pantheon, 1981), p. 267.
2   John Berger, 'Another Way of Telling,' *Journal of Social Reconstruction* 1 (January–March 1980): 64.

Section 4

Criticism and Knowledge

One of the most fierce and vigorously fought critical debates in the last decade has been what is sometimes referred to as the 'culture wars' and sometimes the 'science wars'. Since the 1960s, critiques of scientific method (beginning with the work of Gadamer and Kuhn, already considered), developments in science itself (particularly in the areas of molecular biology and quantum physics), and postmodern and constructivist assaults on epistemology, have seemed to erode the boundaries between the sciences and the humanities, with implications for the discipline of literary criticism. Some commentators have viewed postmodernism as an attempt to end the epistemic hegemony of science. In the so-called 'culture wars', a triumphalist postmodern aestheticism encounters perhaps its most ferocious rival yet: a rejuvenated scientism unabashed by the earlier romantic–humanist critique of science as value and armed and ready to take on the more radical postmodern assault on science as knowledge. (Not only can science explain all the things it has always explained, science can now give a 'true' account of all those things that the humanities has floundered over with its imprecise and inadequate vocabularies: things like mind, consciousness, values, ethics, beauty.) The ire of scientists such as Lewis Wolpert, Richard Dawkins and Alan Sokal has been drawn not so much by the on-going and value-oriented Romantic–hermeneutic critique of scientism (reaching back as far as Schiller's indictment of Newtonian mechanics as plunging the world into a monotonous round of ends), but most emphatically by the far more radical postmodern critique of the epistemological foundations of science.

Postmodernists speak of the 'aestheticization' of science, rhetoricians have pointed out the metaphorical nature of scientific language. The now infamous volume of the journal *Social Text* (1996) provoked impassioned debate about the intrusion of literary theorists onto the terrain of science and prompted defences of scientific 'objectivity' and 'scientific realism' as the true base of knowledge against what is regarded by scientists as the dangerous and decadent creeping nihilisms and relativisms of contemporary theory. The immediate controversy in 1996 grew out of an article, by the mathematical physicist Alan Sokal, written as a hoax in order to expose what its author regarded as the intellectual pretension and ideological bias of the journal. The article claimed to 'prove' mathematically the source of a number of theoretically fashionable concepts (such as uncertainty, indeterminacy, non-linearity) and pastiched the kind of arguments put forward by theorists like Lyotard who claim the end of scientific realism and the demise of certain knowledge. Sokal's aim was to expose the hubris of literary theory in its attempts to displace the classic scientific model of knowledge with a model derived from the aesthetic, but claimed by such theorists to be derived from the new sciences themselves. What enrages Sokal is that such arguments are not made as whimsical and poetic speculations, but are claimed in the more narrowly epistemological spirit of science. For him, their effect is to erode all distinction between science and fiction and plunge us into a condition of dangerous anti-rationalism.

Sokal's aim was partly to resist the recently formulated rainbow coalition of anti-science radicals who have been drawn less from the ranks of literary criticism than from those of sociology and social theory, but also to counter what he sees as a pervasive drift towards epistemological relativism which has affected all the human sciences, literary criticism included. Sociologists of science persuaded of the cultural situatedness of all knowledge have recently joined forces with more traditional philosophers of science who have sought to demonstrate the unverifiability of the reality affirmed by scientific claims. From this perspective, scientific theory begins to look indistinguishable from literary theory: scientific theory, it is argued, may be empirically adequate without necessarily describing the world at all. Scientific discourses, moreover, use models and metaphors from everyday language which are inevitably already imbued with ideological constructions and slants. The objectivity of science is at best a flattering illusion which convinces us of our human autonomy by affirming our instrumental power over nature. At worst, it is another and powerful ideological state apparatus whose very rhetoric of truth and understanding and authority preserves our political quietude by conferring on scientists the status of priestly diviners.

What has shifted in this 'two cultures' debate about the relations between the humanities and the sciences is a move from the Romantic critique inherited by F.R. Leavis, which opposed the embodied experience of art and humanistic criticism to the abstract calculations of science, to a postmodern critique where science itself is aestheticized and where both science and art, mathematics and literary criticism, quantum theory and aesthetic theory, are brought into the same arena of ideological critique. All deny the possibility of transcendental experience or of an epistemological 'view from nowhere'. Scientific knowledge can be no more 'objective' than aesthetic knowledge; just as criticism constructs the 'literariness'of the text, so science constructs the shape of nature. If literary theory cannot be tested against theory-independent facts, neither can scientific theory. It is impossible to offer final proof that any scientific theory is actually in contact with what it purports to explain. Contexts of discovery which shape knowledge and questions of intentionality now enter into the scientific account. Fictionality moves from the demesne of literature to that of science. If logic cannot proceed from the empirical data to the postulates of a deductively formulated theory, but only vice versa, then the same data can be used to support competing theories; we cannot say that one theory is more true than another.

For Richard Rorty, then, there is no difference between protons and poems or between what he refers to in the essay reprinted here as texts and lumps. Scientists, like poets, like literary critics, all impose their fictions upon the world (though at least poets acknowledge what they are about).

Modern literary theory has stood in a relation of reciprocal influence to the sociology of science over these questions of epistemology. In many ways, it is not surprising that literary criticism has been so receptive to the constructivist turn. As we have seen, there always has been a problem for an increasingly professionalized discipline in the disjunction between a 'scientific' model of criticism and scholarship which urged the critic, on the one hand, to treat the text 'objectively' as an object in the world and, on the other, to recognize the 'autonomy' of art, to regard the text as the product of a unique intentional consciousness and occupying its own ontological space. There is bound to be a problem about reducing consciousness to an entity available to the procedures of 'objective' research. So the relativist and constructivist turn in epistemology becomes attractive not only because it suggests that aesthetic knowing is the only valid kind of knowledge, but also because it does away with the difficulty of trying to resolve the tension between idealist and empiricist currents within the discipline of literary criticism itself as it has developed within the modern academy. Rorty's pragmatist argument is also that of Stanley Fish: knowledge is about usefulness, is always construction within the framework of the knowledge community.

The two essays reprinted here by Rorty and Haraway represent different facets of this debate and both have been immensely influential. They have been chosen not so much to represent the debate in terms of traditional humanist (believing that both art and science 'know' the world but in different ways) versus postmodernist nihilist (there is no knowledge, no truth, no self), positions, both of which have become caricatures of themselves of late. Rorty and Haraway stand on the same 'turf' in the culture wars but their orientations are different: Rorty's pragmatism is of the textualist variety, but in the service of a concept of 'solidarity'which is drawn from the bourgeois–liberal tradition he openly proclaims to be his own; Haraway's more fully-fledged postmodern irony is put in the service of a utopian and apocalyptic imagination which foresees a future in which the entire organicist base of human understanding has eroded and been abandoned. She imagines a future already embryonic, when humans and machines and animals are no longer distinct categories, and when feminism can truly embrace the new technologies which will make this possible. Feminism is poised to embrace a postmodern science where text and real are truly indistinguishable in a reinvented 'cyborg' world, a world beyond nature.

Although Rorty's textualism puts him broadly in the postmodern camp in that he believes that the world can be changed and improved through the manipulation of vocabularies, he has always been critical of the kind of post-structuralism evident in Haraway's essay. Rorty views this kind of ironic idealism (as he sees it) as a distraction from that piecemeal, practical social reform which has been the real engine of progress. For Rorty, there is a need for publicly shared vocabularies, a linguistic *sensus communis* which can create and maintain a detheoreticized sense of community. Haraway's textualism is stronger, colonizing science itself and not just philosophy of science, and is put in the service of a radical politics which aims to break down and abandon older forms of social consensus which have always, in her view, functioned as categories of exclusion. Her argument is that the very foundation of the new sciences is itself radically textual: genetic coding, artificial intelligence, artificial life, have created a world in which we are on the verge of destroying completely the traditional dualisms of mind and body, animal and human, fact and value, male and female, human and machine, text and real. This new 'textualist' science promises to destroy forever the old organicist picture of nature and the belief in the desirability of organic wholes. Haraway's essay calls on feminists to recognize the liberatory potential in this newest picture of nature, to seize the potential of new technologies to destroy the old categories and to resist the tendency to fall back on old myths of unity and consensus (like Rorty's). Science now offers the capacity to complete that liberation of the 'Eternal Feminine' begun by cultural critics such as de Beauvoir in the middle of the last century.

46 | Richard Rorty,

'Texts and Lumps' in *Objectivity, Relativism and Truth* (1991), pp. 78–92

Like most other disciplines, literary criticism swings back and forth between a desire to do small-scale jobs well and carefully and a desire to paint the great big picture. At the moment it is at the latter pole, and is trying to be abstract, general, and theoretical. This has resulted in literary critics taking more of an interest in philosophy, and philosophers returning the compliment. This exchange has been useful to both groups. I think, however, that there is a danger that literary critics seeking help from philosophy may take philosophy a bit too seriously. They will do this if they think of philosophers as supplying 'theories of meaning' or 'theories of the nature of interpretation', as if 'philosophical research' into such topics had recently yielded interesting new 'results'.

Philosophy too swings back and forth between a self-image modeled on that of Kuhnian 'normal science', in which small-scale problems get definitively solved one at a time, and a self-image modeled on that of

Kuhnian 'revolutionary science', in which all the old philosophical problems are swept away as pseudoproblems and philosophers busy themselves redescribing the phenomena in a new vocabulary. The field presently called 'literary theory' has profited primarily from the latter sort of philosophy (which has lately been fashionable in France and Germany). Unfortunately, however, it has often tried to describe itself as if it were profiting from philosophy of the former sort. It has employed the scientistic rhetoric characteristic of the early period of analytic philosophy. One often finds critics using sentences beginning 'Philosophy has shown . . .' to formulate a justification for taking a certain favored approach to a literary text, or to literary history, or to literary canon-formation.

I think critics would do better to realize that philosophy is no more likely to produce 'definitive results' (in the sense in which microbiology can show how to create immunity to a certain disease, or nuclear physics how to build a better bomb) than is literary criticism itself. This should not be viewed as undesirable 'softness' on the part of either discipline, but simply as an illustration of the fact that there are lots of areas in which desiderata are not as well agreed upon as they are in medicine or in the munitions industry. It would be better for critics to simply have favorite philosophers (and philosophers to have favorite literary critics)—favorites picked by consonance with their own desiderata. If a literary critic wants to see the great big picture, tell a great big story, then he or she is going to have to engage in the same sort of canon-formation in respect to philosophers as he or she does in respect to novelists or poets or fellow critics. As Geoffrey Hartman sensibly puts it, 'Theory itself is just another text; it does not enjoy a privileged status'.[2]

The need to have a general theory (of something as grand as 'interpretation' or 'knowledge' or 'truth' or 'meaning') is the sort of need which James and Dewey tried to put in perspective by insisting, with Hegel, that theory follows after, rather than being presupposed by, concrete accomplishment. On this pragmatical view, a 'theoretical' style—the 'Aristotelian' style which depends heavily on definitions or the 'Galilean' style which depends on generalizations—is useful principally for pedagogic purposes, to provide succinct formulations of past achievements. When applied to literary criticism, pragmatism offers reasons why critics need not worry about being 'scientific', and why they should not be frightened of the appearance of 'subjectivity' which results from the adoption of an untheoretical, narrative style. It suggests that we neither be afraid of subjectivity nor anxious for methodology, but simply proceed to praise our heroes and damn our villains by making invidious comparisons. It urges that we not try to show that our choice of heroes is imposed upon us by, or underwritten by, antecedently plausible principles. For pragmatists, telling stories about how one's favorite and least favorite literary texts hang together is not to be distinguished from—is simply a species of—the 'philosophical' enterprise of telling stories about the nature of the universe which highlight all the things one likes best and least. The misguided attempt to be 'scientific' is a confusion between a pedagogical device–the device of summarizing the upshot of one's narrative in pithy little formulae–and a method for discovering truth.

In what follows, I shall first offer a general account of pragmatism's view of the nature of truth and of science, in order to fill out the sketch I have just offered. Then I shall turn to the question of what the notion of 'meaning' looks like when seen from a pragmatist point of view. In both sections, I shall be urging that we avoid Dilthey's suggestion that we set up distinct parallel metavocabularies, one for the *Geistes*–and one for the *Naturwissenschaften*. We should instead assume that if a philosophical doctrine is not plausible with respect to the analysis of lumps by chemists, it probably does not apply to the analysis of texts by literary critics either.

Pragmatists say that the traditional notion that 'truth is correspondence to reality' is an uncashable and outworn metaphor. Some true statements–like 'the cat is on the mat'–can be paired off with other chunks of reality so as to associate parts of the statement with parts of the chosen chunk. Most true statements–like 'the cat is *not* on the mat' and 'there are transfinite numbers' and 'pleasure is better than pain'–cannot. Furthermore, we will be no better off even if we construct a metaphysical scheme which pairs off something in the world with each part of *every* true statement, and some first-order relation with every relevant metalinguistic relation. For we should still be faced with the question of whether the first-order language we use *itself* 'corresponds to reality'. That is, we should still wonder whether talk of cats or numbers or goodness is the right way to break up the universe into chunks, whether our language cuts reality at the joints. The pragmatists conclude that the intuition that truth is correspondence should be extirpated rather than explicated.[3] On this view, the notion of reality as having a 'nature' to which it is our duty to correspond is simply one more variant of the notion that the gods can be placated by chanting the right words. The notion that some one among the languages mankind has used to deal with the universe is the one the universe prefers–the one which cuts things at the joints–was a pretty conceit. But by now it has become too shopworn to serve any purpose.

This line of argument about truth is usually met by changing the subject from truth to factuality. Science, it is said, deals with hard facts, and other areas of culture should either imitate, or confess their inability to imitate, the scientists' respect for brute factuality. Here the pragmatist invokes his second line of argument. He offers an analysis of the nature of science which construes the reputed hardness of facts as an artifact produced by our choice of language game. We construct games in which a player loses or wins if something definite and uncontrollable happens. In some Mayan ball game, perhaps, the team associated with a lunar deity automatically loses, and is executed, if the moon is eclipsed during play. In poker, you know you've won if you're dealt an ace-high straight flush. In the laboratory, a hypothesis may be discredited if the litmus paper turns blue, or the mercury fails to come up to a certain level. A hypothesis is agreed to have been 'verified by the real world' if a computer spits out a certain number.

The hardness of fact in all these cases is simply the hardness of the previous agreements within a community about the consequences of a certain event. The same hardness prevails in morality or literary criticism if, and only if, the relevant community is equally firm about who loses and who wins. Some communities do not take cheating at cards, or intertribal marriage, too seriously; others may make one or the other decisive for their treatment of their fellow humans. Some of Stanley Fish's 'interpretive communities' throw you out if you interpret 'Lycidas' as 'really' about intertextuality. Others will take you in only if you do so.

This pragmatist analysis of the hardness of data may seem to confuse the causal, physical force of the event with the merely social force of the consequences of the event. When Galileo saw the moons of Jupiter through his telescope, it might be said, the impact on his retina was 'hard' in the relevant sense, even though its consequences were, to be sure, different for different communities. The astronomers of Padua took it as merely one more anomaly which had somehow to be worked into a more or less Aristotelian cosmology, whereas Galileo's admirers took it as shattering the crystalline spheres once and for all. But the datum *itself*, it might be argued, is utterly real quite apart from the interpretation it receives.

The pragmatist meets this point by differentiating himself from the idealist. He agrees that there is such a thing as brute physical resistance – the pressure of light waves on Galileo's eyeball, or of the stone on Dr. Johnson's boot. But he sees no way of transferring this nonlinguistic brutality to *facts*, to the truth of sentences. The way in which a blank takes on the form of the die which stamps it has no analogy to the relation between the truth of a sentence and the event which the sentence is about. When the die hits the blank something causal happens, but as many *facts* are brought into the world as there are languages for describing that causal transaction. As Donald Davidson says, causation is not under a description, but explanation is. Facts are hybrid entities; that is, the causes of the assertibility of sentences include both physical stimuli and our antecedent choice of response to such stimuli. To say that we must have respect for facts is just to say that we must, if we are to play a certain language game, play by the rules. To say that we must have respect for unmediated causal forces is pointless. It is like saying that the blank must have respect for the impressed die. The blank has no choice, nor do we.

The philosophical tradition has yearned for a way of approximating the total passivity of the blank. It has seen language as interposed, like a cushion, between us and the world. It has regretted that the diversity of language games, of interpretive communities, permits us so much variation in the way in which we respond to causal pressures. It would like us to be machines for cranking out true statements in 'direct' response to the pressures of reality upon our organs. Pragmatists, by contrast, think the metaphor of language as cushioning the effect of causal forces is not one which can fruitfully be spun out any further. But if that metaphor goes, so does the traditional notion of an ideal language, or of the ideal empirical theory, as an ultrathin cushion which translates the brutal thrust of reality into statement and action as directly as possible.

The metaphors which the pragmatist suggests we put in the place of all this masochistic talk about hardness and directness are those of linguistic behavior as tool-using, of language as a way of grabbing hold of causal forces and making them do what we want, altering ourselves and our environment to suit our aspirations. The pragmatist thus exalts spontaneity at the cost of receptivity, as his realist opponent did the reverse. In doing so, he shows his indebtedness to Romanticism and Absolute Idealism. But the pragmatist does not try to justify his metaphors by philosophical argument – by claiming to have made some new discovery about the nature of the universe or of the universe or of knowledge which shows that the nature of truth is quite different than had been thought. He abjures Aristotelian appeals to the nature of this and that. Instead, like Dewey, he tells stories about how the course of Western thought has been stultified by the metaphors he dislikes. His own technique in philosophy is that same Homeric, narrative style which he recommends to the literary critic. His recommendation to the critic is thus not grounded in a theory about literature or about criticism, but in a narrative whose details he hopes the literary critic will help him fill in. The pragmatist philosopher has a story to tell about his favorite, and least favored, books – the texts of, for example, Plato, Descartes, Hegel, Nietzsche, Dewey, and Russell. He would like other people to have stories to tell about other sequences of texts, other genres – stories which will fit together with his. His appeal is not to the latest philosophical discoveries about the nature of science or language, but to the existence of views on these matters which chime with certain views other people (for example, contemporary critics looking for the big picture) hold about other matters.

In what I have said so far I have been concurring with Walter Michaels, whose work links American pragmatism with a Fish-like account of the nature of interpretation. Michaels sums up this attitude by saying, 'Our beliefs are not obstacles between us and meaning, they are what makes meaning possible in the first place.[4] My account of pragmatism is designed to show that this claim can best be seen as a corollary of the more general claim that our beliefs, our theories, our languages, our concepts – everything which Kant located on the side of 'spontaneity' – are not to be seen as defenses against the hardness of data, much less veils between us and objects, but as ways of putting the causal forces of the universe to work for us. In the case of texts, these forces merely print little replicas on our retinas. From there on it is up to us to make something out of these replicas by telling a story about their relation to other texts, or the intentions of its author, or what makes life worth living, or the events of the century in which the poem was written, or the events of our own century, or the incidents of our own lives, or whatever else seems appropriate in a given situation. The question of whether any of these stories *really is* appropriate is like the question of whether Aristotelian hylomorphism or Galilean mathematization is *really* appropriate for describing planetary motion. From the point of view of a pragmatist philosophy of science, there is no point to such a question. The only issue is whether describing the planets in one language or the other lets us tell stories about them which will fit together with all the other stories we want to tell.

Anybody who argues from a pragmatist philosophy of science to a Fish-like philosophy of literary interpretation is, however, going to have to account for the *apparent* difference between chemistry and criticism. There *seems* to be a difference between the hard objects with which chemists deal and the soft ones with which literary critics deal. This apparent difference is the occasion for all the neo-Diltheyan theories which insist on a distinction between explanation and understanding, and all the neo-Saussurean theories which insist upon a distinction between lumps and texts. The pragmatist objects to both distinctions, but he has to admit that there is a prima facie difference to be accounted for. For when chemists say that gold is insoluble in nitric acid, there's an end on it. Yet when critics say that the problem of *The Turn of the Screw*, or *Hamlet*, or whatever, is insoluble with the apparatus of New, or psychoanalytic, or semiotic criticism, this is just an invitation to the respective critical schools to distill even more powerful brews.

Kant's idealist way of dealing with this difference has become canonical. He thought that hard objects were ones which we constituted according to *rules*–rules laid down by unavoidable concepts wired into our transcendental faculties–whereas soft objects were those which we constituted without being bound by any rules. This distinction–the transcendental underpinning of the traditional cognitive versus aesthetic distinction–is unsatisfactory for the dialectical reasons offered by Hegel and the evolutionary ones offered by Dewey. One cannot formulate a rule without saying what it would be like to break the rule. As soon as one does so, the question of whether to stick to the rule becomes of interest. When, with Hegel, we begin to view rules as historical stages or cultural products, we blur the Kantian distinction between rule-governed and playful behavior. But whereas Hegel has to see natural science as a rather early and primitive form of Spirit's self-consciousness, Dewey can see chemistry and literary criticism and paleontology and politics and philosophy all striding along together– equal comrades with diverse interests, distinguished *only* by these interests, not by cognitive status. James and Dewey appreciated Kant's point that you can't compare your beliefs with something that isn't a belief to see if they correspond. But they sensibly pointed out that doesn't mean that there is nothing out there to have beliefs *about*. The *causal* independence of the gold or the text from the inquiring chemist or critic does not mean that she either can or should perform the impossible feat of stripping her chosen object bare of human concerns, seeing it as it is in itself, and then seeing how our beliefs measure up to it. So Kant's distinction between constituting gold by rule-governed synthesis and constituting texts by free and playful synthesis must be discarded.

The pragmatists replace this idealist formulation with a wholehearted acceptance of the brute, inhuman, causal stubbornness of the gold or the text. But they think this should not be confused with, so to speak, an *intentional* stubbornness, an insistence on being *described in a certain way*, its *own way*. The object can, given a prior agreement on a language game, cause us to hold beliefs, but it cannot suggest beliefs for us to hold. It can only do things which our practices will react to with preprogrammed changes in beliefs. So when he is asked to interpret the felt difference between hard objects and soft objects, the pragmatist says that the difference is between the rules of one institution (chemistry) and those of another (literary criticism). He thinks, with Stanley Fish, that 'all facts are institutional, are facts only by virtue of the prior institution of some such [socially conceived dimensions of assessment].[5] The only way to get a noninstitutional fact would be to find a language for describing an object which was as little ours, and as much the object's own, as the object's causal powers. If one gives up that fantasy, no object will appear softer than any other. Rather, some institutions will appear more internally diverse, more complicated, more quarrelsome about ultimate desiderata than others.

So much for the pragmatist's view of truth and of science. I turn now to a discussion of some issues raised by my colleague E. D. Hirsch, Jr. Hirsch has argued for the possibility of objective interpretation by making a distinction between isolating the meaning of a text (a task to which the normal tests of historical objectivity apply) and relating that meaning to something else. The latter activity Hirsch calls finding *significance* in the text, as opposed to finding its *meaning*. I agree with Hirsch that we need some such distinction as this. I also agree with him that, in his words, 'the much-advertised cleavage between thinking in the sciences and the humanities does not exist'.[6] I think he is right in suggesting that philosophy of science and literary theory ought to carry over into each other. But I think that his distinction between 'meaning' and 'significance' is misleading in certain respects. My holistic strategy, characteristic of pragmatism (and in particular of Dewey), is to reinterpret every such dualism as a momentarily convenient blocking-out of regions along a spectrum, rather than as recognition of an ontological, or methodological, or epistemological divide. So I shall construct such a spectrum and use it as a heuristic device for commenting on Hirsch's dualism.

In the table below there is a column for texts and one for lumps, a division which corresponds roughly to things made and things found. Think of a paradigmatic text as something puzzling which was said or written by a member of a primitive tribe, or by Aristotle, or by Blake. Nonlinguistic artifacts, such as pots, are borderline cases of texts. Think of a lump as something which you would bring for analysis to a natural scientist rather than to somebody in the humanities or social sciences – something which might turn out to be, say, a piece of gold or the fossilized stomach of a stegosaurus. A wadded-up plastic bag is a borderline case of a lump. Most philosophical reflection about objectivity – most epistemology and philosophy of science–has concentrated on lumps. Most discussion of interpretation has concentrated on texts. A lot of controversies about the objectivity of interpretation can, I think, be smoothed out by insisting, as far as possible, on the text-lump parallelism. In particular, I think that if one starts from a Kuhnian philosophy of science, one can preserve most of what Hirsch wants to say about validity in interpretation. So I should like to convince Hirsch that his view can be reconciled with the Dewey-Wittgenstein-Davidson-Kuhn sort of pragmatism which I am advocating.

Texts	Lumps
I. The phonetic or graphic features of an inscription (philology is in point here).	I. The sensory appearance and spatio-temporal location of a lump (avoidance of perceptual illusion is in point here).
II. What the author would, under ideal conditions, reply to questions about his inscription which are phrased in terms which he can understand right off the bat.	II. The real essence of the lump which lurks behind its appearances–how God or Nature would describe the lump.
III. What the author would, under ideal conditions, reply to *our* questions about his inscription– questions he would have to be reeducated to understand (think of a Cambridge-educated primitive, an Aristotle who had assimilated Freud and Marx) but which are easily intelligible to a present-day interpretive community.	III. The lump as described by that sector of *our* 'normal' science which specializes in lumps of that sort (for example, a routine analysis performed by a chemist, or routine identification performed by a biologist).
IV. The role of the text in somebody's revolutionary view of the sequence of inscriptions to which the text belongs (including revolutionary suggestions about which sequence that is)–for example, the role of an Aristotle text in Heidegger or a Blake text in Bloom.	IV. The lump as described by a scientific revolutionary, that is, somebody who wants to redo chemistry, or entomol- ogy, or whatever, so that the currently 'normal' chemical analyses or biological taxonomies are revealed as 'mere appearances'.
V. The role of the text in somebody's view of something other than the 'kind' to which the text belongs– for example, its relation to the nature of man, the purpose of my life, the politics of our day, and so forth.	V. The place of the lump, or of that *sort* of lump, in some- body's view of something other than the science to which the lump has been as- signed (for example, the role of gold in the international economy, in sixteenth-century alchemy, in Alberich's fantasy life, my fantasy life, and so forth, as opposed to its role in chemistry).

Numbers II–V under 'texts' can be thought of as four possible meanings of 'meaning'; the same numbers under 'lumps' can be thought of as so many meanings of 'nature'. One can think of the bottom four-fifths of the table as four definitions of each term, arranged in levels. The point which the pragmatist brings over from philosophy of science, the point that conditions his attitude toward questions in literary theory, is his claim that the definition under 'lumps' at Level II is not a useful notion. The *anti* pragmatist in philosophy of science and philosophy of language (for example, Kripke, Boyd) is the philosopher who thinks that there are such things as 'real natures' or 'real essences'. But for the pragmatist, we can only distinguish better and worse nominal essences–more and less useful descriptions of the lump. For him, there is no need for the notion of a convergence of scientific inquiry toward what the lump really, truly, is in itself. So the pragmatist philosopher of science may be tempted to interpret Hirsch's distinction between 'meaning' and 'significance' as a distinction between meaning *in se* and meaning *ad nos*, and to dismiss Hirsch as a belated Aristotelian who has not yet got the word that all essences are nominal.[7]

Such a dismissal would be overhasty. For there obviously *is* something called 'the author's intention' which we can and do use to give sense to Level II in the case of texts, but which we cannot use to give sense to Level II in the case of lumps. The *only* interesting difference between texts and lumps is that we know how to form and defend hypotheses about the author's intentions in the one case but not in the other. Reinterpreting Hirsch's reinterpretation of Vico, I would claim that the fact that Level II makes sense for texts but not for lumps is the kernel of truth in 'Vico's insight that the human realm is genuinely knowable while the realm of nature is not'.[8] I would also claim that the source of realist, antipragmatist philosophy of science is the attempt, characteristic of the Enlightenment, to make 'Nature' do duty for God–the attempt to make natural science a way of conforming to the will of a power not ourselves, rather than simply facilitating our commerce with the things around us. On my account, our ideal of perfect knowledge is the sympathetic knowledge we occasionally have of the state of mind of another person. Realistic epistemologies have been ill-starred attempts to transfer this sort of knowledge to our knowledge of lumps. As Nietzsche said, 'the concept of substance is a consequence of the concept of the subject; not the reverse'.[9] Realistic interpretations of natural science are thus hopeless attempts to make physical science imitate the *Geisteswissenschaften*. But once we give up primitive animism, and the more sophisticated forms of anthropomorphization of nature essayed by Plato and Aristotle, we can admit that the lumps are just whatever it is presently convenient to describe them as–that they have no 'inside' in the way that persons do. So whereas Hirsch wants to make realistic philosophy of science look good in order to make 'meaning' at Level II look good for texts, I want to do the opposite. I want to admit everything Hirsch says about the objective validity of inquiry into meaning (in that sense) in order to make realistic philosophy of science look bad. I want to insist that we *can* have what Hirsch wants at Level II for texts, just in order to ram home the point that we *cannot* have anything of the sort for lumps.

But even though I agree with Hirsch that we can have the same sort of objectivity about the mind of the author as we can have about the chemical composition of a lump, I want to disagree with the way he draws a distinction between meaning and significance. Hirsch defines these terms in the following passage: 'Meaning' refers to the whole verbal meaning of a text, and 'significance' to textual meaning in relation to another context, i.e., another mind, another era, a wider subject matter, an alien system of values, and so on. In other words, 'significance' is textual meaning as related to some context, indeed any context, beyond itself.[10] These definitions permit him to say that 'from the standpoint of knowledge, valid criticism is dependent on valid interpretation',[11] where 'criticism' means the discovery of significance and 'interpretation' the discovery of meaning. These intertwined distinctions are backed up by Hirsch's claim that 'if we could not distinguish a content of consciousness from its contexts, we could not know any object at all in the world'.[12]

From my Wittgensteinian point of view, Hirsch's Husserlian talk of contents of consciousness and of intentional objects can be replaced by talk about our ability to agree on what we are thinking about – that is, to agree on what propositions using the same referring expressions we accept, even while disagreeing about the truth-value of others. With Wittgenstein, I regard talk of 'intuition' (and of 'consciousness' and 'intentionally') as an unnecessary shuffle – incapable of explaining our use of language and unneeded if we take that use as primitive.[13] Pragmatism views knowledge not as a relation between mind and an object, but, roughly, as the ability to get agreement by using persuasion rather than force. From this point of view, the distinction between an object X and the context in which it is put is never more than a distinction between two batches of propositions – roughly, the ones using the word X which are currently presupposed and undoubted, and those which are currently being debated. There is no way to identify an object save by talking about it – putting it in the context of some other things you want to talk about. (This I take to be one of the morals of Wittgenstein's criticism of the idea of ostensive definition.) What we know of both texts and lumps is nothing more than the ways these are related to the other texts and lumps mentioned in or presupposed by the propositions which we use to describe them. At Level I a text of Aristotle is just the thing which is found on a certain page, has this visual form when printed in that font, and so on. At Level II the meaning of a text of Aristotle is whatever, for example, an un-reeducated Aristotle would say about it. At Level III it is what somebody like Werner Jaeger says about it; at level IV it is what, for example, Heidegger says about it; at Level V it is, for example, what I am saying about it here.

It is a mistake to ask what it is that is the *same* at each level, as if we were in quest of an enduring substrate of changing descriptions. All that is needed to make communication and persuasion, and thus knowledge, possible is the linguistic know-how necessary to move from level to level. An account of the acquisition of that know-how does not require that we postulate an object – the very text itself, or the true meaning of the text, or the very lump itself, or the real essence of the lump – which is present to consciousness at each level. All that is required is that agreement should be obtainable about what we are talking about – and this just means agreement on a reasonable number of propositions using the relevant term. Propositions at *any* level will do the job. The epistemological tradition common to Hirsch and to the 'theory of semantic autonomy' (which Hirsch attributes to the New Critics and the deconstructionists) insists that one of these levels has to be picked out as 'what we are *really* talking about' at each of the other levels. Both insist that knowledge of meaning at that level is the foundation of discussion at other levels. But this common doctrine is, it seems to me, the analogue of the doctrine common to phenomenalistic empiricism and to the current realistic reaction against phenomenalism – namely, the doctrine that either Level I (for phenomenalism) or Level II (for realism) is privileged (in the case of lumps) as that which 'determines reference'. From a pragmatist angle, this whole notion of privileging a level and putting it forward as a foundation of inquiry is one more unhappy attempt to save the notion of truth as correspondence. Hirsch and his opponents are both too preoccupied with the distinctive textuality of texts, just as both Kripke and his opponents are too preoccupied with the distinctive lumpishness of lumps. Rather than trying to locate sameness, we should dissolve both texts and lumps into nodes within transitory webs of relationships.

Criticism of attempts to privilege levels has, unfortunately, given rise to a kind of silly relativism which says that the views of idiosyncratic nature mystics about lumps are somehow 'on a par with' the views of professors of chemistry (as in Feyerabend) or that free-association interpretations of texts are 'on a par with' ordinary philological or historic ones. All that 'on a par with' means in such contexts is 'epistemologically on a par'. So interpreted, the claim is true but trivial. Anybody, no matter how kooky he sounds, may, for all we know merely on *epistemological* grounds, be the originator of a brilliant new account of the meanings of some texts or the natures of some lumps. Time will tell, but epistemology won't – nor will philosophy of science, nor semiotics, nor any other theory which purports to give a taxonomy of all possible bright new ideas, all possible futures. We had, after all, to dream up a brand new philosophy of science to take care of Galileo and his friends, and a whole new aesthetics to take care of Duchamp and *his* friends. In the future we shall have to redo our narratives of how scientific theories or paintings or poems or literary essays fit together just as often as somebody does something so original and striking that it won't fit into the stories we have been accustomed to tell.

The recent prevalence of what I have called 'silly relativism' – the bad inference from 'no epistemological difference' to 'no objective criterion of choice' – has led writers like Hirsch to try to form general theories of interpretation, theories which will help us retain the idea of 'the right interpretation of the text' as opposed to that of a 'good interpretation for certain purposes'. I agree with Fish that the latter notion is all we need, and I do not see, *pace* Hirsch, that a meaning at level II has to be assigned to a text before we can assign meanings at other levels. I think of objectivity as a matter of ability to achieve agreement on whether a particular set of desiderata has or has not been satisfied. So I think that we can have objective knowledge at any level without necessarily having it at any other.

In the preceding discussion of Hirsch I have tried to suggest that philosophy of language and epistemology not be taken as seriously as both he and his opponents take them. I do not think philosophers have discovered or will discover something about the nature of knowledge or language or intentionality or reference which is going to make life startlingly different for critics or historians or anthropologists. They do not have independent expertise, they just have stories which can be used to complement or buttress other stories. A discipline swinging toward atomism, for example, will want atomistic theories of meaning, and one swinging toward holism will want holistic theories. I agree with Geoffrey Hartman that we should not try very hard to separate philosophy from literary criticism, nor the figure of the philosopher from that of the critic. The way in which Derrida, Hartman, Bloom, and de Man weave together 'literary' and 'philosophical' texts and considerations, disregarding the frontiers between the traditional genres, seems to me just the right way to proceed. This is because I think the test of philosophical truth consists neither in 'correct analyses' of individual concepts (for example, 'meaning', 'intentionality') nor in the internal coherence among hundreds of such analyses linked together in a philosophical system, but only in the coherence of such a system with the rest of culture, a culture which one hopes will continue to be as *ondoyant et divers* as is that of the Western democracies at the present time.

This means that the test of a philosophical theory of justice or meaning or truth (or, for that matter, of philosophy) is how well it coheres with the best work currently being done in, for example, both biochemistry and literary criticism. Precisely because philosophy deals with concepts which are used all over the place – places where people are analyzing texts as well as those where they are analyzing lumps – it is not in a position to lay down the law to any of them. The idea that philosophy is a matter of give and take with the 'hard' sciences is familiar enough. The idea that the give-and-take extends to softer areas, combined with skepticism about the hard/soft distinction, begins with Hegel and is, to my mind, best developed in Dewey's naturalized Hegelianism. This idea is resisted by people on both sides of the artificial boundary drawn by Dilthey (a boundary pencilled in, alas, by Hegel, in his own distinction between Nature and Spirit – the distinction which Dewey did his best to blur). On the 'lump' side (a side where one finds many 'analytic' philosophers), it is still widely believed, with Quine, that 'philosophy of [fairly hard] science is philosophy enough'. On the 'text' side (where one finds a lot of 'Continental' philosophers) it is still widely believed that it would be simplemindedly 'positivist'–neglectful of the textuality of texts–to think that the same battery of concepts will work on both sides. But recently both 'Analytic' and 'Continental' philosophers have been suggesting that, once the holism common to Quine and Gadamer is pushed along a few more steps, it cannot confine itself to one side of the text/lump distinction, but blurs that distinction. This seems to me the upshot of work by, for example, Donald Davidson and Mary Hesse on one side of the Channel and Lorenz Krüger and Wolf Lepenies on the other. If this work is followed up, then the French and the German philosophers might stop using 'positivism' as a bogeyman to frighten their students, and the British and American philosophers might be able to stop giggling nervously at the mention of the word 'hermeneutics'.

In this essay I have been citing lots of debatable philosophical views – Davidson-like views of meaning, Kuhn-like views of science, Dennett-like views of intentionality–in order to support something like Fish's debatable view of literary interpretation. I think the degree of debatability is about the same on both sides of the philosophy/criticism divide, and that if literary theorists recognize this they may be able to make a freer and more flexible use of philosophical texts, rather than treating them as lumps to be swallowed or spit out. They could do so by getting in on the philosophical arguments rather than assuming that specialized, technical, philosophical research will produce something comparable to an assayer's report.

If this shift in attitude became general, it would help us to accept Hartman's view that literary criticism is as respectable and nonparasitic a genre as the lyric, or as the contributions to *Chemical Abstracts*. It might also help us see that critics are no more or less in need of a 'general theory of interpretation' than poets are of aesthetics, or chemists of philosophy of science. The Deweyan pragmatism I am preaching develops this holistic way of seeing things by reclassifying culture in terms of genres, as opposed to 'subject matters' and 'methods'. The tradition asked itself what joints the world wanted to be cut at and what methods were suitable for examining the various disjointed bits. Pragmatism treats every such division of the world into 'subject matters' as an experiment, designed to see if we can get what we want at a certain historical moment by using a certain language.

Each new language creates or modifies a genre–that is, a sequence of texts, the later members of which take earlier members into account. These sequences may intertwine–as do, for example, poetry and criticism, or science and the history of science, or criticism and philosophy, or criticism and the history of criticism. But there are no rules for whether they should or shouldn't intertwine–no necessities lying in the nature of a subject or a method. There is nothing general and epistemological to be said about how the contributors to the various genres should conduct themselves. Nor is there any ranking of these disciplines according to degrees or kinds of truth. There is, in short, nothing to be said about the relation of these genres to 'the world', only things to be said about their relations to each other. Further, there are no ahistorical things to be said about the latter sort of relations. There is no synoptic view of culture which is more than a narrative account of how various cultures managed to get to where they now are. All of us who want big broad pictures are contributing to such an account. If we could see ourselves *as* doing that, then we would worry less about having general principles which justify our procedures. Pragmatism declines to provide us with such principles. But it does tell a story about why we thought we needed such principles, and it offers some suggestions about what a culture might be like in which we did *not* think this.

Notes

1 See my 'The Historiography of Philosophy: Four Genres', *in Philosophy in History: Essays in the Historiography of Philosophy*, ed. Richard Rorty, J.B. Schneewind, and Quentin Skinner (Cambridge, 1984), for a defense of the claim that *Geistesgeschichte*, because of its role in creating canons, has taken over in our culture the role that philosophical systems (of the sort exemplified by Leibniz and Kant) had played earlier.

2 Geoffrey Hartman, *Criticism in the Wilderness* (New Haven, 1980), p. 242.

3 See my 'Pragmatism, Davidson and Truth'. I argue there that Davidson's holism in the theory of meaning coincides with the outcome of pragmatism, once pragmatism renounces the attempt to define *true* (by, for example, invoking the Peircean notion of the 'ideal end of inquiry').

4 Walter Michaels, 'Saving the Text', *Modern Language Notes*, 93 (1978), 780. See also Jeffrey Stout, 'What Is the Meaning of a Text? *New Literary History*, 14 (1982), 1–12.

5 Stanley Fish, *Is There a Text in This Class?* (Cambridge, Mass., 1980), p. 198. Of course, neither the gold nor the text is institutional when considered as a locus of causal power – to resist the attacks of an acid, or to cause certain patterns to appear on the retina. Using a causal vocabulary we can say that the same object is the stimulus for manifold uses of language. But as soon as we ask for *facts* about the object, we are asking how the object should be described is a particular language, and that language is an institution. The fact that the same object is commented on by many different communities does not, *pace* Richard Wollheim's criticism of Fish, show that the object can help us decide which community to belong to.

6 E.D. Hirsch, Jr., *Validity in Interpretation* (New Haven, 1967), p. 264.

7 For discussion of the realism-pragmatism issue in the philosophy of science, see, e.g., W.H. Newton-Smith, *The Rationality of Science* (London, 1981), and a useful collection of essays on Kuhn, *Paradigms and Revolutions*, ed. Gary Gutting (Notre Dame, 1980). The best recent statement of the pragmatist case is Hilary Putnam's *Reason, Truth, and History* (Cambridge, 1981).

8 Hirsch, *Validity in Interpretation*, p. 273.

9. Friedrich Nietzsche, *The Will to Power*, tr. Walter Kaufmann (New York, 1967), par. 485.

10 E.D. Hirsch, Jr., *Aims of Interpretation* (Chicago, 1976), p. 3.

11 Hirsch, *Validity in Interpretation*, p. 162.

12 Hirsch, *Aims of Interpretation*, p. 3.

13 Whether one can be so blithe about consciousness and intentionality is a matter of dispute between, for example, Daniel Dennett and John Searle. I defend Dennett against Searle in 'Contemporary Philosophy of Mind' and 'Comments on Dennett', and Dennett demurs from some parts of my defense in 'Comments on Rorty', all in *Synthèse*, 53 (1982). A related dispute is how seriously to take the notion of

'reference'. Kripke is the best example of a philosopher who takes it very seriously. For the anti-Kripke case, see Donald Davidson, 'Reality Without Reference', in his *Inquiries into Truth and Interpretation* (Oxford: Oxford University Press, 1984); Putnam, *Reason, Truth, and History*; and my 'Is There a Problem about Fictional Discourse?' in *Consequences of Pragmatism* (Minneapolis, 1982).

47 | Donna Haraway,

'A Manifesto for Cyborgs: Science, Technology and Socialist Feminism in the 1980s', 'in *Feminism/Postmodernism*, L. Nicholson ed., (1990), pp. 190–204; 219–20; 223

An Ironic Dream of a Common Language for Women in the Integrated Circuit

This chapter is an effort to build an ironic political myth faithful to feminism, socialism, and materialism. Perhaps more faithful as blasphemy is faithful, than as reverent worship and identification. Blasphemy has always seemed to require taking things very seriously. I know no better stance to adopt from within the secular-religious, evangelical traditions of U.S. politics, including the politics of socialist feminism. Blasphemy protects one from the Moral Majority within, while still insisting on the need for community. Blasphemy is not apostasy. Irony is about contradictions that do not resolve into larger wholes, even dialectically, about the tension of holding incompatible things together because both or all are necessary and true. Irony is about humor and serious play. It is also a rhetorical strategy and a political method, one I would like to see more honored within socialist feminism. At the center of my ironic faith, my blasphemy, is the image of the cyborg.

A cyborg is a cybernetic organism, a hybrid of machine and organism, a creature of social reality as well as a creature of fiction. Social reality is lived social relations, our most important political construction, a world-changing fiction. The international women's movements have constructed 'Women's experience', as well as uncovered or discovered this crucial collective object. This experience is a fiction and fact of the most crucial, political kind. Liberation rests on the construction of the consciousness, the imaginative apprehension, of oppression, and so of possibility. The cyborg is a matter of fiction and lived experience that changes what counts as women's experience in the late twentieth century. This is a struggle over life and death, but the boundary between science fiction and social reality is an optical illusion.

Contemporary science fiction is full of cyborgs – creatures simultaneously animal and machine, who populate worlds ambiguously natural and crafted. Modern medicine is also full of cyborgs, of couplings between organism and machine, each conceived as coded devices, in an intimacy and with a power that was not generated in the history of sexuality. Cyborg 'sex' restores some of the lovely replicative baroque of ferns and invertebrates (such nice organic prophylactics against heterosexism). Cyborg replication is uncoupled from organic reproduction. Modern production seems like a dream of cyborg colonization of work, a dream that makes the nightmare to Taylorism seem idyllic. Modern war is a cyborg orgy, coded by C^3 I, command-control-communication-intelligence, an $84 billion item in 1984's U.S. defense budget. I am making an argument for the cyborg as a fiction mapping our social and bodily reality and as an imaginative resource suggesting some very fruitful couplings. Foucault's biopolitics is a flaccid premonition of cyborg politics, a very open field.

By the late twentieth century, our time, a mythic time, we are all chimeras, theorized and fabricated hybrids of machine and organism; in short, we are cyborgs. The cyborg is our ontology; it gives us our politics. The cyborg is a condensed image of both imagination and material reality, the two joined centers structuring any possibility of historical transformation. In the traditions of Western science and politics – the tradition of racist, male-dominant capitalism; the tradition of progress; the tradition of the appropriation of nature as resource for the productions of culture; the tradition of reproduction of the self from the reflections of the other – the relation between organism and machine has been a border war. The stakes in the border war have been the territories of production, reproduction, and imagination. This chapter is an argument for pleasure in the confusion of boundaries and for responsibility in their construction. It is also an effort to contribute to socialist-feminist culture and theory in a postmodernist, nonnaturalist mode and in the utopian tradition of imagining a world without gender, which is perhaps a world without genesis, but maybe also a world without end. The cyborg incarnation is outside salvation history. Nor does it mark time on an Oedipal calendar, attempting to heal the terrible cleavages of gender in oral symbiotic utopia or post-Oedipal apocalypse. As Zoe Sofoulis argues in her unpublished manuscript on Lacan, Klein, and nuclear culture, *Lacklein*, the most terrible and perhaps the most promising monsters in cyborg worlds are embodied in non-Oedipal narratives with a different logic of repression, which we need to understand for our survival.

The cyborg is a creature in a postgender world; it has no truck with bisexuality, pre-Oedipal symbiosis, unalienated labor, or other seductions to organic wholeness through a final appropriation of all the powers of the parts into a higher unity. In a sense, the cyborg has no origin story in the Western sense; a 'final' irony since the cyborg is also the awful apocalyptic telos of the West's escalating dominations of abstract individuation, an ultimate self untied at last from all dependency, a man in space. An origin story in the Western humanist sense depends on the myth of original unity, fullness, bliss, and terror, represented by the phallic mother from whom all humans must separate, the task of individual development and of history, the twin potent myths inscribed most powerfully for us in psychoanalysis and Marxism. Hilary Klein has argued that both Marxism and psychoanalysis, in their concepts of labor and of individuation and gender formation, depend on the plot of original unity out of which difference must be produced and enlisted in a drama of escalating domination of woman/nature. The cyborg skips the step of original unity, of identification with nature in the Western sense. This is its illegitimate promise that might lead to subversion of its teleology as Star Wars.

The cyborg is resolutely committed to partiality, irony, intimacy, and perversity. It is oppositional, utopian, and completely without innocence. No longer structured by the polarity of public and private, the cyborg defines a technological polis based partly on a revolution of social relations in the oikos, the household. Nature and culture are reworked; the one can no longer be the resource for appropriation or incorporation by the other. The relationships for forming wholes from parts, including those of polarity and hierarchical domination, are at issue in the cyborg world. Unlike the hopes of Frankenstein's monster, the cyborg does not expect its father to save it through a restoration of the garden, that is, through the fabrication of a heterosexual mate, through its completion in a finished whole, a city and cosmos. The cyborg does not dream of community on the model of the organic family, this time without the Oedipal project. The cyborg would not recognize the Garden of Eden; it is not made of mud and cannot dream of returning to dust. Perhaps that is why I want to see if cyborgs can subvert the apocalypse of returning to nuclear dust in the manic compulsion to name the Enemy. Cyborgs are not reverent; they do not remember the cosmos. They are wary of holism, but needy for connection – they seem to have a natural feel for united front politics, but without the vanguard party. The main trouble with cyborgs, of course, is that they are the illegitimate offspring of militarism and patriarchal capitalism, not to mention state socialism. But illegitimate offspring are often exceedingly unfaithful to their origins. Their fathers, after all, are inessential.

I will return to the science fiction of cyborgs at the end of the chapter, but now I want to signal three crucial boundary breakdowns that make the following political fictional (political scientific) analysis possible. By the late twentieth century in United States, scientific culture, the boundary between human and animal, is thoroughly breached. The last beachheads of uniqueness have been polluted, if not turned into amusement parks – language, tool use, social behavior, mental events. Nothing really convincingly settles the separation of human and animal. Many people no longer feel the need of such a separation; indeed, many branches of feminist culture affirm the pleasure of connection with human and other living creatures. Movements for animal rights are not irrational denials of human uniqueness; they are clear-sighted recognition of connection across the discredited breach of nature and culture. Biology and evolutionary theory over the last two centuries have simultaneously produced modern organisms as objects of knowledge and reduced the line between humans and animals to a faint trace re-etched in ideological struggle or professional disputes between life and social sciences. Within this framework, teaching modern Christian creationism should be fought as a form of child abuse.

Biological-determinist ideology is only one position opened up in scientific culture for arguing the meanings of human animality. There is much room for radical political people to contest for the meanings of the breached boundary.[2] The cyborg appears in myth precisely where the boundary between human and animal is transgressed. Far from signaling a walling off of people from other living things, cyborgs signal disturbingly and pleasurably tight coupling. Bestiality has a new status in this cycle of marriage exchange.

The second leaky distinction is between animal-human (organism) and machine. Pre-cybernetic machines could be haunted; there was always the specter of the ghost in the machine. This dualism structured the dialogue between materialism and idealism that was settled by a dialectical progeny called spirit or history, according to taste. But basically machines were not self-moving, self-designing, autonomous. They could not achieve man's dream, only mock it. They were not man, an author of himself, but only a caricature of that masculinist reproductive dream. To think they were otherwise was paranoid. Now we are not so sure. Late twentieth-century machines have made thoroughly ambiguous the difference between natural and artificial, mind and body, self-developing an externally designed, and many other distinctions that used to apply to organisms and machines. Our machines are disturbingly lively, and we ourselves frighteningly inert.

Technological determinism is only one ideological space opened up by the reconceptions of machine and organism as coded texts through which we engage in the play of writing and reading the world.[3] 'Textualization' of everything in poststructuralist, postmodernist theory has been damned by Marxists and socialist feminists for its utopian disregard for lived relations of domination that ground the 'play' of arbitrary reading.[4,5] It is certainly true that postmodernist strategies, like my cyborg myth, subvert myriad organic wholes (e.g., the poem, the primitive culture, the biological organism). In short, the certainty of what counts as nature – a source of insight and a promise of innocence – is undermined, probably fatally. The transcendent authorization of interpretation is lost and with it the ontology grounding Western epistemology. But the alternative is not cynicism or faithlessness, that is, some version of abstract existence, like the accounts of technological determinism destroying 'man' by the 'machine' or 'meaningful political action' by the 'text'. Who cyborgs will be is a radical question; the answers are a matter of survival. Both chimpanzees and artifacts have politics, so why shouldn't we?[6]

The third distinction is a subset of the second: The boundary between physical and nonphysical is very imprecise for us. Pop physics books on the consequences of quantum theory and the indeterminacy principle are a kind of popular scientific equivalent to the Harlequin romances as a marker of radical change in American white heterosexuality: they get it wrong, but they are on the right subject. Modern machines are quintessentially microelectronic devices: they are everywhere and they are invisible. Modern machinery is an irreverent upstart god, mocking the Father's ubiquity and spirituality. The silicon chip is a surface for writing; it is etched in molecular scales disturbed only by atomic noise, the ultimate interference for nuclear scores. Writing, power, and technology are old partners in Western stories of the origin of civilization, but miniaturization has changed our experience of mechanism. Miniaturization has turned out to be about power; small is not so much beautiful as preeminently dangerous, as in Cruise missiles. Contrast the TV sets of the 1950s or the news cameras of the 1970s with the TV wristbands or hand-sized video cameras now advertised. Our best machines are made of sunshine; they are all light and clean because they are nothing but signals, electromagnetic waves, a section of a spectrum. These machines are eminently portable, mobile – a matter of immense human pain in Detroit and Singapore. People are nowhere near so fluid, being both material and opaque. Cyborgs are ether, quintessence.

The ubiquity and invisibility of cyborgs is precisely why these Sunshine Belt machines are so deadly. They are as hard to see politically as materially. They are about consciousness – or its simulation.[7] They are floating signifiers moving in pickup trucks across Europe, blocked more effectively by the witch-weavings of the displaced and so unnatural Greenham women, who read the cyborg webs of power very well, than by the militant labor of older masculinist politics, whose natural constituency needs defense jobs. Ultimately, the 'hardest' science is about the realm of greatest boundary confusion, the realm of pure number, pure spirit, C^3 I, cryptography, and the preservation of potent secrets. The new machines are so clean and light. Their engineers are sun worshipers mediating a new scientific revolution associated with the night dream of post industrial society. The diseases evoked by these clean machines are 'no more' than the minuscule coding changes of an antigen in the immune system, 'no more' than the experience of stress. The 'nimble' fingers of 'Oriental' women, the old fascination of little Anglo-Saxon Victorian girls with dollhouses, and women's enforced attention to the small take on quite new dimensions in this world. There might be a cyborg Alice taking account of these new dimensions. Ironically, it might be the unnatural cyborg women making chips in Asia and spiral dancing in Santa Rita jail after an antinuclear action whose constructed unities will guide effective oppositional strategies.

So my cyborg myth is about transgressed boundaries, potent fusions, and dangerous possibilities which progressive people might explore as one part of needed political work. One of my premises is that most American socialists and feminists see deepened dualisms of mind and body, animal and machine, idealism and materialism in the social practices, symbolic formulations, and physical artifacts associated with high technology and scientific culture. From *One-Dimensional Man* to *The Death of Nature*,[8] the analytic resources developed by progressives have insisted on the necessary domination of technics and recalled us to an imagined organic body to integrate our resistance. Another of my premises is that the need for unity of people trying to resist worldwide intensification of domination has never been more acute. But a slightly perverse shift of perspective might better enable us to contest for meanings, as well as for other forms of power and pleasure in technologically mediated societies.

From one perspective, a cyborg world is about the final imposition of a grid of control on the planet, about the final abstraction embodied in a Star Wars apocalypse waged in the name of defense, about the final appropriation of women's bodies in a masculinist orgy of war.[9] From another perspective, a cyborg world might be about lived social and bodily realities in which people are not afraid of their joint kinship with animals and machines, not afraid of permanently partial identities and contradictory standpoints. The political struggle is to see from both perspectives at once because each reveals both dominations and possibilities unimaginable from the other vantage point. Single vision produces worse illusions than double vision or many-headed monsters. Cyborg unities are monstrous and illegitimate; in our present political circumstances, we could hardly hope for more potent myths for resistance and recoupling. I like to imagine the Livermore Action Group, LAG, as a kind of cyborg society, dedicated to realistically converting the laboratories that most fiercely embody and spew out the tools of technological apocalypse, and committed to building a political form that actually manages to hold together witches, engineers, elders, perverts, Christians, mothers, and Leninists long enough to disarm the state. Fission Impossible is the name of the affinity group in my town. (Affinity: related not by blood but by choice, the appeal of one chemical nuclear group for another, avidity.)[10]

Fractured Identities

It has become difficult to name one's feminism by a single adjective—or even to insist in every circumstance upon the noun. Consciousness of exclusion through naming is acute. Identities seem contradictory, partial, and strategic. With the hard-won recognition of their social and historical constitution, gender, race, and class cannot provide the basis for belief in 'essential' unity. There is nothing about being female, that naturally binds women. There is not even such a state as 'being' female, itself a highly complex category constructed in contested sexual scientific discourses and other social practices. Gender, race, or class consciousness is an achievement forced on us by the terrible historical experience of the contradictory social realities of patriarchy, colonialism, racism and capitalism. Who counts as 'us' in my own rhetoric? Which identities are available to ground such a potent political myth called 'us', and what could motivate enlistment in this collectivity? Painful fragmentation among feminists (not to mention among women) along every possible fault line has made the concept of woman elusive, an excuse for the matrix of women's dominations of each other. For me–and for many who share a similar historical location in white, professional, middle-class, female, radical, North American, mid-adult bodies–the sources of a crisis in political identity are legion. The recent history for much of the U.S. Left and the U.S. feminism has been a response to this kind of crisis by endless splitting and searches for a new essential unity. But there has also been a growing recognition of another response through coalition–affinity, not identity.[11]

Chela Sandoval, from a consideration of specific historical moments in the formation of the new political voice called women of color, has theorized a hopeful model of political identity called 'oppositional consciousness', born of the skills for reading webs of power by those refused stable member-ship in the social categories of race, sex, or class.[12] 'Women of color', a name contested at its origins by those whom it would incorporate, as well as a historical consciousness marking systematic breakdown of all the signs of Man in Western traditions, constructs a king of postmodernist identity out of otherness, difference, and specificity. This postmodernist identity is fully political, whatever might be said about other possible postmodernisms. Sandoval's oppositional consciousness is about contradictory locations and heterochronic calendars, not about relativisms and pluralisms.

Sandoval emphasizes the lack of any essential criterion for identifying who is a woman of color. She notes that the definition of the group has been by conscious appropriation of negation. For example, a chicana or a U.S. black woman has not been able to speak as a woman or as a black person or as a chicano. Thus, she was at the bottom of a cascade of negative identities, left out of even the 'privileged' oppressed authorial categories called 'women and blacks', who claimed to make the important revolutions. The category 'woman' negated all nonwhite women; 'black' negated all nonblack people, as well as all black women. But there was also no 'she', no singularity, but a sea of differences among U.S. women who have affirmed their historical identity as U.S. women of color. This identity marks out a self-consciously constructed space that cannot affirm the capacity to act on the basis of natural identification, but only on the basis of conscious coalition, of affinity, of political kinship.[13] Unlike the 'woman' of some streams of the white women's movement in the United States, there is no naturalization of the matrix, or at least this is what Sandoval argues is uniquely available through the power of oppositional consciousness.

Sandoval's argument has to be seen as one potent formulation for feminists out of the worldwide development of anti-colonialist discourse, that is, discourse dissolving the West and its highest product–the one who is not animal, barbarian, or woman: that is, man, the author of a cosmos called history. As Orientalism is deconstructed politically and semiotically, the identities of the Occident destabilize, including those of its feminists.[14] Sandoval argues that 'women of color' have a chance to build an effective unity that does not replicate the imperializing, totalizing revolutionary subjects of previous Marxisms and feminisms which had not faced the consequences of the disorderly polyphony emerging from decolonization.

Katie King has emphasized the limits of identification and the political/ poetic mechanics of identification built into reading 'the poem', that generative core of cultural feminism. King criticizes the persistent tendency among contemporary feminists from different 'moments' or 'conversations' in feminist practice to taxonomize the women's movement to make one's own political tendencies appear to be the telos of the whole. These taxonomies tend to remake feminist history to appear to be an ideological struggle among coherent types persisting over time, especially those typical units called radical, liberal, and socialist feminism. Literally, all other feminisms are either incorporated or marginalized, usually by building an explicit ontology and epistemology.[15] Taxonomies of feminism produce epistemologies to police deviation from official women's experience. Of course, 'women's culture,' like women of color, is consciously created by mechanisms inducing affinity. The rituals of poetry, music, and certain forms of academic practice have been preeminent. The politics of race and culture in the U.S. women's movements are intimately interwoven. The common achievement of King and Sandoval is learning how to craft a poetic/political unity without relying on a logic of appropriation, incorporation, and taxonomic identification.

The theoretical and practical struggle against unity-through-domination or unity-through-incorporation ironically not only undermines the justifications for patriarchy, colonialism, humanism, positivism, essentialism, scientism, and other unlamented-isms, but all claims for an organic or natural standpoint. I think that radical and socialist/Marxist feminisms have also undermined their/our own epistemological strategies and that this is a crucially valuable step in imagining possible unities. It remains to be seen whether all epistemologies as Western political people have known them fail us in the task to build effective affinities.

It is important to note that the effort to construct revolutionary standpoints, epistemologies as achievements of people committed to changing the world, has been part of the process showing the limits of identification. The acid tools of postmodernist theory and the constructive tools of ontological discourse about revolutionary subjects might be seen as ironic allies in dissolving Western selves in the interests of survival. We are excruciatingly conscious of what it means to have a historically constituted body. But with the loss of innocence in our origin, there is no expulsion from the Garden either. Our politics lose the indulgence of guilt with the *naïveté* of innocence. But what would another political myth for socialist feminism look like? What kind of politics could embrace partial, contradictory, permanently unclosed constructions of personal and collective selves and still be faithful, effective–and, ironically, socialist feminist?

I do not know of any other time in history when there was greater need for political unity to confront effectively the dominations of race, gender, sexuality, and class. I also do not know of any other time when the kind of unity we might help build could have been possible. None of 'us' have any longer the symbolic or material capability of dictating the shape of reality to any of 'them'. Or at least 'we' cannot claim innocence from practicing such dominations. White women, including Euroamerican socialist feminists, discovered (i.e., were forced kicking and screaming to notice) the noninnocence of the category 'woman'. That consciousness changes the configuration of all previous categories; it denatures them as heat denatures a fragile protein. Cyborg feminists have to argue that 'we' do not want any more natural matrix of unity and that no construction is whole. Innocence, and the corollary insistence on victimhood as the only ground for insight, has done enough damage. But the constructed revolutionary subject must give late twentieth-century people pause as well. In the fraying of identities and in the reflexive strategies for constructing them, the possibility opens up for weaving something other than a shroud for the day after the apocalypse that so prophetically ends salvation history.

But Marxist/socialist feminisms and radical feminisms have simultaneously naturalized and denatured the category 'woman' and consciousness of the social lives of 'women'. Perhaps a schematic caricature can highlight both kinds of moves. Marxian socialism is rooted in an analysis of wage labor which reveals class structure. The consequence of the wage relationship is systematic alienation, as the worker is dissociated from his [sic] product. Abstraction and illusion rule in knowledge; domination rules in practice. Labor is the preeminently privileged category enabling the Marxist to overcome illusion and find that point of view which is necessary for changing the world. Labor is the humanizing activity that makes man; labor is an ontological category permitting the knowledge of a subject, and so the knowledge of subjugation and alienation.

In faithful filiation, socialist feminism advanced by allying itself with the basic analytic strategies of this Marxism. The main achievement of both Marxist feminists and socialist feminists was to expand the category of labor to accommodate what (some) women did, even when the wage relation was subordinated to a more comprehensive view of labor under capitalist patriarchy. In particular, women's labor in the household and women's activity as mothers generally, that is, reproduction in the socialist feminist sense, entered theory on the authority of analogy to the Marxian concept of labor. The unity of women here rests on an epistemology based on the ontological structure of 'labor'. Marxist/socialist feminism does not 'naturalize' unity; it is a possible achievement based on a possible standpoint rooted in social relations. The essentializing move is in the ontological structure of labor or of its analogue, women's activity.[16,17] The inheritance of Marxian humanism, with its preeminently Western self, is the difficulty for me. The contribution from these formulations has been the emphasis on the daily responsibility of real women to *build* unities, rather than to naturalize them.

Catherine MacKinnon's version of radical feminism is itself a caricature of the appropriating, incorporating, totalizing tendencies of Western theories of identity grounding action.[18] It is factually and politically wrong to assimilate all of the diverse 'moments' or 'conversations' in recent women's politics named radical feminism to MacKinnon's version. But the teleological logic of her theory shows how an epistemology and ontology – including their negations – erase or police difference. Only one of the effects of MacKinnon's theory is the rewriting of the history of the polymorphous field called radical feminism. The major effect is the production of a theory of experience, of women's identity, that is a kind of apocalypse for all revolutionary standpoints. That is, the totalization built into this tale of radical feminism achieves its end – the unity of women – by enforcing the experience of and testimony to radical nonbeing. As for the Marxist/socialist feminist, consciousness is an achievement, not a natural fact. MacKinnon's theory eliminates some of the difficulties built into humanist revolutionary subjects, but at the cost of radical reductionism.

MacKinnon argues that feminism necessarily adopted a different analytical strategy from Marxism, looking first not at the structure of class, but at the structure of sex/gender and its generative relationship, men's constitution and appropriation of women sexually. Ironically, MacKinnon's 'ontology' constructs a nonsubject, a nonbeing. Another's desire, not the self's labor, is the origin of 'woman'. She therefore develops a theory of consciousness that enforces what can count as 'women's' experience – anything that names sexual violation, indeed, sex itself as far as 'women' can be concerned. Feminist practice is the construction of this form of consciousness; that is, the self-knowledge of a self-who-is-not.

Perversely, sexual appropriation in this feminism still has the epistemo-logical status of labor, that is, the point from which analysis able to contribute to changing the world must flow. But sexual objectification, not alienation, is the consequence of the structure of sex/gender. In the realm of knowledge, the result of sexual objectification is illusion and abstraction. However, a woman is not simply alienated from her product, but in a deep sense she does not exist as a subject, or even potential subject, since she owes her existence as a woman to sexual appropriation. To be constituted by another's desire is not the same thing as to be alienated in the violent separation of the laborer from his product.

MacKinnon's radical theory of experience is totalizing in the extreme; it does not so much marginalize as obliterate the authority of any other women's political speech and action. It is a totalization producing what Western patriarchy itself never succeeded in doing – feminists' consciousness of the nonexistence of women, except as products of men's desire. I think MacKinnon correctly argues that no Marxian version of identity can firmly ground women's unity. But in solving the problem of the contradictions of any Western revolutionary subject for feminist purposes, she develops an even more authoritarian doctrine of experience. If my complaint about socialist/Marxian standpoints is their unintended erasure of polyvocal, unassimilable, radical difference made visible in anti-colonial discourse and practice, MacKinnon's intentional erasure of all difference through the device of the 'essential' nonexistence of women is not reassuring.

In my taxonomy, which like any other taxonomy is a reinscription of history, radical feminism can accommodate all the activities of women named by socialist feminists as forms of labor only if the activity can somehow be sexualized. Reproduction had different tones of meanings for the two tendencies, one rooted in labor, one in sex, both calling the consequences of domination and ignorance of social and personal reality 'false consciousness'.

Beyond either the difficulties or the contributions in the argument of any one author, neither Marxist nor radical-feminist points of view have tended to embrace the status of a partial explanation; both were regularly constituted as totalities. Western explanation has demanded as much; how else could the Western author incorporate its others? Each tried to annex other forms of domination by expanding its basic categories through analogy, simple listing, or addition. Embarrassed silence about race among white radical and socialist feminists was one major, devastating political consequence. History and polyvocality disappear into political taxonomies that try to establish genealogies. There was no structural room for race (or for much else) in theory claiming to reveal the construction of the category 'woman' and social group 'women' as a unified or totalizable whole. The structure of my caricature looks like this:

Socialist Feminism—
    structure of class//wage labor//alienation
    labor, by analogy reproduction, by extension sex, by addition race
Radical Feminism—
    structure of gender//sexual appropriation//objectification
    sex, by analogy labor, by extension reproduction, by addition race

In another context, the French theorist Julia Kristeva claimed women appeared as a historical group after World War II, along with groups like youth. Her dates are doubtful, but we are now accustomed to remembering that as objects of knowledge and as historical actors, 'race' did not always exist, 'class' has a historical genesis, and 'homosexuals' are quite junior. It is no accident that the symbolic system of the family of man—and so the essence of woman—breaks up at the same moment that networks of connection among people on the planet are unprecedentedly multiple, pregnant, and complex. 'Advanced capitalism' is inadequate to convey the structure of this historical moment. In the Western sense, the end of man is at stake. It is no accident that woman disintegrates into women in our time. Perhaps socialist feminists were not substantially guilty of producing essentialist theory that suppressed women's particularity and contradictory interests. I think we have been, at least through unreflective participation in the logics, languages, and practices of white humanism and through searching for a single ground of domination to secure our revolutionary voice. Now we have less excuse. But in the consciousness of our failures, we risk lapsing into boundless difference and giving up on the confusing task of making partial, real connection. Some differences are playful; some are poles of world historical systems of domination. Epistemology is about knowing the difference.

The Informatics of Domination

In this attempt at an epistemological and political position, I would like to sketch a picture of possible unity, a picture indebted to socialist and feminist principles of design. The frame for my sketch is set by the extent and importance of rearrangements in worldwide social relations tied to science and technology. I argue for a politics rooted in claims about fundamental changes in the nature of class, race, and gender in a emerging system of world order analogous in its novelty and scope to that created by industrial capitalism; we are living through a movement from an organic, industrial society to a polymorphous, information system – from all work to all play, a deadly game. Simultaneously material and ideological, the dichotomies may be expressed in the following chart of transitions from the comfortable old hierarchical dominations to the scary new networks I have called the informatics of domination:

Representation	Simulation
Bourgeois novel, realism	Science fiction, postmodernism
Organism	Biotic component
Depth, integrity	Surface, boundary
Heat	Noise
Biology as clinical practice	Biology as inscription
Physiology	Communications engineering
Small group	Subsystem
Perfection	Optimization
Eugenics	Population Control
Decadence, *Magic Mountain*	Obsolescence, *Future Shock*
Hygiene	Stress management
Microbiology, tuberculosis	Immunology, AIDS
Organic division of labor	Ergonomics/cybernetics of labor
Functional specialization	Modular construction
Reproduction	Replication
Organic sex role specialization	Optimal genetic strategies
Biological determinism	Evolutionary inertia, constraints
Community ecology	Ecosystem
Racial chain of being	Neo-imperialism, United Nations humanism
Scientific management in home/factory	Global factory/electronic cottage
Family/market/factory	Women in the integrated circuit
Family wage	Comparable worth
Public/private	Cyborg citizenship
Nature/culture	Fields of difference
Cooperation	Communications enhancement
Freud	Lacan
Sex	Genetic engineering
Labor	Robotics
Mind	Artificial intelligence
World War II	Star Wars
White capitalist patriarchy	Informatics of domination

This list suggests several interesting things.[19] First, the objects on the right-hand side cannot be coded as 'natural', a realization that subverts naturalistic coding for the left-hand side as well. We cannot go back ideologically or materially. It's not just that 'god' is dead; so is the 'goddess'. Or both are revivified in the worlds charged with microelectronic and biotechnological politics. In relation to objects like biotic components, one must think not in terms of essential properties, but in terms of design, boundary constraints, rates of flows, systems logics, costs of lowering constraints. Sexual reproduction is one kind of reproductive strategy among many, with costs and benefits as a function of the system environment. Ideologies of sexual reproduction can no longer reasonably call on notions of sex and sex role as organic aspects in natural objects like organisms and families. Such reasoning will be unmasked as irrational, and ironically corporate executives reading *Playboy* and anti-porn radical feminists will make strange bedfellows in jointly unmasking the irrationalism.

* * * * *

To recapitulate, certain dualisms have been persistent in Western traditions; they have all been systemic to the logics and practices of domination of women, people of color, nature, workers, animals – in short, domination of all constituted as others, whose task is to mirror the self. Chief among these troubling dualisms are self/other, mind/body, culture/nature, male/female, civilized/primitive, reality/appearance, whole/part, agent/resource, maker/made, active/passive, right/wrong, truth/illusion, total/partial, God/man. The self is the One who is not dominated, who knows that by the service of the other; the other is the one who holds the future, who knows that by the experience of domination, which gives the lie to the autonomy of the self. To be One is to be autonomous, to be powerful, to be · God; but to be One is to be an illusion and so to be involved in a dialectic of apocalypse with the other. Yet, to be other is to be multiple, without clear boundaries, frayed, insubstantial. One is too few, but two are too many.

High-tech culture challenges these dualisms in intriguing ways. It is not clear who makes and who is made in the relation between human and machine. It is not clear what is mind and what is body in machines that resolve into coding practices. Insofar as we know ourselves in both formal discourse (e.g., biology) and in daily practice, (e.g., the homework economy in the integrated circuit), we find ourselves to be cyborgs, hybrids, mosaics, chimeras. Biological organisms have become biotic systems, communications devices like others. There is no fundamental, ontological separation in our formal knowledge of machine and organism, of technical and organic. The replicant Rachel in the film *Blade Runner* stands as the image of a cyborg culture's fear, love, and confusion.

One consequence is that our sense of connection to our tools is heightened. The trance state experienced by many computer users has become a staple of science-fiction film and cultural jokes. Perhaps paraplegics and other severely handicapped people can (and sometimes do) have the most intense experiences of complex hybridization with other communication devices.[20] Anne McCaffrey's prefeminist *The Ship Who Sang* explored the consciousness of a cyborg, hybrid of girl's brain and complex machinery, formed after the birth of a severely handicapped child. Gender, sexuality, embodiment, skill: all were reconstituted in the story. Why should our bodies end at the skin or include at best other beings encapsulated by skin? From the seventeenth century till now, machines could be animated – given ghostly souls to make them speak or move or to account for their orderly development and mental capacities. Or organisms could be mechanized – reduced to body understood as resource of mind. These machine/organism relationships are obsolete, unnecessary. For us, in imagination and in other practice, machines can be prosthetic devices, intimate components, friendly selves. We don't need organic holism to give impermeable wholeness, the total woman and he feminist variants (mutants?)

* * * * *

Cyborg imagery can help express two crucial arguments in this essay: (1) the production of universal, totalizing theory is a major mistake that misses most of reality, probably always, but certainly now; (2) taking responsibility for the social relations of science and technology means refusing an anti-science metaphysics, a demonology of technology, and so means embracing the skillful taks of reconstructing the boundaries of daily life, in partial connection with others, in communication with all of our parts. It is not just that science and technology are possible means of great human satisfaction, as well as a matrix of complex dominations. Cyborg imagery can suggest a way out of the maze of dualisms in which we have explained our bodies and our tools to ourselves. This is a dream not of a common language, but of a powerful infidel heteroglossia. It is an imagination of a feminist speaking in tongues to strike fear into the circuits of the super savers of the New Right. It means both building and destroying machines, identities, categories, relationships, spaces, stories. Although both are bound in the spiral dance, I would rather be a cyborg than a goddess.

Notes

1 This article was first published in *Socialist Review*, No. 80, 1985. The essay originated as a response to a call for political thinking about the 1980s from socialist-feminist points of view, in hopes of deepening our political and cultural debates in order to renew commitments to fundamental social change in the face of the Reagan years. The cyborg manifesto tried to find a feminist place for connected thinking and acting in profoundly contradictory worlds. Since its publication, this bit of cyborgian writing has had a surprising half life. It has proved impossible to rewrite the cyborg. Cyborg's daughter will have to find its own matrix in another essay, starting from the proposition that the immune system is the biotechnical body's chief system

of differences in late capitalism, where feminists might find provocative extraterrestrial maps of the networks of embodied power marked by race, sex, and class. This chapter is substantially the same as the 1985 version, with minor revisions and correction of notes.

2 Useful references to left and/or feminist radical science movements and theory and to biological/biotechnological issues include Ruth Bleier, *Science and Gender: A Critique of Biology and Its Themes on Women* (New York: Pergamon, 1984); Ruth Bleier, ed., *Feminist Approaches to Science* (New York: Pergamon, 1986); Sandra Harding, *The Science Question in Feminism* (Ithaca, NY: Cornell University Press, 1986); Anne Fausto-Sterling, *Myths of Gender* (New York: Basic Books, 1985): Stephen J. Gould, *Mismeasure of Man* (New York: Norton, 1981); Ruth Hubbard, Mary Sue Henifin, Barbara Fried, eds., *Biological Woman, the Convenient Myth* (Cambridge, MA: Schenkman, 1982); Evelyn Fox Keller, *Reflections on Gender and Science* (New Haven, CT: Yale University Press, 1985); R.C. Lewontin, Steve Rose, and Leon Kamin, *Not in Our Genes* (New York: Pantheon, 1984); *Radical Science Journal* (from 1987, *Science as Culture*), 26 Freegrove Road, London N7 9RQ; *Science for the People*, 897 Main St., Cambridge, MA 02139.

3 Starting points for left and/or feminist approaches to technology and politics include Ruth Schwartz Cowan, *More Work for Mother: The Ironies of Household Technology from the Open Hearth to the Microwave* (New York: Basic Books, 1983; Joan Rothschild, *Machina ex Dea: Feminist Perspectives on Technology* (New York: Pergamon, 1983); Sharon Traweek, *Beantimes and Lifetimes: The World of High Energy Physics* (Cambridge, MA: Harvard University Press, 1988); R.M. Young and Les Levidov, eds, *Science, Technology, and the Labour Process*, Vols. 1–3 (London: CSE Books); Joseph Weizenbaum, *Computer Power and Human Reason* (San Francisco: Freeman, 1976): Langdon Winner, *Autonomous Technology: Technics Out of Control as a Theme in Political Thought* (Cambridge, MA: MIT Press, 1977); Langdon Winner, *The Whale and the Reactor* (Chicago: Chicago University Press, 1986); Jan Zimmerman, ed., *The Technological Woman: Interfacing with Tomorrow* (New York: Praeger, 1983); Tom Athanasiou, 'High-tech Politics. The Case of Artificial Intelligence', *Socialist Review*, No. 92, 1987, pp. 7–35; Carol Cohn, 'Nuclear Language and How We Learned to Pat the Bomb', *Bulletin of Atomic Scientists*, June 1987, pp. 17–24; Terry Winograd and Fernando Flores, *Understanding Computers and Cognition: A New Foundation for Design* (New Jersey: Ablex, 1986); Paul Edwards, 'Border Wars: The Politics of Artificial Intelligence', *Radical America*, Vol. 19, No. 6, 1985, pp. 39–52; *Global Electronics Newsletter*, 867 West Dana St., #204, Mountain View, CA 94041; *Processed World*, 55 Sutter st., San Francisco, CA 94104; *ISIS*, Women's International Information and Communication Service, P.O. Box 50 (Cornavin), 1211 Geneva 2, Switzerland, and Via Santa Maria dell' Anima 30, 00186 Rome, Italy. Fundamental approaches to modern social studies of science that do not continue the liberal mystification that it all started with Thomas Kuhn, include: Karin Knorr-Cetina, *The Manufacture of Knowledge* (Oxford: Pergamon, 1981); K.D. Knorr-Cetina and Michael Mulkay, eds., *Science Observed: Perspectives on the Social Study of Science* (Beverly Hills, CA: Sage, 1983); Bruno Latour and Steve Woolgar, *Laboratory Life: The Social Construction of Scientific Facts* (Beverly Hills, CA: Sage, 1979); Robert M. Young, 'Interpreting the Production of Science', *New Scientist*, Vol. 29, March 1979, pp. 1026–1028. More is claimed than is known about room for contesting productions of science in the mythic/material space of 'the laboratory', the 1984 Directory of the Network for the Ethnographic Study of Science, Technology, and Organizations lists a wide range of people and projects crucial to better radical analysis; available from NESSTO, P.O. Box 11442, Stanford, CA 94305.

4 Fredric Jameson, 'Post Modernism, or the Cultural Logic of Late Capitalism, *New Left Review*, July/August 1984, pp. 53–94. See Marjorie Perloff, 'Dirty' Language and Scramble Systems', *Sulfur* Vol 2, 1984, pp. 178–183; Kathleen Fraser, *Something (Even Human Voices) in the Foreground, a Lake* (Berkeley, CA: Kelsey St. Press, 1984). For feminist modernist/postmodernist cyborg writing, see *How (ever)*, 871 Corbett Ave., San Francisco, CA 94131.

5 A provocative, comprehensive argument about the politics and theories of postmodernism is made by Fredric Jameson, who argues that postmodernism is not an option, a style among others, but a cultural dominant requiring radical reinvention of left politics from within; there is no longer any place from without that gives meaning to the comforting fiction of critical distance. Jameson also makes clear why one cannot be for or against postmodernism, an essentially moralist move. My position is that feminists (and others) need continuous cultural reinvention, postmodernist critique, and historical materialism; only a cyborg would have a chance. The old dominations of white capitalist patriarchy seen nostalgically innocent now: They normalized heterogeneity, e.g., into man and woman, white and black. 'advanced capitalism' and postmodernism release heterogeneity without a norm, and we are flattened, without subjectivity, which requires depth, even unfriendly and drowning depths. It is time to write *The Death of the Clinic*. The clinic's methods required bodies and works; we have texts and surfaces. Our dominations don't work by medicalization and normalization anymore; they work by networking, communications redesign, stress management. Normalization gives way to automation, utter redundancy. Michel Foucault's *Birth of the Clinic, History of Sexuality*, and *Discipline and Punish* name a form of power at its moment of implosion. The discourse of biopolitics gives way to technobabble, the language of the spliced substantive; no noun is left whole by the multinationals. These are their names, listed from one issue of *Science*: Tech-Knowledge, Genentech, Allergen, Hybritech, Compupro, Genen-cor, Syntex, Allelix, Agrigenetics Corp., Syntro, Codon, Repligen; Micro-Angelo from Scion Corp., Percom Data, Inter Systems, Cyborg Corp., Statcom Corp., Intertec. If we are imprisoned by language, then escape from that prison-house requires language poets, a kind of cultural restriction enzyme to cut the code; cyborg heteroglossia is one form of radical culture politics.

6 Frans de Waal, *Chimpanzee Politics: Power and Sex among the Apes* (New York: Harper & Row, 1982); Langdon Winner, 'Do artifacts have politics?', *Daedalus* (Winter 1980): 121–136.

7 Jean Baudrillard, *Simulations*, trans. P. Foss, P. Patton, P. Beitchman (New York: Semiotext(e), 1983). Jameson ('Postmodernism', p. 66) points out that Plato's definition of the simulacrum is the copy for which there is no original, i.e., the world of advanced capitalism, of pure exchange. See *Discourse* 9, Spring/Summer 1987, for a special issue on technology (Cybernetics, Ecology, and the Postmodern Imagination).

8 Herbert Marcuse, *One-Dimensional Man* (Boston: Beacon Press, 1964); Carolyn Merchant, *Death of Nature* (San Francisco: Harper & Row, 1980).

9 Zoe Sofia, 'Exterminating Fetuses', *Diacritics*, Vol. 14, No. 2, Summer 1984, pp. 47–59, and 'Jupiter Space' (Pomona, CA: American Studies Association, 1984).

10 For ethnographic accounts and political evaluations, see Barbara Epstein, 'The Politics of Prefigurative Community: The Non-Violent Direction Action Movement', *The Year Left*, forthcoming, and Noel Sturgeon, qualifying essay on feminism, anarchism, and nonviolent direct-action politics, University of California, Santa Cruz, 1986. Without explicit irony, adopting the spaceship earth/whole earth logo of the planet photographed from space, set off by the slogan 'Love Your Mother', the May 1987 Mothers and Others Day action at the nuclear weapons testing

facility in Nevada nonetheless took account of the tragic contradictions of views of the earth. Demonstrators applied for official permits to be on the land from officers of the Western Shoshone tribe, whose territory was invaded by the U.S. government when it built the nuclear weapons test ground in the 1950s. Arrested for trespassing, the demonstrators argued that the police and weapons facility personnel, without authorization from the proper officials, were the trespassers. One affinity group at the women's action called themselves the Surrogate Others, and in solidarity with the creatures forced to tunnel in the same ground with the bomb, they enacted a cyborgian emergence from the constructed body of a large, nonheterosexual desert worm.

11 Powerful developments of coalition politics emerge from 'third world' speakers, speaking from nowhere, the displaced center of the universe, earth: 'We live on the third planet from the sun' – *Sun Poem* by Jamaican writer Edward Kamau Braithwaite, review by Nathaniel Mackey, *Sulfur*, Vol. 2, 1984, pp. 200–205. *Home Girls*, ed. Barbara Smith (New York: Kitchen Table Women of Color Press, 1983), ironically subverts naturalized identities precisely while constructing a place from which to speak called home. See Bernice Reagan, 'Coalition Politics, Turning the Century', pp. 356–368. Trinh T. Minh-ha, ed., 'She, the Inappropriate/d Other', *Discourse*, Vol. 8, Fall/Winter 1986–1987.

12 Chela Sandoval, 'Dis-Illusionment and the Poetry of the Future: The Making of Oppositional Consciousness', PhD qualifying essay, University of California, Santa Cruz, 1984.

13 bell hooks, *Ain't I a Woman?* (Boston: South End Press, 1981); bell hooks, *Feminist Theory: From Margin to Center* (Boston: South End Press, 1984); Gloria Hull, Patricia Bell Scott, and Barbara Smith, eds, *All the Women Are White, All the Men Are Black, But Some of Us Are Brave*: Black Women's Studies (Old Westbury, NY: Feminist Press, 1982). Toni Cade Bambara, *The Salt Eaters* (New York: Vintage/Random House, 1981), writes an extraordinary postmodernist novel, in which the women of color theater group, The Seven Sisters, explores a form of unity. Elliott Butler-Evans, *Race, Gender, and Desire: Narrative Strategies and the Production of Ideology in the Fiction of Toni Cade Bambara, Toni Morrison and Alice Walker*, Ph.D. dissertation, University of California, Santa Cruz, 1987.

14 On Orientalism in feminist works and elsewhere, see Lisa Lowe, 'Orientation: Representations of Cultural and Sexual 'Others', Ph.D. thesis, Univeristy of California, Santa Cruz; Edward Said, *Orientalism* (New York: Pantheon, 1978). Chandra Talpade Mohanty, 'Under Western Eyes: Feminist Scholarship and Colonial Discourse', *Boundary* Vol. 2, No. 12, and Vol. 3, No. 13, 1984, pp. 333–357; 'Many Voices, One Chant: Black Feminist Perspectives', *Feminist Review*, Vol. 17, Autumn 1984.

15 Katie King has developed a theoretically sensitive treatment of the workings of feminist taxonomies as genealogies of power in feminist ideology and polemic: Katie King, 'Canons without Innocence', Ph.D. thesis, University of California, Santa Cruz, 1987, and 'The Situation of Lesbianism as Feminism's Magical Sign: Contests for Meaning in the U.S. Women's Movement, 1968–72', *Communication* Vol. 9, No. 1, 1985, pp. 65–91. King examines an intelligent, problematic example of taxonomizing feminisms to make a little machine producing the desired final position; Alison Jaggar, *Feminist Politics and Human Nature* (Totowa, NJ: Rowman & Allanheld, 1983). My caricature here of socialist and radical feminism is also an example.

16 The feminist standpoint argument has been developed by Jane Flax, 'Political Philosophy and the Patriarchal Unconsciousness', *Discovering Reality*, ed. Sandra Harding and Merill Hintikka, (Dordrecht: Reidel, 1983); Sandra Harding, 'The Contradictions and Ambivalence of a Feminist Science', ms.; Harding and Hintikka,

Discovering Reality; Nancy Hartsock, *Money, Sex and Power* (New York: Longman, 1983) and 'The Feminist Standpoint: Developing the Ground for a Specifically Feminist Historical Materialism', *Discovering Reality*, ed. S. Harding and M. Hintikka; Mary O'Brien, *The Politics of Reproduction* (New York: Routledge & Kegan Paul, 1981); Hilary Rose, 'Hand, Brain, and Heart: A Feminist Epistemology for the Natural Sciences', *Signs*, Vol. 9, No. 1, 1983, pp. 73–90; Dorothy Smith, 'Women's Perspective as a Radical Critique of Sociology', *Sociological Inquiry* Vol 44, 1974, and 'A Sociology of Women', *the Prism of Sex*, ed. J. Sherman and E. T. Beck, Madison, WI: University of Wisconsin Press, 1979). For rethinking theories of feminist materialism and feminist standpoint in response to criticism, see Chapter 7 in Harding, *The Science Question in Feminism*, op. cit. (note 1); Nancy Hartsock, 'Rethinking Modernism: Minority vs. Majority Theories', *Cultural Critique* 7 (1987): 187–206; Hilary Rose, 'Women's Work: Women's Knowledge', *What is Feminism? A Re-examination*, ed. Juliet Mitchell and Ann Oakley (New York: Pantheon, 1986), pp. 161–83.

17 The central role of object-relations versions of psychoanalysis and related strong universalizing moves in discussing reproduction, caring work, and mothering in many approaches to epistemology underline their authors' resistance to what I am calling postmodernism. For me, both the universalizing moves and these versions of psychoanalysis make analysis of 'women's place in the integrated circuit' difficult and lead to systematic difficulties in accounting for or even seeing major aspects of the construction of gender and gendered social life.

18 Catherine MacKinnon, 'Feminism, Marxism, Method, and the State: An Agenda for Theory', *Signs*, Vol. 7, No. 3, Spring 1982, pp. 515–544. See also MacKinnon, *Feminism Unmodified* (Cambridge, MA: Harvard University Press, 1987). I make a category error in 'modifying' MacKinnon's positions with the qualifier 'radical', thereby generating my own reductive critique of extremely heterogeneous writing, which does explicitly use that label, by my taxonomically interested argument about writing which does not use the modifier and which brooks no limits and thereby adds to the various dreams of a common, in the sense of univocal, language for feminism. My category error was occasioned by an assignment to write from a particular taxonomic position which itself has a heterogeneous history, socialist feminism, for *Socialist Review*. A critique indebted to MacKinnon, but without the reductionism and with an elegant feminist account of Foucault's paradoxical conservatism on sexual violence (rape), is Teresa de Lauretis, 'The Violence of Rhetoric: Considerations on Representation and Gender', *Semiotica*, Vol. 54, 1985, pp. 11–31, and Teresa de Lauretis, ed., *Feminist Studies/Critical Studies* (Bloomington: Indiana University Press, 1986). A theoretically elegant feminist social-historical examination of family violence, that insists on women's, men's, and children's complex agency without losing sight of the material structures of male domination, race, and class, is Linda Gordon, *Heroes of their own Lives* (New York: Viking, 1988).

19 My previous efforts to understand biology as a cybernetic command-control discourse and organisms as 'natural-technical objects of knowledge' are 'The High Cost of Information in Post-World War II Evolutionary Biology', *Philosophical Forum*, Vol. 13, Nos. 2–3, 1979, pp. 206–237; 'Signs of Dominance: From a Physiology to a Cybernetics of Primate Society', *Studies in History of Biology*, Vol. 6, 1983, pp. 129–219; 'Class, Race, Sex, Scientific Objects of Knowledge: A Socialist-Feminist Perspective on the Social Construction of Productive Knowledge and Some Political Consequences', *Women in Scientific and Engineering Professions*, ed. Violet Haas and Carolyn Perucci (Ann Arbor, MI: University of Michigan Press, 1984), pp. 212–229.

20 The convention of ideologically taming militarized high technology by publicizing

its applications to speech and motion problems of the disabled-differently abled takes on a special irony in monotheistic, patriarchal, and frequently anti-Semitic culture when computer-generated speech allows a boy with no voice to chant the Haftorah at his bar mitzvah. See Vic Sussman, 'Personal Technology Lends a Hand', *Washington Post Magazine*, Nov. 9, 1986, pp. 45–46. Making the always context-relative social definitions of 'abledness' particularly clear, military high-tech has a way of making human beings disabled by definition, a perverse aspect of much automated battlefield and Star Wars R&D. See John Noble Welford, 'Pilot's Helmet Helps Interpret High Speed World', *New York Times*, July 1, 1986, pp. 21, 24.

Select Bibliography

Included here are a selection of secondary works on literary theory. General works are historical overviews or retrospective accounts of theory. Works on specific movements or topics have been grouped under appropriate headings though, inevitably, there will be border-crossings and overlaps between these various groupings.

General Works on Literary Theory

Arac, J. and Johnson, B., *The Consequences of Theory* (Baltimore, Johns Hopkins University Press, 1991).
Barry, P., *Beginning Theory: An Introduction to Literary and Cultural Theory* (Manchester, Manchester University Press, 1995).
Culler, J., *Literary Theory: A Very Short Introduction* (Oxford, Oxford University Press, 1997).
Douglas, A. G. and Morrow, L. eds, *Contemporary Literary Theory* (London, Macmillan, 1989).
Eagleton, T., *Literary Theory: An Introduction* (Oxford, Blackwell, 1983).
Green, K. and Le Bihan, J., *Critical Theory and Practice: A Coursebook* (London, Routledge, 1996).
Hawthorn, J., *Unlocking the Text* (London, Edward Arnold, 1987).
Hernandi, P., *What is Literature?* (Bloomington, Indiana University Press, 1978).
Jefferson, A. and Robey, D. eds, *Modern Literary Theory: A Comparative Introduction* (London, Batsford Academic, 1982).
Selden, R., *A Reader's Guide to Contemporary Literary Theory* (Brighton, Harvester Press, 1985).
Selden, R. ed., *The Cambridge History of Literary Criticism*, vol. viii, *From Formalism to Poststructuralism* (Cambridge, Cambridge University Press, 1995).

Russian Formalism

Bann, S. and Bowlt, J.E., eds, *Russian Formalism* (Edinburgh, Scottish Academic Press, 1973).
Bennett, T., *Formalism and Marxism* (London and New York, Methuen, 1979).
Erlich, V., *Russian Formalism: History-Doctrine* (3rd edn) (New Haven and London, Yale University Press, 1981).

Jameson, F., *The Prison-House of Language: A Critical Account of Structuralism and Russian Formalism* (Princeton and London: Princeton University Press, 1972).

Lemon, L.T. and Reis, M.J., *Russian Formalist Criticism: Four Essays* (Lincoln: University of Nebraska Press, 1965).

Matejka, L. and Pomorska, K. eds, *Readings in Russian Poetics: Formalist and Structuralist Views* (Cambridge, Mass. and London, MIT Press, 1971).

Medvedev, P.N. and Bakhtin, M.M., *The Formal Method in Literary Scholarship: An Introduction to Sociological Poetics* (Baltimore, MD, and London, Johns Hopkins University Press, 1978).

Saussure and Structuralism

Barthes, R., *Elements of Semiology*, tr. A. Lavers and C. Smith (London, Jonathan Cape, 1967).

_____ *Writing Degree Zero*, tr. A Lavers and C. Smith (London, Jonathan Cape, 1967).

Culler, J., *Structuralist Poetics: Structuralism, Linguistics and the Study of Literature* (London, Routledge & Kegan Paul, 1975).

_____ *Saussure* (London, Collins, 1976).

_____ *The Pursuit of Signs* (London: Routledge & Kegan Paul, 1981).

Eco, U., *A Theory of Semiotics* (Bloomington and London: Indiana University Press, 1977).

Genette, G., *Narrative Discourse* (Oxford, Blackwell, 1980).

Hawkes, T. *Structuralism and Semiotics* (London, Methuen, 1977).

Jackson, L., *The Poverty of Structuralism: Literature and Structuralist Theory* (London and New York, Longman, 1991).

Lodge, D., *The Modes of Modern Writing: Metaphor, Metonymy and the Typology of Modern Literature* (London, Edward Arnold, 1977).

_____ *Working with Structuralism* (London, Routledge and Kegan Paul, 1981).

Macksey, R. and Donato, E., eds, *The Structuralist Controversy: The Languages of Criticism and the Sciences of Man* (Baltimore, MD, Johns Hopkins University Press, 1972).

Rimmon-Kenan, S., *Narrative Fiction: Contemporary Poetics* (London, Methuen, 1983).

Robey, D., ed, *Structuralism: An Introduction* (Oxford: Clarendon Press, 1973).

Saussure, F. de, *Course in General Linguistics*. tr. W. Baskin (London, Collins, 1974).

Scholes, R., *Structuralism in Literature: An Introduction* (New Haven and London, Yale University Press, 1974).

Todorov, T., The Fantastic: *A Structural Approach to a Literary Genre*, tr. R. Howard (Ithaca, NY, Cornell University Press, 1975).

_____ *The Poetics of Prose*, tr. R. Howard (Oxford, Blackwell, 1977).

Marxism

Althusser, L., *For Marx*, tr. B. Brewster (London, New Left Books, 1977).

_____ *Lenin and Philosophy and Other Essays*, tr. B. Brewster (London, New Left Books, 1977).

Barthes, R., *Mythologies*, tr. A. Lavers (London, Jonathan Cape, 1972).
Bennett, T., *Formalism and Marxism* (London and New York, Methuen, 1979).
Eagleton, T., *Marxism and Literary Criticism* (London, Methuen, 1976).
_____ *Criticism and Ideology* (London, New Left Books, 1976).
_____ *Ideology* (London and New York, Verso, 1991).
Frow, J., *Marxism and Literary History* (Oxford, Blackwell, 1986).
Jameson, F., *Marxism and Form* (Princeton, NJ, Princeton University Press, 1971).
Macherey, P., *A Theory of Literary Production*, tr. G. Wall (London, Routledge & Kegan Paul, 1978).
Williams, R., *Marxism and Literature* (Oxford, Oxford University Press, 1977).

Feminism

Barrett, M., *Women's Oppression Today* (London, New Left Books, 1980).
Beauvoir, S. de, *The Second Sex*, tr. H.M. Parshley (Harmondsworth, Penguin, 1974).
Brunt, R. and Rowan, C., *Feminism, Culture and Politics* (London, Lawrence & Wishart, 1982).
Eisenstein, H., *Contemporary Feminist Thought* (London and Sydney, Unwin, 1984).
Ellman, M., ed., *Thinking about Women* (London, Virago, 1979).
Felski, R., *Beyond Feminist Aesthetics: Feminist Literature and Social Change* (London, Hutchinson, 1989).
Greene, G. and Kahn, C., *Making a Difference: Feminist Literary Criticism* (London and New York, Methuen, 1985).
Humm, M., *Feminist Criticism: Women as Contemporary Critics* (Brighton, Sussex, Harvester, 1986).
Kaplan, C., *Sea Changes: Essays on Culture and Feminism* (London, Verso, 1986).
Jacobus, M., ed., *Women Writing and Writing about Women* (London, Croom Helm, 1979).
Millett, K., *Sexual Politics* (London, Virago, 1977).
Moi, T., *Sexual/Textual Criticism: Feminist Literary Theory* (London, Methuen, 1985).
Showalter, E., *A Literature of Their Own* (Princeton, NJ, Princeton University Press, 1977; London, Virago, 1978).
_____ *The New Feminist Criticism* (London, Virago, 1986).
Warhol, R. and Herndl, D.P., *Feminisms: An Anthology of Literary Theory and Criticism* (New Brunswick and New Jersey, Rutgers University Press.
Waugh, P., *Feminine Fictions: Revisiting the Postmodern* (London and New York, Routledge, 1989).
Wolff, J., *Feminine Sentences: Essays on Women and Culture* (Cambridge, Polity, 1990).

Poststructuralism and Deconstruction

Attridge, D., *Peculiar Language: Literature as Difference from the Romantics to James Joyce* (London, Methuen, 1988).
Belsey, C., *Critical Practice* (London, Methuen, 1980).
Culler, J., *On Deconstruction: Theory and Criticism after Structuralism* (Ithaca, NY, Cornell U.P., 1982).

Easthope, A., *British Post-structuralism since 1968* (New York, Routledge, 1988)

Harari, J.V.,*Textual Strategies: Perspectives in Post-Structuralist Criticism* (Ithaca, NY, Cornell University Press, 1979).

Harland, R., *Superstructuralism* (London, Methuen, 1980).

Hartman, G., ed., *Deconstruction and Criticism* (London, Routledge, Kegan and Paul, 1979).

Johnson, B., *The Critical Difference* (Baltimore, Johns Hopkins University Press 1980).

Leitch, V., *Deconstructive Criticism: An Advanced Introduction* (London, Hutchinson, 1983).

Lentricchia, F., *After the New Criticism* (London, Athlone Press, 1980).

Norris, C., *Deconstruction: Theory and Practice* (London, Methuen, 1982).

Norris, C., *The Contest of Faculties: Philosophy and Theory After Deconstruction* (London and New York, Methuen, 1985).

Ryan, M., *Marxism and Deconstruction: A Critical Articulation* (Baltimore, MD, and London, Johns Hopkins University Press, 1982).

Sturrock, John, *Structuralism and Since: From Lévi-Strauss to Derrida* (Oxford, Oxford University Press, 1979).

Young, R., *Untying the Text: A Post-Structuralist Reader* (Boston, and London, Routledge, Kegan and Paul, 1981).

History and Discourse

Bakhtin, M.M., *The Dialogic Imagination: Four Essays*, tr. M. Holquist and C. Emerson (Austin, University of Texas Press, 1981).

_____ *Rabelais, and his World* (Cambridge, Mass., MIT Press, 1986).

Diamond, I. and Quilby, L., *Feminism and Foucault: Reflections on Resistance* (Boston, Northwestern University Press, 1988).

Dollimore, J. and Sinfield, A., eds, *Political Shakespeare: New Essays in Cultural Materialism* (Ithaca, NY, Cornell University Press, 1985).

Foucault, M., *The Order of Things* (London, Tavistock, 1970).

_____ *Technologies of the Self*, ed. L.H. Martin, H. Gutman, P.H. Hutton (London, Tavistock Press, 1988).

Goldberg, J., *James I and the Politics of Literature: Jonson, Shakespeare, Donne, and their Contemporaries* (Baltimore, MD and London, Johns Hopkins, 1983).

Greenblatt, S., *Renaissance Self-Fashioning: From More to Shakespeare* (Chicago, Chicago University Press, 1980).

Levinson, M. *et al. Rethinking Historicism: Critical Readings in Romantic History* (Oxford, Blackwell, 1989).

McGann, J., *The Beauty of Inflections: Literary Investigations in Historical Method and Theory* (Oxford, Clarendon, 1988).

Said, E., *Orientalism* (London: Routledge & Kegan Paul, 1978).

Stallybrass, P. and White, A. *The Politics and Poetics of Transgression* (London, Methuen, 1986).

Vološinov, V.N. *Marxism and the Philosophy of Language*, tr. L. Matejka and I.R. Titunik (London and New York, Seminar Press, 1973).

Weimann, R., *Structure and Society in Literary History: Studies in the History and Theory of Historical Criticism* (London, Lawrence & Wishart, 1977).

Subjectivity and Gender

Belsey, C., *The Subject of Tragedy* (London, Methuen, 1985).

Butler, J., *Gender Trouble: Feminism and the Subversion of Identity* (New York, Routledge, 1990).

_____ *Bodies That Matter: On the Discursive Limits of Sex* (New York, Routledge, 1993).

Coward R., and Ellis, J., *Language and Materialism: Developments in Semiology and the Theory of the Subject* (London, Routledge, Kegan and Paul, 1977).

Dollimore, J., *Sexual Dissidence: Augustine to Wilde, Freud to Foucault* (Clarendon Press, Oxford, 1991).

Felman, S., ed., *Literature and Psychoanalysis: The Question of Reading: Otherwise*, Yale French Studies, 55/56, (1977).

Flax, J., *Thinking Fragments: Psychoanalysis, Feminism and Postmodernism in the Contemporary West* (Berkeley, California University Press , 1980).

Fuss, D., *Identification Papers* (New York, Routledge, 1995).

Grosz, E., *Sexual Subversions: Three French Feminists* (Sydeny, Allen and Unwin, (1989).

Sedgwick, E.K., *Between Men: English Literature and Male Homosocial Desire* (New York, Columbia University Press, 1985).

_____ *Epistemology of the Closet* (Sussex, Harvester, 1991).

Wright, E., *Psychoanalytic Criticism: Theory and Practice* (London, Methuen, 1984).

Postmodernism

Baudrillard, J. *Simulations* (New York, Semiotext(e), 1983).

_____ *In the Shadow of the Silent Majorities* (New York, Semiotext(e), 1983).

Foster, H., ed., *Postmodern Culture* (London, Pluto Press, 1985).

Jameson, F., *The Ideologies of Theory: Essays 1971–86* (New York, 1989).

Lyotard, J-F., *The Postmodern Condition* (Manchester, Manchester University Press, 1985).

Rorty, R., *Contingency, Irony and Solidarity* (Cambridge, Cambridge University Press, 1989).

Waugh, P., *Practising Postmodernism/Reading Modernism* (London, Edward Arnold, 1992).

Postcolonialism

Adam, I. and Tiffin, H., eds, *Past the Last Post: Theorising Post-Colonialism and Postmodernism* (Hemel Kempstead, Harvster, 1987).

Ahmad, A., *In Theory: Classes, Nations, Literatures* (London, Verso, 1992).

Bennington, G., Bowlby, R., and Young, R., eds, *Oxford Literary Review: Colonialism and Other Essays*, 9/1–2, 1987.

Bhabha, H., ed., *Nation and Narration* (London and New York, Routledge, 1994).

hooks, b., *Ain't I a Woman: Black Women and Feminism* (London, Pluto, 1982).

Spivak, G.C., *The Post-Colonial Critic* (New York and London, Routledge, 1990).

Young, R., *Writing History and the West* (London and New York, Routledge, 1990).

Critical Debates

Canonicity and value

Bloom, H., *The Western Canon: The Books and School of the Ages* (London, Macmillan, 1995).
Eagleton, T., *The Ideology of the Aesthetic* (Oxford, Blackwell, 1990).
Frow, J., *Cultural Studies and Cultural Value* (Oxford, Oxford University Press, 1995).
Hallberg, R. von, *Canons* (Chicago, Chicago University Press, 1985).
Waugh, P., 'Canon', in D. Cooper, ed., *Companion to Aesthetics* (Oxford, Blackwell, (1992), pp. 59–61,

Ethics and criticism

Critchley, S., *The Ethics of Deconstruction* (Oxford, Blackwell, 1992).
Eaglestone, R., *Ethical Criticism: Reading After Levinas* (Edinburgh, Edinburgh University Press, 1997).
MacIntyre, A., *Three Rival Versions of Moral Enquiry* (London, Duckworth, 1990).
Miller, J.H., *The Ethics of Reading* (New York, Columbia University Press, 1987).
Palmer, F., *Literature and Moral Understanding* (Oxford, Clarendon, 1992).

Criticism and the institution

Baldick, C., *Criticism and Literary Theory, 1890 to the Present* (London, Longman, 1996).
Culler, J., *Framing the Sign: Criticism and its Institutions* (Oxford, Blackwell, 1988).
Easthope, A., *Literary into Cultural Studies* (London, Routledge, 1991).
Graff, G., *Professing Literature: An Institutional History* (Chicago, Chicago University Press, 1987).

Criticism and Knowledge

Fuller, D. and Waugh, P., eds, *The Arts and Sciences of Criticism* (Oxford, Oxford University Press, 1999).
Livingstone, P., *Literary Knowledge: Humanistic Inquiry and the Philosophy of Science* (Ithaca and London, Cornell University Press, 1988).
Raval, S., *Metacriticism* (Athens, Georgia University Press, 1981).
Whiteley, R., *Intellectual and Social Organisation of the Sciences* (Oxford, Clarendon, 1984).

Index